THE
BOOK ®

Audi 80, 90 & Coupé
Service and Repair Manual

A K Legg LAE MIMI

(1491-272-1AC3)

Models covered

All Audi 80, 90 & Coupé models with four- & five-cylinder petrol engines, including 20-valve engine
1595 cc, 1781 cc, 1984 cc, 1994 cc, 2226 cc and 2309 cc

Does not cover Diesel engine or Quattro models

ABCDE
FGHIJ
KLMNO
PQRST
2

Printed in the USA

Haynes Publishing
Sparkford, Nr Yeovil, Somerset BA22 7JJ, England

Haynes North America, Inc
861 Lawrence Drive, Newbury Park, California 91320, USA

Editions Haynes S.A.
Tour Aurore - IBC, 18 Place des Reflets,
92975 Paris La Défense 2, Cedex, France

Haynes Publishing Nordiska AB
Box 1504, 751 45 Uppsala, Sverige

Contents

LIVING WITH YOUR AUDI

Roadside Repairs

Routine Maintenance

Contents

Introduction to the Audi

The 'new' Audi 80 was introduced at the 1986 Motor Show, and features a fully-galvanised body, energy-absorbing crumple zones, a new five-speed gearbox, a new ventilation and heating system, and a high level of instrumentation. Audi 80 models are fitted with four-cylinder carburettor or fuel injection engines.

The 'new' Audi 90 was introduced in July 1987, and features as standard equipment power steering, high-quality upholstery, electrically-operated windows and door mirrors, central locking, tinted glass, a four-speaker stereo radio/cassette unit, front foglights and an auto-check system. The 2.2/2.3E has alloy wheels, sports seats and a rear spoiler.

The 'new' Audi Coupé was introduced in December 1988, and features a zinc-galvanised body, the option of a cable-operated safety system called 'Procon-Ten', split-folding rear seats, and on later models, a 20-valve engine, equipped with a catalytic converter.

Acknowledgements

Thanks are due to the Champion Sparking Plug Company Limited who supplied the illustrations showing the spark plug conditions. Thanks are also due to Sykes-Pickavant Limited, who supplied some of the workshop tools and to all those people at Sparkford who assisted in the production of this manual.

We take great pride in the accuracy of information given in this manual, but vehicle manufacturers make alterations and design changes during the production run of a particular vehicle of which they do not inform us. No liability can be accepted by the authors or publishers for loss, damage or injury caused by errors in, or omissions from, the information given.

Project vehicles

The vehicles used in the preparation of this manual, and which appear in many of the photographic sequences, were a 1989 Audi 80 1.8S Saloon and a 1989 Audi 90 2.3E Saloon.

Audi 80 1.8S Saloon (1989 model)

Audi 90 2.3E Saloon (1989 model)

Audi Coupé (1989 model)

Working on your car can be dangerous. This page shows just some of the potential risks and hazards, with the aim of creating a safety-conscious attitude.

General hazards

Scalding

• Don't remove the radiator or expansion tank cap while the engine is hot.
• Engine oil, automatic transmission fluid or power steering fluid may also be dangerously hot if the engine has recently been running.

Burning

• Beware of burns from the exhaust system and from any part of the engine. Brake discs and drums can also be extremely hot immediately after use.

Crushing

• When working under or near a raised vehicle, always supplement the jack with axle stands, or use drive-on ramps. *Never venture under a car which is only supported by a jack.*
• Take care if loosening or tightening high-torque nuts when the vehicle is on stands. Initial loosening and final tightening should be done with the wheels on the ground.

Fire

• Fuel is highly flammable; fuel vapour is explosive.
• Don't let fuel spill onto a hot engine.
• Do not smoke or allow naked lights (including pilot lights) anywhere near a vehicle being worked on. Also beware of creating sparks (electrically or by use of tools).
• Fuel vapour is heavier than air, so don't work on the fuel system with the vehicle over an inspection pit.
• Another cause of fire is an electrical overload or short-circuit. Take care when repairing or modifying the vehicle wiring.
• Keep a fire extinguisher handy, of a type suitable for use on fuel and electrical fires.

Electric shock

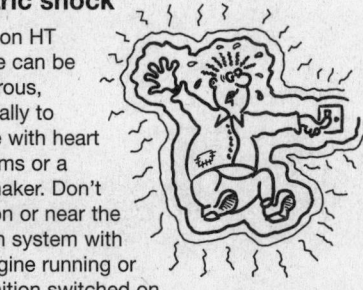

• Ignition HT voltage can be dangerous, especially to people with heart problems or a pacemaker. Don't work on or near the ignition system with the engine running or the ignition switched on.

• Mains voltage is also dangerous. Make sure that any mains-operated equipment is correctly earthed. Mains power points should be protected by a residual current device (RCD) circuit breaker.

Fume or gas intoxication

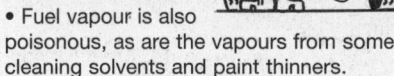

• Exhaust fumes are poisonous; they often contain carbon monoxide, which is rapidly fatal if inhaled. Never run the engine in a confined space such as a garage with the doors shut.
• Fuel vapour is also poisonous, as are the vapours from some cleaning solvents and paint thinners.

Poisonous or irritant substances

• Avoid skin contact with battery acid and with any fuel, fluid or lubricant, especially antifreeze, brake hydraulic fluid and Diesel fuel. Don't syphon them by mouth. If such a substance is swallowed or gets into the eyes, seek medical advice.
• Prolonged contact with used engine oil can cause skin cancer. Wear gloves or use a barrier cream if necessary. Change out of oil-soaked clothes and do not keep oily rags in your pocket.
• Air conditioning refrigerant forms a poisonous gas if exposed to a naked flame (including a cigarette). It can also cause skin burns on contact.

Asbestos

• Asbestos dust can cause cancer if inhaled or swallowed. Asbestos may be found in gaskets and in brake and clutch linings. When dealing with such components it is safest to assume that they contain asbestos.

Special hazards

Hydrofluoric acid

• This extremely corrosive acid is formed when certain types of synthetic rubber, found in some O-rings, oil seals, fuel hoses etc, are exposed to temperatures above 400°C. The rubber changes into a charred or sticky substance containing the acid. *Once formed, the acid remains dangerous for years. If it gets onto the skin, it may be necessary to amputate the limb concerned.*
• When dealing with a vehicle which has suffered a fire, or with components salvaged from such a vehicle, wear protective gloves and discard them after use.

The battery

• Batteries contain sulphuric acid, which attacks clothing, eyes and skin. Take care when topping-up or carrying the battery.
• The hydrogen gas given off by the battery is highly explosive. Never cause a spark or allow a naked light nearby. Be careful when connecting and disconnecting battery chargers or jump leads.

Air bags

• Air bags can cause injury if they go off accidentally. Take care when removing the steering wheel and/or facia. Special storage instructions may apply.

Diesel injection equipment

• Diesel injection pumps supply fuel at very high pressure. Take care when working on the fuel injectors and fuel pipes.

⚠️ *Warning: Never expose the hands, face or any other part of the body to injector spray; the fuel can penetrate the skin with potentially fatal results.*

Remember...

DO

• Do use eye protection when using power tools, and when working under the vehicle.

• Do wear gloves or use barrier cream to protect your hands when necessary.

• Do get someone to check periodically that all is well when working alone on the vehicle.

• Do keep loose clothing and long hair well out of the way of moving mechanical parts.

• Do remove rings, wristwatch etc, before working on the vehicle – especially the electrical system.

• Do ensure that any lifting or jacking equipment has a safe working load rating adequate for the job.

DON'T

• Don't attempt to lift a heavy component which may be beyond your capability – get assistance.

• Don't rush to finish a job, or take unverified short cuts.

• Don't use ill-fitting tools which may slip and cause injury.

• Don't leave tools or parts lying around where someone can trip over them. Mop up oil and fuel spills at once.

• Don't allow children or pets to play in or near a vehicle being worked on.

Dimensions

Overall length:
  80 and 90 .... 4393 mm (173.1 in)
  Coupé .... 4366 mm (172.0 in)
Overall width:
  80 and 90 .... 1695 mm (66.8 in)
  Coupé .... 1716 mm (67.6 in)
Overall height (unladen):
  80 and 90 .... 1397 mm (55.0 in)
  Coupé .... 1368 mm (53.9 in)
Ground clearance (at gross vehicle weight):
  80 .... 120 mm (4.7 in)
  90 with standard suspension .... 127 mm (5.0 in)
  90 with lowered suspension .... 115 mm (4.5 in)
  Coupé .... 129.5 mm (5.1 in)
Wheelbase (unladen):
  80 and 90 .... 2546 mm (100.3 in)
  Coupé .... 2556.5 mm (100.7 in)
Front track (unladen):
  80 and 90 .... 1411 mm (55.6 in)
  Coupé .... 1452 mm (57.2 in)
Rear track:
  80 with drum rear brakes .... 1432 mm (56.4 in)
  80 with disc rear brakes .... 1430 mm (56.3 in)
  90 .... 1431 mm (56.4in)
  Coupé .... 1447 mm (57.0 in)
Turning circle:
  80 with manual steering .... 10.3 m (33.8 ft)
  80 with power steering .... 10.5 m (34.5 ft)
  90 with manual steering .... 11.2 m (36.7 ft)
  90 with power steering .... 11.1 m (36.4 ft)
  Coupé .... 11.05 m (36.3 ft)

Weights

Kerb weight (unladen):
  80 with carburettor engine .... 1020 kg (2249 lb)
  80 with fuel injection engine .... 1050 kg (2315 lb)
  90 .... 1170 to 1200 kg (2580 to 2646 lb)
  Coupé .... 1170 kg (2580 lb)
Gross vehicle weight:
  80 with carburettor engine .... 1480 kg (3263 lb)
  80 with fuel injection engine .... 1510 kg (3330 lb)
  90 .... 1630 to 1660 kg (3594 to 3660 lb)
  Coupé .... 1630 kg (3594 lb)
Maximum roof rack load .... 75 kg (165 lb)
Maximum towing weight (12% gradient):
  80 with carburettor engine .... 750 to 1300 kg (1654 to 2867 lb)
  80 with fuel injection engine .... 1100 to 1200 kg (2426 to 2646 lb)
  90 and Coupé .... 1250 to 1350 kg (2756 to 2977 lb)

Capacities

Engine oil:
  Four-cylinder (with filter) .... 3.0 litres (5.3 pints)
  Four-cylinder (without filter) .... 2.5 litres (4.4 pints)
  Five-cylinder (with filter) .... 4.5 litres (7.9 pints)
  Five-cylinder (without filter) .... 4.0 litres (7.0 pints)
  Difference between engine oil dipstick minimum and maximum marks 1.0 litre (1.8 pints)
Cooling system:
  Four-cylinder .... 6.5 litres (11.4 pints)
  Five-cylinder .... 8.0 litres (14.1 pints)
Fuel tank:
  Except Coupé .... 68 litres (15.0 gallons)
  Coupé .... 70 litres (15.4 gallons)
Manual gearbox .... 2.35 litres (4.1 pints)
Automatic transmission:
  Transmission:
    Total .... 6.0 litres (10.6 pints)
    Drain and refill .... 3.0 litres (5.3 pints)
  Final drive:
    089 .... 0.75 litres (1.3 pints)
    087 .... 1.00 litres (1.8 pints)

Identifying leaks

Puddles on the garage floor or drive, or obvious wetness under the bonnet or underneath the car, suggest a leak that needs investigating. It can sometimes be difficult to decide where the leak is coming from, especially if the engine bay is very dirty already. Leaking oil or fluid can also be blown rearwards by the passage of air under the car, giving a false impression of where the problem lies.

 Warning: Most automotive oils and fluids are poisonous. Wash them off skin, and change out of contaminated clothing, without delay.

 HAYNES HiNT *The smell of a fluid leaking from the car may provide a clue to what's leaking. Some fluids are distinctively coloured. It may help to clean the car carefully and to park it over some clean paper overnight as an aid to locating the source of the leak.*
Remember that some leaks may only occur while the engine is running.

Sump oil

Engine oil may leak from the drain plug...

Oil from filter

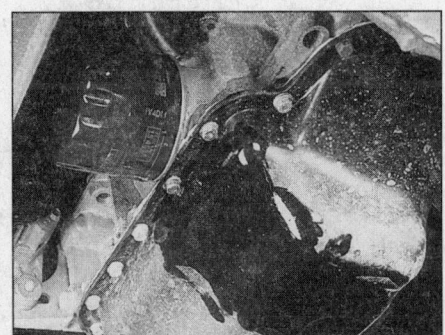

...or from the base of the oil filter.

Gearbox oil

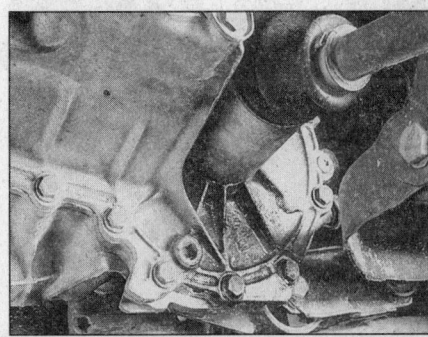

Gearbox oil can leak from the seals at the inboard ends of the driveshafts.

Antifreeze

Leaking antifreeze often leaves a crystalline deposit like this.

Brake fluid

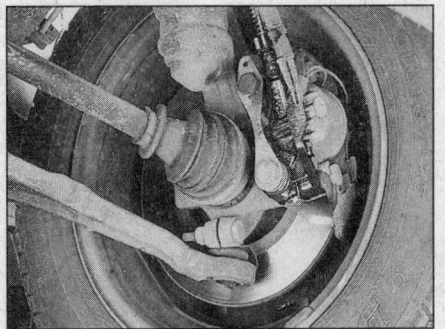

A leak occurring at a wheel is almost certainly brake fluid.

Power steering fluid

Power steering fluid may leak from the pipe connectors on the steering rack.

Jacking, wheel changing and towing

Jacking

The jack supplied with the vehicle should only be used for wheel changing, as described later. When raising the vehicle for repair or maintenance, preferably use a trolley or hydraulic jack, with a wooden block as an insulator, to prevent damage to the underbody. Place the jack under the jacking points, which are located behind the front wheels and in front of the rear wheels, beneath the diamond-embossed marks on the sills (photo). Position axle stands together with wooden blocks under the jacking points. If both front or both rear wheels are to be raised, jack up one side first, and securely support it on an axle stand before raising the other side.

Front towing eye

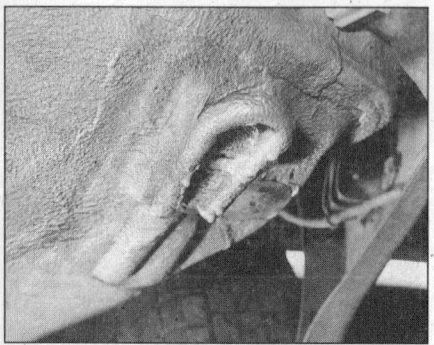

Rear towing eye

To avoid repetition, the procedure for raising the vehicle in order to carry out work beneath it, is not included before each relevant operation described in this manual. Where possible, position the car over an inspection pit, or raise it on a lift. Always support the car on axle stands before working beneath it.

Towing

Towing eyes are provided at the front and rear of the car (photos). The rear eye is welded to the underbody. The front eye is located in the right-hand front air duct, and may be unscrewed and kept in the tool kit. When removing or fitting the front eye, or when fitting a tow rope, the air duct must be removed by pressing down on the middle of the upper rail, then pulling the duct from the bumper.

When being towed, switch on the ignition so that the steering lock is unlocked, and so that the direction indicator, horn and wipers may be used. Note that with the engine stopped, more effort will be required to stop the car, as the brake servo will be inoperative. Similarly on power steering models, more effort will be required to turn the steering wheel. The gear lever should be in neutral on manual gearbox models, or position 'N' on automatic transmission models.

Automatic transmission models should not be towed further than 30 miles (50 km) or faster than 30 mph (50 km/h). If these conditions cannot be met, or if transmission damage has occurred, the front wheels should

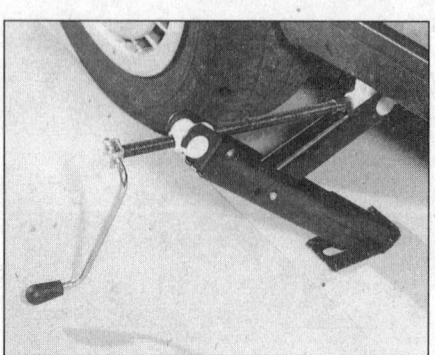

Jacking the car

be off the ground for the duration of the tow.

Wheel changing

To change a roadwheel, first park on a firm level surface if possible. Chock the wheel opposite the one being removed. Apply the handbrake, and engage reverse gear (or 'P' on automatic transmission models). Remove the wheel trim, using a screwdriver where necessary.

Where fitted, unlock and remove the wheel bolt lock. Loosen the wheel bolts half a turn each. Position the jack beneath the jacking point with its pad on the vertical seam. Raise the car until the wheel is just clear of the ground. Remove the uppermost wheel bolt, and screw in the plastic guide from the tool kit. Remove the remaining bolts, and take off the wheel. Fit the spare wheel, and insert the three bolts finger-tight, then unscrew the plastic guide and fit the fourth bolt. Lightly tighten the bolts with the brace. Lower the car to the ground and remove the jack, then tighten the wheel bolts in diagonal sequence. Tighten the bolts as hard as possible using the brace supplied, but have their tightness checked as soon as possible with a torque wrench.

Refit the wheel trim, making sure (where applicable) that the valve is located in the special hole.

Where the temporary lightweight spare wheel is fitted, do not exceed 50 mph (80 km/h), and fit the standard wheel as soon as possible.

Plastic guide screwed into a wheel bolt hole

Jump starting

HAYNES HiNT *Jump starting will get you out of trouble, but you must correct whatever made the battery go flat in the first place. There are three possibilities:*

1 *The battery has been drained by repeated attempts to start, or by leaving the lights on.*

2 *The charging system is not working properly (alternator drivebelt slack or broken, alternator wiring fault or alternator itself faulty).*

3 *The battery itself is at fault (electrolyte low, or battery worn out).*

When jump-starting a car using a booster battery, observe the following precautions:

✔ Before connecting the booster battery, make sure that the ignition is switched off.

✔ Ensure that all electrical equipment (lights, heater, wipers, etc) is switched off.

✔ Take note of any special precautions printed on the battery case.

✔ Make sure that the booster battery is the same voltage as the discharged one in the vehicle.

✔ If the battery is being jump-started from the battery in another vehicle, the two vehicles MUST NOT TOUCH each other.

✔ Make sure that the transmission is in neutral (or PARK, in the case of automatic transmission).

1 Connect one end of the red jump lead to the positive (+) terminal of the flat battery

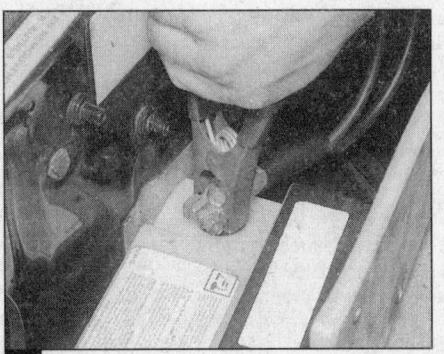

2 Connect the other end of the red lead to the positive (+) terminal of the booster battery.

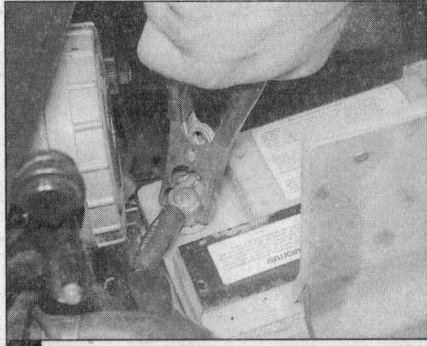

3 Connect one end of the black jump lead to the negative (-) terminal of the booster battery

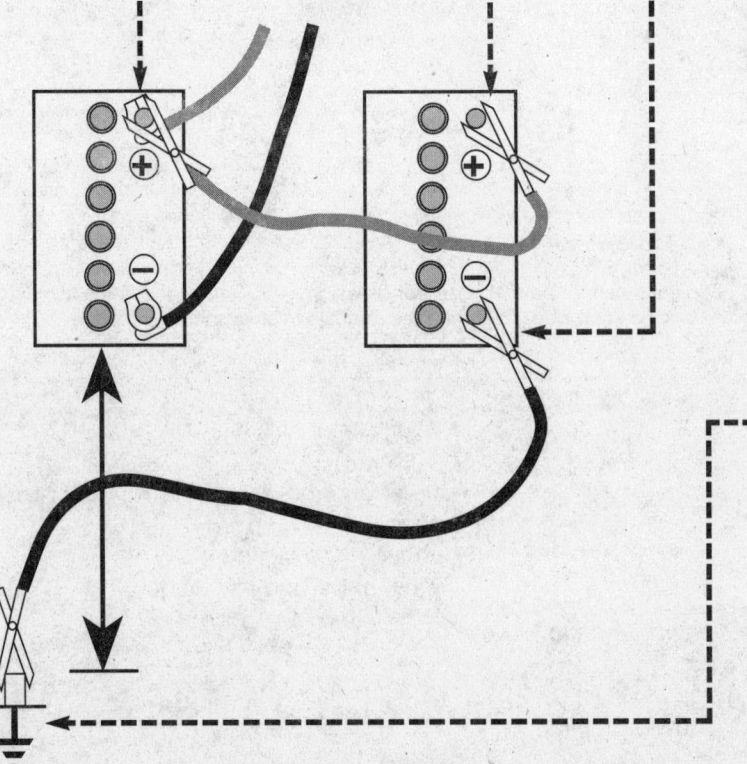

4 Connect the other end of the black jump lead to a bolt or bracket on the engine block, well away from the battery, on the vehicle to be started.

5 Make sure that the jump leads will not come into contact with the fan, drivebelts or other moving parts of the engine.

6 Start the engine using the booster battery and run it at idle speed. Switch on the lights, rear window demister and heater blower motor, then disconnect the jump leads in the reverse order of connection. Turn off the lights etc.

Maintenance is essential for ensuring safety and desirable for the purpose of getting the best in terms of performance and economy from your vehicle. Over the years the need for periodic lubrication – oiling, greasing, and so on – has been drastically reduced if not totally eliminated. This has unfortunately tended to lead some owners to think that because no such action is required, components either no longer exist, or will last for ever. This is certainly not the case; it is essential to carry out regular visual examination as comprehensively as possible in order to spot any possible defects at an early stage before they develop into major expensive repairs.

The following service schedule is a list of the maintenance requirements, and the intervals at which they should be carried out. Where applicable, these procedures are covered in greater detail throughout this manual, in Section 2 of each Chapter.

Vehicles which operate under adverse conditions (eg in extremes of temperature, or full-time trailer towing, or mainly on short journeys) may benefit from more frequent maintenance than specified. If in doubt, consult an Audi dealer.

Weekly, or before a long journey

- [ ] Check engine oil level
- [ ] Check coolant level
- [ ] Check the tyre pressures (cold), including the spare
- [ ] Top up the washer reservoir(s), adding a screen

Every 10 000 miles (15 000 km)

- [ ] Change engine oil and renew oil filter

Note: *Frequent oil and filter changes are good for the engine. We recommend changing the oil at 5000 miles (7500 km), or at least twice a year if the mileage covered is less.*

- [ ] Check brake pad linings for wear

Every 12 months

- [ ] Check engine for leaks
- [ ] Check cooling system for leaks
- [ ] Check antifreeze strength
- [ ] Check idling speed and CO content
- [ ] Check exhaust system for leaks
- [ ] Check clutch hydraulic circuit for leaks and damage
- [ ] Check clutch hydraulic fluid level
- [ ] Check gearbox for leakage and damage
- [ ] Check automatic transmission and final drive fluid level

Every 12 months (continued)

- [ ] Check CV joint rubber bellows
- [ ] Check braking system hydraulic circuit for leaks and damage
- [ ] Check rear brake shoe linings for wear
- [ ] Check brake fluid level
- [ ] Check tie-rod ends
- [ ] Check front suspension lower balljoints
- [ ] Check the tyres
- [ ] Lubricate the door check straps and bonnet lock
- [ ] Check operation of lights and horn
- [ ] Check wiper and washer systems
- [ ] Check battery electrolyte level
- [ ] Check headlight adjustment

Every 24 months

As for the 12-month schedule plus:
- [ ] Renew coolant
- [ ] Renew brake fluid

Every 20 000 miles (30 000 km)

- [ ] Check water pump drivebelt tension (four-cylinder engine)
- [ ] Renew the in-line fuel filter on the carburettor engine
- [ ] Renew the air cleaner element
- [ ] Renew the spark plugs
- [ ] Renew automatic transmission fluid
- [ ] Check power-assisted steering fluid level
- [ ] Check and adjust the power steering pump drivebelt
- [ ] Check and adjust the air conditioner compressor drivebelt
- [ ] Lubricate the sliding sunroof
- [ ] Check underbody sealant
- [ ] Check alternator drivebelt

Every 40 000 miles (60 000 km)

- [ ] Renew the timing belt

Under-bonnet view of Audi 80 with four-cylinder carburettor engine

1 Front suspension strut upper mounting
2 Fusebox
3 Brake fluid reservoir
4 Brake vacuum servo unit
5 Steering gear
6 Ignition coil
7 Distributor
8 In-line fuel filter

9 Battery
10 Cooling system expansion tank
11 Washer fluid reservoir
12 Top hose
13 Bottom hose
14 Electric cooling fan
15 Engine oil level dipstick
16 Fuel pump

17 Alternator
18 Fuel reservoir
19 Engine oil filler cap
20 Radiator
21 Automatic air temperature unit
22 Air cleaner assembly
23 Vacuum reservoir
24 Brake master cylinder

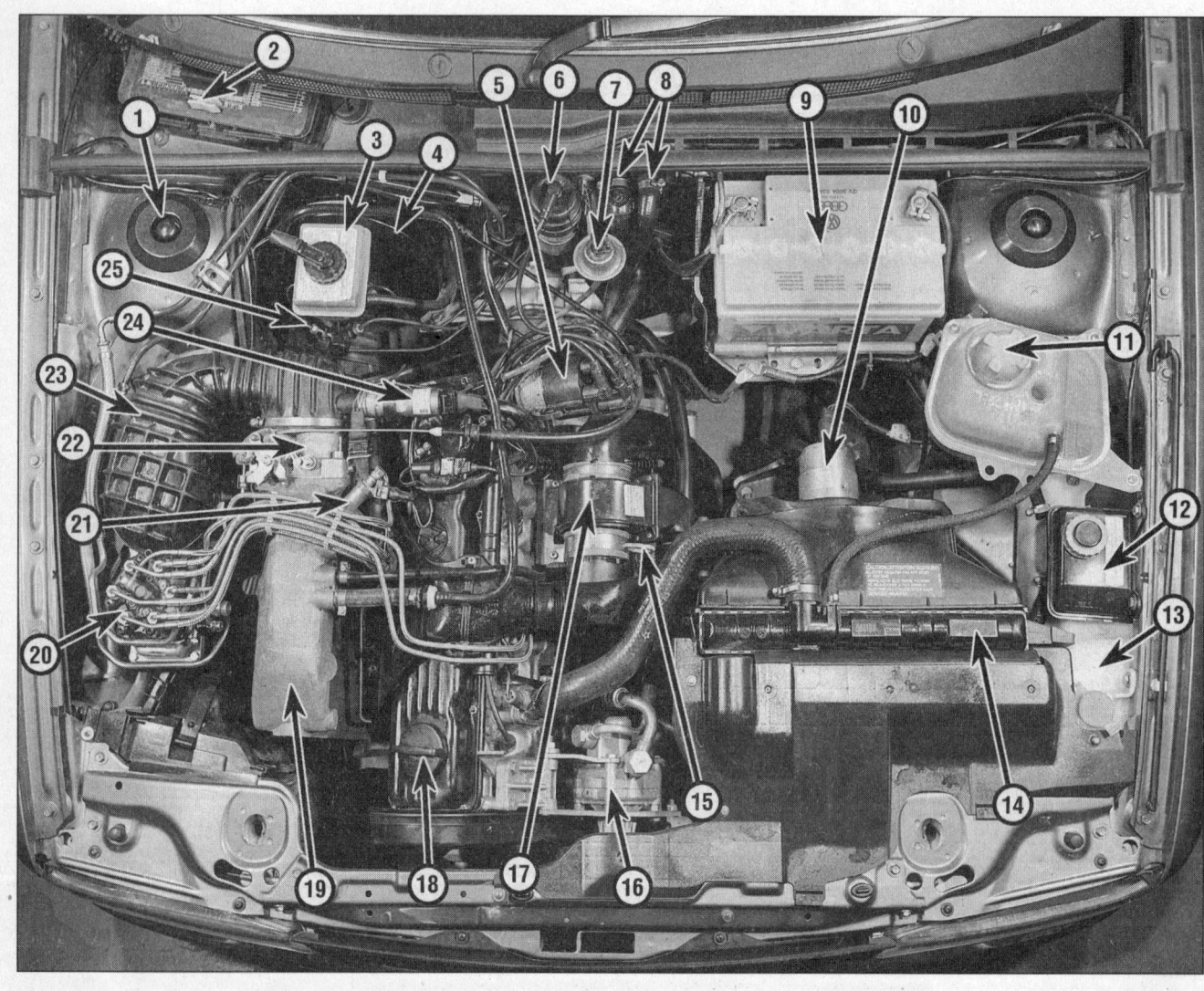

Under-bonnet view of Audi 90 with five-cylinder fuel injection engine

1 Front suspension strut upper mounting
2 Fusebox
3 Brake fluid reservoir
4 Brake vacuum servo unit
5 Distributor
6 Ignition coil
7 Diaphragm pressure switch
8 Heater hoses
9 Battery

10 Electric cooling fan
11 Cooling system expansion tank
12 Power steering fluid reservoir
13 Washer fluid reservoir
14 Radiator
15 Engine oil level dipstick
16 Power steering pump
17 Injector cooling fan motor

18 Engine oil filler cap
19 Inlet manifold
20 Fuel distributor and air flow meter
21 Cold start valve
22 Throttle valve housing
23 Inlet duct
24 Control unit for idle stabilisation
25 Brake master cylinder

Front underbody view of Audi 80 with four-cylinder carburettor engine

1 Driveshaft
2 Gearbox rear mounting
3 Gearbox oil drain plug
4 Exhaust downpipe
5 Cooling fan thermoswitch
6 Engine oil drain plug
7 Water pump
8 Engine mounting
9 Horn
10 Anti-roll bar
11 Lower suspension arm

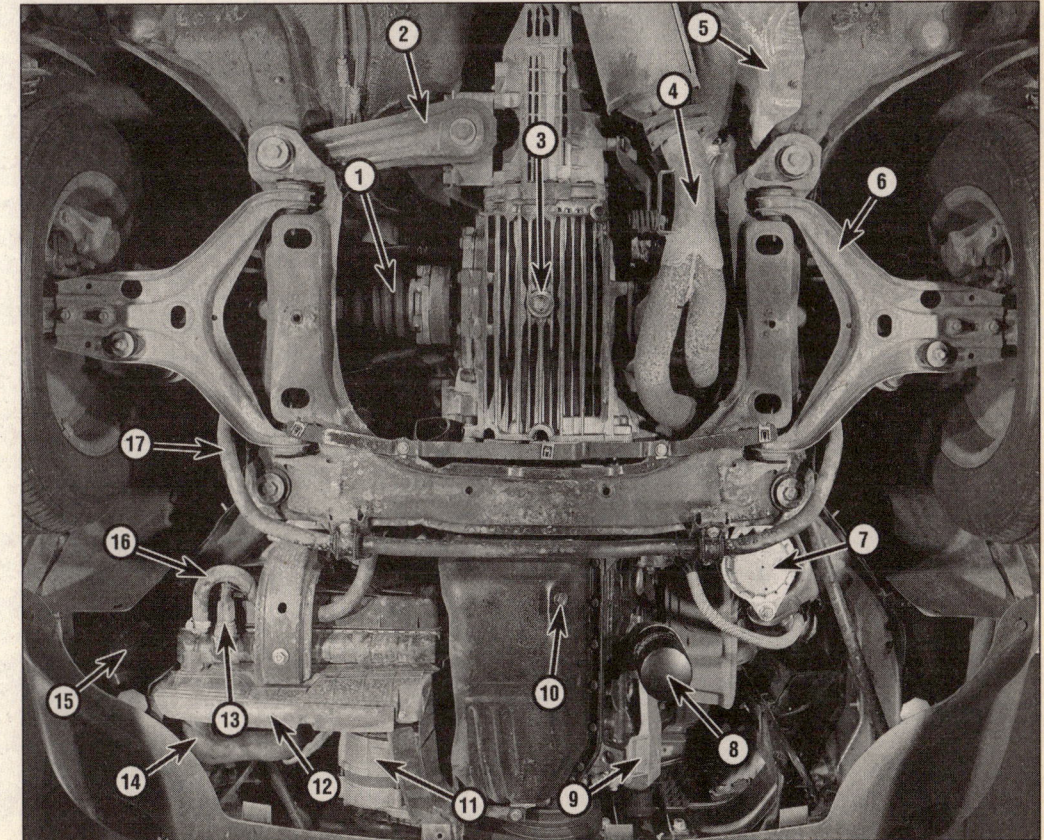

Front underbody view of Audi 90 with five-cylinder fuel injection engine

1 Driveshaft
2 Gearbox rear mounting
3 Gearbox oil drain plug
4 Exhaust downpipe
5 Heatshield
6 Lower suspension arm
7 Engine mounting
8 Oil filter
9 Front engine support bar
10 Engine oil drain plug
11 Alternator
12 Radiator
13 Cooling fan thermoswitch
14 Bottom hose
15 Horn
16 Expansion tank feed hose
17 Anti-roll bar

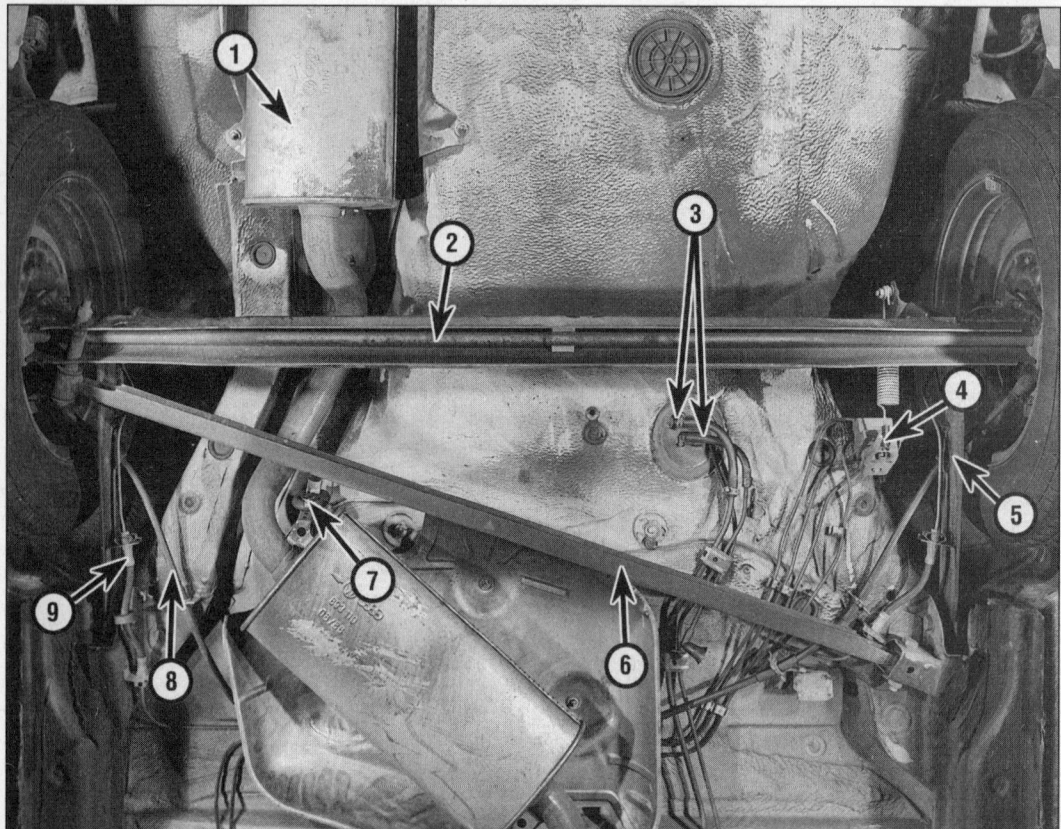

Rear underbody view of Audi 80 with four-cylinder carburettor engine

1 Rear silencer
2 Rear axle torsion bar
3 Fuel tank supply and return pipes
4 Brake pressure regulator
5 Rear axle trailing arm
6 Panhard rod
7 Exhaust mounting rubber
8 Handbrake cable
9 Brake hydraulic flexible hose

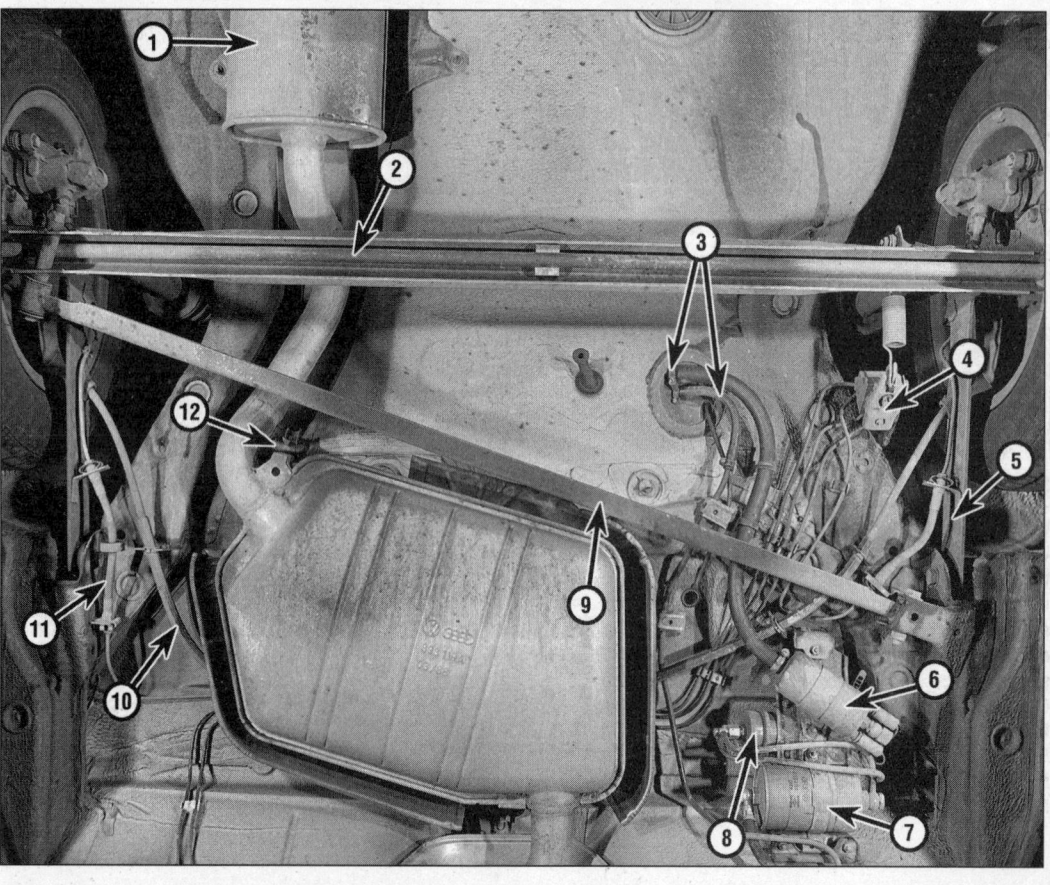

Rear underbody view of Audi 90 with five-cylinder fuel injection engine

1 Rear silencer
2 Rear axle torsion bar
3 Fuel tank supply and return pipes
4 Brake pressure regulator
5 Rear axle trailing arm
6 Fuel pump
7 Fuel filter
8 Fuel accumulator
9 Panhard rod
10 Handbrake cable
11 Brake hydraulic flexible hose
12 Exhaust mounting rubber

Tyre conditon and pressure

It is very important that tyres are in good condition, and at the correct pressure - having a tyre failure at any speed is highly dangerous. Tyre wear is influenced by driving style - harsh braking and acceleration, or fast cornering, will all produce more rapid tyre wear. As a general rule, the front tyres wear out faster than the rears. Interchanging the tyres from front to rear ("rotating" the tyres) may result in more even wear. However, if this is completely effective, you may have the expense of replacing all four tyres at once!

Remove any nails or stones embedded in the tread before they penetrate the tyre to cause deflation. If removal of a nail does reveal that the tyre has been punctured, refit the nail so that its point of penetration is marked. Then immediately change the wheel, and have the tyre repaired by a tyre dealer.

Regularly check the tyres for damage in the form of cuts or bulges, especially in the sidewalls. Periodically remove the wheels, and clean any dirt or mud from the inside and outside surfaces. Examine the wheel rims for signs of rusting, corrosion or other damage. Light alloy wheels are easily damaged by "kerbing" whilst parking; steel wheels may also become dented or buckled. A new wheel is very often the only way to overcome severe damage.

New tyres should be balanced when they are fitted, but it may become necessary to re-balance them as they wear, or if the balance weights fitted to the wheel rim should fall off. Unbalanced tyres will wear more quickly, as will the steering and suspension components. Wheel imbalance is normally signified by vibration, particularly at a certain speed (typically around 50 mph). If this vibration is felt only through the steering, then it is likely that just the front wheels need balancing. If, however, the vibration is felt through the whole car, the rear wheels could be out of balance. Wheel balancing should be carried out by a tyre dealer or garage.

1 Tread Depth - visual check
The original tyres have tread wear safety bands (B), which will appear when the tread depth reaches approximately 1.6 mm. The band positions are indicated by a triangular mark on the tyre sidewall (A).

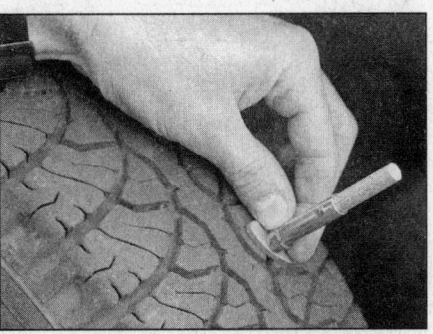

2 Tread Depth - manual check
Alternatively, tread wear can be monitored with a simple, inexpensive device known as a tread depth indicator gauge.

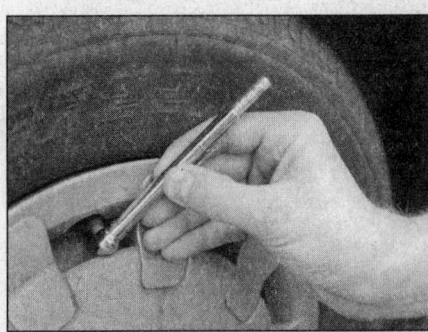

3 Tyre Pressure Check
Check the tyre pressures regularly with the tyres cold. Do not adjust the tyre pressures immediately after the vehicle has been used, or an inaccurate setting will result.

Tyre tread wear patterns

Shoulder Wear
Underinflation (wear on both sides)
Under-inflation will cause overheating of the tyre, because the tyre will flex too much, and the tread will not sit correctly on the road surface. This will cause a loss of grip and excessive wear, not to mention the danger of sudden tyre failure due to heat build-up.
Check and adjust pressures
Incorrect wheel camber (wear on one side)
Repair or renew suspension parts
Hard cornering
Reduce speed!

Centre Wear
Overinflation
Over-inflation will cause rapid wear of the centre part of the tyre tread, coupled with reduced grip, harsher ride, and the danger of shock damage occurring in the tyre casing.
Check and adjust pressures

If you sometimes have to inflate your car's tyres to the higher pressures specified for maximum load or sustained high speed, don't forget to reduce the pressures to normal afterwards.

Uneven Wear
Front tyres may wear unevenly as a result of wheel misalignment. Most tyre dealers and garages can check and adjust the wheel alignment (or "tracking") for a modest charge.
Incorrect camber or castor
Repair or renew suspension parts
Malfunctioning suspension
Repair or renew suspension parts
Unbalanced wheel
Balance tyres
Incorrect toe setting
Adjust front wheel alignment
Note: *The feathered edge of the tread which typifies toe wear is best checked by feel.*

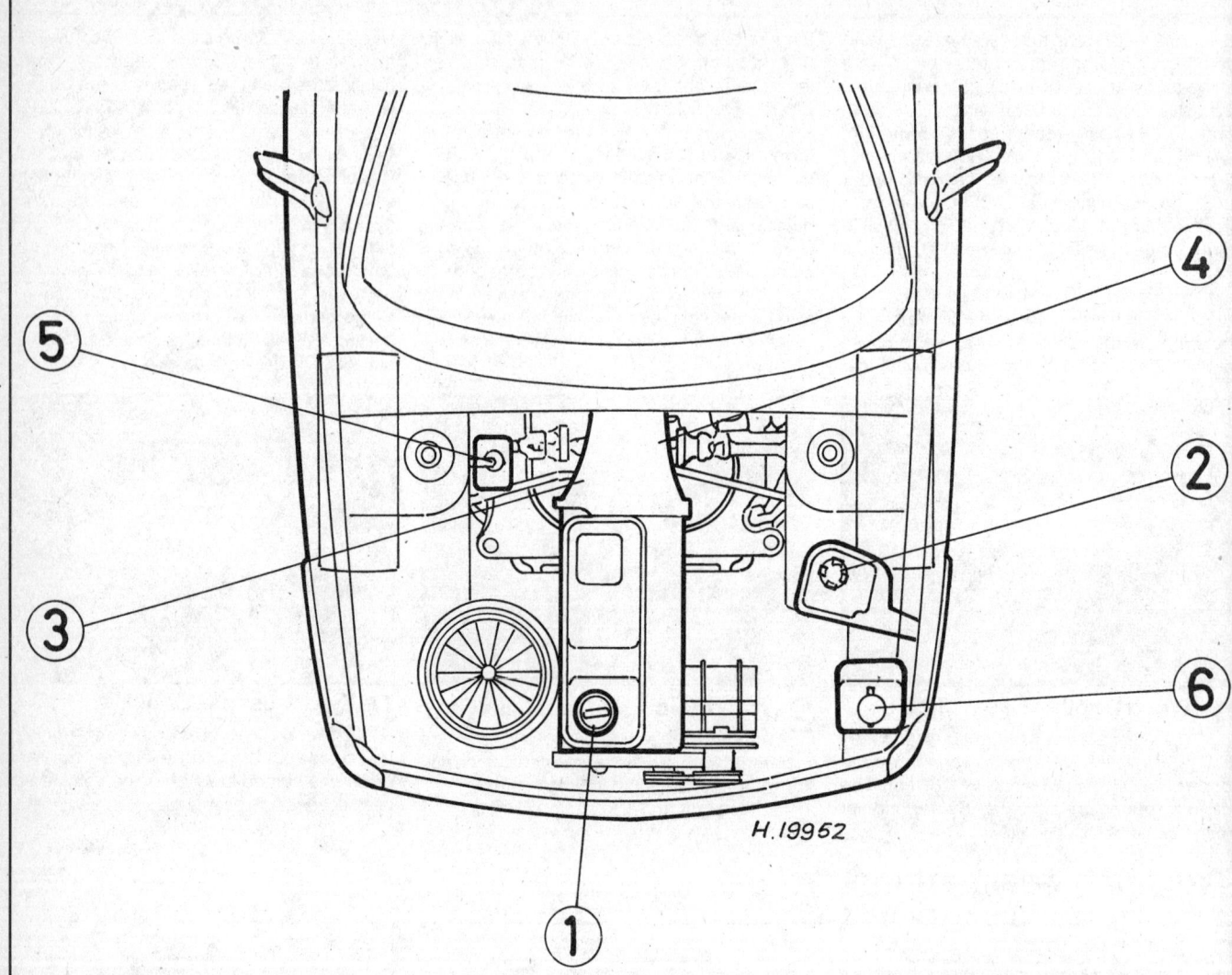

H.19952

Component or system	Lubricant type/specification
Engine (1)	Multigrade engine oil, viscosity SAE 15W/50 or 20W/50 *(Duckhams QXR Premium Petrol Engine Oil, or Duckhams Hypergrade Petrol Engine Oil)*
Cooling system (2)	Ethylene glycol based antifreeze with corrosion inhibitor *(Duckhams Antifreeze & Summer Coolant)*
Manual gearbox and final drive (3)	VW/Audi gear oil G50 (synthetic oil), viscosity SAE 75W/90 *(Duckhams Hypoid Gear Oil 75W-90 GL-4)*
Automatic transmission (4) Transmission Final drive	Dexron type ATF *(Duckhams ATF Autotrans III)* Hypoid gear oil, viscosity SAE 90, to API GL5 *(Duckhams Hypoid Gear Oil 85W-90 GL-5)*
Brake and clutch hydraulic systems (5)	Hydraulic fluid to FMVSS 116 DOT 4 *(Duckhams Universal Brake & Clutch Fluid)*
Power steering (6)	VW/Audi hydraulic oil G 002 000

Chapter 1 Engine

Contents

Degrees of difficulty

Easy, suitable for novice with little experience	**Fairly easy,** suitable for beginner with some experience	**Fairly difficult,** suitable for competent DIY mechanic	**Difficult,** suitable for experienced DIY mechanic 	**Very difficult,** suitable for expert DIY or professional

Specifications

Part A: Four-cylinder engines

General

Code letters:
  1.6 litre . . . . RN
  1.8 litre . . . . RU, DZ, NE, PM, JN
  2.0 litre 3A
Capacity:
  1.6 litre . . . . 1595 cc
  1.8 litre . . . . 1781 cc
  2.0 litre . . . . 1984 cc
Bore/stroke:
  1.6 litre . . . . 81.0/77.4 mm (3.19/3.05 in)
  1.8 litre . . . . 81.0/86.4 mm (3.19/3.40 in)
  2.0 litre . . . . 82.5/92.8 mm (3.25/3.66 in)

General (continued)

Compression ratio:
- 1.6 litre .... 9.0 : 1
- 1.8 litre
  - Code letters RU, PM and JN .... 9.0 : 1
  - Code letters DZ and NE .... 10.0 : 1
- 2.0 litre .... 10.4 : 1

Minimum compression pressure:
- All engines except code NE .... 7.0 bar (102 lbf/in²)
- Engine code NE .... 7.5 bar (109 lbf/in²)

Maximum difference between cylinders .... 3 bar (43.5 lbf/in²)

Firing order .... 1-3-4-2 (No 1 at timing belt end)

Lubrication system

Oil type/specification .... Multigrade engine oil, viscosity SAE 15W/50 or 20W/50

Oil capacity:
- Including filter .... 3.0 litres (5.3 pints)
- Excluding filter .... 2.5 litres (4.4 pints)

Difference between dipstick minimum and maximum marks .... 1.0 litre (1.8 pints)

Oil pressure (minimum) .... 2.0 bar (29 lbf/in²) at 2000 rpm, and oil temperature of 80°C (176°F)

Oil pump
- Gear backlash (maximum) .... 0.20 mm (0.008 in)
- Gear endfloat (maximum) .... 0.15 mm (0.006 in)

Oil filter .... Champion C101

Intermediate shaft

Endfloat .... 0.25 mm (0.010 in)

Crankshaft

Needle bearing depth .... 1.5 mm (0.059 in)

Endfloat:
- New .... 0.07 to 0.17 mm (0.003 to 0.007in)
- Wear limit .... 0.25 mm (0.010 in)

Maximum main bearing running clearance .... 0.017 mm (0.007 in)

Main bearing journal diameter:
- Standard size .... 53.96 to 53.98 mm (2.1244 to 2.1252 in)
- 1st undersize .... 53.71 to 53.73 mm (2.1146 to 2.1154 in)
- 2nd undersize .... 53.46 to 53.48 mm (2.1047 to 2.1055 in)
- 3rd undersize .... 53.21 to 53.23 mm (2.0949 to 2.0957 in)

Big-end bearing journal diameter:
- Standard size .... 45.96 to 45.98 mm (1.8094 to 1.8102 in)
- 1st undersize .... 45.71 to 45.73 mm (1.7996 to 1.8004 in)
- 2nd undersize .... 45.46 to 45.48 mm (1.7898 to 1.7906 in)
- 3rd undersize .... 45.21 to 45.23 mm (1.7799 to 1.7807 in)

Maximum journal out-of-round .... 0.03 mm (0.0012 in)

Pistons and rings

	1.6/1.8	2.0
Piston diameter:		
Standard	80.98 mm (3.1882 in)	82.48 mm (3.2472 in)
1st oversize	81.23 mm (3.1980 in)	82.73 mm (3.2571 in)
2nd oversize	81.48 mm (3.2079 in)	82.98 mm (3.2669 in)
Bore diameter:		
Standard	81.01 mm (3.1894 in)	82.51 mm (3.2484 in)
1st oversize	81.26 mm (3.1992 in)	82.76 mm (3.3484 in)
2nd oversize	81.51 mm (3.2091 in)	83.01 mm (3.2681 in)

Piston-to-bore clearance:
- New .... 0.03 mm (0 0012 in)
- Wear limit .... 0.07 mm (0.0028 in)

Groove-to-ring clearance:
- New .... 0.02 to 0 05 mm (0.0008 to 0.0020in)
- Wear limit .... 0.15 mm (0.0059 in)

Cylinder bore:
- Maximum out-of-round .... 0.04 mm (0.0016 in)

Piston ring endgap clearance (ring 15 mm/0.6 in from bottom of bore):
- New - compression .... 0.30 to 0.45 mm (0.012 to 0.018in)
- New - oil scraper .... 0.25 to 0.45 mm (0.010 to 0.018in)
- Wear limit .... 1.0 mm (0.040 in)

Connecting rods
Maximum big-end endfloat . . . . 0.37 mm (0.015 in)
Big-end bearing running clearance wear limit . . . . 0.12 mm (0.0047 in)

Camshaft
Maximum endfloat . . . . 0.15 mm (0.006 in)
Bearing running clearance . . . . 0.1 mm (0.004 in)
Camshaft run-out (max) . . . . 0.01 mm (0.0004 in)

Valves
Valve head angle . . . . 45°
Valve guides:
    Maximum valve rock (measured at head):
      Inlet . . . . 1.0 mm (0.039 in)
      Exhaust . . . . 1.3 mm (0.051 in)
Valve timing (at 1 mm lift):

Engine code	RN,RU	NE	DZ,3A	JN	PM to 1988	PM from 1989
Inlet opens	TDC	2° BTDC	3° ATDC	2° BTDC	2° ATDC	5° ATDC
Inlet closes	22° ABDC	34° ABDC	43° ABDC	38° ABDC	38° ABDC	41° ABDC
Exhaust opens	28° BBDC	44° BBDC	37° BBDC	40° BBDC	40° BBDC	37° BBDC
Exhaust closes	6° BTDC	8° BTDC	3° ATDC	4° BTDC	4° BTDC	1° BTDC

Cylinder head
Maximum gasket face distortion . . . . 0.1 mm (0.004 in)
Minimum height (between faces) . . . . 132.55 mm (5.2185 in)
Valve seat angle . . . . 45°

Torque wrench settings

	Nm	lbf ft
Cylinder head bolts:		
Stage 1	40	30
Stage 2	60	44
Stage 3	Angle-tighten 180°	Angle-tighten 180°
Camshaft bearing caps	20	15
Camshaft sprocket	80	59
Front engine support to block	25	18
Engine mounting	35	26
Transmission to engine	55	41
Timing cover	10	7
Tensioner nut	45	33
Tensioner stud	30	22
Rear cover bolt	30	22
Water pump pulley	20	15
Crankshaft sprocket bolt (oiled):		
Hexagon head	180	133
Double hexagon head	90 + 180°	66 + 180°
Intermediate shaft sprocket	80	59
Valve cover	10	7
Engine front lifting eye	25	18
Engine mounting bracket	35	26
Main bearing caps	65	43
Intermediate shaft sealing flange	25	18
Front oil seal housing	20	15
Flywheel/driveplate	100	74
Big-end bearing cap nut	30 + 90°	22 + 90°
Oil pressure switch	25	18
Oil pump mounting bolts	20	15
Oil pump cover and suction tube	10	7
Sump drain plug	30	22
Sump bolts	20	15

1

Part B: Five-cylinder engines

General

Code letters:
  2.0 litre .... PS
  2.2 litre .... KV
  2.3 litre:
    10-valve .... NG
    20-valve 7A
Capacity:
  2.0 litre .... 1994 cc
  2.2 litre .... 2226 cc
  2.3 litre .... 2309 cc
Bore/stroke:
  2.0 litre .... 81.0/77.4 mm (3.19/3.05 in)
  2.2 litre .... 81.0/86.4 mm (3.19/3.40 in)
  2.3 litre .... 82.5/86.4 mm (3.25/3.40 in)
Compression ratio 10.0: 1
Minimum compression pressure .... 8.0 bar (116 lbf/in^2)
Maximum difference between cylinders .... 3.0 bar (43.5 lbf/in^2)
Firing order .... 1-2-4-5-3 (No 1 at timing belt end)

Lubrication system

Oil type/specification .... Multigrade engine oil, viscosity SAE 15W/50 or 20W/50
Oil capacity:
  Including filter .... 4.5 litres (7.9 pints)
  Excluding filter .... 4.0 litres (7.0 pints)
Difference between dipstick minimum and maximum marks .... 1.0 litre (1.8 pints)
Oil pressure (minimum) .... 2.0 bar (29 lbf/in^2) at 2000 rpm and oil temperature of 80°C (176°F)
Oil filter .... Champion C101

Crankshaft

Endfloat:
  New .... 0.07 to 0.23 mm (0.003 to 0.009 in)
  Wear limit .... 0.29 mm (0.011 in)
Maximum main bearing running clearance .... 0.16 mm (0.006 in)
Main bearing journal diameter:
  Standard size .... 57.96 to 57.98 mm (2.2819 to 2.2827 in)
  1st undersize .... 57.71 to 57.73 mm (2.2721 to 2.2728 in)
  2nd undersize .... 57.46 to 57.48 mm (2.2622 to 2.2630 in)
  3rd undersize .... 57.21 to 57.23 mm (2.2524 to 2.2532 in)
Big-end bearing journal diameter:
  Standard size .... 47.76 to 47.78 mm (1.8802 to 1.8810 in)
  1st undersize .... 47.51 to 47.53 mm (1.8704 to 1.8712 in)
  2nd undersize .... 47.26 to 47.28 mm (1.8606 to 1.8613 in)
  3rd undersize .... 47.01 to 47.03 mm (1.8507 to 1.8515 in)
Maximum journal out-of-round .... 0.03 mm (0.0012 in)

Pistons and rings

Piston-to-bore clearance:
  New .... 0.025 mm (0.001 in)
  Wear limit .... 0.08 mm (0.0032 in)
Groove-to-ring clearance:
  New:
    Compression rings .... 0.02 to 0.07 mm (0.0008 to 0.0028 in)
    Oil scraper ring .... 0.02 to 0.06 mm (0.0008 to 0.0024 in)
  Wear limit .... 0.15 mm (0.0059 in)
Piston diameter .... As for four-cylinder engine*
Bore diameter .... As for four-cylinder engine*
Cylinder bore:
  Maximum out-of-round .... 0.04 mm (0.0016 in)
Piston ring endgap clearance (ring 15 mm/0.6 in from bottom of bore):
  New compression .... 0.20 to 0.40 mm (0.0079 to 0.0158 in)
  New oil scraper .... 0.25 to 0.50 mm (0.0098 to 0.0197 in)
  Wear limit .... 1.0 mm (0.040 in)
Nominal sizes are 81.0/82.5 mm (3.19/3.25 in)

Connecting rods

Maximum big-end endfloat .... 0.40 mm (0.0158 in)
Big-end bearing running clearance wear limit .... 0.12 mm (0.0047 in)

Camshaft

Maximum endfloat:
  10-valve engine .... 0.15 mm (0.006 in)
  20-valve engine .... 0.20 mm (0.008 in)
Bearing running clearance:
  10-valve engine .... 0.1 mm (0.004 in)
  20-valve engine .... 0.2 mm (0.008 in)
Camshaft run-out (max) .... 0.01 mm (0.004 in)

Valves

Valve head angle .... 45°
Valve guides .... As for four-cylinder engine
Valve timing (at 1 mm lift):

Engine code	PS	KV,NG	7A
Inlet opens	2° ATDC	TDC	6° BTDC
Inlet closes	31° ABDC	41° ABDC	38° ABDC
Exhaust opens	31° BBDC	40° BBDC	42° BBDC
Exhaust closes	2° BTDC	1° ATDC	3° BTDC

Cylinder head

Minimum height:
  Between faces on 10-valve engine .... 132.75 mm (5.2264 in)
  Between bolt contact face and joint face .... 118.1 mm (4.6496 in)

Torque wrench settings

	Nm	lbf ft
Cylinder head bolts:		
Stage 1	40	30
Stage 2	60	44
Stage 3	Angle-tighten 180°	Angle-tighten 180°
Transmission to engine:		
M8	20	15
M10	45	33
M12	65	48
Subframe	70	52
Front support arm	45	33
Engine mounting	45	33
Timing cover	10	7
Camshaft sprocket - 10-valve engine	80	59
Camshaft sprocket - 20-valve engine	65	48
Crankshaft gear bolt (using tool 2079 - see text)	350	258
Valve cover	10	7
Oil pump intake pipe	10	7
Sump drain plug 10-valve engine	40	30
Sump drain plug 20-valve engine	30	22
Flywheel cover	25	19
Sump (10-valve engine)	20	15
Oil pump	10	7
Main bearing caps	65	48
Flywheel/driveplate	100	74
Timing belt idler	20	5
Big-end bearing nut	30 + 90°	22 + 90°
Big-end bearing cap oil jet	10	7
Camshaft bearing caps - 10-valve engine	20	15
Camshaft bearing caps - 20-valve engine	15	11
Rear timing cover	20	15
Crankshaft pulley	20	15
Oil check valve (20-valve engine)	6	4
Oil pressure switch adaptor	50	37
Sump (20-valve engine):		
M6	10	7
M8	20	15

1

Part A: Four-cylinder engines

1 General description

The engine is of four-cylinder, in-line overhead camshaft type, mounted conventionally at the front of the car. The crankshaft is of five-bearing type, and the centre main bearing shells incorporate flanged or separate thrustwashers to control crankshaft endfloat. The camshaft is driven by a toothed belt from the crankshaft sprocket. The belt also drives the intermediate shaft, which is used to drive the distributor, oil pump and on carburettor engines, the fuel pump. The valves are operated from the camshaft through hydraulic bucket type tappets, and the valve clearances are adjusted automatically.

The engine has a full-flow lubrication system from a gear type oil pump mounted in the sump, and driven by an extension of the distributor, which is itself geared to the intermediate shaft. The oil filter is of the cartridge type, mounted on the left-hand side of the cylinder block. Two oil pressure switches are located on the oil filter housing, the lower one operating at 0.3 bar (4.35 lbf/in²) and the upper one at 1.8 bar (26.1 lbf/in²)

2 Routine maintenance

Carry out the following procedures at the intervals given in 'Routine maintenance' at the beginning of the manual.

Change engine oil, and renew oil filter

1 To ensure complete draining of the oil, it is preferable that the engine is warm.
2 Remove the splash guard from under the engine.
3 Position a suitable container beneath the left-hand side of the engine, and unscrew the oil filler cap from the valve cover. Unscrew the drain plug from the sump (photo), and allow the oil to drain.
4 Unscrew the oil filter from the housing, using a filter strap if necessary (photo). Keep it upright to prevent spillage of oil.
5 Clean the mating faces of the new oil filter and the housing, then smear a little engine oil on the filter seal. Screw the filter onto the housing and tighten by hand only (photos).
6 Clean the drain plug, and check that the washer is in good condition. Renew the

washer if necessary, clean the sump around the plug hole, then refit and tighten the drain plug.
7 Pour the correct quantity and grade of oil through the oil filler neck on the valve cover. Refit the cap.
8 Run the engine to check for leaks, then refit the splash guard.

Check engine for leaks

9 Examine the engine for oil leaks, and for leaks from the cooling system, and fuel system.
10 Check all pipes, hoses, and connections for deterioration.

Check engine oil level

11 Position the vehicle on level ground. If the engine has been running allow several minutes for the oil to drain back into the sump.
12 Pull the dipstick from its tube, wipe it clean, then fully re-insert it and pull it out again. The oil level should be at, or near, the maximum level mark. If not, top up with the correct grade of oil after removing the oil filler cap. The difference between the minimum and maximum marks is 1.0 litre (1.76 pints) (photos).
13 Refit the dipstick and filler cap.

2.3 Engine oil drain plug (arrowed) on the sump

2.4 Using a filter strap to unscrew the oil filter

2.5A Oil the filter seal . . .

2.5B . . . then screw the oil filter onto the housing

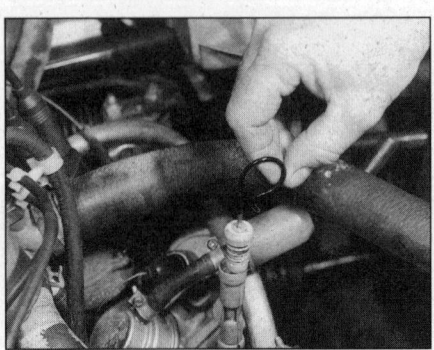
2.1 2A Pulling out the engine oil level dipstick

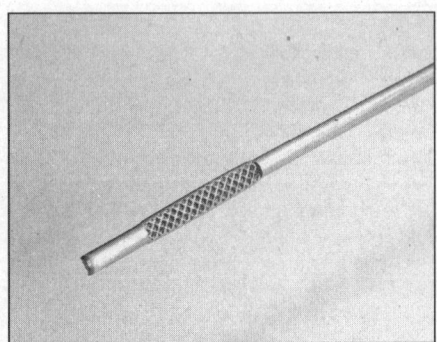
2.1 2B Markings on the engine oil level dipstick

2.1 2C Topping-up the engine oil level

6.7 Disconnecting the crankcase ventilation hose from the valve cover

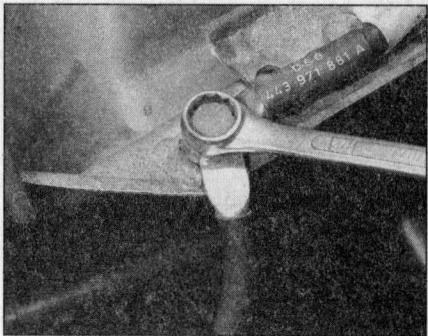

6.8A Unbolt the earth cable from the battery support bracket . . .

3 Major operations possible with the engine in the car

The following operations can be carried out without having to remove the engine from the car:

(a) Removal of the camshaft and timing belt
(b) Removal and servicing of the cylinder head
(c) Removing of the flywheel/driveplate (after first removing the transmission)
(d) Removal of the sump (after first lowering the subframe)
(e) Removal of the oil pump, pistons and connecting rods

4 Major operations only possible after removal of the engine from the car

The following operations can only be carried out after removal of the engine from the car:

(a) Removal of the intermediate shaft
(b) Removal of the crankshaft and main bearings

5 Method of engine removal

The engine can be lifted from the car either separately or together with the manual gearbox.

On automatic transmission models, it is recommended that the engine is removed separately because of the extra weight involved.

6 Engine - removal and refitting

1 Remove the bonnet as described in Chapter 11, and stand it on cardboard in a safe place.
2 Disconnect the battery negative lead.
3 Unbolt and remove the splash shield from under the engine.
4 Position a suitable container beneath the sump, then unscrew the drain plug and drain the engine oil. Clean, refit, and tighten the plug after all the oil has drained.
5 Drain the cooling system as described in Chapter 2.
6 Remove the air cleaner and ducting, and where applicable, the final injection components, with reference to Chapter 3.
7 Disconnect the crankcase ventilation hose from the valve cover (where applicable) (photo).
8 Unbolt the earth cable from the battery support bracket and cylinder head (photos).
9 Disconnect the fuel supply and return hoses at the bulkhead (photos).
10 Disconnect the accelerator and choke cables as applicable, with reference to Chapter 3.
11 Disconnect the heater hoses at the

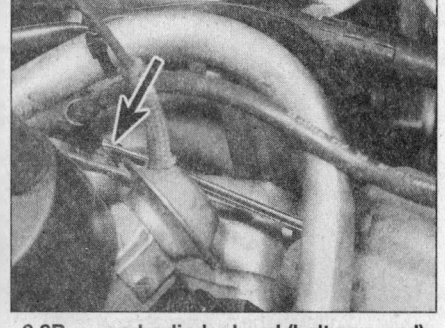

6.8B . . . and cylinder head (bolt arrowed)

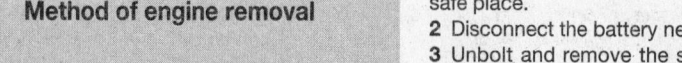

6.9A Disconnecting the fuel supply hose . . .

6.9B . . . and return hose

6.11A Disconnecting the heater hoses from the cylinder head outlet . . .

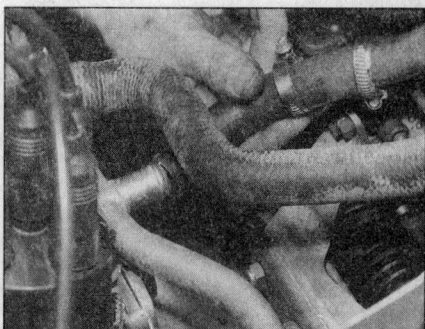

6.11B . . . and the return pipe

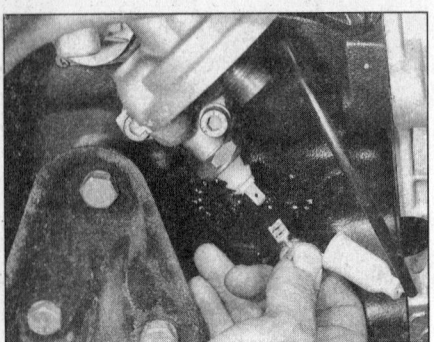

6.1 2A Disconnecting the low oil pressure . . .

6.1 2B . . . and high oil pressure switch wiring . . .

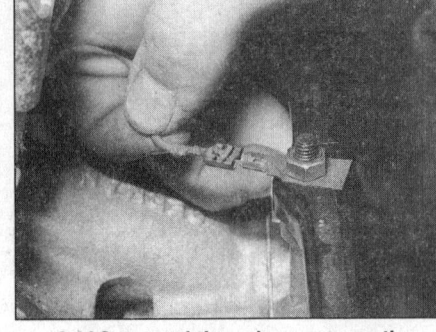

6.12C . . . and the valve cover earth terminal

bulkhead noting their location. Disconnect them from the cylinder head outlet and return pipe, and remove them (photos).

12 Note the routing and location of the engine wiring harness, then disconnect the various wires and remove the harness. To prevent confusion when reconnecting the wires, it is a good idea to identify the location of each wire with a piece of adhesive tape marked accordingly. A list of the wires follows, but this will vary according to model.

Coolant temperature senders
Coil HT lead
Oil pressure switches
Alternator
Gearbox switches and speedo sender
Oil temperature sender
Earth cable from valve cover (photo)

Starter motor
Carburettor or fuel injection equipment
Distributor

13 Disconnect the vacuum hoses from the distributor and inlet manifold as applicable.
14 Remove the radiator as described in Chapter 2.
15 On models equipped with power steering, remove the pump with reference to Chapter 10, but leave the hoses connected, and place the pump on one side.
16 On models equipped with air conditioning, remove the compressor with reference to Chapter 11, but leave the refrigerant pipes connected, and place the unit to one side.
17 Disconnect and remove the bottom hose from the water pump.
18 Disconnect and remove the top hose from

the outlet elbow on the left-hand side of the cylinder head (photo).
19 If necessary, disconnect the bypass hose from the water pump and cylinder head outlet elbow (photo).
20 Disconnect the hose from the inlet manifold, and remove the hose and coolant pipe from the rear of the engine after unscrewing the support bracket bolt (photos).
21 If required, the alternator and drivebelt may be removed at this stage with reference to Chapter 12.
22 Remove the radiator grille with reference to Chapter 11.
23 Release the bonnet catch control cable (Chapter 11), then unbolt and remove the crossmember from the front of the engine compartment (photo).

6.18 Disconnecting the top hose from the cylinder head outlet elbow

6.19 Disconnecting the bypass hose from the cylinder head outlet

6.20A Unscrewing the gearbox-to-engine bolt which also secures the rear engine coolant pipe

6.20B Removing the rear engine coolant pipe and hose

6.23 Engine compartment front crossmember removal

6.26A Engine front support bar . . .

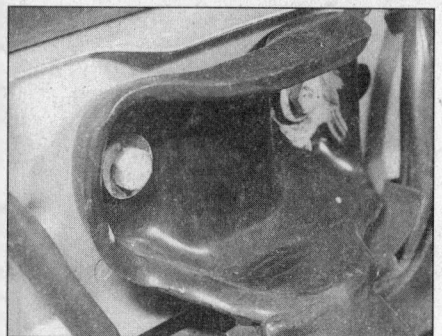

6.26B . . . and support bracket

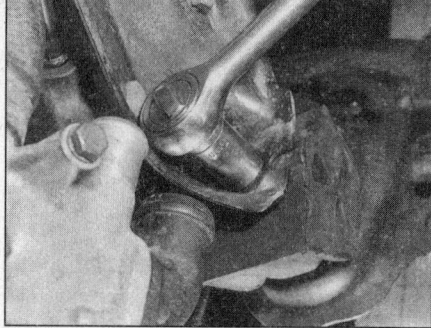

6.39 Unscrewing the engine mounting nuts

6.40 Removing the engine together with the manual gearbox

24 On manual gearbox models, remove the clutch slave cylinder with reference to Chapter 5, but leave the pipe connected, and position the cylinder on the bulkhead.

25 Unscrew the nuts securing the exhaust downpipe to the exhaust manifold.

26 Unbolt the engine front support bar from the cylinder block. If necessary, the support bracket may also be unbolted from the front crossmember (photos).

Removing engine with manual gearbox attached

27 With the handbrake applied, jack up the front of the car and support on axle stands.

28 Unbolt the exhaust downpipe from the bracket on the side of the gearbox. For additional working room, it is recommended that the complete exhaust system is removed, with reference to Chapter 3. If the system is the original one fitted, then it will be necessary to unbolt the left-hand rear shock absorber, and raise the rear of the car in order to remove the system. If a service replacement system is fitted, it can be split above the rear axle, making removal easier. Where applicable, disconnect the wiring from the catalytic converter.

29 Unbolt the earth cable from the gearbox.

30 Unscrew the nuts and remove the crossmember from the underbody behind the gearbox.

31 Where a Procon-Ten safety system is fitted, disconnect the cables from the gearbox, with reference to Chapter 11.

32 Unscrew the locking bolt and slide the gearshift coupling from the gearbox shift rod.

33 Unbolt and remove the gearbox front cover.

34 Where applicable, unbolt the driveshaft cover from under the car.

35 Unscrew and remove the bolts securing the driveshaft inner constant velocity joints to the gearbox drive flanges. Note the location of the bolt plates, and remove the gaskets if fitted. Tie the driveshafts to one side, and wrap the inner joints in plastic bags in order to prevent entry of dust and dirt.

36 Lower the car to the ground if necessary, then support the gearbox with a trolley jack.

37 Unscrew the bolt securing the rear support bar to the rubber mounting on the rear of the gearbox. Loosen the outer bolt, and swing the bar to one side. Alternatively, use an Allen key to unbolt the mounting complete from the gearbox.

38 Connect a hoist, and just take the weight of the engine. The hoist should be positioned so that the weight of the gearbox will tilt the engine slightly backwards when lifted.

39 Unscrew the nuts from the engine mountings (photo).

40 Lift the engine from the mountings and move it forwards, then lower the trolley jack, and lift the engine and gearbox from the engine compartment, turning it as necessary to clear the body (photo).

41 Lower the engine and gearbox to the floor.

42 If necessary, separate the gearbox from the engine by removing the starter motor (Chapter 12), gearbox front cover, and engine-to-gearbox bolts.

Removing engine without transmission

43 With the handbrake applied, jack up the front of the car and support on axle stands.

44 Remove the exhaust downpipe (ie from the exhaust system front section to the exhaust manifold).

45 Unbolt and remove the transmission front cover.

46 Remove the starter motor, as described in Chapter 12.

47 On automatic transmission models, unscrew the bolts securing the torque converter to the driveplate, working through the front cover aperture. It will be necessary to turn the engine to gain access to each bolt, and to do this, either turn the starter ring gear on the driveplate, or use a spanner on the crankshaft pulley bolt. Hold the starter ring gear stationary with a screwdriver while unscrewing the bolts.

48 Also on automatic transmission models, disconnect the kickdown cable.

49 Unscrew and remove the lower bolts securing the transmission to the engine.

50 Lower the front of the car to the ground.

51 Connect a hoist and just take the weight of the engine. The hoist should be positioned centrally over the engine.

52 Support the transmission with a trolley jack.

53 Unscrew and remove the remaining bolts securing the transmission to the engine, noting the location of any brackets and the earth strap.

54 Unscrew the nuts from the engine mountings.

55 Lift the engine from the mountings, and reposition the trolley jack beneath the transmission.

56 Pull the engine from the transmission. Make sure that, on automatic transmission models, the torque converter remains fully engaged with the transmission splines.

57 Position the engine as required and lift it from the engine compartment (photo), then lower it to the floor.

58 On automatic transmission models, make sure that the torque converter remains in position by bolting a piece of bent metal to one of the mounting bolt holes.

Refitting

59 Refitting is a reversal of the removal procedure, but before starting the engine, check that it has been filled with oil, and also that the cooling system has been filled with coolant. Before tightening the engine and gearbox mountings, rock the engine by hand to ensure correct alignment. Make sure that the starter cable is not touching the engine or mounting bracket. Adjust the accelerator and choke cables as applicable, with reference to Chapter 3.

6.57 Removing the engine without the transmission

1

7 Engine dismantling - general

1 If possible, position the engine on a bench or strong table for the dismantling procedure. Two or three blocks of wood will be necessary to support the engine in an upright position.
2 Cleanliness is most important, and if the engine is dirty, it should be cleaned with paraffin before commencing work.
3 Avoid working with the engine directly on a concrete floor, as grit presents a real source of trouble.
4 As parts are removed, clean them in a paraffin bath. However, do not immerse parts with internal oilways in paraffin, as it is difficult to remove.
5 It is advisable to have suitable containers to hold small items according to their use, as this will help when reassembling the engine and also prevent possible losses.
6 Always obtain complete sets of gaskets when the engine is being dismantled, but retain the old gaskets with a view to using them as a pattern to make a replacement if a new one is not available.
7 When possible, refit nuts, bolts, and washers in their location after being removed, as this helps to protect the threads, and will also be helpful when reassembling the engine.
8 Retain unserviceable components in order to compare them with the new parts supplied.

8 Ancillary components - removal and refitting

With the engine removed from the car, the externally mounted ancillary components given in the following list can be removed. The removal sequence need not necessarily follow the order given.

Inlet and exhaust manifolds (Chapter 3)
Fuel pump or fuel injection components (Chapter 3)
HT leads and spark plugs (Chapter 4)
Oil filter (Section 2)
Distributor (Chapter 4)
Dipstick
Alternator (Chapter 12)
Clutch (Chapter 5)
Oil cooler from the oil filter housing (where fitted)

9 Engine - complete dismantling

1 Mark the flywheel in relation to the end of the crankshaft.
2 Have an assistant support the engine, then unscrew the flywheel/driveplate bolts while holding the unit stationary. Temporarily insert a bolt in the cylinder block, and use a screwdriver to hold the flywheel, or make up a holding tool as shown in photo 25.79D.
3 Remove the flywheel/driveplate from the crankshaft (photo).
4 Remove the intermediate plate from the dowels on the rear of the cylinder block (photo). Note the wiring clip location.
5 If necessary, remove the dowels from the block (photo).
6 Unscrew the nuts, and remove the fuel container and bracket from the valve cover (where applicable).
7 Unscrew and remove the oil filter.
8 Unbolt the oil filter housing from the block, and remove the gasket (photos).
9 Un bolt the outlet elbow from the side of the cylinder head. Prise the rubber O-ring from the base of the elbow (photos).
10 Unbolt the outlet housing from the rear of

9.3 Removing the flywheel

9.4 Removing the intermediate plate

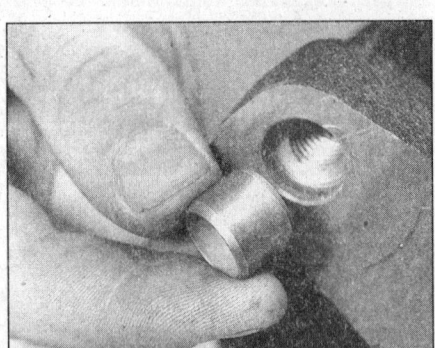

9.5 Removing dowels from rear of block

9.8A Removing the oil filter housing . . .

9.8B . . . and gasket

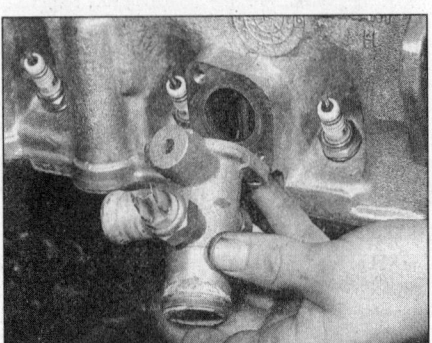

9.9A Remove the outlet elbow . . .

9.9B . . . and prise out the rubber O-ring

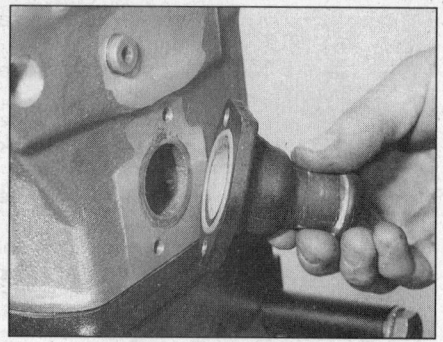

9.10A Remove the outlet housing

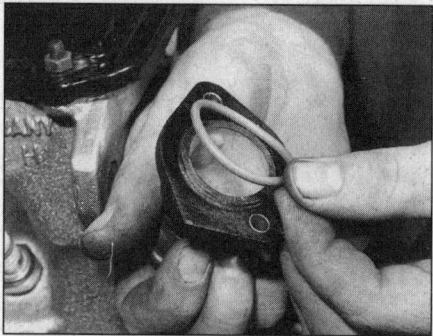

9.10B . . . and prise out the rubber O-ring

9.14A Releasing the upper timing cover clips

the cylinder head. Prise the rubber O-ring from the base of the housing (photos).

11 Using an Allen key, unscrew the bolts and remove the pulley from the water pump.

12 Unscrew the nut and remove the special bolt retaining the lower timing cover to the water pump assembly.

13 Unbolt the water pump assembly from the cylinder block, and remove the sealing O-ring.

14 Release the clips, and (where fitted) unscrew the nut, then remove the upper timing cover (photos).

15 Unscrew the nuts, and remove the timing belt rear upper cover from the front of the valve cover (photo).

16 Unscrew the remaining valve cover nuts, noting the location of the wire retaining straps and the earth terminal (photo).

17 Remove the reinforcement strips, and lift off the valve cover (photos).

18 Remove the oil deflector (photo).

19 Remove the gasket from the studs on the cylinder head (photo).

20 Remove the semi-circular gasket from the groove in the camshaft front bearing cap. Also remove the rubber plug from the rear of the cylinder head (photos).

21 Mark the drivebelt pulley and crankshaft sprocket in relation to each other, then using an Allen key, unscrew the bolts securing the drivebelt pulley to the crankshaft sprocket. Remove the drivebelt pulley (photos).

22 Unscrew the bolts and remove the lower

9.1 4B Removing the upper timing cover

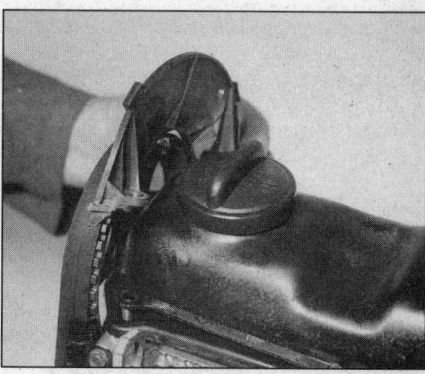

9.15 Timing belt rear upper cover removal

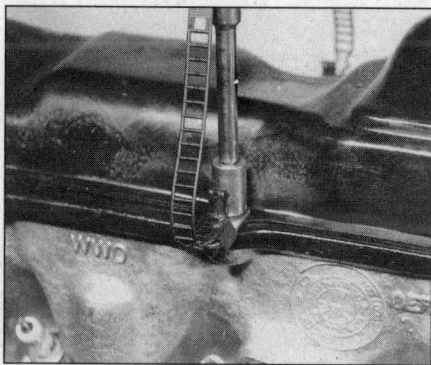

9.16 Unscrewing the valve cover nuts

9.17A Remove the reinforcement strips . . .

1

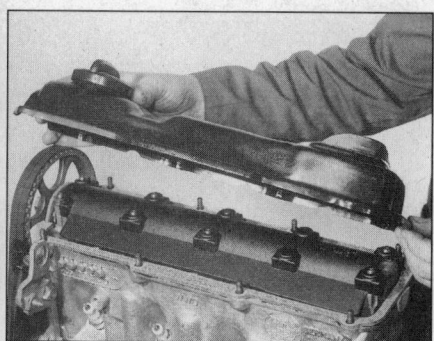

9.17B . . . and lift off the valve cover

9.18 Oil deflector removal

9.19 Valve cover gasket removal

9.20A Removing the valve cover front gasket . . .

9.20B . . . and the rear rubber plug

9.21A Remove the bolts . . .

9.21B . . . and withdraw the pulley

9.22A Lower timing belt cover

timing belt cover. An Allen key will be required for one of the bolts. Recover the special spacer from the top of the cover (photos).

23 Turn the crankshaft clockwise with a socket on the crankshaft pulley bolt, until the mark on the rear of the camshaft sprocket is aligned with the top of the cylinder head on the left-hand side.

24 Loosen the nut, and turn the tensioner hub anti-clockwise to release the tension on the timing belt.

25 Mark the timing belt with an arrow to indicate its normal direction of rotation, then remove it from the tensioner, camshaft sprocket. Intermediate shaft sprocket, and the crankshaft sprocket (photo).

26 Unscrew the nut, remove the washer, and withdraw the tensioner wheel and hub from the stud on the front of the cylinder head (photos).

27 Unscrew the bolt securing the camshaft sprocket to the camshaft, while holding the sprocket stationary. A tool may be used to hold the sprocket stationary as shown in photo 25.53, and this is to be preferred to inserting a tool through a hole in the sprocket. The upper surface of the cylinder head may be damaged if the latter method is used.

28 Remove the bolt and washer, and pull the sprocket from the camshaft. Remove the Woodruff key (photos).

29 Using a screwdriver, prise out the camshaft front oil seal (photo).

9.22B Lower timing belt cover spacer

9.25 Removing the timing belt

9.26A Tensioner wheel and hub

9.26B Remove the nut and washer . . .

9.26C . . . and withdraw the tensioner

9.28A Camshaft sprocket bolt removal

9.28B Woodruff key removal

9.29 Camshaft front oil seal removal

30 Mark the camshaft bearing caps for position, then progressively unscrew the nuts, and remove the caps (photo).

31 Lift the camshaft from the cylinder head (photo).

32 Have ready a box with internal compartments, suitably marked to identify the bucket tappet locations, numbered from the front of the engine.

33 Lift the hydraulic bucket tappets from their locations over the valves (photo). Place the tappets *upside-down* in the box, to prevent the oil draining out.

34 Loosen the bolt securing the sprocket to the intermediate shaft while holding the sprocket stationary. Use the tool shown in photo 25.46.

35 Remove the bolt, and pull the sprocket from the intermediate shaft. Remove the Woodruff key (photos).

36 Unbolt and remove the timing belt rear cover (photos).

37 Unbolt the engine front lifting eye bracket from the cylinder head (photo).

38 Using a splined socket, unscrew the cylinder head bolts a turn at a time in reverse order to that shown in Fig. 1.2.

39 Remove the cylinder head bolts, together with their washers (photo).

40 With all the bolts removed, lift the cylinder head from the block (photo). If it is stuck, tap it free with a wooden mallet. Do not insert a lever into the gasket joint.

9.30 Camshaft bearing cap removal

9.31 Removing the camshaft

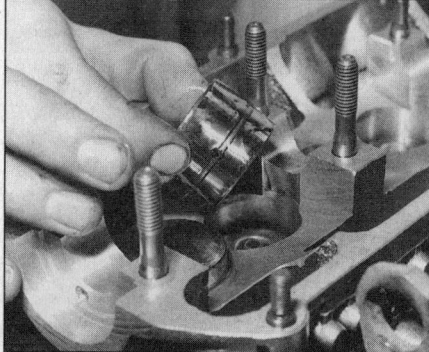

9.33 Removing a bucket tappet

9.35A Unscrew the bolt . . .

9.35B . . . withdraw the intermediate shaft sprocket . . .

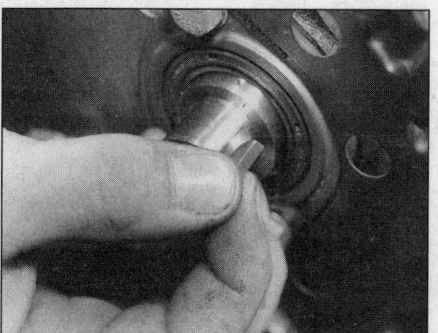

9.35C . . . and remove the Woodruff key

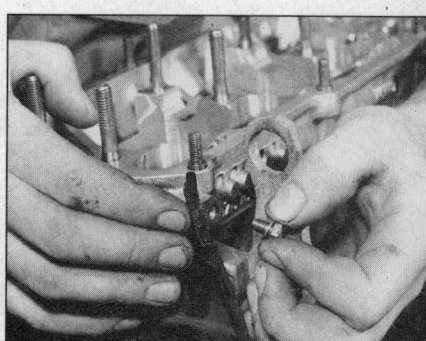

9.36A Removing the timing belt rear cover upper bolt . . .

1

9.36B . . . and lower bolt

9.37 Removing the engine front lifting eye bracket

9.39 Removing the cylinder head bolts

9.40 Lifting the cylinder head from the block

9.41 Cylinder head gasket removal

41 Remove the cylinder head gasket from the block (photo).
42 Unbolt and remove the alternator mounting bracket (photo).
43 Unbolt the engine mounting bracket from the left-hand side of the block (photos).
44 Unbolt the engine mounting bracket and bar from the right-hand side of the block, using an Allen key (photos).
45 Unscrew the two bolts from the intermediate shaft sealing flange. Remove the flange, and prise out the O-ring and oil seal (photos).
46 Withdraw the intermediate shaft from the block (photos).
47 Temporarily insert two flywheel/driveplate

9.42 Alternator mounting bracket removal

9.43A Left-hand engine mounting bracket bolts

9.43B Removing the left-hand engine mounting bracket

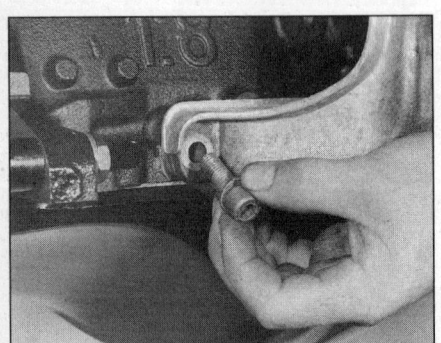

9.44A Unscrew the bolts . . .

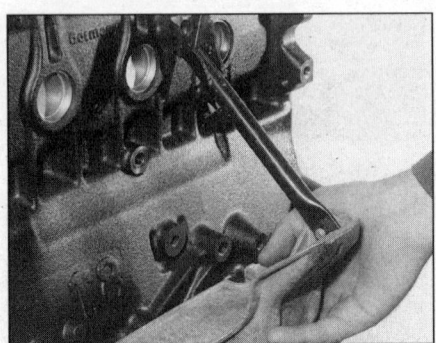

9.44B . . . and remove the right-hand engine mounting bracket and bar

9.45A Remove the intermediate shaft sealing flange . . .

Four-cylinder engines 1•15

9.45B . . . remove the O-ring . . .

9.45C . . . and prise out the oil seal

9.46A Withdrawing the intermediate shaft
from the block

bolts in the rear of the crankshaft, and use a long
bar to hold the crankshaft stationary. Unscrew
the crankshaft sprocket bolt (very tight), and
remove the sprocket from the crankshaft (photo).
48 Hold the dipstick tube with a pair of grips,
and tap it carefully from the hole in the block
(photo).
49 Invert the engine, then unscrew and
remove the sump bolts.
50 Remove the sump and gasket (photos).
51 Unbolt and remove the crankshaft front
and rear oil seal housings, and remove the
gaskets (photo).
52 Using an Allen key, unscrew the bolts and
remove the suction pipe from the oil pump.
Remove the O-ring seal (photos).

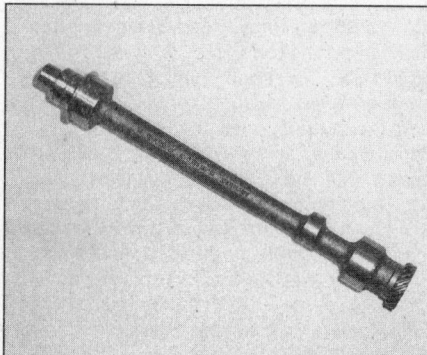

9.46B Intermediate shaft removed

9.47 Crankshaft sprocket removal

9.48 Dipstick tube removal

9.50A Removing the sump . . .

9.50B . . . and gasket

9.51 Removing the crankshaft front oil seal
housing and gasket

9.52A Removing the oil pump suction
pipe . . .

9.52B . . . and O-ring seal

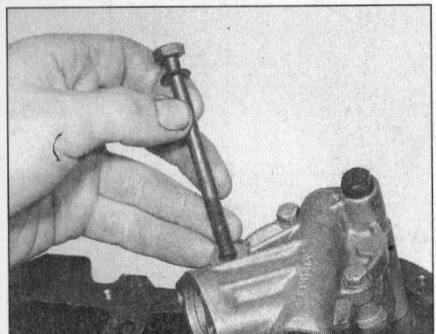

9.53A Unscrew and remove the large oil pump mounting bolts . . .

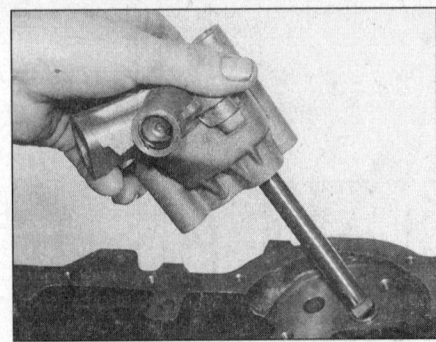

9.53B . . . and withdraw the oil pump

9.54 Centre-punch markings (arrowed) on No 4 cylinder connecting rod and big-end cap

53 Unscrew and remove the large oil pump mounting bolts, then withdraw the pump from the block (photos).

54 Mark each connecting rod and big-end cap in relation to its cylinder and position, using a centre-punch (photo).

55 Turn the crankshaft so that No 1 piston is at the bottom of its bore, then unscrew the nuts and remove the big-end bearing cap (photo).

56 With the block on its side, use the handle of a hammer to push the connecting rod and piston out of the top of the cylinder. Put the bearing cap with its connecting rod. If any of the bearing shells become detached while removing the connecting rod and big-end cap, ensure that they are placed with their matching components.

57 Repeat the procedure given in paragraphs 55 and 56 to remove the remaining pistons and connecting rods.

58 Check that each main bearing cap is numbered for position (photo), numbering from the front of the engine.

59 Unscrew and remove the bolts from caps 1, 2, 4 and 5, then remove the caps.

60 With cap No 3 still in position, determine the crankshaft endfloat with a feeler blade inserted between the thrustwasher and the crankshaft web (photo). This will give an indication of the wear in the thrustwashers by comparison with the endfloat given in the Specifications.

61 Unbolt and remove No 3 main bearing cap.

62 Make sure that each bearing shell is kept with its corresponding cap.

63 Lift the crankshaft from the crankcase (photo).

64 Remove the bearing shells from the crankcase, keeping them identified for location (photo).

65 The engine is now completely dismantled.

10 Timing belt and sprockets - removal, examination and refitting

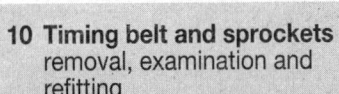

1 Remove the radiator (Chapter 2), and the drivebelts for the alternator, power steering pump and air conditioner compressor (as applicable) .

2 Disconnect the battery negative lead.

3 Unbolt and remove the splash shield from under the engine.

4 For better access, the alternator, power steering pump and air conditioner compressor may be removed, leaving the lines connected to the pump and compressor.

5 Using an Allen key, unscrew the bolts and remove the pulley from the water pump.

6 Unscrew the nut, and remove the special bolt retaining the lower timing cover to the water pump assembly.

7 Release the clips, and (where fitted) unscrew the nut, then remove the upper timing cover.

8 Mark the drivebelt pulley and crankshaft sprocket in relation to each other, then unbolt the pulley using an Allen key.

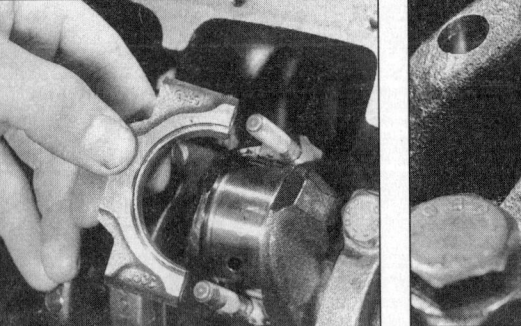

9.55 Big-end bearing cap removal

9.58 No 2 main bearing cap

9.60 Checking the crankshaft endfloat with a feeler blade

9.63 Lifting the crankshaft from the crankcase

9.64 Removing the upper main bearing shells from the crankcase

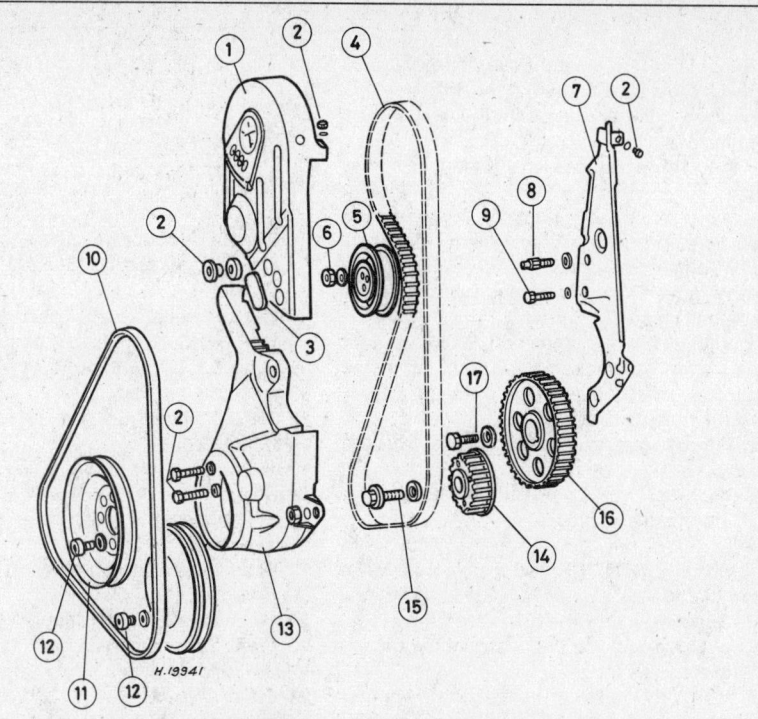

Fig 1.1 Timing belt components (Sec 10)

1 Upper timing cover	7 Rear timing belt cover	13 Lower timing cover
2 Nut	8 Stud	14 Crankshaft sprocket
3 Plug	9 Bolt	15 Bolt
4 Timing belt	10 Drivebelt	16 Intermediate shaft
5 Tensioner	11 Pulley	sprocket
6 Nut	12 Bolt	17 Bolt

9 Unscrew the bolts, and remove the lower timing belt cover. An Allen key will be required for one of the bolts. Recover the special spacer from the top of the cover.

10 Turn the crankshaft clockwise with a socket on the crankshaft pulley bolt, until the mark on the rear of the camshaft sprocket is aligned with the top of the cylinder head on the left-hand side. As the valve cover and reinforcement strips are still in place, extra care will be necessary.

11 Loosen the nut, and turn the tensioner hub anti-clockwise to release the tension on the timing belt.

12 Mark the timing belt with an arrow to indicate its normal direction of rotation, then remove it from the tensioner, camshaft sprocket, intermediate shaft sprocket, and the crankshaft sprocket.

13 Unscrew the nut, remove the washer, and withdraw the tensioner wheel and hub from the stud on the front of the cylinder head.

14 Unscrew the camshaft sprocket bolt, while holding the sprocket stationary using a tool as shown in photo 25.53. Remove the bolt, washer, sprocket and key.

15 Unscrew the intermediate shaft sprocket bolt in the same manner. Remove the bolt, sprocket and key.

16 Unscrew the crankshaft sprocket bolt, and remove the sprocket. The bolt is very

tight, and the crankshaft must be held stationary. On manual gearbox models, engage top gear and apply the handbrake firmly. On automatic transmission models, unbolt the transmission front cover and use a wide-bladed screwdriver in the ring gear to hold the crankshaft stationary.

17 Clean all the sprockets, and examine them for wear and damage. Spin the tensioner, and check that it runs smoothly.

18 Examine the timing belt for wear and deterioration, particularly at the base of the teeth. Audi do not specify a renewal interval for the belt, but if it has covered approximately 40 000 miles (60 000 km) or more it should be renewed as a precaution.

19 Refitting is a reversal of removal, but note the following additional points:

(a) Tighten all nuts and bolts to the specified torque
(b) Refer to Section 25 paragraphs 29 and 30 when refitting the crankshaft sprocket but hold the crankshaft stationary as described in paragraph 16 in this Section
(c) Refer to Section 25 paragraphs 55 to 62 for the timing belt tensioning procedure
(d) Adjust the tension of the alternator power steering pump and air conditioner compressor drivebelts with reference to Chapters 12, 10 and 11 respectively

11 Camshaft and tappets - removal, examination and refitting

1 If the hydraulic tappets are noisy when the engine has reached normal operating temperature, the following method will determine which tappets are defective, so that they may be renewed. Irregular noises when starting the engine from cold are quite normal.
2 Run the engine to normal temperature, until the electric cooling fan has switched on once.
3 Run the engine for a further two minutes at 2500 rpm, and check the tappets for noise. If still evident, proceed as follows after stopping the engine.
4 Remove the valve cover, then turn the crankshaft with a socket on the front sprocket bolt until the cam over the tappet to be checked is pointing upwards.
5 Using a non-metallic tool, press the tappet downwards. If the free travel is more than 0.1 mm (0.004 in) before the valve opens, the tappet should be renewed as follows.
6 Remove the air cleaner or fuel injection components as applicable, with reference to Chapter 3.
7 Unscrew the nuts, and remove the fuel container and bracket from the valve cover (where applicable).
8 Remove the timing belt with reference to Section 10. Do not remove the tensioner or the sprockets from the intermediate shaft and crankshaft.
9 Unscrew the nuts, and remove the timing belt rear upper cover from the front of the valve cover.
10 Unscrew the remaining valve cover nuts, noting the location of the wire retaining straps and the earth terminal. Disconnect the crankcase ventilation hose.
11 Remove the reinforcement strips, and lift off the valve cover.
12 Remove the oil deflector.
13 Remove the gasket from the studs on the cylinder head.
14 Remove the semi-circular gasket from the groove in the camshaft front bearing cap. Also remove the rubber plug from the rear of the cylinder head.
15 Using a screwdriver, prise out the camshaft front oil seal.
16 Mark the camshaft bearing caps for position and orientation, then progressively unscrew the nuts and remove the caps.

11.20 The camshaft removed

17 Lift the camshaft from the cylinder head.
18 Have ready a box with internal compartments, suitably marked to identify the bucket tappet locations, numbered from the front of the engine.
19 Remove the hydraulic bucket tappets, and place them *upside-down* in the box, to prevent the oil draining out.
20 Clean the camshaft (photo), and examine it for wear and damage, in particular on the peaks of the cams and on the bearing journals. Obtain a new oil seal.
21 Commence reassembly by oiling the hydraulic bucket tappets, and insert them in their previously-noted positions over the valves.
22 Oil the bearing journals on the camshaft, then lower the camshaft into position on the bucket tappets, making sure that the cams for No 1 cylinder are pointing upwards.
23 Refit bearing caps 2 and 5 (No 4 position is blanked off). Fit the nuts, and tighten them progressively to the specified torque. Make sure that the caps are fitted the same way round as noted on removal, because they are slightly offset.
24 Refit bearing caps 1 and 3, fit the nuts, and tighten progressively to the specified torque.
25 Smear a little oil on the lips and outer rim of the new oil seal. Locate it on the front of the camshaft, and use a socket and mallet to drive it squarely into position until flush with the cylinder head.
26 Fit a new rubber plug and semi-circular gasket to the head and front bearing cap, then locate a new gasket on the studs.
27 Refit the oil deflector, valve cover, and associated parts. Fit and tighten the nuts.
28 Refit the timing belt, with reference to Section 10.
29 Refit the fuel container and bracket to the valve cover (if applicable).
30 Refit the air cleaner or fuel injection components as applicable, with reference to Chapter 3.
31 If any of the hydraulic tappets have been renewed, **do not** start the engine, or turn the engine, until at least thirty minutes have elapsed. This is to allow time for any excess oil in the tappets to drain off. If this precaution is not taken, there is the danger of a valve striking a piston.

12 Cylinder head - removal and refitting

1 Disconnect the battery negative lead.
2 Drain the cooling system, as described in Chapter 2.
3 Remove the inlet and exhaust manifolds (see Chapter 3), and the HT leads and spark plugs (Chapter 4).
4 Remove the camshaft and tappets with reference to Section 11. Remove the alternator (Chapter 12).

5 Unbolt the earth cable from the cylinder head.
6 Disconnect the heater hose, top hose, and bypass hose from the cylinder head.
7 Disconnect the wiring from the temperature senders.
8 Unbolt and remove the timing belt rear cover.
9 Using a splined socket, unscrew the cylinder head bolts a turn at a time, in reverse order to that shown in Fig. 1.2.
10 Remove the cylinder head bolts, together with their washers.
11 With all the bolts removed, lift the cylinder head from the block. If it is stuck, tap it free with a wooden mallet. Do not insert a lever into the gasket joint.
12 Remove the cylinder head gasket from the block.
13 Thoroughly clean the contact faces of the cylinder head and block.
14 Locate a new gasket on the block, with the words 'OBEN TOP' facing upwards. Make sure that the location dowels are in position.
15 Carefully lower the head onto the block. Do not use any jointing compound on the cylinder head joint.
16 Insert the cylinder head bolts, together with their washers, and initially hand-tighten them using a splined socket.
17 Using the sequence shown in Fig. 1.2, tighten all the bolts to the stage 1 torque given

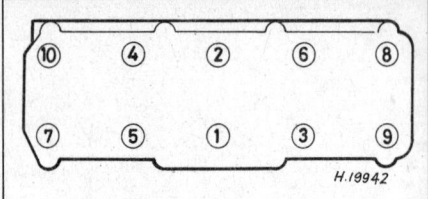

Fig 1.2 Cylinder head bolt tightening sequence (Sec 12)

in the Specifications. Tighten them to the stage 2 torque, and finally angle-tighten by half a turn (180°) without stopping (two 90° turns are permissible).
18 Refit the timing belt rear cover. Insert and tighten the bolts.
19 Re-connect the wiring to the temperature senders.
20 Re-connect the heater hose, top hose and bypass hose.
21 Refit the earth cable. Insert and tighten the bolt.
22 Refit the alternator (Chapter 12).
23 Refit the camshaft and tappets, with reference to Section 11.
24 Refit the HT leads and spark plugs (Chapter 4), and the inlet and exhaust manifolds (Chapter 3).
25 Refill the cooling system (Chapter 2).
26 Re-connect the battery negative lead.

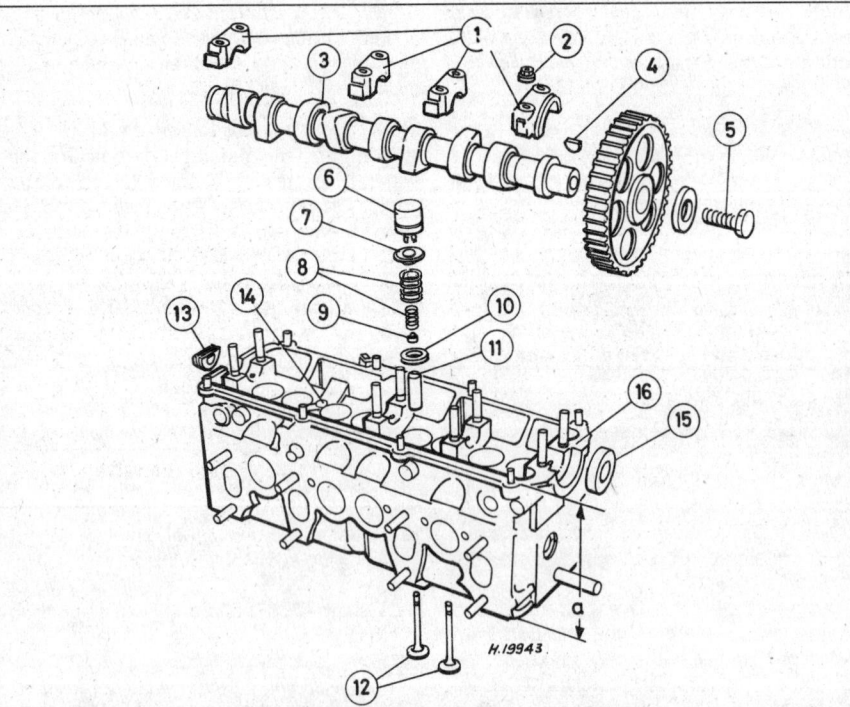

Fig 1.3 Cylinder head components (Sec 13)

1 Camshaft bearing cap	7 Valve spring cover	13 Plug
2 Nut	8 Valve springs	14 Oil return cut-off
3 Camshaft	9 Valve stem oil seal	15 Oil seal
4 Woodruff key	10 Valve spring seat	16 Cylinder head
5 Bolt	11 Valve guide	a Cylinder head height
6 Hydraulic bucket tappet	12 Valves	(see Specifications)

13.3 Compress the valve spring and remove the collets . . .

13.4A . . . valve spring cover . . .

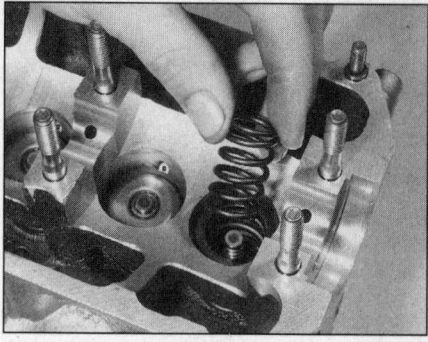

13.4B . . . inner valve spring . . .

13 Cylinder head - overhaul

1 With the cylinder head removed as previously described, the valves can be removed as follows. The valves are deeply recessed into the top of the cylinder head and consequently, their removal requires a valve spring compressor with long claws, or the use of some ingenuity in adapting other types of compressor. One method which can be employed is to use a piece of tubing of roughly the same diameter as the valve spring cover, and long enough to reach above the top of the cylinder head. To remove the valve collets, either cut a window in the tube on each side, or cut a complete section away, so that the tube is about three-quarters of a circle.

2 Have ready a board with holes in it, into which each valve can be fitted as it is removed, or have a set of labelled containers so that each valve and its associated parts can be identified and kept separate. Inlet valves are Nos. 2-4-5-7, exhaust valves are Nos 1-3-6-8, numbered from the timing belt end of the engine.

3 Compress each valve spring until the collets can be removed (photo) . Take out the collets, release the spring compressor and remove it.

4 Remove the valve spring cover, the inner and outer springs, and the valve (photos). It is good practice, but not essential, to keep the valve springs the same way up, so that parts are refitted exactly as they were before removal.

5 Prise off the valve stem seals, or pull them off with pliers and discard them, then remove the valve spring seats (photos).

6 Examine the heads of the valves for pitting and burning, paying particular attention to the heads of the exhaust valves (photo). The valve seats should be examined at the same time. If the pitting on the valve and seat is only slight, the marks can be removed by grinding the seats and valves together with coarse, and then fine, grinding paste. Where bad pitting has occurred, it will be necessary to renew the valve and have the valve seat re-cut. Do not re-cut the valve heads.

7 If the valve seat is re-cut, it is important to calculate the maximum amount that can be removed from the seat. If an excessive amount is removed, the hydraulic tappets may not function correctly. Insert the valve in its guide, and press firmly against its seat. Now measure the distance from the end of the valve stem to the upper face of the cylinder head (Fig. 1.4). The minimum distance

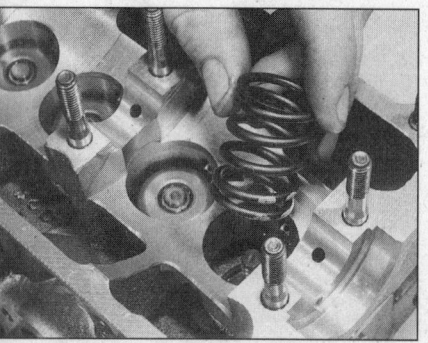

13.4C . . . outer valve spring . . .

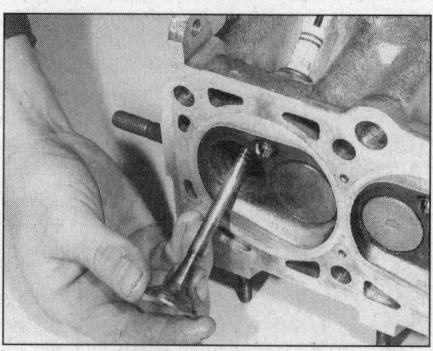

13.4D . . . and the valve

13.5A Removing the valve spring seat

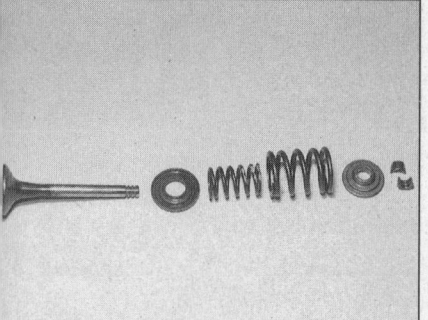

13.5B Valve and spring components

13.6 Inlet valve (left) and exhaust valve (right)

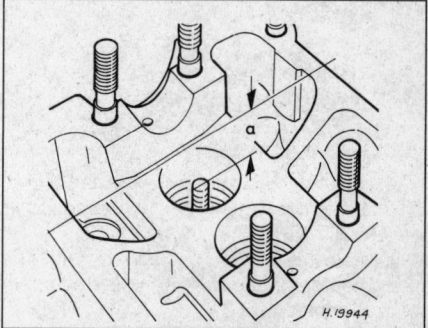

Fig 1.4 Minimum valve depth dimension 'a' (Sec 13)

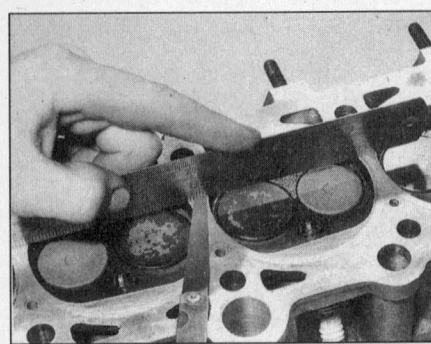

13.10 Checking the cylinder head for distortion

13.15A Fit the special plastic sleeve on the valve stem . . .

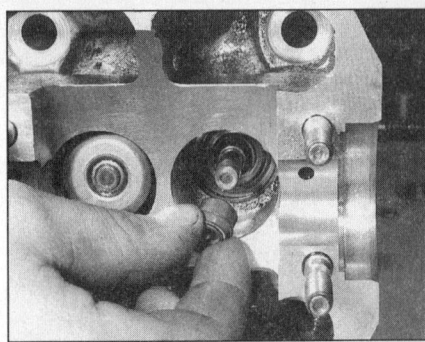

13.15B . . . then fit the valve stem seal . . .

allowed is 33.80 mm (1.331 in) for inlet valves, and 34.10 mm (1.343 in) for exhaust valves. Before re-cutting the seat, it is therefore possible to calculate the maximum amount to be removed. Where a valve seat is worn excessively, and re-cutting is not possible, the cylinder head should be renewed.

8 Valve grinding is carried out as follows. Smear a small quantity of coarse carborundum paste around the contact surface of the valve or seat, and insert the valve into its guide. Apply a suction grinder tool to the valve head, and grind in the valve by semi-rotary motion. This is produced by rolling the valve grinding tool between the palms of the hands. When grinding action is felt to be at an end, extract the valve, turn it and repeat the operation as many times as is necessary to produce a uniform matt grey surface over the whole seating area of the valve head and valve seat. Repeat the process using fine grinding paste.

9 Scrape away all carbon from the valve head and valve stem. Carefully clean away every trace of grinding paste, take care to leave none in the ports, or in the valve guides. Wipe the valves and valve seats with a paraffin-soaked rag, and then with a clean dry rag.

10 Thoroughly clean the cylinder head, then check it for distortion, by placing a straight edge across it at a number of points, lengthwise, crosswise and diagonally, and measuring the gap beneath it with feeler gauges (photo). If the gap exceeds the limit given in the Specifications, the head must be

13.15C . . . and tap it onto the guide with a socket and mallet

re-faced by a workshop which is equipped for this work. Re-facing must not reduce the cylinder head height below the minimum dimension given in the Specifications.

11 Examine the cylinder head for cracks. If there are minor cracks of not more than 0.5 mm (0.020 in) width between the valve seats, or at the bottom of the spark plug holes, the head can be re-used, but a cylinder head cannot be repaired or new valve seat inserts fitted.

12 Check the valve guides for wear. First clean out the guide, and then insert the stem of a new valve into the guide. Because the stem diameters are different, ensure that only an inlet valve is used to check the inlet valve guides, and an exhaust valve for the exhaust valve guides. With the end of the valve stem flush with the top of the valve guide, measure the total amount by which the rim of the valve head can be moved sideways. If the movement exceeds the maximum amount given in the Specifications, new guides should be fitted, but this is a job for an Audi dealer or specialist workshop, as it involves the use of a press and a hand reamer.

13 To refit the valves, oil the valve stem, and insert the valve into its guide.

14 Locate the valve spring seat over the guide.

15 Locate the special plastic sleeve on the end of the valve stem, then dip the new valve stem seal in oil, and press it over the valve stem onto the guide. If there is no plastic sleeve, wrap a piece of thin adhesive tape round the top of the valve stem, so that it covers the recess for the collets. This will prevent damage to the seal. Remove the sleeve or tape after fitting the seal. A socket and light mallet may be used to tap the seal onto the guide (photos).

16 Fit the inner and outer valve springs, then the valve spring cover. If renewing springs, they must only be renewed as a pair on any valve.

17 Fit the spring compressor, and compress the spring just enough to allow the collets to be fitted. If the spring is pressed right down, there is a danger of damaging the stem seal.

18 Fit the collets, release the spring compressor slightly, and check that the

collets seat properly, then remove the compressor.

19 Tap the top of the valve stem with a soft-headed hammer, to ensure that the collets are seated.

20 Repeat the procedure for all the valves.

14 Flywheel/driveplate - removal, examination and refitting

1 On manual gearbox models, remove the gearbox (Chapter 6) and clutch (Chapter 5).

2 On automatic transmission models, remove the automatic transmission (Chapter 7).

3 The flywheel/driveplate bolts are offset to ensure correct fitment. Unscrew the bolts while holding the flywheel/driveplate stationary. Temporarily insert a bolt in the cylinder block, and use a screwdriver to hold the flywheel/driveplate, or make up a holding tool as shown in photo 25.79D.

4 Lift the flywheel/driveplate from the crankshaft. If removing a driveplate, note the location of the shim and spacer.

5 Check the flywheel/driveplate for wear and damage. Examine the starter ring gear for excessive wear to the teeth. If the driveplate or its ring gear are damaged, the complete driveplate must be renewed. The flywheel ring gear, however, may be renewed separately

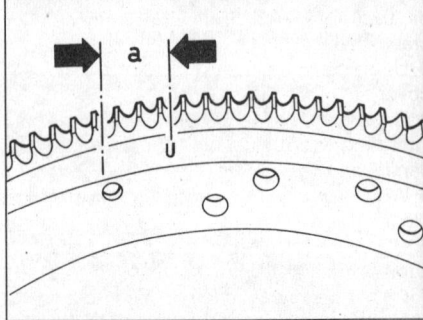

Fig 1.5 Ignition timing mark dimension 'a' (Sec 14)

Ignition setting	Dimension 'a'
6° BTDC	14.0 mm (0.55 in)
18° BTDC	42.0 mm (1.65 in)

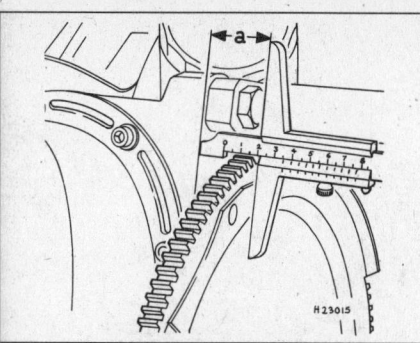

Fig 1.6 Driveplate position dimension 'a' (Sec 14)

from the flywheel, but the work should be entrusted to an Audi dealer. If the clutch friction face is discoloured or scored excessively, it may be possible to regrind it, but this work should also be entrusted to an Audi dealer.

6 Note that if the flywheel/driveplate is renewed, the new part will only have a TDC mark on it. It will be necessary to put an ignition timing mark on it in accordance with the information given in Fig. 1.5.

7 Refitting is a reversal of removal, but coat the threads of the (new) bolts with locking fluid before inserting them and tightening them to the specified torque. If a replacement driveplate is to be fitted, its position must be checked and adjusted if necessary. The distance from the rear face of the block to the torque converter mounting face on the driveplate (Fig. 1.6) must be between 30.5 and 32.1 mm (1.20 and 1.26 in). If necessary, remove the driveplate, and fit a spacer behind it to achieve the correct dimension.

15 Intermediate shaft - removal, examination and refitting

1 Remove the distributor (Chapter 4), and on carburettor models, the fuel pump (Chapter 3).
2 Remove the timing belt with reference to Section 10, but do not remove the tensioner or the sprockets from the camshaft or crankshaft.
3 Unbolt and remove the timing belt rear cover.
4 Unscrew the two bolts from the intermediate shaft sealing flange. Remove the flange, and prise out the O-ring and oil seal.
5 Withdraw the intermediate shaft from the block.
6 Clean the intermediate shaft, and examine it for wear and damage.
7 Oil the bearing journals on the intermediate shaft. Carefully insert the shaft into the block.
8 Smear a little engine oil on the sealing lips and outer rim of the new intermediate shaft oil seal. Place the sealing flange on the bench, and use a socket and mallet to drive the oil seal squarely into position.

9 Locate a new O-ring on the flange. Fit the flange on the block, insert the bolts, and tighten to the specified torque.
10 Using a dial gauge, check that the intermediate shaft endfloat is as given in the Specifications.
11 Refit the timing belt rear cover. Insert and tighten the bolts.
12 Refit the timing belt, with reference to Section 10.
13 Refit the fuel pump (Chapter 3) and distributor (Chapter 4).

16 Sump - removal and refitting

1 Apply the handbrake, then jack up the front of the car and support on axle stands positioned beneath the underbody.
2 Unbolt and remove the splash shield from under the engine.
3 Position a suitable container beneath the sump, then unscrew the drain plug and drain the engine oil. Clean, refit, and tighten the plug after all the oil has drained.
4 Support the weight of the engine with a hoist.
5 Unbolt and remove the transmission front cover.
6 Unscrew the engine mounting lower nuts.
7 Support the front suspension crossmember on a trolley jack, then unscrew the crossmember front mounting bolts and lower the crossmember a little.
8 Unscrew and remove the sump bolts.
9 Remove the sump and gasket. If it is stuck, tap it gently with a mallet to free it.
10 Clean the contact faces of the sump and block.
11 Locate a new gasket on the sump, then offer it up to the block and fit the bolts. Do not use any jointing compound. Tighten the bolts to the specified torque in diagonal sequence.
12 The remaining procedure is a reversal of removal, but fill the engine with the correct quantity and grade of oil.

17 Crankshaft front and rear oil seals - renewal

Front oil seal

1 Remove the timing belt and crankshaft sprocket, with reference to Section 10.
2 If an extractor tool is available, the seal may be renewed without removing the housing, otherwise unbolt and remove the housing (including the relevant sump bolts) and remove the gasket. If the sump gasket is damaged while removing the housing, it will be necessary to remove the sump and fit a new gasket. However, refit the sump after fitting the housing.
3 Drive the old seal out of the housing, then

dip the new seal in engine oil and drive it into the housing with a block of wood or a socket until flush. Make sure that the closed end of the seal is facing outwards.
4 Fit the housing, together with a new gasket, and tighten the bolts evenly in diagonal sequence.
5 Refit the timing belt and crankshaft sprocket, with reference to Section 10.

Rear oil seal

6 Remove the flywheel/driveplate, with reference to Section 14.
7 Follow paragraphs 2 to 4 inclusive.
8 Refit the flywheel/driveplate, with reference to Section 14.

18 Oil pump - removal, examination and refitting

1 Remove the sump as described in Section 16.
2 Using an Allen key, unscrew the bolts and remove the suction pipe from the oil pump. Remove the O-ring seal.
3 Unscrew and remove the large oil pump mounting bolts, then withdraw the pump from the block.
4 Unscrew the two bolts, and lift off the cover. Note that the cover incorporates the pressure relief valve.
5 Clean the components, and check them for wear and damage.
6 Using a feeler blade as shown (photo), check the backlash between the gears, and compare with that given in the Specifications. Similarly check the endfloat of the gears, using a straight edge across the end face of the pump (photo). If outside the specified limits, the pump should be renewed, otherwise refit the cover and tighten the bolts (photo).
7 Prime the pump with oil by immersing it in oil and turning the driveshaft.
8 Clean the contact faces, then fit the oil pump to the block, insert the mounting bolts, and tighten them to the specified torque.
9 Locate a new O-ring seal on the end of the suction tube. Fit the tube to the oil pump,

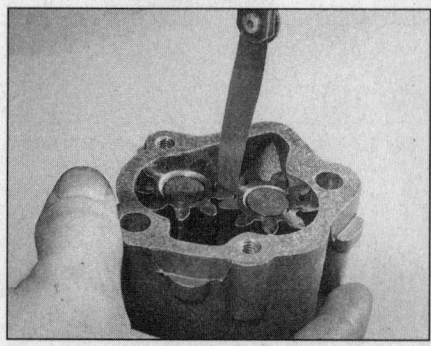

18.6A Checking the oil pump gear backlash . . .

18.6B . . . and gear endfloat

18.6C Tightening the oil pump cover bolts

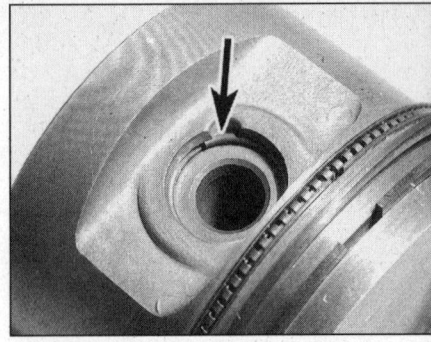

19.7 Gudgeon pin retaining circlip (arrowed)

insert the bolts and tighten them to the specified torque.
10 Refit the sump with reference to Section 16.

19 Pistons and connecting rods - removal and dismantling

1 Remove the cylinder head (Section 12), sump (Section 16), and oil pump (Section 18).
2 Turn the engine with a spanner on the crankshaft sprocket bolt, so that No 1 crankpin is at its lowest point. Mark the connecting rod and big-end cap in relation to its cylinder and position, using a centre-punch.
3 Unscrew the nuts, and remove the big-end bearing cap.
4 Using the handle of a hammer, push the connecting rod and piston out of the top of the cylinder. Put the bearing cap with its connecting rod. If the upper big-end shell becomes detached from the connecting rod, recover it and refit it. Keep all the components together.
5 Repeat the procedure given in paragraphs 2 to 4 inclusive, to remove the remaining pistons and connecting rods.
6 Before removing the pistons from the connecting rods, mark the connecting rods, if necessary, to show which side is towards the front of the engine. The casting marks on the rod and cap face towards the front of the engine (see Fig 1.7).
7 Remove the circlips from the grooves in the gudgeon pin holes (photo), and push the pin out enough for the connecting rod to be removed. Do not remove the pins completely unless new ones are to be fitted, to ensure that the pin is not turned end for end when the piston is refitted. If the pin is difficult to push out, heat the piston by immersing it in hot water.
8 New bushes can be fitted to the connecting rods, but as they need to be reamed to size

after fitting, the job is best left to an Audi agent.
9 Using old feeler gauges, or pieces of rigid plastic inserted behind the piston rings, carefully ease each ring in turn off the piston. Lay the rings out so that they are kept the right way up, and so that the top ring can be identified. Carefully scrape the rings free of carbon, and clean out the ring grooves on the pistons, using a piece of broken piston ring.

20 Pistons and cylinder bores - examination

1 Examine the pistons and the bores for obvious signs of damage and excessive wear. If they appear to be satisfactory, make the following checks.
2 Measure the piston diameter at a position 10 mm (0.4 in) from the lower edge of the skirt, and at 90° to the gudgeon pin axis. Compare this with the information in the Specifications (photo). Maximum wear of 0.04 mm (0.0016 in) is allowed.
3 Push a piston ring into the cylinder bore, and use a piston to push the ring down the bore so that it is square in the bore, and about 15 mm (0.6 in) from the bottom of the cylinder. Measure the ring endgap using a feeler gauge (photo). If the gap is above the top limit, look for obvious signs of bore wear, or if a new

Fig 1.7 Exploded view of the pistons and connecting rods (Sec 19)

1 Piston rings	9 Big-end bearing
2 Piston	cap
3 Gudgeon pin	10 Big-end nut
4 Circlip	A Cylinder number
5 Connecting rod	markings
6 Big-end bolt	B Casting marks
7 Bearing shell	must face front of
8 Cylinder block	engine

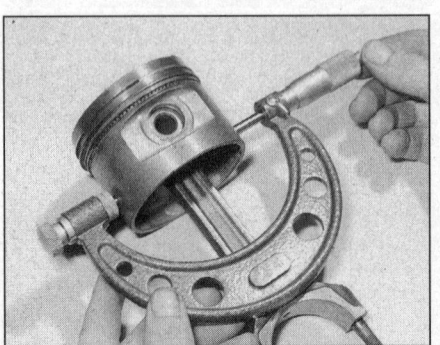

20.2 Measuring the piston diameter with a micrometer

20.3 Measuring the ring endgap with a feeler blade

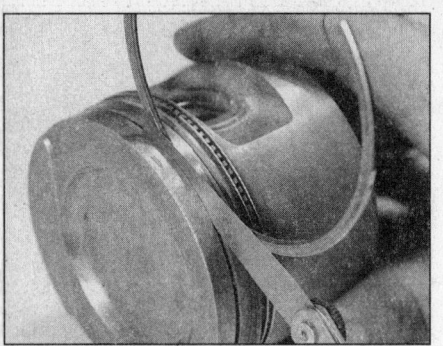

20.6 Measuring the piston ring-to-groove clearance

21.1 Connecting rod small end and piston

piston ring is available, measure the gap when a new piston ring is fitted to the bore.

4 To measure the bore diameter directly, a dial gauge with an internal measuring attachment is required. If one is available, measure each bore in six places, and compare the readings with the wear limit given. Bore diameter should be measured 10 mm (0.4 in) from the top of the bore, 10 mm (0.4 in) from the bottom, and at the mid-point. At each of the three stations, measure in-line with the crankshaft, and at right angles to it. If the bores are worn beyond the limit, they will need to be rebored and new pistons fitted.

5 If one bore is oversize, all four must be rebored, and a new set of pistons fitted, otherwise the engine will not be balanced. Connecting rods must only be fitted as complete sets, and not be replaced individually.

6 Measure the gap between each piston ring and the side of its groove as shown (photo). If the gap is excessive, it is more likely that the groove is worn rather than the ring, and a new piston will be required. If new piston rings are fitted, the wear ridge at the top of the cylinder bore must be removed, or a stepped top ring used.

21 Pistons and connecting rods - reassembly and refitting

1 Heat each piston in hot water, then insert the connecting rod and push in the pin until central (photo). Make sure that the casting marks on the connecting rod and the arrow on the piston crown are facing the same way, then refit the circlips.

2 Before refitting the piston rings, or fitting new rings, check the endgap of each ring in turn in its correct cylinder bore, using a piston to push the ring down the bore, as described in the previous Section. Measure the gap between the ends of the piston ring, using feeler gauges. The gap must be within the limits given in the Specifications.

3 When fitting piston rings, look for the word TOP etched on one side of the ring, and fit this side so that it is towards the piston crown.

4 Unless the big-end bearing shells are known to be almost new, it is worth fitting a new set when reassembling the engine. Clean the connecting rods and bearing caps thoroughly, and fit the bearing shells so that the tang on the bearing engages in the recess in the connecting rod, or cap, and the ends of the bearing are flush with the joint face.

5 To refit the pistons, first space the joints in the piston rings so that they are at 120° intervals. Oil the rings and grooves generously, and fit a piston ring compressor over the piston. The big-end bearing shells must also be oiled liberally.

6 Turn the engine so that No 1 crankpin is at its lowest point.

7 Oil the cylinder bore, then insert the piston and connecting rod, with the arrow on the piston crown pointing towards the front of the engine.

8 Using the handle of a hammer, gently tap the piston through the compressor into the bore, while guiding the connecting rod onto the crankpin.

9 Oil the bearing shell, then fit the big-end bearing cap on the connecting rod studs. Oil the contact surfaces, and fit the nuts. Tighten them first to the specified torque, then angle-tighten them a further 90°. Make sure that the cap is the correct way round, with the previously made marks adjacent to each other.

10 Turn the crankshaft to check for free movement.

11 Repeat the procedure given in para-

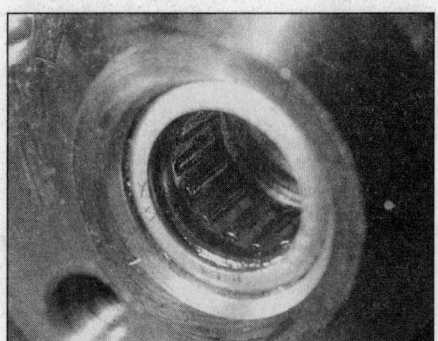

22.4 Needle bearing in the rear of the crankshaft

graphs 6 to 10 inclusive to fit the remaining pistons and connecting rods.

12 Refit the oil pump (Section 18), sump (Section 16), and cylinder head (Section 12).

22 Crankshaft and main bearings - examination

1 Clean the crankshaft, and examine it for wear and damage.

2 Check the crankpins and main bearing journals for scoring. If the engine has done a high mileage, and it is suspected that the crankshaft requires attention, it is best to seek the opinion of an Audi dealer or crankshaft refinishing specialist for advice on the need for regrinding. Unless the bearing shells (and thrustwashers if applicable) are known to be almost new, it is worth fitting a new set when the crankshaft is refitted.

3 If available, Plastigage may be used to check the running clearance of the existing bearings - a strip of Plastigage is placed across the crankshaft journal and then the bearing is assembled and tightened to the specified torque. After dismantling the bearing, the width of the strip is measured with a gauge supplied with the strip, and the running clearance read off.

4 On manual gearbox models, examine the needle bearing in the rear of the crankshaft for excessive wear (photo). To renew it, an extractor tool will be required. Clean the recess, then drive in the new bearing using metal tubing or a socket. The lettered side of the bearing must face outwards, and the bearing must be recessed to a depth of 1.5 mm (0.059 in).

5 Note that short engines are supplied with crankshafts fitted with a needle bearing. Where the engine is to be fitted to an automatic transmission model, the bearing must first be removed, in order to accommodate the torque converter.

Fig 1.8 Crankshaft needle bearing fitting dimension 'a' (Sec 22)

a = 1.5 mm (0.059 in)

23.3A Right-hand engine mounting

23.3B Left-hand engine mounting

25.2 Oiling the upper main bearing shells

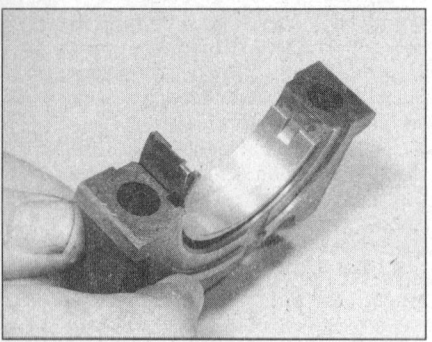

25.4A Fitting the main bearing shell to No 3 cap

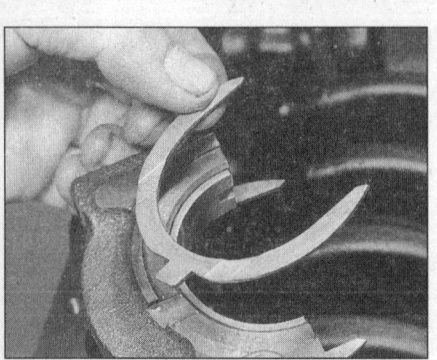

25.4B Fitting the main bearing shell to No 4 cap

23 Engine mountings - renewal

1 Unbolt the front support bar from the block.
2 Support the weight of the engine with a hoist.
3 Unscrew the mounting nuts, then raise the engine and remove the mountings (photos).
4 Refitting is a reversal of removal, but before tightening the nuts, rock the engine by hand to ensure correct alignment.

24 Engine reassembly - general

To ensure maximum life with minimum trouble from a rebuilt engine, not only must all parts be correctly assembled, but they must be spotlessly clean. All oilways must be clear of debris. Oil all bearings and other working surfaces thoroughly with clean engine oil during assembly. Renew any nuts, bolts or studs with damaged threads.

25 Engine - complete reassembly

1 Position the cylinder block on the bench, with the crankcase uppermost.

2 Locate the upper main bearing shells in the crankcase, so that the tags engage with the cut-outs. Oil the bearing shells (photo). If the old shells are being refitted, make sure that they are in their correct locations.
3 Lower the crankshaft into the crankcase.
4 Locate the lower main bearing shells in the main bearing caps, noting that for caps 1, 2 and 5 they are plain, but for cap 4 an oil groove is provided. No 3 bearing shell is plain, but service replacements incorporate a shoulder (photos).
5 Position the thrustwashers on each side of No 3 cap, using a little grease to hold them in place (photo). Make sure that the oil grooves face outwards.
6 Oil the bearing shell, then fit No 3 main bearing cap, insert the bolts, and tighten them to the specified torque.
7 Using a feeler blade (photo 9.60), or a dial gauge, check that the endfloat is as given in the Specifications (photo).
8 Oil the remaining main bearing shells, then fit the caps in their correct locations, insert the bolts, and tighten them to the specified torque (photo).
9 Check that the crankshaft rotates freely.
10 With the block on its side, turn the crankshaft so that the No 1 crankpin is at the bottom of its stroke.
11 Locate the big-end bearing shell in the connecting rod so that the tag engages with the cut-out (photo). Oil the bearing shell.
12 Space the piston ring gaps so that they

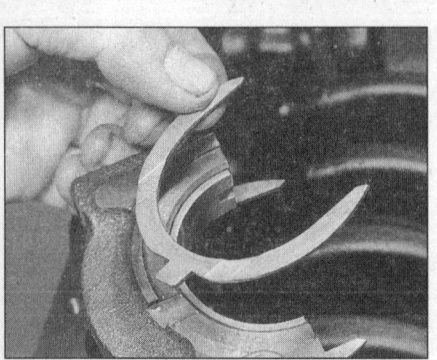

25.5 Positioning the thrustwashers on No 3 main bearing cap

25.7 Checking the crankshaft endfloat

25.8 Tightening the main bearing cap bolts

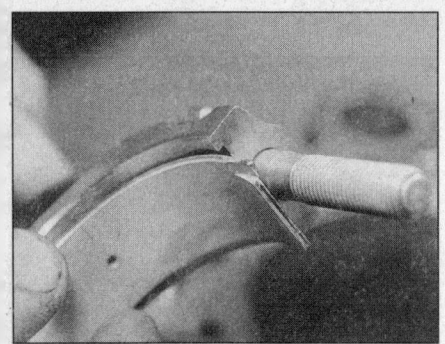

25.11 Fitting the big-end bearing shell to the connecting rod

25.14 Using a hammer handle to tap the piston through the compressor and into the bore

25.16A Initial tightening of big-end bearing nuts

25.16B Angle-tightening the big-end bearing nuts

1

are at 120° intervals. Oil the rings and grooves generously, and fit a piston ring compressor over the piston.

13 Oil the cylinder bore, then insert the piston and connecting rod, with the arrow on the piston crown pointing towards the front of the engine.

14 Using the handle of a hammer, gently tap the piston through the compressor into the bore, while guiding the connecting rod onto the crankpin (photo).

15 Locate the big-end bearing shell in the big-end cap, so that the tag engages the cut-out. Oil the bearing shell.

16 Fit the big-end bearing cap, complete with bearing shell, on the connecting rod studs, then oil the contact surfaces and fit the nuts. Tighten the nuts first to the specified torque, then angle-tighten them a further 90° (photos). Make sure that the cap is the correct way round, with the previously-made marks adjacent to each other.

17 Repeat the procedure given in para-graphs 10 to 16 for the remaining piston and connecting rod assemblies.

18 Temporarily insert two bolts in the rear of the crankshaft, and use a bar to turn the engine, in order to check for free movement.

19 Fit the oil pump to the block, insert the mounting bolts, and tighten them to the specified torque (photo).

20 Locate a new O-ring seal on the end of the suction tube. Fit the tube to the oil pump,

insert the bolts, and tighten them to the specified torque (photo).

21 Fit the crankshaft front oil seal housing (without the oil seal), together with a new gasket. Insert the bolts and tighten to the specified torque (photo).

22 Smear a little engine oil on the sealing lips and outer rim of the new seal. Locate the oil seal over the nose of the crankshaft. Using a suitable socket and mallet, drive the oil seal squarely into the housing, until flush with the outer edge (photos).

23 Fit the crankshaft rear oil seal housing (without the oil seal) together with a new gasket. Insert the bolts and tighten to the specified torque (photos).

25.19 Tightening the oil pump mounting bolts

25.20 Tightening the oil pump suction tube bolts

25.21 Tightening the crankshaft front oil seal housing bolts

25.22A Locate the oil seal on the crankshaft . . .

25.22B . . . and use a socket and mallet to drive it in flush

25.23A Fit the crankshaft rear oil seal housing and gasket . . .

25.23B . . . and tighten the bolts

25.24 Fitting the crankshaft rear oil seal

24 Smear a little engine oil on the sealing lips and outer rim of the new seal. Locate the oil seal over the crankshaft rear flange (photo), and carefully tap it squarely into the housing until flush with the outer edge. Use metal tubing or a block of wood to ensure the seal enters correctly.

25 With the engine inverted, locate a new gasket on the bottom of the block.

26 Fit the sump, then insert the bolts and tighten them to the specified torque in diagonal sequence (photo).

27 Support the engine in an upright position.

28 Apply suitable sealant to the lower end of the dipstick tube on the outer surface. Using a mallet, tap the dipstick tube into the block.

29 Fit the sprocket on the front of the crankshaft, making sure that the location shoulder engages with the cut-out.

30 Oil the threads of the bolt, then insert it and tighten to the specified torque (photos). Hold the crankshaft stationary during tightening, with a long bar positioned between two bolts in the rear of the crankshaft. An assistant will be required, as the bolt must be tightened to a very high torque.

31 Oil the bearing journals on the intermediate shaft. Carefully insert the shaft into the block.

32 Smear a little engine oil on the sealing lips and outer rim of the new intermediate shaft oil seal. Place the sealing flange on the bench, and use a socket and mallet to drive the oil seal squarely into position (photo).

33 Locate a new O-ring on the flange. Fit the flange on the block, insert the bolts and tighten to the specified torque (photo).

34 Using a dial gauge, check that the intermediate shaft endfloat is as given in the Specifications (photo).

35 Fit the right-hand engine mounting bracket and bar to the block, insert the bolts, and tighten to the specified torque.

36 Fit the left-hand engine mounting bracket to the block, insert the bolts, and tighten to the specified torque.

37 Fit the alternator mounting bracket, insert the bolts and tighten.

38 Check that the top of the block is perfectly clean, then locate a new gasket on it, with the words 'OBEN TOP' facing upwards.

25.26 Tightening the sump bolts

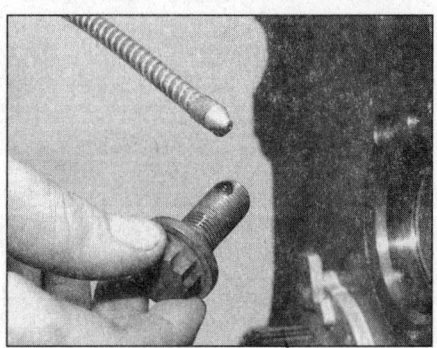

25.30A Oil the threads of the crankshaft sprocket bolt . . .

25.30B . . . then insert and tighten it

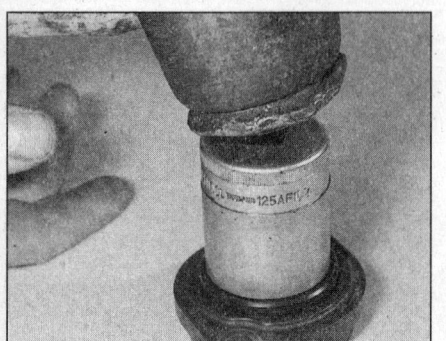

25.32 Driving the oil seal into the intermediate shaft sealing flange

25.33 Tightening the intermediate shaft sealing flange bolts

25.34 Checking the intermediate shaft endfloat

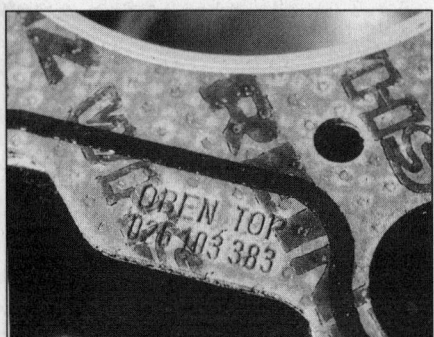

25.38A 'OBEN TOP' marking on the head gasket

25.38B Cylinder head location dowel

25.39 Oiling the cylinder bores

Make sure that the location dowels are in position (photos).

39 Turn the engine clockwise on the front sprocket bolt so that all the pistons are in their mid-bore positions, with Nos 1 and 4 pistons moving up their bores. Squirt a little oil into each cylinder (photo).

40 Check that the cylinder head face is perfectly clean. Carefully lower the head onto the block. Do not use any jointing compound on the cylinder head joint.

41 Insert the cylinder head bolts, together with their washers, and initially hand-tighten them, using a splined socket.

42 Using the sequence shown in Fig. 1.9, tighten the bolts to the stage 1 torque given in the Specifications. Tighten them to the

stage 2 torque, and finally angle-tighten by half a turn (180°) without stopping (two 90° turns are permissible) (photos).

43 Fit the engine front lifting eye bracket and tighten the bolt.

44 Fit the timing belt rear cover, insert the bolts and tighten.

45 Turn the intermediate shaft so that the Woodruff key slot is facing upwards. Insert the key in the slot.

46 Fit the sprocket to the intermediate shaft, and engage it with the Woodruff key. Insert the bolt and tighten to the specified torque. Hold the sprocket stationary, using a tool made as shown (photo) or a similar tool.

47 If necessary, check the endfloat of the

camshaft before inserting the hydraulic bucket tappets. Follow paragraphs 49 and 50, then use a dial gauge to check that the endfloat is as given in the Specifications. Remove the camshaft again, and proceed from the next paragraph.

48 Oil the hydraulic bucket tappets, then insert them in their previously-noted positions over the valves.

49 Oil the bearing journals on the camshaft, then lower the camshaft into position on the bucket tappets, making sure that the cams for No 1 cylinder are pointing upwards.

50 Refit bearing caps 2 and 5 (No 4 position is blanked off). Fit the nuts, and tighten them progressively to the specified torque (photo). Make sure that the caps are the same way

1

25.42A Initial tightening of the cylinder head bolts

25.42B Angle-tightening the cylinder head bolts

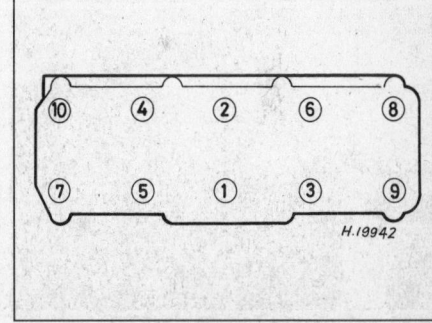

Fig 1.9 Cylinder head bolt tightening sequence (Sec 25)

H.19942

25.46 Tightening the intermediate shaft sprocket bolt

25.50 Tightening the camshaft bearing cap nuts

25.52 Fitting the camshaft front oil seal

25.53 Tightening the camshaft sprocket bolt

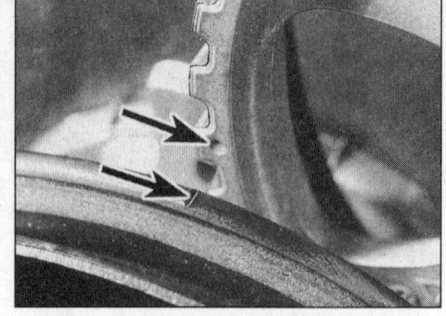

25.57 Timing marks (arrowed) on the crankshaft pulley and intermediate shaft sprocket

25.58 Timing belt located on the intermediate shaft sprocket

round as noted during removal, because they are slightly offset.

51 Refit bearing caps 1 and 3, fit the nuts, and tighten progressively to the specified torque.

52 Smear a little engine oil on the oil seal lips and outer rim. Locate the oil seal over the front of the camshaft, and use a socket and mallet to drive it squarely into position, until flush with the cylinder head (photo).

53 Press the Woodruff key into the slot in the front of the camshaft. Locate the sprocket on the camshaft, insert the bolt and washer, and tighten to the specified torque, while holding the sprocket stationary with a tool as shown (photo) or similar.

54 Fit the timing belt tensioner wheel and hub to the stud on the front of the cylinder

head, followed by the washer and nut.

55 Temporarily fit the drivebelt pulley to the crankshaft sprocket in the previously-noted position. Insert and tighten two diagonally opposite bolts.

56 Align the mark on the rear of the camshaft sprocket with the top of the cylinder head on the left-hand side.

57 Turn the intermediate shaft sprocket until the mark is level with the drivebelt pulley. Turn the engine clockwise until the mark on the pulley is aligned with the mark on the sprocket (photo).

58 Locate the timing belt on the crankshaft sprocket and the intermediate shaft sprocket, making sure that if the old belt is refitted, it is the correct way round as noted previously (photo).

59 Fit the belt up over the camshaft sprocket, then feed it onto the tensioner wheel, and turn the hub clockwise to hold the belt in position (photo).

60 Using circlip pliers or a suitable tool in the holes provided, turn the tensioner hub clockwise. Continue to turn until the tension of the belt is such that it is just possible to twist the belt through 90° at a point midway between the camshaft and intermediate shaft sprockets. Tighten the tensioner nut, check again that the tension is correct and that the timing marks are still aligned (photos).

61 Unbolt the water pump pulley from the crankshaft sprocket. Locate the special spacer in the lower timing belt cover, then fit the cover, insert the bolts, and tighten them (photo).

62 Refit the water pump pulley to the crankshaft sprocket in the previously-noted position. Insert and tighten the bolts.

63 Fit the rubber plug to the rear of the cylinder head, and the semi-circular gasket to the groove in the camshaft front bearing cap.

64 Fit a new gasket over the studs on the top of the cylinder head.

65 Fit the oil deflector.

66 Fit the valve cover and reinforcement strips.

67 Locate the earth terminal and wire retaining straps in their previously-noted positions. Fit and tighten the nuts.

68 Fit the timing belt rear upper cover. Fit and tighten the nuts.

25.59 Locating the timing belt on the tensioner wheel

25.60A Using circlip pliers to turn the tensioner hub

25.60B It should just be possible to twist the timing belt through 90°

25.60C Tightening the tensioner nut

25.61 Tightening the lower timing belt cover bolts

69 Fit the upper timing cover and nut (where fitted). Secure with the clips.
70 Fit the water pump assembly, together with a new O-ring. Insert and tighten the bolts.
71 Fit the special bolt retaining the lower timing cover to the water pump assembly, and tighten the nut.
72 Fit the pulley to the water pump. Insert and tighten the bolts.
73 Fit the outlet housing to the rear of the cylinder head, together with a new O-ring. Insert and tighten the bolts.
74 Fit the outlet elbow to the side of the cylinder head, together with a new O-ring. Insert and tighten the bolts.
75 Fit the oil filter housing to the block, together with a new gasket. Insert and tighten the bolts.
76 Clean the mating faces of the new oil filter and the housing, then smear a little engine oil on the filter seal. Screw the filter into the housing, and tighten by hand only.
77 Fit the fuel container and bracket to the valve cover. Fit and tighten the nuts.
78 Make sure that the dowels are fitted to the rear of the block. Fit the intermediate plate over the dowels.
79 Locate the flywheel/driveplate on the crankshaft. Audi recommend that the flywheel/driveplate bolts are always renewed after removal. Apply locking fluid to the bolt threads, then insert the bolts. Tighten the bolts to the specified torque, while holding the flywheel/driveplate stationary. Fit a bolt in the cylinder block, and use a screwdriver in the ring gear to hold the flywheel/driveplate stationary. Alternatively, make up a holding tool as shown (photos). Make sure that the previously-made marks are aligned.
80 If any of the hydraulic tappets have been renewed, do not start the engine, or turn the engine, until at least thirty minutes have elapsed. This is to allow time for any excess oil in the tappets to drain off. If this precaution is not taken, there is the danger of a valve striking a piston.

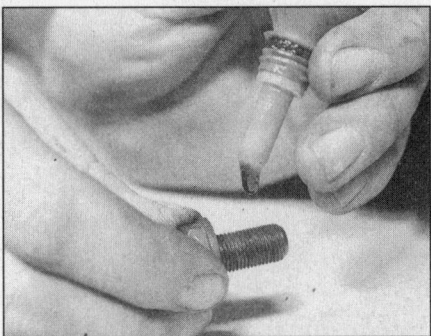
25.79A Apply locking fluid to the flywheel/driveplate bolts . . .

25.79B . . . insert them . . .

25.79C . . . and tighten to the specified torque

25.79D Tool for holding the flywheel/driveplate stationary

26 Engine - initial start-up after major overhaul

Note: *Refer to Section 25, paragraph 80, before starting the engine*
1 With the engine refitted, check that everything has been reconnected, and that no rags or tools are left in the engine compartment.
2 If new pistons or crankshaft bearings have been fitted, it may be necessary to increase the idle speed temporarily, where this is possible.
3 Start the engine, and allow it to idle. Check that the oil light goes out, then check the engine for oil, fuel and water leaks.
4 Initially there may be some noise from the hydraulic tappets, but this should disappear by the time that the car has been driven for a few miles.
5 Run the engine to normal operating temperature, and where possible adjust the idling speed (Chapter 3).
6 If new pistons and crankshaft bearings have been fitted, the engine should be run-in for the first 500 miles. Do not operate the engine at full throttle or allow the engine to labour in any gear.

Part B: Five-cylinder engines

27 General description

The engine is of five-cylinder, in-line, overhead camshaft type, mounted conventionally at the front of the car. The crankshaft is of six-bearing type, and the No 4 (from front) main bearing shells incorporate flanged or separate thrustwashers to control crankshaft endfloat. The camshaft is driven by a toothed belt from the crankshaft sprocket, and the belt also drives the water pump mounted on the left-hand side of the block.

The 20-valve engine incorporates double overhead camshafts, linked at the front by a chain and sprockets. The exhaust camshaft is driven by a sprocket from the toothed belt. A gear on the rear of the camshaft (or inlet camshaft on 20-valve engines) drives the distributor.

The valves are operated from the camshaft(s) through hydraulic bucket type tappets.

The engine has a full-flow lubrication system. A gear-and-crescent type oil pump is mounted on the front of the crankshaft. The oil filter is of the cartridge type, mounted on the right-hand side of the cylinder block.

28.0 Oil filter location

28 Routine maintenance

Refer to Part A, Section 2. The oil filter is located on the right-hand side of the engine (photo).

29 Major operations possible with the engine in the car

Refer to Part A, Section 3, but note that both camshafts may be removed on the 20-valve engine.

30 Major operation only possible after removal of the engine from the car

The following operation can only be carried out after removal of the engine from the car:
(a) *Removal of the crankshaft and main bearings*

31 Method of engine removal

The engine must be disconnected from the transmission, then lifted from the car.

32 Engine - removal and refitting

1 Remove the bonnet as described in Chapter 11, and stand it on cardboard or rags in a safe place.
2 Disconnect the battery negative lead.
3 Unbolt and remove the splash shield from under the engine.
4 Position a suitable container beneath the sump, then unscrew the drain plug (photo) and drain the engine oil. Clean, refit, and tighten the plug after all the oil has drained.
5 Drain the cooling system, as described in Chapter 2.
6 Remove the fuel injection components with reference to Chapter 3.
7 On models equipped with power steering, remove the pump with reference to Chapter 10, but leave the hoses connected, and place the pump on one side.
8 On models equipped with air conditioning remove the compressor with reference to Chapter 11, but leave the refrigerant pipes connected, and place the unit to one side.
9 Remove the radiator grille with reference to Chapter 11. Also unbolt the radiator front upper cowl (photo).
10 Remove the front bumper, with reference to Chapter 11.

32.4 Oil drain plug on the sump

11 Release the bonnet catch control cable (Chapter 11), then unbolt and remove the crossmember from the front of the engine compartment (photo).
12 Remove the auxiliary radiator (where applicable).
13 On manual gearbox models, remove the clutch slave cylinder with reference to Chapter 5, but leave the pipe connected, and position the cylinder on the bulkhead.
14 Remove the lower crossmember from the front valance.
15 Remove the intake hose housing.
16 Where necessary, remove the right-hand headlight and the right-hand lock carrier plate.
17 Disconnect the wiring from the air mass sensor and the idle stabiliser valve.
18 Disconnect the air cleaner pre-heater hose, and remove the air cleaner housing, complete with air mass sensor and air duct.
19 Note the routing and location of the engine wiring harness, then disconnect the various wires and remove the harness (photo). To prevent confusion when reconnecting the wires, identify them with adhesive tape marked accordingly.
20 Unbolt the earth cable from the battery support bracket and cylinder head.
21 Remove the distributor cap.
22 Disconnect the heater hoses at the bulkhead.
23 Remove the fuel pressure regulator.
24 Remove the cruise control unit.
25 Identify, then disconnect, all vacuum hoses.

32.9 Removing the radiator front upper cowl

26 Remove the radiator, with reference to Chapter 2.
27 Disconnect the fuel supply and return hoses at the bulkhead.
28 Unbolt the ignition timing sender unit and rpm sensor.
29 Disconnect the coolant hoses from the oil cooler, cylinder head and block.
30 With the handbrake applied, jack up the front of the car and support on axle stands.
31 Remove the exhaust downpipe with reference to Chapter 3.
32 Unbolt and remove the transmission front cover.
33 Remove the starter motor, as described in Chapter 12.
34 Unbolt the heat deflector from the right-hand driveshaft. Also unbolt the engine front support bar.
35 On automatic transmission models, unscrew the bolts securing the torque converter to the driveplate, working through the front cover aperture. It will be necessary to turn the engine to gain access to each bolt. To do this, either turn the starter ring gear on the driveplate, or use a spanner on the crankshaft pulley bolt. Hold the starter ring gear stationary with a screwdriver while unscrewing the bolts. Also disconnect the kickdown cable.
36 Unscrew and remove the lower bolts securing the transmission to the engine.
37 Lower the front of the car to the ground.
38 Connect a hoist, and just take the weight of the engine. The hoist should be positioned centrally over the engine.

32.11 Front engine compartment crossmember bolts (arrowed)

32.19 Wiring disconnected from the oil pressure switch

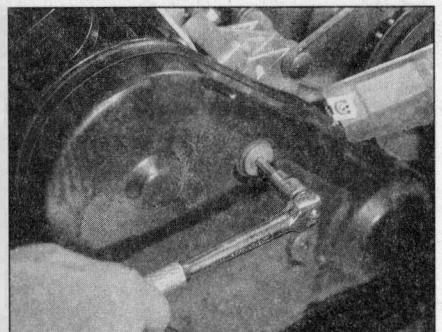

35.2A Unscrew the nuts with an Allen key . . .

35.2B . . . remove the nuts . . .

35.2C . . . and withdraw the upper timing belt cover . . .

39 Support the transmission with a trolley jack.

40 Unscrew and remove the remaining bolts securing the transmission to the engine, noting the location of any brackets and the earth strap.

41 Unbolt and remove the right-hand engine mounting, followed by the left-hand engine mounting.

42 Raise the engine slightly, and reposition the trolley jack beneath the transmission.

43 Pull the engine from the transmission. Make sure that, on automatic transmission models, the torque converter remains fully engaged with the transmission splines.

44 Raise the engine from the engine compartment, taking care not to damage the surrounding components. Pull the engine forwards, and lower it to the floor.

45 On automatic transmission models, make sure that the torque converter remains in position, by bolting a piece of bent metal to one of the mounting bolt holes.

46 Refitting is a reversal of the removal procedure, but before starting the engine, check that it has been filled with oil, and also that the cooling system is full. Before tightening the engine mountings, rock the engine by hand to ensure correct alignment. Adjust the accelerator cable and if applicable, the kickdown cable, with reference to Chapter 3.

33 Engine dismantling - general

Refer to Part A, Section 7 of this Chapter.

34 Ancillary components - removal and refitting

Refer to Part A, Section 8 of this Chapter, with the following change.
Oil filter (Section 28)

35 Camshaft and hydraulic tappets - removal

Note: *If the engine is still in the car, first carry out the following operations:*
(a) Disconnect the battery negative lead
(b) emove the air cleaner and fuel injection components (Chapter 3)
(c) Disconnect all relevant wiring, cables and hoses
(d) Remove the distributor (Chapter 4)
(e) Remove the upper radiator cowl and upper section of the inlet manifold
(f) Disconnect the drivebelts from the crankshaft pulley

(g) Where fitted, remove the power steering pump leaving the hoses connected (Chapter 10)
(h) Where fitted, remove the air conditioning compressor, leaving the hoses connected (Chapter 11)

1 Unscrew the nuts/bolts, and lift off the valve cover. Recover the reinforcement strips (where fitted), and the gaskets. Note the location of the cable holders.

2 Unscrew the nuts, and remove the upper timing belt cover and spacers (photos). An Allen key is required for this. The lower cover need not be removed.

3 Using a socket on the crankshaft pulley bolt, turn the engine so that the piston in No 1 cylinder is at TDC (top dead centre) on its compression stroke.

4 The notch in the crankshaft pulley must be in line with the pointer on the oil pump housing or lower timing cover (photo). Alternatively, the 'O' mark (TDC) on the flywheel/driveplate must be aligned with the pointer in the bellhousing aperture.

5 The valves on No 1 cylinder must be closed, with the cam peaks pointing upwards.

6 On 10-valve engines, the indentation on the rear of the camshaft gear must be in line with the upper surface of the valve cover gasket (photo), (temporarily refit the gasket if necessary).

7 On 20-valve engines, the indentation on the rear of the camshaft gear must be in line with the upper edge of the cylinder head between

1

35.2D . . . and spacers

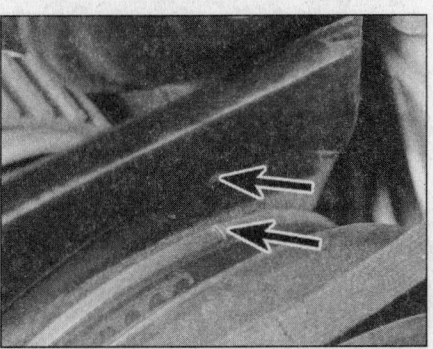

35.4 Crankshaft pulley timing marks (arrowed)

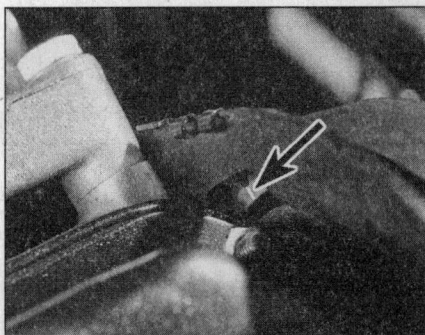

35.6 Camshaft gear timing mark (arrowed)

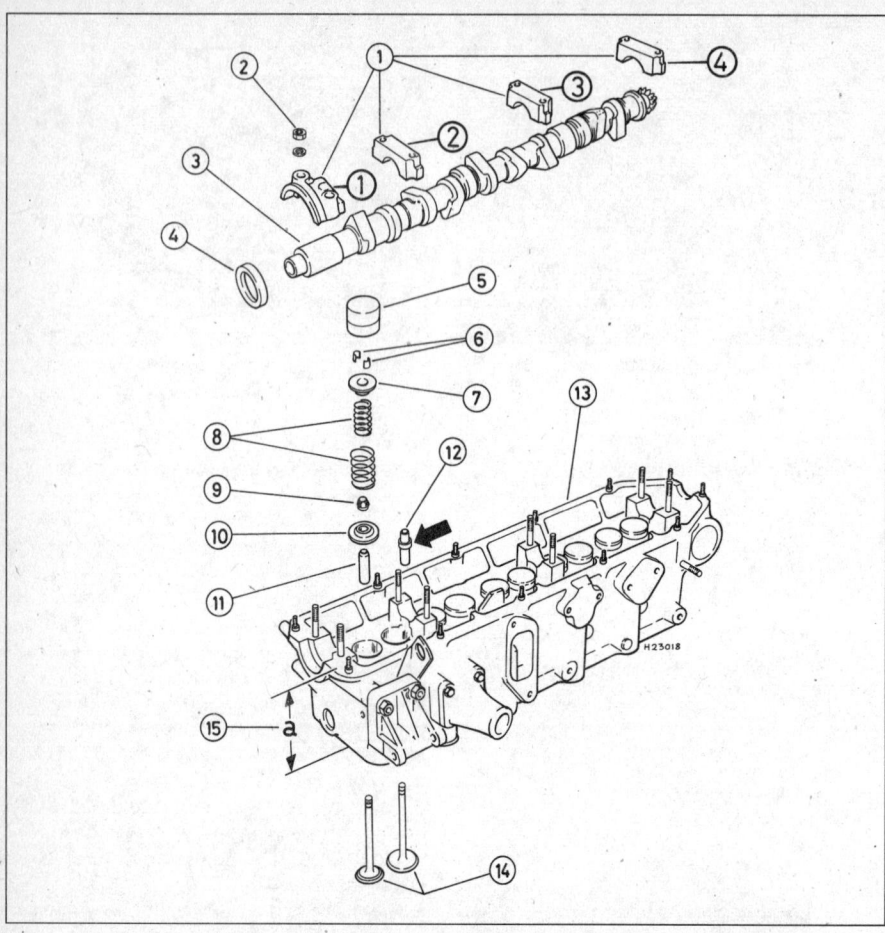

35.8 Water pump and one of the mounting bolts

35.14 Removing No 3 camshaft bearing cap

Fig 1.10 Camshaft and valve components on the 10-valve engine (Sec 35)

1 Bearing cap	7 Cover	12 Service valve guide with collar
2 Nut	8 Valve springs	
3 Camshaft	9 Valve stem oil seal	13 Cylinder head
4 Oil seal	10 Valve spring seat	14 Valves
5 Hydraulic bucket tappet	11 Valve guide	15 Minimum height
6 Collets		a = 132.75 mm (5.226 in)

the camshafts. Alternatively, the indentation on the front of the gear must be in line with the mark on the valve cover (temporarily refitted).

8 Loosen the water pump mounting and adjustment bolts, and rotate the pump clockwise to release the tension on the timing belt (photo).

9 Remove the timing belt from the camshaft gear, and move it to one side.

10 Unscrew the centre bolt from the camshaft gear, at the same time holding the gear stationary using the method shown in photo 25.53 (Part A).

11 Withdraw the gear from the camshaft, and extract the Woodruff key.

12 Check that each bearing cap has its number stamped on it; if not, make an identifying mark to ensure that each cap is put back where it was originally. Note that the caps are offset, and can only be fitted one way round.

13 It is important that the camshaft is removed exactly as described, so that there is no danger of it becoming distorted.

10-valve engines

14 Unscrew the nuts of bearing caps 1 and 3, and remove them (photo).

15 Unscrew the nuts of bearing caps 2 and 4 progressively and in diagonal sequence, then remove the caps.

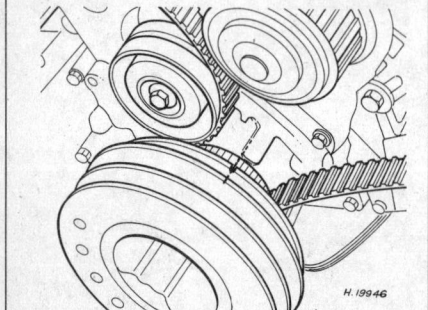

Fig 1.11 Crankshaft pulley TDC marks (Sec 35)

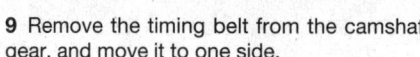
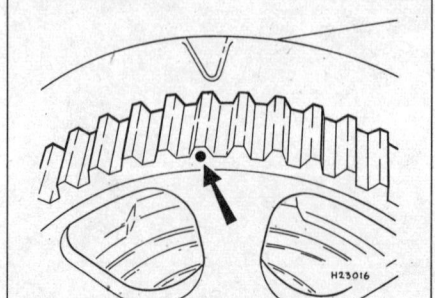

Fig 1.12 Camshaft gear outer timing marks on the 20-valve engine (Sec 35)

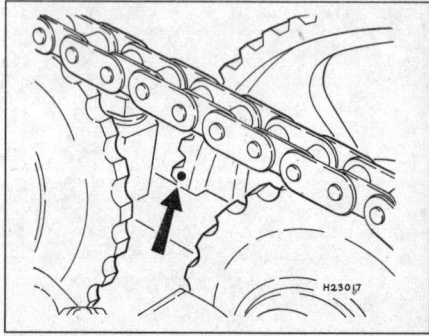

Fig 1.13 Camshaft gear inner timing mark (arrowed) on the 20-valve engine (Sec 35)

35.16 Camshaft removal

16 Lift out the camshaft, and discard the oil seal (photo).

20-valve engine

17 Unscrew the nuts of the exhaust camshaft bearing caps 2 and 4 (Fig. 1.14) and remove them.
18 Unscrew the nuts of bearing caps 1, 3 and 5 progressively and in diagonal sequence, then remove the caps.
19 Lift out the exhaust camshaft, and disconnect it from the chain.
20 Unscrew the nuts of the inlet camshaft bearing caps 7 and 9 (Fig. 1.14), and remove them.
21 Unscrew the nuts of bearing caps 6, 8 and 10 progressively and in diagonal sequence, then remove the caps.
22 Lift out the inlet camshaft, and remove the chain.

All engines

23 Have ready a box with internal compartments marked to identify the bucket tappet locations.
24 Remove the hydraulic bucket tappets, and place them *upside-down* in the box, to prevent the oil draining out.

36 Cylinder head - removal

Note: *If the engine is still in the car, first carry out the following operations:*
(a) *Disconnect the battery negative lead*
(b) *Drain the cooling system (Chapter 2)*
(c) *Remove the inlet and exhaust manifolds (Chapter 3)*
(d) *Remove the distributor, HT leads and spark plugs (Chapter 4)*
(e) *Disconnect the drivebelts from the crankshaft pulley*
(f) *Disconnect all relevant wiring, cables and hoses*
(g) *Remove the upper radiator cowl*
(h) *Where fitted, remove the power steering pump, leaving the hoses connected (Chapter 10)*
(i) *Where fitted, remove the air conditioning compressor, leaving the refrigerant pipes connected (Chapter 11)*

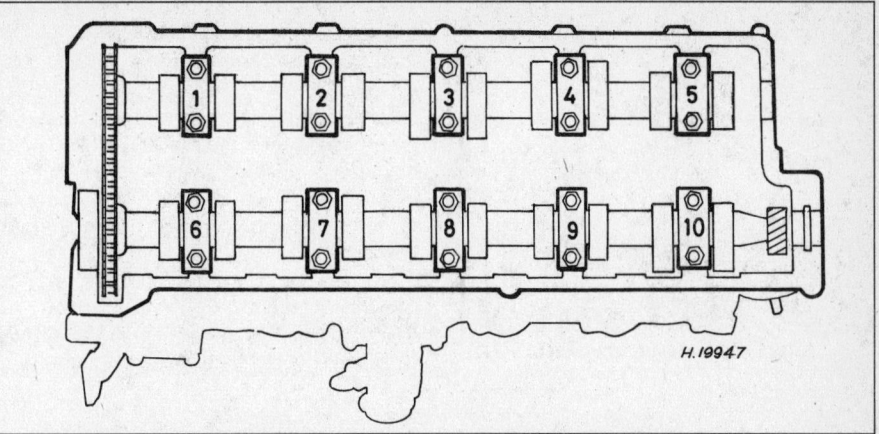

Fig 1.14 Camshaft bearing cap numbering on the 20-valve engine (Sec 35)

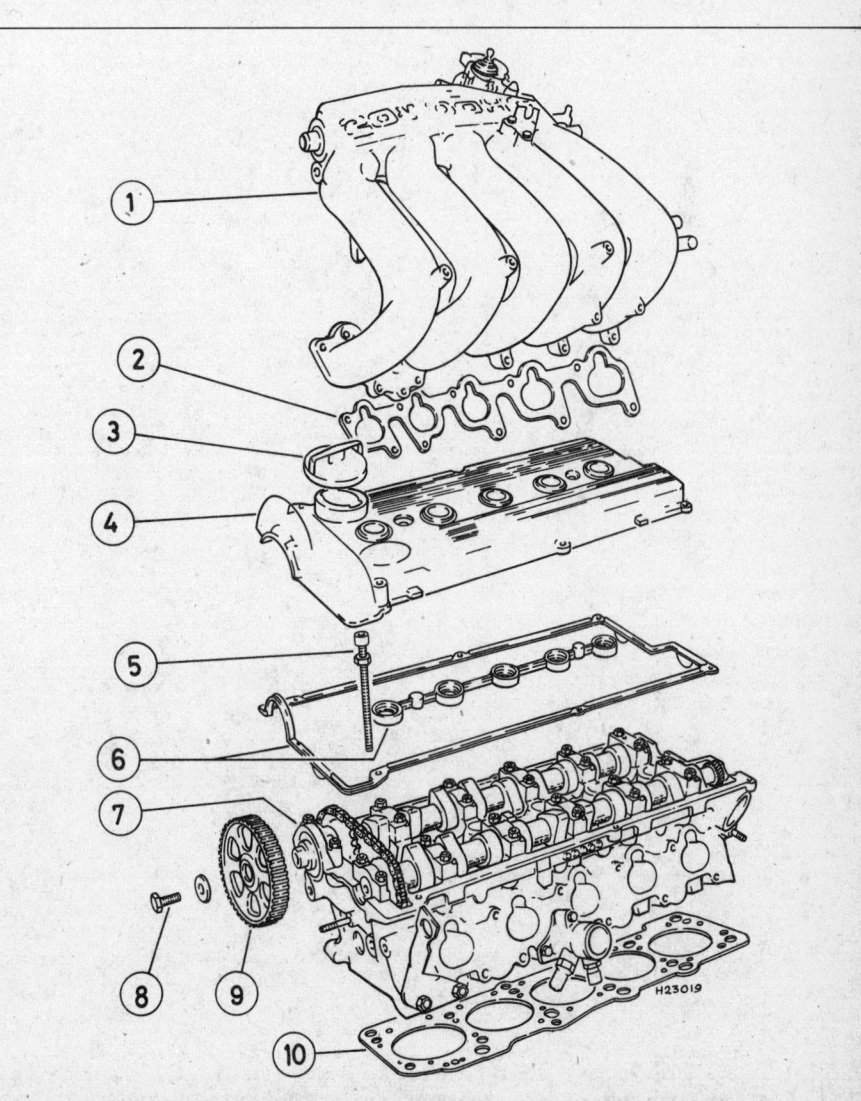

Fig 1.15 Cylinder head components on the 20-valve engine (Sec 36)

1 Inlet manifold	5 Cylinder head bolt	8 Bolt
2 Gasket	6 Valve cover gasket	9 Camshaft gear
3 Oil filler cap	7 Cylinder head	10 Cylinder head gasket
4 Valve cover		

36.6 Cylinder head removal

1 Remove the camshaft(s) and hydraulic tappets, as described in Section 35.
2 Remove the water pump, as described in Chapter 2.
3 Unbolt and remove the timing belt rear cover, and remove the spacers.
4 Using a splined socket, unscrew the cylinder head bolts a turn at a time, in reverse order to that shown in Fig. 1.18 or 1.19 (as applicable).
5 Remove the cylinder head bolts, together with their washers.
6 With all the bolts removed, lift the cylinder head from the block (photo). If it is stuck, tap it free with a wooden mallet. Do not insert a lever into the gasket joint.
7 Remove the cylinder head gasket from the block.

37 Cylinder head - overhaul

1 Follow the procedure given in Part A, Section 13, but note the following.
2 On the 10-valve engine, the inlet valves are 2-4-5-7-9, and the exhaust valves 1-3-6-8-10, numbered from the timing belt end of the engine.
3 On the 10-valve engine, the minimum distance from the end of the valve stems to the upper face of the cylinder head is the same as for the four-cylinder engine. On the 20-valve engine, the minimum distance is 36.0 mm (1.417 in) for inlet valves, and 36.3 mm (1.429 in) for exhaust valves.
4 The exhaust valves on the 20-valve engine are sodium-filled, and if the valves are being scrapped, they should ideally be rendered safe as follows.
5 Using a hacksaw, cut the valves in two, making sure that no water is allowed to contact them.
6 The valves must now be thrown into a bucket of water. Since a violent chemical reaction will occur, safety clothing and goggles must be worn.
7 When the reaction is complete, the valves may be scrapped as normal.

38 Cylinder head - refitting

1 Check that the top of the block is perfectly clean, then locate a new gasket on it, with the part number or 'OBEN TOP' marking facing upwards.
2 Check that the cylinder head face is perfectly clean. Insert two long rods, or pieces of dowel, into the cylinder head bolt holes at

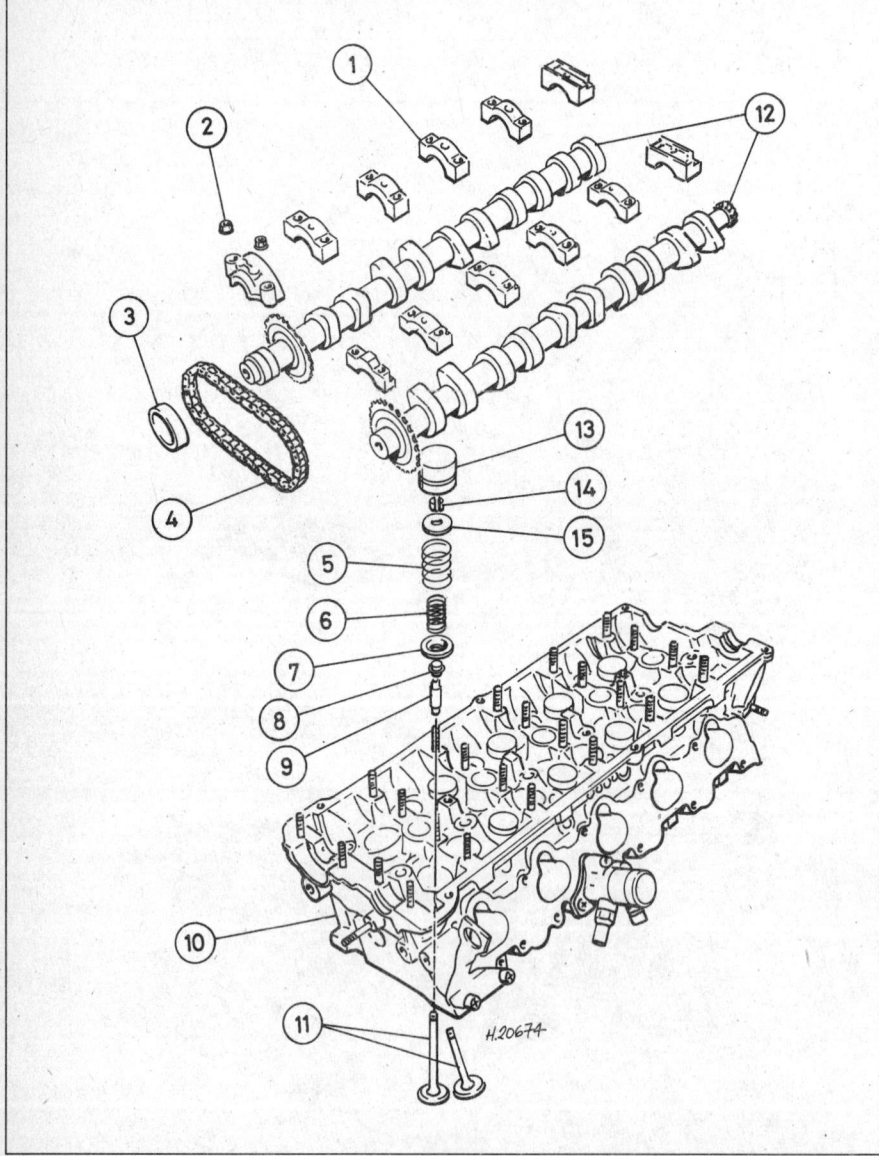

Fig 1.16 Camshaft and valve components on the 20-valve engine (Sec 37)

1 Bearing cap	6 Inner valve spring	11 Valves
2 Nut	7 Valve spring seat	12 Camshafts
3 Oil seal	8 Valve stem oil seal	13 Hydraulic bucket tappet
4 Drive chain	9 Valve guide	14 Collets
5 Outer valve spring	10 Cylinder head	15 Cover

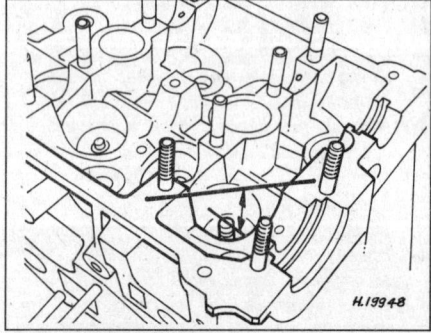

Fig 1.17 Minimum valve depth dimension on the 20-valve engine (Sec 37)

Inlet valve = 36.0 mm (1.42 in)
Exhaust valve = 36.3 mm (1.43 in)

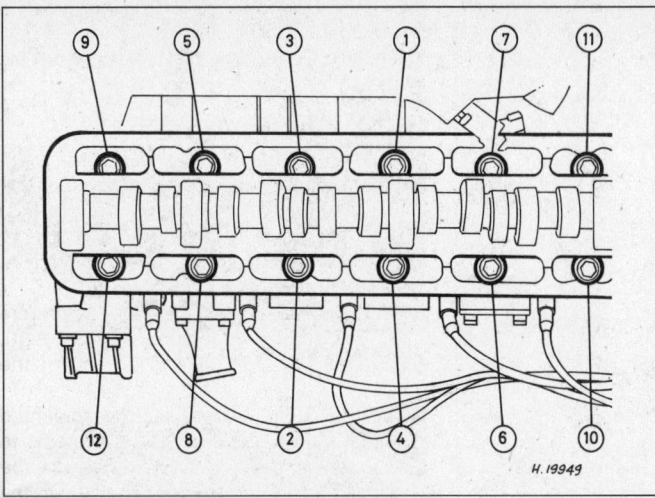

Fig 1.18 Cylinder head bolt tightening sequence on the 10-valve engine (Sec 38)

Fig 1.19 Cylinder head bolt tightening sequence on the 20-valve engine (Sec 38)

opposite ends of the block, to position the gasket and to give a location for fitting the cylinder head (photo). Lower the head on to the block, remove the guide dowels and insert the bolts and washers. Do not use jointing compound on the cylinder head joint.

3 Tighten the bolts using the sequence shown in Fig. 1.18 or 1.19, in the three stages given in the Specifications, to the specified torque.

4 Locate the timing belt rear cover and spacers on the front of the cylinder head and block, and tighten the retaining bolts and studs, as applicable.

5 Refit the water pump with reference to Chapter 2.

6 Refit the camshaft(s) and hydraulic tappets as described in Section 39.

39 Camshaft and hydraulic tappets - refitting

Note: *If necessary, temporarily refit the camshaft(s) before refitting the hydraulic tappets, and check that the camshaft endfloat is as given in the Specifications.*

1 Oil the hydraulic bucket tappets, and insert

them in their previously-noted positions over the valves.

10-valve engines

2 Oil the bearing journals on the camshaft, then lower the camshaft into position on the bucket tappets, making sure that the cams for No 1 cylinder are pointing upwards.

3 Fit bearing caps 2 and 4, and tighten the nuts progressively and in diagonal sequence to the specified torque. Make sure that the caps are the same way round as noted on removal, because they are slightly offset.

4 Similarly fit bearing caps 1 and 3.

20-valve engine

5 Oil the bearing journals on the camshafts.

6 Fit the chain over the sprockets so that the marks are as shown in Fig. 1.20, then lower the camshafts into position.

7 Fit the bearing caps 6, 8 and 10, and tighten the nuts progressively and in diagonal sequence to the specified torque.

8 Similarly fit bearing caps 7 and 9, followed by bearing caps 1, 3 and 5, then caps 2 and 4.

All engines

9 Smear a little oil on the lips and outer rim of the new oil seal. Locate it on the front of the camshaft, and use a socket and mallet to

drive it squarely into position, until flush with the cylinder head. Do not position the oil seal over the oil return drilling.

10 Locate the Woodruff key, then refit the camshaft gear. Insert and tighten the centre bolt to the specified torque.

11 Refit the timing belt, with reference to Section 40.

12 Refit the valve cover, together with new gaskets.

13 Reverse the preliminary procedure given at the beginning of Section 35. If any of the hydraulic tappets have been renewed, do not start the engine or turn it until thirty minutes have elapsed. Excess oil may still be trapped in the tappet, with the resulting possibility of the valve striking the piston.

40 Timing belt and gears - removal and refitting

Note: *If the engine is still in the car, first carry out the following operations:*

(a) Disconnect the battery negative lead

(b) Where fitted, remove the power steering pump, leaving the hoses connected (Chapter 10)

(c) Remove the alternator drivebelt (Chapter 12) and, if fitted, the air conditioning compressor drivebelt (Chapter 11)

(d) Remove the radiator grille

1 Using Audi tool 2084 lock the vibration damper on the front of the crankshaft stationary, then using Audi tool 2079 loosen the centre bolt. The bolt is tightened to a high torque, and it is recommended that these tools are used if at all possible. However, it may be possible to loosen the bolt while holding the starter ring gear stationary using a wide bladed screwdriver, or the method shown (photo).

2 Follow paragraphs 1 to 11 inclusive of

38.2 Guide rod positions when fitting the cylinder head

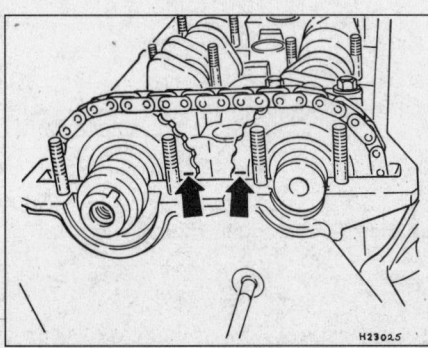

Fig 1.20 Camshaft sprocket timing marks (arrowed) on the 20-valve engine (Sec 39)

1

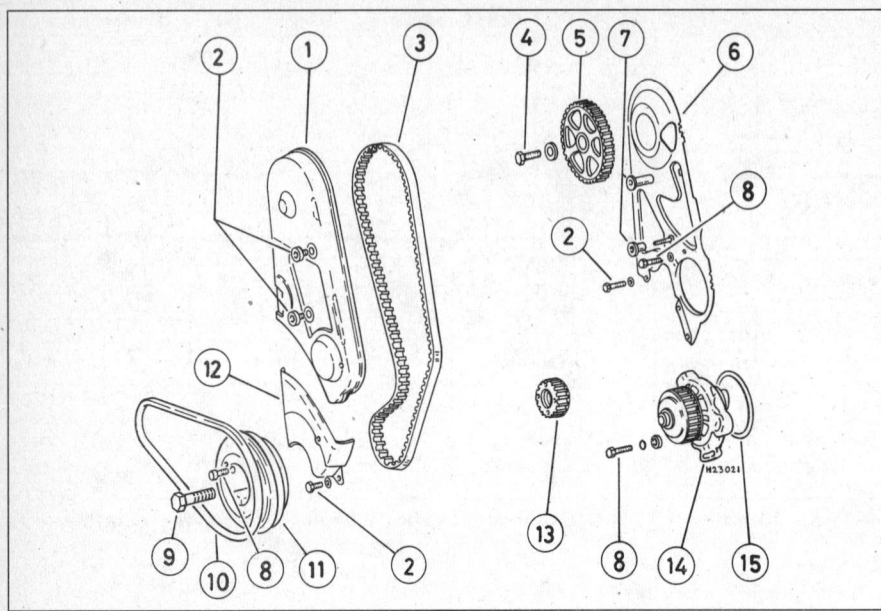

Fig 1.21 Timing belt components on the 10-valve engine (Sec 40)

1 Upper timing cover	6 Rear cover	11 Vibration damper
2 Nuts/bolts	7 Spacers	12 Lower timing cover
3 Timing belt	8 Bolt	13 Crankshaft gear
4 Bolt	9 Crankshaft gear bolt	14 Water pump
5 Camshaft gear	10 Drivebelt	15 O-ring seal

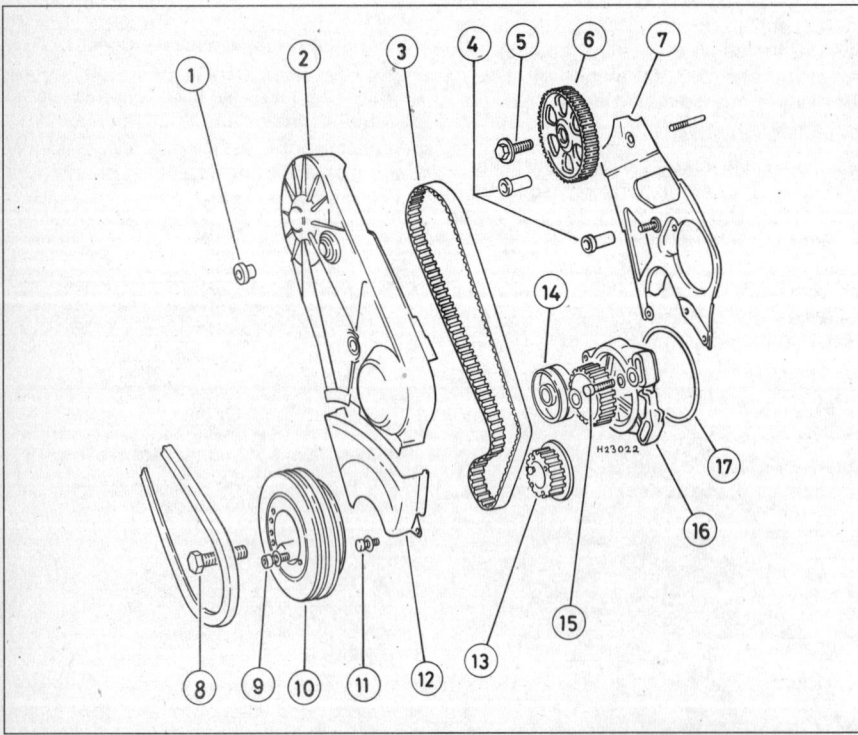

Fig 1.22 Timing belt components on the 20-valve engine (Sec 40)

1 Nut	7 Rear cover	13 Crankshaft gear
2 Upper timing cover	8 Crankshaft gear bolt	14 Idler pulley
3 Timing belt	9 Bolt	15 Bolt
4 Spacers	10 Vibration damper	16 Water pump
5 Bolt	11 Bolt	17 O-ring seal
6 Camshaft gear	12 Lower timing cover	

40.1 One method of locking the starter ring gear

40.9 Fitting the crankshaft gear and vibration damper to the crankshaft – note the location key (arrowed), which is an integral part of the gear

Section 35 (remove both timing covers where applicable).

3 Unscrew the centre bolt, and withdraw the vibration damper, together with the crankshaft gear and timing belt.

4 Separate the vibration damper from the crankshaft gear by removing the bolts using an Allen key, then reinserting two diagonally-opposite bolts on a few threads, and tapping them through the damper.

5 Do not *turn the crankshaft with the timing belt removed.*

6 If necessary, unbolt and remove the timing belt rear cover.

7 Commence refitting by locating the timing belt rear cover on the front of the cylinder head and block, and tighten the retaining bolts and studs, as applicable.

8 Reassemble the vibration damper to the

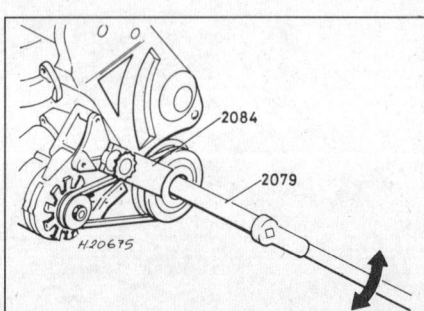

Fig 1.23 Special tools for tightening the crankshaft gear centre bolt (Sec 40)

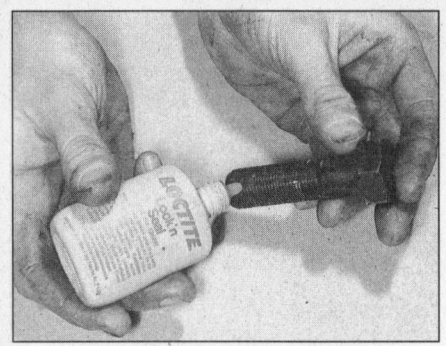

40.10 Applying locking fluid to the crankshaft centre bolt

40.14 Checking the timing belt tension

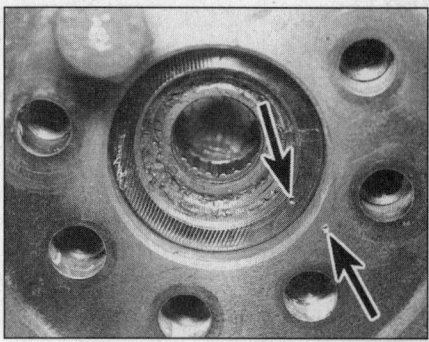

41.1 Centre-punch alignment marks on the crankshaft and flywheel

crankshaft gear, then fit and tighten the bolts.
9 Align the key on the crankshaft gear with the slot in the crankshaft, then locate the timing belt on the crankshaft gear and fit the gear to the crankshaft (photo). Take care not to trap the belt between the gear and the oil pump housing.
10 Coat the threads of the centre bolt with locking fluid (photo), then insert the bolt and tighten it while holding the crankshaft stationary.
Note that the torque wrench setting given for this bolt is only applicable when using Audi tool 2079; if you are not using this tool, tighten the bolt to at least the specified torque, and have your Audi dealer check its tightness on completion (the special tool increases the leverage of the standard torque wrench).
11 Fit the Woodruff key and gear to the camshaft. Insert the bolt and washer, and tighten to the specified torque.
12 Check that the timing marks are as given in Section 35, paragraphs 4 to 7 (as applicable).
13 Locate the timing belt on the crankshaft, camshaft and water pump gears, and over the idler. Turn the water pump anti-clockwise to pretension the belt, then check that the TDC timing marks are still aligned.
14 Turn the water pump anti-clockwise, and tension the timing belt until it can just be twisted through 90° with the thumb and forefinger, midway between the camshaft and water pump gears (photo). Tighten the water pump mounting and adjustment bolts when the adjustment is correct.

15 Turn the crankshaft two complete turns, then re-check the timing belt setting and adjustment.
16 Refit the timing belt covers.
17 Refit the valve cover, together with new gaskets.
18 If the engine is in the car, reverse the preliminary procedures at the beginning of this Section.

41 Flywheel/driveplate - removal, examination and refitting

1 The procedure is as given in Part A, Section 14, but mark the flywheel/ driveplate in relation to the crankshaft, as the retaining bolt holes are not offset (photo).

2 If the flywheel is renewed on the 20-valve engine, two new ignition timing point pins must be fitted. Additionally, the ignition sender and engine speed sender must be adjusted so that they are between 0.50 and 1.25 mm (0.020 and 0.049 in) from the timing point pin and starter ring gear respectively. Use a feeler gauge to make the adjustment.

42 Sump - removal and refitting

Refer to Part A, Section 16, but on the 20-valve engine, remove the dipstick and turn the engine until the cut-out sections in the sump and flywheel are aligned, in order to unscrew the two rear sump bolts.

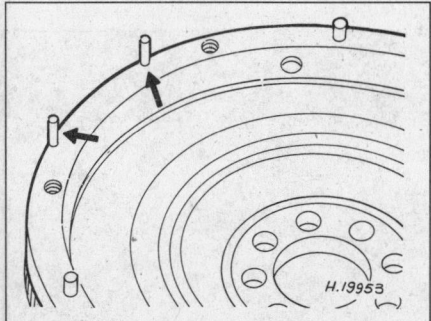

Fig 1.24 Ignition timing point pins fitted to the flywheel on the 20-valve engine (Sec 41)

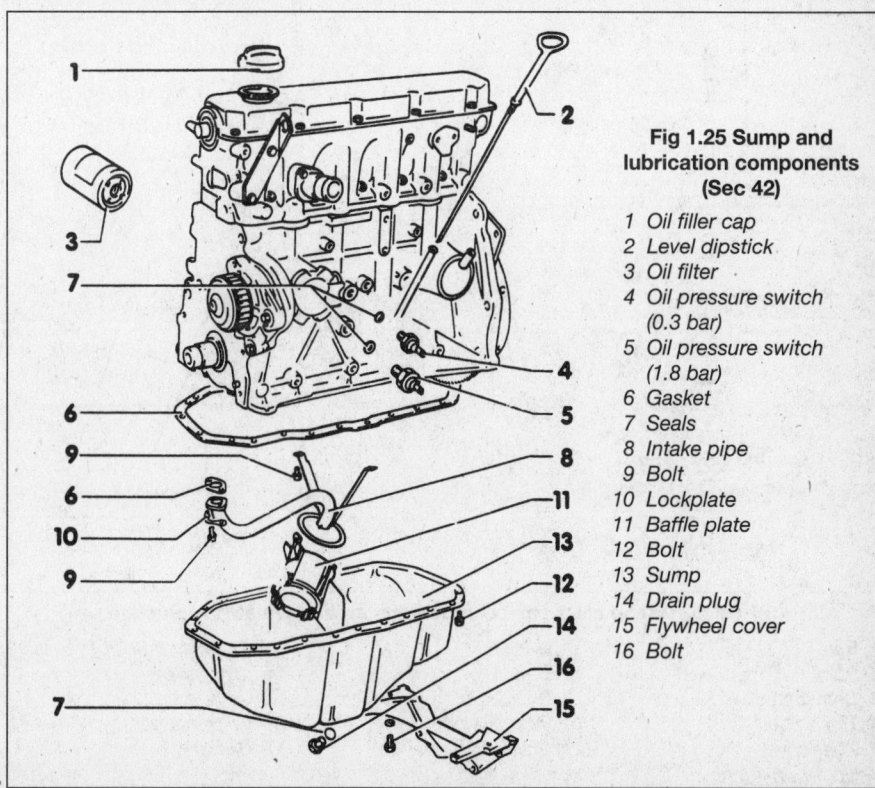

Fig 1.25 Sump and lubrication components (Sec 42)

1 Oil filler cap
2 Level dipstick
3 Oil filter
4 Oil pressure switch (0.3 bar)
5 Oil pressure switch (1.8 bar)
6 Gasket
7 Seals
8 Intake pipe
9 Bolt
10 Lockplate
11 Baffle plate
12 Bolt
13 Sump
14 Drain plug
15 Flywheel cover
16 Bolt

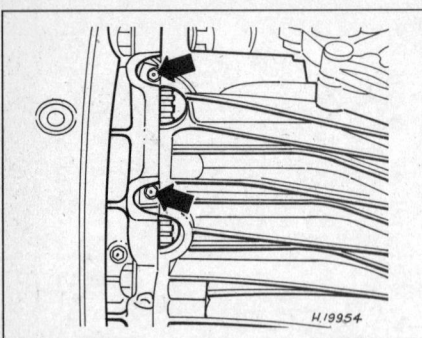

Fig 1.26 Rear sump bolts (arrowed) on the 20-valve engine (Sec 42)

43 Crankshaft front and rear oil seals - renewal

Front oil seal

1 Remove the timing belt and crankshaft gear, as described in Section 40.
2 If an extractor tool is available, the seal may be renewed without removing the oil pump, otherwise refer to Section 44. It is also recommended that Audi tool 2080 together with a guide sleeve be used to install the new seal: Dip the seal in engine oil before fitting, and if the old seal has scored the crankshaft,

43.5 Removing the crankshaft rear oil seal and housing

position the new seal on the unworn surface.
3 Refit the crankshaft gear and timing belt, as described in Section 40.

Rear oil seal

4 Remove the flywheel or driveplate, as described in Section 41.
5 If an extractor tool is available, the seal may be renewed without removing the housing, otherwise unbolt and remove the housing (including the two sump bolts) and remove the gasket (photo). If the sump gasket is damaged while removing the housing, it will be necessary to remove the sump and fit a new gasket. However, refit the sump after fitting the housing.

6 Drive the old seal out of the housing, then dip the new seal in engine oil and drive it into the housing with a block of wood or a socket, until flush. Make sure that the closed end of the seal is facing outwards.
7 Fit the housing together with a new gasket, and tighten the bolts evenly in diagonal sequence.
8 Refit the flywheel or driveplate, as described in Section 41.

44 Oil pump - removal, examination and refitting

1 Remove the timing belt and crankshaft gear, as described in Section 40.
2 Remove the sump, with reference to Section 42.
3 Remove the dipstick.
4 Remove the two bolts securing the oil intake pipe stay to the crankcase (photo). Knock back the tabs of the lockplate on the intake pipe flange (photo), remove the bolts and the intake pipe.
5 Remove the bolts securing the oil pump, and take off the oil pump and gasket (photo).
6 Remove the countersunk screws securing the pump backplate, and lift the backplate off, exposing the gears (photo).
7 Check that there is a mark on the exposed face of the gears and if not, make a mark to show which side of the gears is towards the engine before removing them.
8 Unscrew the pressure relief valve and

44.4A Oil pump intake pipe

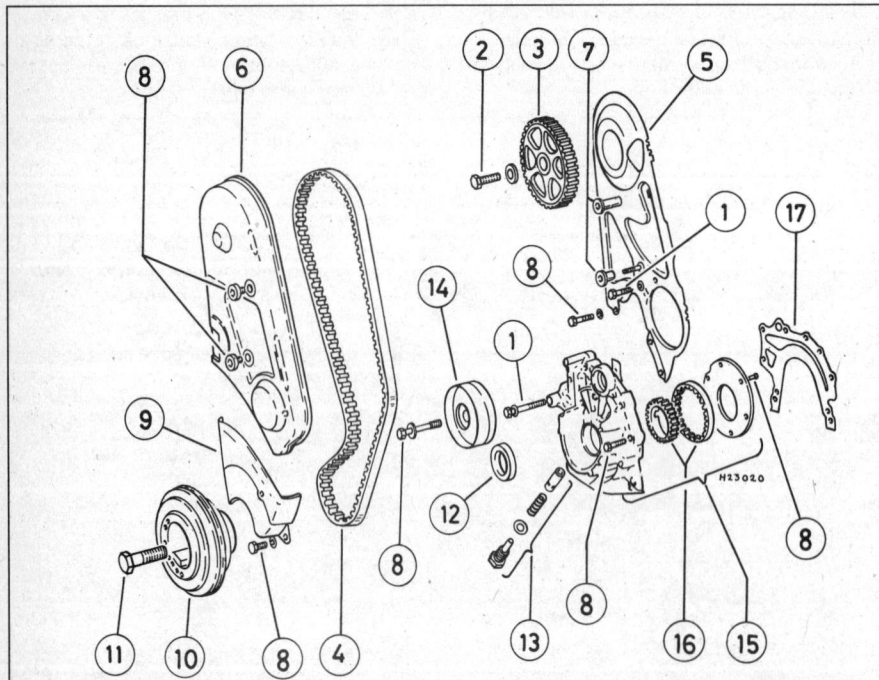

Fig 1.27 Oil pump and timing belt components on the 10-valve engine (Sec 44)

1 Bolt	7 Spacers	13 Oil pressure relief valve
2 Bolt	8 Bolt	14 Idler pulley
3 Camshaft gear	9 Lower timing cover	15 Oil pump
4 Timing belt	10 Vibration damper	16 Oil pump gears
5 Rear cover	11 Crankshaft gear bolt	17 Gasket
6 Upper timing cover	12 Oil seal	

44.4B Oil pump intake pipe flange

44.5 Oil pump removal

44.6 Oil pump with backplate removed

44.8 Removing the oil pressure relief valve

remove the plug, sealing ring, spring and plunger (photo).

9 Clean all the parts thoroughly, and examine the pump casing and backplate for signs of wear or scoring. Examine the pressure relief valve plunger and its seating for damage and wear, and check that the spring is not damaged or distorted. Check the gears for damage and wear. New gears may be fitted, but they must be fitted as a pair.

10 Prise out the oil seal from the front of the pump. Oil the lip of the new seal, enter the seal with its closed face outwards, and use a block of wood to tap the seal in flush. If there is any scoring on the crankshaft in the area on which the lip of the seal bears, the seal may be pushed to the bottom of its recess so that the lip bears on an undamaged part of the crankshaft.

11 Reassemble the pump by fitting the gears and the backplate. The inner gear has its slotted end towards the crankshaft, and although the outer gear can be fitted either way round, it should be fitted the same way round as it was before removal. Some gears have a triangle stamped on them, and this mark should be towards the front.

12 Refit the oil pump, together with a new gasket, making sure that the slot on the inner gear engages the dog on the crankshaft.

13 Insert the bolts and tighten them in diagonal sequence to the specified torque.

14 Fit the oil intake pipe, together with a new gasket, tighten the bolts, and bend the lockplate tabs onto the flange bolts.

15 Refit the dipstick, sump (Section 42), and timing belt and crankshaft gear (Section 40).

45 Pistons and connecting rods
- removal and dismantling

Refer to Part A, Section 19 of this Chapter. Removal of the cylinder head is described in Section 36, and the timing belt in Section 40. Instead of removing the oil pump, remove the sump as described in Section 42, then unbolt the oil intake pipe as described in Section 44. Note that on the 20-valve engine, the big-end caps are fitted with an oil spray jet to cool the piston.

46 Pistons and cylinder bores -
examination

Refer to Part A, Section 20 of this Chapter.

47 Pistons and connecting rods
- reassembly and refitting

Refer to Part A, Section 21 of this Chapter. With the pistons fitted, refit the oil intake pipe, together with a new gasket, tighten the bolts, and bend the lockplate tabs onto the flange bolts. Refitting of the sump is described in Section 42, the timing belt in Section 40, and the cylinder head in Section 36.

48 Crankshaft - removal,
examination and refitting

1 With the engine removed from the car, remove the pistons and connecting rods as described in Section 45. Keep the big-end bearings with their matching connecting rods, to ensure correct refitting.

2 Remove the oil pump (Section 44) and rear oil seal, complete with housing (Section 43).

3 Check that each main bearing cap is numbered for position from the front of the engine.

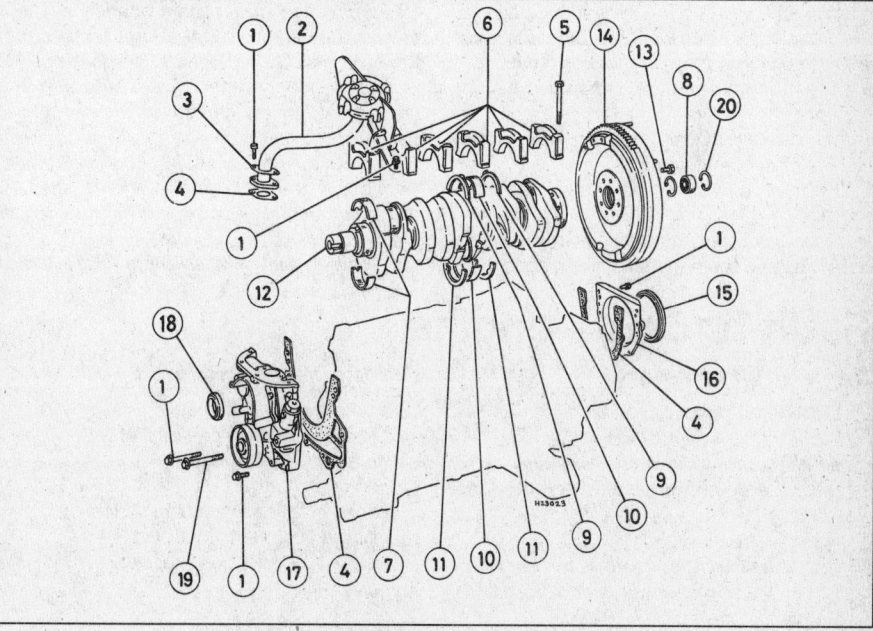

Fig 1.28 Crankshaft components (Sec 48)

1 Bolt
2 Intake pipe
3 Lockplate
4 Gasket
5 Bolt
6 Main bearing caps
7 Main bearing shells
8 Ball-bearing
9 Thrustwasher (lower)
10 No 4 main bearing shell
11 Thrustwasher (upper)
12 Crankshaft
13 Bolt
14 Flywheel
15 Rear oil seal
16 Housing
17 Oil pump
18 Front oil seal
19 Bolt
20 Circlip

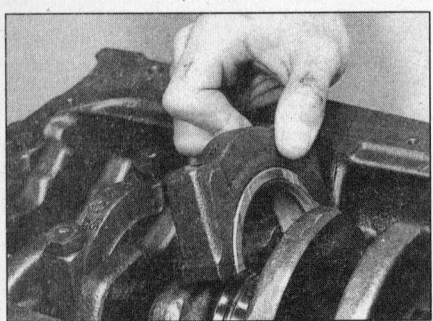

48.6 Removing No 4 main bearing cap

48.8 Removing the crankshaft

49.0A Engine front support bar

49.0B Top view of the left-hand engine mounting

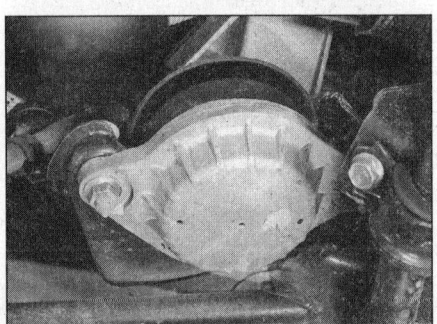

49.0C Bottom view of the right-hand engine mounting

4 Unscrew and remove the bolts from caps 1, 2, 3, 5 and 6, then remove the caps.

5 With cap No 4 still in position, determine the crankshaft endfloat with a feeler blade inserted between the thrustwasher and the crankshaft web. This will give an indication of the wear in the thrustwashers, by comparison with the endfloat given in the Specifications.

6 Unbolt and remove the No 4 main bearing cap (photo).

7 Make sure that each bearing shell is kept with its corresponding cap.

8 Lift the crankshaft from the crankcase (photo).

9 Remove the bearing shells from the crankcase, keeping them identified for location.

10 Refer to Part A, Section 22, but note that on some models, the rear spigot bearing is retained in the flywheel by two circlips.

11 Position the cylinder block on the bench, with the crankcase uppermost.

12 Locate the upper main bearing shells in the crankcase, so that the tags engage with the cut-outs. Oil the bearing shells. If the old shells are being refitted, make sure that they are in their correct locations. They should all have oil grooves.

13 Lower the crankshaft into the crankcase.

14 Locate the lower main bearing shells in the main bearing caps, noting that they are all plain.

15 Position the thrustwashers on each side

of No 4 cap, using a little grease to hold them in place. Make sure that the oil grooves face outwards.

16 Oil the bearing shell, then fit No 4 main bearing cap, insert the bolts, and tighten them to the specified torque.

17 Using a feeler blade or a dial gauge, check that the endfloat is as given in the Specifications.

18 Oil the remaining main bearing shells, then fit the caps in their correct locations, insert the bolts, and tighten them to the specified torque.

19 Check that the crankshaft rotates freely.

20 Refit the rear oil seal and housing (Section 43), the oil pump (Section 44), and the pistons and connecting rods (Section 47).

49 Engine mountings - renewal

Refer to Part A, Section 23 (photos).

50 Engine - initial start-up after major overhaul

Refer to Part A, Section 26.

Fault finding - engine

Engine fails to start
- [ ] Discharged battery
- [ ] Loose battery connection
- [ ] Loose or broken ignition leads
- [ ] Moisture on spark plugs, distributor cap, or HT leads
- [ ] Incorrect spark plug
- [ ] Cracked distributor cap or rotor
- [ ] Dirt or water in carburettor (as applicable)
- [ ] Empty fuel tank
- [ ] Faulty fuel pump
- [ ] Faulty starter motor
- [ ] Low cylinder compression

Engine stalls
- [ ] Idling adjustments incorrect
- [ ] Intake manifold air leak
- [ ] Ignition timing incorrect

Engine idles erratically
- [ ] Intake manifold air leak
- [ ] Leaking cylinder head gasket
- [ ] Worn camshaft lobes
- [ ] Faulty fuel pump
- [ ] Loose crankcase ventilation hoses
- [ ] Idling adjustments incorrect
- [ ] Uneven cylinder compressions

Engine misfires
- [ ] Spark plugs gap incorrect
- [ ] Faulty coil or transistorised ignition component
- [ ] Dirt or water in carburettor (as applicable)
- [ ] Burnt out valve
- [ ] Leaking cylinder head gasket
- [ ] Distributor cap cracked
- [ ] Uneven cylinder compressions
- [ ] Idling adjustments incorrect

Engine backfires
- [ ] Idling adjustments incorrect
- [ ] Ignition timing incorrect
- [ ] Intake manifold air leak
- [ ] Sticking valve

Excessive oil consumption
- [ ] Worn pistons and cylinder bores
- [ ] Valve guides and valve stem seals worn
- [ ] Oil leaking from crankshaft oil seals, valve cover gasket, etc

Engine lacks power
- [ ] Incorrect ignition timing
- [ ] Incorrect spark plug gap
- [ ] Low cylinder compression
- [ ] Excessive carbon build-up in engine
- [ ] Air filter choked

Chapter 2 Cooling system

Contents

Degrees of difficulty

Easy, suitable for novice with little experience	Fairly easy, suitable for beginner with some experience	Fairly difficult, suitable for competent DIY mechanic 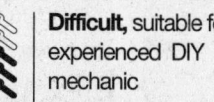	Difficult, suitable for experienced DIY mechanic 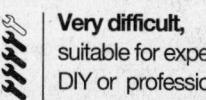	Very difficult, suitable for expert DIY or professional 

Specifications

System type . . . . Pressurized radiator and expansion tank, belt-driven water pump, thermostatically-controlled electric cooling fan

Expansion tank cap opening pressure . . . . 1.2 to 1.5 bar (17.4 to 21.8 lbf/in²)

Thermostat
Starts to open:
  Four-cylinder . . . . 85°C (185°F)
  Five-cylinder . . . . 87°C (188°F)
Fully open:
  Four-cylinder . . . . 105°C (221°F)
  Five-cylinder . . . . 102°C (216°F)
Stroke (minimum):
  Four-cylinder . . . . 7.0 mm (0.28 in)
  Five-cylinder (10-valve) . . . . 7.0 mm (0.28 in)
  Five-cylinder (20-valve) . . . . 8.0 mm (0.32 in)

Electric cooling fan
Thermo-switch operating temperatures:
  Single-speed (two-pin plug):
    Switches on . . . . 92 to 97°C (198 to 207° F)
    Switches off . . . . 84 to 91°C (183 to 196° F)
  Two-speed (three-pin plug):
    1st speed switches on . . . . 92 to 97°C (198 to 207°F)
    1st speed switches off . . . . 84 to 91°C (183 to 196°F)
    2nd speed switches on . . . . 99 to 105°C (210 to 221°F)
    2nd speed switches off . . . . 91 to 98°C (196 to 208°F)
Run-on switch (injector cooling):
  Switches on . . . . 110°C (120°F)
  Switches off . . . . 103°C (217°F)
Run-on relay (injector cooling):
  Timed period . . . . 10 to 12 minutes

Antifreeze
Type . . . . Ethylene glycol, with corrosion inhibitor
Concentration percentage for protection down to:
  -25°C (-13°F) 40%
  -30°C (-22°F) 45%
  -35°C (-31°F) 50%
System capacity:
  Four-cylinder . . . . 6.5 litres (11.4 pints)
  Five-cylinder . . . . 8.0 litres (14.1 pints)

2

Torque wrench settings

	Nm	lbf ft
Radiator mountings (four-cylinder)	10	7
Radiator mountings (five-cylinder)	20	15
Thermostat cover	10	7
Temperature sender unit	10	7
Water pump to housing (four-cylinder)	10	7
Water pump housing to block (four-cylinder)	20	15
Water pump pulley (four-cylinder)	20	15
Electric cooling fan cowl	10	7
Electric cooling fan	10	7
Water pump to block (five-cylinder)	20	15

1 General description

The cooling system is of pressurized type and includes a front (four-cylinder) or side (five-cylinder) mounted radiator, a water pump driven by an external V-belt on four-cylinder engines, or by the timing belt on five-cylinder engines, and an electric cooling fan. On certain models, a second fan is driven by a belt from the first fan, and on models fitted with air conditioning, automatic transmission and trailer towing, a small auxiliary radiator may be fitted. On models with air conditioning, a condenser is fitted in front of the radiator. A remote expansion tank is fitted to all models. The cooling system thermostat is located in the water pump housing on four-cylinder models, and in the inlet on the left-hand side of the cylinder block on five-cylinder models.

The system functions as follows. With the engine cold, the thermostat is shut, and the water pump forces the water through the internal passages, then via the bypass hose and heater circuit over the thermostat capsule, and to the water pump inlet again. This circulation of water cools the cylinder bores, combustion surfaces and valve seats. However, when the coolant reaches the predetermined temperature, the thermostat begins to open. The coolant now circulates through the top hose to the top of the radiator. As it passes through the radiator matrix, it is cooled by the inrush of air when the car is in forward motion supplemented by the action of the electric cooling fan when necessary. Finally, the coolant is returned to the water pump via the bottom hose, and through the open thermostat.

The electric cooling fan is controlled by a thermo-switch, located in the bottom of the radiator. Additionally on some four-cylinder fuel injection engines, a thermo-switch is located near the injectors in the cylinder head. Water temperature is monitored by a sender unit in the cylinder head.

⚠ **Warning: The electric cooling fan will operate when the temperature of the coolant in the radiator (and cylinder head on some models)** *reaches the predetermined level even if the ignition is switched off. Therefore extreme caution should be exercised with a hot engine, when working in the vicinity of the fan blades.*

2 Routine maintenance

Carry out the following procedures at the intervals given in 'Routine maintenance' at the beginning of the manual.

Check cooling system for leaks

1 Inspect all coolant hoses, including the heater hoses, for deterioration and damage. Also check that the hose clips are secure.

Check coolant level

2 The coolant level can be checked by looking through the translucent expansion tank. There is no need to remove the filler cap.
3 There is normally only one level mark on the side of the expansion tank, just below the seam, with a 'minimum' arrow pointing down to it. There is no 'maximum' mark.
4 With the engine cold, the coolant should be on the level mark, but with the engine hot, the coolant should be slightly higher.
5 If necessary, remove the filler cap and top up to the correct level with the correct antifreeze mixture (photo). Note that if the engine is hot, the filler cap should be covered with a cloth, then turned one turn anti-clockwise, to release the system pressure before removing it. If a lot of coolant is required, allow the engine to completely cool before topping up, otherwise there is a risk of damage to the cylinder head.
6 Refit and tighten the filler cap after topping-up.
7 Where frequent topping-up is required, but there is no obvious leak in the system, it is recommended that a pressure test is carried out, using a cooling system tester. An Audi dealer should have this equipment, which will confirm or negate any internal leaks in the engine.

Check antifreeze strength

8 It is important to maintain the correct antifreeze strength throughout the year. Besides preventing freezing of the coolant, the antifreeze also raises its boiling point, and therefore helps to prevent boiling. The recommended antifreeze mixture also incorporates a corrosion inhibitor, which prevents the formation of rust and scale in the engine's internal waterways.
9 The antifreeze strength may be checked using a special hydrometer, obtainable from motor accessory shops.

Check water pump drivebelt tension (four-cylinder engine)

10 Refer to Chapter 12 under the checking and adjustment of the alternator drivebelt.

Renew coolant

11 Audi do not specify an interval for renewing the coolant if their recommended additive is used. If any other antifreeze is used, refer to Sections 3, 4 and 5, and renew it at the interval given in 'Routine maintenance' at the beginning of the manual.

3 Cooling system - draining

1 It is preferable to drain the cooling system when the engine is cold. If this is not possible, place a cloth over the expansion tank filler cap, then unscrew the cap slowly, and allow all pressure to escape before completely removing it. Refer to the warning in Section 1.
2 Have ready a suitable container to catch the coolant as it is drained.

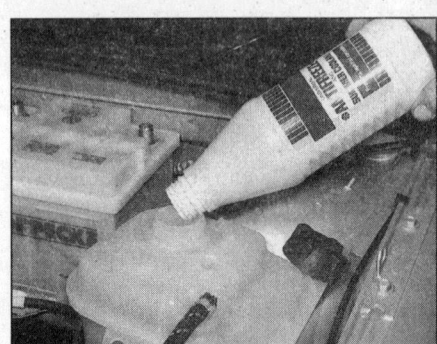

2.5 Topping-up the cooling system

3.3A Loosen the clip . . .

3.3B . . . and disconnect the bottom hose

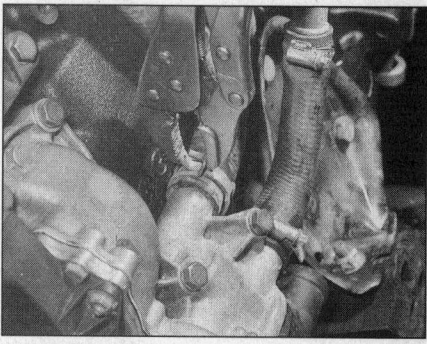
3.3C Disconnecting the bypass hose from the water pump

Four-cylinder engines

3 Disconnect the bottom hose, and the bypass hose from the thermostat and water pump housing on the left-hand side of the engine (photos). Alternatively, unbolt the thermostat cover and remove the thermostat.

Five-cylinder engines

4 Disconnect the heater supply hose from the outlet stub on the rear of the cylinder block.
5 Disconnect the bottom hose from the front of the radiator (photo).
6 Either remove the thermostat (Section 8), or disconnect the short hose leading from the coolant pipe to the block inlet union on the left-hand side of the engine (photo).

4 Cooling system - flushing

1 Whenever the cooling system is drained, it should be flushed through with clean water, in order to clear away any accumulations of rust, scale or sediment. If the coolant has not been regularly changed, there may be a severe accumulation of sediment, and reverse-flushing may then be necessary to clear the system.
2 Drain the cooling system, as described in Section 3.
3 Disconnect the top hose from the radiator, then insert a garden hose in the radiator, and allow the water to circulate through the matrix and out of the bottom of the radiator until it runs clear.
4 Insert the hose in the expansion tank, and allow water to run through the supply hose.
5 Insert the hose in the top hose, and allow water to run through the cylinder head and block.
6 In severe cases of contamination, remove the radiator, invert it, and flush with water until clear water runs out of the top hose stub.
7 To flush the heater, disconnect the hoses at the bulkhead, and insert the water hose.
8 If, after a reasonable period, the water still does not run clear, the system can be flushed with a good proprietary cleaning agent.

3.5 Bottom hose connection to the radiator

5 Cooling system - filling

1 Reconnect all hoses, and tighten the retaining clips.

Four-cylinder engines

2 Pour coolant into the expansion tank, until level with the mark just below the seam.

Five-cylinder engines

3 Unscrew the bleed screw, located on the heater return hose leading from the bulkhead to the coolant pipe on the left-hand side of the engine.
4 Pour coolant into the expansion tank, until level with the mark just below the seam.
5 Tighten the bleed screw when the escaping coolant is free of air bubbles.
6 Top up the coolant to the level mark below the seam (marked 'minimum' on some models).

All engines

7 Refit and tighten the expansion tank cap.
8 Run the engine at a fast idling speed until the electric cooling fan cuts in, indicating that the engine is at normal operating temperature.
9 Switch off the engine, then check the level of the coolant in the expansion tank. At normal operating temperature, the coolant should be slightly higher than the level mark, but with the engine cold, it should be on the level mark.

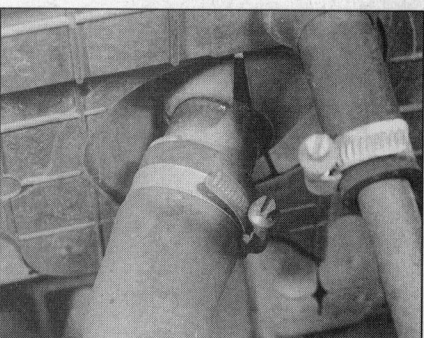
3.6 Bottom hose and coolant pipe viewed from front of radiator

10 If necessary, allow the engine to cool, then top up the coolant to the level mark. Refit and tighten the filler cap.

6 Antifreeze mixture

1 The cooling system is filled at the factory with an antifreeze mixture which contains a corrosion inhibitor. The antifreeze mixture prevents freezing, raises the boiling point of the coolant, and so delays the tendency of the coolant to boil, while the corrosion inhibitor reduces corrosion and the formation of scale. For these reasons, the cooling system should be filled with antifreeze all the year round.
2 The concentration of antifreeze should be adjusted to give the required level of protection selected from the table given in the Specifications.
3 When topping-up the cooling system, always use the same mixture of water and antifreeze which the system contains. Topping-up using water only will gradually reduce the antifreeze concentration and lower the level of protection against both freezing and boiling.
4 At the beginning of the winter season, check the coolant for antifreeze concentration, and add neat antifreeze if necessary.
5 Antifreeze mixture should not be left in the system for longer than its manufacturer's recommendation, which does not usually exceed three years. At the end of this time, drain the system and refill with fresh mixture.

2

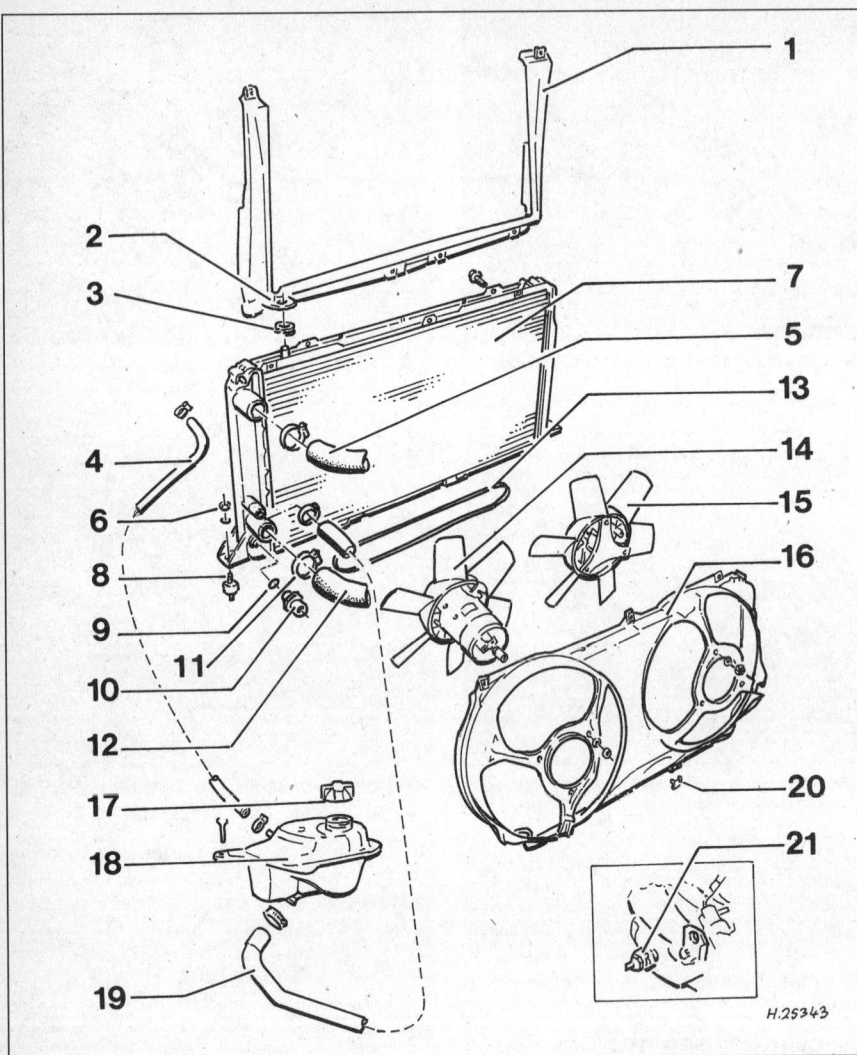

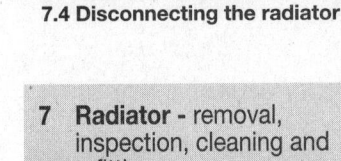

7.4 Disconnecting the radiator top hose

7 Radiator - removal, inspection, cleaning and refitting

1 Disconnect the battery negative lead.
2 Drain the cooling system as described in Section 3.

Four-cylinder engines

3 On models equipped with air conditioning, remove the front grille with reference to Chapter 11, Section 24, then detach the condenser from the radiator by removing the screws.
4 Loosen the clips, and disconnect the top and bottom hoses from the radiator (photo).
5 Loosen the clips, and disconnect the expansion tank hoses from the radiator (photo).
6 Unscrew the bolts retaining the upper mounting brackets to the front panel (photo). Lift the brackets and rubber grommets from the radiator location pins.
7 Disconnect the wiring from the thermo-switch located on the lower right-hand corner of the radiator (photo).
8 Disconnect the wiring from the electric fan motor, and release the wiring harness from the clip (photos).
9 Unscrew the nuts retaining the radiator lower corner brackets to the rubber mountings.
10 Lift the radiator from the lower mountings,

Fig 2.1 Radiator and electric cooling fan components (Sec 7)

1 Shroud	9 Washer	15 2nd cooling fan (where fitted)
2 Top mounting bracket	10 Thermo-switch	16 Fan cowling
3 Rubber mounting	11 Clip	17 Filler cap
4 Breather pipe	12 Radiator bottom hose	18 Expansion tank
5 Radiator top hose	13 Drivebelt for 2nd fan (where fitted)	19 Supply hose
6 Mounting nut	14 Electric cooling fan and motor	20 Spring clip
7 Radiator		21 Temperature sender
8 Mounting rubber		

H.25343

7.5 Disconnecting the expansion tank supply hose from the radiator

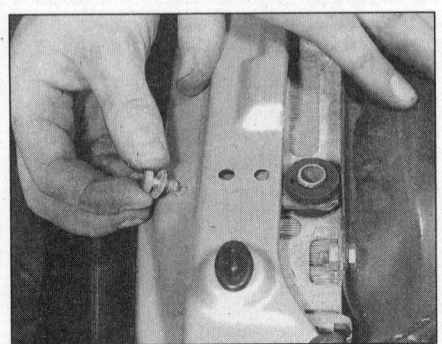

7.6 Removing the radiator upper mounting bracket bolts

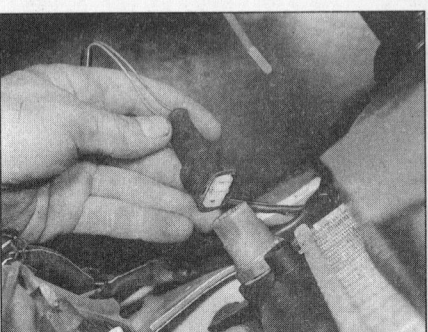

7.7 Disconnecting the thermo-switch wiring

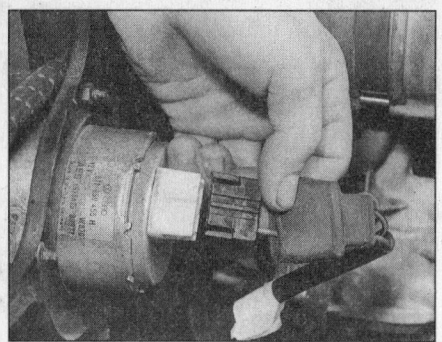

7.8A Disconnecting the electric fan motor wiring

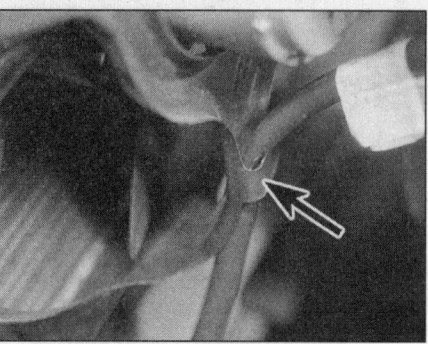

7.8B Release the harness from the clip (arrowed)

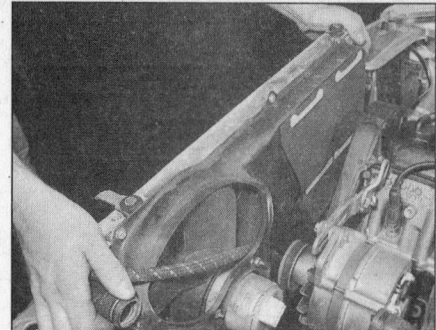

7.10 Removing the radiator

and withdraw it from the engine compartment, complete with the electric cooling fan(s) and cowling (photo).

Five-cylinder engines

11 On models equipped with air conditioning, detach the condenser from the radiator by removing the screws.

12 Unbolt and remove the upper radiator cowl (photos).

13 Loosen the clips and disconnect the top hose and the upper and lower expansion tank hoses from the radiator (photo). On models fitted with air conditioning, automatic transmission and trailer towing, also disconnect the auxiliary radiator hose from the top front of the radiator.

14 Disconnect the wiring from the thermo-switch located on the bottom left of the radiator (photo).

15 Disconnect the wiring from the electric fan motor (photo).

16 Unscrew the radiator mounting nuts (photo).

17 Unbolt the right-hand radiator cowl.

18 On 20-valve models equipped with ABS (anti-lock braking), loosen the fan motor mounting nuts and push the motor forwards.

19 Lift the radiator from the mountings, and withdraw it from the engine compartment, complete with the electric cooling fan and cowling.

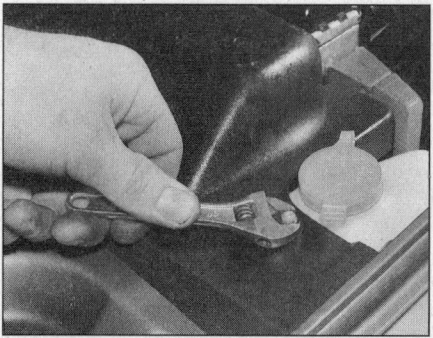

7.12A Unscrewing the upper radiator cowl left-hand . . .

7.12B . . . and right-hand bolts

7.13 Top hose and expansion tank hose connections to the radiator

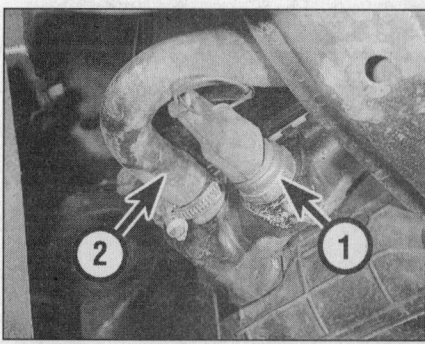

7.14 Thermo-switch (1) and expansion tank hose (2) on the bottom of the radiator

7.15 Disconnecting the electric fan motor wiring

7.16 Radiator lower mounting nut

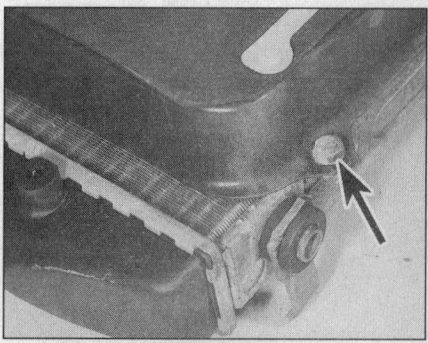

7.20A Cowling retaining bolt (arrowed)

2

7.20B Cowling retaining clip

7.20C Electric fan motor and mounting nuts

7.23 Radiator mounting rubber

All models

20 If necessary, unbolt and unclip the cooling fan and cowling from the radiator, then unscrew the nuts and separate the fan and motor from the cowling (photos). Unscrew the thermo-switch, and remove the gasket if necessary.
21 Radiator repair is best left to a specialist,

although minor leaks may be stopped using a proprietary coolant additive. Clean the radiator matrix of flies and small leaves with a soft brush, or by hosing with water.
22 Reverse-flush the radiator as described in Section 4, and renew the hoses and clips if they are damaged or deteriorated.

23 Refitting is a reversal of removal, but fill the cooling system as described in Section 5. If the thermo-switch was removed, fit a new gasket when refitting it. Check the mounting rubbers, and renew them if necessary (photo).

8 Thermostat - removal, testing and refitting

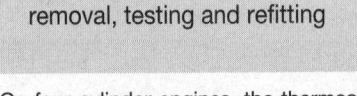

1 On four-cylinder engines, the thermostat is located in the bottom of the water pump housing, but on five-cylinder engines, it is located behind the water pump on the left-hand side of the cylinder block.
2 To remove the thermostat first drain the cooling system, as described in Section 3.
3 Unbolt and remove the thermostat cover, and prise out the O-ring (photos).
4 Prise the thermostat from its housing (photo).
5 To test whether the unit is serviceable, suspend it with a piece of string in a container of water. Gradually heat the water, and note the temperatures at which the thermostat starts to open, and at which it is fully open. Remove the thermostat from the water, and check that it is fully closed when cold. Renew the thermostat if it fails to operate in accordance with the information given in the Specifications.
6 Clean the thermostat housing and cover faces.

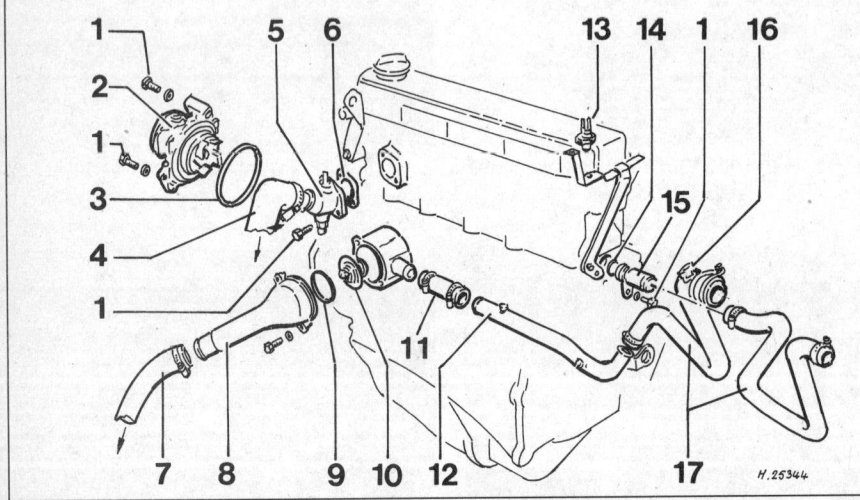

Fig 2.2 Water pump and thermostat components (Sec 8)

1 Bolt
2 Water pump
3 O-ring
4 Radiator top hose
5 Connecting tube
6 Gasket
7 Radiator bottom hose
8 Inlet elbow
9 O-ring
10 Thermostat
11 Connecting hose
12 Coolant pipe
13 Fan run-on thermoswitch
14 O-ring
15 Outlet stub
16 Bleed screw
17 Heater hoses

8.3A Removing the thermostat cover . . .

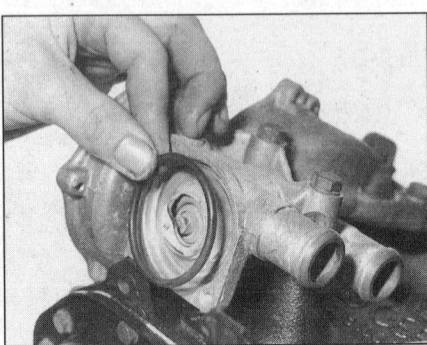

8.3B . . . and O-ring (four-cylinder engine)

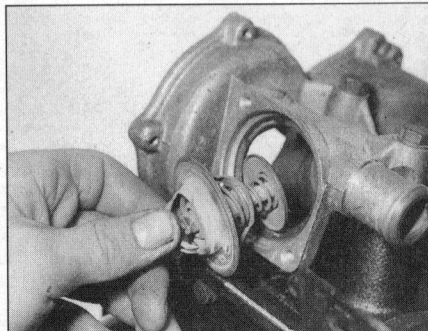

8.4 Removing the thermostat (four-cylinder engine)

9.3A Unscrew the Allen screws . . .

9.3B . . . and remove the water pump drive pulley (four-cylinder engine)

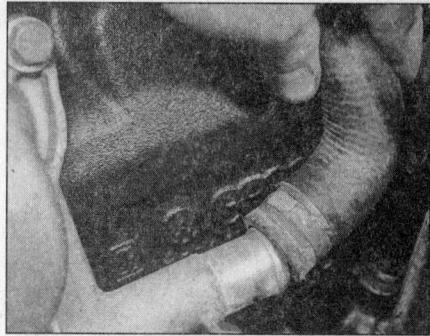

9.4 Disconnecting the bypass hose

7 Locate the thermostat in the housing. On four-cylinder engines, the arrow on the crosspiece must point away from the engine, but on five-cylinder engines, the arrow must point downwards.
8 Locate a new O-ring on the thermostat or cover (as applicable), then fit the thermostat cover, and tighten the bolts to the specified torque.
9 Fill the cooling system as described in Section 5.

9 Water pump - removal and refitting

1 Drain the cooling system as described in Section 3.

Four-cylinder engines

2 Remove the alternator and drivebelt, as described in Chapter 12, Sections 5 and 6.
3 Unbolt the pulley from the water pump drive flange, using an Allen key (photos).
4 Loosen the clips, and disconnect the hoses from the water pump housing (photo).
5 Unscrew the nut, and remove the special bolt retaining the lower timing cover to the water pump assembly (photo).
6 Unbolt the water pump assembly from the cylinder block, and remove the sealing O-ring (photos).
7 Unscrew the bolts, and remove the water pump from its housing (photos). If it is tight, carefully tap it free using a wooden mallet. Remove the gasket.

Five-cylinder engines

8 On models equipped with power steering, remove the pump with reference to Chapter 10, leaving the hoses connected, and place it to one side.
9 Using an Allen key, unscrew the nuts and withdraw the upper timing cover.
10 Set the engine to TDC compression on No 1 cylinder, with reference to Chapter 1.
11 Loosen the water pump mounting/ adjustment bolts, and rotate the water pump clockwise to release the tension on the timing belt.
12 Disconnect the timing belt from the camshaft and water pump pulleys, and from the idler, and tie it loosely to one side.
13 On single overhead camshaft engines, remove the camshaft timing belt sprocket and

9.5 Removing the lower timing cover-to-water pump bolt

9.6A Remove the mounting bolts . . .

9.6B . . . withdraw the water pump . . .

9.6C . . . and remove the O-ring

9.7A Removing the water pump from its housing

9.7B Water pump assembly

2

timing belt rear cover, with reference to Chapter 1.

14 On double overhead camshaft engines, remove the timing belt rear cover, with reference to Chapter 1.

15 Unscrew the remaining water pump bolts, noting the location of the stay (where fitted).

16 Withdraw the water pump from the cylinder block, and remove the sealing ring. Do not move the crankshaft or camshaft with the timing belt disconnected.

All engines

17 If the water pump is faulty, renew it complete, as individual components are not available. Clean the mating faces of the water pump and housing (four-cylinder engines) or block (five-cylinder engines).

18 Refitting is a reversal of removal, but use a new gasket or sealing ring as applicable. On five-cylinder engines, refit and tension the timing belt as described in Chapter 1. Fill the cooling system as described in Section 5. Tension the alternator and power steering pump drivebelts (as applicable), with reference to Chapters 12 and 10 respectively.

---

10 Cooling fan thermo-switch - testing, removal and refitting

1 If the thermo-switch located in the bottom of the radiator develops a fault, it is most likely to fail open-circuit. This will cause the fan motor to remain stationary even though the coolant reaches the operating temperature.

2 To test the thermo-switch for an open-circuit fault, disconnect the wiring, and connect a length of wire or suitable metal object between the earth and live wires. The fan should operate (even without the ignition switched on), in which case the thermo-switch is proved faulty and must be renewed.

3 To remove the thermo-switch, first drain the cooling system, as described in Section 3.

4 Disconnect the battery negative lead.

5 Disconnect the wiring, then unscrew the thermo-switch from the radiator and remove the sealing washer.

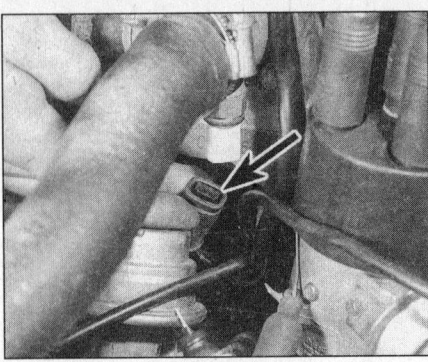

11.3 Disconnecting the wiring (arrowed) from the coolant temperature sender unit

6 To check the operating temperature of the thermo-switch, suspend it in a pan of water so that only the screwed end of the switch is immersed and the electrical contacts are clear of the water. Either connect an ohmmeter between the switch terminals, or connect up a torch battery and bulb in series with the switch. With a thermometer placed in the pan, heat the water, and note the temperature at which the switch contacts close, so that the ohmmeter reads zero, or the bulb lights. Allow the water to cool, and note the temperature at which the switch contacts open. Discard the switch and fit a new one if the operating temperatures are not within the specified limits.

7 Refitting is a reversal of removal, but always fit a new sealing washer. Fill the cooling system, as described in Section 5.

---

11 Coolant temperature sender unit - removal and refitting

1 The coolant temperature sender unit is located on the underside of the coolant outlet elbow, on the left-hand side of the cylinder head on four-cylinder carburettor engines. On four-cylinder fuel-injected engines, it is located on the top of the outlet elbow, and is the smaller of the two units. On five-cylinder engines, it is located on the underside of the outlet elbow.

12.1 Core plugs on the right-hand side of the cylinder block (four-cylinder engine)

2 To remove the unit, first drain half of the cooling system with reference to Section 3.

3 Disconnect the wiring, and unscrew the sender unit from the outlet elbow (photo). Remove the sealing washer.

4 Refitting is a reversal of removal, but always fit a new sealing washer. Top up the cooling system with reference to Section 5.

---

12 Core plug - renewal

1 In the event of a core plug (photo) leaking, it may be renewed as follows. First drain the cooling system, as described in Section 3.

2 Record the fitted depth of the core plug.

3 Drill one or two small holes through the core plug, and use self-tapping screws and a pair of grips to pull out the plug. If the plug is rusted in position, drill a larger hole, and use a lever to remove it.

4 Clean the seating in the cylinder block, then smear a little non-setting sealant around it. Use sealant suitable for use on cooling system components.

5 Using a large socket or piece of metal tubing, tap the new core plug squarely into the block, to the previously-recorded depth.

6 Fill the cooling system, as described in Section 5.

Fault finding - cooling system

Overheating

☐ Low coolant level
☐ Faulty pressure cap
☐ Thermostat sticking shut
☐ Drivebelt broken (four-cylinder engines only)
☐ Thermo-switch faulty (open-circuit)
☐ Cooling fan motor faulty
☐ Clogged radiator matrix

Slow warm-up

☐ Thermostat sticking open
☐ Thermo-switch faulty (short-circuit)

Coolant loss

☐ Deteriorated hose
☐ Leaking water pump or cooling system joint
☐ Blown cylinder head gasket
☐ Leaking radiator
☐ Leaking core plug

Chapter 3
Fuel, exhaust and emission control systems

Contents

Degrees of difficulty

Easy, suitable for novice with little experience	**Fairly easy,** suitable for beginner with some experience 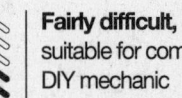	**Fairly difficult,** suitable for competent DIY mechanic	**Difficult,** suitable for experienced DIY mechanic	**Very difficult,** suitable for expert DIY or professional

Specifications

Air cleaner

Type . . . . Renewable paper element type, with automatic air temperature control on most models

Filter element:
  Carburettor engines . . . . Champion W102
  1.6 litre fuel injection engine . . . . Champion U506
  All other fuel injection engines . . . . Champion U501

Fuel system

Fuel pump:
  Carburettor engine . . . . Mechanical, diaphragm type operated by eccentric on intermediate shaft
  Fuel injection engine . . . . Electrically-operated roller cell
Operating pressure on carburettor engine . . . . 0.35 to 0.40 bar (5.08 to 5.8 lbf/in²)

Fuel tank capacity

All models except Coupe . . . . 68 litres (15 gallons)
Coupe . . . . 70 litres (15.4 gallons)

Carburettor system

System application
Engine code:
  RN and NE . . . . Keihin I
  RU . . . . Keihin II

Carburettor (Keihin I)

Type	Twin progressive choke downdraught, manual choke	
Jets and settings:	**Engine code RN**	**Engine code NE**
Fast idle speed	3200 ± 200 rpm	3200 ± 200 rpm
Accelerator pump injection	0.78 ± 0.12 cc/stroke	0.78 ± 0.12 cc/stroke
Choke valve gap	4.6 ± 0.15 mm	4.6 ± 0.15 mm
Idling speed	900 ± 50 rpm	900 ± 50 rpm
CO content	1.0 – 0.5%	1.0 – 0.5%
Venturi – stage 1/2	20/26	20/26
Main jet – stage 1/2	108/150	110/150
Air correction jet – stage 1/2	90/120	90/120
Idling fuel jet	52	52
Idling air jet	115	115
Float needle valve	2.5	2.5

Carburettor (Keihin II)

Type	Twin progressive choke downdraught, manual choke
Jets and settings:	**Engine code RU**
Fast idle speed	3500 ± 200 rpm
Accelerator pump injection	0.85 ± 0.15 cc/stroke
Choke valve gap	2.2 ± 0.15 mm
Idling speed	900 ± 50 rpm
CO content	1.0 – 0.5%
Venturi – stage 1/2	22/26
Main jet – stage 1/2	100/140
Air correction jet – stage 1/2	90/100
Idling fuel jet – stage 1	50
Idling air jet – stage 1	100
Float needle valve	2.5
Discharge pipe – stage 1	40
Enrichment – stage 1	35

Fuel injection system

System application

Engine code:	
PS (to 1989), DZ and KV	K-Jetronic
PS (1989 on) and JN	KE-Jetronic
PM	Mono-Jetronic
NG	KE III-Jetronic
3A	KE-Motronic
7A	Multipoint injection (MPI)

Engine code DZ – K-Jetronic

Idling speed	950 ± 30 rpm
CO content	1.3 ± 0.2%
Idling speed boost:	
Switch-in speed	700 rpm
Switch-out speed	1050 rpm
Cut-out speed of fuel pump relay	6500 to 6700 rpm
System pressure	5.2 to 5.9 bar
Holding pressure after ten minutes	3.3 bar

Engine codes PS (to 1989) and KV – K-Jetronic

Idling speed	750 to 850 rpm
Idling control current	430 to 440 mA
CO content	1.0 to 1.2 %
System pressure	5.4 to 6.2 bar
Holding pressure after ten minutes	3.4 bar

Engine code PM – Mono-Jetronic

Speed limitation	6300 rpm
Idling speed	750 to 950 rpm
CO content	0.2 to 1.2%
System pressure	0.8 to 1.2 bar
Holding pressure after five minutes	0.5 bar minimum
Injector resistance	1.2 to 1.6 ohms

Engine code JN – KE-Jetronic

Idling speed	900 ± 30 rpm
CO content	0.3 to 1.2%
Idling speed boost:	
Switch-in speed	700 rpm
Switch-out speed	1050 rpm
Speed limitation (by fuel pump relay)	6270 to 6330 rpm
System pressure	5.2 to 5.6 bar
Holding pressure after ten minutes	2.6 bar
Injector injection pressure	3.5 to 4.1 bar

Engine code PS (1989 on) – KE-Jetronic

Idling speed	750 to 850 rpm
CO content	0.3 to 1.2%
System pressure	6.1 to 6.5 bar
Holding pressure after ten minutes	3.4 bar
Injector injection pressure	4.3 to 4.6 bar

Engine code NG – KE III-Jetronic

Idling speed	720 to 860 rpm
CO content:	
Lambda probe disconnected	0.8 ± 0.3%
Lambda probe connected	0.3 to 1.2%
Speed limitation (by control unit)	6500 to 6700 rpm
System pressure	6.1 to 6.5 bar
Holding pressure:	
After ten minutes	3.5 bar
After twenty minutes	3.4 bar
Injector injection pressure	4.3 to 4.6 bar

Engine code 3A – KE-Motronic

Idling speed	780 to 900 rpm
CO content	0.2 to 1.2%
CO content control current	0 to 5 mA
Speed limitation	6300 to 6500 rpm
System pressure	6.1 to 6.5 bar
Holding pressure:	
After ten minutes	3.3 bar
After twenty minutes	3.2 bar
Injector injection pressure	3.7 to 4.8 bar

Engine code 7A – Multipoint injection (MPI)

Idling speed	800 ± 50 rpm
CO content	0.75 to 0.25%
System pressure	3.8 to 4.2 bar
Holding pressure:	
After ten minutes	3.2 bar
After twenty minutes	3.0 bar

Torque wrench settings

	Nm	lbf ft
Front exhaust pipe mounting	30	22
Mechanical fuel pump mounting bolts	20	15
Fuel tank	25	18
Exhaust manifold	25	18
Exhaust pipe connecting sleeve	40	30
Warm-up valve	10	7
Cold start valve	10	7
Fuel filter union	20	15
CO measuring pipe union	30	22
Exhaust downpipe to manifold	35	26
Lambda probe to catalytic converter	50	37
Carburettor flange	13	10
Inlet manifold	25	18
Inlet to exhaust manifold bracket	20	15
Intake air preheater	10	7
Carburettor cover	5	4
Warm-up regulator union	20	15
Thermo time switch	30	22
Throttle housing	20	15
Diaphragm pressure regulator union	20	15

3

1 General description

The fuel system comprises a fuel tank mounted behind the rear seat, and either a mechanical fuel pump and downdraught carburettor, or a Bosch fuel injection system. The air cleaner incorporates a renewable paper element, and on most models, an automatic temperature control. The exhaust system is in four sections, and on some models, incorporates a catalytic converter.

To discourage unqualified adjustment of the fuel system, in particular the setting of idle speeds and CO content, all adjusting screws are fitted with tamperproof caps or plugs. These must be removed in order to make adjustments. The caps must be crushed, and the plugs drilled with a 2.5 mm (0.10 in) drill. A 3.0 mm (0.120 in) self-tapping screw should then be used to pull out the plug. Make sure that no infringement of warranty or legal requirements is made.

When working on the fuel system, it is important to be constantly aware of the fire hazard (refer to 'Safety first!'). Carry out the work only in a well-ventilated area. As fuel vapour is heavier than air, do not carry out work over an inspection pit.

2 Routine maintenance

Carry out the following procedures at the intervals given in 'Routine maintenance' at the beginning of the manual.

Check idling speed and CO content

1 Refer to Section 16 or 23. Make sure that the engine is at normal operating temperature, and that the ignition timing is correctly adjusted. Also ensure that the crankcase ventilation system and, where fitted, the EGR, catalytic converter, and lambda probe are functioning correctly. The air cleaner element must also be in good condition.

Renew the in-line fuel filter on carburettor engine

2 Refer to Section 7.

Renew the air cleaner element

3 Refer to Section 3.

Check exhaust system for leaks

4 With the car over an inspection pit or on car ramps, run the engine at idling speed and check the complete exhaust system for leaks. Also check the system for damage and deterioration, and check the mountings.

3 Air cleaner element - renewal

1 A dirty air cleaner element will cause a loss of performance and an increase in fuel consumption, and therefore it must always be renewed at the specified intervals. If the car is operated in dusty conditions, renew the element more frequently.

Carburettor models (and PM engine with Mono-Jetronic)

2 Release the spring clips at the edge of the air cleaner cover. Unscrew the single screw and withdraw the cover from the air cleaner body (photos).
3 Lift out the air cleaner element.
4 Wipe clean the inside of the air cleaner body and cover.
5 Locate the new element in the body, then refit the cover. Insert and tighten the single screw, and snap the spring clips into position.

Fuel injection models (except PM engine)

6 Release the rubber strap on the right-hand front corner of the engine compartment, then pull out the intake cover and disconnect the intake hose (photos).

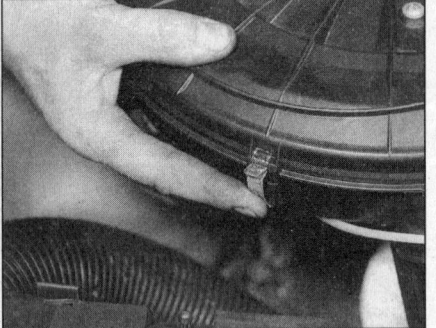
3.2A Release the spring clips . . .

3.2B . . . unscrew the single screw . . .

3.2C . . . and remove the air cleaner cover

3.6A Release the rubber strap . . .

3.6B . . . pull out the intake cover . . .

3.6C . . . and disconnect the intake hose

3.7 Removing the side cover

3.8A Release the spring clips (one arrowed) . . .

3.8B . . . lift the cover, for access to the air cleaner element

7 Remove the screw and withdraw the side cover (photo).
8 Release the spring clips securing the air cleaner cover, and lift the cover from the airflow meter (photos).
9 Remove the air cleaner element from the main body.
10 Wipe clean the inside of the air cleaner body and cover.
11 Locate the new element in the body, then refit the cover and snap the spring clips into position.
12 Refit the side cover, the intake hose, and the intake cover, and secure with the rubber strap.

4 Air cleaner - removal and refitting

Carburettor models (and PM engine with Mono-Jetronic)

1 Remove the element, as described in Section 3.
2 Remove the intake cover from the right-hand front corner of the engine compartment (photo).
3 Unscrew the lower mounting nut and the

upper mounting screw, then remove the intake tube from the front panel and air cleaner (photos).
4 As a precaution against dropping a mounting nut down into the carburettor (or Monojet unit), position a rag over the top of it.
5 Unscrew and remove the three nuts and washers securing the air cleaner body to the carburettor (or Monojet unit) and remove the adaptor or retaining ring if fitted (photo).
6 Lift the air cleaner, and disconnect it from the crankcase ventilation hose (where fitted) and from the warm air duct over the exhaust manifold shroud. Disconnect the vacuum pipe (photos).

3

4.2 Right-hand front intake cover removal

4.3A Unscrew the air cleaner lower mounting nut . . .

4.3B . . . the upper mounting screw . . .

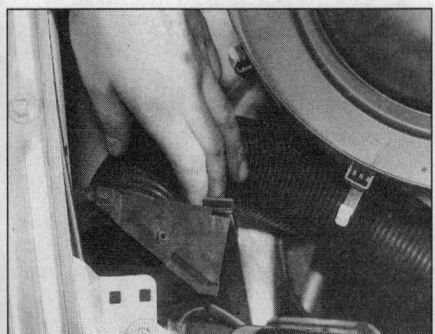

4.3C . . . then remove the intake tube from the front panel . . .

4.3D . . . and air cleaner

4.5 Removing the air cleaner body mounting nuts

4.6A Exhaust manifold warm air duct (arrowed)

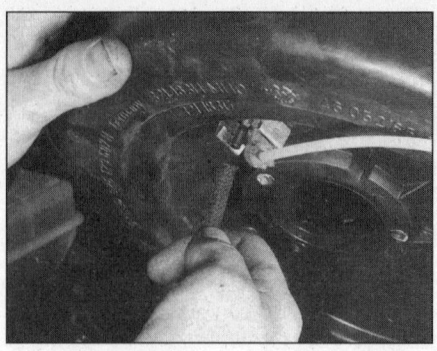

4.6B Disconnecting the vacuum pipe

Fuel injection models (except PM engine)

7 Remove the element, as described in Section 3.

8 Unbolt the air cleaner body from the body panel.

All models

9 Refitting is a reversal of removal.

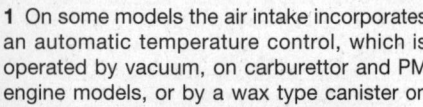

5 Automatic air temperature control - general

1 On some models the air intake incorporates an automatic temperature control, which is operated by vacuum, on carburettor and PM engine models, or by a wax type canister on all other fuel injection models. A flap in the air intake directs warm air from the exhaust manifold, or cold air from the front of the car, according to the temperature of the air.

2 *To check the control on carburettor and PM engines,* disconnect the regulator hose from the adaptor in the brake servo vacuum hose, and plug the adaptor. Start the engine (cold), and run it at a fast idle speed for several minutes. Remove the air cleaner cover, and reconnect the regulator hose to the adaptor - the control flap should move to the fully open position, to admit warm air only. If the flap remains shut, connect a hose direct from the adaptor to the vacuum unit - the flap should now open. If it does, the temperature control valve within the air cleaner has proved faulty, but if it is stays shut the vacuum unit is faulty.

3 *On all other fuel injection engines,* the flap control must be removed to check its operation. Remove the cross-head screws from the control, and withdraw the unit from the air cleaner body. Dip the thermostat in water at a temperature below 30°C (86°F), and check that the flap moves to the warm air position. Increase the temperature of the water to above 38°C (100°F), and check that the flap moves, to close off the warm air. If necessary, the thermostat can be removed by unhooking the flap and pushing the thermostat through the bracket.

4 On both types check that the flap moves freely.

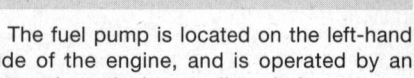

6 Mechanical fuel pump - removal and refitting

1 The fuel pump is located on the left-hand side of the engine, and is operated by an eccentric on the intermediate shaft.

2 Loosen the clips, and disconnect the inlet and outlet hoses (photo).

3 Using an Allen key, unscrew the mounting bolts, then withdraw the fuel pump from the cylinder block (photo).

4 Remove the sealing flange and the O-ring (photos).

5 The pump may be checked by temporarily reconnecting it to the fuel supply hose, and operating the lever by hand, while directing the outlet into a suitable container. Well-defined spurts of fuel should be evident. If the pump is proved faulty, renew it, as it cannot be serviced.

6 Clean the contact faces, then refit the pump, together with a new O-ring and sealing flange. Make sure that the lever locates on top of the camshaft eccentric. Insert and tighten the mounting bolts to the specified torque (photo).

7 In-line fuel filter - renewal

1 A disposable fuel filter is fitted in the fuel line. On carburettor engines, it is located near the fuel pump in the supply line. On some fuel

6.2 Disconnecting the fuel pump outlet hose

6.3 Removing the fuel pump

6.4A Fuel pump sealing flange . . .

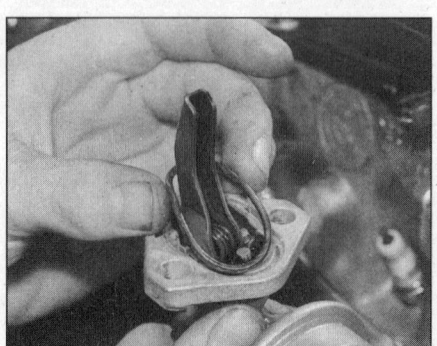

6.4B . . . and O-ring

6.6 Tightening the fuel pump mounting bolts

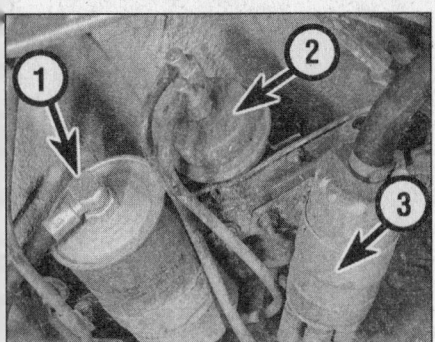

8.3 Fuel filter (1), accumulator (2), and fuel pump (3)

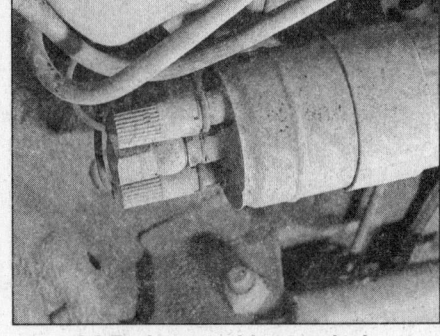

8.8 Fuel pump wiring terminals

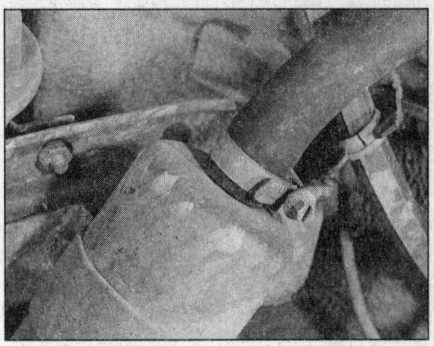

8.10 Fuel pump inlet hose

injection engines, it is located in the supply line from the fuel tank to the fuel pump - in addition, fuel injection engines have a canister type filter, located in the supply line to the metering unit and positioned on the bulkhead.

2 To renew the filter, disconnect the fuel lines and, where necessary, remove the nut from the mounting clip. It will be necessary to jack up the rear of the car to renew the filter near the fuel tank on fuel injection engines.

3 Fit the new filter, making sure that the arrow points in the direction of flow of the fuel (ie towards the engine). Fit new clips and washers, as applicable; *do not allow any dirt or foreign matter to enter the fuel lines.*

8 Fuel pump (fuel injection models) - testing, removal and refitting

1 Check that the fuse supplying the fuel pump circuit is intact.

2 Disconnect the HT wire from the ignition coil, and connect it to earth with a bridging wire.

3 Chock the front wheels, then jack up the rear of the car and support on axle stands, for access to the fuel pump (photo).

4 Operate the starter briefly, and check that the fuel pump is heard to be operating. On engines PM and 3A, it will operate as soon as the ignition is switched on.

5 Should the fuel pump not run, remove the fuel pump relay from the relay board, and connect a bridging wire from the battery

positive terminal to the relay terminal 52 in the board. If the pump now runs, the relay is proved faulty. If not, check the supply wiring to the fuel pump.

6 Note that if the pump is working, but the fuel supply is insufficient, the filter may be blocked.

7 To remove the fuel pump, disconnect the battery negative lead.

8 Unscrew the nuts (where fitted) and disconnect the wiring from the pump (photo).

9 Fit a hose clamp to the fuel supply hose.

10 Position a suitable receptacle beneath the pump to catch spilled fuel, then disconnect the hose and union (photo). Plug the two pipes.

11 Unscrew the nut and release the mounting clamp. Withdraw the pump.

12 If necessary, remove the mounting clamp from the pump.

13 Refitting is a reversal of removal, but make sure that the lug engages with the recess in the clamp.

9 Fuel filter (fuel injection models) - renewal

1 Chock the front wheels, then jack up the rear of the car and support on axle stands.

2 Fit hose clamps to the fuel filter input and output hoses.

3 Unscrew the union bolts, and disconnect the hoses (photo). Recover the sealing washers.

4 Unscrew the nuts, remove the mounting bracket, and withdraw the fuel filter (photo).

5 Refitting is a reversal of removal, but make sure that the arrow points in the direction of flow of the fuel, renew the sealing washers, and tighten the union bolts to the specified torque.

10 Fuel tank - removal and refitting

Note: *For safety, the fuel tank must always be removed in a well ventilated area, never over a pit*

1 Disconnect the battery negative lead.

2 Chock the front wheels, then jack up the rear of the car and support on axle stands. Remove the tank filler cap.

3 Position a suitable container beneath the fuel tank to receive the fuel. Loosen the clips, and disconnect the supply and return hoses from the tank (photo).

4 Prise out the rubber grommet, and disconnect the breather pipe.

5 Remove the trim from inside the luggage compartment.

6 Disconnect the wiring from the fuel gauge sender unit.

7 Disconnect the breather pipe from the top of the tank (photo), and unclip from the side.

8 Unscrew the mounting bolts and screw, and remove the clamping plates (photos). Lift the fuel tank from the luggage compartment.

9 If the tank is contaminated with sediment or

3

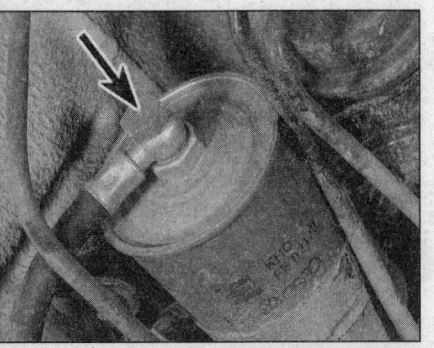

9.3 Fuel filter banjo union bolt (arrowed)

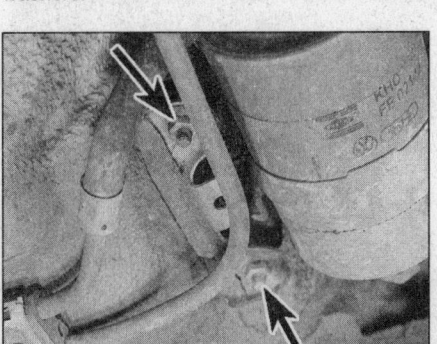

9.4 Fuel filter mounting nuts (arrowed)

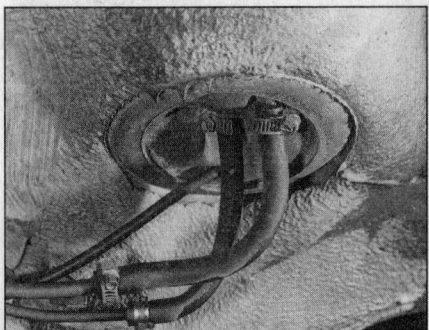

10.3 Fuel tank supply and return hoses

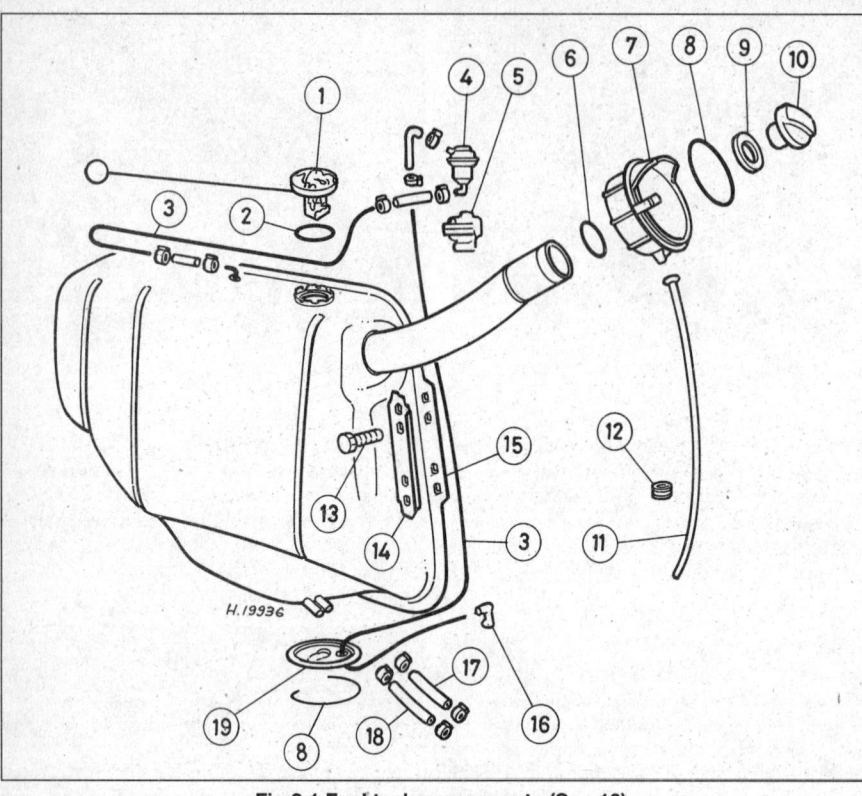

Fig 3.1 Fuel tank components (Sec 10)

1 Fuel gauge sender	6 O-ring seal	11 Overflow pipe	16 End fitting
2 O-ring seal	7 Rubber boot	12 Rubber grommet	17 Return pipe
3 Breather pipe	8 O-ring seal	13 Bolt	18 Supply pipe
4 Gravity valve	9 Gasket	14 Strip	19 Grommet
5 Retainer	10 Cap	15 Fuel tank	

water, remove the gauge sender unit as described in Section 11, and swill the tank out with clean fuel. If the tank is damaged or leaks, it should be repaired by specialists, or alternatively, renewed.

10 With the tank removed, it is a good time to check the gravity valve (photo). Disconnect the hoses, and pull the valve up from the retainer. With the valve in a vertical position and the right way up, the valve should be open, but with it tilted by 45°, it should be closed.

11 Refitting the fuel tank is a reversal of removal, but new cushioning strips should be fitted.

11 Fuel gauge sender unit - removal and refitting

Note: *For safety reasons, the fuel gauge sender unit must always be removed in a well-ventilated area.*

1 Disconnect the battery negative lead.
2 Remove the trim from inside the luggage compartment.
3 Disconnect the wiring from the fuel gauge sender unit (photo).
4 Using two crossed screwdrivers, turn the unit anti-clockwise, and withdraw it together with the float. Remove the sealing O-ring.
5 Refitting is a reversal of removal, but use a new sealing ring, and smear it with a little glycerine. The moulded arrow on the unit should face forwards.

12 Accelerator cable - removal, refitting and adjustment

1 On automatic transmission models, refer to Chapter 7 where necessary.
2 On carburettor models, remove the air cleaner as described in Section 4.
3 Working inside the car, release the cable from the top of the accelerator pedal.
4 Working inside the engine compartment, prise off the clips, then disconnect the inner cable from the quadrant on the carburettor, throttle housing or relay bracket (photos).

10.7 Fuel tank breather pipe

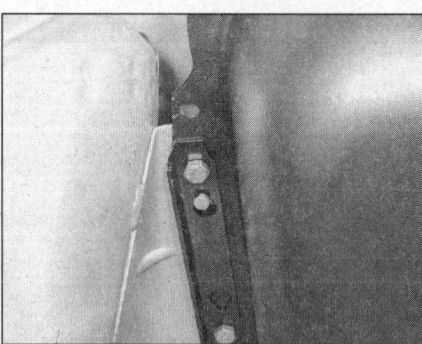

10.8A Fuel tank mounting bolts . . .

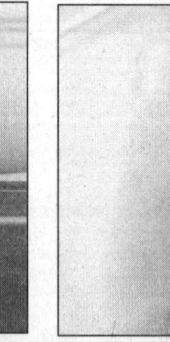

10.8B . . . and mounting screw (arrowed)

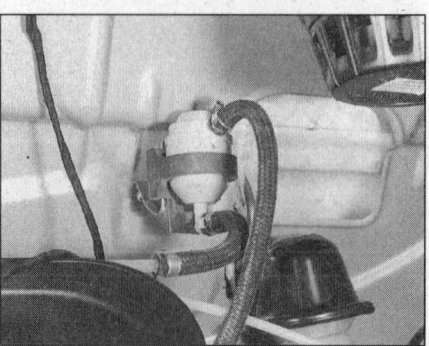

10.10 Fuel tank gravity valve

11.3 Fuel gauge sender unit and wiring

12.4A Accelerator cable end clip (carburettor engine)

12.4B Accelerator cable quadrant clip (carburettor engine)

12.4C Disconnecting the accelerator inner cable (carburettor engine)

5 Release the cable end fitting from the bracket (photos).
6 Disconnect the cable from the bulkhead, and withdraw it from the engine compartment.
7 Refitting is a reversal of removal, but make sure that the cable is not kinked.
8 Adjustment of the cable on automatic transmission models is described in Chapter 7. On manual gearbox models, the clip must be positioned on the ferrule so that the throttle is fully open when the accelerator pedal is fully depressed. With the pedal fully released, there must be no more than 1.0 mm (0.04 in) clearance on the inner cable. On models with cruise control, with the throttle valve in its idling position, adjust the control linkage so a clearance of between 0.1 and 0.3 mm (0.004 and 0.012 in) exists between the bushing and stop plate at the final control element.

12.4D Accelerator cable quadrant (fuel injection engine)

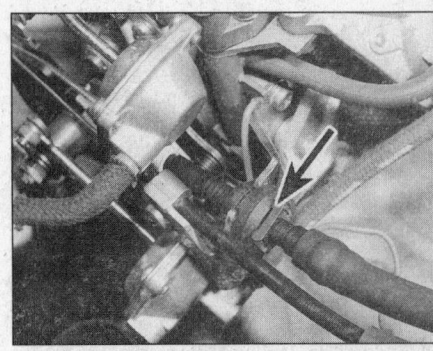

12.5A Accelerator cable end fitting (carburettor engine) – arrowed

3

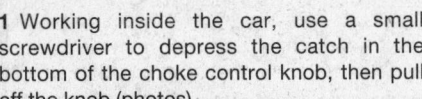

13 Choke cable - removal, refitting and adjustment

1 Working inside the car, use a small screwdriver to depress the catch in the bottom of the choke control knob, then pull off the knob (photos).
2 Unbolt and remove the lower facia panel (photo).
3 Unscrew the nut, and remove the cable end fitting from the bracket (photo). Disconnect the wiring for the warning lamp.

12.5B Accelerator cable end fitting (fuel injection engine) – arrowed

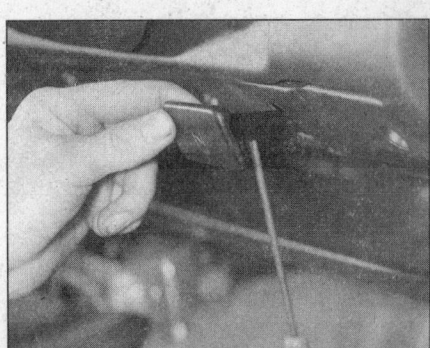

13.1A Depress the catch . . .

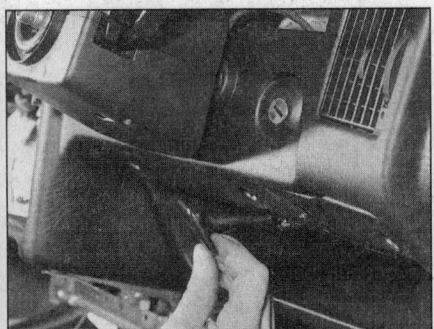

13.1B . . . and remove the choke control knob

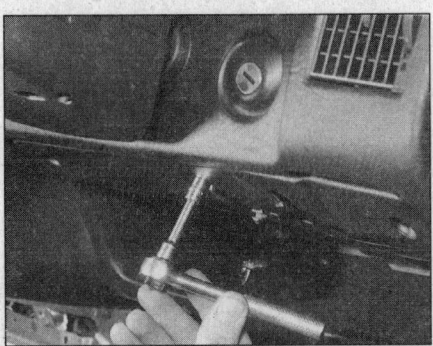

13.2 Lower facia panel removal

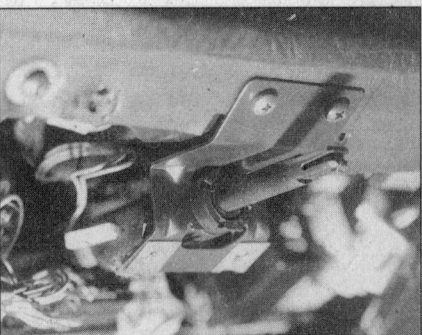

13.3 Choke cable end fitting and bracket

13.5A Extract the circlip . . .

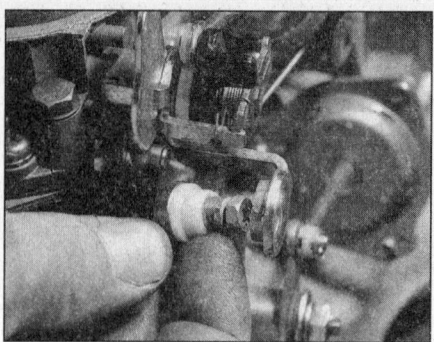

13.5B . . . and release the choke cable end fitting

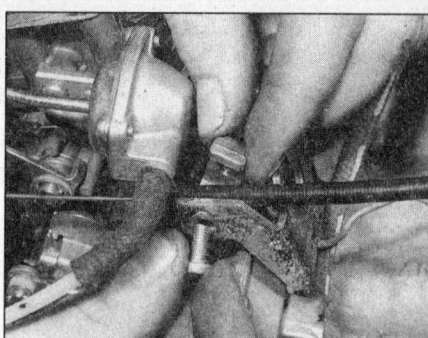

13.6 Choke cable outer cable clamp removal

4 Remove the air cleaner as described in Section 4.

5 If the choke cable is to be refitted, the carburettor end fitting may be left on the inner cable. In this case, extract the circlip and release the end fitting from the choke lever (photos). Otherwise, unscrew the crosshead screw and pull out the inner cable.

6 Unscrew the bolt, and remove the clamp from the outer cable (photo). Withdraw the cable from the car.

7 Refitting is a reversal of removal, but adjust it as follows.

8 Push the control knob fully onto its stop.

9 Refer to Fig. 3.2, and adjust the outer cable until the dimension 'a' is approximately 10.0 mm (0.4 in).

10 Fully open the choke lever, then tighten the cross-head screw on the end fitting.

11 Operate the choke control, and check that the choke flap functions correctly. With the choke fully open, there must be a gap 'b' between the throttle valve lever and stop.

14 Accelerator pedal - removal and refitting

1 Disconnect the cable from the top of the pedal.

2 Using a pair of pliers, break off the mounting lugs and remove the pedal (photo).

3 Remove the remains of the lugs then obtain new ones and fit the pedal in reverse order.

15 Carburettor - description

The carburettor is a Keihin twin progressive choke downdraught type, fitted with a manual choke control. The primary throttle valve is opened mechanically, but the secondary throttle valve is opened by vacuum developed in the primary venturi. A vacuum-operated choke pulldown unit is fitted, to open the choke during acceleration and full-throttle conditions with a cold engine. On the Keihin I carburettor, the vacuum system includes a spherical vacuum reservoir. An idling speed cut-off valve is fitted to both carburettors, and the Keihin II carburettor includes a main jet cut-off solenoid (photos).

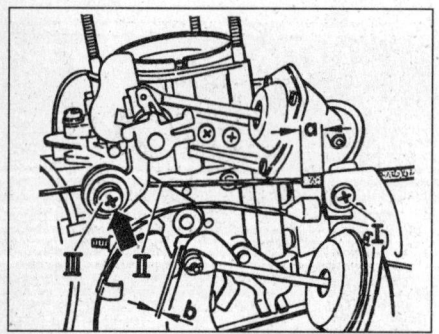

Fig 3.2 Choke cable adjustment (Sec 13)

a = 10 mm (0.4 in)
b Refer to text
I Clamp screw
II Inner cable
III Adjustment screw

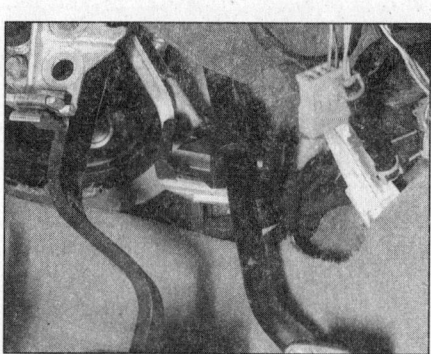

14.2 Accelerator pedal and mounting

15.0A Right-hand view of the Keihin I carburettor

15.0B Left-hand view of the Keihin I carburettor

15.0C Rear view of the Keihin I carburettor

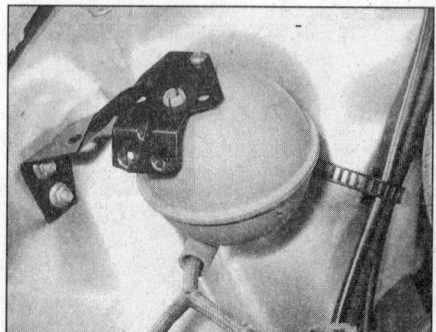

15.0D Vacuum reservoir for the Keihin I carburettor

16.6 Tamperproof caps (arrowed) fitted to the carburettor idling adjustment screws

Fig 3.3 Keihin I idling speed (A) and CO content (B) adjusting screws (Sec 16)

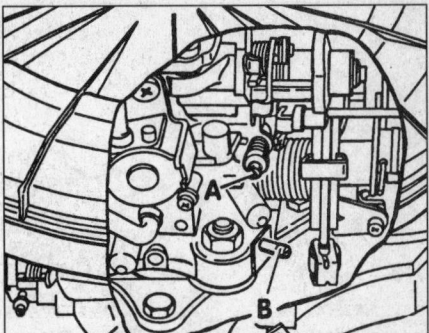

Fig 3.4 Keihin II idling speed (A) and CO content (B) adjusting screws (Sec 16)

16 Carburettor - idle speed and mixture adjustment

Note: *A tachometer (rev counter) and an exhaust gas analyser (CO meter) are required for accurate adjustment*

1 Adjustment should be made with the air cleaner fitted, the accelerator cable correctly adjusted, and the engine at normal temperature. On automatic transmission models, the selector lever should be in position 'P'.
2 Disconnect the crankcase ventilation hose from the valve cover, and plug it.
3 Switch off all electrical components, and make the adjustments when the radiator fan is not running. Make sure that the choke control is fully pushed in.
4 Connect the tachometer and exhaust gas analyser to the engine in accordance with the equipment manufacturer's instructions. On engines fitted with a catalytic converter, connect the analyser to the CO measuring pipe in the engine compartment, making sure that the connecting pipe is a good fit.
5 Run the engine at idling speed, and check that the idling speed and CO content are as given in the Specifications.
6 If necessary, alternately adjust the screws shown in Figs. 3.3 or 3.4 until the readings are

correct. Remove the tamperproof caps first if necessary (photo).
7 Reconnect the crankcase ventilation hose. If the CO content now increases, do not make an adjustment, as this is caused by oil dilution in the crankcase. A long, fast drive will reduce the amount of fuel in the oil, or alternatively, an oil change will return the CO content to normal.
8 Switch off the engine, and disconnect the tachometer and exhaust gas analyser.

17 Carburettor - removal and refitting

1 Disconnect the battery negative lead.
2 Remove the air cleaner as described in Section 4.
3 Disconnect the accelerator cable and choke cable with reference to Sections 12 and 13.
4 Disconnect the fuel inlet hose (photo).
5 Identify the vacuum pipes for location, then disconnect them (photos).
6 Identify the wiring for location, then disconnect it (photos).
7 Unscrew the through-bolts, and lift the carburettor from the inlet manifold (photos). If necessary, unbolt the flange.
8 Refitting is a reversal of removal, but clean the contact faces, and renew the flange if necessary. Tighten the mounting bolts evenly.

17.4 Disconnecting the fuel inlet hose

17.5A Disconnecting the vacuum pipe from the overrun boost control valve

17.5B Disconnecting the vacuum pipe from the pulldown unit

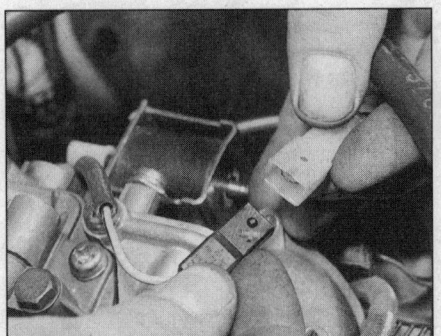

17.6A Disconnecting the idling speed cut-off valve wiring

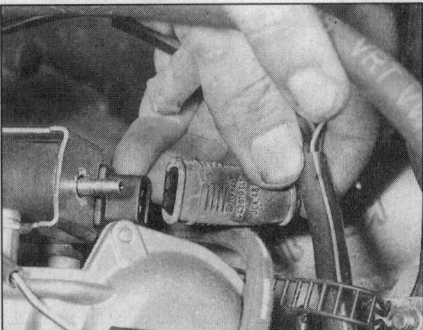

17.6B Disconnecting the wiring from the overrun boost control valve

17.7A Unscrew the through-bolts . . .

17.7B . . . and remove the carburettor

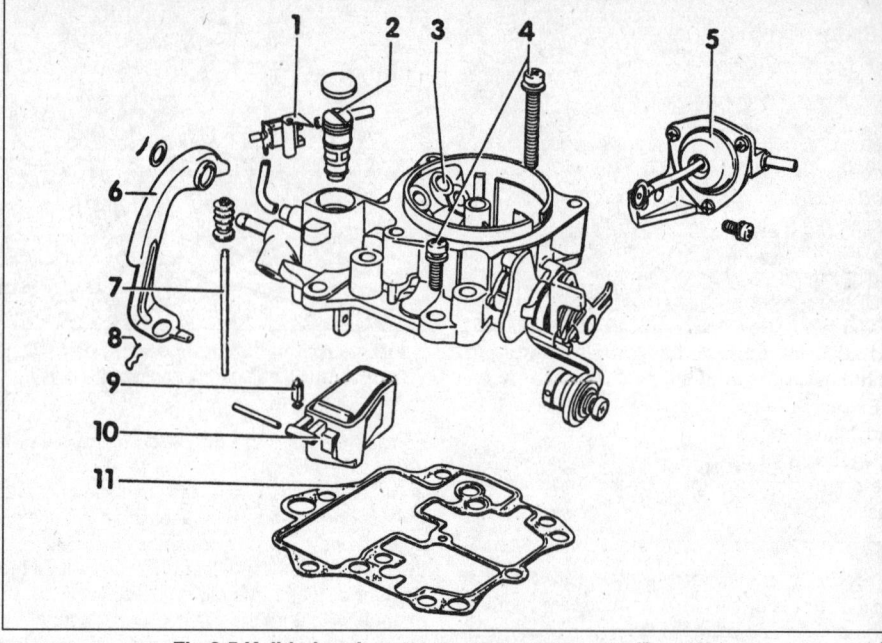

Fig 3.5 Keihin I carburettor cover components (Sec 18)

1 Control valve	4 Screws	7 Accelerator pump
2 Needle valve seat	5 Pulldown unit	plunger
3 Cover	6 Lever	8 Clip
		9 Needle
		10 Float
		11 Gasket

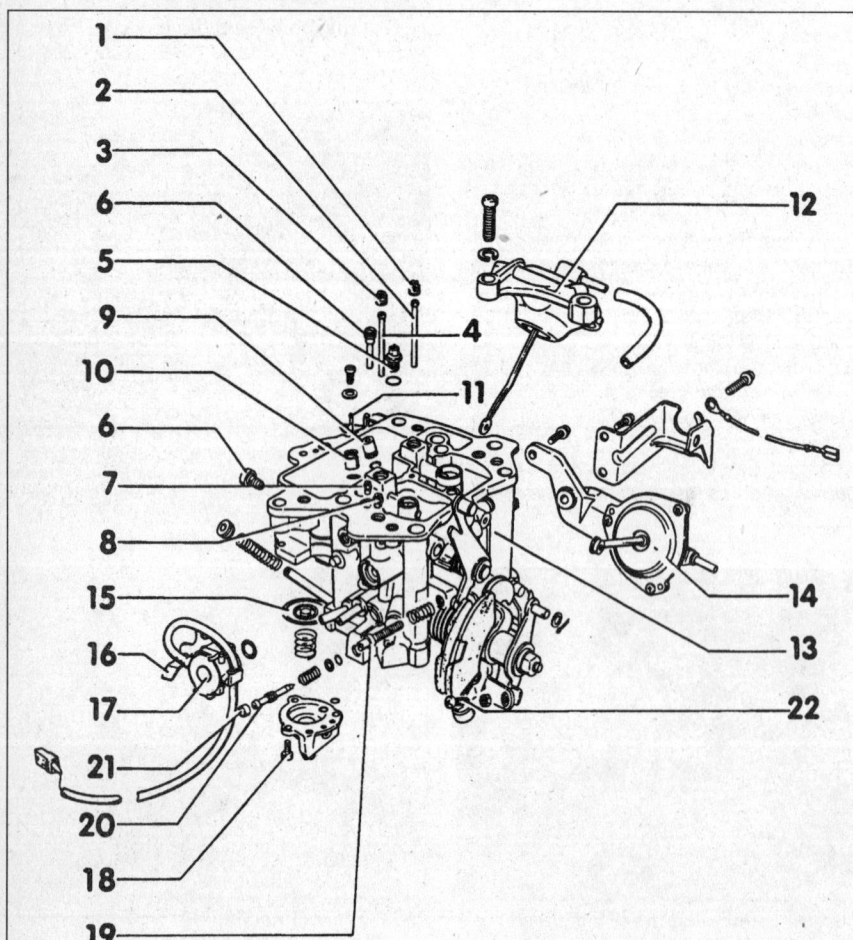

Fig 3.6 Keihin I carburettor main body components (Sec 18)

1 Air correction jet, stage 2
2 Emulsion tube, stage 2
3 Air correction jet, stage 2
4 Emulsion tube, stage 1
5 Enrichment valve
6 Plug
7 Idling fuel jet
8 Idling air jet
9 Main jet, stage 2
10 Main jet, stage 1
11 Retaining plate
12 Vacuum unit, stage 2
13 Main body
14 Throttle valve positioner
15 Accelerator pump diaphragm
16 Stop
17 Idling speed cut-off valve
18 Screw
19 Idling adjusting screw
20 CO content adjusting screw
21 Anti-tamper cap
22 Overrun boost adjusting screw

18 Carburettor - dismantling, cleaning and reassembly

Note: *The following paragraphs describe procedures on the Keihin I carburettor. The procedures for the Keihin II carburettor are similar, but make reference to Figs. 3.5 to 3.9*

1 With the carburettor removed from the engine, clean its exterior surfaces.

2 Disconnect the accelerator pump linkage by extracting the spring clip, separating the rod, and collecting the nylon bush and spring (photos).

3 Extract the split pin, and remove the washer and linkage (photos).

4 Unscrew the cross-head screws, and lift the cover from the main body. Remove the gasket (photos).

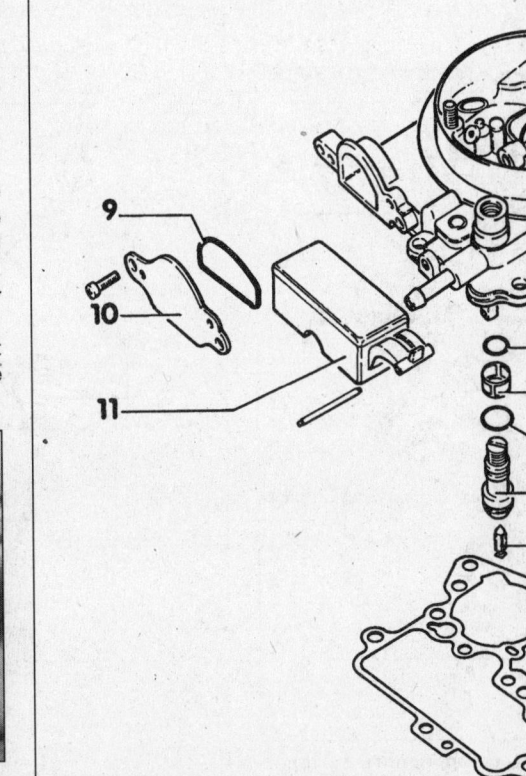

Fig 3.7 Keihin II carburettor cover components (Sec 18)

1 Cover
2 Choke lever
3 Screw
4 Split pin
5 Washer
6 Connecting rod
7 Screw
8 Air correction jet
9 Gasket
10 Cover plate
11 Float
12 O-ring
13 Filter
14 Needle valve seat
15 Needle

18.2A Accelerator pump linkage and spring clip . . .

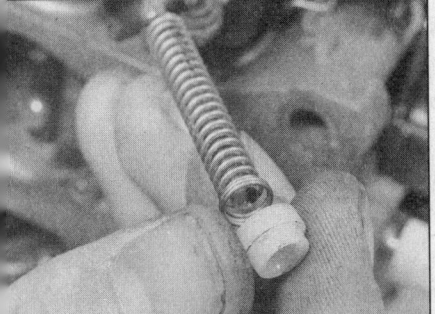

18.2B . . . nylon bush . . .

18.2C . . . and spring

18.3A Extract the split pin . . .

18.3B . . . and remove the linkage

18.4A Unscrew the cross-head screws. . .

18.4B . . . remove the screws . . .

3

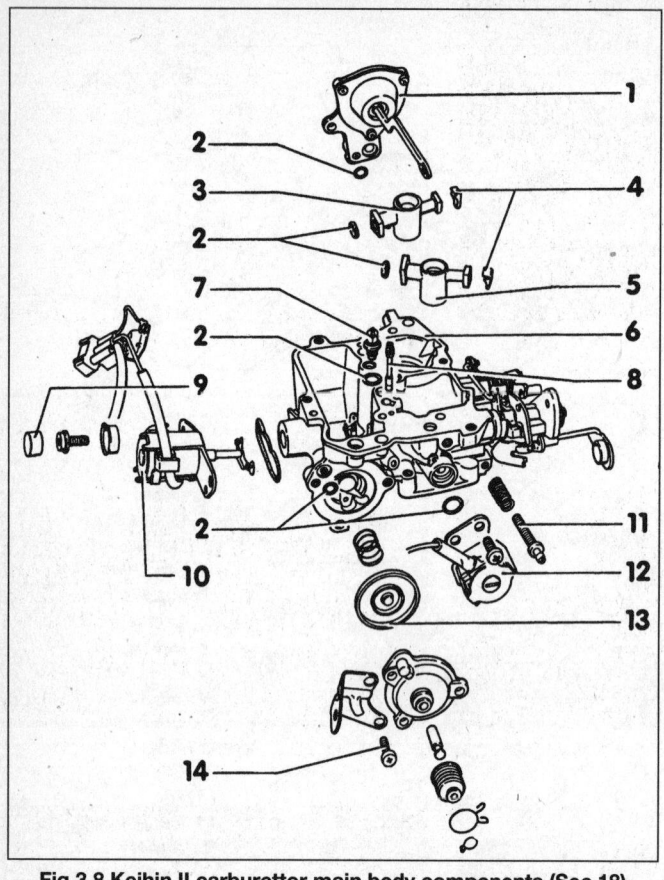

Fig 3.8 Keihin II carburettor main body components (Sec 18)

1 Pulldown unit
2 O-ring
3 Stage 2 atomizer
4 Clip
5 Stage 1 atomizer
6 Main body
7 Enrichment valve
8 Idling emulsion tube
9 Cap
10 Main jet cut-off solenoid
11 Idling speed adjustment screw
12 Idling speed cut-off valve
13 Accelerator pump diaphragm
14 Screw

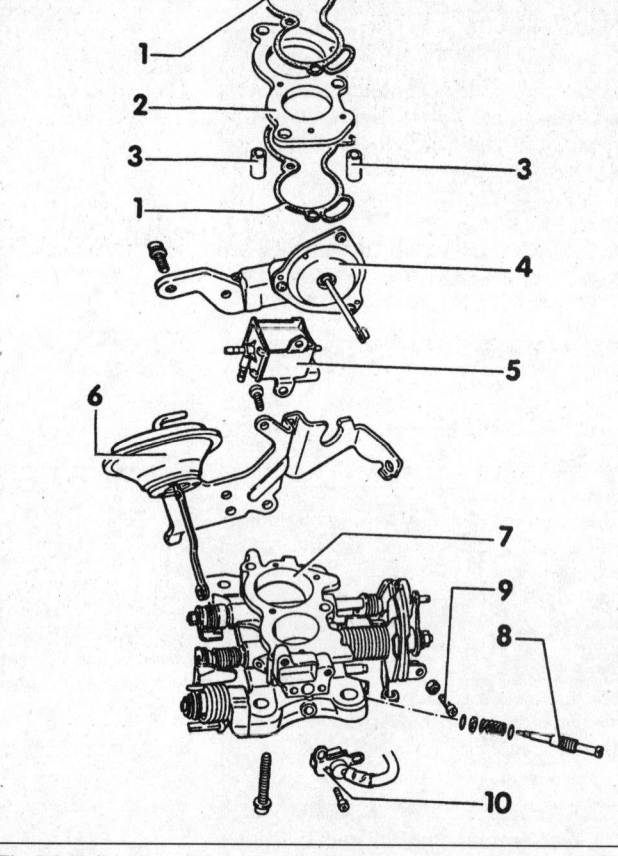

Fig 3.9 Keihin II carburettor throttle housing components (Sec 18)

1 Gasket
2 Intermediate flange
3 Sleeve
4 Throttle valve positioner
5 Overrun boost control valve
6 Vacuum unit, stage 2
7 Housing
8 CO content adjusting screw
9 Overrun boost adjusting screw
10 Part-throttle channel heating

5 Unscrew the cross-head screw in the bottom of the float chamber, and remove the main jet holder (photos).
6 Carefully remove the main jets, keeping them identified for location. Remove the O-ring seals if necessary (photos).
7 Unscrew and remove the air correction jets, and remove the emulsion tubes, keeping them

identified for location (photos).
8 Unscrew the enrichment valve from the bottom of the float chamber.
9 Unscrew the idling air jet, then unscrew the plug and remove the idling fuel jet.
10 Press out the float pivot pin, and remove the float and needle valve. Unhook the valve.
11 For normal cleaning purposes, this is the

limit of the dismantling procedure. Clean a the components with fuel, and if possibl blow through the internal passageways wit an air hose or foot pump. Similarly clean th jets, but **do not** probe them with wire. Chec the needle valve for wear, and the float fo puncturing, and renew them if necessary.
12 Reassembly is a reversal of dismantlin

18.4C . . . lift the cover from the main body . . .

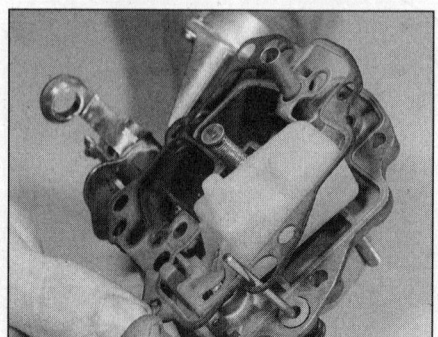

18.4D . . . and remove the gasket

18.5A Unscrew the cross-head screw (arrowed) . . .

18.5B . . . and remove the main jet holder

18.6A Removing the main jets

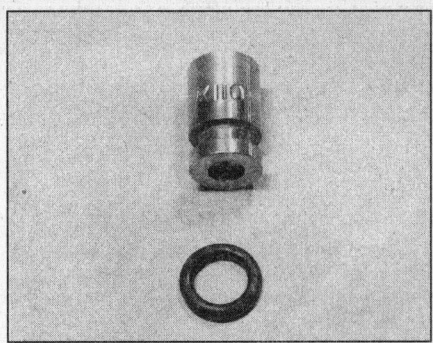

18.6B Main jet and O-ring seal

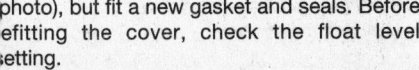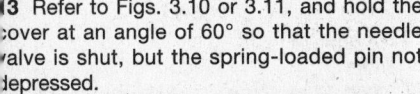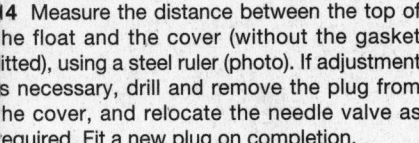

photo), but fit a new gasket and seals. Before refitting the cover, check the float level setting.

13 Refer to Figs. 3.10 or 3.11, and hold the cover at an angle of 60° so that the needle valve is shut, but the spring-loaded pin not depressed.

14 Measure the distance between the top of the float and the cover (without the gasket fitted), using a steel ruler (photo). If adjustment is necessary, drill and remove the plug from the cover, and relocate the needle valve as required. Fit a new plug on completion.

15 Apply locking fluid to the threads of the cover retaining screws before inserting and tightening them (photo), and lubricate all joints with molybdenum disulphide grease.

18.7A Unscrew the air correction jets . . .

18.7B . . . remove them . . .

3

18.7C . . . and extract the emulsion tubes

18.12 Carburettor main body with jets fitted

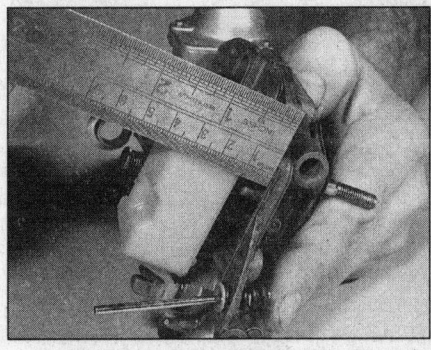

18.14 Checking the float level setting

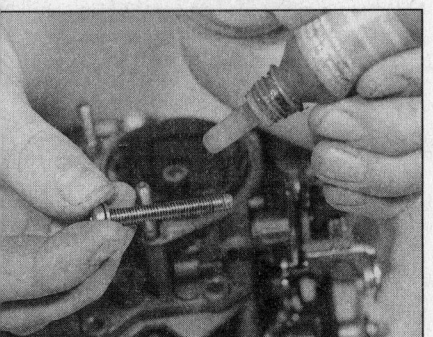

18.15 Applying locking fluid to the cover retaining screws

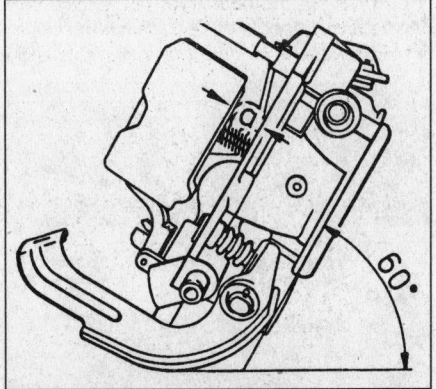

Fig 3.10 Float level adjustment on the Keihin I carburettor (Sec 18)
a = 9 ± 1 mm (0.36 ± 0.04in)

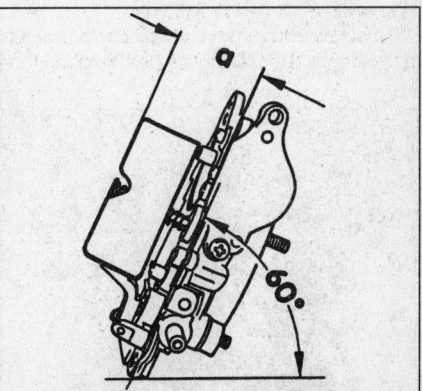

Fig 3.11 Float level adjustment on the Keihin II carburettor (Sec 18)
a = 36 ± 1 mm (1.42 ± 0.04 in)

19 Carburettor - additional adjustments and tests

Fast idling speed

1 Connect a tachometer to the engine. Run the engine to normal operating temperature.
2 Remove the air cleaner, and plug the vacuum hose for the air temperature control.
3 Pull the choke control fully out, so that the choke lever on the carburettor is fully on.
4 Using a screwdriver, fully open the choke on the carburettor, but leave the choke lever on.
5 Start the engine, and check that it runs at the specified fast idle speed. If necessary, adjust by bending the interconnecting lever.

Choke pulldown unit (Keihin I)

6 Pull the choke control fully out.
7 Apply a vacuum of 400 mbar to the pulldown unit (photo), then use a drill to check that the gap between the lower edge of the choke valve and the carburettor wall is as given in the Specifications. If necessary, bend the operating lever.

Choke pulldown unit (Keihin II)

8 Pull the choke control fully out.
9 Press the operating rod into the pulldown unit, then use a drill to check that the gap between the lower edge of the choke valve and the carburettor wall is as given in the Specifications. If necessary, bend the operating lever.
10 The pulldown unit may be checked after removal by pushing in the rod and sealing the vacuum hole with a finger. If the rod moves out, the internal diaphragm is proved faulty.

Stage 2 basic throttle valve setting

11 The adjusting screw (photo) is set at the factory and should not normally require adjustment. If the screw has been disturbed, carry out the following procedure.
12 With the carburettor removed, fully open the Stage 2 throttle, leaving the Stage 1 throttle closed.
13 Loosen the nut, and unscrew the

19.7 Choke pulldown unit (arrowed)

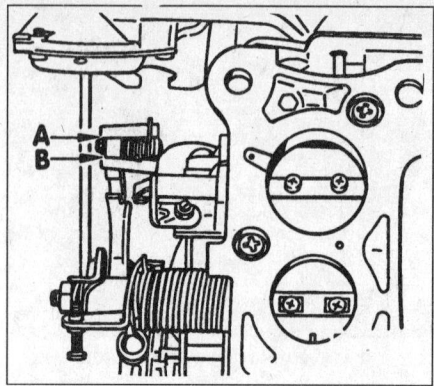

Fig 3.12 Keihin II carburettor stage 2 locking lever clearances (Sec 19)
A = 0.25 ± 0.05mm (0.010 ± 0.002in)
B = 0.20 ± 0.05 mm (0.008 ± 0.002 in)

adjusting screw so that there is a gap between the lever and stop, then turn the screw clockwise until it just touches the stop. The point of contact is best judged by using a thin piece of paper, to determine when it is just trapped. From this point, turn the screw three quarters of a turn clockwise. Apply locking fluid to the nut threads, then tighten it while holding the screw stationary.
14 Check the idling speed after making an adjustment.

Stage 2 locking lever clearance (Keihin II)

15 With the carburettor removed, fully open the choke so that the throttle valve is shut.
16 Refer to Fig. 3.12, and check that the clearances are as stated. If not, bend the arm as required. Fit a new plug on completion.

Accelerator pump capacity

17 With the carburettor removed and the float chamber filled with fuel to the correct level, hold the carburettor over a calibrated container.
18 Fully open the choke. Fully close the Stage 1 throttle valve by unscrewing the idle screw.
19 On the Keihin II carburettor, check that the accelerator pump lever is in contact with the plunger - no clearance is permitted.
20 Open the throttle lever slowly and fully ten

19.11 Stage 2 basic throttle valve setting adjusting screw (arrowed)

times, allowing a minimum of three second per stroke.
21 Divide the amount of fuel injected by ten and compare with the amount given in Specifications. If necessary bend the stop.

Part-throttle channel heating (Keihin II)

22 Unscrew the heater element then switch on the ignition.
23 Connect a diode test lamp between the yellow/black wire and the carburettor body The lamp should light up.
24 With the element suspended, connect the test lamp between the element body and the carburettor body. The test lamp should light up

Overrun boost (models with manual gearbox)

25 Run the engine to normal operating temperature, then switch off.
26 Connect a tachometer (rev counter) to the engine.
27 Start the engine, increase the speed to 4000 rpm, then release the throttle. The engine speed should drop slowly to approximately 1800 rpm, pause, then drop quickly to idling speed. If not, check the following:
(a) Throttle valve positioner
(b) Voltage for control valve
(c) Control valve

Throttle valve positioner

28 The throttle valve positioner is located below the choke pulldown unit. With the engine at normal operating temperature, connect a vacuum pump to the positioner, and apply 350 mbar (Keihin I) or 400 mbar (Keihin 11).
29 Check that the engine speed is 1200 to 1250 rpm. If not, adjust the screw provided.
30 Check the vacuum pipes for leaks.

Voltage for control valve

31 Run the engine to normal operating temperature, then switch off.
32 Connect a tachometer (rev counter) to the engine.
33 Disconnect the plug from the control valve, and connect a voltmeter to the two terminals in the plug.
34 Start the engine, and run at idling speed. The voltmeter should indicate battery voltage. If not, check that battery voltage is available on the plug black wire. Similarly connect the voltmeter between the brown/red wire and the battery positive terminal. No voltage indicates a break in the wiring.
35 Increase, and then decrease, the engine speed slowly, to check the switching point of the control unit, with the voltmeter connected across the two terminals. Above 1900 rpm, the voltmeter should read zero, but below 1750 rpm, it should read battery voltage. Renew the control unit if necessary.

Control valve

36 Remove the air cleaner, then start the engine and run at idling speed.

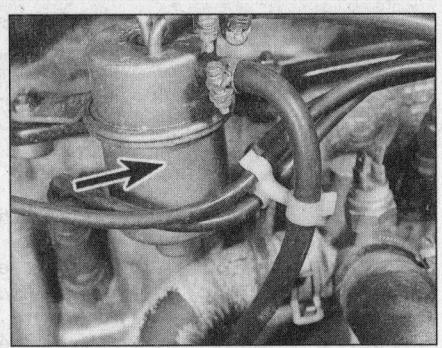

20.1 Fuel reservoir (carburettor engines) – arrowed

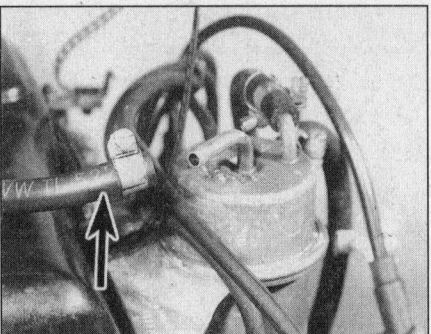

20.3 Disconnecting the outlet pipe (arrowed) from the carburettor

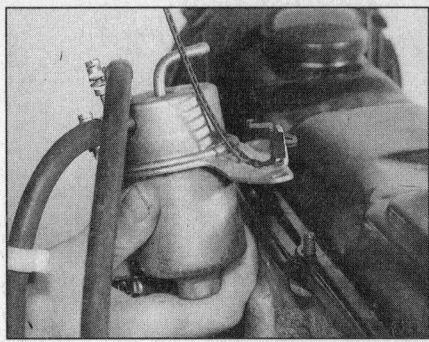

20.4 Removing the fuel reservoir

37 Disconnect the control valve wiring, and pull off the vacuum pipe.

38 On the Keihin I carburettor, disconnect the vacuum hose from the brake servo hose.

39 Remove the control valve breather cap, and fit an extension hose to the control valve. Blow into the extension hose, and check that it is blocked.

40 Now connect the wiring plug while blowing through the hose, and check that the valve opens up audibly.

41 From the vacuum unit side, the valve must always be open.

Idle speed boost (automatic transmission models)

42 Run the engine to normal operating temperature, then switch off.

43 Connect a tachometer (rev counter) to the engine.

44 Apply the handbrake firmly, then run the engine at idling speed.

45 Switch on the heated rear window, main beam headlights, and the heater fan at maximum speed.

46 Depress the footbrake pedal and select 'D'. At this point, the throttle positioner should open the throttle slightly. If not, check the vacuum unit for leaks, and check the control valve as follows.

47 Disconnect the wiring plug from the control valve, and connect a test lamp to the terminals in the plug.

48 Switch on the ignition and select 'N'. The test lamp should light up.

49 Select 'R', 'D', '2' and '1', and check that the test lamp goes out.

50 Check the control valve as described in paragraphs 38 to 41 inclusive.

20 Fuel reservoir (carburettor engine) - removal and refitting

1 The fuel reservoir is mounted on the valve cover studs, on the left-hand side of the engine (photo).

2 Identify the three fuel pipes for location. The outlet stub without a marking goes to the carburettor; the inlet stub with an arrow

comes from the fuel pump; the outlet stub marked 'R' is the return line to the fuel pump.

3 Loosen the clips and disconnect the fuel pipes, then plug the pipes (photo).

4 Unscrew the nuts, and lift the mounting bracket from the studs (photo). Where necessary, release the cable strap.

5 Refitting is a reversal of removal.

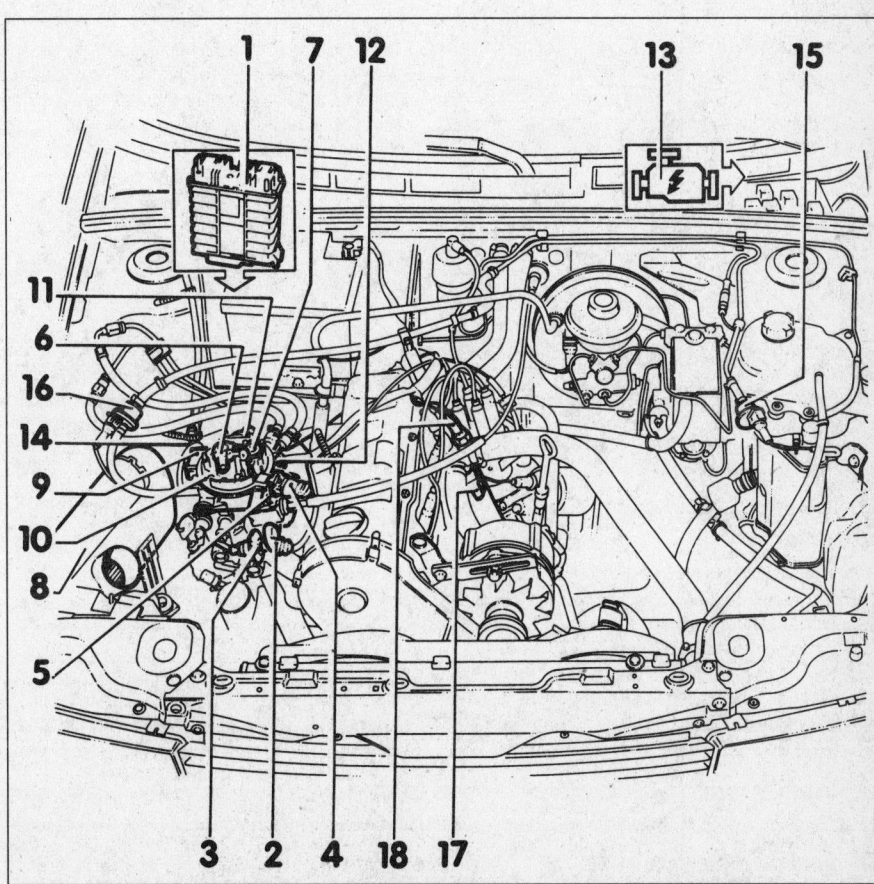

Fig 3.13 Mono-Jetronic fuel injection system components (Sec 21)

1 Control unit	6 Injector and intake air temperature sender	13 Fault warning lamp
2 Connector for throttle valve positioner and idling switch	7 Fuel pressure regulator	14 Lambda probe connector
3 Throttle damper	8 Intake noise damper	15 Activated charcoal filter solenoid (1)
4 Connector for injector and intake air temperature sender	9 Control valve for ignition timing vacuum control	16 Activated charcoal filter solenoid (2)
5 Throttle valve positioner and idling switch	10 Injection unit	17 Coolant temperature sender
	11 Throttle valve potentiometer	18 Intake manifold preheating thermoswitch
	12 Water deflector	

3

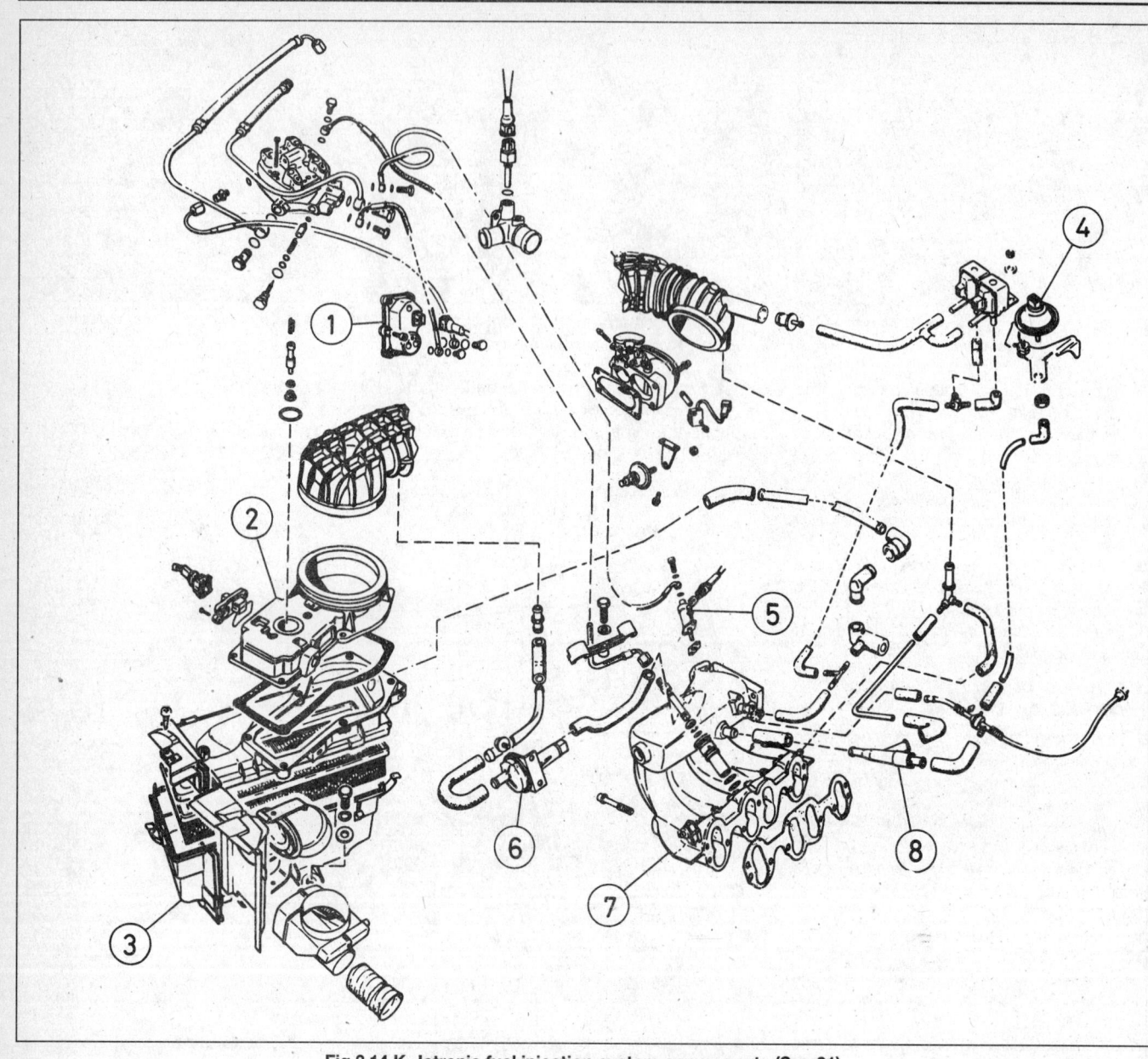

Fig 3.14 K-Jetronic fuel injection system components (Sec 21)

1 Warm-up regulator
2 Airflow meter
3 Air cleaner
4 Diaphragm pressure switch
5 Cold start valve
6 Auxiliary air valve
7 Inlet manifold
8 Vacuum boost

21 Fuel injection system - description and precautions

A Bosch fuel injection system is fitted, and according to engine code, this may be K-Jetronic, Mono-Jetronic, KE-Jetronic, KE III-Jetronic, KE-Motronic or Multipoint injection (MPI).

The basic K-Jetronic system consists of an airflow meter to monitor the volume of air entering the engine, a fuel distributor integral with the airflow meter, a cold start valve and auxiliary air device for cold starting, and a warm-up regulator to lean out the mixture gradually during the warm-up period. A thermotime switch energises the cold start valve during initial cold starting, the length of period depending on the engine temperature.

The KE-Jetronic system uses the same basic system, but in addition, sensors are used to monitor the engine speed, load and temperature. The signals from the sensors are processed by an electronic control unit (ECU), which activates a fuel pressure control unit in the fuel distributor. This effectively varies the quantity of fuel injected by the injectors. Should the electronic system fail with the engine warm, the system will operate as the K-Jetronic system, thus enabling the car to be driven home. The KE-Motronic system operates in a similar way.

The Multipoint injection system (MPI) is a fully-electronic engine management system, employing sensors to monitor engine speed, load and temperature. An electronic air volume sensor is fitted, and the injectors are operated electrically.

The Mono-Jetronic system consists of a single injector unit mounted on the inlet

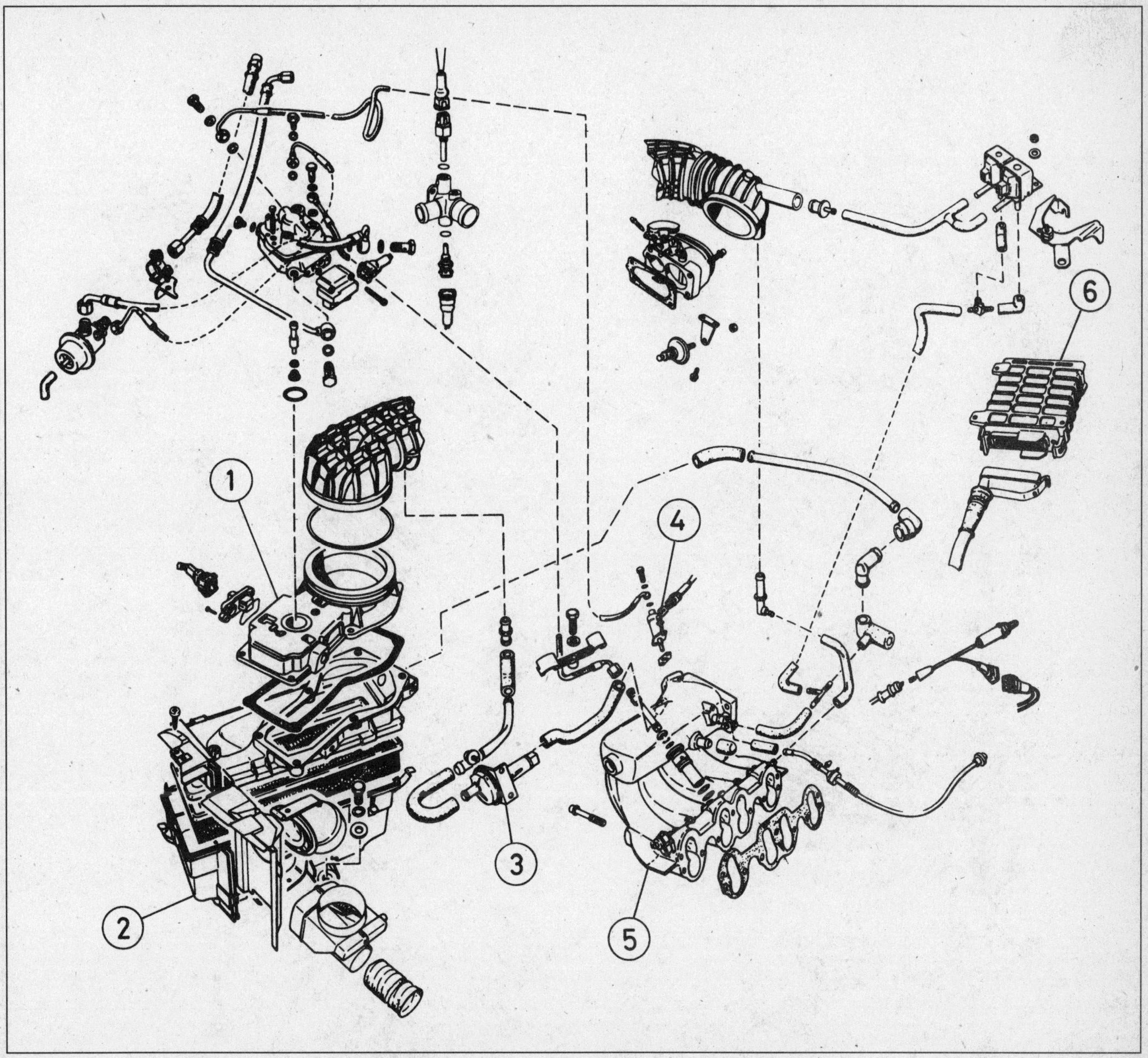

Fig 3.15 KE-Jetronic fuel injection system components (Sec 21)

1 Airflow meter   2 Air cleaner   3 Auxiliary air valve   4 Cold start valve   5 Inlet manifold   6 Electronic control unit

manifold, rather like a carburettor. Electronic sensors monitor the engine speed, load and temperature, and the signals are processed by an electronic control unit in a similar manner to the KE-Jetronic system.

Because of the complex electronic circuitry in many of these systems, certain precautions must be observed in order to prevent damage.

(a) Do not disconnect the battery with the engine running
(b) Do not use a boost charger as a starting aid

(c) Do not disconnect or reconnect wiring plugs with the ignition switched on
(d) Remove the control unit if the temperature will exceed 80°C (176°F), as for example in a paint-drying oven
(e) Before performing a cylinder compression test, unplug the control relay to disable the fuel pump

It is recommended that only the tasks given in the following Sections are attempted by the home mechanic, and that in the event of a major fault, the services of an Audi dealer are enlisted.

22 Fuel injection system components - removal and refitting

Airflow meter

1 With the ignition switched off, place some rag beneath the fuel inlet hose in the engine compartment, then loosen the union to depressurise the system (photo).
2 Identify each fuel line on the distributor, and thoroughly clean the surrounding area (photo). Disconnect the fuel lines.

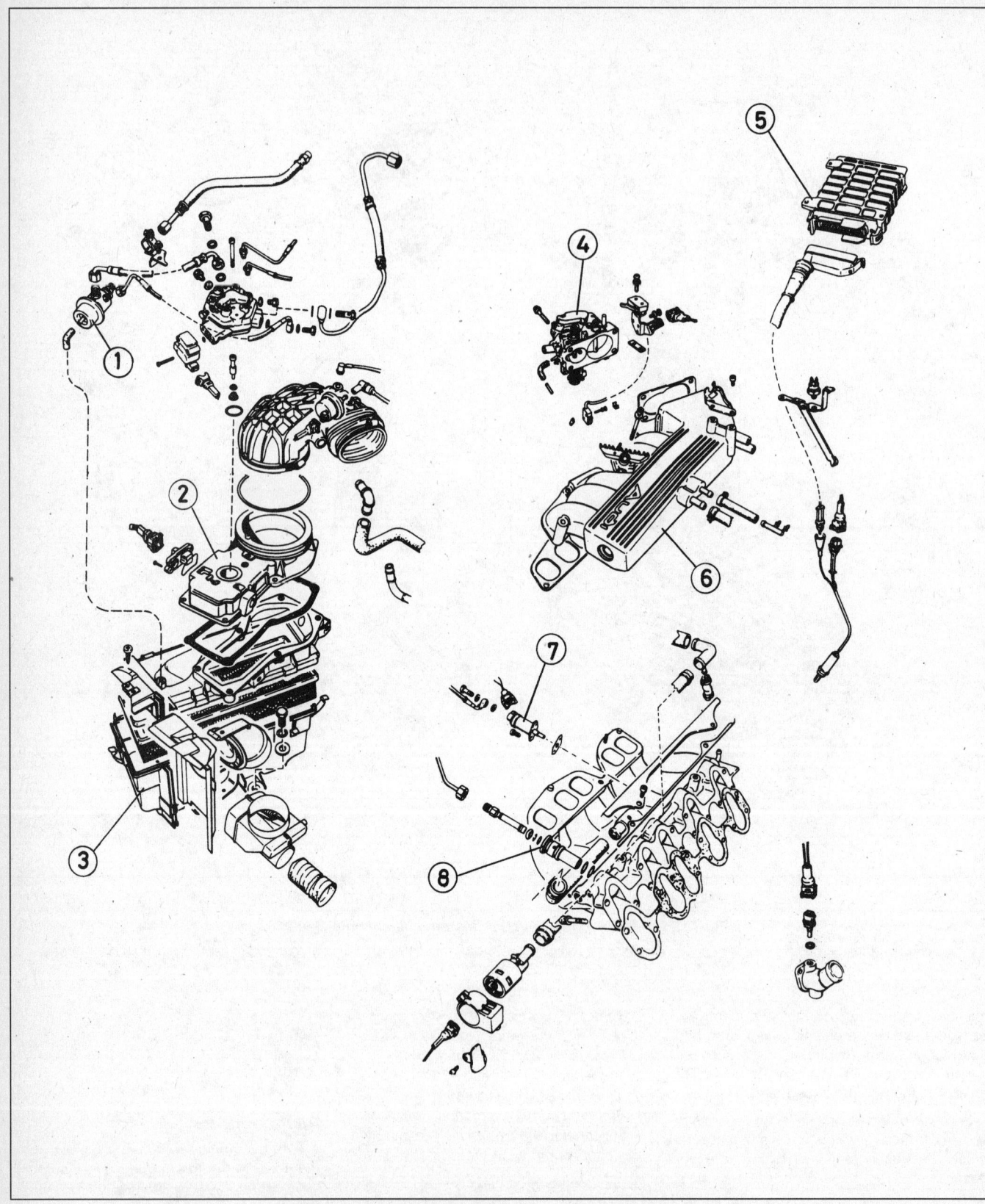

Fig 3.16 KE III-Jetronic fuel injection system components (Sec 21)

1 Diaphragm pressure regulator
2 Airflow meter
3 Air cleaner
4 Throttle valve housing
5 Electronic control unit
6 Inlet manifold
7 Cold start valve
8 Injector and insert

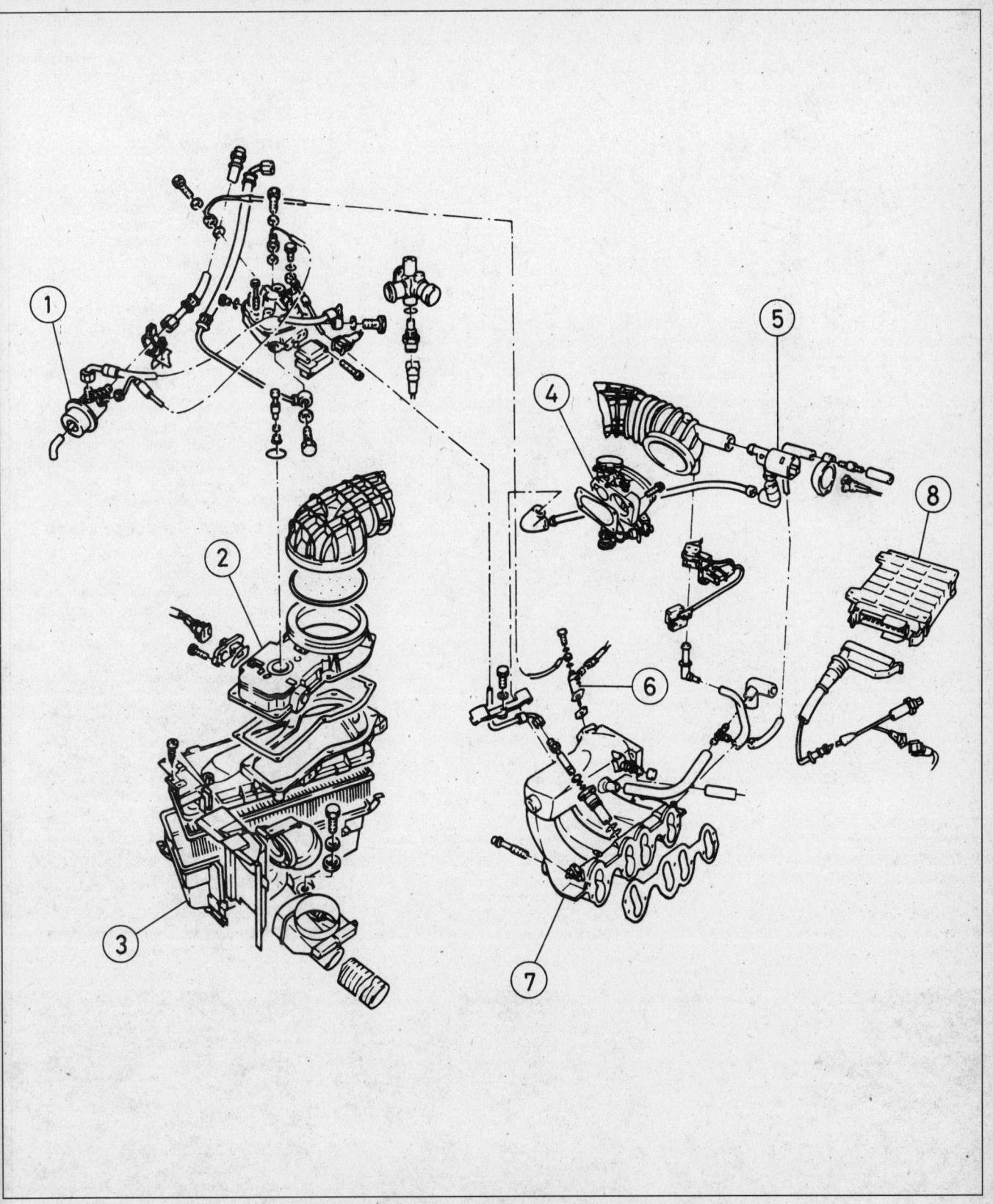

Fig 3.17 KE-Motronic fuel injection system components (Sec 21)

1 Diaphragm pressure regulator   3 Air cleaner   5 Idling stabilization control valve   7 Inlet manifold
2 Airflow meter   4 Throttle valve housing   6 Cold start valve   8 Electronic control unit

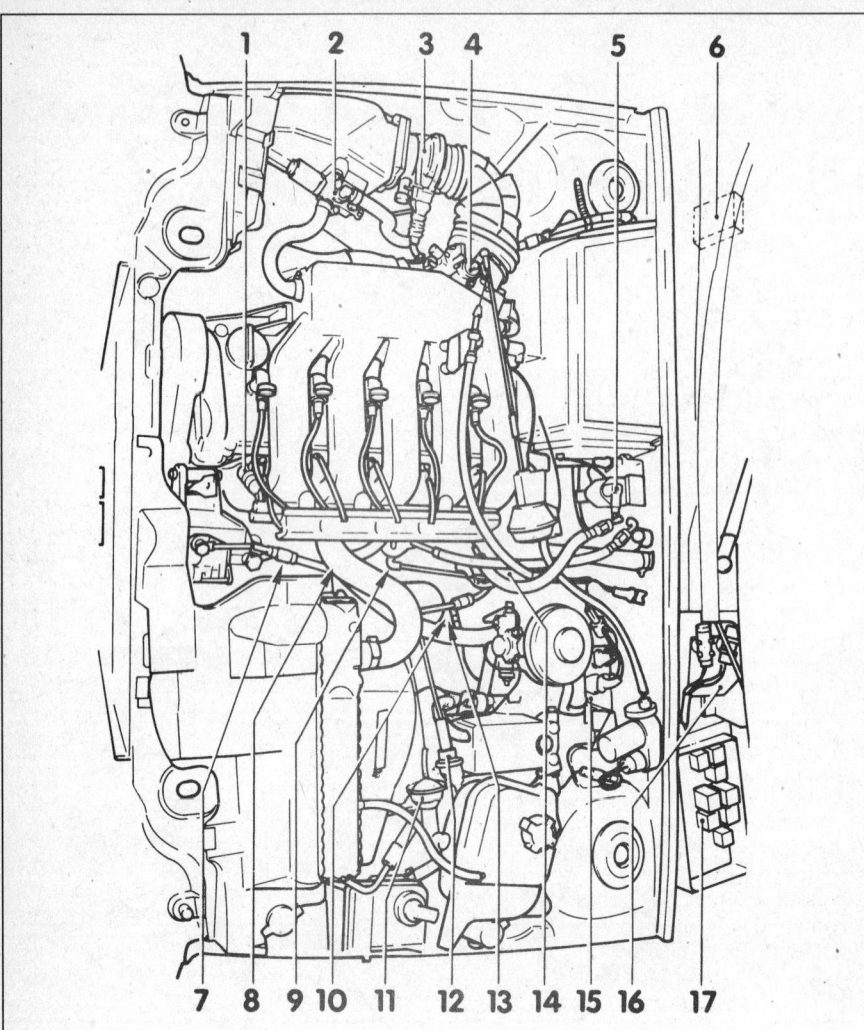

Fig 3.18 MPI fuel injection system components (Sec 21)

1 *Injector*
2 *Idle stabilizing valve*
3 *Air volume sensor*
4 *Throttle valve housing*
5 *Ignition coil with power stage*
6 *MPI control unit*
7 *Knock sensor 1*
8 *Coolant temperature sensor*
9 *Knock sensor 2*

10 *Ignition timing sender*
11 *Check valve*
12 *Activated charcoal filter valve*
13 *Engine speed sensor*
14 *Distributor*
15 *Bracket for plug connector*
16 *Series resistor for injectors*
17 *Fuel pump relay*

3 Loosen the clip and disconnect the air inlet duct.
4 Remove the air cleaner element (Section 3).
5 Disconnect the wiring plugs (where fitted).
6 Withdraw the airflow meter (photo).
7 Refitting is a reversal of removal.

Warm-up regulator

8 Refer to paragraph 1.
9 Identify each fuel line, then unscrew the union bolts and disconnect the fuel lines.
10 Disconnect the wiring plug.
11 Unscrew the mounting bolts, and remove the warm-up regulator.
12 Refitting is a reversal of removal.

Throttle valve housing

13 Disconnect the accelerator cable (Section 12).
14 Loosen the clip, and disconnect the air inlet duct (photo).
15 Disconnect the throttle switch wiring.
16 Disconnect the auxiliary air device hose.
17 Unscrew the nuts, and withdraw the throttle valve housing from the inlet manifold. Remove the gasket.
18 Refitting is a reversal of removal.

Fuel injectors (except Mono-Jetronic)

19 Refer to paragraph 1.
20 Where applicable, disconnect the wiring plugs from the injectors. Remove the cooling duct (where fitted).
21 Remove the fuel distribution rail (where

22.1 Depressurising the fuel injection system

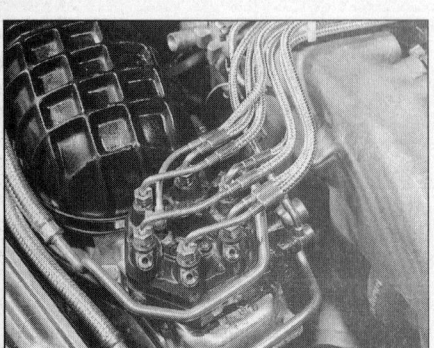

22.2 Fuel lines on the fuel distributor

22.6 Removing the airflow meter

22.14 Disconnecting the inlet duct from the throttle valve housing

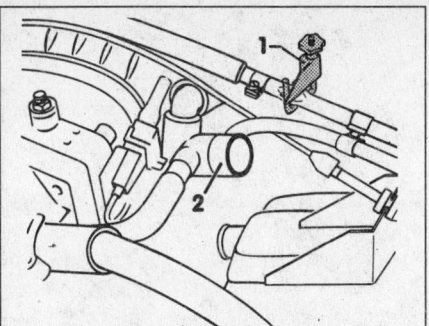

Fig 3.19 Clamp (1) fitted to idling speed boost hose, and crankcase ventilation hose (2) disconnected (Sec 23)

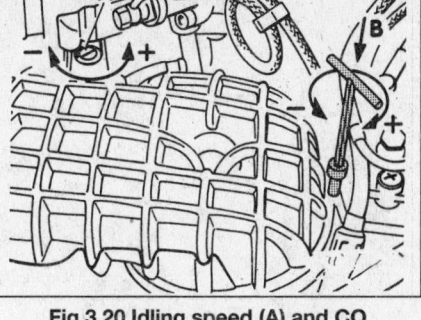

Fig 3.20 Idling speed (A) and CO content (B) adjustment screws on the DZ engine (Sec 23)

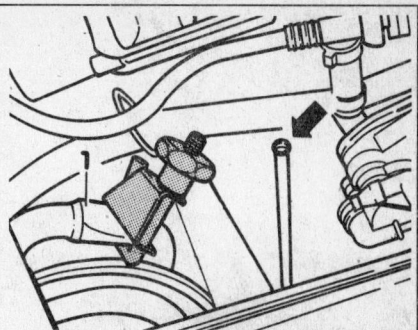

Fig 3.21 Clamp fitted to the crankcase ventilation hose (1) on the NG engine (Sec 23)
Arrow indicates dipstick tube

applicable), then unscrew the union nuts and disconnect the injector pipes.

22 Ease the injectors from their inserts. Prise out the sealing O-rings.

23 Refitting is a reversal of removal, but fit new O-rings and moisten them with fuel before inserting.

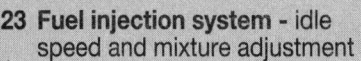

23 Fuel injection system - idle speed and mixture adjustment

Adjustment conditions

1 The engine must be at normal operating temperature.

2 All electrical components must be switched off, and the radiator cooling fan must not be running during the adjustment.

3 The exhaust system must be in good condition.

4 The ignition timing must be correct.

5 Where fitted, the lambda control must be operating correctly.

6 On automatic transmission models, the kickdown cable must be correctly adjusted.

7 If the injector pipes have been detached, the engine must be run at 3000 rpm several times, then allowed to idle for at least two minutes prior to making adjustments.

8 The air conditioning system (where fitted) must be switched off.

9 Where fitted, remove the tamperproof cap

from the activated charcoal canister adjustment screw.

10 The throttle valve must be at the idling position.

Engine code DZ

11 Fit a clamp to the idling speed boost hose (Fig. 3.19).

12 Disconnect the crankcase ventilation hose from the valve cover and position it to draw in fresh air.

13 With the ignition switched off, connect a tachometer and exhaust gas analyser to the engine.

14 Start the engine, and allow it to idle, then check that the idling speed and CO content are as given in the Specifications. If necessary, adjust the screws shown in Fig. 3.20, using a special key for the CO content adjustment. Do not press down on the CO adjustment key, and do not rev the engine with the key in position.

15 Refer to Section 16, paragraph 7 after reconnecting the crankcase ventilation hose.

Engine code PM

16 With the ignition switched off, connect a tachometer to the engine and an exhaust gas analyser to the CO measuring pipe.

17 No adjustment is possible, but if the results are incorrect, check all vacuum connections and the frequency valve grey solenoid, and if necessary recall the fault memory.

Engine codes PS (1989 on) and JN

18 Refer to paragraphs 11 to 15, but connect the exhaust gas analyser to the measuring pipe in the front of the exhaust manifold.

Engine code NG

19 With the ignition switched off, connect a tachometer to the engine, and an exhaust gas analyser to the CO measuring pipe.

20 Fit a clamp to the crankcase ventilation hose (Fig. 3.21). Remove the dipstick, and drape a cloth rag over the tube.

21 Start the engine, and allow it to idle, then check that the idling speed and CO contents are as given in the Specifications.

22 Note that the idling speed cannot be adjusted, and the screw in the throttle housing must be completely screwed in.

23 Check the ignition timing with reference to Chapter 4.

24 Disconnect the wiring to the lambda probe, then check the CO content. If necessary, use a special key to adjust the setting (Fig. 3.22).

25 Reconnect the lambda probe wiring, and check the CO content.

26 Pull the line from the activated charcoal canister outlet, and check that the CO content drops. Now crimp the line, and check that the CO content rises and drops back. If not, check the lambda control.

3

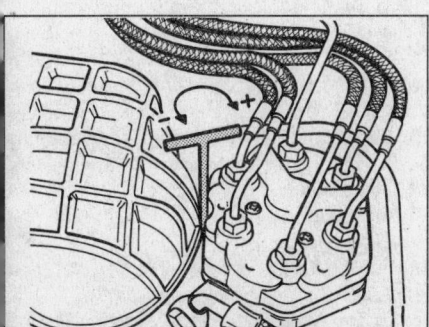

Fig 3.22 Adjusting the CO content on the NG engine (Sec 23)

Fig 3.23 Digital multimeter connection on the PS engine (Sec 23)

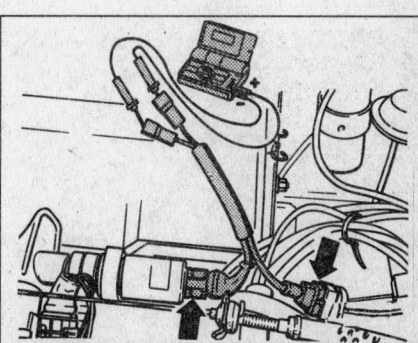

Fig 3.24 Digital multimeter connection on the KV engine (Sec 23)

23.27 Disconnecting the wiring plug from the control unit for idle stabilisation

23.31A Adjusting the idling control current on the KV engine

23.31B Adjusting the CO content on the KV engine

Engine code PS (up to 1989) and KV

27 With the ignition switched off, connect a tachometer and exhaust gas analyser to the engine. Also connect a digital multimeter to the control unit for idle stabilisation (photo) - see also Figs. 3.23 and 3.24.

28 On the KV engine, disconnect and plug the crankcase ventilation hoses.

29 On the PS engine, fit a clamp to the crankcase ventilation hose, then remove the dipstick, and drape a cloth rag over the tube.

30 Start the engine, and allow it to idle.

31 Check that the control current and CO content are as given in the Specifications. If necessary, adjust the screws shown in

Figs. 3.26 and 3.27 (photos). If the control current remains constant at approximately 470 mA, check the idle stabilisation.

32 Refer to paragraphs 14 and 15.

Engine code 3A

33 Check the ignition timing as described in Chapter 4.

34 With the ignition switched off, connect a tachometer to the engine. Also connect an exhaust gas analyser to the CO measuring pipe on the exhaust manifold.

35 Start the engine, and allow it to idle. Check that the idling speed is as given in the Specifications.

36 On models fitted with air conditioning, the idling speed should increase by approxi-

mately 70 rpm when the air conditioning is switched on.

37 Check that the CO content is as specified. If adjustment is necessary, remove the cap from the activated charcoal filter, and disconnect the crankcase ventilation hose from the valve cover.

38 With the ignition switched off, disconnect the wiring plug from the differential pressure regulator, and connect a digital multimeter using an adaptor wire. Switch on the ignition, and check that the control current indicates positive. If not, change the wiring around.

39 Start the engine, and allow it to idle.

40 Adjust the CO screw using a special key, until the control current fluctuates between 0 and 5 mA. Do not press down on the CO adjustment key, and do not rev the engine with the key in position. After removing the key, briefly accelerate the engine before checking the CO content.

41 If necessary, cancel the fault memory.

Engine code 7A

42 With the ignition switched off, connect a tachometer and exhaust gas analyser to the engine.

43 Fit a clamp to the crankcase ventilation hose, located behind the fuel pressure regulator. Remove the dipstick, and drape a cloth rag over the tube.

44 Start the engine, and allow it to idle.

45 Remove the cover from the fusebox, and connect a known good fuse across the fuel pump relay contacts. Wait approximately three seconds, then check that the idling speed is as given in the Specifications. If necessary, adjust the idling speed screw shown in Fig. 3.28.

46 Check that the CO content reading is as given in the Specifications, and if necessary adjust the screw.

47 After adjusting the CO content, read just the idling speed.

48 Pull the fuse from the fuel pump relay, and briefly rev the engine to 2000 rpm. If the idle speed and CO readings now deviate from the Specifications, ascertain the faulty component from the vehicle self-diagnosis system.

Fig 3.25 Disconnect and plug the crankcase ventilation hoses on the KV engine (Sec 23)

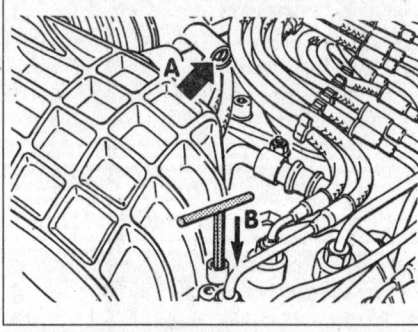

Fig 3.26 Idling control current (A) and CO meter (B) adjusting screws on the PS engine (Sec 23)

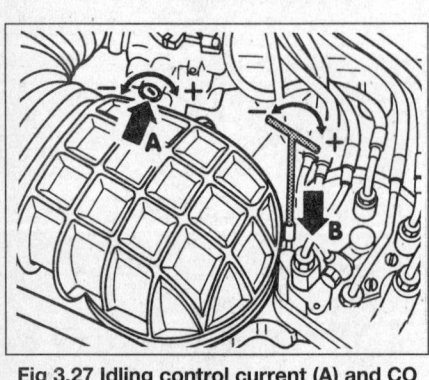

Fig 3.27 Idling control current (A) and CO meter (B) adjusting screws on the KV engine (Sec 23)

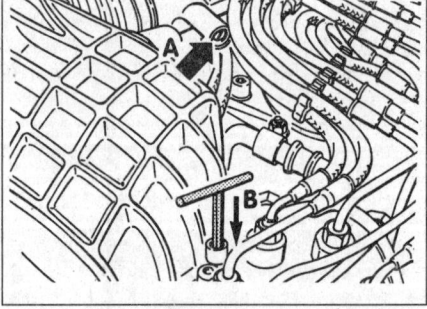

Fig 3.28 Idling speed (1) and CO content (2) adjusting screws on the 7A engine (Sec 23)

24 Fuel injection (K-Jetronic) - additional adjustments and tests

Idle speed boost (engine code DZ)

1 The two-way valve I (Fig. 3.29) increases the engine speed when it drops below 700 rpm. The control unit is located beneath the facia.

2 The two-way valve II increases the engine speed when the air conditioner is switched on.

3 To check valve I, lower the engine speed on the adjustment screw, and check that the engine speed increases at 700 rpm. Now squeeze the hose 1 (Fig. 3.29), and check that the speed drops.

4 With the hose still clamped, adjust the idling speed to the specified value, then unclamp the hose. Check that the engine speed increases to 1050 rpm, that the valve then closes, and the speed drops to the normal idling speed.

5 To check valve II, allow the engine to idle, then squeeze the hose. The engine speed must not alter. Switch on the air conditioning, and repeat the test. This time the engine speed must drop.

Airflow meter plate

6 Remove the air duct from the airflow meter. Disconnect and earth the coil HT lead, then operate the starter for ten seconds.

7 Lift the plate, and check that it has the same resistance over the full range of movement.

8 Check the dimension shown in Fig. 3.30. If necessary, the position may be adjusted by bending the wire clip under the plate.

9 The free travel of the plate should be 0.5 to 3.0 mm (0.02 to 0.12 in) on the DZ engine, and on the KV and PS engines, free travel should be detectable, up to a maximum of 2.1 mm (0.08 in). The free travel is adjusted at the control plunger stop.

Cold start valve and thermotime switch

10 Disconnect and earth the HT cable from the ignition coil.

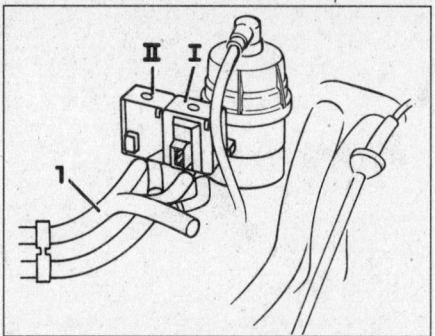

Fig 3.29 Idling speed boost two-way valves on the DZ engine (Sec 24)
1 Hose connection

11 Disconnect the wiring plug from the cold start valve, and connect a diode test lamp to the terminals in the plug.

12 Disconnect the wiring plug from the thermotime switch, and earth the terminal from the green/white wire. Do not earth the terminal from the red/black wire.

13 Operate the starter, and check that the test lamp lights up.

14 Refit the plug to the switch, leaving the green/white wire still earthed.

15 Remove the cold start valve, and hold it over a measuring glass. Operate the starter, and check that the spray pattern from the valve is an even cone shape.

16 Wipe the valve dry, and check that it remains dry for at least a minute.

17 With the cold start valve refitted, but the wiring plug disconnected, connect a diode test lamp across the two terminals of the plug.

18 Operate the starter for ten seconds, and check that the test lamp is lit for one to eight seconds, depending on the temperature of the coolant (maximum of 30°C (86°F) for the test).

Cold acceleration enrichment

19 The cold acceleration enrichment operates when the thermotime switch, diaphragm pressure switch, and throttle valve switch are closed.

20 Follow the procedure in paragraphs 11 and 12, then start the engine, and let it idle. The test lamp must not light up.

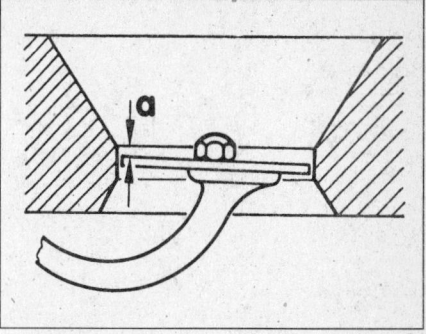

Fig 3.30 Airflow meter plate adjustment dimension (Sec 24)
a (DZ engine) = 1.9 + 1.1 mm (0.07 + 0.04 in)
a (KV/PS engines) = 1.9 + 2.0mm (0.07 + 0.08in)

21 Quickly open the throttle, and check that the test lamp lights briefly (0.4 seconds).

Diaphragm pressure switch

22 Disconnect the wiring from the pressure switch (photo).

23 Run the engine at idling speed.

24 Connect an ohmmeter to the two terminals on the switch (photo), and check that the resistance is infinity, proving that the contacts are open.

25 Quickly open the throttle, and check that the resistance drops briefly.

Throttle valve switch

26 Disconnect the wiring plug from the throttle valve switch, and connect an ohmmeter to the two terminals.

27 With the throttle closed, infinity resistance should be registered.

28 Slowly open the throttle until the switch contacts are heard to close. At this point, the resistance must be infinity, and the gap between the idling stop and throttle lever must be between 0.2 and 0.6 mm (0.008 and 0.024 in). If necessary adjust the switch as required.

Auxiliary air valve

29 Disconnect and earth the HT lead from the ignition coil.

30 Disconnect the wiring plug from the auxiliary air valve, and connect a diode test lamp across the plug terminals.

24.22 Diaphragm pressure switch (arrowed)

24.24 Ohmmeter test on the diaphragm pressure switch

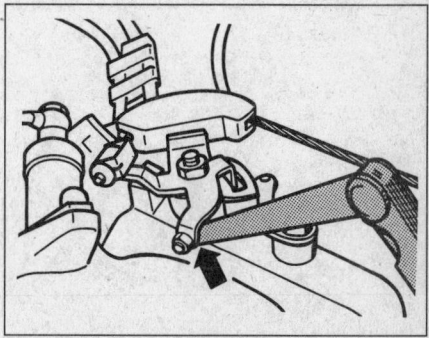

Fig 3.31 Throttle valve switch adjustment (Sec 24)

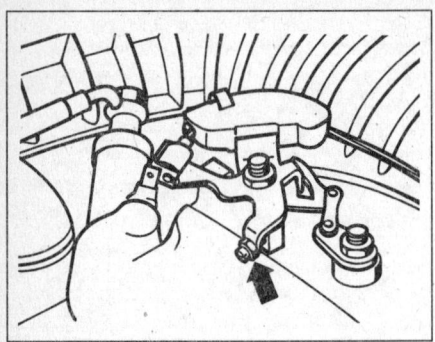

Fig 3.32 Basic throttle valve setting (Sec 24)

31 Operate the starter motor, and check that the test lamp lights up.

32 Switch off the ignition, and connect a tachometer.

33 Start the engine, and let it idle (HT lead reconnected).

34 Squeeze the hose between the auxiliary air valve and inlet manifold, and check that the engine speed drops.

35 Reconnect the wiring plug, and repeat the test with the engine warm. The engine speed must not alter.

Warm-up valve

36 Disconnect and earth the HT lead from the ignition coil.

37 Disconnect the wiring plug from the warm-up valve, and connect a diode test lamp across the plug terminals.

38 Operate the starter motor, and check that the test lamp lights up.

Basic throttle valve setting

39 The adjusting screw is set at the factory, and should not normally require adjustment. If the screw has been disturbed, carry out the following procedure.

40 Loosen the nut, and unscrew the adjusting screw so that there is a gap between the screw and stop, then turn the screw clockwise until it just touches the stop. The point of contact is best judged by using a thin piece of paper, to determine when it is just trapped. From this point, turn the screw in a further half-turn. Apply locking fluid to the

nut threads, then tighten the nut while holding the screw stationary.

41 Check the idling settings after making an adjustment.

25 Fuel injection (Mono-Jetronic) - additional adjustments and tests

Fault memory

1 The Mono-Jetronic system is equipped with a fault memory, which may be recalled for a coded read-out. A warning lamp on the instrument panel lights up in the event of a fault, and the same lamp is used to recall the fault memory code.

2 If the engine will not start, operate the starter for approximately six seconds, then leave the ignition switched on. If the engine will start, start it and let it idle.

3 Connect a known good fuse across the fuel pump relay test contacts for at least five seconds.

4 Remove the fuse, then count the number of flashing impulses given by the warning lamp. If no fault is found, the code 4444 (four groups of four flashes) will be given.

5 Note the code, then repeat the test by connecting and disconnecting the fuse until the code 0000 appears, indicating the end of the test.

6 The flashing code functions are as follows:

1111	Control unit
1232	Throttle valve positioner
2121	Throttle valve switch
2122	No speed signal
2212	Throttle valve potentiometer
2312	Coolant temperature sender
2322	Intake air temperature sender
2341	Lambda control
2342	Lambda probe
2343	Mixture control adjustment limit lean
4431	As code 1232

7 To cancel codes 2341 and 2343, disconnect the control unit wiring for a minimum of thirty seconds with the ignition switched off.

8 To cancel the fault memory, switch off the ignition, then connect the fuse across the fuel

pump relay test contacts. Switch on the ignition, wait a minimum of five seconds, then remove the fuse.

Note: *On 1989-on models, a test cable is required, as described in Chapter 4, Section 10.*

Idling switch/control valve

9 Switch on the ignition, then open and close the throttle valve. The control valve should click twice. If not, disconnect the wiring plug, and connect a diode test lamp across the plug terminals. With the throttle closed, the test lamp should light up, but with the throttle open, it should go out.

10 Run the engine at idling speed, then disconnect the wiring plug and reconnect it. The engine speed should increase, then drop. If not, renew the control valve.

11 Switch off the ignition, then disconnect the wiring plug from the throttle valve positioner.

12 Connect battery voltage and an earth wire to the positioner terminals until the plunger is fully pulled in. Remove the wires.

13 Press the plunger onto the stop, then use a feeler blade to check that the clearance indicated in Fig. 3.34 is 0.5 mm (0.02 in). Adjust the screw nut if necessary.

14 Connect an ohmmeter as shown. With the feeler blade in position, the switch must be open, with it removed, the switch must be closed (zero ohms indicated).

Throttle positioner

15 With the ignition switched off, disconnect the wiring plug from the throttle positioner.

16 Refer to Fig. 3.35, and use an ohmmeter to check the resistances given.

Throttle valve potentiometer

17 Disconnect the wiring plug from the potentiometer.

18 Refer to Fig. 3,35, and use an ohmmeter to check the resistances given. When checking between terminals 1 and 2, the resistance will change during the first quarter-throttle opening, then remain constant. Between terminals 1 and 4, the resistance will be constant during the first quarter-throttle opening, then change.

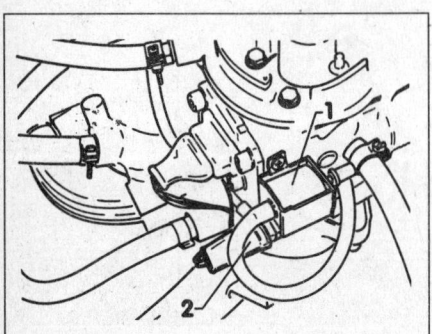

Fig 3.33 Idling switch/control valve (1) and wiring connector 12) (Sec 25)

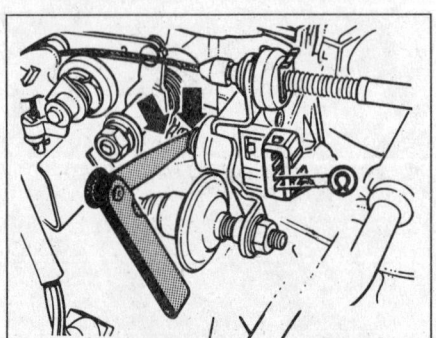

Fig 3.34 Idling switch/control valve adjustment (Sec 25)

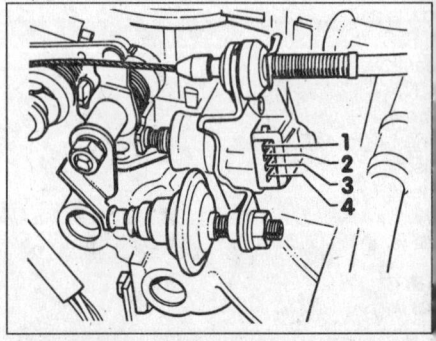

Fig 3.35 Throttle positioner resistances (Sec 25)

1 to 2 = 3 to 200 ohms
3 to 4 = 0.5 ohms maximum or infinity (throttle open)

Injector

19 Run the engine to normal operating temperature, then remove the air cleaner.

20 With the engine idling, check that the spray 'cone' pattern onto the throttle valve is even. Increase the engine speed to 3000 rpm, then quickly release the throttle. The spray cone should be interrupted briefly, indicating that the overrun cut-off is functioning correctly.

21 With the ignition switched off, check that the injector does not leak more than two drops per minute.

22 Remove the intake elbow from the injection unit.

23 Operate the starter, and check that the spray cone is visible on the throttle valve. If not, disconnect the injector wiring plug, and use an ohmmeter to check that the injector resistance is between 1.2 and 1.6 ohms at an ambient temperature of 15 to 30°C (59 to 86°F).

24 Connect a diode test lamp across the plug central terminals, then operate the starter. The test lamp should flicker, indicating that the supply to the injector is good.

Throttle damper (manual gearbox models)

25 Check that, when the throttle is closed, the lever pushes the plunger into the damper by a minimum of 4.0 mm (0.16 in). If not, loosen the adjusting nut, and adjust the damper until the lever just touches the plunger. From this position, turn the damper 4 1/4 turns towards the lever, then tighten the nut.

26 Fuel injection (KE-Jetronic) - additional adjustments and tests

Idle speed boost (engine code JN)

1 Refer to Section 24.

Lambda control (engine code JN)

2 With the engine at normal operating temperature, connect an exhaust gas analyser to the CO measuring pipe.

3 Start the engine, and allow it to idle for at least two minutes.

4 Note the CO content, then clamp hose 2 shown in Fig. 3.36. The CO content must briefly increase, then decrease. If not, disconnect the lambda probe wires, and hold the green wire to earth for approximately twenty seconds. If the CO content now alters, the lambda probe is proved faulty.

Lambda control (engine code PS)

5 Refer to Section 27, paragraphs 2 to 4.

Cold acceleration enrichment

6 Connect a multimeter to the differential pressure regulator.

---

7 Disconnect the plug from the lower temperature sender.

8 Remove the air intake elbow from the airflow meter.

9 Turn on the ignition. Check that the control current is 80 to 100 mA.

10 Lift the airflow meter plate quickly. The control current must briefly rise to over 100 mA.

Re-start and warm-up enrichment

11 Disconnect and earth the HT lead from the ignition coil.

12 Connect a multimeter to the differential pressure regulator.

13 Disconnect the plug from the lower temperature sender.

14 Operate the starter for approximately two seconds, then leave the ignition switched on. The control current must reach 120 mA for 30 to 60 seconds, then within 20 to 50 seconds, fall to 80 to 100 mA.

Cold start valve and thermotime switch

15 Refer to Section 24, paragraphs 10 to 18.

Auxiliary air valve

16 Refer to Section 24, paragraphs 29 to 35.

Basic throttle valve setting

17 Refer to Section 24, paragraphs 39 to 41.

27 Fuel injection (KE III-Jetronic) - additional adjustments and tests

Fault memory

1 The KE III-Jetronic system is equipped with a fault memory, covering both the fuel injection system and ignition system. The self-check procedure is described in Chapter 4, Section 8.

Lambda control

2 Connect a digital multimeter to the differential pressure regulator.

3 With the engine at normal operating temperature, allow the engine to idle for two minutes.

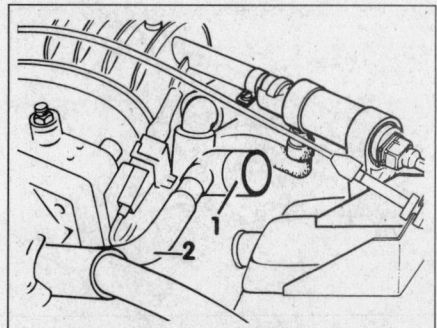

Fig 3.36 Crankcase ventilation hoses (1 and 2) on the JN engine (Sec 26)

---

4 Note the control current, then remove the dipstick, and check that the control current increases. If not, disconnect the lambda probe wires, and hold the green wire to earth for approximately twenty seconds. If the control current now changes, the lambda probe is proved faulty.

Cold acceleration enrichment

5 Disconnect the temperature sender wiring plug, and connect a digital potentiometer with a resistance of 3 kilohms. VAG digital potentiometer 1630 satisfies these conditions.

6 Run the engine at idling speed, and note the control current.

7 Quickly open and close the throttle valves, and check that the control current increases briefly to at least 6 mA.

Cold start valve

8 Refer to paragraph 5.

9 Remove the cold start valve, and hold it over a measuring beaker (photo).

10 Operate the starter, and check that it sprays in an even 'cone' pattern for two to three seconds.

11 Wipe the valve dry, and check that the valve remains dry for at least a minute.

Throttle valve switches

12 Throttle valve switch 1 monitors the closed position of the throttle; switch 2 the fully-open position of the throttle.

13 Special test leads are required to test the switches, and this job is best entrusted to an Audi dealer.

Diaphragm pressure switch

14 Refer to Section 24, paragraphs 22 to 25.

28 Fuel injection (KE-Motronic) - additional adjustments and tests

Fault memory

1 The KE-Motronic system is equipped with a fault memory, covering both the fuel injection system and ignition system. The self-check procedure is described in Chapter 4, Section 10.

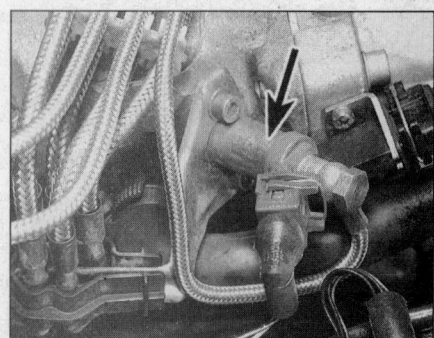

27.9 Cold start valve (arrowed) on the KV engine

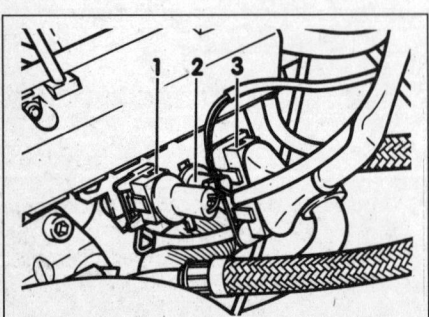

Fig 3.37 Lambda control tests on the 3A engine (Sec 28)

1 Connecting hose
2 Adaptor
3 Connection to earth

Lambda control

2 Connect a digital multimeter to the differential pressure regulator.

3 With the engine at normal operating temperature, allow the engine to idle for two minutes.

4 Note the control current, then disconnect hose 1 shown in Fig. 3.37. The control current should increase. If not, disconnect the lambda probe wires, and hold the green wire to earth for approximately twenty seconds. If the control current now changes, the lambda probe is proved faulty.

Start enrichment

5 Connect a digital multimeter to the differential pressure regulator.

6 Disconnect the wiring plug from the ignition coil power stage.

7 Remove fuse 13.

8 Operate the starter, and check that the control current drops to 35 to 45 A for a maximum of three seconds, then moves to zero.

Overrun cut-off

9 Connect a digital multimeter to the differential pressure regulator.

10 Switch on the ignition, and note the control current.

11 Start the engine, and increase the speed to over 3000 rpm.

12 Quickly close the throttle, and check that the control current briefly indicates negative.

Cold start valve

13 Disconnect the ignition coil power stage wiring.

14 Disconnect the wiring from the temperature sender, and connect a 15 kilohm resistance in series to the plug.

15 Remove the cold start valve, and hold it over a measuring beaker.

16 Operate the starter, and check that it sprays in an even 'cone' pattern for approximately eight seconds.

17 Wipe the valve dry, and check that the valve remains dry for at least a minute.

18 Disconnect the wiring, and connect an ohmmeter to the valve terminals. A reading of 10 ohms should be registered.

Airflow meter plate

19 Refer to Section 24, paragraphs 6 to 9.

Throttle valve switches

20 Special test leads are required to test the switches, and this job is best entrusted to an Audi dealer.

Basic throttle valve setting

21 Refer to Section 24, paragraphs 39 to 41.

29 Fuel injection (Multipoint injection/MPI) - additional adjustments and tests

Fault memory

1 The Multipoint injection system (MPI) is equipped with a fault memory, covering both the fuel injection system and ignition system. The self-check procedure is described in Chapter 4, Section 12.

Lambda probe

2 Disconnect the wiring plug located next to the inlet manifold (Fig. 3.38) and connect a voltmeter to the two terminals in the plug.

3 Start the engine, and check that the voltage is 12 volts. If not, check for an open-circuit.

4 If the lambda probe is removed from the exhaust manifold, its threads must be coated with fitting paste before fitting it. However, the paste must not be allowed to contact the slots on the probe.

System check

5 The MPI control unit incorporates a sequential test function for checking the fuel pump relay, the individual injectors, the idle stabilising valve, and the activated charcoal filter valve. However, a special fault read-out unit is required, and therefore this work is beyond the scope of the home mechanic. As the test is made with the engine stopped, it is possible to listen for the operation of each individual component in the correct order, or alternatively feel the component for vibration.

Coolant temperature sender (models up to 1988)

6 With the coolant temperature above 20°C (68°F), disconnect the wiring plug '3' shown in Fig. 3.38.

7 Connect an ohmmeter between contacts 6 and 7 on the plug (Fig. 3.39), and check that the resistance is approximately 2400 ohms. If not, check the wiring plug on the sender.

Throttle valve potentiometer

8 Disconnect the wiring plug from the throttle valve housing.

9 With the ignition switched on, connect a voltmeter between terminals 2 and 4, then 3 and 4 (see Fig. 3.40), and check that 5 volts is registered. If not, check the wiring between the yellow control unit plug and the four-pin plug. Otherwise, check the potentiometer itself, or the idling switch.

10 To check the potentiometer, disconnect the wiring plug, and remove the air intake elbow.

11 Connect an ohmmeter between contacts 2 and 4, and check that the resistance is between 3500 and 6500 ohms. Between contacts 2 and 3, the resistance should be between 3000 and 6000 ohms. Fully open the throttle, and check that the resistance is between 0 and 600 ohms.

Throttle valve switch

12 Disconnect the wiring plug, and connect an ohmmeter between contacts 1 and 2 or

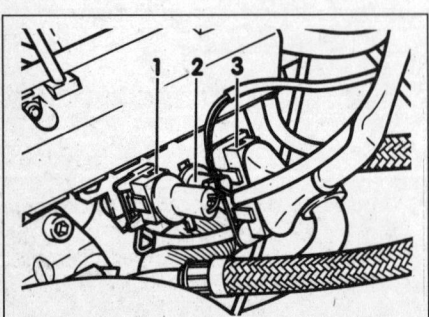

Fig 3.38 Connectors for lambda probe (1), lambda control (2), and coolant temperature sender (3) plugs on the 7A engine (Sec 29)

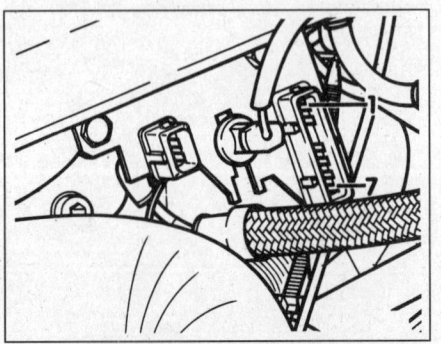

Fig 3.39 Contact numbering on the coolant temperature sender plug (Sec 29)

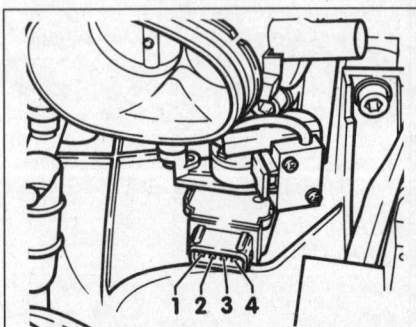

Fig 3.40 Throttle valve potentiometer contacts on the 7A engine (Sec 29)

pre-January 1989 models, or 3 and 4 on models from January 1989 on.

13 Loosen the switch mounting screws, and adjust its position so that the switch just opens at the point where a 0.75 mm (0.03 in) feeler blade can be inserted between the basic setting screw and the stop. Tighten the screws.

Idling switch

14 Disconnect the wiring plug, and connect an ohmmeter between the two contacts on the switch.

15 Insert a 0.5 mm (0.02 in) feeler blade between the basic setting screw and the stop. The resistance should be infinity. Pull out the feeler blade, and allow the throttle valve to close. The resistance should be zero.

Air volume sensor

16 Disconnect the wiring plug from the air volume sensor and connect a voltmeter between contact 3 and the engine earth.

17 Switch on the ignition, and check for approximately 12 volts. If not, check the wiring.

18 Connect the voltmeter between contacts 3 and 2, and check for approximately 12 volts.

19 Connect the voltmeter between contacts 2 and 4, and check for approximately 8 volts.

20 Reconnect the plug, and pull back the rubber cover.

21 With the ignition on, connect the voltmeter between contacts 2 and 4, and check for approximately 1.0 to 7.5 volts. Between contacts 2 and 1, the reading should be 0.3 to 1.1 volts.

22 With all electrical accessories switched off, start the engine and vary its speed repeatedly between idling and 4000 rpm. The voltage reading must vary between 1.5 and 3.4 volts.

Coolant temperature sender (1989-on models)

23 Allow the engine to cool to room temperature.

24 Disconnect the wiring plug, and connect an ohmmeter between the contacts 1 and 2 shown in Fig. 3.41. The resistance should be approximately 2500 ohms with the coolant temperature at 20°C (68°F). If it is

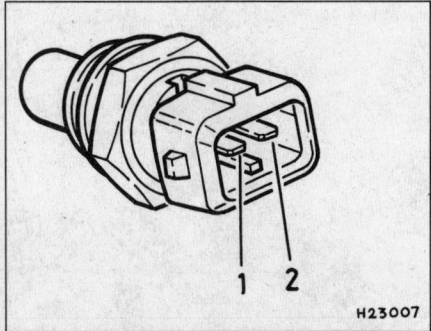

Fig 3.41 Coolant temperature sender contacts on 1989 on models (Sec 29)

inconvenient to cool the engine, the resistance should be approximately 330 ohms with the coolant temperature at 80°C (176°F).

30 Injector cooling fan motor - removal and refitting

1 Disconnect the battery negative lead.

2 Disconnect the air ducts from each end of the motor (photo).

3 Disconnect the wiring plug.

4 Unscrew the mounting screws, and withdraw the motor from the engine.

5 If necessary, the ducting may be removed from the cylinder head by unscrewing the screws.

6 Refitting is a reversal of removal. Note that if the engine is still warm, the thermoswitch may be in its 'on' position.

31 Emission control systems - general

Although careful attention to the correct ignition and mixture settings minimises the amount of harmful gases released by the exhaust system, the increasingly stringent legislation has made the introduction of additional systems necessary.

Crankcase ventilation system

Some of the products of combustion blow past the piston rings and enter the crankcase, from whence they would escape to the atmosphere if special precautions were not taken.

To prevent these gases from escaping to the atmosphere, the crankcase breather is connected by a hose to the air cleaner, so that the crankcase gases mix with the air/fuel mixture in the manifold, and are consumed by the engine.

Catalytic converter

This consists of an additional component in the exhaust pipe and silencer system.

30.2 Injector cooling fan motor and ducting

The converter contains a catalyst, which induces a chemical reaction to turn the carbon monoxide and hydrocarbons in the exhaust gas into carbon dioxide and water.

The converter does not require any maintenance, but should be examined periodically for signs of physical damage.

The catalyst in the converter can be rendered ineffective by lead and other fuel additives, so it is important that only unleaded fuel is used, and that the fuel contains no harmful additives.

The catalytic converter contains a ceramic insert, which is fragile, and is liable to fracture if the converter is hit, or dropped.

Evaporative fuel control

To prevent fuel vapour escaping to the atmosphere, the fuel tank is vented to a carbon canister. The fuel tank has an expansion chamber and vent lines, which are arranged so that no fuel or vapour can escape, even though the car may be at a very high temperature, or may be driven or parked on a very steep incline.

The vent lines are connected to a canister containing carbon, which absorbs the hydrocarbon vapours. When the engine is not running, fuel vapour collects in the carbon canister. When the engine is running, fresh air is sucked through the canister, and the vapours are drawn from the canister through the air cleaner and into the engine, where they are burnt. The canister is sometimes referred to as an activated carbon or charcoal filter.

Lambda probe

Models equipped with a catalytic converter are able to monitor the amount of oxygen present in the exhaust gases, either using the catalytic converter itself, or a lambda probe in the exhaust manifold. From this information, the electronic control unit maintains the air/fuel ratio at a constant level, in order to give complete combustion.

Exhaust gas recirculation (EGR)

Models fitted with the PS engine and automatic transmission are equipped with an EGR system, where some of the exhaust gases are returned to the inlet manifold and burnt, in order to reduce the emission of nitrogen oxides.

32 Inlet manifold - removal and refitting

1 Remove the carburettor or throttle valve assembly, as applicable.

2 On carburettor models, drain the cooling system, then disconnect and plug the coolant and vacuum hoses. Disconnect the wiring from the preheater (photos).

3 On fuel injection models, remove the auxiliary air valve and cold start valve.

32.2A Disconnecting the coolant hose . . .

32.2B . . . and vacuum hose

32.2C Disconnecting the preheater wiring

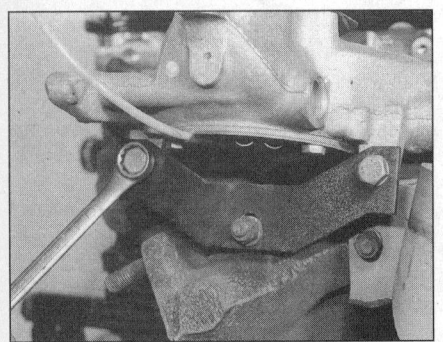

32.4A Unscrew the bolts . . .

32.4B . . . and remove the support bracket . . .

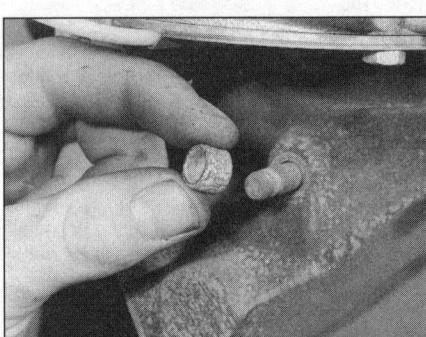

32.4C . . . spacer. . .

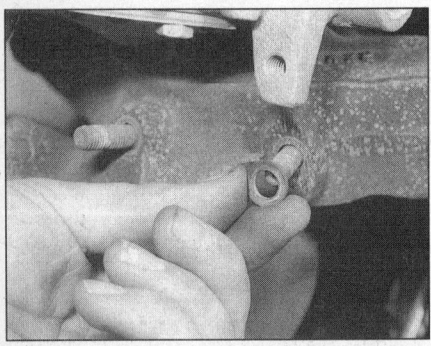

32.4D . . . and washer

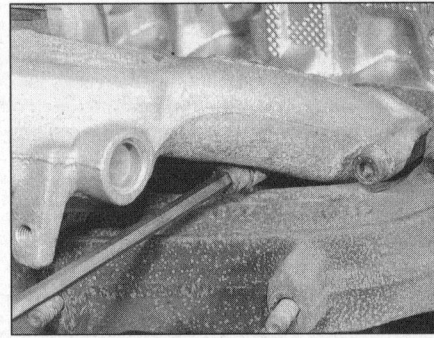

32.5A Unscrew the mounting bolts with an Allen key. . .

32.5B . . . remove the bolts . . .

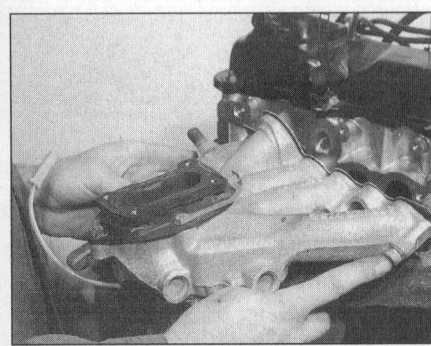

32.5C . . . withdraw the inlet manifold . . .

32.5D . . . and remove the gasket

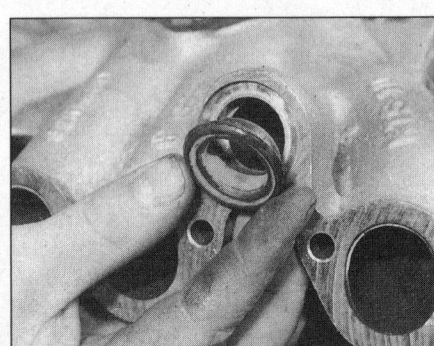

32.6A Removing the sealing ring (carburettor models)

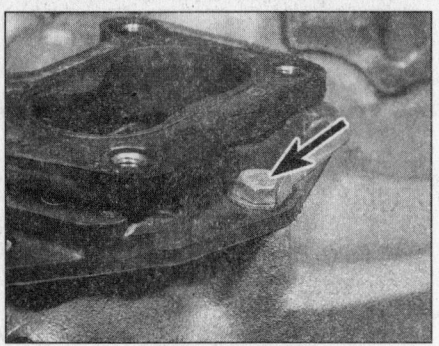

32.6B Carburettor flange bolt – note locktab (arrowed)

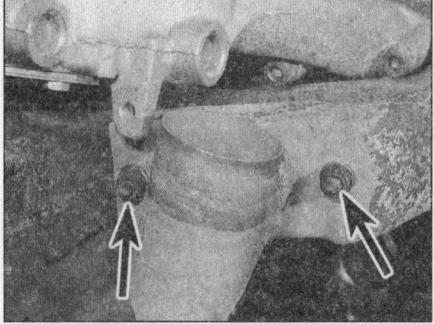

33.2A Unscrew the nuts . . .

33.2B . . . and withdraw the exhaust manifold shroud (carburettor engine)

4 Unscrew the bolts and nut, and remove the support bracket from the inlet and exhaust manifolds. Remove the spacer and washer from the exhaust manifold studs (photos).
5 Unscrew the mounting bolts, using an Allen key where necessary, and withdraw the inlet manifold from the cylinder head. Remove the gasket (photos).
6 On carburettor models, remove the sealing ring, and unbolt the carburettor flange (photos).
7 Refitting is a reversal of removal, but make sure that the contact faces are clean, and fit a new gasket. Tighten all nuts and bolts to the specified torque. Refill the cooling system, with reference to Chapter 2.

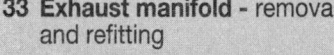

33 Exhaust manifold - removal and refitting

1 Remove the inlet manifold (Section 32).
2 Unscrew the nuts, and remove the exhaust manifold shroud (photos). Disconnect the warm air hose.
3 Unbolt the exhaust downpipe from the manifold, and remove the gasket (photo). Where applicable, disconnect the lambda probe wiring.
4 Unscrew the mounting nuts, and withdraw the exhaust manifold from the cylinder head. Remove the gaskets (photos).

5 Refitting is a reversal of removal, but fit new gaskets, and tighten all nuts and bolts to the specified torque (photo).

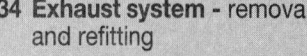

34 Exhaust system - removal and refitting

1 The exhaust systems are shown in Figs. 3.42, 3.43 and 3.44.
2 Position the car over an inspection pit, or on car ramps. Before trying to unscrew the system's nuts and bolts, soak them in penetrating oil to ease their removal.
3 The original system fitted by the

3

33.2C Lower view of the exhaust manifold and shroud (five-cylinder fuel injection engine)

33.3 Lower view of the exhaust manifold-to-downpipe joint (four-cylinder carburettor engine) – arrowed

33.4A Removing the exhaust manifold . . .

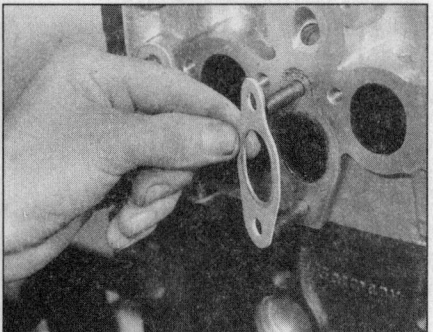

33.4B . . . and gasket

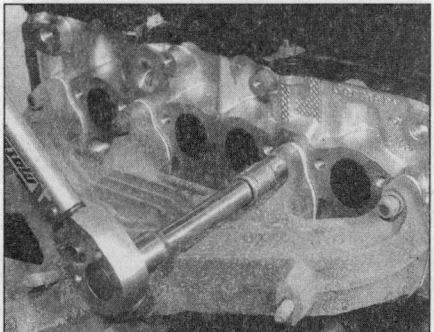

33.5 Tightening the exhaust manifold nuts

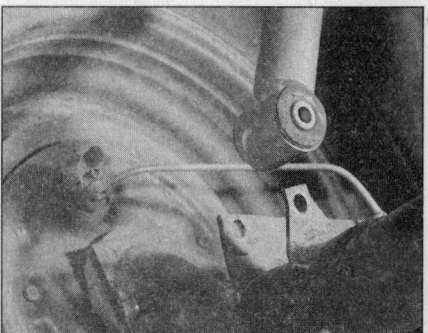

34.3 Left-hand rear shock absorber lower mounting disconnected, to remove the original exhaust system

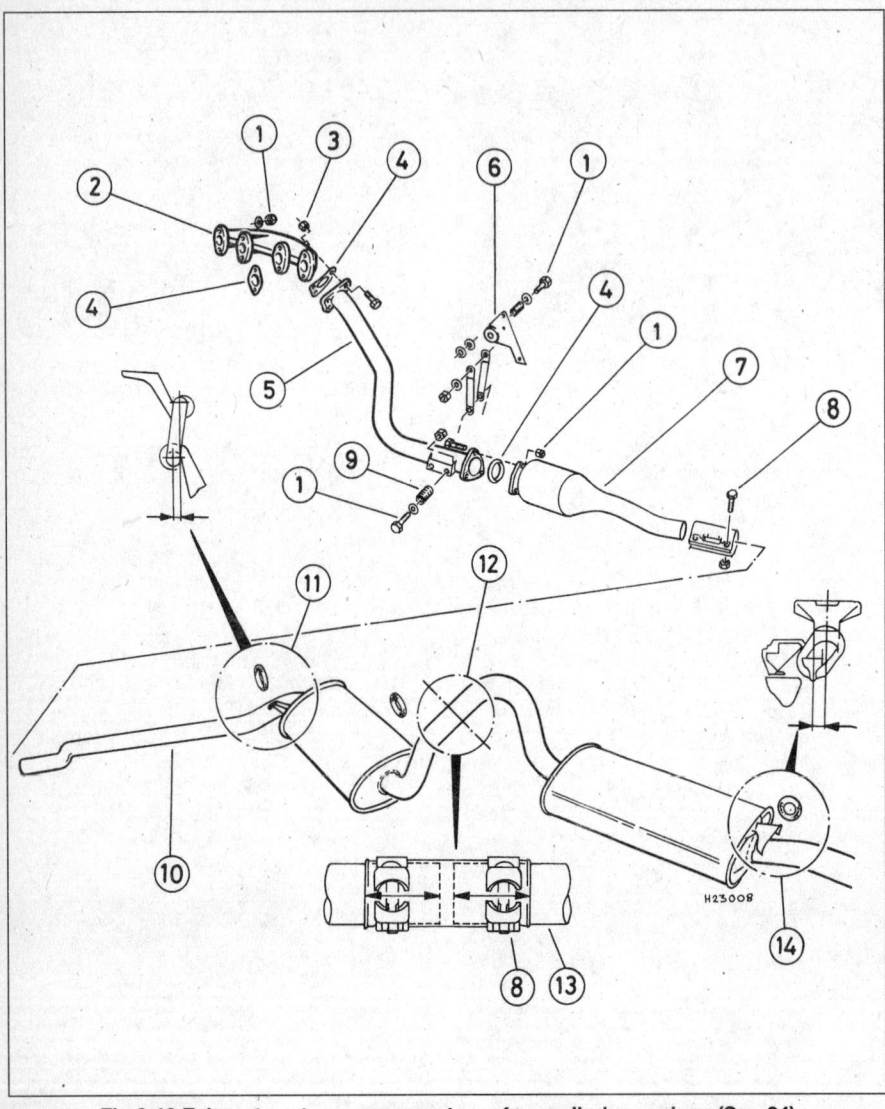

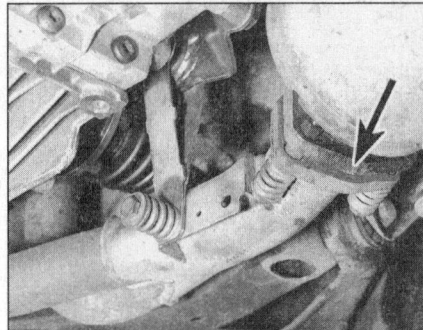

34.4 Downpipe flange-to-front silencer joint (arrowed)

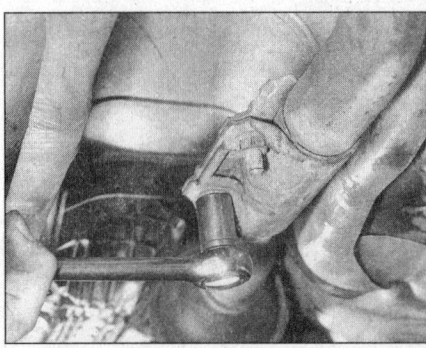

34.5 Exhaust system connecting sleeve removal

Fig 3.42 Exhaust system components on four-cylinder engines (Sec 34)

1 Bolt	7 Front silencer or catalytic converter	11 Mounting rubber (front)
2 Exhaust manifold	8 Bolt	12 Separating point for repairs
3 Nut	9 Spring	13 Clamping sleeve
4 Gasket	10 Intermediate	14 Mounting rubber (rear)
5 Front downpipe		
6 Bracket		

manufacturer is a one-piece unit from the lower end of the downpipe. To remove it, the rear body must be raised, and the rear axle lowered, after disconnecting the left-hand rear shock absorber lower mounting bolt (photo). The service repair system is in two pieces, joined with a connecting sleeve over the rear axle.

4 To remove the system, unscrew and remove the bolts and springs securing the downpipe flange to the front silencer or catalytic converter (photo).

5 Where applicable, unbolt the connecting sleeve (photo).

6 Bend back the mounting bracket lugs, and unhook the mounting rubber rings. To do this, a length of wire may be inserted through the

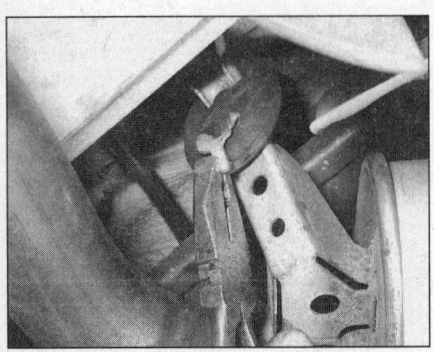

34.6A Bending back the mounting bracket lugs

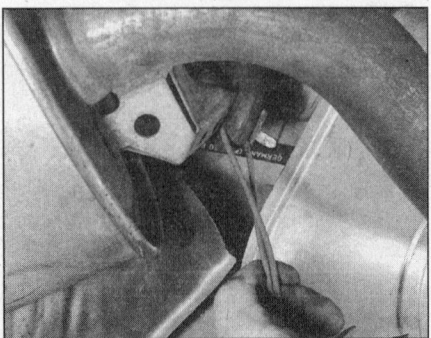

34.6B Using a length of wire to release the mounting rubbers

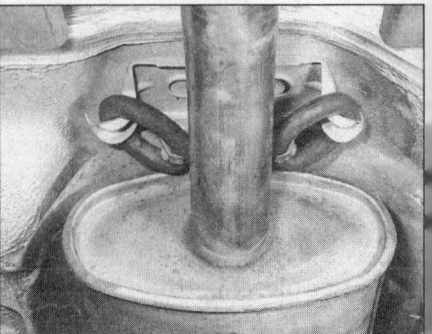

34.6C Front silencer mounting rubbers

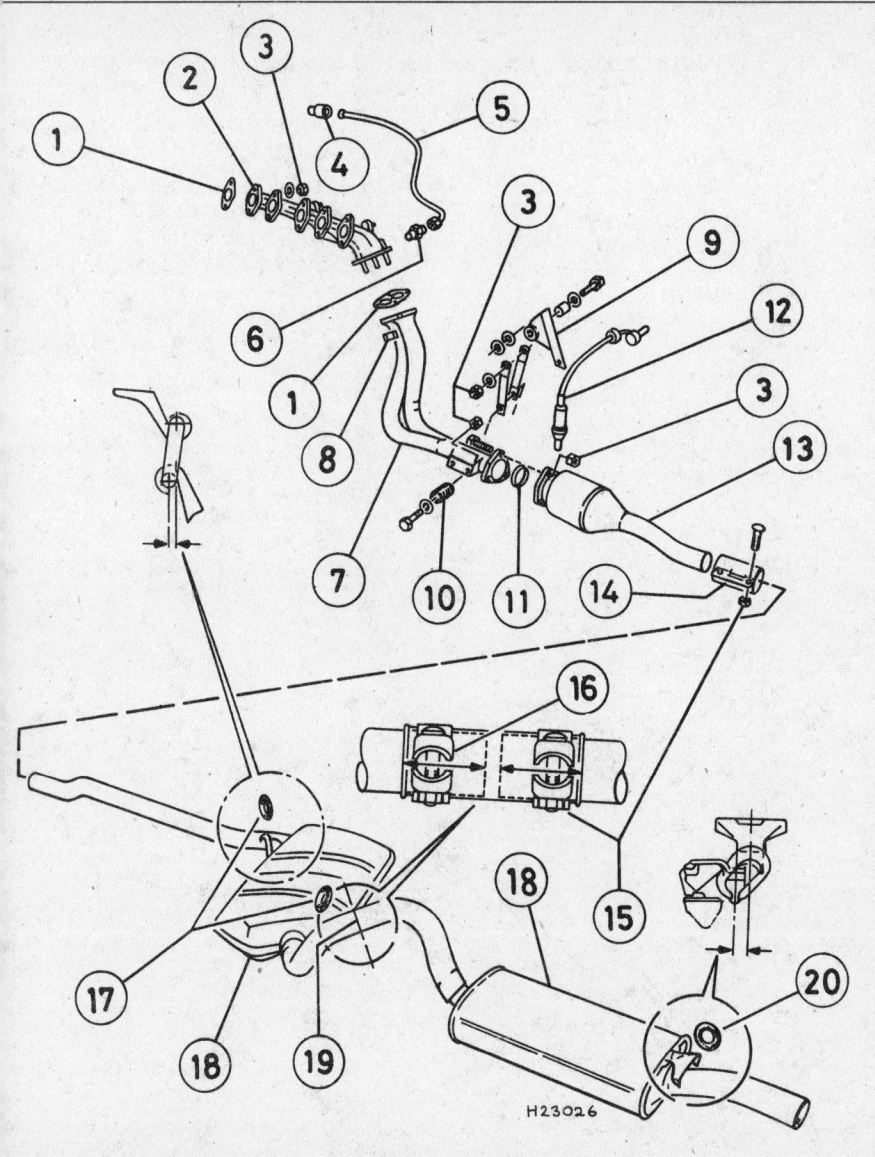

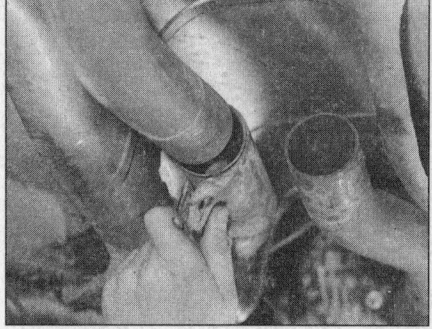

34.7 Removing the rear exhaust system and connecting sleeve

34.8A Front downpipe lower mounting (four-cylinder carburettor engine)

34.8B Front downpipe lower mounting (five-cylinder fuel injection engine)

Fig 3.43 Exhaust system components on five-cylinder engines – except 20-valve (Sec 34)

1 Gasket	9 Bracket	15 Clamp
2 Exhaust manifold	10 Spring	16 Connecting sleeve
3 Nut	11 Seal	17 Mounting rubber
4 Anti-tamper cap	12 Lambda probe	18 Intermediate pipe
5 CO measuring pipe	13 Front silencer or catalytic	19 Separating point for
6 Union	converter	repairs
7 Front downpipe	14 Connecting sleeve	20 Mounting rubber
8 Nut		

...ing (photos). Where applicable, also ...disconnect the lambda probe wiring.

... Withdraw the rear exhaust system, and ...ecover the connecting sleeve (photo).

... Unbolt the front downpipe at the lower ...mounting and at the exhaust manifold, then ...emove it and recover the gasket (photos).

... Refit the system a piece at a time, starting ...with the downpipe (with a new gasket).

10 Clear all joints, and smear with a proprietary exhaust sealing compound.

11 Assemble the system loosely to start with, then make sure that it is not under any strain. A stressed exhaust system will have a much shorter lifespan. When satisfied with its position, the nuts and bolts should be tightened securely.

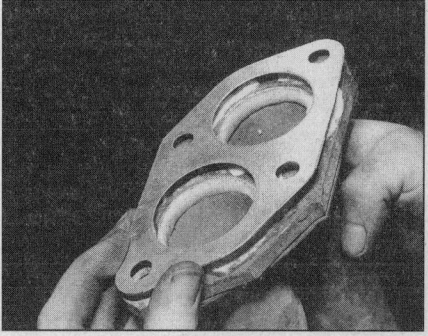

34.8C Removing the exhaust manifold-to-front downpipe gasket

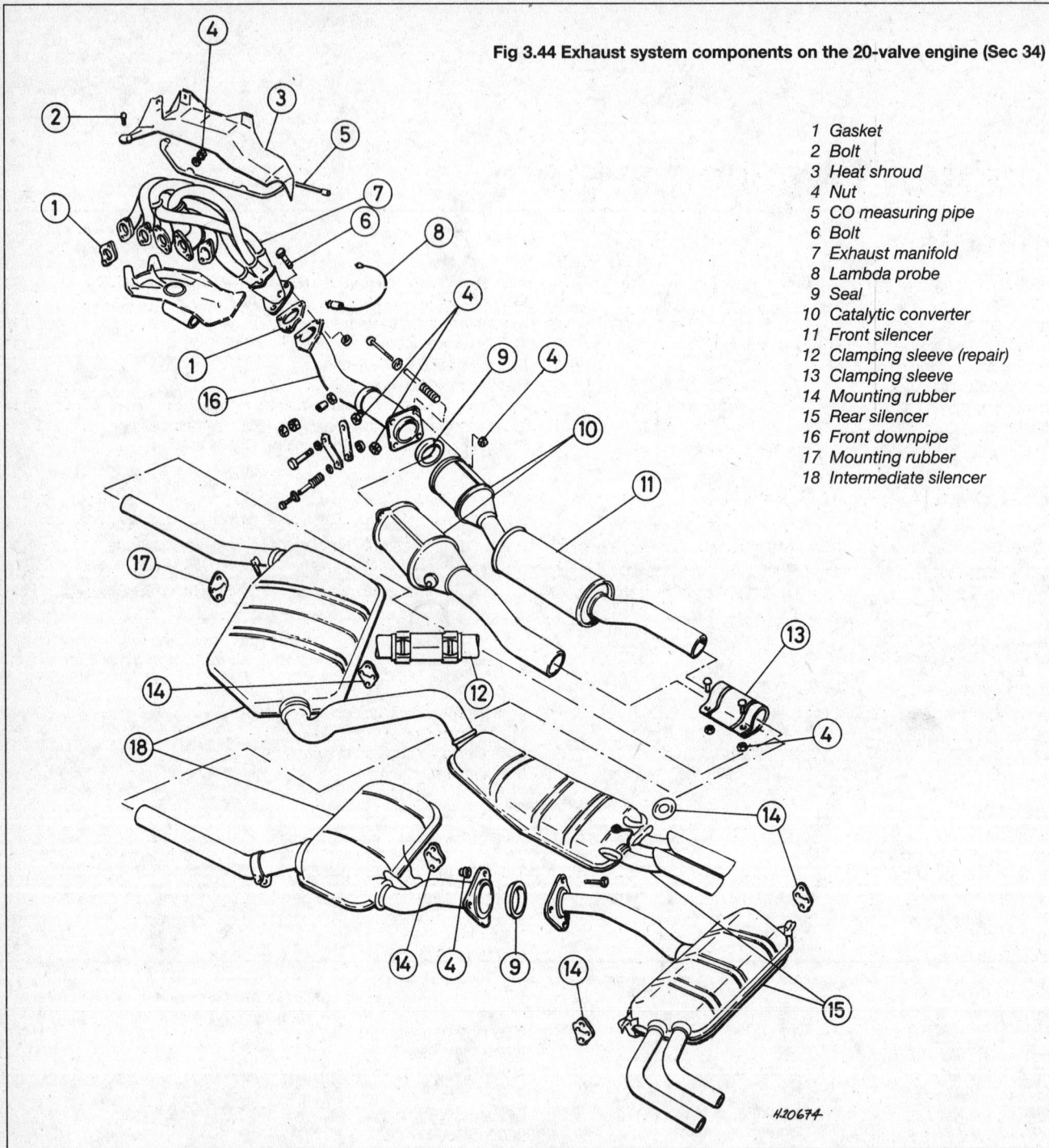

Fig 3.44 Exhaust system components on the 20-valve engine (Sec 34)

1 Gasket
2 Bolt
3 Heat shroud
4 Nut
5 CO measuring pipe
6 Bolt
7 Exhaust manifold
8 Lambda probe
9 Seal
10 Catalytic converter
11 Front silencer
12 Clamping sleeve (repair)
13 Clamping sleeve
14 Mounting rubber
15 Rear silencer
16 Front downpipe
17 Mounting rubber
18 Intermediate silencer

Fault finding - fuel, exhaust and emission control systems

Excessive fuel consumption

- ☐ Mixture setting incorrect (where applicable)
- ☐ Air cleaner element blocked
- ☐ Fuel leak
- ☐ Incorrect float level (carburettor)
- ☐ Warm-up regulator or fuel metering unit faulty (fuel injection)

Insufficient fuel supply or weak mixture

- ☐ Fuel pump faulty
- ☐ Mixture setting incorrect (where applicable)
- ☐ Fuel filter blocked
- ☐ Fuel leak
- ☐ Sticking needle valve (carburettor)
- ☐ Cold start valve faulty (fuel injection)

Chapter 4 Ignition system

Contents

Degrees of difficulty

Easy, suitable for novice with little experience	Fairly easy, suitable for beginner with some experience	Fairly difficult, suitable for competent DIY mechanic	Difficult, suitable for experienced DIY mechanic	Very difficult, suitable for expert DIY or professional

Specifications

System type

Engine code KV, and 1.6/1.8 litre engines	Transistorised coil ignition system (TCI-H)
Engine code 3A	Motronic ignition system
Engine codes PS and NG	Fully electronic ignition system (FEI)
Engine code 7A	MPI ignition system

Distributor

Rotor rotation	Clockwise
Firing order:	
Four cylinder engines	1-3-4-2 (No 1 at timing belt end)
Five-cylinder engines	1-2-4-5-3 (No 1 at timing belt end)
Rotor arm resistance	
Engine code 7A	1000 ohms
All other engines	600 to 1400 ohms

Coil

Primary resistance:	
Engine code KV, and 1.6/1.8 litre engines	0.52 to 0.76 ohms
Engine codes 3A, PS and NG	0.5 to 1.5 ohms
Engine code 7A	Approximately 0 to 1.0 ohm,
Secondary resistance:	
Engine code KV, and 1.6/1.8 litre engines	2400 to 3500 ohms
Engine codes 3A, PS and NG	5000 to 9000 ohms
Engine code 7A	6500 to 8000 ohms
HT lead resistance:	
Coil connector	600 to 1400 ohms
Plug connector	4000 to 6000 ohms

Spark plugs

Type:	
Engine code:	
RN	Champion N9BYC or N9YCC
DZ, NE, PM, RU, JN, PS, NG, 3A, KV	Champion N7BYC or N7YCC
7A	Champion C6BYC or C6YCC
Electrode gap (all models)	0.8 mm (0.032 in)

4

Ignition timing

Engine code	Vacuum hoses on/off	Setting
RN	On	18° ± 1° BTDC at 950 ± 50 rpm
NE	On	With leaded petrol, 18° ± 1° BTDC at 950 ± 50 rpm
		With unleaded petrol, 10° ± 1° BTDC at 825 to 975 rpm
RU	On	18° ± 1° BTDC at 950 ± 50 rpm
DZ	Off and plugged	With leaded petrol, 6° ± 1° BTDC at 800 to 1000 rpm
		With unleaded petrol, 0° ± 1° at 800 to 1000 rpm
PM	Off and plugged	6° ± 1° BTDC at 950 (maximum)
JN	Off and plugged	6° ± 1° BTDC at 900 ± 50 rpm
3A	-	6° ± 1° BTDC at 780 to 900 rpm
NG	-	15° ± 1° BTDC at 720 to 860 rpm
PS	-	18° ± 1° BTDC at 750 to 850 rpm
KV	On	With leaded petrol, 18° ± 1° BTDC at 800 ± 50 rpm
		With unleaded petrol, 9° ± 1° BTDC at 750 to 850 rpm
7A	-	TDC static

Torque wrench settings

	Nm	lbf ft
Spark plugs	20	15
Distributor clamp bolt	11	8

1 General description

The ignition system comprises the battery, coil, electronic switch unit or control unit, distributor, and spark plugs. There are four different systems described in this Chapter the TCI-H, FEI, Motronic and MPI systems. Each system consists of a low tension (LT) and high tension (HT) circuit. The low tension circuit is interrupted regularly by a Hall sender unit in the distributor, and this action causes the magnetic field around the coil primary windings to collapse. The coil secondary windings are located over the primary windings, and the magnetic field induces a high tension current. The current is fed to the spark plug via the distributor cap and rotor.

The exact timing of the HT spark is dependent on the speed of, and load on, the engine, to give the most efficient setting.

The distributor is positioned in the cylinder block on four-cylinder engines, and at the right-hand rear of the cylinder head on five-cylinder engines.

2 Routine maintenance

Carry out the following procedure at the intervals given in 'Routine maintenance' at the beginning of the manual.

Renew the spark plugs

1 Refer to Section 16.

3 Distributor - removal and refitting

1 Before removing the distributor, the engine must be positioned at TDC compression on No 1 cylinder. To do this, remove the spark plugs, then turn the engine clockwise with a spanner on the crankshaft pulley bolt. Turn the engine until compression can be felt in No 1 cylinder (front of the engine), using a finger or rubber plug over the spark plug hole.
2 Continue turning the engine clockwise until the TDC marks are aligned on the crankshaft pulley and lower timing cover (photo). On the 20-valve engine (code 7A), it will be necessary to align the 'O' mark on the flywheel with the corresponding mark on the transmission housing timing aperture, so there is no mark on the pulley. This procedure may also be carried out on all other engines.
3 As a further check, the upper timing cover may be removed and the TDC mark on the camshaft sprocket aligned with the pointer on the 20-valve engine, or the upper edge of the cylinder head on other engines (see Chapter 1).
4 Mark the distributor body and engine block or cylinder head (as applicable) accurately in relation to each other, using a scriber or pin punch.
5 Disconnect the vacuum pipe from the vacuum capsule on the distributor where applicable (photo).
6 Squeeze the spring clip together, and disconnect the wiring plug (photo).
7 Remove the interference screen (if fitted), then prise off the clips and lift the cap from the distributor (photos).

3.2 TDC timing marks on the crankshaft pulley and lower timing cover

3.5 Disconnecting the vacuum pipe from the distributor vacuum capsule on the four-cylinder engine

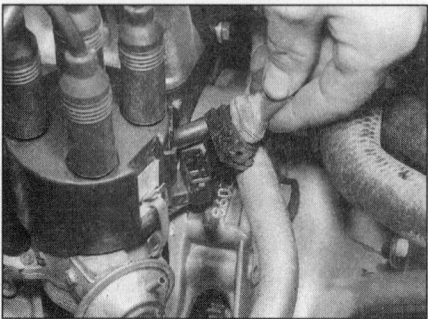

3.6 Disconnecting the distributor wiring plug

3.7A Release the clips . . .

3.7B . . . and lift off the distributor cap

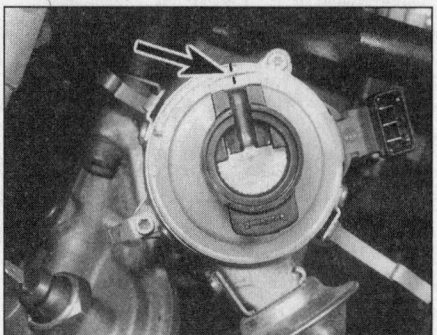

3.8 TDC marks on the distributor body and rotor arm (arrowed)

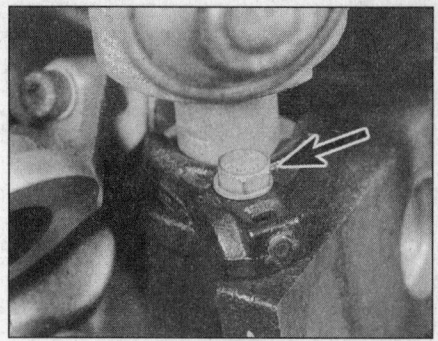

3.9 Distributor clamp and bolt (arrowed) on the four-cylinder engine

8 Check if the upper rim of the distributor body has a mark which coincides with the centre of the rotor arm. If not, make a mark with a pencil (photo). On the 20-valve engine, the special tool shown in Fig. 4.21 is used by Audi technicians to align the rotor arm. If necessary, a similar tool may be made out of card or an old distributor cap.

9 Unscrew the clamp bolt or nut, and remove the clamp (photo). An anti-tamper cap may be fitted on the bolt.

10 Withdraw the distributor from the block or head (photo).

11 Check the condition of the rubber O-ring on the base of the distributor, and if necessary prise it out and renew it (photo). If fitted, also renew the gasket.

12 Check that the crankshaft is still on the TDC position.

3.10 Removing the distributor from the block on the four-cylinder engine

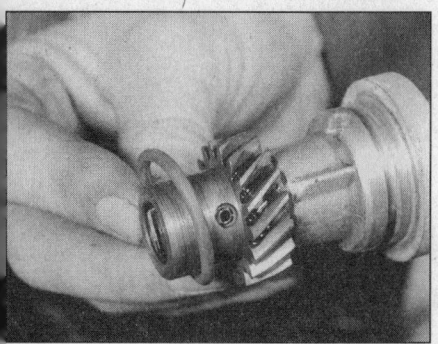

3.11 Distributor rubber O-ring removal

13 Turn the rotor arm slightly clockwise from the TDC position, then locate the distributor over the aperture in the block or head, with the previously-made marks on the body and block or head aligned.

14 Lower the distributor into position, and check that, as the drive gears engage, the rotor arm moves anti-clockwise to its original position. On the four-cylinder engine, if the distributor will not seat fully, withdraw the unit, and use a screwdriver to turn the oil pump driveshaft slightly, then try again (photo).

15 Check that the previously-made marks are aligned, then fit the clamp and tighten the bolt or nut.

16 Refit the distributor cap, wiring plug, and vacuum pipe. If removed, also refit the timing cover.

17 Check and if necessary adjust the ignition timing, as described in Sections 13, 14 or 15.

4 Distributor - dismantling, inspection and reassembly

Caution: *The rotor arm on some 20-valve engines is permanently bonded to the shaft, and if damaged, it will be necessary to renew the complete distributor. Do not exert undue effort on the rotor arm on these engines in an attempt to remove it.*

1 Wipe clean the exterior of the distributor.

2 Pull the rotor arm from the driveshaft, then

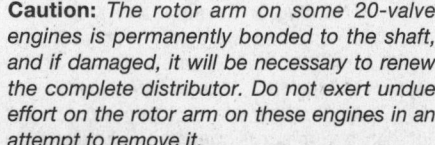

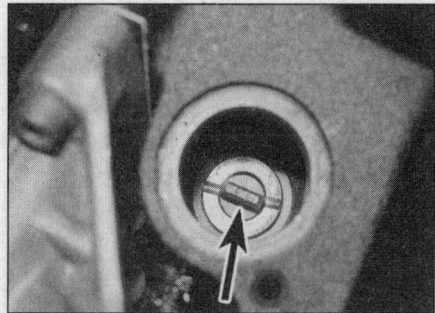

3.14 Distributor locating segment on the oil pump driveshaft on the four-cylinder engine (arrowed)

lift off the dust cap. Do not allow the cap retaining clips to foul the Hall rotor.

3 Mark the Hall rotor in relation to the driveshaft, then extract the circlip and withdraw the Hall rotor, together with the locating pin.

4 Remove the plain and spring washers, noting their fitted locations.

5 Where fitted, remove the screws and withdraw the vacuum unit, after disconnecting the operating arm.

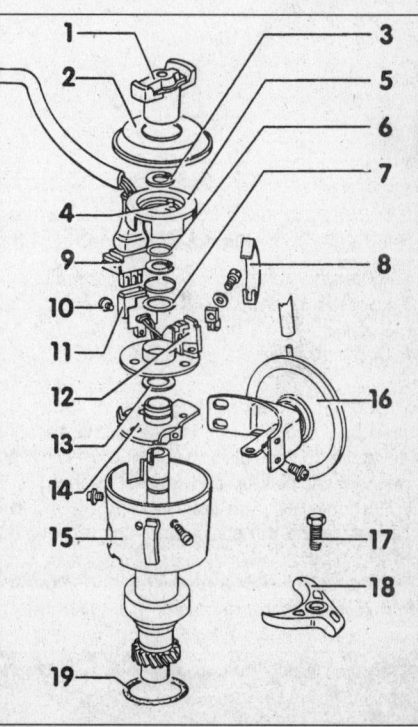

Fig 4.1 Exploded view of the distributor on the TCI-H ignition system (Sec 4)

1 Rotor arm	11 Socket
2 Dust cap	12 Hall sender
3 Circlip	13 Washer
4 Pin	14 Baseplate
5 Hall rotor	15 Distributor
6 Spring washer	16 Vacuum unit
7 Washer	17 Bolt
8 Clip	18 Clamp
9 Connector	19 O-ring
10 Retaining button	

4

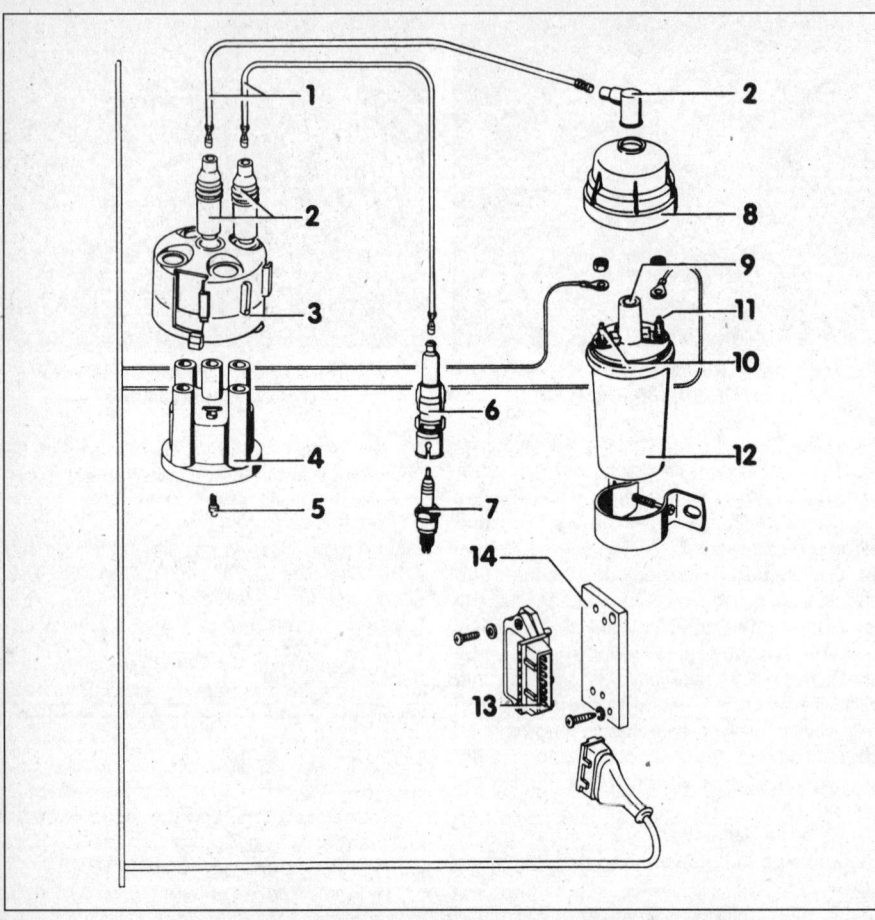

Fig 4.2 Components of the TCI-H ignition system (Sec 5)

1 HT leads	5 Carbon brush	9 Terminal 4	12 Ignition coil
2 Suppressor cap	6 HT connector	10 Terminal 1	13 Switch unit
3 Screen	7 Spark plug	11 Terminal 15	14 Heat sink
4 Distributor cap	8 Cap		

6 Extract the circlip and washer from the baseplate, and also remove the screws securing the socket to the side of the distributor. Withdraw the magnetic pick-up and socket together.

7 Remove the side screws, and lift out the baseplate and thrust-washer. Also remove the spring clips.

8 Clean all the components, and examine them for wear and damage.

9 Inspect the inside of the distributor cap for signs of burning or tracking. Make sure that the carbon brush in the centre of the cap is in good condition, and that it moves freely against the tension of the spring.

10 Check that the rotor arm is not damaged. Use an ohmmeter to measure the resistance between the brass contact in the centre of the rotor arm and the brass contact at the edge of the arm. The resistance should be between 600 and 1400 ohms.

11 Where applicable, suck on the pipe connection to the vacuum diaphragm, and check that the operating rod of the diaphragm unit moves. Retain the diaphragm under vacuum to check that it is not perforated.

12 Reassemble the distributor in reverse order, but smear a little grease on the bearing surface of the baseplate. On completion, spin the driveshaft to check that the Hall rotor is free and not bent.

5 Transistorised coil ignition system (TCI-H) - description

The TCI-H ignition system employs a Hall sender in the distributor which switches the low tension coil circuit on and off by a remotely located transistorised switch unit. The ignition timing is advanced and retarded by centrifugal weights and a vacuum capsule on the distributor. These mechanisms provide the most efficient engine performance for the prevailing conditions.

6 Transistorised coil ignition system (TCI-H) - testing

Note: *Audi recommend the use of their digital multimeter VAG 1315 A, or hand multimeter VAG 1526 for accurate readings on the following tests, as the internal resistance of some meters can influence the results obtained.*

Ignition coil

1 Disconnect the wiring and cap from the ignition coil (photo). If necessary identify each wire for location.

2 Connect an ohmmeter between terminals 1 - and 15 +, and check that the resistance of the primary windings is as given in the Specifications.

3 Connect the ohmmeter between terminals 4 (HT) and 15+, and check that the resistance of the secondary windings is as given in the Specifications.

4 Reconnect the wiring.

6.1A Disconnecting the HT lead from the ignition coil

6.1B Ignition coil with cap removed

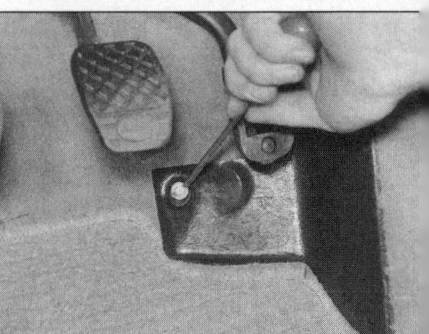

6.6A Unscrew the nut . . .

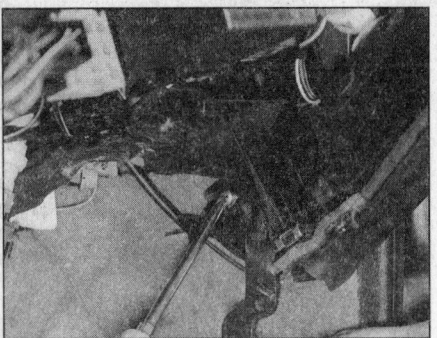

6.6B . . . and screws . . .

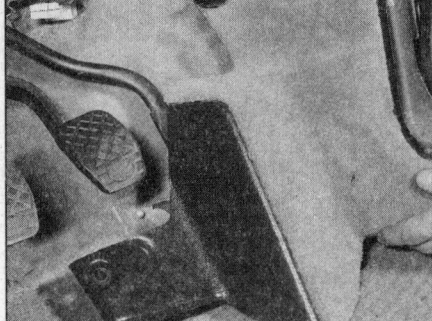

6.6C . . . and withdraw the trim from the right footwell

6.7 Transistorised ignition switch unit – spring clip arrowed

Switch unit

5 Check the ignition coil as described in paragraphs 1 to 4.

6 Working inside the car, remove the trim from the left or right footwell (according to model) (photos).

7 Squeeze together the spring clip and disconnect the wiring plug from the switch unit (photo).

8 Connect a voltmeter between terminals 2 and 4 on the plug (Fig. 4.3),

9 Switch on the ignition, and check that the voltmeter registers battery voltage. If not, check the supply wiring for an open-circuit.

10 Switch off the ignition, then disconnect the voltmeter and reconnect the plug.

11 Squeeze together the spring clip, and disconnect the wiring plug from the distributor.

12 Connect a voltmeter between terminals 1- and 15+ on the ignition coil.

13 Switch on the ignition, and check that the initial reading is 2 volts, dropping to zero after approximately one to two seconds. If not, renew the switch unit, and also check whether sealing compound has escaped from the ignition coil. Renew the ignition coil as well, if necessary.

14 Connect a length of wire briefly between the centre terminal of the distributor wiring plug and earth. Check that the voltage rises briefly to 2 volts. If not, check the centre terminal wire for an open-circuit, or renew the switch.

15 Switch off the ignition.

16 Connect the voltmeter between the outer terminals of the distributor wiring plug.

17 Switch on the ignition, and check that the voltmeter reading is at least 5 volts.

18 Disconnect the voltmeter, and re-connect the wiring plug to the distributor.

19 If a fault still exists, check the wiring between the distributor and switch unit for an open-circuit, and if the wiring proves to be intact, renew the switch.

20 Disconnect the voltmeter, and re-connect the wiring plug. Refit the trim to the left or right footwell.

Distributor Hall sender

21 Before checking the Hall sender, first check the switch unit and ignition coil as previously described, and make sure that the relevant wiring is secure and in good condition.

22 Disconnect the HT king lead from the distributor cap, and connect it to a suitable earthing point using a length of wire.

23 Working inside the car, remove the trim from the left or right footwell.

24 Connect a voltmeter between terminals 6 and 3 on the switch unit wiring plug, leaving the plug still connected to the switch (see Fig. 4.4).

25 Switch on the ignition.

26 Using a spanner on the crankshaft pulley bolt, turn the engine slowly clockwise (from the front) while observing the voltmeter. The voltage should alternate between zero and at least 2 volts. If not, renew the Hall sender unit.

27 Switch off the ignition, disconnect the voltmeter, refit the trim, and reconnect the HT king lead.

7 Fully electronic ignition system (FEI) - description

In common with the TCI-H ignition system, the FEI system employs an ignition coil, distributor with Hall sender, a power output stage (in the switch unit on TCI-H), wiring, connectors and spark plugs. The difference is that the FEI control unit supplies voltage to the Hall sender unit, and the signal from the Hall sender is supplied to terminal 2 on the power output stage via the control unit.

The ignition timing is determined by the FEI control unit, which is programmed with a ROM (Read Only Memory), and is supplied with the current status of the engine by the following components.

Engine code PS

Knock sensor, Hall sender, temperature sender, throttle valve switches (idling and full-load), and intake manifold pressure

Engine code NG

Knock sensor, Hall sender, temperature sender throttle valve switches (idling and full-load), air flow meter, and altitude sensor (where fitted)

The control unit incorporates a self-check feature, which is specific for the particular engine.

8 Fully electronic ignition system (FEI) - testing

⚠️ *Caution: Before disconnecting any wiring (including HT wiring) from the ignition system, the ignition must always be switched off. If this precaution is not taken, there is a risk of damage to the integrated circuit components, and of an HT shock to the person.*

Self-check system

1 The FEI control unit is equipped with a fault memory, which functions only when the

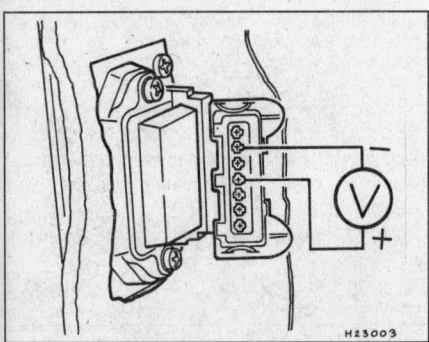

Fig 4.3 Voltage test on terminals 2 and 4 of the switch unit (Sec 6)

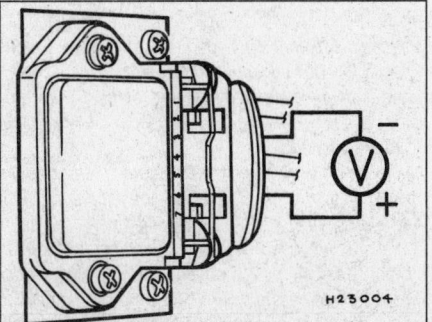

Fig 4.4 Voltage test on terminals 6 and 3 of the Hall sender switch unit (Sec 6)

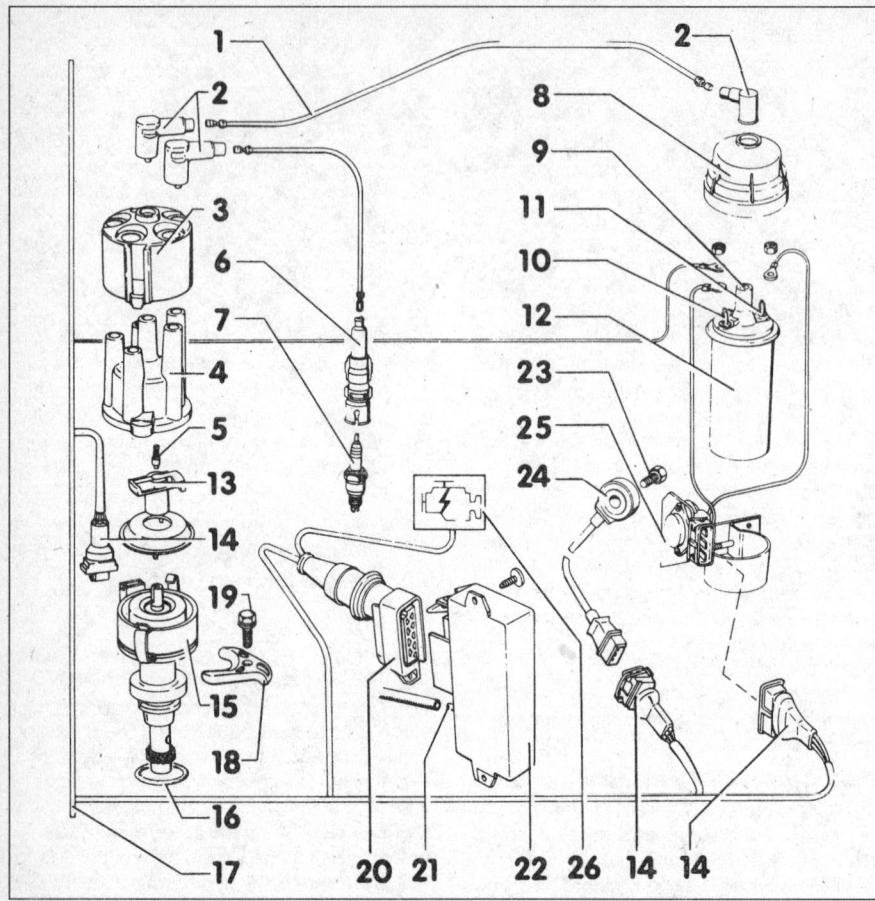

Fig 4.5 Components of the FEI ignition system (Sec 7)

1 HT lead	10 Terminal 1	19 Bolt
2 Suppressor cap	11 Terminal 15	20 Multi-plug
3 Screen	12 Ignition coil	21 Vacuum connection
4 Distributor cap	13 Rotor arm	22 FEI control unit
5 Carbon brush	14 Connector	23 Bolt
6 HT connector	15 Distributor	24 Knock sensor
7 Spark plug	16 O-ring	25 Power output stage
8 Cap	17 Wiring loom	26 Fault warning lamp
9 Terminal 4	18 Clamp	

ignition is switched on. The fault memory is cancelled when the ignition is switched off. If a fault occurs which is likely to lead to engine damage, a warning lamp on the instrument panel will light up. The lamp should come on whenever the ignition is switched on, but should go out when the engine starts. If it does not go out, there is a fault in the engine's electronic circuit. However, it may come on if fuel with too low an octane number is used, as the knock sensor will be continuously activated at its control limit.

2 If the warning lamp does not come on, remove the cover from the fusebox, and connect a known good fuse across the fuel pump relay contacts. The lamp should light up for as long as the fuse is in place. If not, check the wiring for an open-circuit.

3 To initiate a fault scan, first check that fuses 13, 24 and 28 are intact and the warning lamp

functional. Also check that the intake manifold earth wire is secure. Switch off the air conditioning (if fitted), then switch on the ignition.

4 Start the engine and drive the car for at least five minutes, during which time the engine speed should exceed 3000 rpm several times, and the accelerator pedal should be briefly fully depressed.

5 Run the engine at idling speed. Do not increase the engine speed during the following tests.

6 Connect a known good fuse across the fuel pump relay test contacts for at least four seconds.

7 Remove the fuse, then count the number of flashing impulses given by the warning lamp. The sequence starts with a signal lasting 2.5 seconds and a pause lasting 2.5 seconds, then the impulses are given in 0.5 second flashes. Count each group of flashes and the

result will be a four-figure number, after which four 2.5 second flashes and pauses indicate the end of the fault output. If no fault is found, the code 4444 (four groups of four flashes) will be given.

8 Check if there are more faults by repeating the procedure from paragraph 6, until the flashes and pauses indicate the end of the fault output.

9 The KE III-Jetronic control unit (engine code NG) fault memory may also be scanned in the same manner.

10 The flashing code explanations for the NG engine are given in the following table.

1111 Control unit
2121 Throttle valve switch I
2122 Speed signal from FEI control unit
2123 Throttle valve switch II
2141 Knock control at control limit
2142 Knock sensor
2223 Altitude sensor
2232 Airflow meter potentiometer or load signal from KE III control unit
2233 Reference voltage for load and altitude signals from KE III control unit
2312 Coolant temperature sender
4431 Control valve for idling speed stabilization
4444 No fault detected
0000 End of fault output

11 The flashing code explanations for the PS engine are given in the following table.

2141 Knock control at control limit
2142 Knock sensor defective
2222 EFI control unit pressure sensor defective or throttle valve switch II defective
2221 Vacuum hose from intake manifold to FEI control unit defective
2312 Coolant temperature sender
4444 No fault detected
0000 End of fault output

12 Testing of individual components is given in the following paragraphs. Before attempting to remove any components, the associated wiring should first be checked. Note that incorrect ignition timing may cause the knock sensor to reach its control limit and cause a corresponding fault output.

Ignition coil

13 Refer to Section 6, paragraphs 1 to 4, but note the resistances given in the Specifications.

FEI control unit

14 Where the self-check procedure shows a fault in the control unit, it should be renewed. However, on the PS engine, the following procedure may be followed.

15 First check that the knock sensor is working.

16 Start the engine and run at idling speed.

17 With a timing light connected, check the ignition timing setting, and note it.

18 With the engine running, pull the white vacuum hose from the throttle valve housing

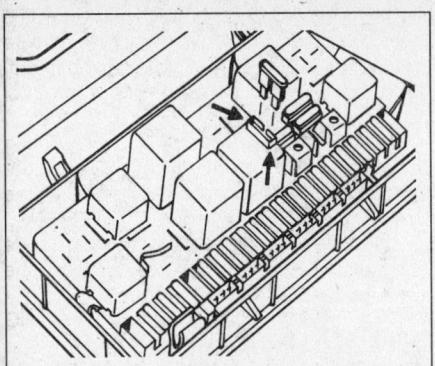

Fig 4.6 Fuel pump relay contacts (arrowed) for starting the FEI self-check system (Sec 8)

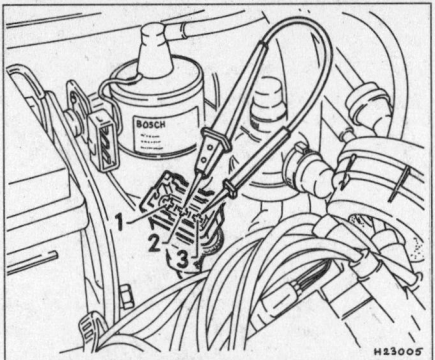

Fig 4.7 Checking the Hall sender output with a diode tester (Sec 8)
Terminal numbers indicated

(ie the FEI control unit hose), then increase the engine speed to 3000 rpm.

19 Note the ignition timing setting, and deduce from it the value noted in paragraph 17. The result should be approximately 7°.

20 Renew the control unit if the value in paragraph 19 is not obtained.

Distributor Hall sender

21 The following test is only necessary if there is no HT spark from the ignition coil.

22 Squeeze together the spring clip, and disconnect the wiring plug from the power output stage on the ignition coil.

23 Connect a diode tester between terminals 2 and 3 on the plug.

24 Spin the engine on the starter, and check that the LED flashes, indicating that the Hall sender is functioning correctly.

25 If there is no output, disconnect the wiring plug from the Hall sender on the distributor, then connect a voltmeter (preferably digital) between the two outer terminals on the plug. With the ignition switched on, a minimum of 9 volts should be recorded.

26 Re-connect the plug, then pull back the rubber boot to expose the terminals.

27 Connect a diode tester between the plug central terminal and the battery position (+) terminal.

28 Spin the engine on the starter, and check that the LED flashes, indicating that the Hall sender is functioning correctly. If there is no output, either the Hall sender or the FEI control unit is faulty.

Power output stage

29 First check that the ignition coil is in good condition, with reference to Section 6.

30 Squeeze together the spring clip, and disconnect the wiring plug from the power output stage next to the ignition coil.

31 Switch on the ignition then connect a voltmeter (preferably digital) between the two outer terminals on the plug. If battery voltage is not registered, check the associated wiring.

32 Connect a diode tester between terminals 2 and 3 on the plug.

33 Spin the engine on the starter, and check that the LED flashes, indicating that the Hall

sender is functioning correctly. If not, check the Hall sender.

34 Switch off the ignition and re-connect the plug.

35 Disconnect the wiring plug from the Hall sender at the distributor.

36 Connect a voltmeter (preferably digital) between terminals 1- and 15+ on the ignition coil, then switch on the ignition.

37 On the PS engine, 2 volts should be recorded initially, dropping to zero after one to two seconds.

38 Using a short length of wire, briefly connect the centre terminal of the Hall sender wiring plug to earth. Check that the voltage increases initially to 2 volts, then drops to zero after one to two seconds.

39 If the voltage does not drop, fit a new power output stage or control unit, and also check the ignition coil for leakage of sealing compound. If evident, renew the coil as well.

FEI control unit multi-plug

40 The following tests require the use of a digital multimeter, which must be set to the measuring range **before** connection to the terminals. Failure to observe this precaution may result in the destruction of electronic components.

41 Make sure that the battery is in good condition. Switch off the ignition.

42 Remove the trim from the right-hand side of the driver's footwell.

43 Remove the screws and lower the unit.

44 Disconnect the multi-plug, and if necessary the vacuum hose.

45 Referring to Fig. 4.8, connect the voltmeter between terminals 3 and 5. With the ignition on, battery voltage should be registered.

46 Connect the voltmeter between terminals 3 and 6. With the ignition on and the throttle shut, battery voltage should be registered.

47 Connect the voltmeter between terminals 3 and 8. With the ignition on and the throttle fully open, battery voltage should be registered.

48 Connect the voltmeter between terminals 3 and 10. With the ignition on, battery voltage should be registered.

49 Connect the voltmeter between terminals 4 and 5. With the ignition on and the fuel pump relay contacts bridged, battery voltage should be registered.

50 Switch to the ohmmeter range. Disconnect the multi-plug from the KEJetronic control unit, then connect the ohmmeter between terminal 2 on the FEI control unit and terminal 25 on the KE-Jetronic control unit. There must be continuity (zero ohms).

51 Disconnect the power output stage multi-plug and bridge terminals 2 and 3. Connect the ohmmeter between terminals 3 and 12. There must be continuity (zero ohms).

52 Disconnect the knock sensor wiring plug, and bridge all three terminals. Connect the ohmmeter between terminals 13 and 14. There must be continuity (zero ohms).

53 Disconnect the wiring plug from the Hall sender, and bridge the outer terminals. Connect the ohmmeter between terminals 7 and 15. There must be continuity (zero ohms).

54 Bridge the centre and brown/white leads on the Hall sender. Connect the ohmmeter between terminals 7 and 9. There must be continuity (zero ohms).

55 Check that the connector is attached to the temperature sender. Connect the ohmmeter between terminals 3 and 1. The resistance must be within the tolerances shown in Fig. 4.9 according to the temperature.

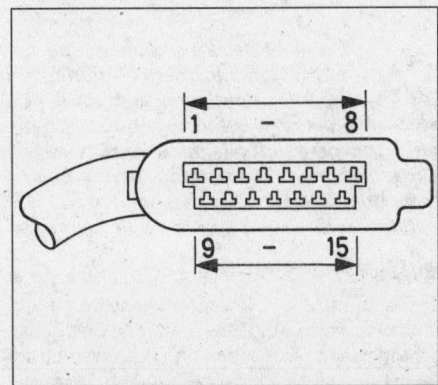

Fig 4.8 FEI control unit multi-plug terminals (Sec 8)

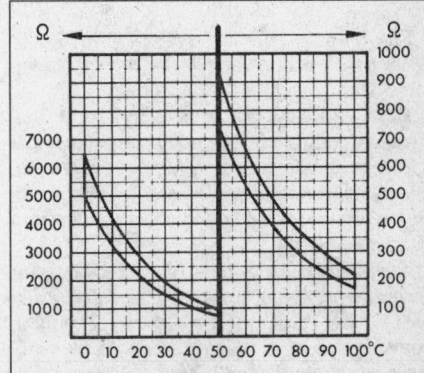

Fig 4.9 Temperature sender resistance graph (Sec 8)

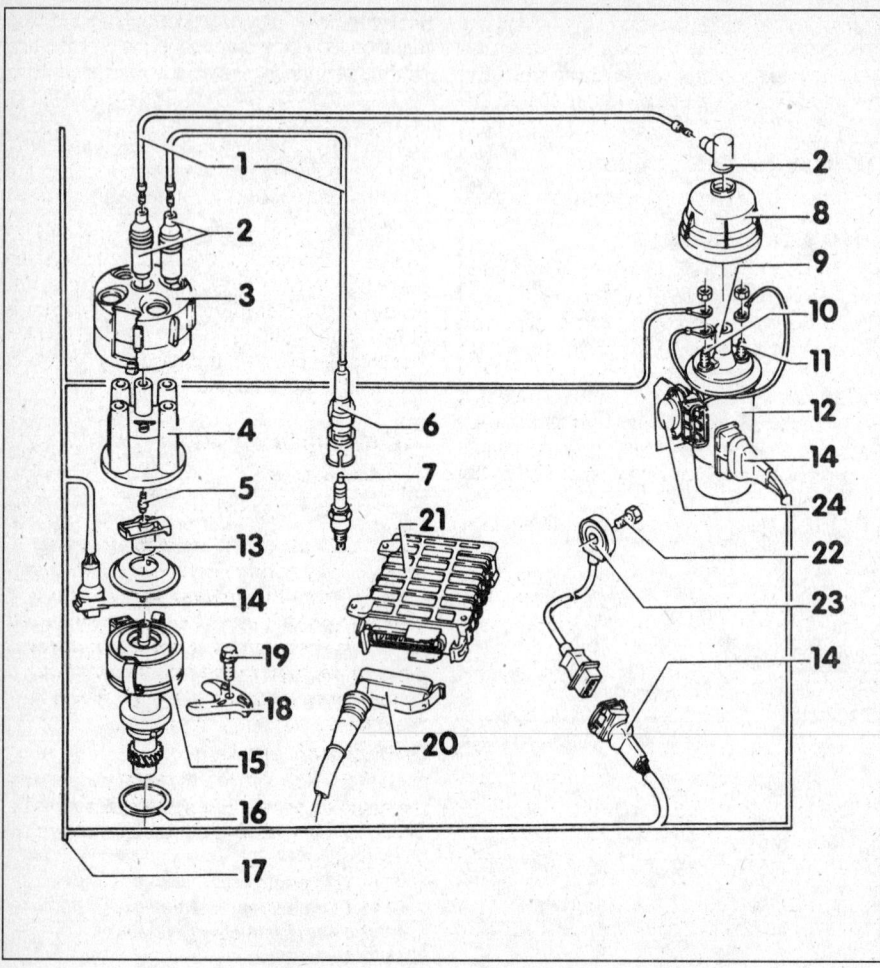

Fig 4.10 Components of the Motronic ignition system (Sec 9)

1 HT leads	7 Spark plug	13 Rotor arm	19 Bolt
2 Suppressor cap	8 Cap	14 Connector	20 Multi-plug
3 Screen	9 Terminal 4	15 Distributor	21 Motronic control unit
4 Distributor cap	10 Terminal 1	16 O-ring	22 Bolt
5 Carbon brush	11 Terminal 15	17 Wiring loom	23 Knock sensor
6 HT connector	12 Ignition coil	18 Clamp	24 Power stage

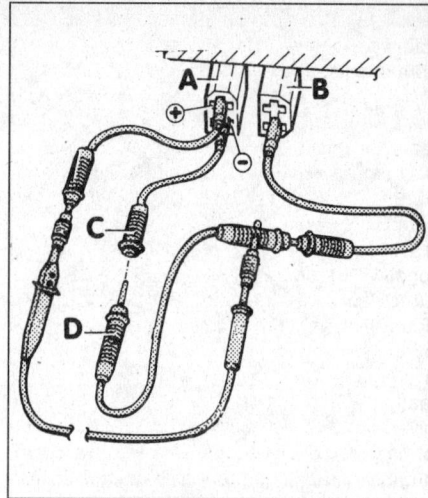

Fig 4.11 Diode tester and cables for recalling a fault read-out on the Motronic ignition system (Sec 10)

A Test connection (black)   C Socket
B Test connection (brown)   D Plug

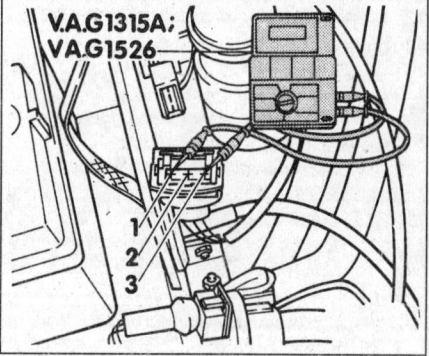

Fig 4.12 Checking the voltage between terminals 1 and 3 on the power output stage (Sec 10)

9 Motronic ignition system - description

The Motronic ignition system fitted to the 3A engine functions in a similar manner to the FEI system described in Section 7.

Both the ignition control unit and fuel injection control unit are combined in a single control unit. Unlike some Motronic systems, this system employs a distributor with a Hall sender unit, and not an inductive sender from the crankshaft.

The system uses signals from the following components to control the ignition timing, in order to give the optimum engine performance.

Knock sensor, Hall sender, temperature sender, throttle valve switches, and airflow meter.

10 Motronic ignition system - testing

Caution: Before disconnecting any wiring (including HT wiring) from the ignition system, the ignition must always be switched off. If this precaution is not taken, there is a risk of damage to the integrated circuit components, and of an HT shock to the person.

Self-check system

1 The control unit is equipped with a fault memory, which functions when the ignition is switched on. Emission and safety-related faults are stored in a permanent memory, which must be cleared after remedying the faults. Other faults are stored in an additional memory which is retained even if the ignition is switched off, but is automatically cancelled when the engine is restarted.

2 The following paragraphs describe recalling a fault read-out using a diode tester. Audi dealers use a special electronic fault reader, but this will not normally be available to the home mechanic.

3 Obtain a diode tester, jack plugs and wiring, and make up a test cable as shown in Fig. 4.11.

4 Check that fuses 13, 21, 27 and 28 are intact and secure. Switch off the air conditioner where applicable, and check that the cylinder head earth cable is secure.

5 Start the engine, and drive the car for at least five minutes, during which time the engine speed should exceed 3000 rpm several times and the accelerator pedal should be briefly fully depressed.

6 Run the engine at idling speed. Do not

increase the engine speed during the following tests. The engine should be at normal operating temperature.

7 If the engine will not start, operate the starter for approximately six seconds, then leave the ignition switched on.

8 Locate the two test connectors at the front of the driver's footwell, and connect the cables as shown.

9 Connect the plug and socket C and D together for a minimum of four seconds.

10 Disconnect the plug and socket, then count the number of flashing impulses given by the diode tester. The sequence starts with a signal lasting 2.5 seconds and a pause lasting 2.5 seconds, then the impulses are given in 0.5 second flashes. Count each group of flashes and the result will be a four-figure number, after which four 2.5 second flashes and pauses indicate the end of the fault output. If no fault is found, the code 4444 (four group of four flashes) will be given.

11 Check if there are more faults by repeating the procedure from paragraph 9, until the flashes and pauses indicate the end of the fault output.

12 Further testing of the KE-Motronic system is described in Chapter 3.

13 The flashing code explanations for the 3A engine are given in the following table.

  1111 Control unit
  2113 Engine speed signal, sticking airflow
        meter plate, Hall sender defective
  2121 Throttle valve idling switch I
  2123 Throttle valve full open switch II
  2141 Knock control at control limit
  2142 Knock sensor
  2231 Setting limits of idling stabilization
        exceeded
  2232 Air flow meter potentiometer
  2312 Coolant temperature sender
  2341 Lambda control at control limit
  2342 Lambda control
  2343 Mixture control unit adjustment limit,
        lean
  2344 Mixture control unit adjustment limit,
        rich
  4431 Idling stabilisation control valve
  4444 No fault detected
  0000 End of fault output

14 Testing of individual components is given in the following paragraphs. Before attempting to remove any components, the associated wiring should first be checked. Note that incorrect ignition timing may cause the knock sensor to reach its control limit, and cause a corresponding fault output. After repairing a fault from the *permanent* memory, the memory must be cancelled as described in paragraphs 28 to 32. The *basic* memory will be cancelled when the engine is restarted.

Ignition coil

15 Refer to Section 6, paragraphs 1 to 4.

Control unit

16 Where the self-check procedure shows a fault in the control unit, it should be renewed.

Access to the unit is gained by removing the trim behind the glove compartment, pressing in the locking pins, withdrawing the unit downwards, and disconnecting the multi-plug.

Distributor Hall sender

17 Refer to Section 8, paragraphs 21 to 28.

Power output stage

18 First check that the ignition coil is in good condition, with reference to Section 6.

19 Squeeze together the spring clip, and disconnect the wiring plug from the power output stage next to the ignition coil.

20 Switch on the ignition, then connect a digital multimeter (set to read volts) between the two outer terminals (1 and 3) on the plug. if battery voltage is not registered, check the associated wiring.

21 Connect a diode tester between terminals 2 and 3 on the plug.

22 Spin the engine on the starter, and check that the LED flashes, indicating that the Hall sender is functioning correctly. If not, check the Hall sender.

23 Switch off the ignition and re-connect the plug.

24 Disconnect the wiring plug from the Hall sender at the distributor.

25 Connect a digital multimeter (set to record volts) between terminals 1 - and 15 + on the ignition coil, then switch on the ignition.

26 Using a short length of wire, briefly connect the centre terminal of the Hall sender wiring plug to earth. Check that the voltage increases initially to 2 volts, then drops to zero after one to two seconds.

27 If the voltage does not drop, fit a new power output stage or control unit, and also check the ignition coil for leakage of sealing compound. If evident, renew the coil as well.

Permanent fault memory - cancellation

28 Connect the special test cable as shown in Fig. 4.11 with the ignition switched off.

29 Connect the plug and socket C and D together.

30 Switch on the ignition, and check that the LED lights up.

31 Separate the plug and socket C and D for a minimum of four seconds, and check that the flash code is 0000.

32 Reconnect the plug and socket for five

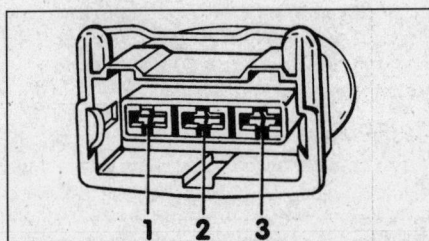

Fig 4.13 Power output stage plug terminals (Sec 12)

seconds, then disconnect them and check that the LED lights up continuously, indicating that the permanent memory is cancelled.

11 MPI ignition system - description

The MPI ignition system fitted to the 7A engine is similar to the Motronic system described in Section 9. In addition to a Hall sender in the distributor, the MPI system is fitted with a firing point sender, which monitors the crankshaft position by means of a rotating toothed segment.

12 MPI ignition system - testing

Caution: Before disconnecting any wiring (including HT wiring) from the ignition system, the ignition must always be switched off. If this precautions is not taken, there is a risk of damage to the integrated circuit components, and also of an HT shock to the person.

Self-check system

1 The procedures for pre-1989 models are the same as for the FEI system described in Section 8. The flashing code explanations are as follows.

  1111 MPI control unit
  2111 Engine speed sender (grey)
  2112 Firing point sender (black)
  2113 Hall sender
  2114 Distributor adjustment
  2121 Idling switch
  2141 or 2143
       Knock sensor, or too low fuel octane
  2142 or 2144
       Knock sensor
  2212 Throttle valve potentiometer
  2242 Air volume sensor CO potentiometer
  2232 Air volume sensor (G70)
  2233 Air 2114 Di sensor (G19)
  2234 Battery voltage
  2312 Coolant temperature sender
  2342 Lambda probe
  4431 Idle stabilising valve
  4444 No fault detected
  0000 End of fault output

2 The procedures for models from 1989 onwards are the same as for the Motronic system described in Section 10. The flashing code explanations are the same as given in paragraph 1 of this Section.

Ignition coil (and power stage)

3 Disconnect the plug from the power output stage.

4 Connect a voltmeter between terminal 1 on the plug and a suitable earth. Switch on the ignition, and check that 12 volts is registered.

5 Repeat the test between terminals 1 and 3. If there is no reading, check the wiring for an open-circuit.

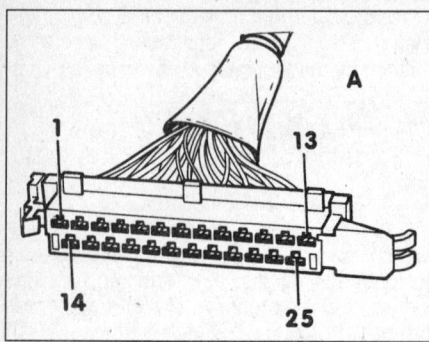
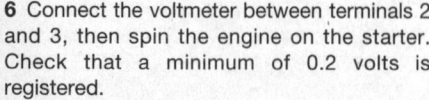

Fig 4.14 MPI control unit multi-plug terminals (Sec 12)

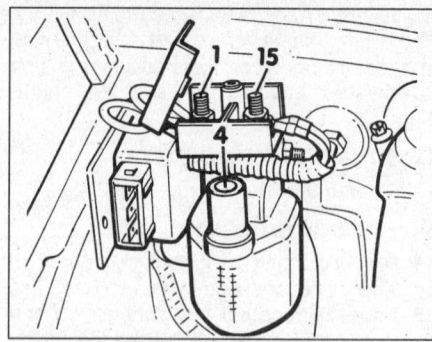

Fig 4.15 Ignition coil terminal numbers on MPI ignition system (Sec 12)

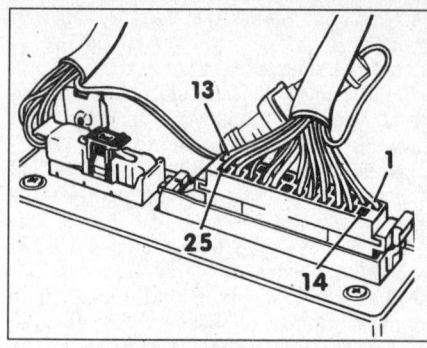

Fig 4.16 MPI control unit multi-plug terminals when fitted (Sec 12)

6 Connect the voltmeter between terminals 2 and 3, then spin the engine on the starter. Check that a minimum of 0.2 volts is registered.

7 If the reading is incorrect, remove the glove compartment, detach the MPI control unit, and disconnect the multi-plug (black). Using an ohmmeter, check for continuity between terminal 2 on the power stage plug and terminal 9 on the multi-plug.

8 Check the wiring between the power stage and ignition coil, and between the power stage and the engine.

9 Disconnect the HT lead from the coil, and the plug from the power stage. Detach the terminal cover.

10 Connect an ohmmeter between the HT terminal and terminal 1(-). The resistance should be between 5000 and 9000 ohms.

11 Connect the ohmmeter between terminals 1- and 15+. The resistance should be between 0.5 and 1.5 ohms.

12 Renew the ignition coil and power stage if the readings are incorrect.

MPI control unit

13 Remove the glove compartment, detach the MPI control unit, and disconnect the black multi-plug.

14 Switch on the ignition, then connect a voltmeter in turn between terminals 25 and 1, 25 and 2, 25 and 13, and 25 and 21 on the multiplug. A reading of 12 volts should be recorded in each case.

15 Switch off the ignition, re-connect the plug, then switch on the ignition.

16 Connect the voltmeter between terminals 18 and 1, and check that the reading is 12 volts. If not, check the wiring for an open-circuit, or renew the control unit.

Firing point sender

17 Locate the black plug and socket on the left-hand side of the bulkhead in the engine compartment, separate the plug, and pull it from the bracket.

18 Connect an ohmmeter between terminals 1 and 2 on the plug, and check that the resistance is 1000 ohms.

19 Connect the ohmmeter in turn between terminals 1 and 3, then 2 and 3, and check that the reading is infinity.

20 Check the associated wiring.

21 Release the black clip, and disconnect the small multi-plug from the control unit. Check that the small pins are in good condition.

Distributor Hall sender

22 Disconnect the HT king lead from the distributor cap, and connect it to earth with a length of wire.

23 Disconnect the plug from the distributor Hall sender, and connect a voltmeter between the two outer terminals on the plug.

24 Switch on the ignition, and check that the reading is 9 volts. If not, check the wiring.

25 Re-connect the plug, but pull up the rubber boot.

26 Connect the voltmeter between terminals 1 and 2.

27 Remove the distributor cap, then turn the engine until the rotor arm is aligned with the TDC mark (Section 3 and also Fig. 4.21).

28 Check that the reading is 4 volts.

29 Turn the engine to the firing point, and check that the reading is 0 to 0.5 volts.

30 If the readings are incorrect, check the wiring. Renew the Hall sender if necessary.

13 Ignition timing (engine code KV, and 1.6/1.8 litre engines) - adjustment

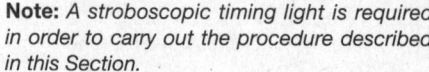

Note: *A stroboscopic timing light is required in order to carry out the procedure described in this Section.*

1 Run the engine to normal operating temperature.,

2 Stop the engine and connect the timing light in accordance with the equipment manufacturer's instructions.

3 On engine codes DZ, PM and JN, disconnect the vacuum hose from the distributor, and plug it. On all other engines, leave the hose connected.

4 Run the engine at idling speed, then point the timing light through the timing window on the left-hand side of the clutch housing (photo). If the ignition timing is correct, the notch on the flywheel will appear in line with the lower edge of the window.

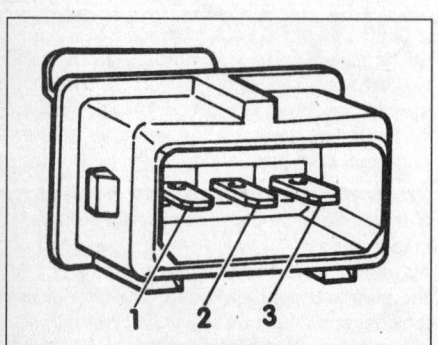

Fig 4.17 Firing point sender plug terminals (Sec 12)

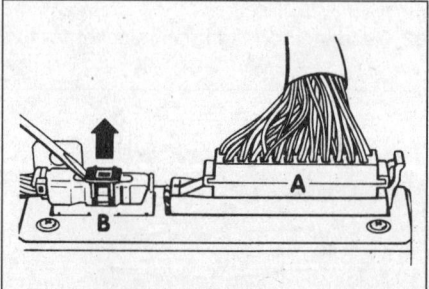

Fig 4.18 Small multi-plug removal from the MPI control unit (Sec 12)

A Large multi-plug   B Small multi-plug

13.4 Timing window (arrowed) in the clutch housing on the four-cylinder engine

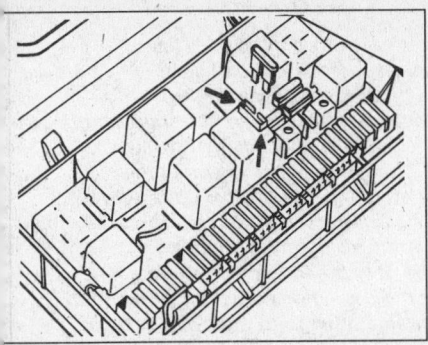

Fig 4.19 Inserting a fuse in the fuel pump relay contacts on engine code NG (Sec 14)

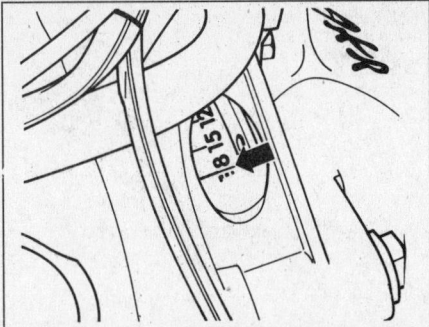

Fig 4.20 Ignition timing marks on engine code PS (Sec 14)

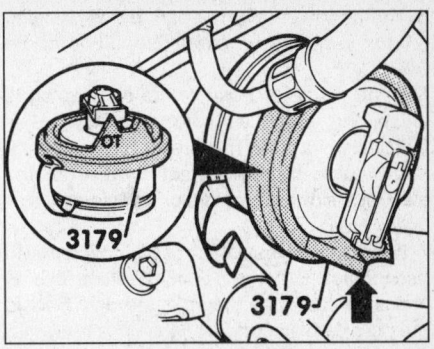

Fig 4.21 Using Audi tool No 3179 to set the distributor to TDC (Sec 15)

5 If adjustment is necessary, remove the tamperproof cap from the distributor clamp bolt, then loosen the bolt and turn the distributor as required. Tighten the bolt after making an adjustment, and refit the cap.
6 Re-connect the vacuum hose where applicable.
7 Stop the engine, and remove the timing light.

14 Ignition timing (engine codes PS and NG) - adjustment

Note: A stroboscopic timing light is required in order to carry out the procedure described in this Section.
1 Run the engine to normal operating temperature.
2 Stop the engine, and connect the timing light in accordance with the equipment manufacturer's instructions.
3 Using the self-check system, ascertain that the knock sensor is not faulty.
4 Switch off the air conditioning (where fitted).
5 On the PS engine, make sure that the throttle valve idle switch is on.
6 On the NG engine, remove the fusebox cover, and have ready a known good fuse to insert in the fuel pump relay contacts.
7 Run the engine at idling speed.
8 On the NG engine, insert the fuse in the fuel pump relay contacts. Allow four seconds before checking the ignition timing.

9 Point the timing light through the timing window on the left-hand side of the clutch housing. If the ignition timing is correct, the applicable notch on the flywheel will appear in line with the lower edge of the window.
10 If adjustment is necessary, remove the tamperproof cap from the distributor clamp bolt, then loosen the bolt and turn the distributor as required. Tighten the bolt after making an adjustment, and refit the cap.
11 Stop the engine, and remove the timing light. Remove the fuse from the fuel pump relay contacts, where applicable.

15 Ignition timing (engine code 7A) - adjustment

Note: Audi special tool No 3179 is required in order to carry out the procedure described in this Section.
1 This engine is fitted with the MPI ignition system, described in Section 11. The ignition timing is determined by a sender which monitors a signal from a rotating segment on the crankshaft. However, the distributor must be set statically to TDC (top dead centre), as a reference position, using Audi tool No 3179.
2 Set the engine to TDC compression on No 1 cylinder as follows. Remove the spark plugs, then turn the engine clockwise with a spanner on the crankshaft pulley bolt, until compression can be felt in No 1 cylinder (front of the engine), using a finger or rubber plug over the spark plug hole.

3 Look through the ignition timing windows on the transmission housing, then continue turning the engine clockwise until the 'O' mark on the flywheel is aligned with the corresponding mark on the housing.
4 As a further check, remove the upper timing cover, and check that the TDC mark on the camshaft sprocket is aligned with the pointer on the valve cover.
5 Remove the distributor cap, then use the tool No 3179 to check that the centre of the rotor arm is exactly aligned with the TDC point (marked OT) on the tool. The slightly lower point on the tool is used to check the Hall sender, as described in Section 12.
6 If necessary remove the anti-tamper cap, loosen the clamp bolt, and turn the distributor body as necessary to align the pointer and rotor arm.
7 Tighten the bolt, and refit the cap.
8 Refit the distributor cap and upper timing cover.

16 Spark plugs - removal, servicing and refitting

1 The correct functioning of the spark plugs is vital for the correct running and efficiency of the engine. It is essential that the plugs fitted are appropriate for the engine, and the suitable type is specified at the beginning of this chapter. if this type is used and the engine is in good condition, the spark plugs should not need attention between scheduled replacement intervals. Spark plug cleaning is rarely necessary and should not be attempted unless specialised equipment is available as damage can easily be caused to the firing ends.
2 To remove the spark plugs, first identify the HT leads for location, if not already marked with the cylinder numbers.
3 Carefully pull the leads from each spark plug. Grip the end fittings, not the actual leads, and pull them off squarely (photo).
4 Using a plug socket, unscrew each spark plug and remove it from the cylinder head (photo).

16.3 Disconnecting the spark plug leads

16.4 Removing a spark plug

4

5 The condition of the spark plugs will also tell much about the overall condition of the engine.

6 If the insulator nose of the spark plug is clean and white, with no deposits, this is indicative of a weak mixture, or too hot a plug. (A hot plug transfers heat away from the electrode slowly - a cold plug transfers it away quickly).

7 If the tip and insulator nose is covered with hard black-looking deposits, then this is indicative that the mixture is too rich. Should the plug be black and oily, then it is likely that the engine is fairly worn, as well as the mixture being too rich.

8 If the insulator nose is covered with light tan to greyish-brown deposits, then the mixture is correct, and it is likely that the engine is in good condition.

9 The spark plug gap is of considerable importance, as, if it is too large or too small,

HAYNES HINT

It is very often difficult to insert spark plugs into their holes without cross-threading them. To avoid this possibility, fit a short length of 5/16 inch internal diameter rubber hose over the end of the spark plug. The flexible hose acts as a universal joint to help align the plug with the plug hole. Should the plug begin to cross-thread, the hose will slip on the spark plug, preventing thread damage to the cylinder head.

the size of the spark and its efficiency will be seriously impaired. The spark plug gap should be set to the figure given in the Specifications at the beginning of this Chapter.

10 To set it, measure the gap with a feeler gauge, and then bend open, or close the *outer* plug electrode until the correct gap is

achieved. The centre electrode should *never* be bent, as this may crack the insulation and cause plug failure, if nothing worse.

11 When fitting the plugs, always insert them by hand until the threads are started, then fully tighten them to the specified torque using the plug socket.

Fault finding - ignition system

1 There are two distinct symptoms of ignition faults. Either the engine will not start or fire, or it starts with difficulty and does not run normally. If the engine will not start, the fault may be either in the LT (low tension) or HT (high tension) circuits. However, if the engine starts but does not run satisfactorily, the fault is more likely to be in the HT circuit.

2 If the engine fails to start due to either damp HT leads or wet distributor cap, a moisture dispersant can be very effective.

LT (low tension) circuit

3 Follow the procedures given in Sections 6, 8 or 10.

HT (high tension) circuit

4 A fault in the HT circuit will be confined to the spark plugs, HT leads, distributor cap, rotor arm, or ignition coil.

5 Disconnect an HT lead from a spark plug, and connect it to a spare plug held in good contact with the cylinder head. The spare plug should be in good condition, and may if necessary be earthed to the cylinder head or suitable earthing point with a jumper lead. It is not advisable to hold the HT lead a short distance away from the head, as this may result in damage to the electronic ignition components.

6 Spin the engine on the starter motor, and check that a good HT spark occurs at the spark plug. Do not repeat this procedure excessively on models fitted with a catalytic converter.

7 Reconnect the HT lead, and repeat the test on the remaining HT leads.

8 If a good spark occurs on all the leads, remove the spark plugs, and clean or renew them.

9 If there is no spark, check the HT leads for dampness or fractures. Also check the ignition coil and distributor cap.

10 Remove the distributor cap, and examine the surfaces between the HT segments (both inner and outer) for signs of tracking - indicated by thin lines of carbon. If evident, renew the cap.

11 Check the rotor arm in the same way. Note on the 7A engine, the rotor arm is bonded to the driveshaft, and cannot be removed.

12 Check that the spring-tensioned carbon brush in the distributor cap is free to move.

13 Clean any accumulated carbon from the distributor cap and rotor arm segments, but do not remove any metal.

14 Refit the rotor arm and distributor cap, and reconnect the HT leads.

Chapter 5 Clutch

Contents

Degrees of difficulty

Easy, suitable for novice with little experience	Fairly easy, suitable for beginner with some experience	Fairly difficult, suitable for competent DIY mechanic	Difficult, suitable for experienced DIY mechanic 	Very difficult, suitable for expert DIY or professional 

Specifications

Type .... Single dry plate, diaphragm spring pressure plate, hydraulically operated

Friction disc
Diameter .... 210.0 mm (8.3 in)

Clutch cover
Diaphragm spring finger maximum scoring depth .... 0.3 mm (0.012 in)

Hydraulic fluid type/specification .... Hydraulic fluid to FMVSS 116 DOT 4

Torque wrench settings	Nm	lbf ft
Master cylinder	20	15
Slave cylinder	25	18
Hydraulic pipe union	15	11
Release lever ball stud	25	18
Clutch cover	25	18

1 General description

The clutch is of single dry plate type, incorporating a diaphragm spring pressure plate, and is hydraulically operated.

The clutch cover is bolted to the rear face of the flywheel, and the friction disc is located between the cover pressure plate and the flywheel friction surface. The disc hub is splined to the gearbox input shaft and is free to slide along the splines. Friction lining material is riveted to each side of the disc and the disc hub incorporates cushioning springs to absorb transmission shocks and ensure a smooth take-up of drive.

When the clutch pedal is depressed, the slave cylinder pushrod moves the release lever forwards, and the release bearing is forced onto the diaphragm spring fingers. As the centre of the spring is pushed in, the outer part of the spring moves out and releases the pressure plate from the friction disc. Drive then ceases to be transmitted to the gearbox.

When the clutch pedal is released, the diaphragm spring forces the pressure plate into contact with the linings on the friction disc, and at the same time pushes the disc slightly forward along the input shaft splines into engagement with the flywheel. The friction disc is now firmly sandwiched between the pressure plate and flywheel. This causes drive to be taken up.

As the linings wear on the friction disc, the pressure plate rest position moves closer to the flywheel resulting in the 'rest' position of the diaphragm spring fingers being raised. On cable-operated clutches some form of adjustment is required, but the hydraulic system employed here requires no adjustment. The quantity of hydraulic fluid in the circuit automatically compensates for wear every time the clutch pedal is operated.

2 Routine maintenance

Carry out the following procedures at the intervals given in 'Routine maintenance' at the beginning of the manual.

Check hydraulic circuit for leaks and damage

1 Check the clutch hydraulic line and hose for leaks and damage.

Check the security of the connections to the master and slave cylinders.
2 Note that a leak in the clutch hydraulic circuit will cause the fluid level to drop in the brake master cylinder reservoir as the latter is used by both systems.

Check hydraulic fluid level

3 Refer to Chapter 9, Section 2, paragraphs 8 and 9.

3 Clutch pedal - removal and refitting

1 Remove the lower facia panel from under the steering column (Chapter 11).
2 Prise off the clip, and extract the clevis pin securing the master cylinder pushrod to the clutch pedal.
3 Extract the clip from the end of the pivot shaft.
4 Withdraw the pedal, and at the same time disconnect the over-centre spring from the pedal and bracket.
5 Clean the components, and check them for wear and damage. Temporarily refit the pedal, and check the bush for excessive wear.

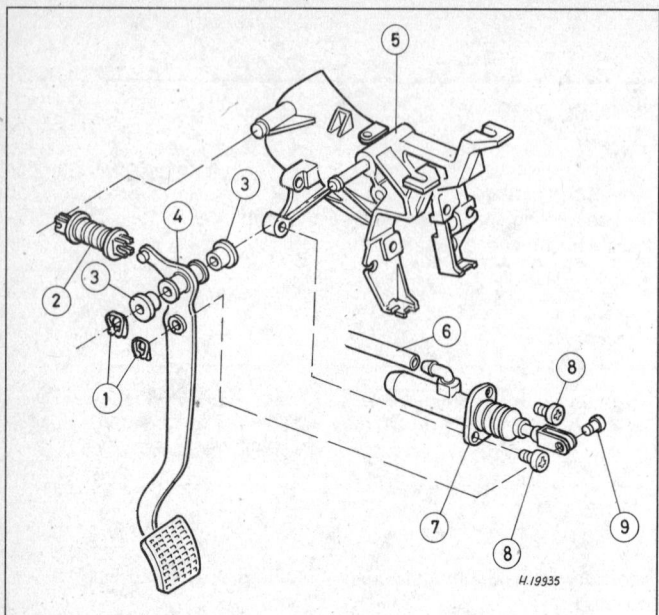

Fig 5.1 Clutch pedal and master cylinder components (Sec 3)

1 Clips	4 Clutch pedal	7 Clutch master
2 Over-centre spring	5 Pedal bracket	cylinder
3 Bushes	6 Hydraulic line	8 Mounting bolts
		9 Clevis pin

Fig 5.2 Clutch master and slave cylinder components (Sec 5)

1 Hydraulic fluid	5 Master cylinder	10 Clip
reservoir	6 Locknut	11 Slave cylinder
2 Pressure line	7 Clevis	12 Bleed screw
3 Grommet	8 Clevis pin	13 Mounting bolt
4 Fluid supply hose	9 Mounting bolt	

Check the rubber foot pad for wear. Renew the components as necessary.

6 Refitting is a reversal of removal, but lubricate the pivot shaft and over-centre spring pivots with a little multi-purpose grease. Check and if necessary adjust the clutch pedal height, with reference to Section 6, paragraph 19.

4 Clutch hydraulic system - bleeding

1 If required, raise the front of the car and support on axle stands, in order to gain better access to the bleed screw on the slave cylinder.
2 Remove the rubber cap from the bleed screw on the top of the slave cylinder, which is located on the left-hand side of the gearbox.
3 Fit a bleed tube onto the bleed screw, and place the other end in a jar with some brake fluid in it.
4 Check that the fluid level is topped up to the maximum level, and have ready some fresh brake fluid for topping-up purposes.
5 Unscrew the bleed screw half a turn, and have an assistant fully depress the clutch pedal several times until the fluid entering the jar is free of air bubbles. Make sure that the fluid level in the reservoir does not drop to the level of the slave cylinder outlet, otherwise air will be drawn into the system.
6 Tighten the bleed screw with the clutch

pedal depressed, release the pedal, then top up the fluid level as necessary.
7 Disconnect the bleed tube, and refit the rubber cap.

5 Clutch slave cylinder - removal, overhaul and refitting

1 The slave cylinder is retained in the clutch housing by a single bolt. Although access is possible from the engine compartment, it may be considered better to raise the front of the car by supporting the car on axle stands.
2 Loosen only the hydraulic pipe union on the slave cylinder.
3 Unscrew the mounting bolt and withdraw the slave cylinder (photo).
4 Unscrew the cylinder from the pipe union, and plug the end of the pipe.
5 Repair kits are not available from Audi, but they may be available from a motor factor.
6 To overhaul the slave cylinder, first clean the exterior surfaces.
7 Prise off the rubber boot and remove the pushrod.
8 Extract the special spring clip from the mouth of the cylinder, and withdraw the piston and spring.
9 Clean the components, and examine them for wear and deterioration. If the piston and bore are worn excessively, or if corrosion is evident, renew the complete cylinder. If they are in good condition, remove the seal from the piston and renew it.

10 Dip the new seal in hydraulic fluid, and fit it on the piston, using the fingers only to manipulate it into position. Make sure that the seal lip faces the spring end of the piston.
11 Insert the spring in the cylinder, then dip the piston in hydraulic fluid and carefully insert it.
12 Hold the piston depressed with a screwdriver then press a new spring clip into the mouth of the cylinder, making sure that the legs of the clip grip the cylinder.
13 Fit the pushrod, followed by the rubber boot.
14 Refitting is a reversal of removal, but finally bleed the system as described in Section 4. The end of the pushrod which contacts the release lever should be lightly lubricated with a molybdenum disulphide grease. Where a plastic support ring is fitted, the outer surface should also be lubricated with the same grease.

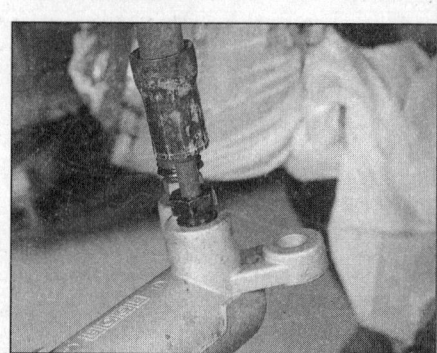

5.3 Clutch slave cylinder connected to hydraulic pipe

6.5 Clutch master cylinder pressure line (arrowed)

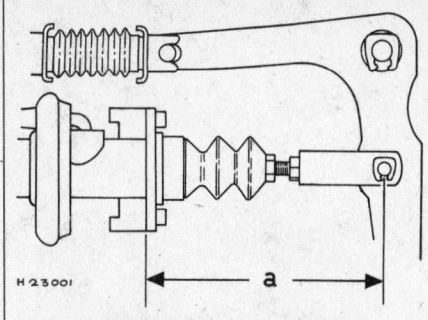

Fig 5.3 Clutch pedal height initial adjustment dimension (Sec 6)

a = 116.0.2 mm (4.57 0.01 in)

6 Clutch master cylinder - removal, overhaul and refitting

1 The clutch master cylinder is located in the engine compartment, on the front of the bulkhead.
2 Working inside the car, remove the lower facia panel from under the steering column.
3 Prise off the clip, and extract the clevis pin securing the master cylinder pushrod to the clutch pedal.
4 In the engine compartment, disconnect the fluid supply pipe from the master cylinder and plug it.
5 Unscrew the union and disconnect the pressure line (photo). Plug the line to prevent the ingress of dust and dirt.
6 Prise the grommet from the bulkhead.
7 Unscrew the mounting bolts from inside the car, then withdraw the master cylinder from inside the engine compartment.
8 Repair kits are not available from Audi, but they may be available from a motor factor.
9 To overhaul the master cylinder, first clean the exterior surfaces.
10 Prise off the rubber boot and remove the pushrod. If necessary loosen the locknut, unscrew the clevis and locknut, and remove the pushrod from the rubber boot.
11 Extract the circlip from the mouth of the cylinder, and withdraw the washer, piston, and spring, noting that the smaller end of the spring contacts the piston.
12 Clean the components with methylated spirit, and examine them for wear and deterioration. If the piston and bore are worn excessively, renew the complete cylinder, but if they are in good condition, remove the seals from the piston and obtain new ones.
13 Dip the new seals in hydraulic fluid, and fit them on the piston, using the fingers only to manipulate them into position. Make sure that the seal lips face the spring end of the piston.
14 Insert the spring into the cylinder, large end first. Dip the piston in hydraulic fluid, locate it on the spring, and carefully insert it.
15 Fit the washer, then locate the circlip in the groove.

16 Apply a little grease to the end of the pushrod, then locate it on the piston and fit the rubber boot. Screw on the locknut and clevis and tighten the locknut.
17 Refitting is a reversal of removal, but finally bleed the hydraulic system as described in Section 4.
18 Lubricate the clevis pin with a little grease.
19 Check that the clutch pedal is approximately 10 mm (0.4 in) higher than the brake pedal in its rest position. If necessary, adjust the pedal position by loosening the locknut, turning the pushrod as required, then retightening the locknut.
20 Check that the dimension between the clevis pin centre and bulkhead is 116.0 ± 0.2 mm (4.57 ± 0.01 in) (Fig. 5.3).
21 Check that the over-centre spring returns the pedal correctly, and that the pedal does not touch the bracket in its rest position. Failure of the pedal to return correctly may be due to air in the hydraulic system, or seizure of the pedal bearing.

7 Clutch - removal, inspection and refitting

1 Access to the clutch is obtained by removing the engine (Chapter 1) or by removing the gearbox (Chapter 6). If it is not intended to carry out major repairs to the engine at the same time, it is preferable to gain

access to the clutch by removing the gearbox.
2 Mark the clutch cover and flywheel in relation to each other.
3 Hold the flywheel stationary, then unscrew the clutch cover bolts progressively in diagonal sequence (photo). With the bolts unscrewed two or three turns, check that the cover is not binding on the dowel pins. If necessary, use a screwdriver to release the cover.
4 Remove all the bolts, then lift the clutch cover and friction disc from the flywheel.
5 Clean the cover, disc, and flywheel. Do not inhale the dust, as it may contain asbestos, which is dangerous to health.
6 Examine the fingers of the diaphragm spring for wear or scoring. If the depth of any scoring exceeds 0.3 mm (0.012 in), a new cover assembly must be fitted.
7 Examine the pressure plate for scoring, cracking and discoloration. Light scoring is acceptable, but if excessive, a new cover assembly must be fitted.
8 Examine the friction disc linings for wear, cracking, and for contamination with oil or grease. The linings are worn excessively if they are worn down to, or near, the rivets. Check the disc hub and splines for wear, by temporarily fitting it on the gearbox input shaft. Renew the friction disc as necessary.
9 Examine the flywheel friction surface for scoring, cracking, and discoloration (caused by overheating). If excessive, it may be possible to have the flywheel machined by an engineering works, otherwise it should be renewed.
10 Ensure that all parts are clean, and free of oil or grease, before reassembling. Apply just a small amount of high-melting-point grease to the splines of the friction disc hub. Note that new pressure plates and clutch covers are coated with protective grease. It is only permissible to clean the grease away from the friction disc lining contact area. Removal of the grease from other areas will shorten the service life of the clutch.
11 Commence reassembly by locating the friction disc on the flywheel, with the raised, torsion spring side of the hub facing outwards (photo).
12 Locate the clutch cover on the disc, and fit it onto the location dowels. Hold the disc in its control position while doing this. If refitting

5

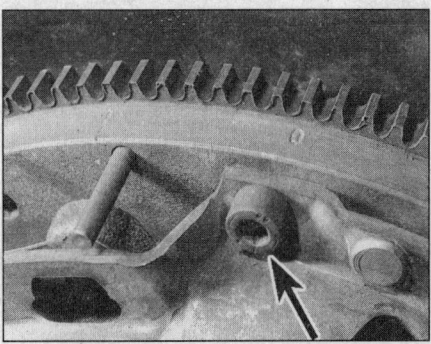

7.3 Clutch cover bolt (arrowed)

7.11 Fitting the friction disc

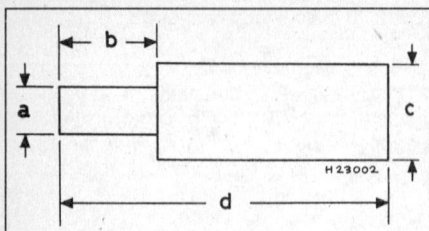

Fig 5.4 Clutch centralising mandrel dimensions (Sec 7)

a = 15.0 mm (0.59 in)
b = 21.0 mm (0.83 in)
c = 23.5 mm (193 in)
d = 150.0 mm (5.91 in) minimum

7.14 Centralising the friction disc

7.15 Tightening the clutch cover bolts

8.1 Release lever plastic pad removal

8.3 Separating the release bearing from the lever

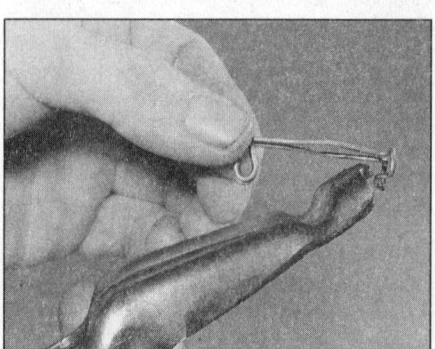

8.6A Fitting the spring to the release lever

8.6B Pressing the release lever onto the ball stud

the original cover, make sure that the previously-made marks are aligned.

13 Insert the bolts finger-tight to hold the cover in position.

14 The friction disc must now be centralised, to ensure correct alignment of the gearbox input shaft with the spigot bearing in the crankshaft. To do this, a proprietary tool may be used, or alternatively, use a wooden mandrel made to the dimensions given in Fig. 5.4. Insert the tool through the friction disc into the spigot bearing, and make sure that it is central (photo).

15 Tighten the clutch cover bolts progressively and in diagonal sequence, until the specified torque setting is achieved, then remove the centralising tool (photo).

16 Check the release bearing in the front of the gearbox for smooth operation, and if necessary renew it with reference to Section 8.

17 Refit the engine or gearbox with reference to Chapters 1 or 6.

8 Release bearing and lever - removal and refitting

1 Using a screwdriver, prise the release lever from the ball stud on the gearbox housing. If this proves difficult, push the spring from the release lever first. Remove the plastic pad from the stud (photo).

2 Slide the release bearing, together with the lever, from the guide sleeve, and withdraw over the gearbox input shaft.

3 Separate the release bearing from the lever (photo).

4 Spin the release bearing by hand, and check it for smooth running. Any tendency to seize or run rough will necessitate renewal of the bearing. If it is to be re-used, wipe it clean with a dry cloth; on no account should the bearing be washed in a liquid solvent, otherwise the internal grease will be removed.

5 Clean the release lever, ball stud, and guide sleeve.

6 Refitting is a reversal of removal, but lubricate the ball stud with molybdenum disulphide grease. Smear a little grease on the release bearing surface which contacts the diaphragm spring fingers in the clutch cover. Fit the spring onto the release lever. Press the release lever onto the ball stud until the spring holds it in position (photos).

Fault finding - clutch

Judder
☐ Friction disc linings contaminated with oil or grease
☐ Loose or worn engine/gearbox mountings
☐ Worn gearbox input shaft or friction disc hub splines
☐ Worn friction disc linings

Clutch slip
☐ Friction disc linings worn or contaminated with oil or grease
☐ Seized clutch pedal or over-centre spring

Clutch drag (failure to disengage)
☐ Air in hydraulic system
☐ Friction disc sticking on input shaft splines
☐ Spigot bearing seized

Noise evident on depressing clutch pedal
☐ Dry or worn release bearing
☐ Worn diaphragm spring

Chapter 6 Manual gearbox and final drive

Contents

Degrees of difficulty

Easy, suitable for novice with little experience	Fairly easy, suitable for beginner with some experience	Fairly difficult, suitable for competent DIY mechanic 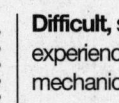	Difficult, suitable for experienced DIY mechanic	Very difficult, suitable for expert DIY or professional

Specifications

Type .... Five forward speeds and reverse, synchromesh on all gears, integral final drive

Gearbox code number 012

Ratios

	AKL	AMR	ATG	AMK	AMV	ALP	ALR
Final drive	4.111:1	4.111:1	4.111:1	3.888:1	3.700:1	3.700:1	3.700:1
1st	3.545:1	3.545:1	3.545:1	3.545:1	3.545:1	3.545:1	3.545:1
2nd	2.105:1	2.105:1	2.105:1	2.105:1	2.105:1	2.105:1	2.105:1
3rd	1.300:1	1.300:1	1.429:1	1.429:1	1.300:1	1.300:1	1.300:1
4th	0.943:1	0.943:1	1.029:1	1.029:1	0.943:1	1.029:1	1.029:1
5th	0.789:1	0.789:1	0.838:1	0.838:1	0.789:1	0.838:1	0.838:1
Reverse	3.500:1	3.500:1	3.500:1	3.500:1	3.500:1	3.500:1	3.500:1

Gearbox code letters

Lubrication

Lubricant type/specification .... VW/Audi gear oil G50 (synthetic oil), viscosity SAE 75W/90
Capacity .... 2.35 litres (4.1 pints)

Torque wrench settings

	Nm	lbf ft
Gear lever to mounting plate	25	18
Gear lever shift fork nut	10	7
Gear lever mounting plate	10	7
Shift rod clamp bolt	25	18
Shift rod coupling bolt	20	15
Rear mounting to gearbox	40	30
Rear mounting to bar	100	74
Gearbox to engine:		
M8	25	18
M10	45	33
M12	65	48
Multi-function sensor	25	18
5th/reverse catch	10	7
Multi-function connector	10	7
Final drive cover	25	18
Clutch release guide sleeve	35	26
Relay shaft Torx bolt	40	30
Reverse gear shaft	35	26
Detent Torx bolt	25	18
Rear housing to main housing	25	18

6

1 General description

The five-speed manual gearbox is bolted to the rear of the engine in the conventional manner. The front-wheel-drive configuration transmits the power to a differential unit located at the front of the gearbox, through driveshafts, to the front wheels. All gears including reverse incorporate a synchromesh engagement. Unlike the conventional floating reverse gear idler arrangement, the reverse gears and idler are in constant mesh.

Gearshift is by a floor-mounted lever, operating a single rod and linkage clamped to the shift rod, which protrudes from the rear of the gearbox.

When overhauling the gearbox, due consideration should be given to the costs involved, since it is often more economic to obtain a service exchange or good secondhand gearbox rather than fit new parts to the existing gearbox. Repairs to the differential are not covered, as the special equipment required is not normally available to the home mechanic.

The gearbox and final drive share a common oil supply. The transmission is 'filled for life', and oil changing is not specified.

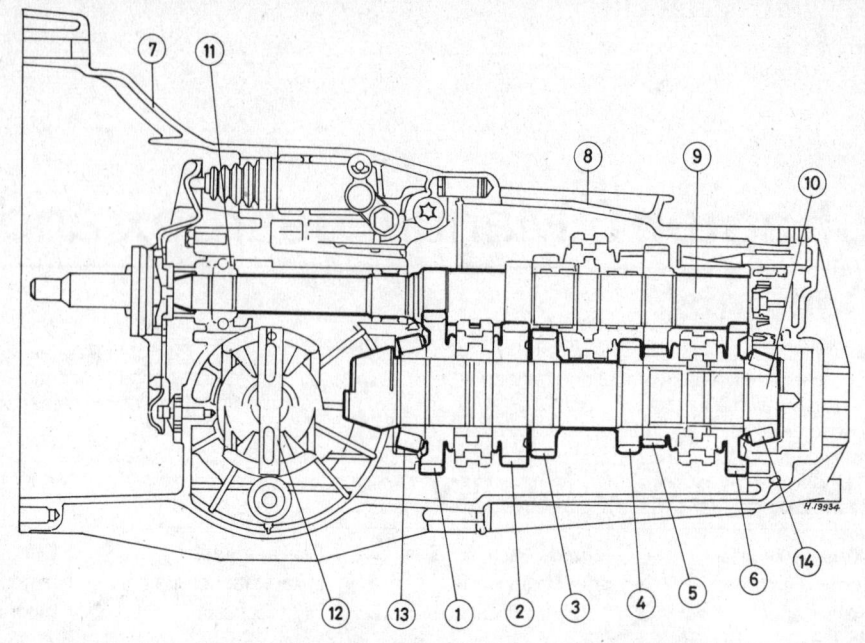

Fig 6.1 Cross-section diagram of the gearbox (Sec 1)

1 1st gear
2 2nd gear
3 3rd gear
4 4th gear
5 5th gear
6 Reverse gear
7 Front housing
8 Rear housing
9 Input shaft
10 Pinion shaft
11 Ball bearing
12 Differential
13 Taper-roller bearing (front)
14 Taper-roller bearing (rear)

2 Routine maintenance

Carry out the following procedure at the intervals given in 'Routine mamtenance' at the beginning of the manual.

Check gearbox for leakage and damage

1 Raise the front of the car and support on axle stands. Alternatively, position the car over an inspection pit or on car ramps.
2 Check the gearbox for signs of oil leakage, and for evidence of damage. In particular check the drive flange oil seals for leakage, and if necessary renew them.

3 Gearbox - removal and refitting

Note: If necessary, the engine and gearbox may be removed together as described in Chapter 1, and the gearbox then separated on the bench. However, this Section describes the removal of the gearbox, leaving the engine in situ.

1 Position the front of the car over an inspection pit or on car ramps, with the handbrake firmly applied. Drain the gearbox oil (see "Routine maintenance").
2 Disconnect the battery negative lead.
3 Unscrew and remove the upper bolts attaching the gearbox to the engine, noting the location of any brackets.

4 Unbolt the earth cable from the gearbox.
5 Disconnect the wiring from the electronic speedometer sender and the connector for the multi-function sensor, by squeezing the spring clips together (photos).
6 Where applicable, release the cable tie, and disconnect the wiring from the catalytic converter.
7 Unbolt and remove the splash guard from under the engine.
8 Unscrew the nuts securing the exhaust downpipe to the manifold. Lower the downpipe and remove the gasket.
9 Disconnect the exhaust pipe behind the front silencer or catalytic converter, with reference to Chapter 3.
10 Unscrew the bolt, and remove the spring securing the exhaust downpipe to the bracket

3.5A Disconnecting the wiring from the electronic speedometer sender . . .

3.5B . . . and the multi-function sensor

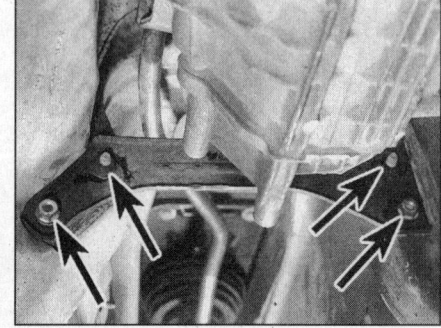

3.11A Unscrew the nuts (arrowed) . . .

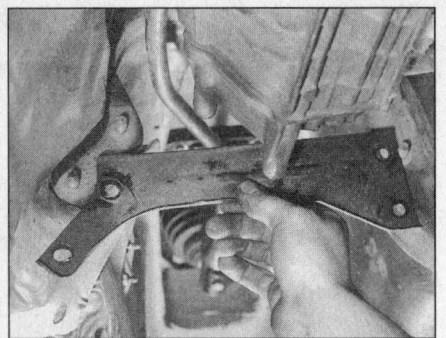

3.11B . . . and remove the underbody crossmember

3.13 Disconnecting the gear shift coupling from the shift rod

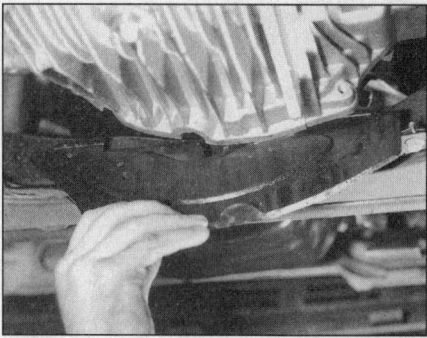

3.14 Removing the gearbox front cover

on the side of the gearbox. Lower the downpipe and front silencer from the car.

11 Unscrew the nuts, and remove the crossmember from the underbody behind the gearbox (photos).

12 Where a Procon-Ten safety system is fitted, disconnect the cables from the gearbox, with reference to Chapter 11, Fig. 11.1.

13 Unscrew the locking bolt, and slide the gearshift coupling from the gearbox shift rod (photo).

14 Unbolt and remove the gearbox front cover (photo).

15 Where applicable, unbolt the driveshaft cover from under the car.

16 Unscrew and remove the bolts securing

the driveshaft inner constant velocity joints to the gearbox drive flanges. Note the location of the bolt plates, and remove the gaskets if fitted. Tie the driveshafts to one side, and wrap the inner joints in plastic bags, in order to prevent entry of dust and dirt (photo).

17 Remove the clutch slave cylinder with reference to Chapter 5, but do not disconnect the hydraulic hose. Tie the slave cylinder to one side.

18 Remove the starter motor as described in Chapter 12.

19 On five-cylinder models, disconnect the steering tie-rod bracket from the steering gear, with reference to Chapter 10.

20 Support the gearbox with a trolley jack or stand.

21 Support the front of the engine using a hoist, or a suitable support bar positioned across the engine compartment.

22 Unbolt the front engine support bar from the cylinder block.

23 Unscrew the bolt securing the rear support bar to the rubber mounting on the rear of the gearbox. Loosen the outer bolt, and swing the bar to one side. Alternatively, use an Allen key to unbolt the mounting complete from the gearbox (photos).

24 Unscrew and remove the lower bolts attaching the gearbox to the engine. Also unbolt the exhaust support bracket (photos).

25 Lower the gearbox slightly and at the same time adjust the engine support.

26 With the held of an assistant, withdraw

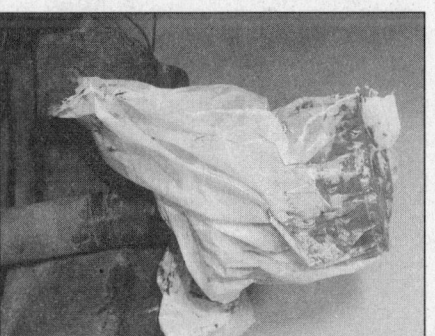

3.16 Inner driveshaft CV joint wrapped in plastic bag, to protect it from dust and dirt

3.23A Unscrew the bolts . . .

3.23B . . . and detach the gearbox rear support mounting

3.23C View of gearbox rear support mounting (with gearbox removed)

3.24A Lower gearbox-to-engine mounting bolt (arrowed)

3.24B Exhaust support bracket (arrowed)

6

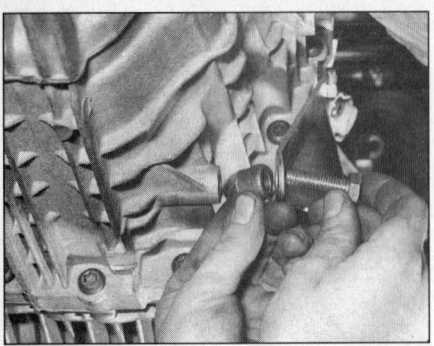

3.24C Removing the exhaust support bracket

3.26 Removing the gearbox

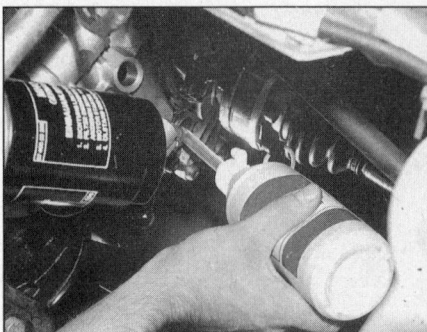

3.28A Topping up the gearbox from the engine compartment . . .

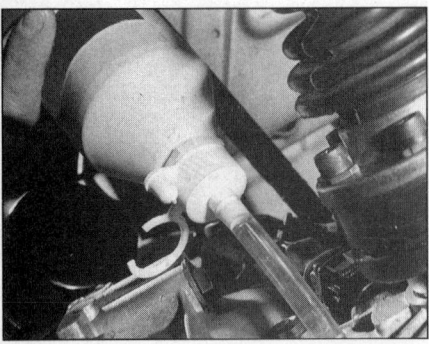

3.28B . . . and from underneath the car

3.28C Tightening the gearbox filler plug

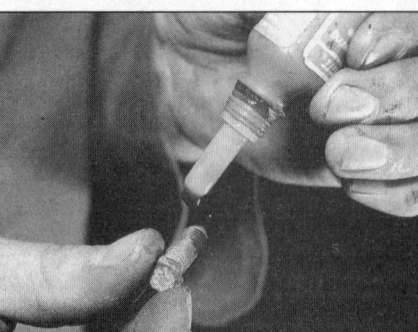

3.28D Applying locking fluid to the gear shift coupling locking bolt

the gearbox from the engine, making sure that the input shaft does not hang on the clutch. Lower the gearbox to the ground (photo).

27 Before refitting the gearbox, make sure that the location dowels are positioned in the engine cylinder block rear face. Lightly lubricate the splines of the input shaft with high-melting point grease.

28 Refitting is a reversal of removal, but if necessary adjust the engine and gearbox mountings as described in Chapter 1. Refill the gearbox with oil of the correct specification (photos). Tighten all nuts and bolts to the specified torque. Apply locking fluid to the gearshift coupling locking bolt before inserting and tightening it (photo).

4 Gearbox - overhaul

Overhauling a manual transmission unit is a difficult and involved job for the DIY home mechanic. In addition to dismantling and reassembling many small parts, clearances must be precisely measured and, if necessary, changed by selecting shims and spacers. Internal transmission components are also often difficult to obtain, and in many instances, are extremely expensive. Because of this, if the transmission develops a fault or becomes noisy, the best course of action is to have the unit overhauled by a specialist

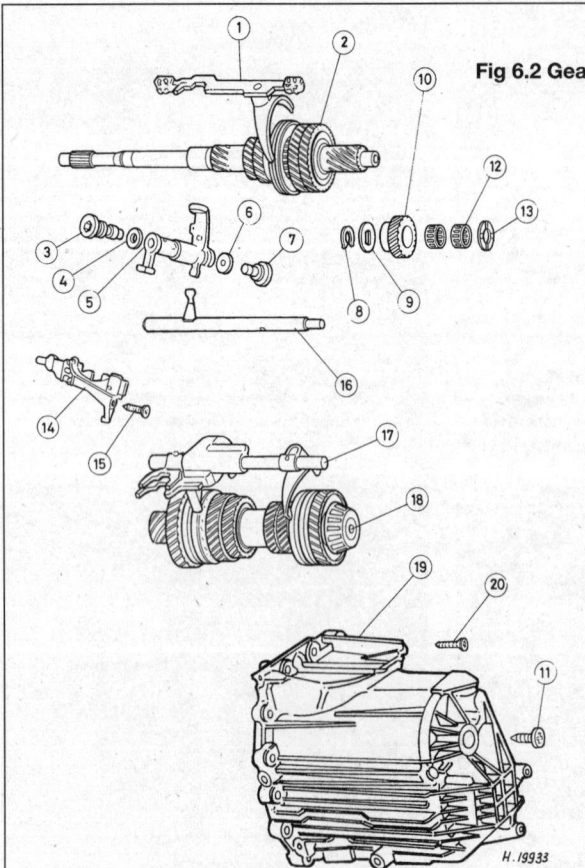

Fig 6.2 Gears and rear housing (Sec 4)

1 3rd/4th selector fork and plate
2 Input shaft assembly
3 Relay shaft Torx bolt
4 Washer
5 Relay shaft
6 Washer
7 Relay shaft Torx bolt
8 Circlip
9 Washer
10 Reverse gear
11 Torx bolt for reverse gear shaft
12 Needle roller bearing
13 Thrustwasher
14 Shift detent
15 Torx bolt
16 Shift rod
17 1st/2nd and 5th/reverse selector shaft assembly
18 Pinion shaft assembly
19 Rear housing
20 Torx bolt

H.19933

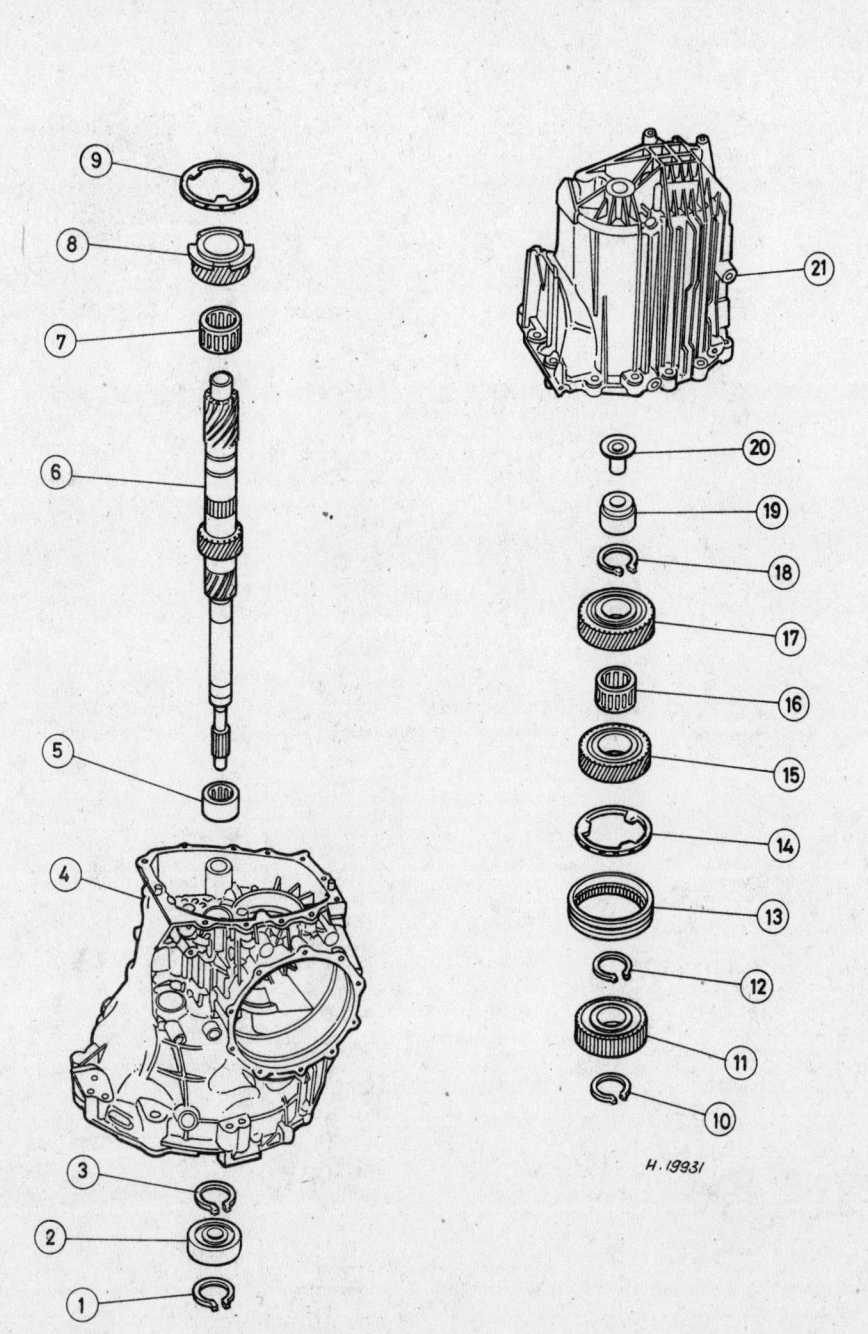

Fig 6.3 Input shaft components (Sec 4)

1 Circlip (outer)
2 Bearing
3 Circlip (inner)
4 Main housing
5 Needle roller bearing
6 Input shaft
7 Needle roller bearing

8 3rd speed gear
9 3rd gear synchro ring
10 Circlip
11 3rd/4th synchro hub
12 Circlip
13 3rd/4th synchro sleeve
14 4th gear synchro ring

15 4th speed gear
16 Needle roller bearing
17 5th speed gear
18 Circlip
19 Needle roller bearing
20 Plastic sleeve
21 Rear housing

H.19931

6

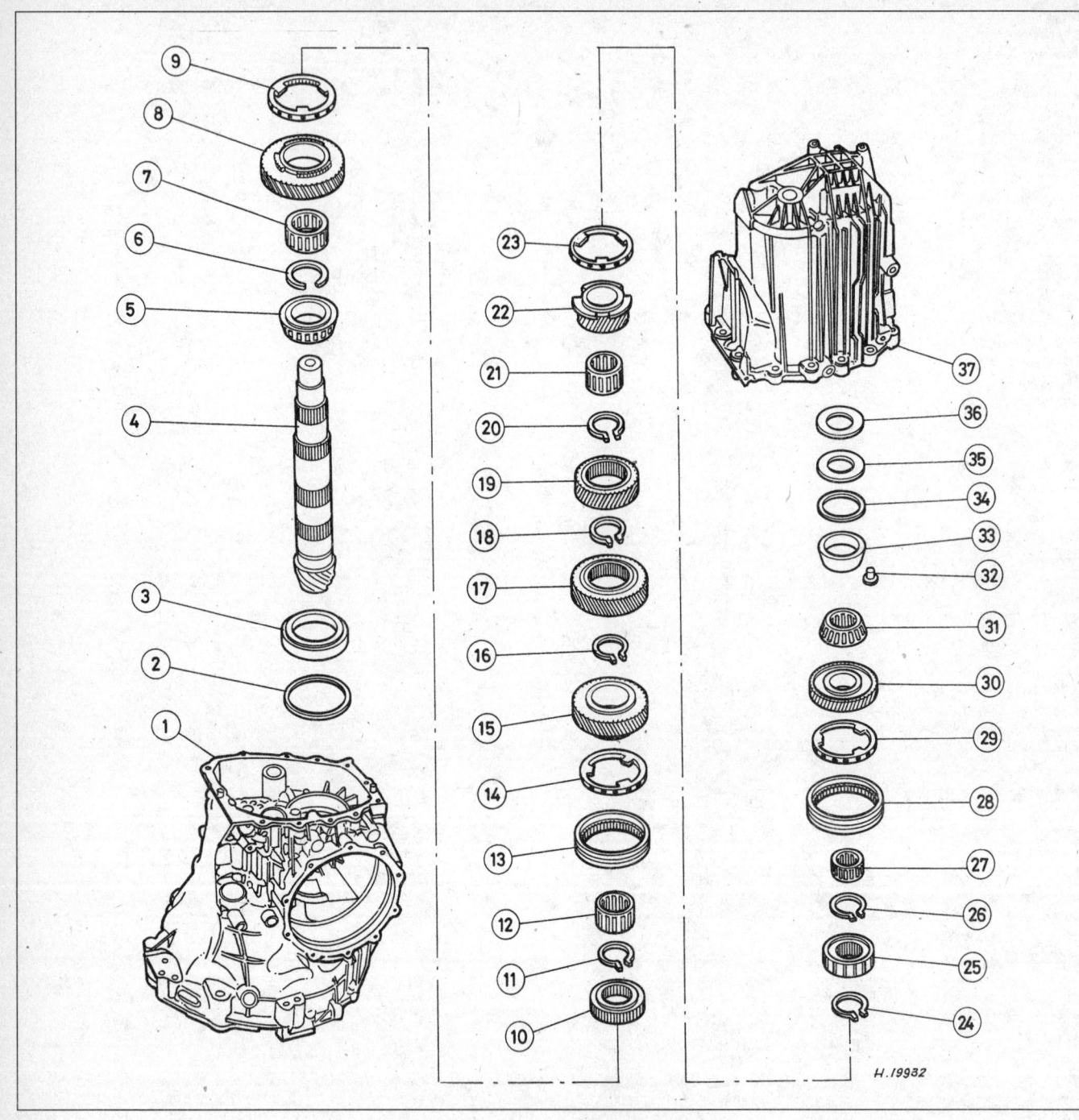

Fig 6.4 Pinion shaft components (Sec 4)

1 Main housing
2 Shim
3 Taper-roller bearing outer race
4 Pinion shaft
5 Taper-roller bearing inner race
6 Circlip
7 Needle roller bearing
8 1st speed gear
9 1st gear synchro ring

10 1st/2nd synchro hubs
11 Circlip
12 Needle roller bearing
13 1st/2nd synchro sleeve
14 2nd gear synchro ring
15 2nd speed gear
16 Circlip
17 3rd speed gear
18 Circlip
19 4th speed gear
20 Circlip

21 Needle roller bearing
22 5th speed gear
23 5th gear synchro ring
24 Circlip
25 5th/reverse synchro hub
26 Circlip
27 Needle roller bearing
28 5th/reverse synchro sleeve
29 Reverse gear synchro ring

30 Reverse gear
31 Taper-roller bearing inner race
32 Locking bush for bearing outer race
33 Taper-roller bearing outer race
34 Shim
35 Thrustplate
36 Washer
37 Rear housing

repairer, or to obtain an exchange reconditioned unit.

Nevertheless, it is not impossible for the more experienced mechanic to overhaul the transmission, provided the special tools are available, and that the job is done in a deliberate step-by-step manner so that nothing is overlooked.

The tools necessary for an overhaul may include internal and external circlip pliers, bearing pullers, a slide hammer, a set of pin punches, a dial test indicator, and possibly a hydraulic press. In addition, a large, sturdy workbench and a vice will be required.

During dismantling of the transmission, make careful notes of how each component is fitted, to make reassembly easier and accurate.

Before dismantling the transmission, it will help if you have some idea which area is mal-functioning. Certain problems can be closely related to specific areas in the gearbox, which can make component examination and replacement easier.

5 Gear lever - removal, overhaul and refitting

1 Apply the handbrake, then jack up the front of the car and support on axle stands.
2 Remove the exhaust system with reference to Chapter 3.
3 Unscrew the nuts and remove the guard plate located behind the gearbox (photo).
4 Mark the position of the adjustment bolt in relation to the shift rod. Unscrew the bolt and lower the rod (photo). Remove the rubber boot.
5 Remove the centre console as described in Chapter 11.
6 Unscrew the bolts securing the gear lever mounting plate to the underbody tunnel (photo). Prise the plate away from the sealing compound, and withdraw the assembly from under the car.
7 Unscrew the nuts and remove the leaf springs and curved spacers, then separate the mounting plate from the gear lever assembly.

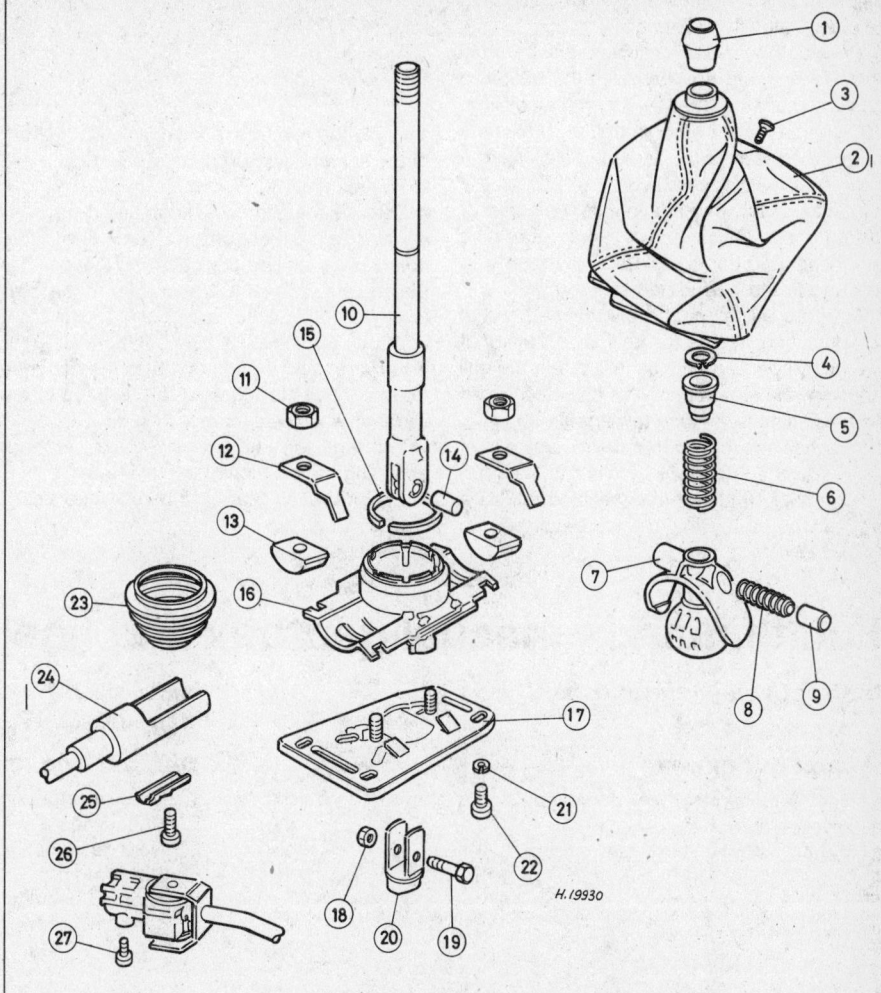

Fig 6.5 Gear lever components (Sec 5)

1 Knob	10 Gear lever	19 Screw
2 Boot	11 Nut	20 Shift fork
3 Screw	12 Leaf spring	21 Washer
4 Circlip	13 Curved spacer	22 Bolt
5 Bush	14 Spacer tube	23 Rubber boot
6 Spring	15 Circlip	24 Shift rod
7 Ball stop	16 Ball housing	25 Clamp plate
8 Spring	17 Mounting plate	26 Adjustment bolt
9 Bush	18 Nut	27 Locking bolt

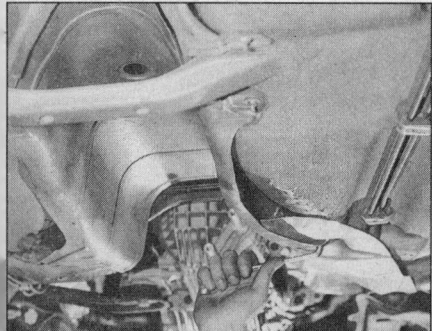

5.3 Removing the guard plate from behind the gearbox

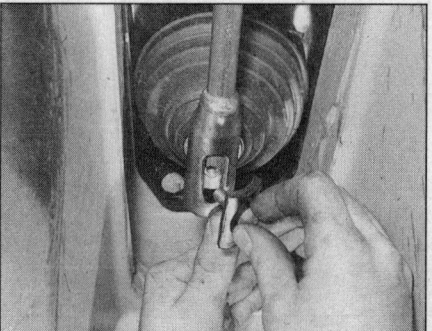

5.4 Unbolting the shift rod from the gear lever

5.6 Gear lever mounting plate bolts (arrowed)

6

8 Extract the circlip from the gear lever, then remove the bush and spring.
9 Prise out the circlip retaining the ball stop to the ball housing, then remove the ball stop and withdraw the gear lever from the housing.
10 Clean all the components, and examine them for wear and damage. Renew the components as necessary.
11 Reassembly and refitting are a reversal of dismantling and removal, but note the following additional points. The bush and spring should be located on the right-hand side of the ball stop, and the rounded end of the bush should face the gear lever. Note that the gear lever can only be inserted in the ball housing one way round. The ball stop circlip rounded side must face towards the bearing. Fit the ball housing so that the reverse detent points to the left. Apply sealant to the gear lever mounting plate before refitting it. Finally adjust the shift linkage as described in Section 6.

6 Gearshift linkage - adjustment

1 Apply the handbrake, then jack up the front of the car and support on axle stands.
2 Engage neutral.
3 Remove the gear lever knob and cover.
4 Using a socket through the hole in the guard plate behind the gearbox, loosen only the adjustment bolt at the bottom of the gear lever.
5 Working inside the car, position the gear lever vertically, then check that the distance from the ball stop lugs to the housing is the same on each side (photo).
6 Tighten the adjustment bolt without changing the position of the gear lever.
7 Check that all gears can be selected freely. Check that the reverse safety catch is effective and if necessary loosen the screws

6.5 Checking central position of the gear lever

and slightly turn the ball housing. Tighten the screws.
8 Refit the gear lever knob and cover, and lower the car to the ground.

Fault finding - manual gearbox and final drive

Ineffective synchromesh

☐ Worn synchro rings

Jumps out of gear

☐ Shift detent spring weak or broken
☐ Worn selector forks or dogs
☐ Worn synchro unit or gears

Noisy operation

☐ Worn bearings or gears

Difficult engagement of gears

☐ Worn selector components
☐ Worn synchro unit
☐ Worn gear engagement dogs
☐ Clutch fault
☐ Incorrect gear shift linkage adjustment
☐ Seized needle roller bearing in end of crankshaft

Chapter 7
Automatic transmission and final drive

Contents

Degrees of difficulty

Easy, suitable for novice with little experience	Fairly easy, suitable for beginner with some experience	Fairly difficult, suitable for competent DIY mechanic	Difficult, suitable for experienced DIY mechanic	Very difficult, suitable for expert DIY or professional 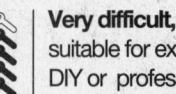

Specifications

Type .... Three or four-speed planetary transmission and torque converter; final drive unit located between torque converter and transmission

Application
Four-cylinder engine models 089
Five-cylinder engine models 087

Ratios

	089	087
Final drive	3.25 : 1 (39 : 12)	3.08 : 1 (37 : 12)
1st	2.71 : 1	2.71 : 1
2nd	1.50 : 1	1.50 : 1
3rd	1.00 : 1	1.00 : 1
Reverse	2.43 : 1	2.43 : 1

Torque converter

	089	087
Maximum diameter of bush	34.25 mm (1.349 in)	34.12 mm (1.344 in)
Maximum out-of-round of bush	0.03 mm (0.001 in)	0.03 mm (0.001 in)
New installed diameter of bush	34.03 to 34.05 mm (1.341 to 1.342 in)	33.90 to 33.92 mm (1.335 to 1.336 in)

Lubrication

Capacity:	Total	Service
Gearbox:		
089	6.0 litres (10.6 pints)	3.0 litres (5.3 pints)
087	6.0 litres (10.6 pints)	3.0 litres (5.3 pints)
Final drive:		
089	0.75 litres (1.3 pints)	
087	1.0 litre (1.8 pints)	

Lubricant type/specification:
  Transmission .... Dexron type ATF
  Final drive .... Hypoid gear oil, viscosity SAE 90, to API GL5

Torque wrench settings

	Nm	lbf ft
Gearchange lever nut	8	6
Selector cable support	15	11
Torque converter to driveplate	30	22
Transmission to engine	55	41
Cooler to transmission	40	30
Final drive housing cover	25	18
Sump pan	20	15
Strainer cover	3	2

7

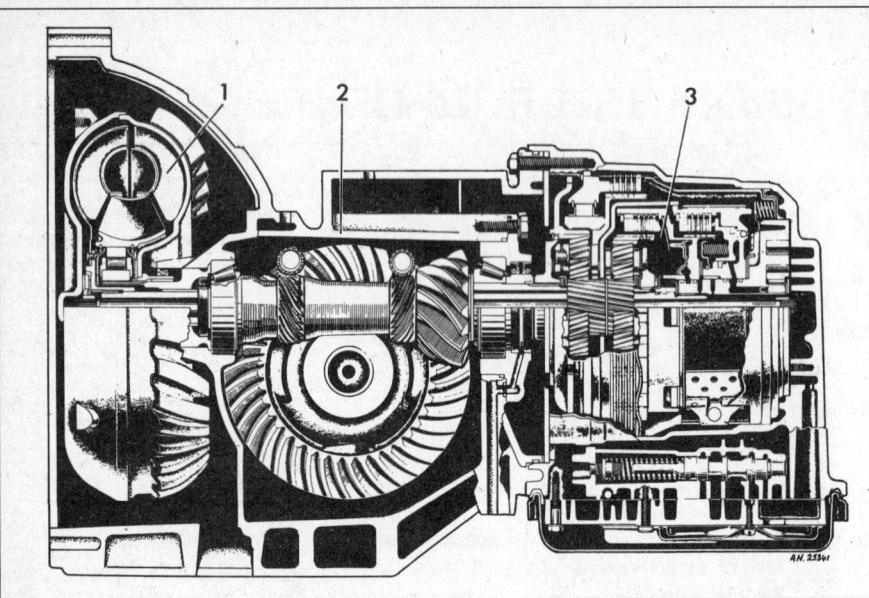

Fig 7.1 Cross-section of the automatic transmission (Sec 1)
1 Torque converter   2 Final drive   3 Planetary gearbox

1 General description and precautions

The automatic transmission consists of three main assemblies, these being the torque converter, which is directly coupled to the engine; the final drive unit which incorporates the differential assembly; and the planetary gearbox with its hydraulically operated multi-disc clutches and brake bands. The gearbox also houses a rear-mounted pump, which is coupled to the torque converter impeller, and this pump supplies automatic transmission fluid to the planetary gears, hydraulic controls and torque converter. The fluid performs a triple function - lubricating the moving parts, cooling the automatic transmission system and providing a torque transfer medium. The final drive lubrication is separate from the transmission lubrication system, unlike the manual gearbox, where the final drive shares a common lubrication system.

The torque converter is a sealed unit which cannot be dismantled. It is bolted to the crankshaft driveplate, and replaces the clutch found on an engine with manual transmission.

The gearbox is of the planetary type, with epicyclic gear trains operated by brakes and clutches through a hydraulic control system. The correct gear is selected by a combination of three control signals; a manual valve operated by the gearshift cable, signals; a manual valve operated by the accelerator pedal, and a governor to control hydraulic pressure. The gearshift cable and selector lever allow the driver to select a specific gear and override the automatic control, if desired. The accelerator control determines the correct gear for the desired rate of acceleration, and the governor determines the correct gear in relation to engine speed.

Because of the need for special test equipment, the complexity of some of the parts, and the need for scrupulous cleanliness when servicing automatic transmissions, the amount which the owner can do is limited. Those operations which can be carried out are detailed in the following Sections. Repairs to the final drive differential are also not recommended.

The automatic transmission has three forward speeds and one reverse, controlled by a six-position lever with the following positions:

P   Park
R   Reverse
N   Neutral
D   Drive
2   Low
1   Low

Coupé models from early 1990 may be fitted with a four-speed automatic transmission, but no information was available on this transmission at the time of writing.

Position 'P'

In the Park position, the transmission is locked mechanically by the engagement of a pawl. This position must only be selected when the car is absolutely stationary. The selector lever must be depressed in order to engage 'P', and when moving out of position 'P' with the engine running, the brake pedal must also be depressed.

Position 'R'

Reverse must only be selected when the car is absolutely stationary, and with the engine running at idling speed. The selector lever must be depressed when engaging position 'R', and additionally the brake pedal must be depressed when moving from 'P' to 'R'.

Position 'D'

This position is for normal driving, and once selected, the three forward gears engage automatically throughout the speed range from zero to top speed.

Position '2'

With the lever in this position, the two lower gears will engage automatically, but the highest gear will not engage. For this reason, position '2' should only be selected when the speed of the car is below 71 mph (115 kph). Selecting position '2' will make use of the engine's braking effect, and the actual change can be made without letting up the accelerator pedal.

Position '1'

The position is needed only rarely, such as on steep inclines or declines. The transmission remains in the lowest gear, and therefore position '1' should only be selected when the car speed is below 40 mph (65 kph).

Precautions when being towed

if the car is being towed, the ignition key must be inserted so that the steering wheel is not locked, and the gear selector must be in position 'N' (neutral). Because the lubrication of the transmission is limited when the engine is not running, the car must not be towed for more than 30 miles (50 km), or at a speed greater than 30 mph (50 kph) unless the front wheels of the car are lifted clear of the road.

2 Routine maintenance

Carry out the following procedures at the intervals given in *'Routine maintenance'* at the beginning of the manual.

Check automatic transmission fluid level

1 To check the fluid level accurately, the transmission should be at normal operating temperature, normally requiring a run of approximately 6 miles (10 km).
2 With the car on level ground and, 'P' selected, apply the handbrake, and with the engine idling, remove and clean the dipstick. Re-insert it, and check that the fluid level is between the minimum and maximum marks. If necessary, top up to the maximum mark. The quantity of fluid required to raise the level from the minimum to maximum marks is 0.23 litres (0.4 pints). Take care not to overfill the transmission.

Renew automatic transmission fluid

3 Refer to Section 3.

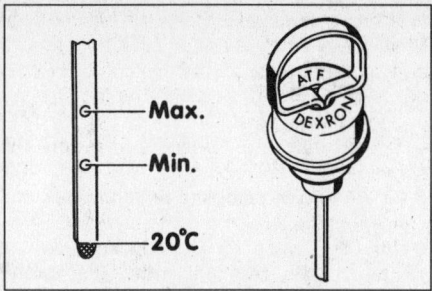

Fig 7.2 Automatic transmission fluid dipstick markings (Sec 2)

3 Automatic transmission fluid - renewal

1 This job should not be attempted unless clean, dust-free conditions can be achieved.
2 With the car standing on level ground, place a container of at least six pints capacity beneath the sump pan of the transmission. For working room beneath the car, jack it up and support it with axle stands, or use car ramps.
3 If necessary, unscrew the bolt securing the dipstick tube bracket to the gearbox.
4 Unscrew the union nut, and remove the dipstick tube from the sump pan. Allow the fluid to drain into the container.
5 Unbolt and remove the sump pan. Remove the gasket.
6 Remove the screws and withdraw the cover, strainer, and gasket.
7 Clean the pan and strainer with methylated spirit and allow to dry.
8 Refit the strainer, cover and pan in reverse order, using new gaskets and tightening the screws to the specified torque.
9 Refit the dipstick tube, and tighten the union nut and mounting bolt.
10 Wipe round the top of the dipstick tube, then remove the dipstick.
11 With the car on level ground, pour 2.5 litres (4.4 pints) of the correct grade of fluid into the transmission, using a clean funnel in the dipstick tube.
12 With the handbrake applied, run the engine at idling speed, then select every gear position once.
13 With the engine still idling, move the selector lever to position 'P'. Remove and clean the dipstick, then re-insert it and check that the fluid is up to the 20°C (68°F) mark. If not, add more fluid. Refit the dipstick.
14 Drive the car approximately 6 miles (10 km) in order to bring the transmission fluid to normal operating temperature.
15 With the car on level ground, and with 'P' selected, apply the handbrake, and with the engine idling, remove and clean the dipstick. Reinsert it, and check that the fluid level is between the minimum and maximum marks. If necessary, top up to the maximum mark. Do not overfill the transmission, because this will

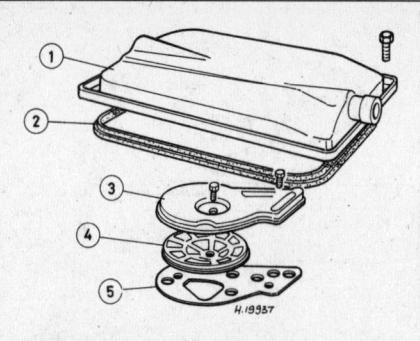

Fig 7.3 Strainer and sump pan (Sec 3)

1 Sump pan	4 Filter screen
2 Gasket	5 Gasket
3 Cover	

upset its operation - any excess fluid added must be drained.
16 Refit the dipstick and switch off the engine.

4 Automatic transmission - removal and refitting

1 Disconnect the battery negative lead.
2 Unscrew and remove the upper transmission-to-engine bolts, working from inside the engine compartment.
3 Unscrew the bolt securing the earth strap to the gearbox.
4 Disconnect the wiring from the speedometer sender unit, and where fitted, the lambda probe.
5 Apply the handbrake, then jack up the front of the car and support on axle stands. Alternatively, raise the front of the car on car ramps.
6 Support the front of the engine with a hoist or engine support bar.
7 Working under the car, unbolt and remove the engine splash guard and transmission front cover plate.
8 Unbolt the stay bar from the front of the engine.
9 Remove the exhaust downpipe completely, with reference to Chapter 3.
10 Remove the starter motor as described in Chapter 12.
11 Working through the front cover aperture, unscrew the bolts securing the torque converter to the driveplate. It will be necessary to turn the engine to gain access to each bolt and to do this, either turn the starter ring gear on the driveplate, or use a spanner on the countershaft pulley bolt. Hold the starter ring gear stationary with a screwdriver while unscrewing the bolts.
12 Position a container beneath the rear of the transmission. Unscrew the union nut, remove the dipstick tube from the sump pan, and drain the fluid.
13 Disconnect the hoses from the fluid cooler on the rear of the transmission. Plug or cap

the open ends to prevent ingress of dust and dirt.
14 Unbolt the right-hand driveshaft splash guard.
15 Unscrew and remove the bolts securing the driveshaft inner constant velocity joints to the transmission drive flanges. Note the location of the bolt plates. Tie the driveshafts to one side. Recover the gaskets where fitted.
16 Unbolt and remove the dipstick/filler tube.
17 Remove the spring clip, and disconnect the kickdown cable from the lever on the side of the transmission.
18 Unbolt the selector cable support bracket, and disconnect the selector cable from the lever on the transmission.
19 Support the weight of the transmission on a trolley jack.
20 Unscrew and remove the transmission mounting bolts.
21 Lower the trolley jack slightly, and raise the front of the engine slightly, in order to position the transmission at a suitable angle for removal.
22 Unscrew and remove the lower transmission-to-engine bolts.
23 With the help of an assistant, withdraw the transmission from the engine, making sure that the torque converter remains fully engaged with the transmission splines. Withdraw the transmission from under the car. To prevent the torque converter from being disengaged from the splines and subsequently losing the fluid, bolt a suitable piece of metal to one of the mounting bolt holes.
24 Refitting is a reversal of removal, but make sure that the torque converter is fully engaged with the transmission pump splines. To check this, position a straight-edge across the bellhousing, and check that the distance to the torque converter boss is approximately 10 mm (0.4 in) for the 087 model, or 30 mm (1.2 in) for the 089 model. Note that the pump driveplate will be damaged beyond repair if the transmission is bolted to the engine with the torque converter incorrectly fitted. Refit the starter motor with reference to Chapter 12, and the exhaust downpipe with reference to Chapter 3. If necessary, adjust the kickdown and selector cables as described in Sections 9, 10 and 11.

5 Torque converter - checking and draining

1 The torque converter is a welded unit, and if it is faulty the complete unit must be replaced. Only the bush can be renewed.
2 Examine the bush for signs of scoring and wear. Checking for wear requires an internal micrometer or dial gauge; if one is available, measure the bore diameter to see if it exceeds the wear limit given in the Specifications.
3 To remove the bush requires a commercial extractor and a slide hammer. After fitting a

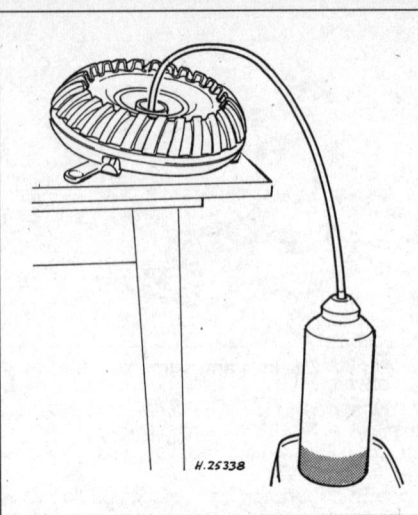

Fig 7.4 Checking the torque converter bush internal diameter with a dial gauge (Sec 5)

Fig 7.5 Syphoning the fluid from the torque converter (Sec 5)

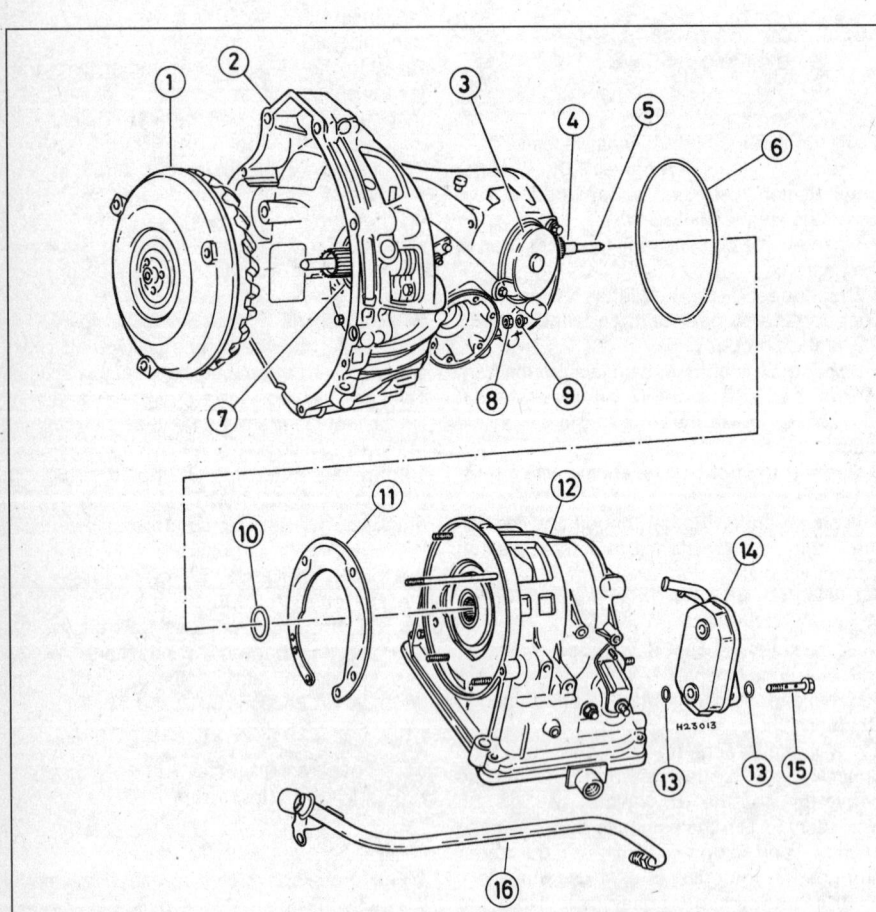

Fig 7.6 Automatic transmission components (Sec 6)

1 Torque converter	7 Torque converter seal	12 Planetary gearbox
2 Final drive housing	8 Nut	13 Seal
3 Governor	9 Washer	14 Fluid cooler
4 Turbine shaft	10 Shim	15 Bolt
5 Pump shaft	11 Gasket	16 Filler pipe and dipstick
6 Seal		

new bush, its diameter must be between the limits given; if not, the bush must be removed and another one fitted. Reaming of the bush is not allowed. For this reason the job is really one for an Audi agent.

4 Check that the cooling vanes on the converter are secure.

5 Fit the turbine shaft into the converter, and check that the turbine turns freely.

6 If the fluid was dirty when drained from the oil pan, drain the fluid from the torque converter before the automatic transmission is refitted.

7 Have ready a container of about half a gallon (2 litres) capacity, a washing-up liquid bottle, and a piece of tubing of not more than 8 mm (0.32 in) outside diameter.

8 Put the torque converter on the bench, and support it so that it is tipped up slightly.

9 Cut one end of the plastic tube on an angle so that the end of the tube will not be blocked if it comes against a flat surface, and push this end into the torque converter hub until it touches the bottom.

10 Connect the spout of the washing up liquid bottle to the other end of the tube, hold the bottle below the level of the torque converter and squeeze the bottle. As the bottle expands again, fluid will be sucked into it, as soon as the fluid begins to syphon, pull the tube end off the bottle, and rest the tube end in the larger container. Syphon as much fluid as possible from the torque converter. On reassembly and installation, the converter will fill with fluid as soon as the engine is started.

6 Automatic transmission – dismantling and reassembly

1 The gearbox may be separated from the final drive housing and the governor may be removed, but dismantling of the gearbox is not recommended, owing to the number of specialised tools and repair techniques required.

2 With the gearbox on the bench, pull out the torque converter if not already removed.

3 Remove the four nuts and washers which secure the gearbox to the final drive housing, and prise away the gearbox. Remove the sealing ring, gasket and the shim.

4 With the gearbox removed, the turbine shaft and pump shaft can be pulled out and examined. When examining the turbine shaft, check that the sealing rings (Fig. 7.7) are seated properly, and that the circlip is correctly seated in the spline groove. Note that the circlip must always be fitted when refitting the turbine shaft, otherwise the needle roller bearing will be damaged.

5 Both the pump shaft and the turbine shaft are available in various lengths, so it is important to take the old shaft when obtaining a new one.

6 When reassembling, be sure to refit the

shim to the front of the gearbox, and use a new gasket and sealing ring. Make sure that the pump shaft is inserted properly (see Section 4).

7 Final drive housing - servicing

1 The removal and dismantling of the differential and final drive assembly is not recommended, owing to the number of specialised tools and repair techniques required.
2 The torque converter oil seal may be renewed as follows. Using the access holes in the side of the final drive housing, drive off the old seal with a hammer and chisel (Fig. 7.8). Fit a new seal over the boss, taking care to keep the seal square and then carefully drive it on fully with a hammer and metal tube. Note that the seal is made of very soft material and should not be cleaned with liquid solvents.

8 Governor - removal and refitting

1 The governor assembly is located on the left-hand side of the final drive housing.
2 Unscrew the two bolts and withdraw the cover. Remove the seal.
3 Withdraw the governor from the housing.
4 If necessary, renew the seal in the housing.
5 If renewing the governor, check the identification letter stamped on the head, and obtain an identical unit.
6 Clean all the parts, then lubricate them with transmission fluid before reassembly.
7 Refitting is a reversal of removal, but renew the cover seal, and tighten the cover bolts evenly.

9 Accelerator and kickdown cables (089 transmission) - removal, refitting and adjustment

Removal and refitting

1 Remove the air cleaner where necessary (Chapter 3).
2 Remove the cover from the relay bracket, then extract the circlip, washer, and ring from the pivot pin.
3 Prise off the special clips, and detach the cable and stop from the quadrant.,
4 Extract the clips and disconnect the outer cable ends from the relay bracket.
5 Remove the quadrant, spring, and washer.
6 Unclip the accelerator cable from the quadrant, and disconnect the outer cable.
7 Remove the lower quadrant.
8 Inside the car, disconnect the kickdown cable from the accelerator pedal, then the outer cable from the bulkhead.

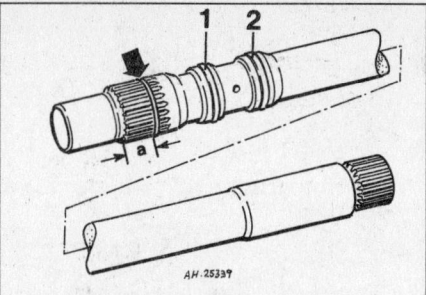

Fig 7.7 Turbine shaft (Sec 6)

1 and 2 Seal positions
a Forward clutch splines
Arrow shows circlip position

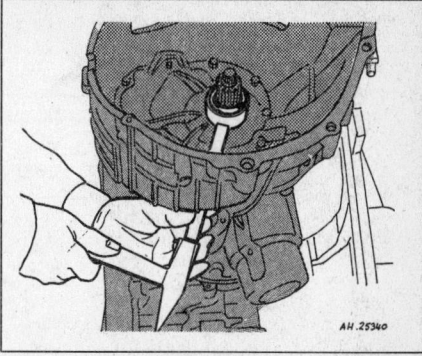

Fig 7.8 Removing the torque converter oil seal from the final drive housing (Sec 7)

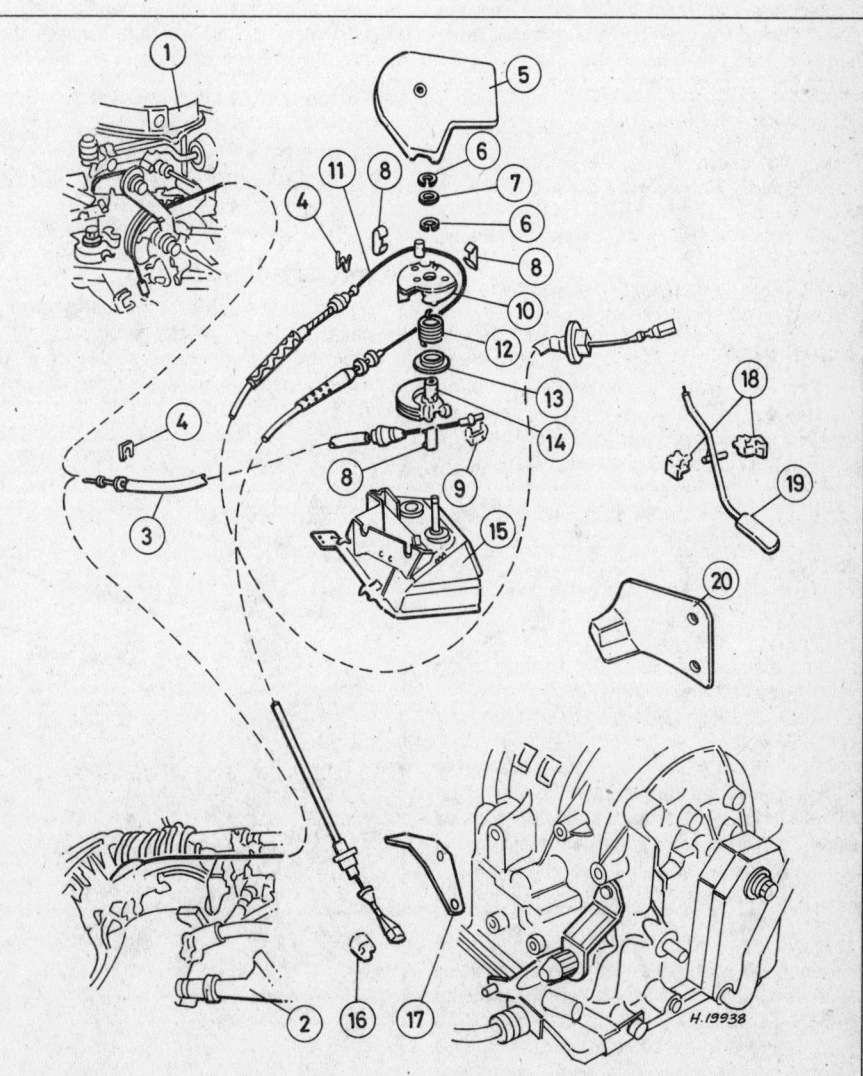

Fig 7.9 Accelerator and kickdown cable components on the 089 transmission (Sec 9)

1 Carburettor	6 Circlip	11 Kickdown cable	16 Clip
2 Fuel injection	7 Washer	12 Spring	17 Bracket
throttle housing	8 Clip	13 Washer	18 Mounting
3 Accelerator cable	9 Clip	14 Lower quadrant	19 Accelerator cable
4 Clip	10 Upper quadrant	15 Relay bracket	20 Pedal stop
5 Cover			

7

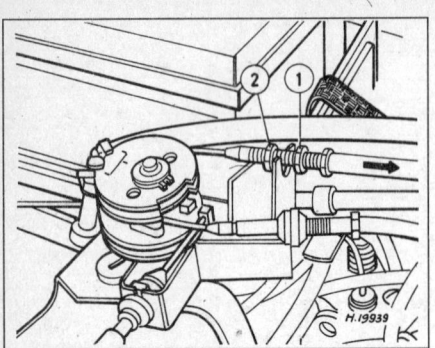

Fig 7.10 Kickdown cable adjustment locknuts (1 and 2) (Sec 9)

Pull outer cable in direction of arrow

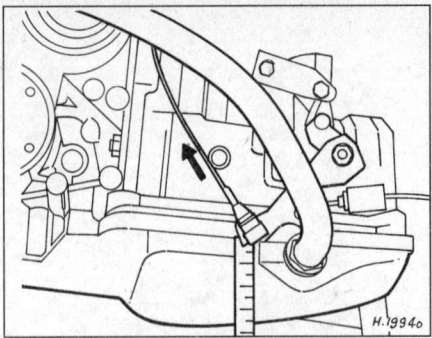

Fig 7.11 Using a steel rule to set the kickdown lever position (See 9)

Pull outer cable in direction of arrow

Fig 7.12 Adjusting the kickdown cable ferrule (Sec 9)

Pull outer cable in direction of arrow

9 Disconnect the accelerator cable from the carburettor or throttle housing as applicable, and also unclip the outer cable.
10 Raise the front of the car, and support on axle stands.
11 Pull off the circlip, and disconnect the kickdown cable from the lever on the transmission. Release the outer cable from the bracket.
12 Withdraw both cables from the engine compartment.
13 Refitting is a reversal of removal, but adjust the cables as follows.

Adjustment

14 The accelerator cable on fuel injection models requires no adjustment. However, on carburettor models, the position of the outer cable at the carburettor should be adjusted so that there is no play on the inner cable with the throttle valve on its stop. Fit the special clip in the groove in the ferrule nearest the bracket.
15 To adjust the kickdown cable, first loosen the two locknuts at the relay bracket.
16 Position the kickdown lever on the transmission 2 mm (0.08 in) off its stop, using a steel rule at the end of the lever. The help of an assistant will be necessary to hold the lever in this position.
17 Pull the outer cable at the relay bracket to eliminate any play, then tighten the two nuts.
18 Position a 90 mm (3.5 in) distance piece beneath the accelerator pedal, then pull the ferrule at the relay bracket to eliminate any play. Fit the special clip in the groove in the ferrule nearest the bracket.
19 Check the adjustment by removing the distance piece and allowing the throttle valve lever to touch its stop. Make sure that the transmission lever is 2 mm (0.08 in) off its stop. Depress the accelerator pedal to the full throttle position (not kickdown), and check that the throttle valve is fully open. Now fully depress the pedal, and check that the transmission lever is on the kickdown stop with the spring under tension.
20 On models fitted with cruise control, disconnect the coupling rod, and, after adjusting the kickdown cable, reconnect the coupling rod, free of any tension.

21 On models fitted with air conditioning, the air conditioner switch must not operate at full throttle, but it must operate at the kickdown position.

10 Accelerator cable (087 transmission) - removal, refitting and adjustment

Removal and refitting

1 To remove the cable, first raise the front of the car and support on axle stands.
2 Disconnect the cable ends from the accelerator pedal and transmission kickdown lever.

3 Unscrew the nut, and remove the cover and return spring from the throttle housing spindle.
4 Disconnect the cable and centre stop from the throttle pulley.
5 Extract the clips, and disconnect the outer cables from the brackets.
6 Withdraw the cable through the bulkhead, and remove from the engine compartment.
7 Refitting is a reversal of removal, but adjust the cable as follows.

Adjustment

8 Adjusting points are provided for the two sections of outer cable. An assistant is required.
9 Locate a 17 mm (0.67 in) spacer beneath

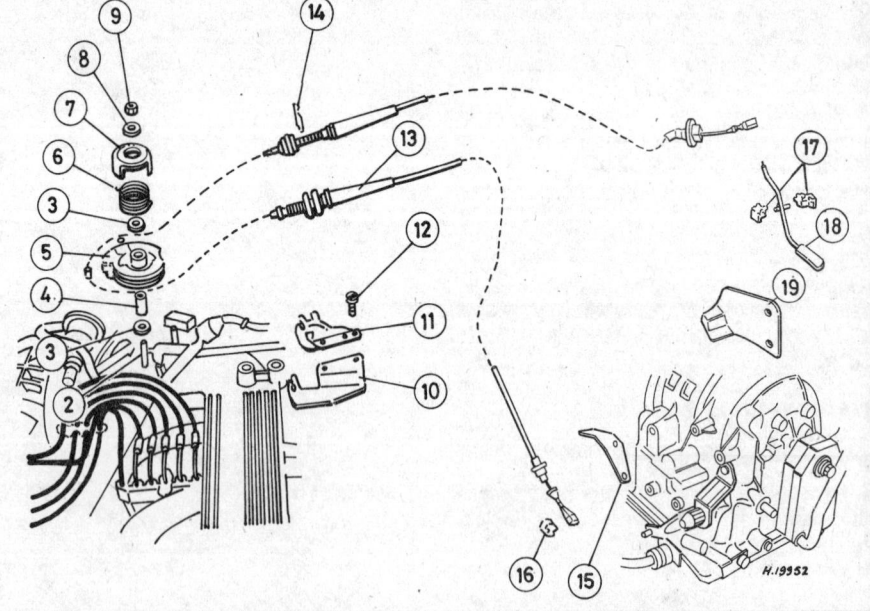

Fig 7.13 Accelerator cable and kickdown linkage component on the 087 transmission (Sec 10)

1 Throttle housing	8 Washer	15 Bracket
2 Throttle valve shaft	9 Nut	16 Clip
3 Washer	10 Bracket	17 Bracket
4 Bush	11 Bracket	18 Accelerator pedal
5 Pulley	12 Bolt	19 Pedal stop
6 Spring	13 Accelerator cable	20 Kickdown lever
7 Cover	14 Clip	21 Spring

the accelerator pedal, and have the assistant hold the pedal down onto the spacer.

10 Loosen the cable adjusting nuts, and remove the adjustment clip.

11 Hold the throttle pulley open. Now pull the pedal outer cable towards the pedal, so that all play is eliminated, and refit the adjustment clip next to the bracket to secure.

12 Pull the transmission outer cable towards the transmission until the kickdown pressure point is felt, then tighten the adjusting nuts against the bracket.

13 Check that, with the pedal released, the throttle lever is contacting the idling stop. Depress the pedal to the full-throttle (not kickdown) position, and check that the throttle lever is contacting the full-throttle stop. Depress the pedal to the kickdown position, and check that the transmission kickdown lever is on the kickdown stop, with the throttle spring under tension.

11 Selector lever and cable - removal, refitting and adjustment

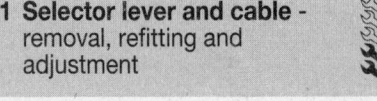

1 Disconnect the battery negative lead.

2 Remove the centre console as described in Chapter 11. Select position 'P'.

3 Unscrew the knob from the selector lever.

4 Remove the screws, and lift off the selector housing. Disconnect the wiring for the illumination lamp and, if applicable, the locking solenoid.

5 Disconnect the wiring from the starter inhibitor switch, and on later models, the locking solenoid.

6 Lift the rubber boot over the selector lever.

7 Raise the front of the car and support on axle stands. Remove the underbody heat shield.

8 Disconnect the cable from the transmission lever, selector lever (one nut), and support bracket.

9 Unbolt the bracket and lever assembly from the floor.

10 Unscrew the locating pin, separate the selector lever from the gearchange lever, and recover the bush and springs.

11 Extract the circlip, and remove the gearchange lever from the bracket. Recover the washer, collar and bush.

12 Where fitted (on later models), unbolt the locking solenoid.

13 Unbolt the inhibitor switch.

14 Clean all the components, and wipe dry.

15 Refitting is a reversal of removal, but note the following additional points. Apply suitable sealant to the bracket before bolting it in position. The cable bracket should be fitted with the angled end towards the selector lever. Apply a little grease to the cable ends before fitting them. Fit the cable in the clamping sleeve first, before fitting the bracket. On models manufactured from August 1988 onwards, adjust the locking

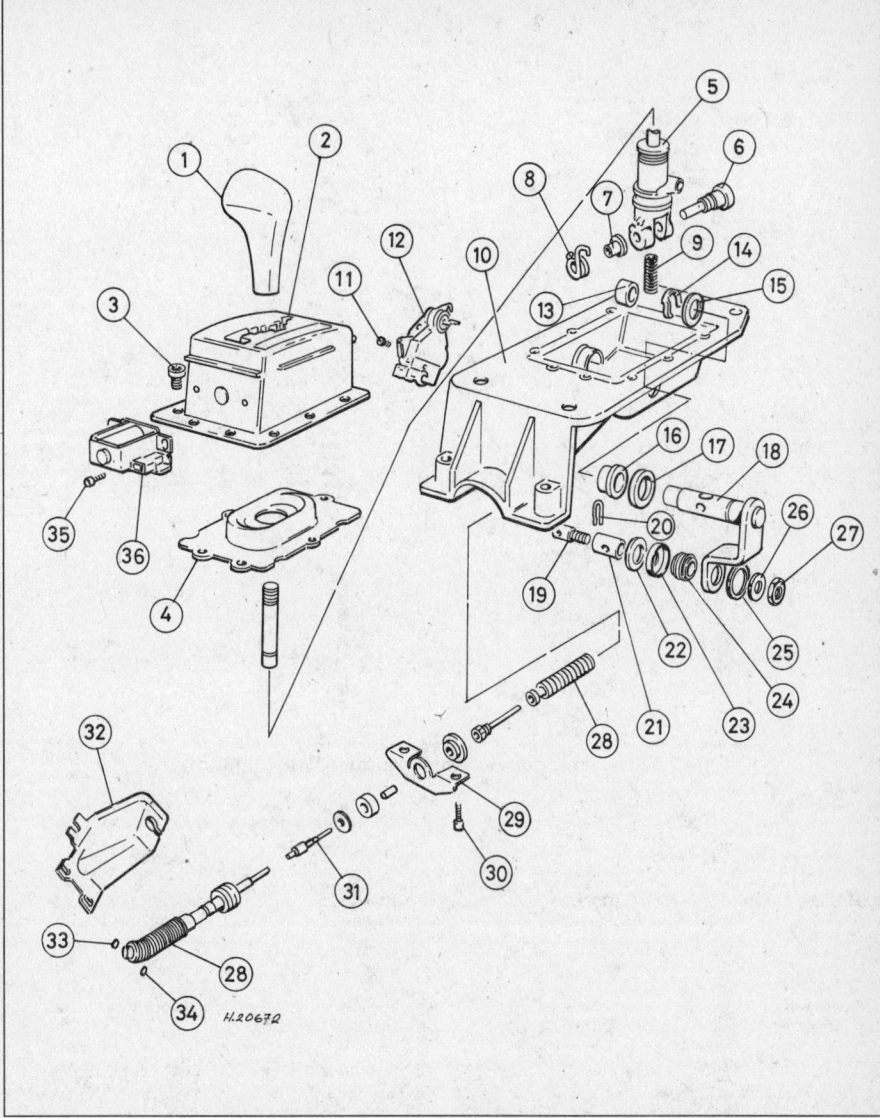

Fig 7.14 Selector components – pre-August 1988 (Sec 11)

1 Knob	11 Bolt	19 Clamping pin	28 Boot
2 Housing	12 Inhibitor switch	20 Spring clip	29 Support bracket
3 Socket-head bolt	assembly	21 Clamping sleeve	30 Bolt
4 Boot	13 Bush	22 Washer	31 Selector cable
5 Selector lever	14 Circlip	23 Collar	32 Bracket
6 Locating pin	15 Washer	24 Bush	33 Seal
7 Bush	16 Bush	25 Collar	34 Circlip
8 Spring	17 Collar	26 Washer	35 Bolt
9 Spring	18 Gearchange lever	27 Nut	36 Solenoid
10 Bracket			

solenoid as follows. Select position 'R', then use a feeler blade to check that the distance between the lever and solenoid is 1 mm (0.04 in). If not, loosen the bolt, push the solenoid against the feeler blade, and tighten the bolt. The selector lever housing should be adjusted after fitting the solenoid as follows. Move the selector lever so that the solenoid pin enters the hole, then fit the housing and align the 'N' mark with the lever. Tighten the bolts, and check that the lever moves an equal distance to positions 'R' and 'D'. Adjust the inhibitor switch with reference to Section 12. Make sure that the selector cable rubber gaiter is in good condition, otherwise there is a risk of water causing the cable to rust and seize. To adjust the cable, select 'P', then loosen the clamping sleeve nut. Move the transmission lever to position 'P' (rear stop), then tighten the nut. Note that the brake pedal must be applied before moving the selector lever from positions 'N' or 'P'.

7

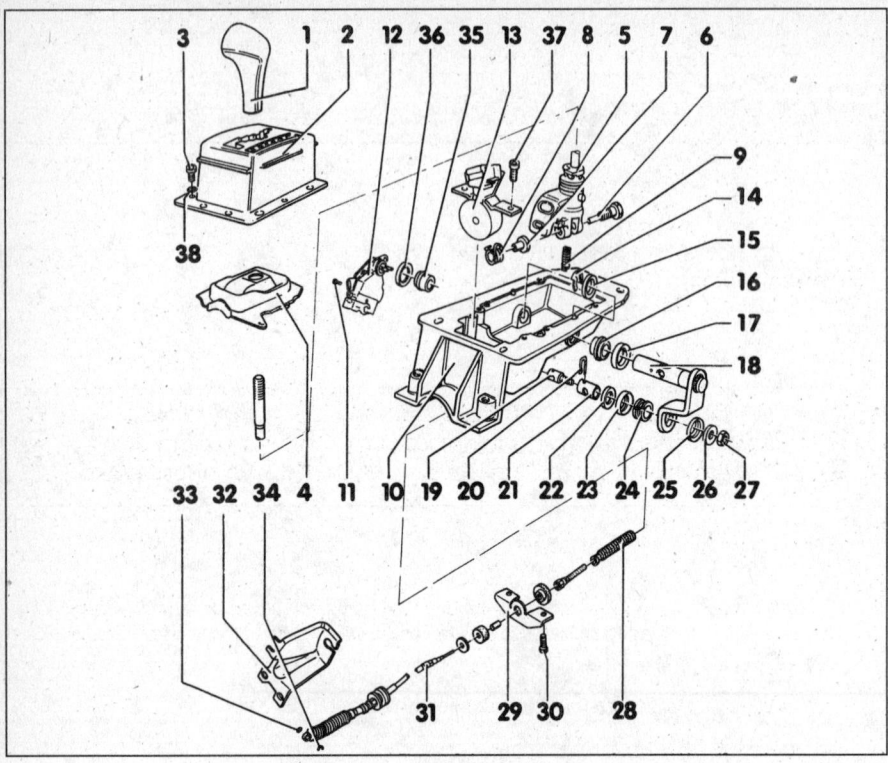

Fig 7.15 Selector components – August 1988 on (Sec 11)

1 Knob	11 Bolt	20 Spring pin	30 Bolt	
2 Housing	12 Inhibitor switch	21 Clamping sleeve	31 Selector cable	
3 Bolt	assembly	22 Washer	32 Bracket	
4 Boot	13 Solenoid	23 Collar	33 Seal	
5 Selector lever	14 Circlip	24 Bush	34 Circlip	
6 Guide pin	15 Washer	25 Collar	35 Bush	
7 Bush	16 Bush	26 Washer	36 Collar	
8 Spring	17 Washer	27 Nut	37 Bolt	
9 Spring	18 Gearchange lever	28 Boot	38 Washer	
10 Bracket	19 Clamping pin	29 Support bracket		

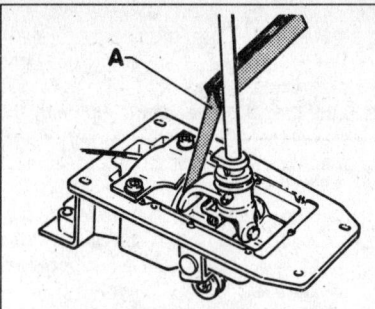

Fig 7.16 Locking solenoid adjustment (August 1988 on) (Sec 11)

A 1 mm (0.04 in) feeler blade

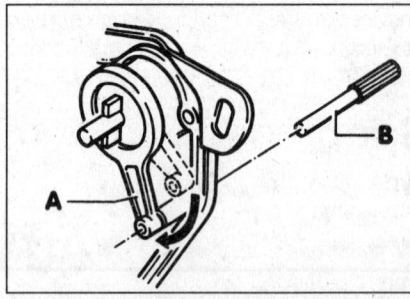

Fig 7.17 Method of locking the switch lever (A) with a pin (B) (Sec 12)

12 Inhibitor switch - removal, refitting and adjustment

1 Disconnect the battery negative lead.
2 Remove the centre console, as described in Chapter 11. Select position 'P'.

3 Unscrew the knob from the selector lever.
4 Remove the screws and lift off the selector housing. Disconnect the wiring for the illumination lamp and, if applicable, the locking solenoid.
5 Disconnect the wiring from the starter inhibitor switch, and on later models, the locking solenoid.

6 Remove the screws and withdraw the switch.
7 Refitting is a reversal of removal, but adjust the switch as follows. On pre-August 1988 models, select 'P', then turn the bracket on the switch towards 'P' until the switch locates in the gearchange lever. On models manufactured from August 1988 onwards, use a 4 mm (0.16 in) diameter drill or pin to lock the switch lever as shown in Fig. 7. 17. Move the selector lever to position 'N', then fit the switch so that the driving dog engages the gearchange lever. Tighten the screws, and remove the drill or pin. After refitting the switch, check that it is only possible to start the engine with positions 'N' or 'P' selected, and that the reversing lights are switched on with position 'R' selected. If the switch does not operate correctly, it may require slight adjustment within the elongated holes.

Fault finding - automatic transmission and final drive

No drive in any gear
☐ Fluid level too low

Erratic drive in forward gears
☐ Fluid level too low
☐ Dirty filter

Gear changes at above normal speed
☐ Accelerator linkage adjustment incorrect
☐ Dirt in governor

Gear changes at below normal speed
☐ Dirt in governor

Gear engagement jerky
☐ idle speed too high

Gear engagement delayed on upshift
☐ Fluid level too low
☐ Accelerator linkage adjustment incorrect

Kickdown does not operate
☐ Accelerator linkage adjustment incorrect

Fluid dirty or discoloured
☐ Brake bands and clutches wearing

Parking lock not effective
☐ Selector lever out of adjustment
☐ Parking lock defective

Chapter 8 Driveshafts

Contents

Degrees of difficulty

| Easy, suitable for novice with little experience | Fairly easy, suitable for beginner with some experience | Fairly difficult, suitable for competent DIY mechanic 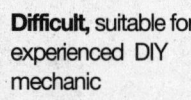 | Difficult, suitable for experienced DIY mechanic | Very difficult, suitable for expert DIY or professional |

Specifications

Type .... Double constant velocity (CV) joints splined to driveshaft, inner joint bolted to gearbox drive flange, outer joint splined to front wheel hub

CV joint lubricant

Type .... Special grease, supplied in repair kit
Capacity:
  Outer joint (except NG and 7A engines) .... 90 g
  Outer joint (NG and 7A engines) .... 120 g
  Inner joint (except KV, NG and 7A engines) .... 90 g
  Inner joint (KV, NG and 7A engines) .... 120 g

Torque wrench settings

	Nm	lbf ft
Inner CV joint to flange:		
M8 bolt	45	33
M10 bolt	80	59
Outer driveshaft nut	265	196
Outer driveshaft bolt:		
M14 bolt	120 + 90°	89 + 90°
M16 bolt	200 + 90°	148 + 90°
Wheel bolts	110	81

1 General description

Drive is transmitted from the gearbox drive flanges to the driveshaft inner and outer constant velocity (CV) joints. The outer CV joints incorporate splined shafts which are attached to the front wheel hubs. Before April 1988, the shafts are secured to the hubs with nuts, while bolts are used on later models. Both the inner and outer CV joints may be renewed separately.

2 Routine maintenance

Carry out the following procedure at the intervals given in 'Routine maintenance' at the beginning of the manual.

Check CV joint rubber bellows

1 Apply the handbrake. Jack up the front of the car and support on axle stands.
2 Turn the driveshafts by hand, and examine the CV joint rubber bellows for signs of leakage, splitting and chafing.
3 Check the bellows clips for security.

3 Driveshafts - removal and refitting

1 Apply the handbrake and prise the trim from the relevant front wheel.
2 Loosen the driveshaft nut or bolt (as applicable) with the weight of the car still on the wheels. The nut/bolt is tightened to a very high torque, and **should not** be loosened with the car raised.
3 Loosen the wheel bolts.
4 Jack up the front of the car and support on axle stands.

5 Remove the wheel.
6 Remove the driveshaft nut and washer, or bolt as appropriate (photo).
7 Unbolt and remove the driveshaft lower cover (where fitted) from the gearbox.
8 Working beneath the car, unscrew and remove the bolts securing the inner constant velocity joint to the gearbox drive flange

3.6 Removing the driveshaft bolt

8

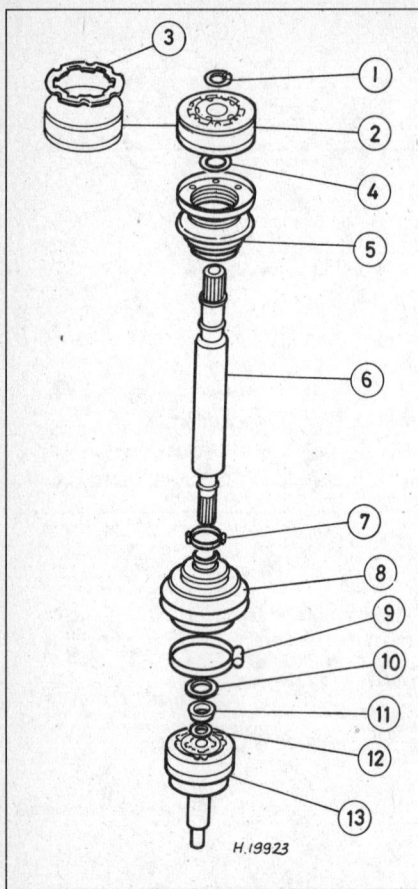

Fig 8.1 Exploded view of the driveshaft
(Sec 1)

1 Circlip
2 Inner constant
  velocity joint
3 Gasket (not fitted
  to all models)
4 Dished washer
5 Rubber bellows
  and cap
6 Driveshaft

7 Clip
8 Rubber bellows
9 Clip
10 Dished washer
11 Spacer
12 Circlip
13 Outer constant
  velocity joint

(photo). Note the location of the bolt plates. Support the inner end of the driveshaft, or temporarily tie it to one side. Recover the gasket if fitted.

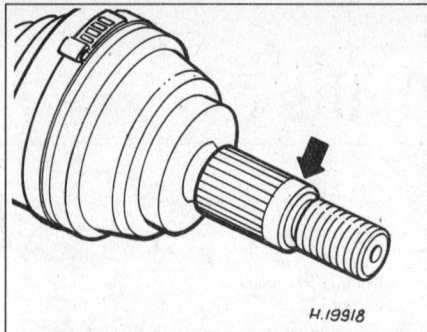

Fig 8.2 Area (arrowed) to apply locking fluid on early driveshafts (Sec 3)

Models with integral strut and wheel bearing housing (up to chassis number F89J373598 - April 1988)

9 On manual steering models, mark the lower suspension balljoint arm in relation to the suspension wishbone - this is necessary in order to retain the wheel camber setting. Unscrew the nuts and release the balljoint arm.
10 On power steering models, disconnect the front anti-roll bar link from the anti-roll bar by unscrewing the nut. Unscrew and remove the wishbone pivot bolts, and swivel the wishbone downwards.
11 Use a hub puller to remove the driveshaft from the front wheel hub, then withdraw the driveshaft from under the car.
12 If it is required to move the car on its wheels before refitting the driveshaft, the wheel bearing inner tracks must be clamped together using a long bolt and washers. If this is not done, the bearing may be damaged. Where applicable, the suspension components must also be reassembled.
13 Clean the splines on the outer end of the driveshaft and inside the hub thoroughly. All traces of old locking fluid must be removed.
14 Apply a 5.0 mm (0.2 in) band of locking fluid to the outer end of the driveshaft splines (Fig. 8.2).
15 Insert the driveshaft in the hub.
16 On power steering models, align the wishbone holes and insert the pivot bolts. Do

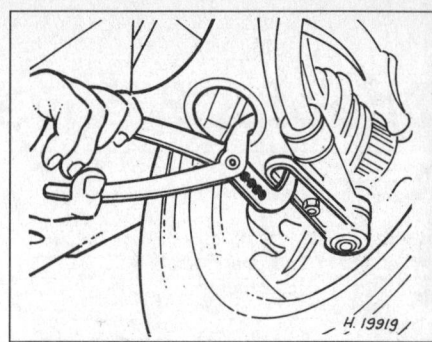

Fig 8.3 Using water pump pliers to pull the lower balljoint arm into position (Sec 3)

not fully tighten the bolts until the weight of the car is on the wheels. Reconnect the anti-roll bar link and tighten the nut.
17 On manual steering models, refit the balljoint arm to the wishbone. Use water pump pliers to pull the arm into its previously-noted position, then tighten the nuts. Take care not to trap the balljoint rubber dust cover.

Models with separate strut and wheel bearing housing (chassis number F89J373599 - April 1988 onwards)

18 Turn the steering to full lock, pull the driveshaft out of the front wheel hub, and withdraw it from under the car (photo). On models with ABS, pull back the speed sensor slightly.
19 If it is required to move the car on its wheels before refitting the driveshaft, the wheel bearing inner tracks must be clamped together using a long bolt and washers. If this is not done, the bearing may be damaged. Where applicable, the suspension components must also be reassembled.
20 Clean the splines on the outer end of the driveshaft and inside the hub thoroughly.
21 With the steering on full lock, insert the driveshaft in the hub. On models with ABS, push the speed sensor fully in.

All models

22 Where applicable, locate a new gasket on

3.8 Removing the inner CV joint-to-gearbox drive flange bolts

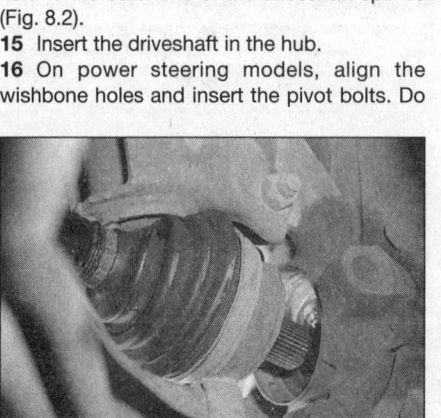

3.12 Pulling the driveshaft out of the front wheel hub

3.23A Position the driveshaft on the gearbox drive flange . . .

3.23B . . . then insert and tighten the bolts

3.29A Tighten the driveshaft bolt to the specified torque . . .

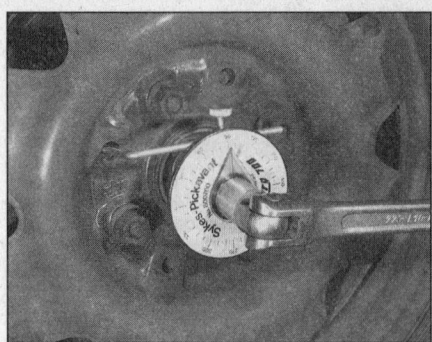

3.29B . . . then angle-tighten by the specified amount

the inner end of the driveshaft, after cleaning the seat. The gasket may have its own adhesive, in which case the backing foil should be removed before fitting it.

23 Position the driveshaft on the gearbox drive flange, then insert the bolts and plates, and tighten to the specified torque (photos).

24 Refit the driveshaft lower cover (where fitted).

25 Where a driveshaft *nut* is fitted, apply locking fluid to its threads, refit it together with the washer and tighten moderately.

26 Where a driveshaft *bolt* is fitted, a new bolt must be used and tightened *moderately*.

27 Refit the wheel and tighten the bolts moderately.

28 Lower the car to the ground.

29 Fully tighten the driveshaft nut or bolt, and the wheel bolts to the specified torques. Note that where a bolt is fitted, it must be tightened to the specified torque, then angle-tightened (photos). Where applicable, also tighten the wishbone pivot bolts. Refit the wheel trim.

30 Where locking fluid was used (in paragraph 14), allow it to harden before using the car on the road.

4 Driveshafts - overhaul

1 Mount the driveshaft (photo) in a vice.

2 Using a suitable drift, drive the cap from the inner constant velocity joint, and pull the rubber bellows towards the middle of the driveshaft.

3 Remove the circlip from the inner end of the driveshaft.

4 Support the inner constant velocity joint in a vice, then press or drive through the driveshaft.

5 Where fitted, remove the dished washer from the end of the driveshaft, noting how it is located.

6 Pull off the inner rubber bellows.

7 Remove the clips from the outer rubber bellows. If the clips are of the crimped type, they will have to be cut free.

8 Remove the bellows from the outer constant velocity joint, and pull towards the middle of the driveshaft.

9 Using a wooden or soft-faced mallet, strike the outer constant velocity joint at the point indicated in Fig. 8.4, in order to release the joint hub from the circlip on the driveshaft. Remove the joint.

10 Remove the circlip, spacer, and dished washer from the end of the driveshaft, noting how they are located.

11 Pull off the outer rubber bellows.

12 Clean all the components and examine them for wear, damage and deterioration. Each joint is available separately as a kit. This contains the rubber bellows, joint, washers, grease, and as applicable, the driveshaft nut/bolt, clips and inner bolts. Alternatively, the bellows is available separately as a kit. Both retaining circlips should be renewed as a matter of course. Do not dismantle the joints if intending to re-use them.

13 Commence reassembly by smearing a little grease on the small inner ends of the bellows, then locate both of them on the driveshaft, towards the middle.

14 Locate the dished washer, spacer and circlip on the outer end of the driveshaft. The circlip should be free to move in its groove. The convex side of the dished washer should be towards the end of the driveshaft.

15 Slide the outer constant velocity joint onto the driveshaft, and drive on the hub using metal tubing until the circlip engages.

16 Fill the outer joint with the specified amount of grease, working it well into both sides of the joint.

17 Slide the outer bellows onto the constant velocity joint, and locate the small diameter end in the driveshaft groove. With a screwdriver, temporarily lift the bellows to dispense any vacuum which may have formed. Fit and tighten new clips.

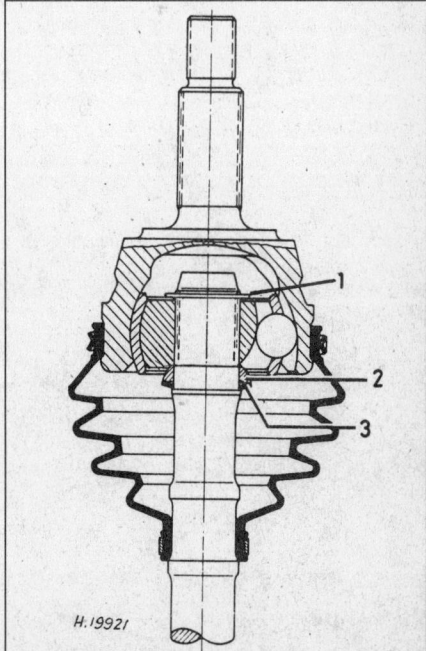

Fig 8.5 Cross-section of the outer constant velocity joint (Sec 4)

1 Circlip   2 Spacer   3 Dished washer

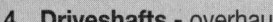

4.1 Driveshaft removed from the car

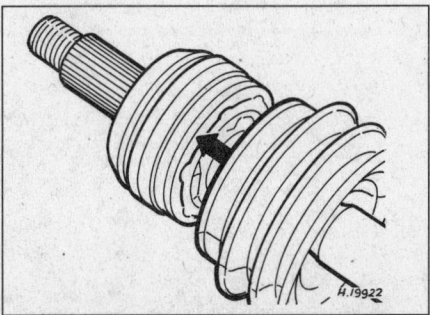

Fig 8.4 Strike the outer constant velocity joint at the point indicated to remove it from the driveshaft (Sec 4)

8

18 Fit the dished washer on the inner end of the driveshaft, with its convex side towards the end of the driveshaft. Note that models with KV, NG and 7A engines are not fitted with the washer. Where it is fitted, the washer may incorporate splines or may be plain, but the correct version must be fitted.

19 Slide the inner constant velocity joint onto the driveshaft, with the chamfer on the hub against the shoulder or dished washer on the driveshaft. Fully drive on the hub using metal tubing, then fit the retaining circlip in its groove.

20 Fill the inner joint with the specified amount of grease, working it well into both sides of the joint.

21 Apply some sealant to the surface of the cap which contacts the joint, then slide the rubber bellows into position, and locate the small diameter end in the driveshaft groove. Lightly tap the cap onto the joint.

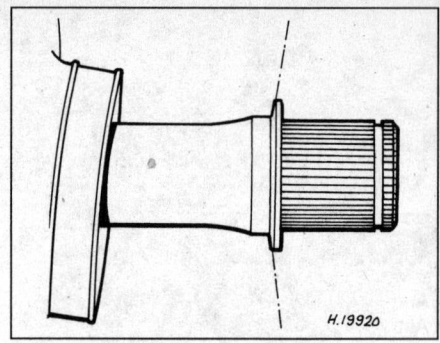

Fig 8.6 Correct location of dished washer on inner end of driveshaft (Sec 4)

Fault finding - driveshafts

Vibration and noise with steering on full lock

☐ Worn driveshaft joints

Noise on taking up drive, or between acceleration and overrun

☐ Worn driveshaft joints
☐ Worn front wheel hub and driveshaft splines
☐ Loose inner CV joint bolts
☐ Loose driveshaft outer nut or bolt

Chapter 9 Braking system

Contents

Degrees of difficulty

Easy, suitable for novice with little experience	Fairly easy, suitable for beginner with some experience	Fairly difficult, suitable for competent DIY mechanic 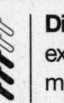	Difficult, suitable for experienced DIY mechanic 	Very difficult, suitable for expert DIY or professional

Specifications

System type .... Front discs, rear drums or discs, dual diagonally-split hydraulic circuit, with vacuum or hydraulic servo assistance. Rear brake pressure regulator, cable-operated handbrake on rear wheels. Anti-lock braking system (ABS) on certain models

Front brake discs

	Single piston calliper	Twin piston calliper
Diameter	256 mm (10.1 in)	276 mm (10.9 in)
Thickness (new):		
Ventilated	22.0 mm (0.87 in)	25.0 mm (0.99 in)
Solid	13.0 mm (0.51 in)	-
Thickness (minimum):		
Ventilated	20.0 mm (0.79 in)	23.0 mm (0.91 in)
Solid	11.0 mm (0.43 in)	-

Front brake pads

	Single piston calliper	Twin piston calliper
Lining thickness (new)	14.0 mm (0.55 in)	13.0 mm (0.51 in)
Lining thickness (minimum)	2.0 mm (0.08 in)	2.0 mm (0.08 in)
Minimum pad thickness (including backing plate)	7.0 mm (0.28 in)	7.0 mm (0.28 in)

Rear brake discs

Diameter	245 mm (9.7 in)
Thickness (new)	10.0 mm (0.39 in)
Thickness (minimum)	8.0 mm (0.32 in)

Rear brake pads

Lining thickness (new)	12.0 mm (0.47 in)
Lining thickness (minimum)	2.0 mm (0.08 in)
Minimum pad thickness (including backing plate)	7.0 mm (0.28 in)

9

Rear brake drums

Drum internal diameter:
New	200.0 mm (7.88 in)
Maximum	201.0 mm (7.92 in)
Drum radial run-out	0.05 mm (0.002 in)
Drum lateral run-out (maximum) on wheel mounting face	0.20 mm (0.008 in)

Rear brake shoes

Lining thickness (new)	5.25 mm (0.21 in)
Lining thickness (minimum)	2.5 mm (0.10 in)

Brake fluid

Type/specification	Hydraulic fluid to FMVSS 116 DOT 4
Brake fluid capacity (approx)	0.6 litre (1.06 pints)

Vacuum servo

Unit size	9.0 in
Hydraulic servo unit factor	4.7 : 1

Hydraulic servo unit accumulator gas pressure (at 20°C):
New	88 to 92 bar (1276 to 1334 lbf/in^2)
Minimum	30 bar (435 lbf/in^2)

Torque wrench settings

	Nm	lbf ft
(ABS) mounting nut	7	5
(ABS) earth lead bolt	20	15
(ABS) earth lead nut	10	7
(ABS) wheel speed sensor bolt	10	7
Girling front brake calliper:		
Guide pin bolt	35	26
Frame bolt	125	92
Teves front brake calliper:		
Guide pin	25	18
Frame bolt	125	92
Rear wheel cylinder	10	7
Girling rear brake calliper:		
Guide pin bolt	35	26
Frame bolt	65	48
Teves rear brake calliper:		
Guide pin	25	18
Frame bolt	65	48
Hydraulic servo unit:		
Mounting nut	25	18
Bracket nut	10	7
Hydraulic servo accumulator union bolt	35	26
Master cylinder bolt	25	18

1 General description

The braking system is of dual hydraulic circuit type, with discs at the front, and either drum or disc brakes at the rear. The dual circuit is split diagonally, so that in the event of a failure in one circuit, the remaining circuit still functions. The handbrake operates by cable on the rear wheels. Both the footbrake and handbrake are self-adjusting in use. A vacuum or hydraulic servo unit is fitted between the brake pedal and master cylinder. Certain models are fitted with an anti-lock braking system (ABS), consisting of a hydraulic modulator, electronic control unit, relays and wheel speed sensors. The system prevents the roadwheels locking when braking, particularly in emergencies.

Warning lamps are provided for the handbrake, low brake fluid level, and the ABS system.

2 Routine maintenance

Carry out the following procedures at the intervals given in 'Routine maintenance' at the beginning of the manual.

Check brake pad linings for wear

1 Check the thickness of the front brake pad linings as described in Section 3.

2 On models with rear disc brakes, also check the rear brake pad linings as described in Section 10.

Check hydraulic circuit for leaks and damage

3 Support the car in a raised position, and remove all the roadwheels.

4 Check the brake lines and hoses for leaks and damage. Check the brake lines for excessive corrosion.

5 Check the flexible hoses for splits and chafing. Check that the hoses are not twisted, and that they are not touching the surrounding bodywork or components.

6 Check the master cylinder, servo unit, brake pressure regulator, brake callipers, wheel cylinders, and where applicable the ABS hydraulic modulator, for leaks and

damage. Check all mounting nuts and bolts for tightness.

Check rear brake shoe linings for wear

7 On models with rear drum brakes, check the thickness of the rear brake shoe linings as described in Section 7.

Check brake hydraulic fluid level

8 Check that the brake fluid level in the translucent reservoir is between the 'MIN' and 'MAX' marks. Note that it is quite normal for the level to drop slightly as the brake pad linings wear. If the level drops quickly over a short period, or if it reaches the 'MIN' mark, the hydraulic circuit should be checked for leaks.

9 After repairs or bleeding the system, top up the level to the 'MAX' mark, using the recommended fluid.

Renew the hydraulic brake fluid

10 Remove the filler cap from the reservoir, and draw out the fluid using a syringe or pipette.

11 Connect a bleed tube to each bleed screw in turn, with reference to Section 17, and pump the brake pedal until all fluid is removed from the system. Tighten each bleed screw before progressing to the next one.

12 Fill the system with new brake fluid by following the procedure described in Section 17.

13 On manual transmission models, it is recommended that the clutch hydraulic circuit is bled at the same time, otherwise the new fluid will be contaminated with the old fluid.

3 Front brake pads -
inspection, removal and refitting

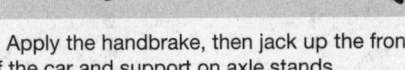

1 Apply the handbrake, then jack up the front of the car and support on axle stands.

2 The thickness of the outer front brake pads may be checked by looking through the holes in the wheels, using a torch if necessary. The inner pads may be checked using a mirror and torch, and looking through the holes in the rear of the brake callipers.

3 If any pad is worn down to the specified minimum thickness, all the front brake pads should be renewed together. If the pads are not yet at their limits, allow approximately 600 miles (1000 km) for every 1 mm (0.04 in) thickness remaining. This determines whether the pads will wear below the limit before the next service.

4 If there is any doubt as to the thickness of the pads, remove both front wheels for a more thorough investigation (photos).

5 To remove the pads, first remove the wheels. If the pads are to be re-used, mark them to ensure refitting in their original positions,

Teves calliper

6 Prise the cap from the inner end of the lower guide pin. If the cap is tight, use a pair of grips to remove it.

7 Using an Allen key, unscrew and remove the lower guide pin.

8 Unclip the flexible brake hose from the wheel bearing housing, then swing the calliper upwards, and tie it to the coil spring.

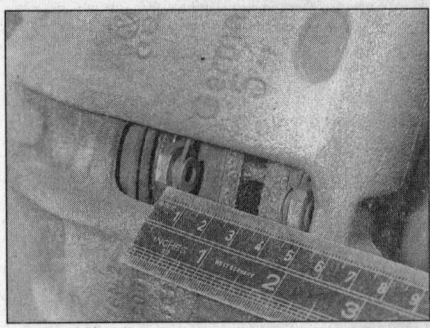

3.4A Checking the front brake pad lining thickness with a ruler, through the calliper window

3.4B Using a ruler against the disc to check the pad thickness

9 Remove the brake pads from the calliper frame.

10 Check that the heat shield cover is correctly located in the piston recess. Push the piston fully into the cylinder, in order to accommodate the new pads.

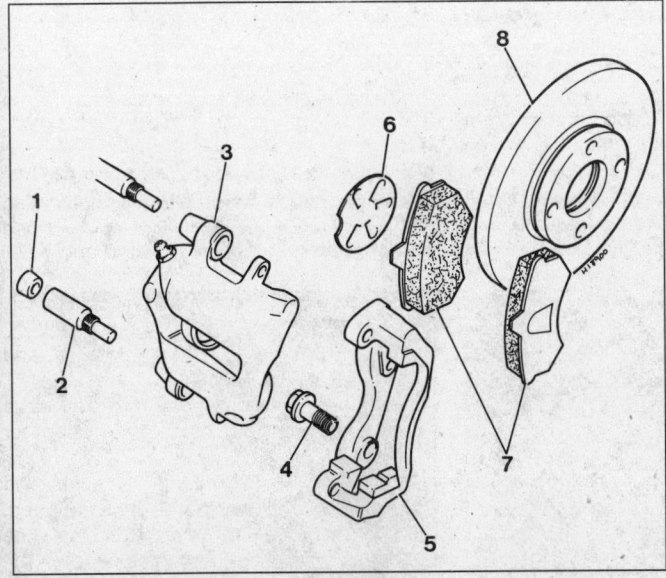

Fig 9.1 Teves front brake components (Sec 3)

1 Cap	4 Frame bolt	7 Brake pads
2 Guide pin	5 Frame	8 Brake disc
3 Calliper	6 Heatshield cover	

Fig 9.2 Girling front brake components (Sec 3)

1 Guide pin bolt	4 Calliper	6 Frame and guide
2 Frame bolt	5 Heat shield cover	pins
3 Brake disc		7 Brake pads

9

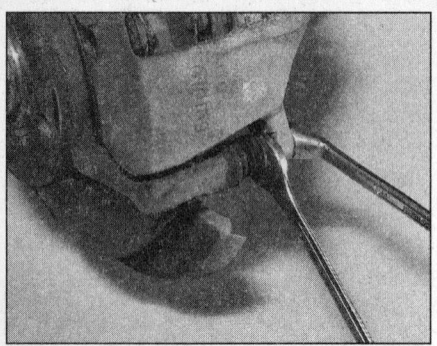

3.11A Unscrew the lower guide pin bolt. . .

3.11 B . . . and remove it

3.12A Swing the calliper up (90 model shown) . . .

Girling calliper

11 Hold the lower guide pin stationary with an open-ended spanner, and unscrew the securing bolt (photos).

12 Swing the calliper upwards. and tie it to the coil spring (photos).

13 Remove the brake pads from the calliper frame (photos).

14 Check that the heat shield cover is correctly located in the piston recess (photo). Push the piston(s) fully into the cylinder(s), in order to accommodate the new pads.

Teves and Girling callipers

15 Brush the dust and dirt from the calliper, piston(s), disc and pads, but do not inhale it, as it is injurious to health. Scrape any scale or rust from the disc and pad backing plates.

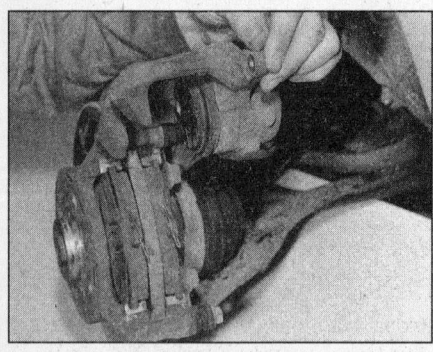

3.12B . . . for access to the brake pads (80 model shown)

16 The set of new brake pads includes two self-locking bolts, which are for fitting to the Girling callipers only.

17 Refitting is a reversal of removal, but tighten the guide pins or bolts to the specified torque. On completion, the brake pedal should be depressed firmly several times with the car stationary, so that the brake pads take up their normal running position. Also check the brake fluid level, as described in Section 2.

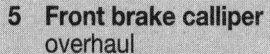

4 Front brake calliper - removal and refitting

1 Apply the handbrake, then jack up the front of the car and support on axle stands.

2 Remove the appropriate front wheel. Fit a brake hose clamp to the flexible hose leading to the brake calliper. Alternatively, remove the brake fluid reservoir filler cap, and tighten it down onto a piece of polythene sheeting placed over the reservoir filler hole. This will reduce the loss of fluid in the following procedure.

3 Loosen the hydraulic hose union, but do not unscrew it at this stage.

4 On the Teves calliper, prise the caps from the guide pins, then unscrew the pins with an Allen key.

5 On the Girling calliper, hold each guide pin in turn with an open-ended spanner, and unscrew the securing bolts.

6 Lift away the calliper, and unscrew it from the hydraulic hose. Plug the end of the hose.

7 If necessary, unbolt the calliper bracket frame from the wheel bearing housing.

8 Refitting is a reversal of removal, but make sure that all mating faces are clean, and tighten the bolts to the specified torques. Tighten the hydraulic hose union securely. Before refitting the calliper bracket bolts, clean the special serrations on the bolts. Finally bleed the hydraulic system as described in Section 17. If the loss of hydraulic fluid has been minimal, it may be sufficient to bleed just the one calliper.

5 Front brake calliper - overhaul

1 Clean the exterior of the calliper, taking care not to allow any foreign matter to enter the hydraulic hose aperture.

2 Mount the calliper in a vice.

3 Prise the dust cap(s) from the groove(s) in the calliper.

4 Place a piece of wood in the calliper jaws, opposite the piston(s).

5 Using air pressure from a foot pump through the hydraulic fluid inlet, force the piston(s) from the bore(s). Where twin pistons are fitted, remove each piston separately by first blocking one with a piece of wood. Use a pad of rubber on a piece of wood and a G-

3.13A Front brake pad removal (80 model shown)

3.13B Front brake pad removal (90 model shown)

3.14 Locating the heat shield in the piston recess

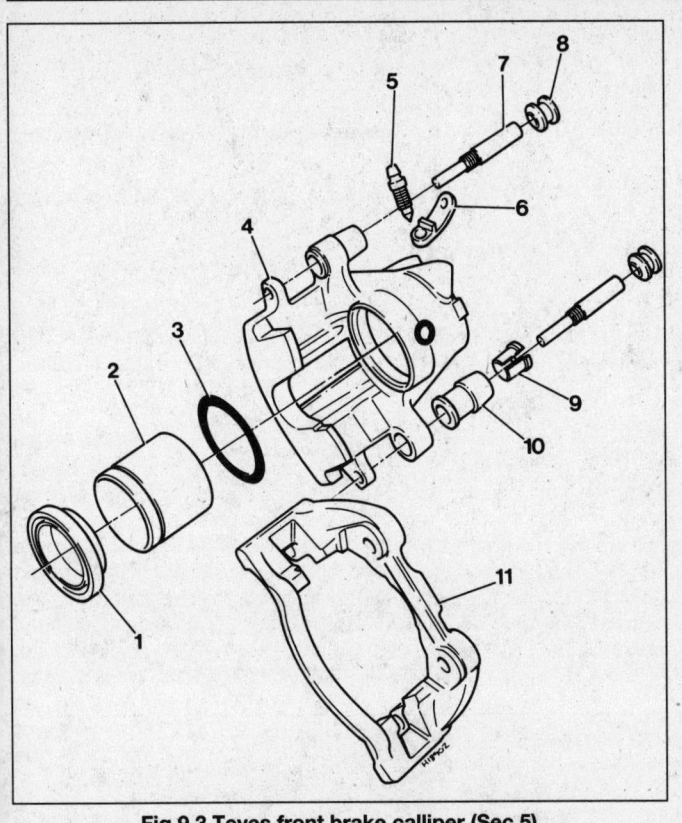

Fig 9.3 Teves front brake calliper (Sec 5)

1 Dust cap
2 Piston
3 Seal
4 Calliper

5 Bleed screw
6 Bleed screw cap
7 Guide pin
8 Cap

9 Teflon bush
10 Rubber bush
11 Frame

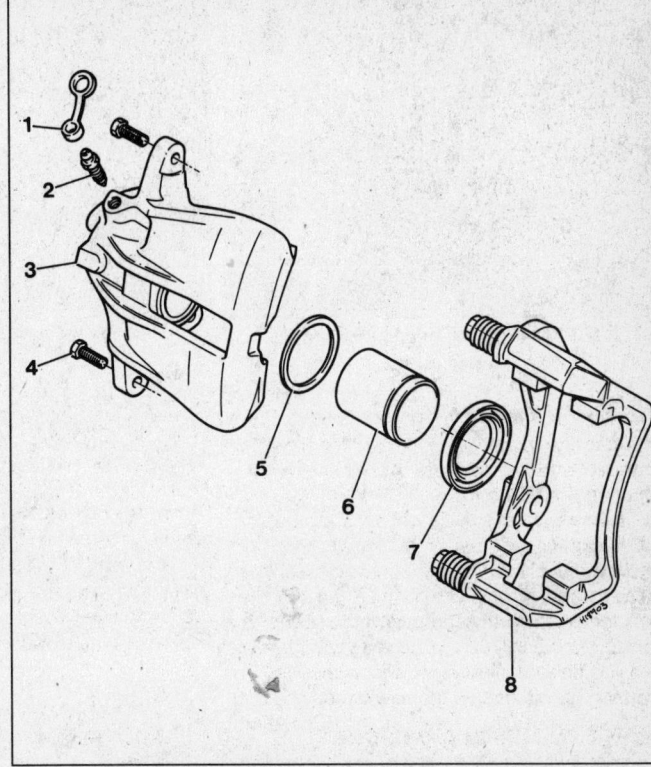

Fig 9.4 Girling front brake calliper (Sec 5)

1 Bleed screw cap
2 Bleed screw
3 Calliper

4 Guide pin bolt
5 Seal
6 Piston

7 Dust cap
8 Frame

clamp to cover the open cylinder while the remaining piston is removed.

6 Prise the piston seal(s) from the bore(s), taking care not to scratch the bore surface. Remove the dust cap(s) from the piston(s).

7 Unscrew the bleed screw.

8 Clean all the components with methylated spirit, and allow to dry.

9 Examine the surface of the piston and bore for signs of corrosion and scoring. Where evident the calliper should be renewed complete, however if the surfaces are good

Fig 9.5 Twin piston front brake calliper (Sec 5)

1 Guide pin bolt
2 Bleed screw
3 Bleed screw cap
4 Calliper
5 Piston seal
6 Piston
7 Dust cap
8 Frame
9 Guide pin
10 Protective cap

Fig 9.6 Removing a piston seal – take care not to scratch the bore surface (Sec 5)

9

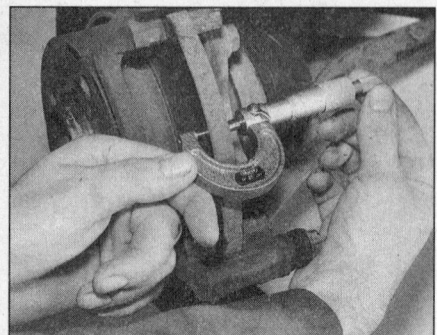

6.4 Checking the front brake disc thickness

obtain a repair kit containing new seals.

10 Commence reassembly by smearing a little brake cylinder fluid on the surface of the bore(s) and piston(s).

11 Locate the piston seal(s) in the bore groove(s).

12 To refit the piston, position the dust cap on the plain end of the piston, then offer the piston to the calliper, and use a screwdriver to lift the dust cap into the calliper groove. Now press the piston into the bore until the dust cap snaps into the groove on the outer end of the piston.

13 Fit a new rubber cap on the bleed screw. Apply a little brake fluid to the threads, then tighten the bleed screw into the calliper.

14 On the Girling calliper, apply a little grease to the guide pins before inserting them.

15 On the Teves calliper, check the guide pin bushes (which are made of Teflon), and if necessary renew them. Also check the rubber bushes.

6 Brake discs - examination, removal and refitting

1 Jack up the front or rear of the car and support on axle stands. Remove the roadwheel.
2 Rotate the disc and examine it for deep scoring or grooving. Light scoring is normal, but if excessive, the disc should be removed and renewed, or reground within the specified limits by a suitably-equipped engineering works. To ensure even braking both front or both rear brake discs should be renewed or reground at the same time.
3 Remove the front or rear brake calliper and bracket as described in Section 4 or 11. Do not disconnect the hydraulic hose but suspend the calliper by wire from the coil spring, making sure that the hose is not strained.
4 Remove the brake pads, then use a micrometer in several positions to check the disc thickness (photo). If it is worn down to the specified minimum thickness, again, both front or both rear discs should be renewed or reground together.

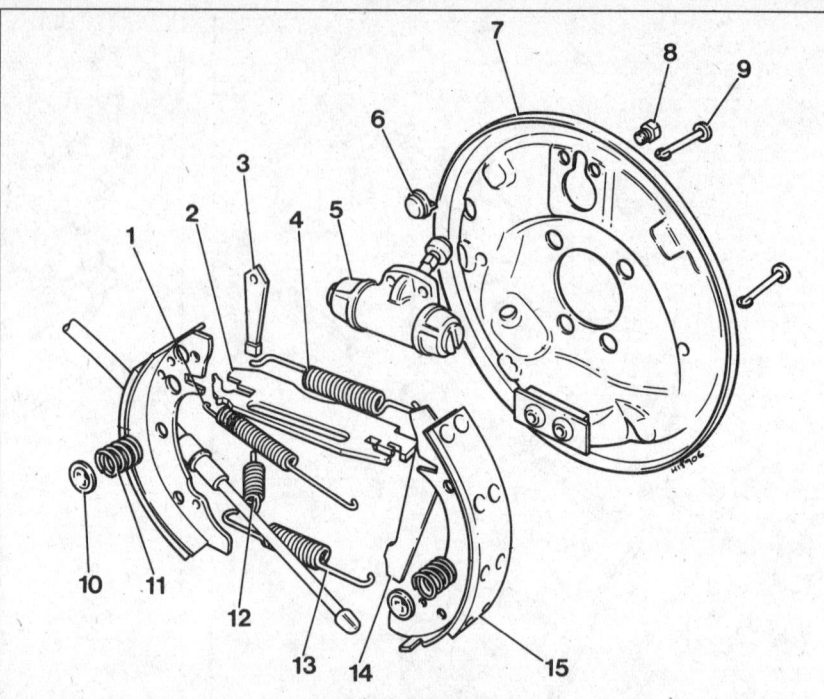

Fig 9.7 Rear brake drum components (Sec 7)

1 Upper return spring	6 Plug	11 Anti-rattle spring
2 Pushrod	7 Backplate	12 Wedge spring
3 Wedge	8 Bolt	13 Lower return spring
4 Tensioning spring	9 Anti-rattle spring pin	14 Handbrake operating lever
5 Wheel cylinder	10 Cap	15 Brake shoe

5 Remove the countersunk cross-head screw, and withdraw the brake disc from the hub.
6 Refitting is a reversal of removal, but make sure that the mating faces of the hub and disc are clean.

7 Rear brake shoes - inspection and renewal

1 The thickness of the rear brake linings can be checked without removing the brake drums. Remove the rubber plug which is above the handbrake cable entry on the brake backplate (photo). Use a torch to increase visibility and check the thickness of friction material remaining on the brake shoes. If the amount remaining is close to the minimum given in the Specifications, a more thorough examination should be made by removing the brake drum.
2 Chock the front wheels, then jack up the rear of the car and support it on axle stands. Remove the rear wheels and release the handbrake.
3 Remove the cap from the centre of the brake drum by tapping it on alternate sides with a screwdriver or blunt chisel.
4 Extract the split pin and remove the locking ring.
5 Unscrew the nut and remove the thrustwasher.

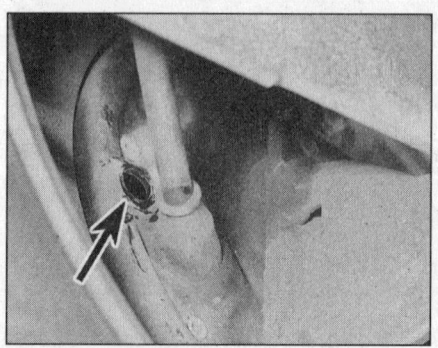

7.1 Rear brake shoe lining inspection hole (arrowed)

7.7 Rear brake shoe assembly

7.8 Brake shoe steady spring and cap

7.9 Brake shoe lower return spring (arrowed)

7.22 Brake shoes located on the wheel

6 Withdraw the brake drum, making sure that the outer wheel bearing does not fall out. If the brake drum binds on the shoes, insert a small screwdriver through a wheel bolt hole and lever up the wedged key in order to release the shoes.

7 Note the position of the brake shoes and springs, and mark the webs of the shoes, if necessary, to aid refitting (photo).

8 Using pliers, depress the spring retainer caps, turn them through 90° and remove them, together with the springs (photo).

9 Unhook the lower return spring from the shoes (photo).

10 Detach the bottom of the shoes from the bottom anchor, then release the top of the shoes from the wheel cylinder and swivel down to reveal the rear of the shoes.

11 Disconnect the handbrake cable, then clamp the bottom of the shoes in a vice.

12 Unhook the upper return spring and wedged key spring.

13 Separate the trailing shoe from the leading shoe and pushrod.

14 Unhook the tensioning spring, and remove the pushrod from the leading shoe, together with the wedged key.

15 Brush the dust from the brake drum, brake shoes, and backplate, *but do not inhale it, as it is injurious to health*. Scrape any scale or rust from the drum.

16 Measure the brake shoe lining thickness.

If it is worn down to the specified minimum amount, renew all four rear brake shoes.

17 Clean the brake backplate. If there are any signs of loss of grease from the rear hub bearings, the oil seal should be renewed, with reference to Chapter 10. If hydraulic fluid is leaking from the wheel cylinder, it must be repaired or renewed, as described in Section 8. Do not touch the brake pedal while the shoes are removed. Position an elastic band over the wheel cylinder pistons to retain them.

18 Apply a little brake grease to the contact areas of the pushrod and handbrake lever.

19 Clamp the pushrod in a vice, then hook the tensioning spring on the pushrod and leading shoe and position the shoe slot over the pushrod .

20 Fit the wedged key between the shoe and pushrod.

21 Locate the handbrake lever on the trailing shoe in the pushrod, and fit the upper return spring.

22 Connect the handbrake cable to the handbrake lever, swivel the shoes upwards, and locate the top of the shoes on the wheel cylinder pistons (photo).

23 Fit the lower return spring to the shoes, then lever the bottom of the shoes onto the bottom anchor.

24 Fit the spring to the wedged key and leading shoe.

25 Fit the retaining springs and caps.

26 Press the wedged key upwards to give the maximum shoe clearance.

27 Fit the brake drum and adjust the wheel bearings, with reference to Chapter 10.

28 Depress the brake pedal once firmly in order to adjust the rear brakes.

29 Repeat the procedure on the remaining rear brake, then lower the car to the ground.

8 Rear wheel cylinder - removal, overhaul and refitting

1 Remove the brake shoes, as described in Section 7.

2 Remove the brake fluid reservoir filler cap, and tighten it down onto a piece of polythene sheeting placed over the reservoir filler hole, in order to prevent the loss of fluid in the following procedure. Alternatively, fit a brake hose clamp on the hydraulic hose between the rear axle and underbody.

3 Loosen the brake pipe union on the rear of the wheel cylinder (photo).

4 Using an Allen key, unscrew the wheel cylinder mounting bolts.

5 Unscrew the brake pipe union and withdraw the wheel cylinder from the backplate. Plug the end of the hydraulic pipe, if necessary.

6 Clean the exterior of the wheel cylinder, taking care not to allow any foreign matter to enter the hydraulic pipe aperture.

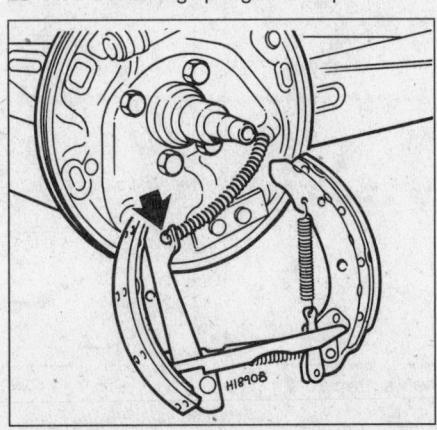

Fig 9.8 Method of fully retracting brake shoes to remove a tight brake drum (Sec 7)

Fig 9.9 Disconnecting the handbrake cable (Sec 7)

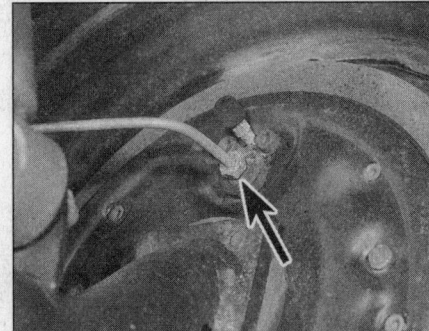

8.3 Brake pipe union connection (arrowed) to the rear of the wheel cylinder

9

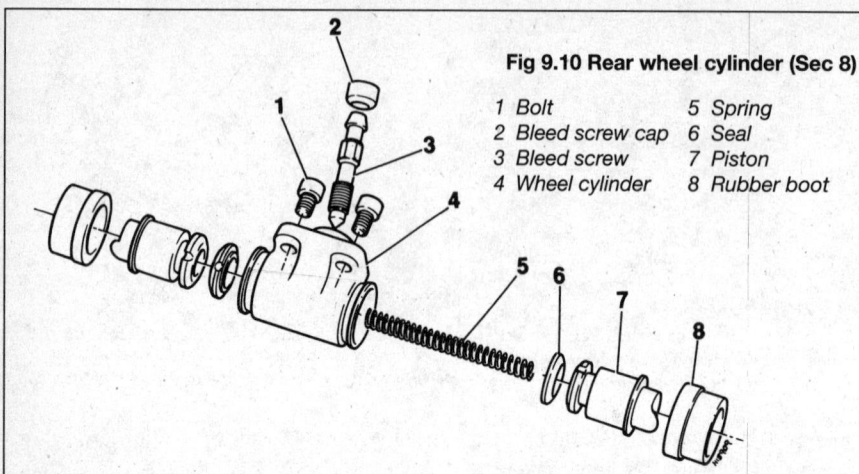

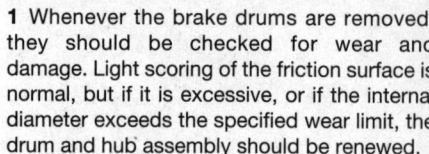

Fig 9.10 Rear wheel cylinder (Sec 8)

1 Bolt	5 Spring
2 Bleed screw cap	6 Seal
3 Bleed screw	7 Piston
4 Wheel cylinder	8 Rubber boot

7 Remove the rubber boots from the ends of the cylinder, and extract the two pistons and the spring between them.

8 Inspect the cylinder bore for signs of scoring and corrosion, and the pistons and seals for wear. If the cylinder is satisfactory, a repair kit can be used; otherwise the cylinder should be discarded and a new complete assembly fitted. If servicing a cylinder, use all the parts in the repair kit. Clean all the metal parts, using methylated spirit if necessary, *but never petrol or similar solvents,* then leave the parts to dry in the air, or dry them with a lint-free cloth.

9 Apply brake fluid to the seals, and fit them, so that their larger diameter end is nearest to the end of the piston.

10 Smear brake fluid on to the pistons and into the bore of the cylinder. Fit a piston into one end of the cylinder, and then the spring and other piston into the other end. Take care not to force the pistons into the cylinders, because this can twist the seals.

11 Locate the rubber boots over the pistons and into the grooves of the wheel cylinder.

12 Refitting is a reversal of removal, but bleed the hydraulic system as described in Section 17.

9 Brake drum - inspection and renovation

1 Whenever the brake drums are removed, they should be checked for wear and damage. Light scoring of the friction surface is normal, but if it is excessive, or if the internal diameter exceeds the specified wear limit, the drum and hub assembly should be renewed.

2 After a high mileage, the friction surface may become oval. Where this has occurred, it may be possible to have the surface ground true by a qualified engineering works. However, it is preferable to renew the drum and hub assembly.

10 Rear brake pads - inspection, removal and refitting

1 Chock the front wheels, then jack up the rear of the car and support on axle stands.

2 The thickness of the outer rear brake pads may be checked by looking through the holes in the wheels, using a torch if necessary. The inner pads may be checked using a mirror and torch, and looking through the holes in the rear of the brake callipers.

3 If any pad is worn down to the specified

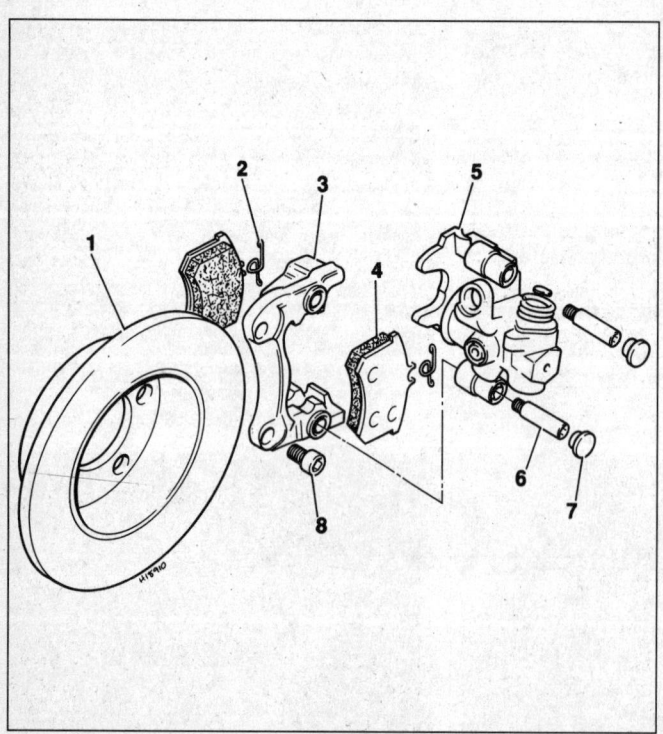

Fig 9.11 Teves rear disc brake components (Sec 10)

1 Brake disc	4 Brake pads	7 Cap
2 Spring	5 Calliper	8 Frame bolt
3 Frame	6 Guide pin	

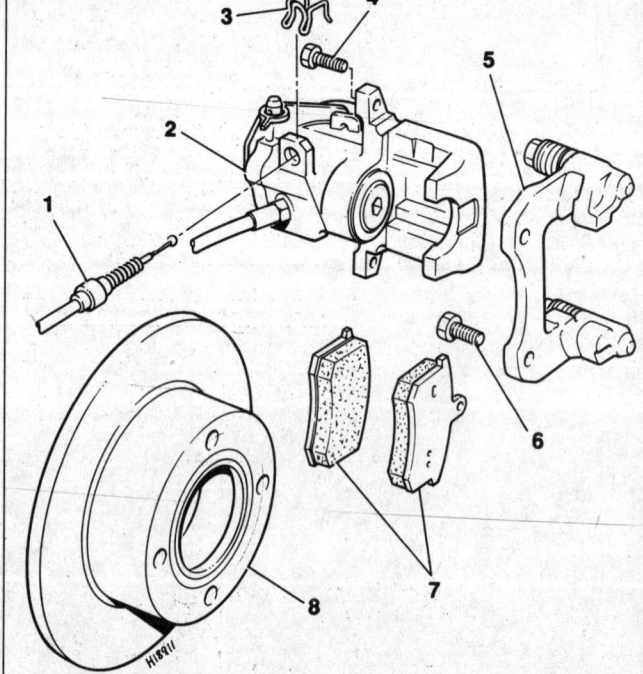

Fig 9.12 Girling rear disc brake components (Sec 10)

1 Handbrake cable	4 Bolt	7 Brake pads
2 Calliper	5 Frame	8 Brake disc
3 Spring clip	6 Frame bolt	

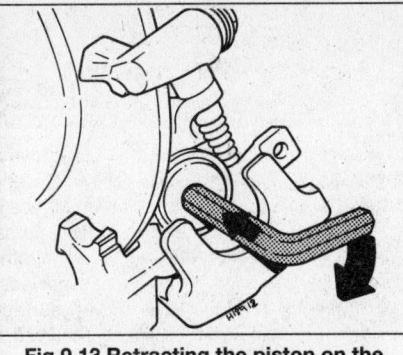

Fig 9.13 Retracting the piston on the Girling rear calliper (Sec 10)

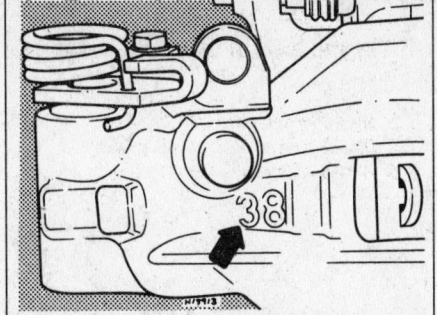

Fig 9.14 Rear calliper piston diameter identification (Sec 10)

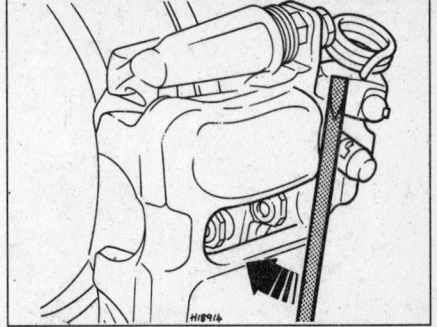

Fig 9.15 Levering the rear calliper handbrake arm against its stop (Sec 10)

minimum thickness, renew all the rear brake pads together.

4 If there is any doubt as to the thickness of the pads, remove both rear wheels for a more thorough investigation (photo).

5 To remove the pads, first remove the wheels. If the pads are to be re-used, mark them so that they may be refitted in their original positions.

Teves calliper

6 Prise the caps from the inner ends of the guide pins. If the caps are tight, use a pair of grips to remove them.

7 Using an Allen key, unscrew both guide pins, but do not remove them from the rubber bushes.

8 Pull the calliper slightly outwards, in order to force the piston into its bore and provide some clearance for the pads.

9 Swing the calliper to the rear and support to one side, taking care not to strain the hydraulic hose.

10 Remove the brake pads from the calliper frame.

Girling calliper

11 Unscrew and remove both guide pin bolts, while holding the guide pins with an open-ended spanner (photo).

12 Swing the calliper to the rear and support to one side, taking care not to strain the hydraulic hose (photo).

13 Remove the brake pads from the calliper frame. Also remove the heat shield (photos).

Teves and Girling callipers

14 Brush the dust and dirt from the calliper, piston, disc and pads, but *do not inhale it, as it is injurious to health*. Scrape any scale or rust from the disc and pad backing plates.

Teves calliper

15 Push the piston fully into the cylinder using a G-clamp and block of wood.

16 Locate the brake pads on the calliper frame.

17 Note that the set of new brake pads includes four self-locking bolts, which are for fitting to the Girling callipers **only**.

18 Locate the calliper over the pads, then insert and tighten the two guide pins.

19 Fit the caps on the guide pins.

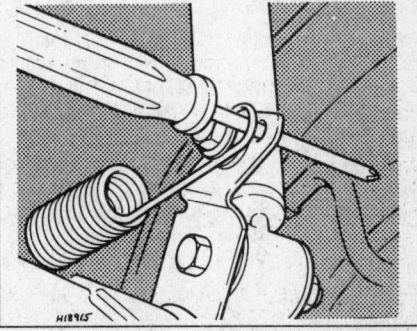

Fig 9.16 Setting the rear brake pressure regulator with a 6 mm (minimum diameter) screwdriver, when checking the rear brake adjustment (Sec 10)

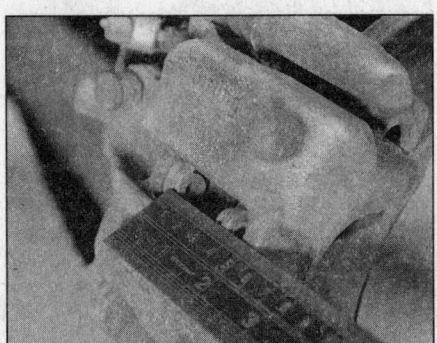

10.4 Checking the rear brake pad lining thickness

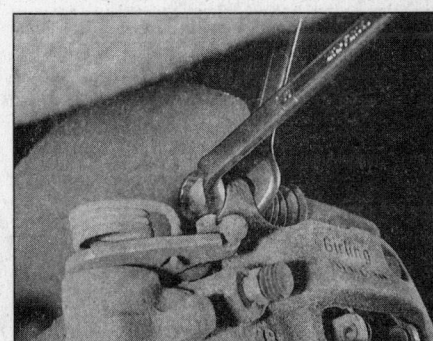

10.11 Guide pin bolt removal

10.12 Swing the calliper to the rear . . .

10.13A . . . remove the brake pads . . .

10.13B . . . and the heat shield

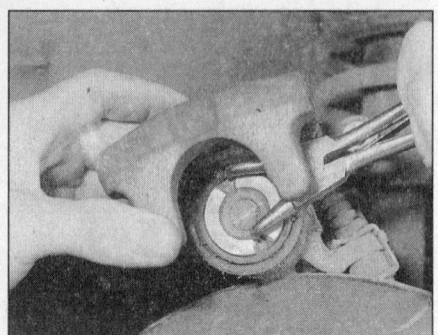

10.20 Using angled circlip pliers to screw in the piston

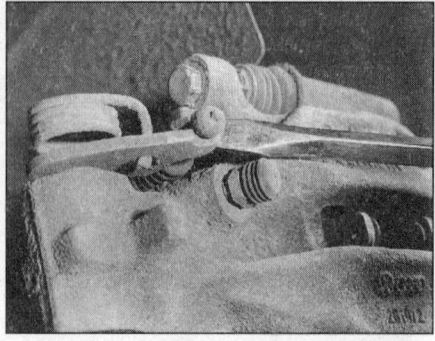

10.25 Using a screwdriver to lever the handbrake arm against its stop

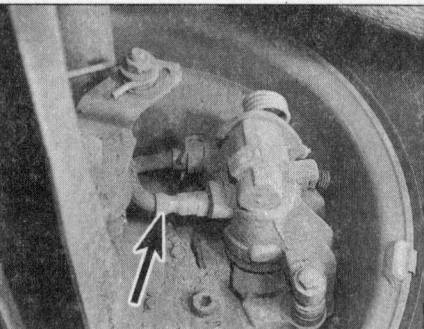

11.3 Hydraulic hose connection to the rear brake calliper

Girling calliper

20 Screw the piston into the cylinder, in order to accommodate the new brake pads. Use an Allen key to do this, while pushing firmly on the piston (see Fig. 9.13). On callipers with a 38 mm diameter piston (chassis number 89JA225957 on) identified with the number 38 instead of 36, Audi recommend the use of their tool number 3131. An alternative tool would be a pair of angled circlip pliers (photo). Refit the heat shield.

21 Locate the brake pads on the calliper frame.

22 Position the calliper over the pads.

23 Insert the new guide pin bolts (supplied with the new set of pads) and tighten them to the specified torque while holding the guide pins with an open-ended spanner.

Teves and Girling callipers

24 Fully release the handbrake.

25 Using a screwdriver, lever the handbrake arm on one of the rear callipers against its stop (photo). Now repeat the procedure on the opposite calliper, and check if the first lever remains on its stop. If it does not, the handbrake cable is adjusted too tightly, and the adjustment nut on the equalizer should be loosened as necessary.

26 Insert a screwdriver (of at least 6 mm diameter) between the rear spring hook and roller of the rear brake pressure regulator (Fig. 9.16).

27 With the engine switched off, pump the brake pedal forty times on callipers with 36 mm diameter pistons, or just once on callipers with 38 mm diameter pistons.

28 Check that both rear wheels rotate freely, then remove the screwdriver from the brake pressure regulator spring.

29 Lower the car to the ground.

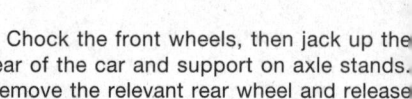

11 Rear brake calliper - removal and refitting

1 Chock the front wheels, then jack up the rear of the car and support on axle stands. Remove the relevant rear wheel and release the handbrake.

2 Fit a brake hose clamp to the flexible hose leading to the brake calliper. Alternatively, remove the brake fluid reservoir filler cap and tighten it down onto a piece of polythene sheeting placed over the reservoir filler hole. This will reduce the loss of fluid in the following procedure.

3 Loosen the hydraulic hose union, but do not unscrew it at this stage (photo).

4 Follow the procedure for removing the brake pads given in Section 10.

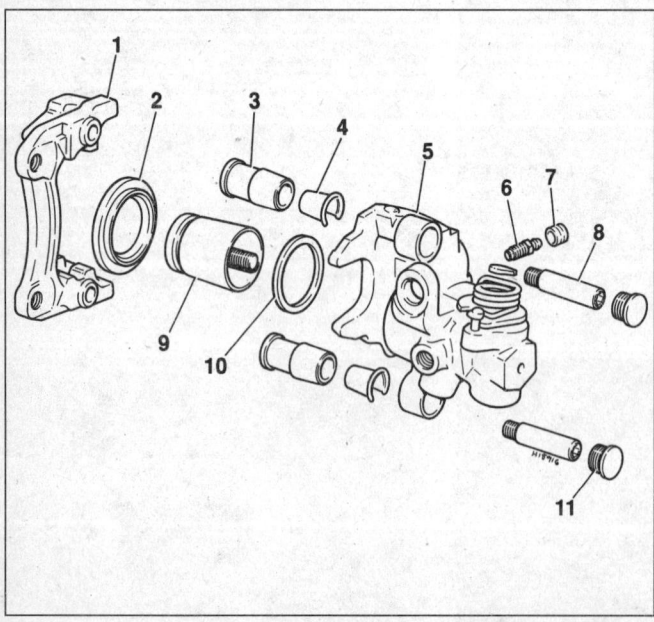

Fig 9.17 Teves rear brake calliper (Sec 12)

1 Frame	5 Calliper	9 Piston
2 Dust cap	6 Bleed screw	10 Seal
3 Rubber bush	7 Bleed screw cap	11 Cap
4 Teflon bush	8 Guide pin	

Fig 9.18 Girling rear brake calliper (Sec 12)

1 Guide pin bolt	4 Bleed screw dust cap	7 Guide pin
2 Calliper	5 Seal	8 Dust cap
3 Bleed screw	6 Piston	9 Rubber boot
		10 Frame

5 On the Girling calliper, remove the handbrake cable retaining spring clip.

6 Turn the handbrake operating arm, unhook the inner cable, and withdraw the outer cable from the calliper.

7 Unscrew the calliper from the hydraulic hose. Plug the end of the hose.

8 If necessary, unbolt the calliper bracket frame from the rear axle.

9 Refitting is a reversal of removal, but make sure that all mating faces are clean, and tighten the bolts and union to the specified torques. Finally bleed the hydraulic system as described in Section 17. If the loss of hydraulic fluid has been minimal, it may be sufficient to bleed just the one calliper.

12 Rear brake calliper - overhaul

1 Clean the exterior of the calliper. Do not allow any foreign matter to enter the hydraulic hose aperture.

2 Mount the calliper in a vice, with the piston facing upwards.

3 Prise the piston dust cap from the groove in the calliper.

4 On the Teves calliper, place a piece of wood in the calliper jaws opposite the piston, then using air pressure from an air line or foot pump, force the piston from the bore. Apply the air pressure through the hydraulic fluid inlet.

5 On the Girling calliper, use an Allen key to unscrew the piston from the bore.

6 Prise the piston seal from the bore, taking care not to scratch the bore surface. Remove the dust cap from the piston.

7 Unscrew the bleed screw.

8 Clean all the components with methylated spirit, and allow to dry.

9 Examine the surface of the piston and bore for signs of corrosion and scoring. Check the automatic adjuster threads for wear and damage. Check the calliper housing for signs of fluid leakage around the handbrake operating arm. Check the guide pins, seals and bushes as applicable for wear. Renew the components as required. On the Girling calliper, the bracket frame is supplied together with the guide pins already greased.

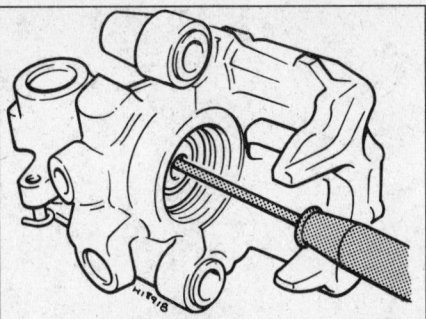

Fig 9.19 Pressing in the clamping piece on the Teves rear calliper (Sec 12)

10 If the calliper and piston are in good condition, obtain a repair kit of seals.

11 Commence reassembly by smearing a little brake fluid on the surface of the bore and piston.

12 Locate the piston seal in the bore groove.

13 To refit the piston on the Teves calliper, first press the clamping piece inside the calliper against its stop using a screwdriver (see Fig. 9.19). Check that the threaded insert turns freely. Position the dust cap on the plain end of the piston, then offer the piston to the calliper, and turn it slightly so that the automatic thread engages. Using a screwdriver, lift the dust cap into the calliper groove. Press the piston fully into its bore, making sure that it enters centrally and squarely to avoid damage to the automatic adjuster. The Audi tool for doing this is shown in Fig. 9.20. The careful use of a G-clamp will serve the same purpose. As the piston enters the bore, the dust cap will snap into the groove on the outer end of the piston.

14 To refit the piston on the Girling calliper, position the dust cap on the plain end of the piston, then offer the piston to the calliper. Use a screwdriver to lift the dust cap into the calliper groove. Using an Allen key, screw the piston into the bore while pressing on it firmly. The dust cap will snap into the groove on the outer end of the piston.

15 Fit a new rubber cap on the bleed screw. Apply a little brake fluid to the threads, then tighten the bleed screw into the calliper.

16 New Girling callipers are supplied already filled with brake fluid. Audi also recommend filling and bleeding a Girling calliper after

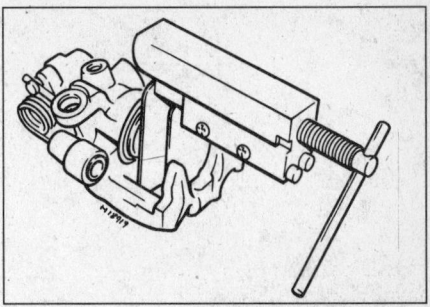

Fig 9.20 Using the special Audi tool to press the piston into the Teves rear calliper (Sec 12)

overhaul. The procedure can also be carried out on Teves callipers.

17 Mount the calliper in a vice, with the hydraulic inlet uppermost. Loosen the bleed screw and connect a brake fluid supply to it. Fill the calliper until the fluid emerges free of air bubbles, then tighten the bleed screw. Plug the fluid inlet if necessary.

13 Master cylinder - removal and refitting

1 Depress the footbrake pedal several times to dissipate the vacuum in the vacuum servo unit, or release the pressure in the hydraulic servo unit (as applicable).

2 Remove the brake fluid reservoir filler cap (photo), and draw off the fluid using a syringe or flexible plastic bottle. Take care not to spill the fluid on the car's paintwork - if some is accidentally spilled, wash it off immediately with copious amounts of cold water.

3 Where applicable, disconnect the clutch supply tube from the reservoir (photo).

4 Identify the hydraulic brake pipes for location using adhesive tape.

5 Place some rags beneath the master cylinder, then unscrew the union nuts and pull the brake pipes just clear of the master cylinder. Plug the ends of the pipes, or cover them with masking tape.

6 Unscrew the mounting nuts or bolts (as applicable), and withdraw the master cylinder from the front of the servo unit (photo). Remove the seal for the servo unit.

13.2 Brake fluid reservoir and filler cap

13.3 Clutch supply tube (arrowed)

13.6 Brake master cylinder and mounting nuts (arrowed)

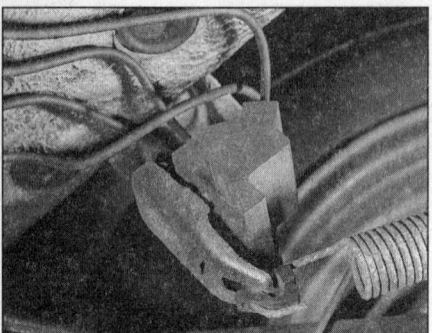

15.1 Brake pressure regulator

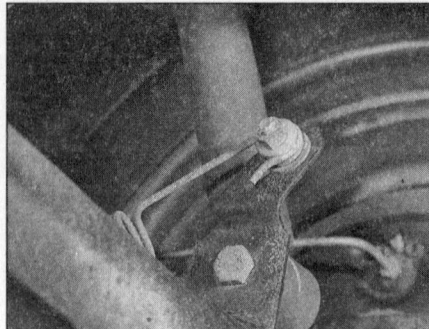

15.5 Brake pressure regulator control spring, roller, and adjustment bolt

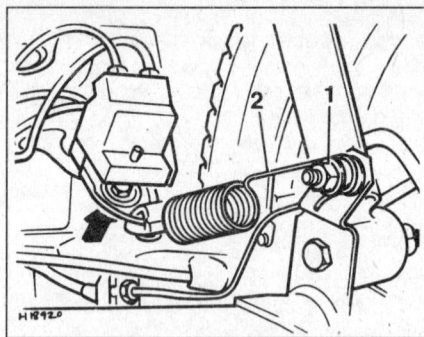

Fig 9.21 Adjusting the rear brake pressure regulator (Sec 15)

1 Adjustment nut and bolt   2 Spring

7 Refitting is a reversal of removal, but fit a new seal to the servo unit, and finally bleed the hydraulic system as described in Section 17. The brake pipe union nuts should be tightened firmly, but not overtightened, otherwise the flange on the end of the pipe may be damaged.

14 Master cylinder - overhaul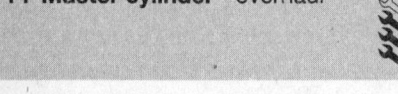

1 The master cylinder is sealed, and it is therefore not possible to dismantle it, or to fit new seals. If faulty, renew it complete.
2 The reservoir may be removed by pulling it from the rubber grommets. Prise out the grommets with a screwdriver.
3 Clean the master cylinder inlet ports. Dip the grommets in clean brake fluid, and press them into the master cylinder, then press the reservoir into the grommets.

15 Brake pressure regulator - testing and adjustment

1 The brake pressure regulator is located on the right-hand side of the rear axle, and is controlled by the up-and-down movement of the rear axle (photo).
2 To test the operation of the regulator, have an assistant depress the footbrake firmly, then release it quickly. With the weight of the car

on the suspension, the arm on the regulator should move, indicating that the unit is not seized.
3 To test the regulator for leakage, pressure gauges must be connected to the left-hand front calliper and right-hand rear wheel cylinder or calliper as applicable. As the equipment will not normally be available to the home mechanic, this work should be entrusted to an Audi dealer. However, an outline of the procedure is as follows. Depress the brake pedal so that the pressure in the left-hand front calliper is 100 bar (1450 lbf/in²). Hold this pressure for five seconds, and check that the pressure in the right-hand rear wheel cylinder or calliper varies by no more than 10 bar (145 lbf/in²).
4 Note that it is normal for a small quantity of brake fluid to seep out of the outlet drilling in the regulator over a period of time.
5 Before adjusting the regulator, unscrew the nut, unhook the control spring and remove the plastic roller from the adjustment bolt (photo). Clean the bush and apply a little grease to it, then refit the roller, nut and spring, leaving the nut loose.
6 The car should be at normal kerb weight, and the rear suspension at normal height. Bounce the rear of the car several times to settle the suspension.
7 Press the regulator lever fully to the rear so that it is on its stop.
8 On Audi 90 models, position a 1.0 mm drill between the hooked end of the spring and the plastic roller. On Coupe models, use a 7.0 mm drill instead .

9 Move the adjustment bolt so that all slack is taken up without stretching the coil spring, then tighten the nut to lock it.
10 Remove the drill where applicable, and push the spring fully onto the plastic roller.

16 Hydraulic brake lines and hoses - removal and refitting

1 Before removing a brake line or hose, unscrew the brake fluid reservoir filler cap and tighten it down onto a piece of polythene sheeting placed over the reservoir filler hole, in order to reduce the loss of fluid. Alternatively, fit a brake hose clamp on the rear brake hose if a rear brake line is being removed.
2 To remove a rigid line, unscrew the union nuts at each end, prise open the clips (where fitted) and withdraw the line (photo). Refitting is a reversal of removal.
3 To remove a flexible brake hose, unscrew the union nut securing the rigid brake line to the end of the flexible hose, while holding the end of the flexible hose stationary (photos). Remove the clip and withdraw the hose from the bracket. Unscrew the remaining end from the component or rigid pipe according to position. Refitting is a reversal of removal.
4 Bleed the hydraulic system as described in Section 17 after fitting a rigid brake line or flexible brake hose.

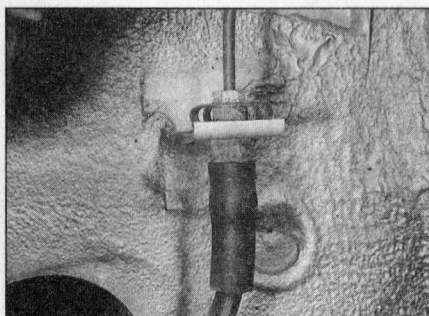

16.2 Front brake lines and bracket

16.3A Rear flexible brake hose

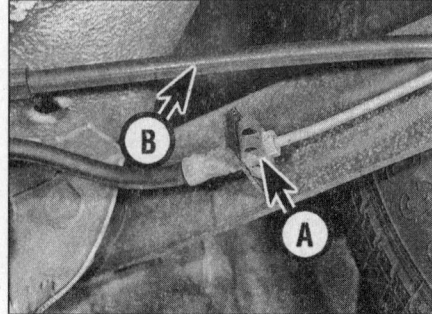

16.3B Rear brake lines and bracket (A), and handbrake cable (B)

17 Hydraulic system - bleeding

1 If any of the hydraulic components in the braking system have been removed or disconnected, or if the fluid level in the master cylinder has been allowed to fall appreciably, it is inevitable that air will have been introduced into the system. The removal of all this air from the hydraulic system is essential if the brakes are to function correctly, and the process of removing it is known as bleeding.

2 There are a number of one-man, do-it-yourself, brake bleeding kits currently available from motor accessory shops. It is recommended that one of these kits should be used whenever possible, as they greatly simplify the bleeding operation, and also reduce the risk of expelled air and fluid being drawn back into the system.

3 If one of these kits is not available, then it will be necessary to gather together a clean jar and a suitable length of clear plastic tubing which is a tight fit over the bleed screw, and also to engage the help of an assistant.

4 Before commencing the bleeding operation, check that all rigid pipes and flexible hoses are in good condition, and that all hydraulic unions are tight. Take great care not to allow hydraulic fluid to come into contact with the car's paintwork, otherwise the finish will be seriously damaged. Wash off any spilled fluid immediately with cold water.

5 If hydraulic fluid has been lost from the master cylinder, due to a leak in the system, ensure that the cause is traced and rectified before proceeding further, or a serious malfunction of the braking system may occur

6 To bleed the system, clean the area around the bleed screw to be bled. If the hydraulic system has only been partially disconnected on one of the wheel circuits, and suitable precautions taken to prevent further loss of fluid, it should only be necessary to bleed that part of the system. However, if the entire system is to be bled, the following sequence must be adhered to:
- (1) The brake master cylinder on models with ABS only
- (2) Right-hand rear wheel cylinder or calliper
- (3) Left-hand rear wheel cylinder or calliper
- (4) Right-hand front calliper
- (5) Left-hand front calliper

7 When bleeding the rear wheel cylinders or callipers on models with a brake pressure regulator, have an assistant push the regulator lever fully to the rear.

8 Remove the brake fluid reservoir filler cap, and top up the fluid level (photo). Periodically check the fluid level during the bleeding operation and top up as necessary.

9 With all the bleed screws tight, pump the brake pedal quickly several times in order to build up initial pressure in the system.

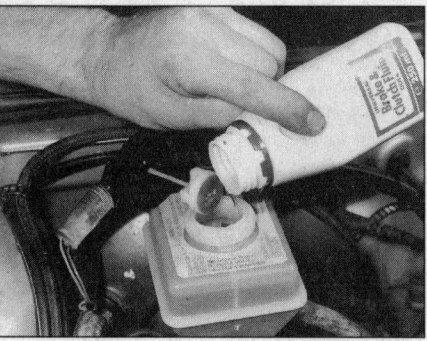

17.8 Topping-up the brake fluid level

10 If a one-man brake bleeding kit is being used, connect the outlet tube to the bleed screw and then open the screw half a turn (photo). If possible, position the unit so that it can be viewed from the car, then depress the brake pedal to the floor and slowly release it. The one-way valve in the kit will prevent expelled air from returning to the system at the end of each stroke. Repeat this operation until clean hydraulic fluid, free from air bubbles, can be seen coming through the tube. Now tighten the bleed screw and remove the outlet tube.

11 If a one-man brake bleeding kit is not available, connect one end of the plastic tubing to the bleed screw and immerse the other end in the jar containing sufficient clean hydraulic fluid to keep the end of the tube submerged. Open the bleed screw half a turn, and have your assistant depress the brake pedal to the floor and then slowly release it.

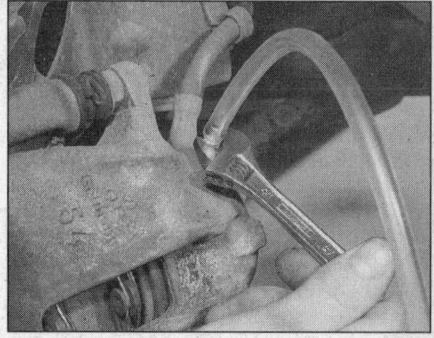

17.10 Bleeding a brake calliper

Tighten the bleed screw at the end of each downstroke, to prevent expelled air and fluid from being drawn back into the system. Repeat this operation until clean hydraulic fluid, free from air bubbles, can be seen coming through the tube. Now tighten the bleed screw and remove the plastic tube.

12 If the entire system is being bled the procedures described above should now be repeated at each wheel. Do not forget to recheck the fluid level in the reservoir at regular intervals, and top up as necessary.

13 When completed, recheck the fluid level in the reservoir, top up if necessary, and refit the cap. Check the 'feel' of the brake pedal; this should be firm, and free from any 'sponginess', which would indicate air still present in the system.

14 Discard any expelled hydraulic fluid, as it is likely to be contaminated with moisture, air and dirt, making it unsuitable for further use.

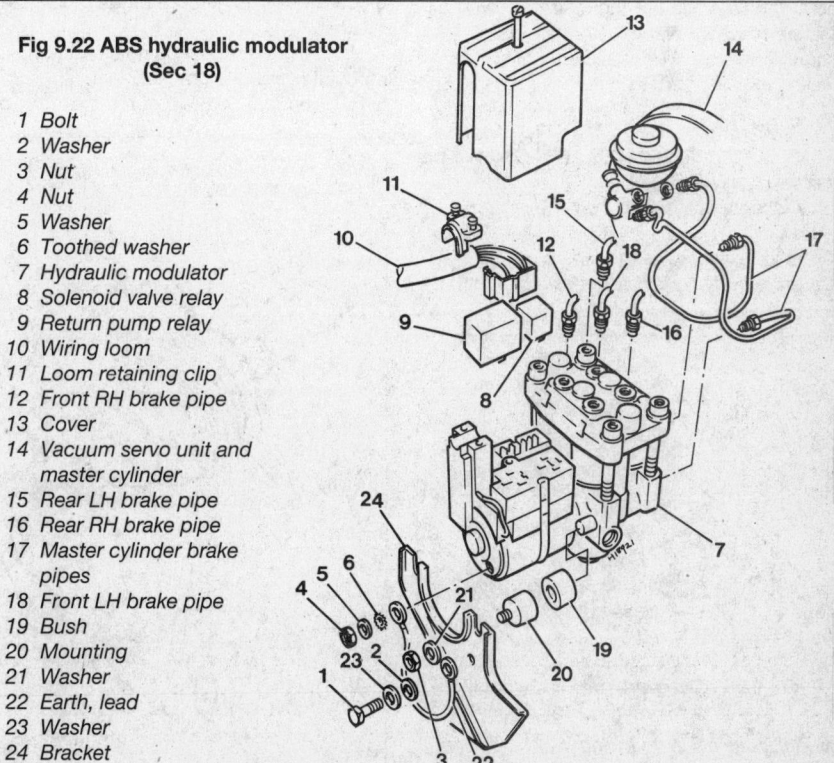

Fig 9.22 ABS hydraulic modulator (Sec 18)

1 Bolt
2 Washer
3 Nut
4 Nut
5 Washer
6 Toothed washer
7 Hydraulic modulator
8 Solenoid valve relay
9 Return pump relay
10 Wiring loom
11 Loom retaining clip
12 Front RH brake pipe
13 Cover
14 Vacuum servo unit and master cylinder
15 Rear LH brake pipe
16 Rear RH brake pipe
17 Master cylinder brake pipes
18 Front LH brake pipe
19 Bush
20 Mounting
21 Washer
22 Earth, lead
23 Washer
24 Bracket

18 Anti-lock braking system (ABS) - general

The anti-lock braking system (ABS) is available as a factory-fitted option on certain models. The system is maintenance-free.

The system prevents the roadwheels locking, even under heavy braking on slippery roads, thereby enabling the driver to retain full steering control.

Wheel speed sensors monitor the rotational speed of each roadwheel. As soon as a wheel is on the point of locking, pressure regulators reduce the hydraulic pressure to that wheel until it starts to rotate again, at which point braking pressure is re-applied. This process is repeated many times each second, ensuring that maximum braking effort is available.

The driver is made aware of the operation of the system by oscillation felt through the brake pedal, and an audible warning. This is intended to warn the driver of potential wheel lock-up under braking, and road speed should be reduced accordingly.

The system switches on automatically when the engine is started, and a warning lamp is fitted. This lamp should normally go out with the engine running, but if it does not, or if it comes on during driving, test the system by switching off and on with the main control switch. If the lamp is still lit, it indicates a fault with the ABS system - normal braking only is available.

The main control switch provided on the facia enables the ABS system to be switched off at the discretion of the driver, for driving in certain road conditions. Normally the system should not be switched off unless brake testing is being carried out.

Precautions

On cars equipped with ABS, observe the following precautions.
(a) Disconnect the plug from the system electronic control unit before carrying out any electric welding to the body
(b) If the bodywork is to be 'baked' after paint refinishing, the temperature may be allowed to reach 85°C (185°F) for up to two hours, or 95°C (203° F) for brief periods
(c) Always disconnect the battery before removing the modulator

19 Anti-lock braking system (ABS) components - removal and refitting

Note: *After carrying out any of the procedures described in this Section, it is recommended that the anti-lock braking system is completely tested by an Audi dealer, who will have the special test equipment and rolling road necessary.*

Hydraulic modulator

1 Disconnect the battery negative lead.
2 Where applicable, remove the cooling system expansion tank with reference to Chapter 2, and position it to one side.
3 Accurately identify each brake pipe for its location on the hydraulic modulator.
4 Unscrew the brake fluid reservoir cap, and tighten it down onto a piece of polythene sheeting placed over the reservoir filler hole, in order to reduce the loss of fluid. Alternatively, the fluid may be syphoned out of the reservoir into a container.
5 Unscrew the union nuts and disconnect the brake pipes. Plug the ends of the pipes, or cover them with masking tape, to prevent entry of dust and dirt.
6 Lift the cover from the modulator, and disconnect the wiring plugs and harness retainer.
7 Unscrew the mounting nuts and remove the modulator from its bracket.
8 Refitting is a reversal of removal, but bleed the complete hydraulic system as described in Section 17.

Electronic control unit

9 This is located beneath the left-hand side of the rear seat cushion.
10 Check that the ignition is switched off.
11 Remove the seat cushion (Chapter 11).
12 Depress the retaining spring, and disconnect the wiring multi-plug.
13 Unscrew both retaining screws and remove the electronic control unit.
14 Refitting is a reversal of removal, but make sure that the retaining spring is fully engaged to secure the multi-plug.

Relays

15 There are two relays on the hydraulic modulator, one for the solenoid valve, and one for the return pump. There is also a combination relay located in an additional relay board below the facia panel.
16 Switch off the ignition before removing a relay.
17 To remove the relays from the modulator, first remove the cover then pull the relay direct from its socket.
18 Refer to Chapter 12 for the removal of the relay from the additional relay board.
19 Refitting is a reversal of removal.

Wheel speed sensors

20 Jack up the front or rear of the car and support on axle stands. Remove the roadwheel.
21 On early models, the sensor is retained by a socket-head bolt. Using a dab of paint, mark the exact position of the bolt in its elongated hole if the sensor is to be re-used. Unscrew the bolt and remove the sensor from the sleeve in the wheel bearing housing or rear axle as applicable. Recover the seal.

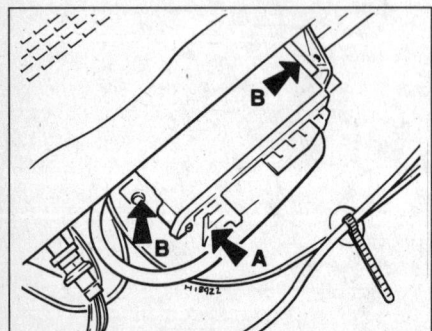

Fig 9.23 ABS electronic control unit removal (Sec 19)

A Multiplug retaining spring
B Retaining screws

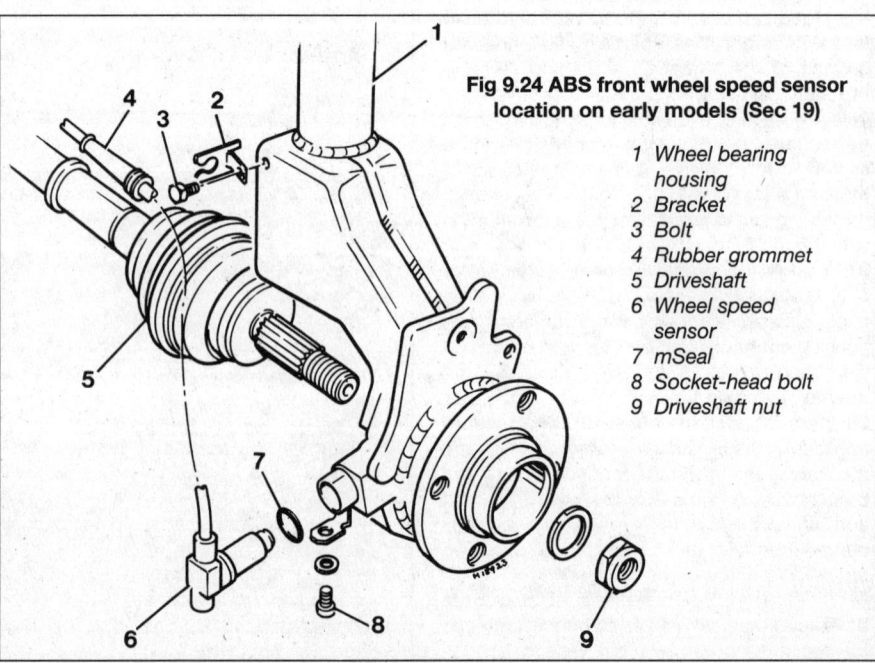

Fig 9.24 ABS front wheel speed sensor location on early models (Sec 19)

1 Wheel bearing housing
2 Bracket
3 Bolt
4 Rubber grommet
5 Driveshaft
6 Wheel speed sensor
7 mSeal
8 Socket-head bolt
9 Driveshaft nut

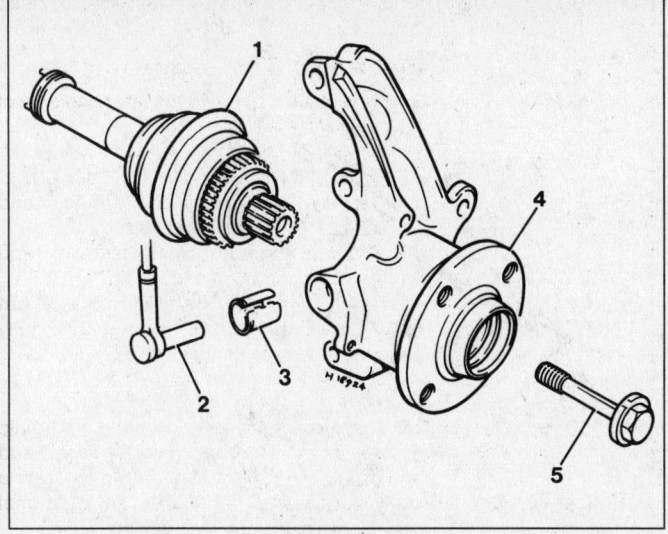

Fig 9.25 ABS front wheel speed sensor on later models (Sec 19)

1 Driveshaft
2 Wheel speed sensor
3 Clamping sleeve
4 Wheel bearing housing
5 Driveshaft bolt

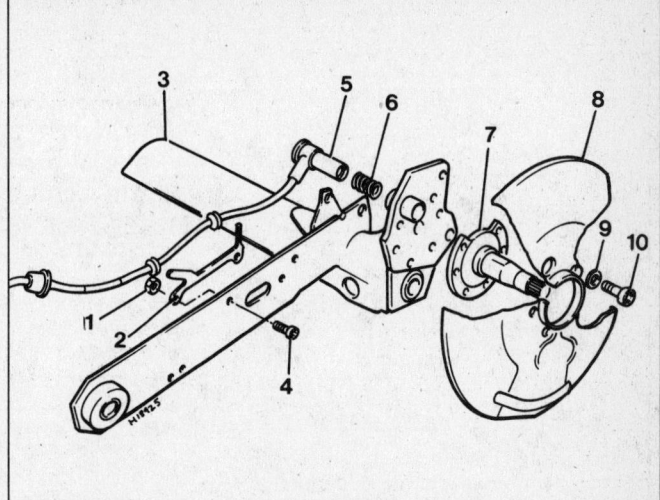

Fig 9.26 ABS rear wheel speed sensor location on later models (Sec 19)

1 Nut
2 Bracket
3 Rear axle
4 Bolt
5 Wheel speed sensor
6 Clamping sleeve
7 Stub axle
8 Backplate
9 Washer
10 Socket-head bolt

22 On later models, the sensor is retained by a clamping sleeve. Pull out the sensor, then remove the clamping sleeve from the wheel bearing housing or rear axle as applicable.

23 Release the sensor wiring from the bracket by pulling out the rubber grommet.

24 Separate the wiring connector located either in the engine compartment or beneath the rear seat cushion. On fuel injection models, first disconnect the air duct from the airflow meter and move it to one side.

25 Before refitting a *rear* sensor, check and if necessary adjust the rear wheel bearing play as described in Chapter 10.

26 To refit the sensor on early models, it is recommended that a new PVC tip is obtained and fitted to the end of the sensor. If, however, the sensor can be refitted in its exact original position, this should not be necessary. Fit a new seal, and coat the seal and sensor with brake cylinder paste. Insert the sensor and tighten the bolt, while pressing on the sensor to keep the PVC tip in contact with the rotor.

27 To refit the sensor on later models, first coat the clamping sleeve with brake cylinder paste, and press it fully into the wheel bearing housing or rear axle. Push the sensor fully into the clamping sleeve. Refit the rubber boot on the rear sensor (if fitted).

28 Re-connect the wiring, and where applicable, the air duct.

29 Press the rubber grommet into the bracket to secure the wiring.

30 Refit the roadwheel and lower the car to the ground.

Wheel speed sensor rotors

31 The front sensor rotors are incorporated in the driveshaft outer CV joints. The joints may be renewed separate to the driveshaft if necessary, with reference to Chapter 8.

32 To remove a rear sensor rotor, first remove the hub with reference to Chapter 10.

33 Mount the hub in a vice, and use a drift through the wheel bolt holes to drive off the rotor. Tap the rotor alternately on opposite sides to prevent it jamming on the hub.

34 A metal tube should be used to drive the rotor onto the hub, taking care not to damage the special sensor serrations.

35 Refit the hub with reference to Chapter 10.

20 Anti-lock braking system (ABS) - pressure test

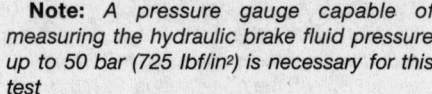

Note: *A pressure gauge capable of measuring the hydraulic brake fluid pressure up to 50 bar (725 lbf/in²) is necessary for this test*

1 Apply the handbrake, then raise the front of the car and support on axle stands.

2 Unscrew the bleed screw from one of the front brake callipers, and connect the pressure gauge to it. Bleed the gauge as necessary.

3 Using an adjustable brake pedal depresser between the driver's seat and pedal, depress the pedal until the pressure gauge indicates 50 bar (725 lbf/in²)

4 Check that over a period of 45 seconds, the pressure drops by no more than 4 bar (58 lbf/in²). If it does, first check for leaks in the hydraulic circuit, master cylinder and callipers. If these are not proved faulty, renew the hydraulic modulator.

5 Reduce the brake pedal pressure until the gauge indicates 6 bar (87 lbf/ in²),

6 Check that over the next three minutes, the pressure drops by no more than 1 bar (14.5 lbf/in²). If it does, renew the hydraulic modulator.

7 Remove the gauge, and refit the bleed screw.

8 Bleed the hydraulic system as described in Section 17.

9 Lower the car to the ground.

21 Brake pedal - removal and refitting

1 Working inside the car, unhook the return spring from the brake pedal and servo pushrod clevis. Remove the lower facia panel if necessary.

2 Extract the clip and remove the clevis pin securing the servo pushrod to the pedal.

3 Extract the clip from the end of the pivot shaft, and withdraw the pedal.

4 Clean the components, and check them for wear and damage. Temporarily refit the pedal, and check the bush for excessive wear. Check that the return spring and retaining clips are not damaged. Check the rubber foot pad for wear. Renew the components as necessary.

5 Refitting is a reversal of removal, but lubricate the pivot shaft with a little multi-purpose grease. Make sure that the pedal return spring is fitted with its bent end located on the pedal bracket. Its straight end should be located in the hole in the servo pushrod clevis.

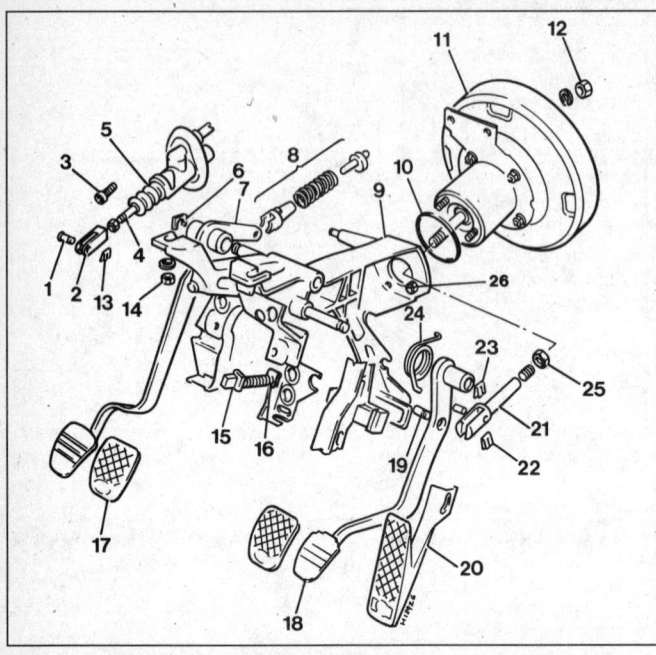

Fig 9.27 Pedal bracket components (Sec 21)

1	Clevis pin	9	Pedal bracket	18	Brake pedal
2	Clevis	10	O-ring	19	Clevis pin
3	Socket-head bolt	11	Vacuum servo unit	20	Accelerator pedal
4	Pushrod	12	Nut	21	Clevis
5	Clutch master	13	Clip	22	Clip
	cylinder	14	Nut	23	Clip
6	Circlip	15	Stop-light switch	24	Return spring
7	Clutch pedal	16	Clip	25	Locknut
8	Overcentre spring	17	Pedal pad	26	Nut

Fig 9.28 Handbrake lever components (Sec 22)

1	Hand grip	9	Toothed segment	17	Nut
2	Release button	10	Pivot pin	18	Leaf spring
3	Spring	11	Pivot pin	19	Handbrake
4	Handbrake lever	12	Roller		warning lamp
5	Soot	13	Washer		switch
6	Pivot pin	14	Pullrod	20	Self-tapping
7	Pushrod	15	Rubber boot		screw
8	Locking pawl	16	Compensator bar	21	Circlip

22 Handbrake lever -
removal and refitting

1 Working inside the car, prise out the plastic cover from the front of the tray beneath the handbrake lever. Remove the screw.
2 Remove the rear ashtray and unscrew the two screws retaining the rear of the centre console. On taxi models, the ashtray is secured with screws, and the centre console screws are external.
3 Remove the centre console over the handbrake lever.

4 Chock the front wheels, then jack up the rear of the car and support on axle stands. Remove the heat shield, where fitted (photo).
5 Unscrew the adjusting nut from the end of the handbrake lever rod, and remove the cable compensator bar (photo).
6 Remove the rubber bellows.
7 Working inside the car, extract the circlip and remove the lever pivot pin (photo).
8 Move the handbrake lever slightly to the rear, then withdraw it from the bracket.
9 If necessary, the handbrake lever may be dismantled as follows. Pull off the hand grip and unscrew the release button. Remove the spring. Pull off the rubber boot. To remove the

pawl, ratchet, pushrod, pullrod, and roller, it is necessary to grind off the two pivot pins.
10 Examine the components for wear, in particular the pawl and ratchet, and renew them as necessary. The pawl and ratchet should be renewed together.
11 Reassemble the handbrake lever in reverse order, using pivot pins riveted in position.
12 Refitting is a reversal of removal, but lubricate the pivots with a little multi-purpose grease. Make sure that the slot in the ratchet is engaged with the front of the bracket. Finally adjust the handbrake as described in Section 23.

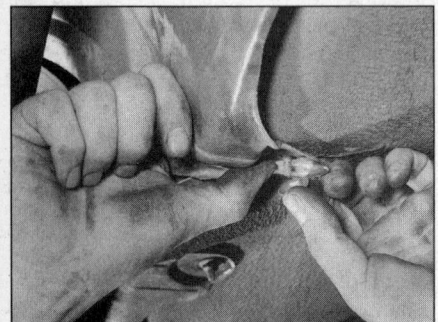

22.4 Removing the underbody heat shield

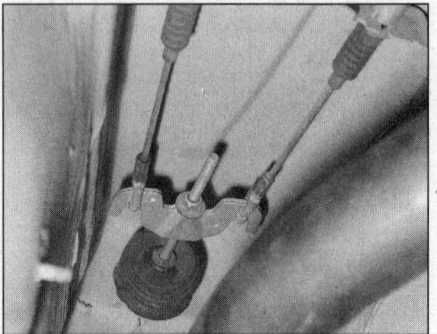

22.5 Handbrake lever rod, cables and compensator bar

22.7 Top view of the handbrake lever

23 Handbrake - adjustment

1 Routine adjustment of the handbrake is not necessary, since the rear brakes (both drum and disc types) are self-adjusting. Adjustment will only be required after renewal of the handbrake components or brake linings, or if the cables have stretched as a result of the car completing a high mileage.
2 Chock the front wheels, then jack up the rear of the car and support on axle stands. Remove the heat shield where fitted.

Rear drum brakes

3 Fully release the handbrake.
4 Working beneath the car, loosen the cable adjusting nut on the handbrake lever pullrod until it is clear of the equalizer bar.
5 Fully depress the brake pedal once.
6 Apply the handbrake lever by two notches.
7 Tighten the adjusting nut until it is only just possible to turn the rear wheels by hand.
8 Release the handbrake, and check that both rear wheels turn freely.
9 Apply the handbrake and lower the car to the ground.

Rear disc brakes

10 Carry out the procedure described in Section 10, paragraphs 24 to 28 inclusive.
11 Tighten the adjusting nut on the handbrake lever pull rod until the operating arms on each of the rear callipers just lift off their stops. The help of an assistant will be necessary to determine the exact point when the arms lift.
12 Back off the adjusting nut two complete turns.
13 Using a screwdriver, lever the handbrake arm on one of the rear callipers against its stop. Now repeat the procedure on the opposite calliper, and check if the first lever remains on its stop. If it does not, the handbrake cable is adjusted too tightly, and the adjustment nut should be loosened as necessary.
14 Fully apply, then fully release, the handbrake, and check that both rear wheels turn freely.
15 Apply the handbrake and lower the car to the ground.

24 Vacuum servo unit - description and testing

1 The vacuum servo unit is located between the brake pedal and the master cylinder, and provides assistance to the driver when the brake pedal is depressed. With the exception of 1994 cc automatic transmission models, the vacuum for the unit is obtained from the inlet manifold.
2 On 1994 cc automatic transmission models, a vacuum pump is fitted on the cylinder head, and is operated by a plunger in contact with the camshaft.
3 On 1781 cc automatic transmission models, a vacuum booster is incorporated in the hose from the inlet manifold to the vacuum servo unit.
4 The vacuum servo unit basically comprises a diaphragm and non-return valve. With the brake pedal released, vacuum is channelled to both sides of the diaphragm, but when the pedal is depressed, one side is opened to the atmosphere. The resultant unequal pressures are harnessed to assist in depressing the master cylinder pistons.
5 Normally, the vacuum servo unit is very reliable, but if the unit becomes faulty, it should be renewed. In the event of a failure, the hydraulic system is in no way affected, except that high pedal pressures will be necessary.
6 To test the vacuum servo unit, depress the brake pedal several times with the engine switched off to dissipate the vacuum. Apply moderate pressure to the brake pedal, then start the engine. The pedal should move down slightly if the servo unit is operating correctly.

25 Vacuum servo unit - removal and refitting

1 Remove the master cylinder as described in Section 13.
2 Pull the non-return valve and vacuum hose from the servo unit.
3 Working inside the car, unhook the return spring from the brake pedal and servo pushrod clevis. Extract the clip, and remove the clevis pin.
4 Unscrew the mounting nuts securing the

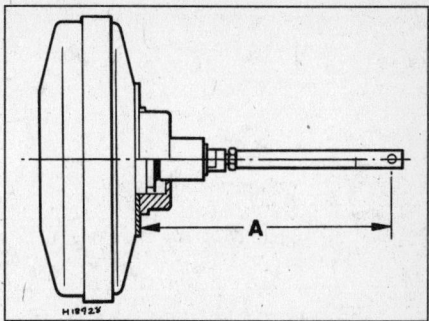

Fig 9.29 Vacuum servo unit pushrod adjustment dimension (Sec 25)
$A = 228.0 \pm 0.5$ mm (8.98 ± 0.02 in)

servo unit to the pedal bracket and bulkhead.
5 Withdraw the servo unit into the engine compartment. Remove the rubber O-ring from the unit, and renew if necessary.
6 Before refitting the servo unit, check that the pushrod dimension is as shown in Fig. 9.29. If necessary, loosen the locknut, reposition the clevis, then re-tighten the locknut.
7 Refitting is a reversal of removal, but lubricate the clevis pin with a little multi-purpose grease. On completion, roll the rubber O-ring against the bulkhead to seal the hole.

26 Vacuum pump (1994 cc automatic transmission models) - removal and refitting

1 Disconnect the spark plug HT leads and the crankcase ventilation hose as necessary for access to the vacuum pump, which is located on the left-hand side of the cylinder head.

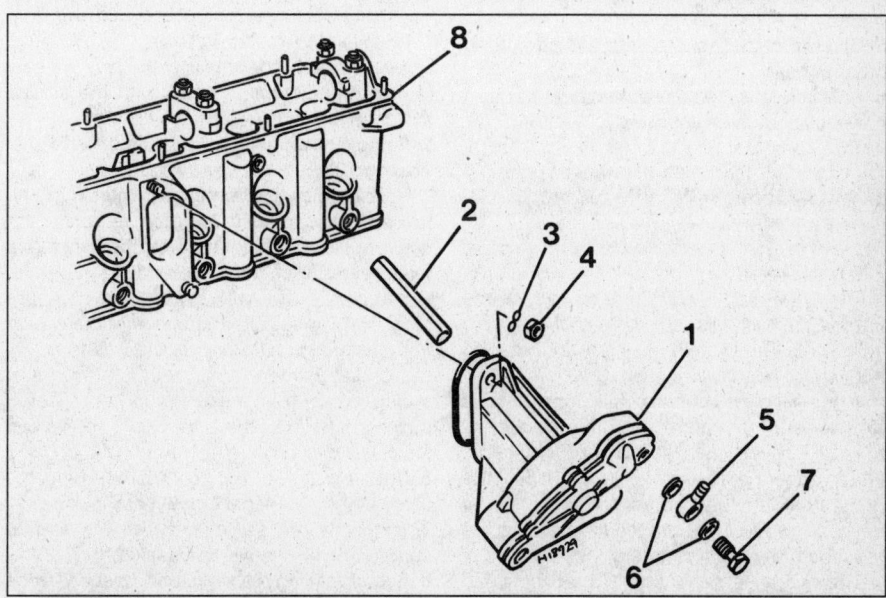

Fig 9.30 Vacuum pump fitted to 1994 cc automatic transmission models (Sec 26)

1 Vacuum pump	3 Washer	5 Union	7 Union nut
2 Plunger	4 Nut	6 Washers	8 Cylinder head

9

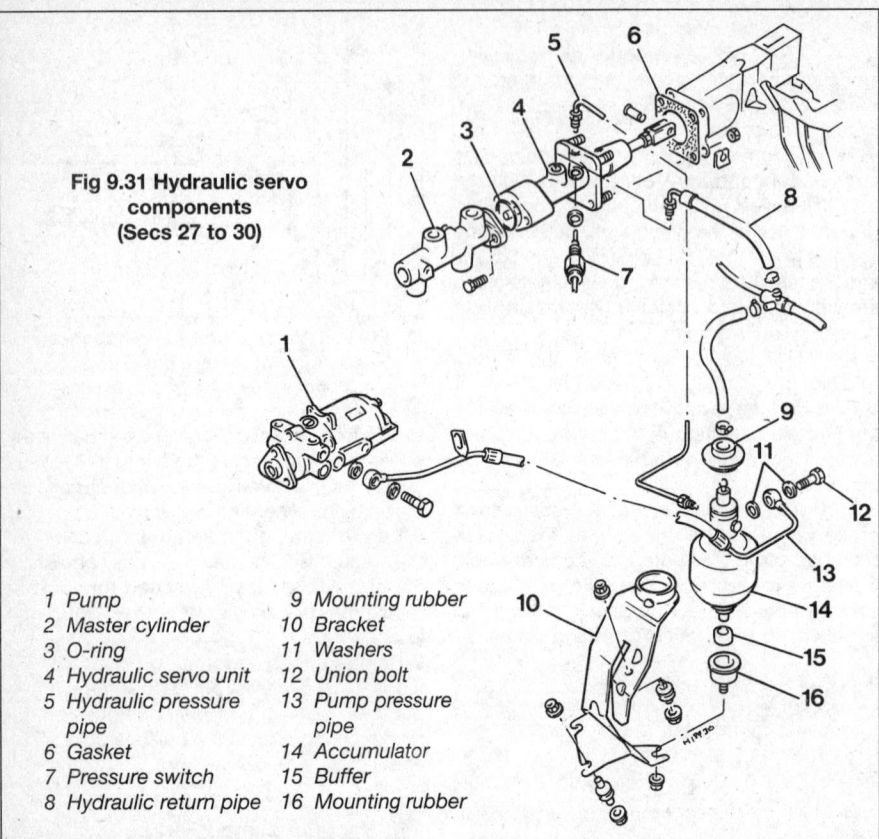

Fig 9.31 Hydraulic servo components (Secs 27 to 30)

1 Pump
2 Master cylinder
3 O-ring
4 Hydraulic servo unit
5 Hydraulic pressure pipe
6 Gasket
7 Pressure switch
8 Hydraulic return pipe
9 Mounting rubber
10 Bracket
11 Washers
12 Union bolt
13 Pump pressure pipe
14 Accumulator
15 Buffer
16 Mounting rubber

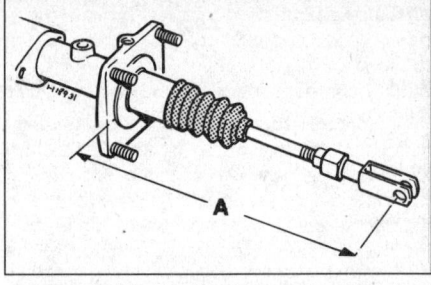

Fig 9.32 Hydraulic servo unit pushrod adjustment dimension (Sec 28)
A = 226.0 ± 0.5mm (8.90 ± 0.02 in)

2 Unscrew the union bolt and detach the vacuum hose union from the pump. Recover the sealing washers.
3 Unscrew the two nuts and withdraw the vacuum pump from the cylinder head. Recover the seal.
4 Remove the plunger from the vacuum pump.
5 Clean the contact faces of the pump and cylinder head.
6 Refitting is a reversal of removal, but fit a new seal and union washers.

27 Hydraulic servo unit - description

The 1990 model year 2309 cc models are fitted with a hydraulic servo instead of a vacuum servo unit. The system uses pressurized fluid from the power-assisted steering system.

A gas-filled pressure accumulator maintains a reserve of pressure and incorporates a pressure relief valve and non-return valve. Fluid under pressure is taken from the accumulator to the servo unit, where it is used, to provide assistance in reducing the required braking effort for the driver.

The hydraulic servo unit is fitted between the brake pedal and the master cylinder. Each component works on an entirely separate hydraulic circuit, supplied by separate fluid reservoirs.

The removal and refitting procedure for the pump is given in Chapter 10.

28 Hydraulic servo unit - removal and refitting

1 Relieve all pressures from the hydraulic servo circuit, by depressing the brake pedal approximately twenty times with the engine switched off.
2 Remove the master cylinder as described in Section 13.
3 Position a container beneath the servo unit to catch escaping fluid, then unscrew the union nuts and disconnect the pressure and return pipes. Plug the pipe ends.
4 Disconnect the wiring from the pressure drop warning switch, and unscrew the switch from the servo unit. Recover the washer.
5 Working inside the car, unhook the return spring from the brake pedal and servo pushrod clevis. Extract the clip, and remove the clevis pin.
6 Unscrew the mounting nuts securing the servo unit to the pedal bracket and bulkhead.
7 Withdraw the servo unit into the engine compartment. Recover the gasket.
8 Before refitting the servo unit, check that the pushrod dimension is as shown in Fig. 9.32. If necessary, loosen the locknut, reposition the clevis, then re-tighten the locknut.
9 Refitting is a reversal of removal, but fit a new

gasket, and tighten all nuts and bolts to the specified torque. On completion, top up the servo/power steering reservoir with the specified fluid (refer to Chapter 10 if necessary). Position the front wheels straight-ahead and run the engine at idling speed for approximately two minutes. Switch off, and immediately check the fluid level in the reservoir. Top up to the maximum mark if necessary.

29 Hydraulic servo pressure accumulator - removal and refitting

1 Relieve all pressure from the hydraulic servo circuit, by depressing the brake pedal approximately twenty times with the engine switched off.
2 Unscrew the union bolt and disconnect the inlet pressure line. Note that the union bolt incorporates a strainer and restrictor. Recover the washers.
3 Unscrew the union nut and disconnect the outlet pressure line.
4 Loosen the clip and disconnect the return hose.
5 Unscrew the lower mounting nut, and remove the accumulator from the bracket. Recover the mounting rubbers.
6 If the accumulator is to be discarded, it should be depressurized by drilling a 3.0 mm (0.118 in) diameter hole in the bottom of the unit opposite the pipe connection end. Goggles should be worn when carrying out this procedure, for protection against escaping gas.
7 Refitting is a reversal of removal, but top up the fluid level as described in Section 28, paragraph 9.

30 Hydraulic servo system - testing

1 To check the hydraulic servo unit for leaks, switch off the engine, then disconnect the *return* pipe from the unit. Only a few drops of fluid should escape. If a continual flow of fluid escapes, the unit is faulty and should be renewed. Refit the return pipe after the check.

2 The remaining checks require the use of a pressure gauge, therefore an Audi garage is best equipped for this work. However, for those who have access to this gauge, an outline of the procedures is given in the following paragraphs.

3 Relieve all pressure from the hydraulic servo circuit, by depressing the brake pedal approximately twenty times with the engine switched off.

4 Disconnect the wiring from the pressure drop warning switch, then unscrew the switch and recover the washer. Connect the pressure gauge in its place.

5 Run the engine at idling speed until the pressure is approximately 140 bar (2030 lbf/in²).

6 Switch off the ignition, then pump the brake pedal while watching the pressure gauge. The gauge should drop slowly at first, then suddenly drop to zero. The pressure just before dropping to zero is the accumulator gas pressure, and if less than 30 bar (435 lbf/in²), the accumulator should be renewed.

7 If the pressure given in paragraph 5 cannot be reached, first check the pump drivebelt tension, with reference to Section 2 of Chapter 10.

8 If the drivebelt tension is correct, check the pump delivery rate, by connecting a special hose and limiter (VAG 1354/1) to the pump pressure outlet. With the engine idling, the delivery rate should be at least 0.3 litres/min. Renew the pump if not.

9 Remove the special hose and limiter, and refit the pump outlet pipe.

10 The accumulator includes a pressure relief valve and a non-return valve. If the pump delivery rate is correct, but it is not possible to reach the pressure given in paragraph 5, the pressure relief valve is faulty, and the accumulator should be renewed.

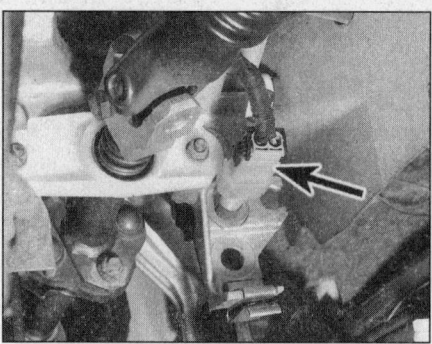

31.3 Brake stop-light switch (arrowed)

32.3 Front mounting of the handbrake outer cables

11 To check the non-return valve, run the engine at idling speed until maximum pressure is reached. Switch off the ignition, and pump the brake pedal until the pressure is approximately 135 bar (1958 lbf/in²). Check that the pressure does not drop below 130 bar (1885 lbf/in²) after five minutes. If it does, the non-return valve is faulty, and the accumulator should be renewed.

12 On completion of the checks, remove the pressure gauge and refit the pressure drop warning switch, together with a new washer if necessary. Re-connect the wiring.

31 Brake stop-light switch - removal and refitting

1 Working inside the car, disconnect the wiring from the stop-light switch on the pedal bracket (photo).

2 Pull the switch from the special clip. If necessary, remove the shim and the special clip.

3 Refitting is a reversal of removal, but adjust the switch as follows. Depress the brake pedal and hold it down, then fully press in the switch through the special clip. Pull up the brake pedal to its stop by hand.

32 Handbrake cables - removal and refitting

1 Chock the front wheels, then jack up the rear of the car and support on axle stands. Remove the heat shield where fitted.

2 Unscrew the adjusting nut from the end of the handbrake lever rod, and remove the cable compensator bar.

3 Disconnect the front ends of the outer cables from the underbody bracket (photo).

4 Disconnect the rear ends of the cables, with reference to Section 7 or 11.

5 Release the cables from the underbody clips.

6 Refitting is a reversal of removal, but adjust the handbrake as described in Section 23.

Fault finding - braking system

Excessive pedal travel
☐ Air in hydraulic system
☐ Brake fluid leak

Uneven braking and pulling to one side
☐ Disc pads or brake shoes contaminated with oil or brake fluid
☐ Seized calliper or wheel cylinder
☐ Unequal tyre pressures

Brake judder
☐ Worn discs or drums
☐ Disc pads or brake shoes contaminated with oil or brake fluid

Brake pedal feels 'spongy'
☐ Air in hydraulic system
☐ Faulty master cylinder

Excessive effort to stop car
☐ Faulty servo unit
☐ Excessively worn brake linings
☐ Seized calliper or wheel cylinder
☐ Disc pads or brake shoes contaminated with oil or brake fluid
☐ Failure of one hydraulic circuit

9

Notes

Chapter 10 Suspension and steering

Contents

Degrees of difficulty

Easy, suitable for novice with little experience	Fairly easy, suitable for beginner with some experience	Fairly difficult, suitable for competent DIY mechanic	Difficult, suitable for experienced DIY mechanic	Very difficult, suitable for expert DIY or professional

Specifications

Front suspension

Type . . . . Independent, with coil spring struts incorporating telescopic shock absorbers; lower suspension arms and anti-roll bar

Rear suspension

Type . . . . Transverse torsion beam with trailing arms, Panhard rod; telescopic shock absorbers with externally-mounted coil springs

Steering

Type . . . . Rack and pinion, tie-rods connected to carrier plate on rack; power assistance on some models, manual steering version fitted with damper

Power steering fluid type/specification . . . . VW/Audi hydraulic oil G 002 000

Front wheel alignment*

Total toe-in	+ 10' ± 10'
Camber	-45' ± 30'
Track angle difference at 20° lock:	
Saloon	-55' ± 30'
Coupe	-1°5' ± 30'
Castor:	
Saloon	+ 1° 15' ± 30'
Coupe	+1° 25' ± 30'
Maximum camber difference side-to-side	30'
Maximum castor difference side-to-side	30'

*Note: *A 'heavy duty' suspension may be fitted in production, in which case the wheel alignment figures will differ from those quoted here. Consult your Audi dealer for details.*

Rear wheel alignment

Total toe-out . . . . + 20' ± 20'
Maximum toe difference side-to-side . . . . 25'
Camber . . . . -1° ± 20'
Maximum camber difference side-to-side . . . . 30'

Wheels

Type . . . . Pressed-steel or light alloy
Size . . . . 5 1/2J x 14 (steel), 5 1/2J x 15 (steel). 6J x 14 (alloy), 6J x 15 (alloy), or 7J x 15 (alloy)

Tyres

Size . . . . 175/70 SR 14, 175/70 HR 14, 175/70 TR 14,195/60 HR 14, 195/60 VR 14, 205/50 VR 15, 205/60 R 15

Pressures (cold) - lbf/in² (bar):	Front	Rear
175/70 SR/HR/TR 14, 1.6/1.8/2.0 models:		
Normal load	31 (2.1)	31 (2.1)
Full load	38 (2.6)	38 (2.6)
175/70 SR/HR/TR 14, 2.2/2.3 models:		
Normal load	33 (2.3)	33 (2.3)
Full load	39(2.7)	41 (2.8)
195/60 HR 14:		
Normal load	31 (2.1)	31 (2.1)
Full load	36 (2.5)	36 (2.5)
195/60 VR 14:		
Normal load	33 (2.3)	33 (2.3)
Full load	39(2.7)	41 (2.8)
205/50 VR 15:		
Normal load	33 (2.3)	33 (2.3)
Full load	39 (2.7)	41 (2.8)

Torque wrench settings	Nm	lbf ft
Front suspension		
Balljoint-to-wheel bearing housing	65	48
Anti-roll bar front mounting	35	26
Lower suspension arm pivot	40 + 90°	30 + 90°
Anti-roll bar side mounting	25	18
Balljoint-to-lower suspension arm and strut	65	48
Anti-roll bar link nut	20	15
Crossmember mounting bolt	35 + 90°	26 + 90°
Strut top mounting nut	60	44
Wheel bearing housing to strut	80 + 90°	59 + 90°
Shock absorber piston slotted nut	50	37
Shock absorber cap	150	111
Rear suspension		
Trailing arm front mounting	100	74
Panhard rod to body	80	59
Shock absorber lower mounting	60	44
Panhard rod to rear axle	90	66
Shock absorber top mounting	20	15
Steering		
Column mounting	35	26
Steering lock housing	6	4
Column to pinion clamp	20	15
Column flange to coupling	7	5
Coupling to pinion	25	18
Tie-rod carrier plate to rack	45	33
Steering damper to tie-rod carrier plate	35	26
Steering gear centre mounting	40	30
Steering damper to steering gear	35	26
Steering gear side mounting	20	15
Steering gear cover bolt	20	15
Tie-rod end nut	30	22
Tie-rod adjuster locknut	40	30
Steering wheel retaining nut	40	30
Power steering union bolt	50	37
Roadwheel bolts	110	81

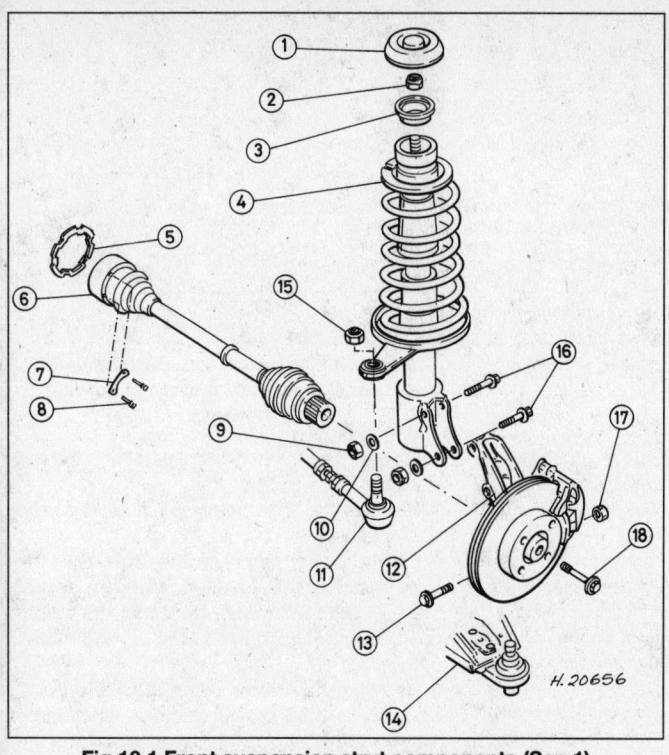

Fig 10.1 Front suspension strut components (Sec 1)

1 Plastic cover	7 Locking plate	13 Bolt
2 Nut	8 Bolt	14 Lower suspension
3 Bump stop	9 Nut	arm
4 Strut and coil	10 Washer	15 Nut
spring	11 Track rod	16 Bolt
5 Gasket	12 Wheel bearing	17 Nut
6 Driveshaft	housing	18 Driveshaft bolt

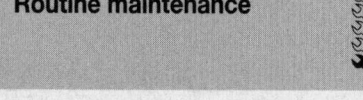

Fig 10.2 Rear suspension components (Sec 1)

1 Nut	6 Panhard rod	9 Nut
2 Bush	7 Rear axle	10 Shock absorber
3 Nut	8 Brake pressure	11 Nut
4 Handbrake cable	regulator spring	12 Nut
5 Rubber bush		

1 General description

The front suspension is of independent type, incorporating coil spring struts and lower suspension arms. Telescopic shock absorbers are fitted to the struts, and the lower suspension arms are mounted on the front crossmember.

The rear suspension comprises a transverse torsion beam, with trailing arms bushed to the underbody. Telescopic shock absorbers are attached to the transverse beam, and they incorporate mountings for the coil springs, forming a strut configuration. Side-to-side movement of the transverse beam is controlled by a Panhard rod.

The steering is of rack-and-pinion type. Unlike the normal arrangement, only one end of the rack is used to move the tie-rods from side to side. Manual steering models are fitted with a hydraulic damper, which dampens the effects of road irregularities. Power assistance is fitted to most models.

The Procon-Ten (Programmed Contraction/Tension) safety system may be fitted as an optional extra. It consists of two steel cables attached to the seat belt reels and the steering column tube. The cables are routed round the rear of the gearbox. In the event of a severe frontal impact, the engine and gearbox move rearwards towards the passenger compartment. This tensions the two cables, which pull the seat belt reels and steering column tube forwards. This provides improved seat belt support, and also pulls the steering column away from the driver. The system is the result of much experimentation with accident simulation tests.

2 Routine maintenance

Carry out the following procedures at the intervals given in 'Routine maintenance' at the beginning of the manual.

Check and adjust power steering pump drivebelt

1 Examine the full length of the drivebelt for fraying, deterioration and cracks, and for glazing of the pulley contact surfaces.
2 Check that the drivebelt deflection halfway between the two pulleys is approximately 10.0 mm (0.4 in), under firm thumb pressure.
3 If necessary, renew and/or adjust the drivebelt, with reference to Section 21.

Check tie-rod ends

4 Apply the handbrake, then raise the front of the car and support on axle stands.
5 With the steering column lock unlocked, move each front wheel by hand, and check the tie-rod ends for excessive movement. It should not be possible to detect any side movement in the balljoint.
6 Check the rubber tie-rod end dust covers for damage.
7 If necessary, renew the tie-rod end, with reference to Section 14.

Check front suspension lower balljoints

8 Apply the handbrake, then raise the front of the car and support on axle stands.
9 Using a lever, attempt to move the wheel bearing housing sideways and upwards from the lower suspension arm, while observing the balljoint. There should be no movement evident.
10 Check both balljoints and renew as necessary.

10

3.16 Front suspension strut upper mounting – note Allen-type fitting in piston rod (arrowed)

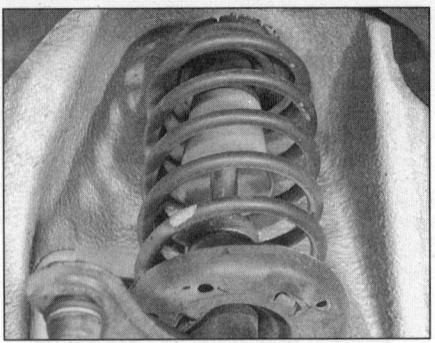

3.17 Front suspension strut removal

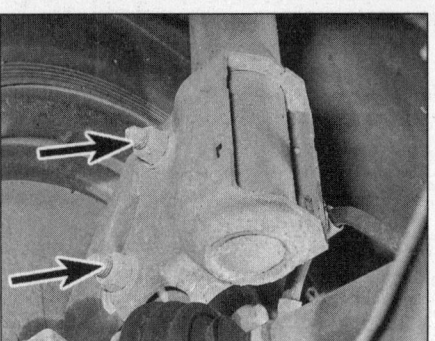

3.18 Bolts (arrowed) securing the front suspension strut to the wheel bearing housing

Check the tyres

11 Refer to Section 23. The originally-fitted tyres incorporate tread wear indicators, which are 1.6 mm (0.063 in) thick.
12 Check and adjust the tyre pressures.

Check power-assisted steering fluid level

13 Set the front wheels in the straight-ahead position.
14 With the engine idling, check that the fluid level is on the maximum mark. Top up if necessary. If frequent topping-up is required, check the system for leaks.

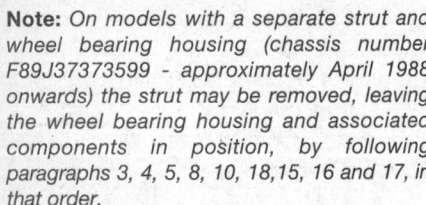

3 Front suspension strut - removal and refitting

Note: *On models with a separate strut and wheel bearing housing (chassis number F89J37373599 - approximately April 1988 onwards) the strut may be removed, leaving the wheel bearing housing and associated components in position, by following paragraphs 3, 4, 5, 8, 10, 18, 15, 16 and 17, in that order.*
1 Apply the handbrake and prise the trim from the relevant front wheel.
2 Loosen the driveshaft nut or bolt (as applicable) with the weight of the car still on the wheels. The nut/bolt is tightened to a very high torque, and **should not** be loosened with the car raised.
3 Loosen the wheel bolts.
4 Jack up the front of the car and support on axle stands.
5 Remove the wheel.
6 Remove the driveshaft nut and washer, or bolt, as appropriate.
7 Remove the brake disc, with reference to Chapter 9.
8 Unbolt the brake hydraulic hose bracket from the strut.
9 Unscrew and remove the pinch-bolt securing the lower suspension balljoint to the wheel bearing housing.
10 Disconnect the steering tie-rod from the strut, with reference to Section 1 4.

11 On power steering models, unscrew the nut securing the anti-roll bar link to the lower suspension arm, and recover the washer and rubber.
12 Pull the lower suspension arm downwards, and disconnect the balljoint from the strut.
13 On models with manual steering, remove the anti-roll bar completely, as described in Section 6.
14 Using a puller, press the driveshaft through the hub, and support it on an axle stand.
15 Working in the engine compartment, pull the plastic cover from the top of the strut.
16 Support the bottom of the strut, then unscrew the nut from the top of the piston rod, while holding the rod stationary with an Allen key (photo).
17 Lower the front suspension strut from the top mounting, and withdraw it from under the wing (photo).
18 If the complete strut has been removed on models from April 1988 onwards, mark the position of the wheel bearing housing in relation to the strut, then unscrew the two bolts and separate the housing. Note that the bolt heads face forwards (photo).
19 Refitting is a reversal of removal, but tighten all nuts and bolts to the specified torque. Refer to Chapter 8 when installing the driveshaft, Chapter 9 when installing the brake disc, and Section 6 of this Chapter when installing the anti-roll bar.

4 Front suspension strut - dismantling and reassembly

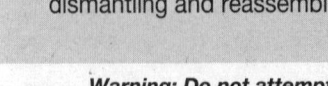

⚠️ *Warning: Do not attempt to dismantle the suspension strut unless a spring compressor has been fitted. If you have no spring compressor, take the strut to a garage for dismantling.*

1 Fit the spring compressor securely to the spring, then mount the strut in a vice.
2 Compress the spring until the upper spring retainer is free. Unscrew the slotted nut from

the top of the piston rod, while holding the rod stationary with an Allen key.
3 Remove the strut bearing, followed by the spring retainer.
4 Lift the coil spring from the strut, with the compressor still in position. Mark the top of the spring for reference. Note that the colour code on the bottom of the spring faces outwards.
5 Remove the rubber bump stop and boot. On models with heavy duty suspension, there is an additional cup and washer. Note the position of each component before removing it.
6 To check the efficiency of the shock absorber, operate the piston rod fully over its complete stroke, and check that the resistance is even and smooth. without any signs of seizing. On hydraulic shock absorbers, check for excessive leakage of fluid. Disregard slight traces of fluid, which is normal. On gas-filled shock absorbers, there is no easy way of detecting a leak.
7 The shock absorber may be 'renewed' by fitting a new cartridge, however on the hydraulic type, the original piston and rod must be removed and the hydraulic fluid discarded.
8 To remove the shock absorber cartridge or piston rod, unscrew the cap from the top of the strut using Audi tool No 40-201 A or a similar tool. The cap is very tight, so a close-fitting tool is required.
9 Withdraw the cartridge or piston from the strut, and clean the recess thoroughly.
10 If applicable, remove the hub and bearing, and the splash guard, with reference to Section 5.
11 Check the strut top mounting ball bearing for excessive wear by spinning it by hand, and obtain a new bearing if necessary.
12 Reassembly is a reversal of dismantling, but tighten the cap and the slotted nut to the specified torque. On models with heavy duty suspension, make sure that the convoluted rubber boot is fitted onto the cap. If fitting a new shock absorber, the piston rod should be operated over its full stroke in a vertical position several times before refitting the strut.

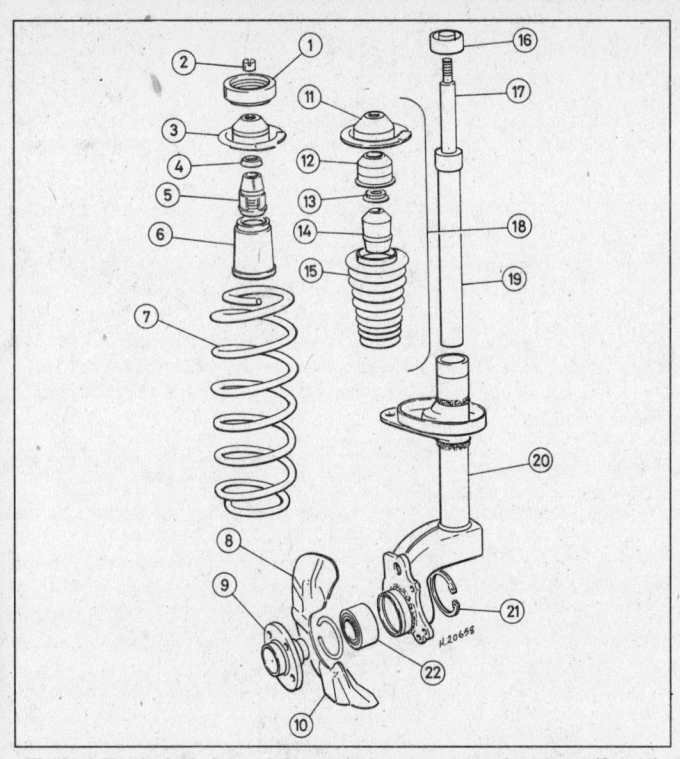

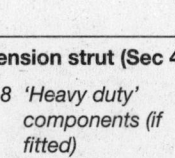

Fig I0.3 Exploded view of the early front suspension strut (Sec 4)

1 Upper mounting	10 Bolt	18 'Heavy duty'
2 Slotted nut	11 Spring seat	components (if
3 Spring seat	12 Cup	fitted)
4 Washer	13 Washer	19 Shock absorber
5 Bump stop	14 Bump stop	20 Wheel bearing
6 Boot	15 Boot	housing
7 Coil spring	16 Cap	21 Circlip
8 Splash guard	17 Piston rod	22 Wheel bearing
9 Hub		

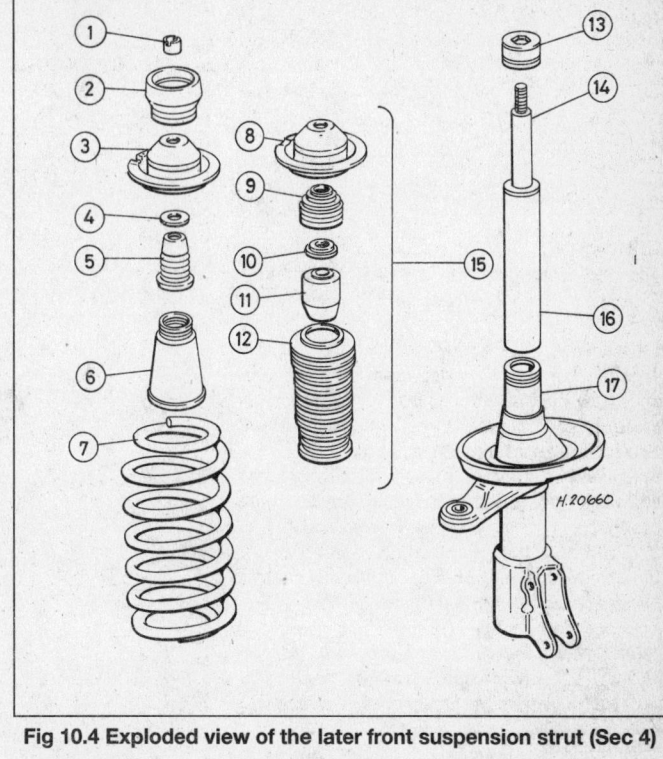

Fig 10.4 Exploded view of the later front suspension strut (Sec 4)

1 Slotted nut	8 Sprint seat	15 'Heavy duty'
2 Upper mounting	9 Cup	components
3 Spring seat	10 Washer	(if fitted)
4 Washer	11 Bump stop	16 Shock absorber
5 Bump stop	12 Boot	17 Strut/shock
6 Boot	13 Screw cap	absorber housing
7 Coil spring	14 Piston rod	

5 Front hub and bearing - removal and refitting

1 Remove the front suspension strut, complete with the wheel bearing housing, as described in Section 3.
2 Remove the countersunk cross-head screw, and withdraw the brake disc from the hub.

3 Remove the screws and withdraw the splash guard.
4 Support the wheel bearing housing, with the hub facing downwards (photo), and press or drive out the hub using a suitable mandrel. The bearing inner race will remain on the hub and therefore once removed, it is not possible to re-use the bearing. Use a puller to remove the inner race from the hub.
5 Extract the circlips, then, while supporting the wheel bearing housing, press or drive out

the bearing, using a large socket or metal tubing on the outer race.
6 Clean the hub and the recess in the wheel bearing housing.
7 Fit the outer circlip, then support the wheel bearing housing and press or drive in the new bearing, using a metal tube on the outer race only. Fit the inner circlip.
8 Position the hub with its bearing shoulder facing upwards, then press or drive on the bearing and housing, using a metal tube on the inner race only.
9 Refit the splash guard and brake disc, tighten the disc screw, then refit the front suspension strut with reference to Section 3.

6 Front anti-roll bar - removal and refitting

1 Apply the handbrake, then jack up the front of the car and support on axle stands. Remove the front wheels.
2 Unscrew the bolts and remove the front mounting clamps (photo). On some models, a stud and nut may be fitted instead of the lower bolt.

10

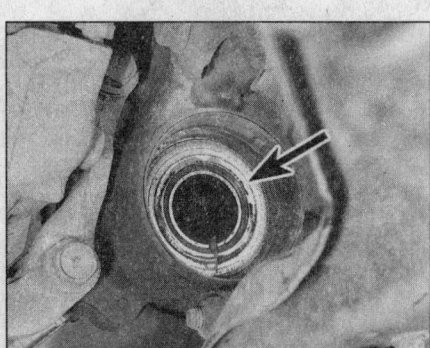

5.4 Front hub and bearing (arrowed)

6.2 Front anti-roll bar mounting clamp (arrowed)

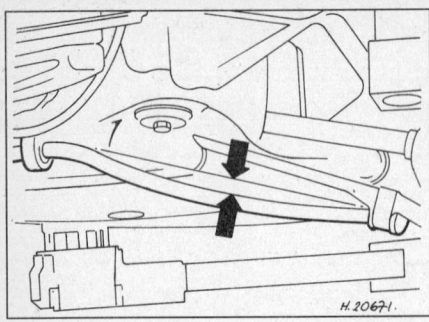

Fig 10.5 Correct fitting of the front anti-roll bar (Sec 6)

3 Unscrew the nuts or bolts securing the side mountings to the lower suspension arms, and withdraw the anti-roll bar from under the car.

4 Recover the mounting rubbers, washers and spacers, noting their positions.

5 On power steering models, detach the side links by unscrewing the nuts. Recover the mounting rubbers, washers and spacers.

6 Examine the mounting rubbers for deterioration and damage, and renew them if necessary.

 **It is helpful to apply talcum powder to the rubbers, to make centralising them easier.**

7 Refitting is a reversal of removal, but make sure that the anti-roll bar is fitted the correct way round, with the offset away from the lower suspension arm. Delay fully tightening the anti-roll bar mountings until the full weight of the car is on the wheels.

7 Front lower suspension arm - removal, overhaul and refitting

1 Apply the handbrake, then jack up the front of the car and support on axle stands. Remove the relevant front wheel.

2 On manual steering models, remove the anti-roll bar completely, as described in Section 6. On power steering models, unscrew the nut securing the side link to the lower suspension arm.

3 Unscrew and remove the lower suspension balljoint clamp bolt, noting that its head faces forwards.

4 Tap the suspension arm downwards, to release the balljoint from the wheel bearing housing.

5 Unscrew and remove the pivot bolts (photo) from the subframe, noting that the nuts face each other, then lower the arm and withdraw it from under the car.

6 Check the balljoint for excessive wear, and check the pivot bushes for deterioration. Also examine the suspension arm for damage. If necessary, renew the balljoint and bushes as follows.

7 To renew the balljoint, first outline its exact position on the suspension arm (photo). This

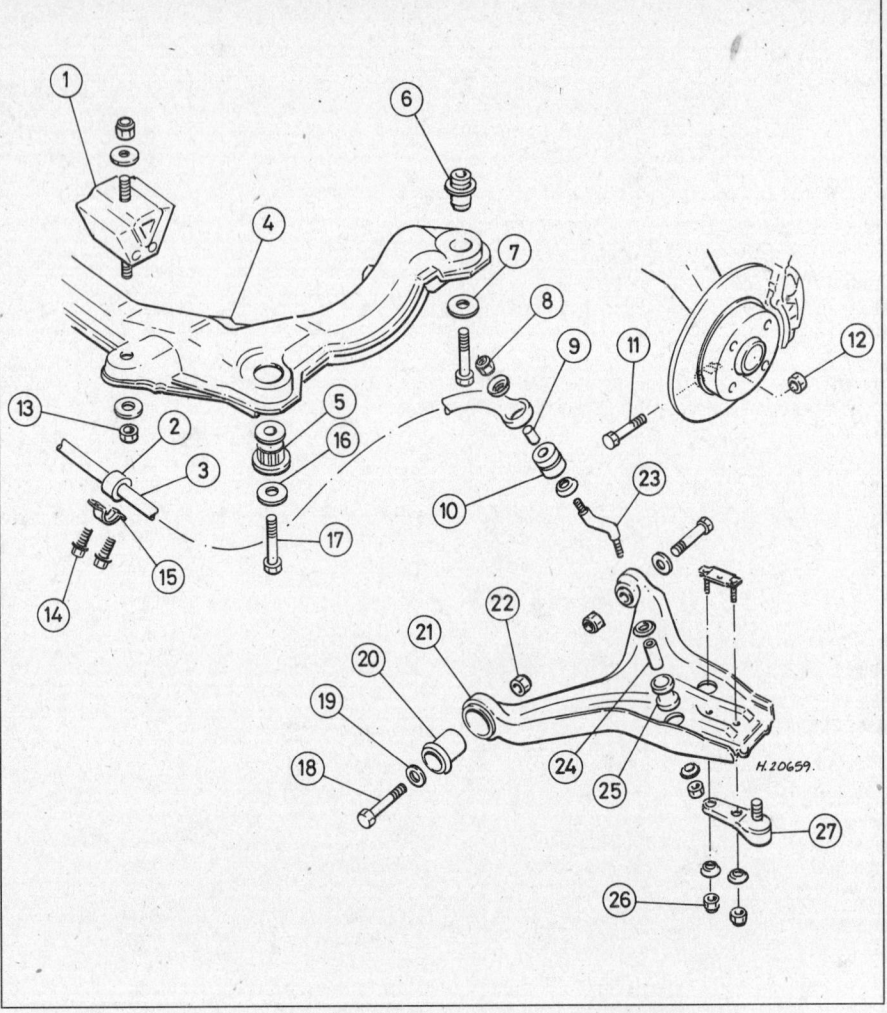

Fig 10.6 Front lower suspension arm components (Sec 7)

1 Rubber mounting	10 Mounting	19 Washer
2 Mounting	11 Bolt	20 Bush
3 Anti-roll bar	12 Nut	21 Lower suspension arm
4 Crossmember	13 Nut	22 Nut
5 Mounting	14 Bolt	23 Link
6 Mounting	15 Clamp	24 Spacer
7 Washer	16 Washer	25 Mounting
8 Nut	17 Bolt	26 Nut
9 Spacer	18 Bolt	27 Lower balljoint

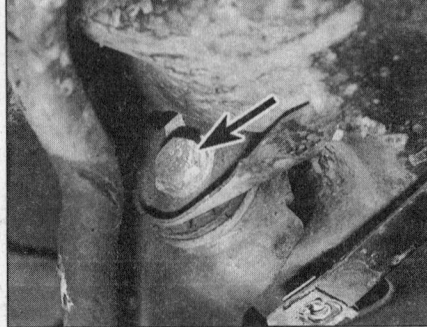

7.5 Front lower suspension arm pivot bolt (arrowed)

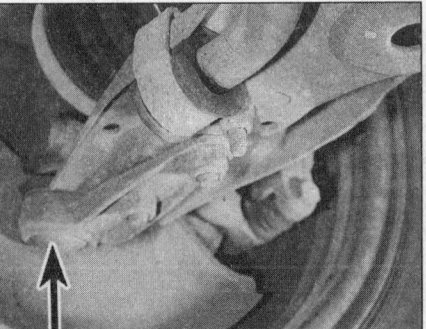

7.7 Front lower suspension arm balljoint (arrowed)

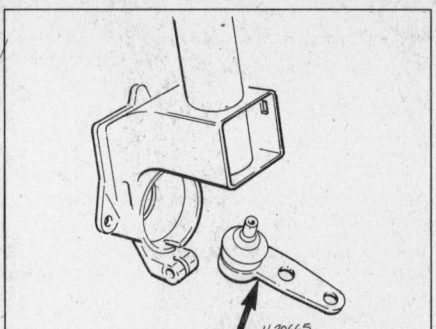

Fig 10.7 Balljoint recess (arrowed) must be at front (Sec 7)

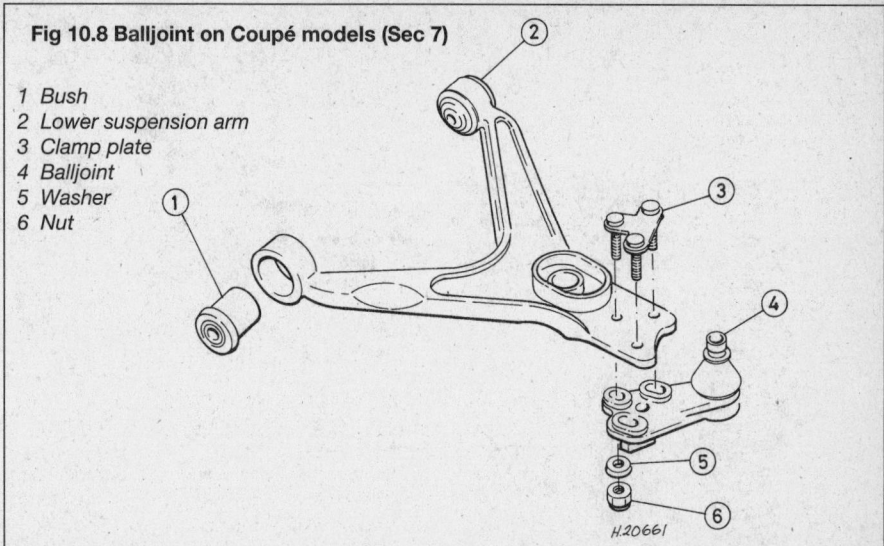

Fig 10.8 Balljoint on Coupé models (Sec 7)

1 Bush
2 Lower suspension arm
3 Clamp plate
4 Balljoint
5 Washer
6 Nut

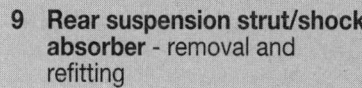
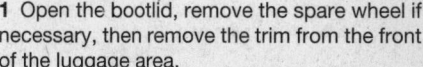

is important, as the holes in the arm are elongated to allow camber adjustment. Unscrew the nuts and remove the balljoint and clamp plate. Locate the new balljoint on the exact outline, fit the clamp plate and tighten the nuts. **New** nuts should be fitted. Note that on non-Coupé models, the offset side of the balljoint should face to the front (ie the balljoints are handed). On Coupé models, the balljoint with the *uneven* part number should be on the *left-hand* side, and with the *even* part number on the *right-hand* side.

8 To renew the pivot bushes, use a long bolt together with a metal tube and washers to pull out each bush. Fit the new bushes using the same method, but first dip them in soapy water.

9 Refitting the suspension arm is a reversal of removal, but delay tightening the pivot bolts until the weight of the car is on the suspension.

10 Refer to Section 6 when refitting the anti-roll bar.

11 Tighten all nuts and bolts to the specified torque, noting that the inner pivot bolts are additionally angle-tightened. All self-locking nuts should be renewed.

12 Have the front wheel camber angle checked, and if necessary, adjusted by an Audi dealer on completion.

8 Rear axle - removal and refitting

1 Chock the front wheels, then jack up the rear of the car and support on axle stands. Remove the rear wheels and release the handbrake.

2 Working under the car, unscrew the adjusting nut and remove the equalizer bar from the rear of the handbrake operating bar.

3 Unclip the handbrake cables from the brackets and supports.

4 Fit brake hose clamps to the two flexible hoses leading to the rear brakes, then unscrew the union nuts and disconnect the two rigid brake lines.

5 Unscrew and remove the nuts from the pivot bolts at the front of the rear axle trailing

arms. Do not remove the bolts at this stage.

6 Unhook the brake pressure regulator control spring from the rear axle.

7 Unscrew the nut and remove the bolt securing the Panhard rod to the rear axle.

8 Support the rear axle on a trolley jack, or on axle stands.

9 Unscrew and remove both rear shock absorber lower mounting bolts.

10 With the help of an assistant, remove the pivot bolts, then lower the rear axle to the ground while guiding the handbrake cable over the exhaust system.

11 If necessary, remove the stub axles (Section 11), brake lines and handbrake cables (Chapter 9). The pivot bushes may be renewed using a long bolt and nut, metal tube, and parking washers. When fitting the new bushes, make sure that the two gaps in the rubber are horizontal, and in line with the trailing arm. Press the bushes in until flush with the arm.

12 Refitting is a reversal of removal, but delay fully tightening the mounting bolts until the weight of the car is on the suspension.

13 Tighten all nuts and bolts to the specified torque. All self-locking nuts should be renewed.

14 Bleed the hydraulic system and adjust the handbrake cable as described in Chapter 9.

9 Rear suspension strut/shock absorber - removal and refitting

1 Open the bootlid, remove the spare wheel if necessary, then remove the trim from the front of the luggage area.

2 Pull the plastic cap from the top of the shock absorber.

3 Chock the front wheels. Jack up the rear of the car and support on axle stands positioned beneath the underbody.

4 Support the rear axle on a trolley jack.

5 Unscrew the nut from the top of the shock absorber, and remove the cup and upper mounting rubber (photo). Note that it is not recommended to remove both shock absorbers at the same time, otherwise there is a possibility of damaging one or both of the flexible hydraulic brake hoses.

6 Lower the rear axle sufficiently to release all tension from the coil spring.

7 Unscrew and remove the shock absorber lower mounting bolt. The shock absorber may now be lowered from the car, together with the coil spring, damper ring, and mounting components (photo). Note the fitted position of the mounting rubbers.

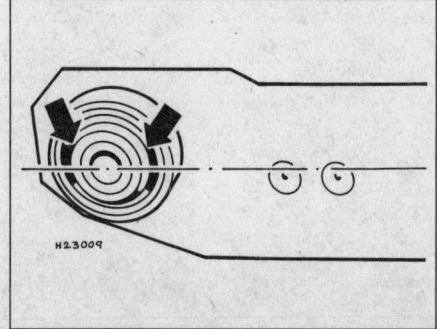

Fig 10.9 Correct position of gaps for pivot bushes on rear axle trailing arms (Sec 8)

9.5 Rear suspension strut upper mounting

10

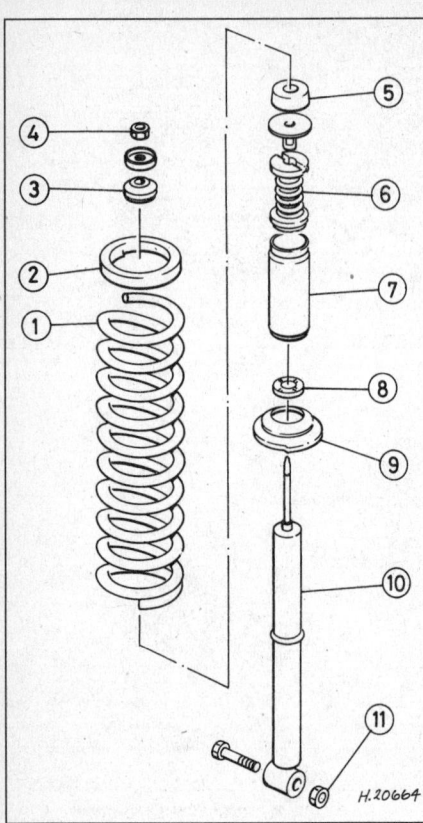

Fig 10.10 Rear suspension strut components (Sec 9)

1 Coil spring
2 Damper ring
3 Mounting
4 Nut
5 Mounting
6 Bump stop
7 Sleeve
8 Plate
9 Spring seat
10 Shock absorber
11 Nut

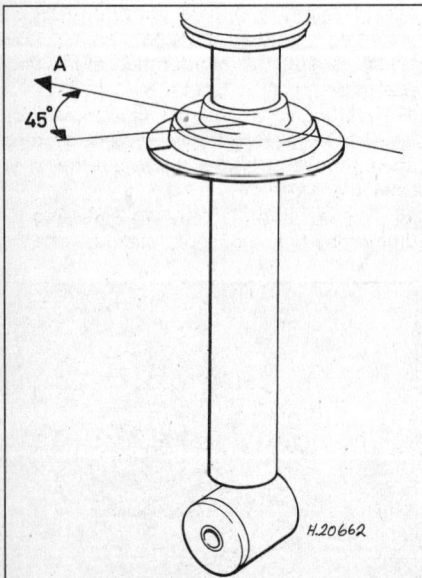

Fig 10.11 Correct positioning of rear spring seat on shock absorber (Sec 9)

A Front

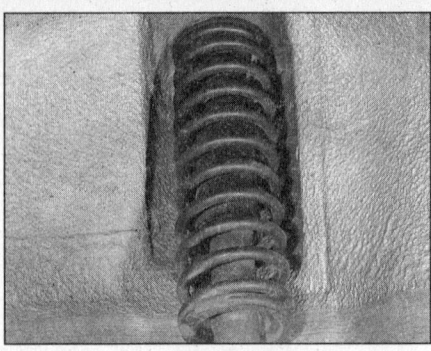

9.7 Rear suspension strut removal

8 Remove the coil spring, damper ring, lower spring seat, mounting and bump stop rubbers.

9 Clean all the components, and check them for wear and damage. Check the shock absorber with reference to Section 4, paragraph 6. Both the shock absorber and coil spring are individually colour-coded, and new units must always bear the same colour as those removed. Before fitting a *new* shock absorber, the piston rod should be operated over its full stroke in a vertical position several times before refitting the strut, in order to purge any trapped air.

10 Refitting is a reversal of removal, but position the spring lower seat as shown in Fig. 10.11, and dust the upper rubber mounting rubbers with talcum powder before fitting them. Delay fully tightening the shock absorber lower mounting bolt until the weight of the car is on the suspension. All self-locking nuts should be renewed.

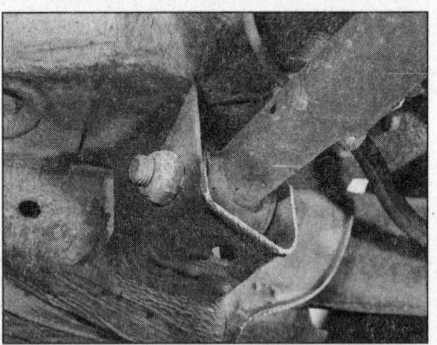

10.2A Panhard rod-to-underbody mounting

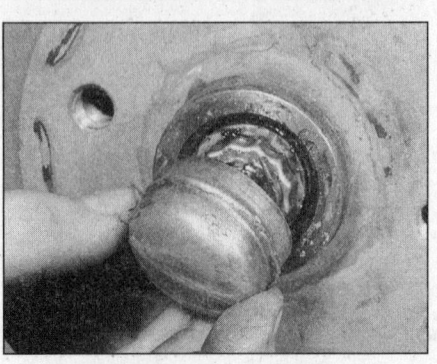

11.2 Removing the rear hub cap . . .

10 Panhard rod - removal, overhaul and refitting

1 Chock the front wheels, then jack up the rear of the car and support on axle stands. If required, for better access, remove the rear wheels.

2 Unscrew and remove the bolts attaching the Panhard rod to the underbody and rear axle, noting that the bolt heads are adjacent to the rod (photos). Withdraw the rod from under the car.

3 Examine the rod and bushes for damage and deterioration. If necessary, the bushes can be renewed using a long bolt, metal tube and washers. Dip the bushes in soapy water before installing them.

4 Refitting is a reversal of removal, but delay fully tightening the mounting bolts until the weight of the car is on the suspension.

11 Rear wheel bearings and stub axle - removal, refitting and adjustment

1 Chock the front wheels, then jack up the rear of the car and support it on axle stands. Remove the rear roadwheel, and release the handbrake. Remove the rear brake duct, if applicable (Chapter 9).

2 Remove the cap from the centre of the hub by tapping it on alternate sides with a screwdriver or blunt chisel (photo).

3 Extract the split pin and remove the locking ring (photo).

10.2B Panhard rod-to-rear axle mounting

11.3 . . . split pin and locking ring . . .

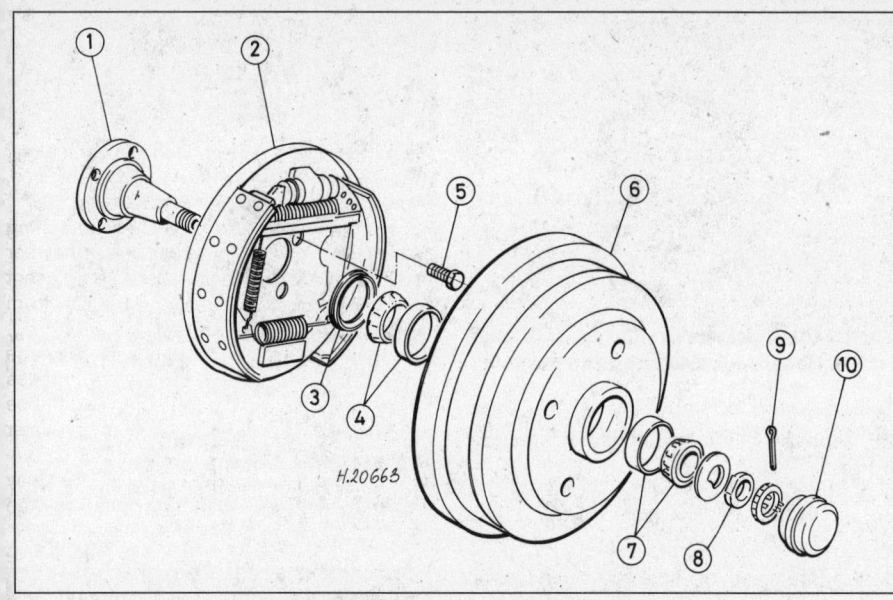

11.4A . . . nut . . .

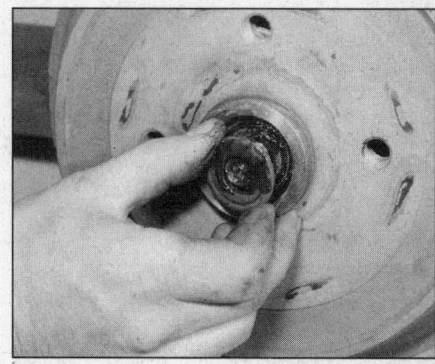

11.4B . . . and thrustwasher

Fig 10.12 Rear hub and bearings (Sec 11)

1 Stub axle	5 Bolt	8 Nut
2 Brake backplate	6 Brake drum	9 Split pin
3 Oil seal	7 Outer wheel bearing	10 Grease cap
4 Inner wheel bearing		

4 Unscrew the nut and remove the thrust washer (photos).

5 Withdraw the brake drum hub, making sure that the outer wheel bearing does not fall out. If the brake drum (where applicable) binds on the shoes, insert a small screwdriver through a wheel bolt hole, and lever up the wedged key in order to release the shoes (photo) - refer to Chapter 9, if necessary.

6 Remove the outer wheel bearing inner race and rollers from the brake drum/hub (photo).

7 Lever the oil seal from the inner side of the brake drum/hub (photo), and withdraw the inner wheel bearing inner race and rollers.

8 Using a soft metal drift, drive the outer races from each side of the brake drum/hub.

9 Clean the bearings and brake drum/hub with paraffin, and also wipe the stub axle clean. Examine the tapered rollers, inner and outer races, brake drum/hub, and stub axle for wear and damage. If the bearing surfaces

are pitted, renew them. Obtain a new oil seal.

10 Pack the bearing cages and tapered rollers with a lithium based grease, and also pack the grease into the brake drum/hub inner cavity.

11 Using a length of metal tube, drive the outer races fully into the brake drum/hub.

12 Insert the inner bearing inner race and rollers, then locate the oil seal with the sealing lip facing inwards, and drive it in with a block of wood until flush. Smear a little grease on the oil seal lip, then wipe clean the outer face of the seal.

Drum brake models

13 Remove the rear brake shoes with reference to Chapter 9.

14 Remove the brake fluid reservoir filler cap, and tighten it down onto a piece of polythene sheeting over the reservoir filler hole, in order to prevent the loss of fluid in the following

procedure. Alternatively, fit a brake hose clamp on the hydraulic hose between the rear axle and underbody.

15 Unscrew the brake pipe union on the rear of the wheel cylinder.

All models

16 Unscrew the bolts and withdraw the brake backplate and stub axle from the rear axle mounting plate, at the same time disconnecting the handbrake cable where applicable.

17 Refitting is a reversal of removal, but bleed the brake hydraulic system on drum brake models (Chapter 9). Adjust the wheel bearing as follows.

18 Tighten the nut firmly while turning the drum/hub, then back off the nut until the

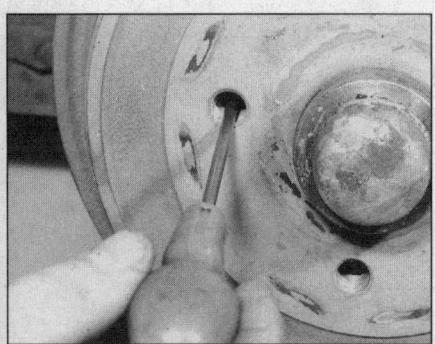

11.5 Releasing the rear brake shoe wedged key

11.6 Outer wheel bearing inner race removal

11.7 Rear hub oil seal

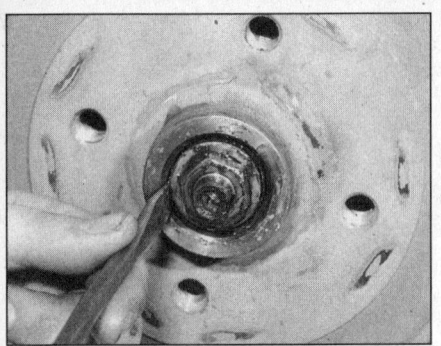

11.18 Checking the rear hub wheel bearing adjustment

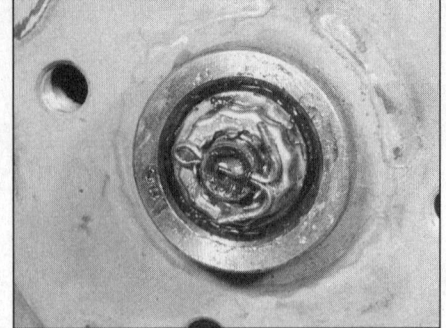

11.19 Rear hub locking ring and split pin

12.1 Horn pad removal

thrust washer can just be moved by pressing on its edge with a screwdriver. Do not lever or twist the screwdriver in an attempt to move the thrust washer (photo).
19 Fit the locking ring without moving the nut, and install a new split pin (photo).
20 Tap the grease cap onto the drum/hub.

12 Steering wheel - removal and refitting

1 Pull the horn pad from the centre of the steering wheel by releasing the top, then bottom of the pad (photo). Do this carefully, otherwise the plastic retaining claws may be broken.

2 Disconnect the horn wiring, and withdraw the pad.
3 Set the front wheels in the straight-ahead position, and put the direction indicator lever in 'neutral' ('off' position).
4 Mark the steering wheel and inner column in relation to each other then unscrew and remove the retaining nut and washer (photos).
5 Withdraw the steering wheel from the inner column splines (photo). If it is tight, ease it off by rocking from side to side.
6 Refitting is a reversal of removal, but align the previously-made marks, and tighten the retaining nut to the specified torque. Make sure that the direction indicator lever is in 'neutral', otherwise the switch arm may be damaged.

13 Steering column - removal, overhaul and refitting

1 Disconnect the battery negative lead.
2 Remove the trim panel covering the steering column .
3 Remove the steering wheel, as described in Section 12.
4 Remove the shroud covers from the steering column. On some models, these are retained by several screws, but on other models a clamp secures the cover unit to the column, and a hole is provided for access to the clamp screw (photos).
5 Disconnect the multi-plugs from the ignition switch and combination switch.

12.4A Hold the steering wheel stationary, and unscrew the nut . . .

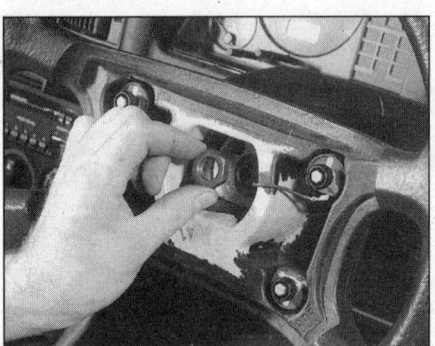

12.4B . . . remove the nut . . .

12.4C . . . and remove the washer

12.5 Removing the steering wheel

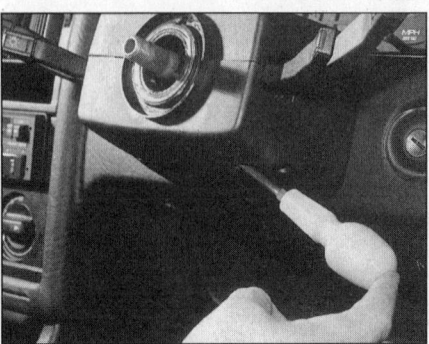

13.4A Loosen the clamp screw . . .

13.4B . . . and remove the steering column shroud

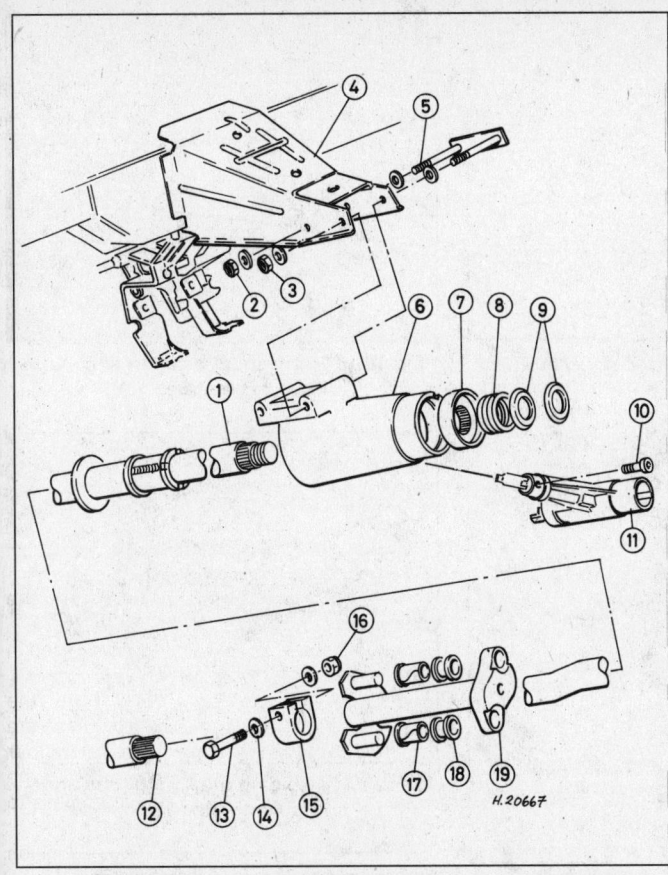

Fig 10.13 Steering column components on manual steering models (Sec 13)

1 Inner column	8 Spring	14 Washer
2 Nut	9 Lockwashers	15 Clamp
3 Washer	10 Bolt	16 Nut
4 Bracket	11 Lock housing	17 Bush
5 Shackle	12 Pinion	18 Bush
6 Tube	13 Clamp bolt	19 Flange tube
7 Bearing		

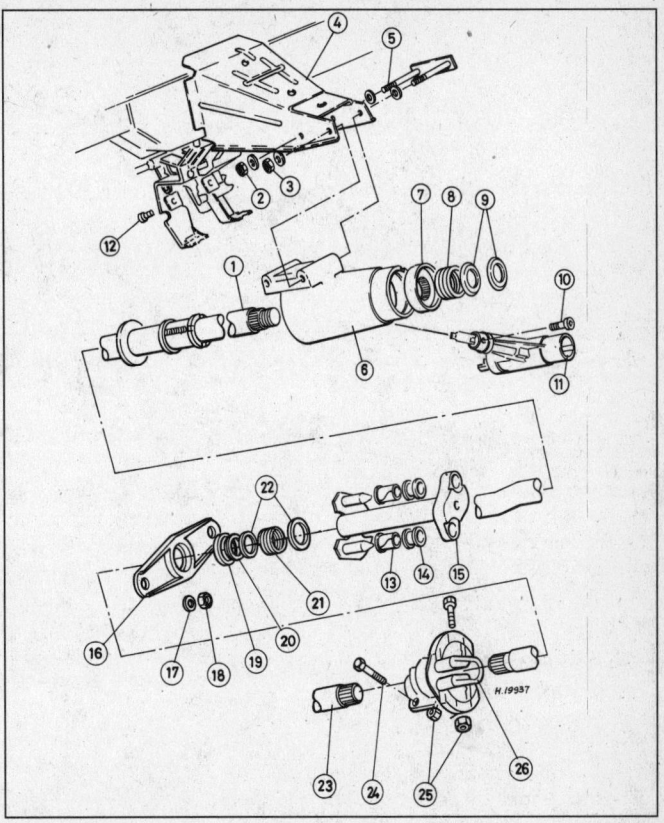

Fig 10.14 Steering column components on power steering models (Sec 13)

1 Inner column	10 Bolt	18 Nut
2 Nut	11 Lock housing	19 Bearing
3 Washer	12 Square-headed	20 Support ring
4 Bracket	bolt	21 Spring
5 Shackle	13 Bush	22 Washers
6 Tube	14 Bush	23 Pinion
7 Bearing	15 Flange tube	24 Clamp bolt
8 Spring	16 Bearing flange	25 Nut
9 Lockwashers	17 Washer	26 Coupling

6 Remove the screw(s) and withdraw the combination switch.

7 Remove the instrument panel, with reference to Chapter 12.

8 On manual steering models, prise out the rubber boot from the bulkhead at the base of the column (photo).

9 On power steering models, unbolt the column mounting flange from the pedal bracket.

10 Unscrew and remove the clamp bolt, and pull the flange tube or coupling from the steering gear pinion.

11 Unscrew the mounting bolts from the upper column (photo).

12 Release the column from the bracket, and remove the threaded shackle.

13 Unbolt the lock housing from the column using a Torx key.

14 Lower the column through the bulkhead, and withdraw it from under the facia. On models fitted with the Procon-Ten safety

system, it will be necessary to disconnect the cable first. Take care with the Procon-Ten type column tube, as it consists of two halves bonded together. On models from October 1988 onwards, the two halves are sealed with a spot of red paint which, if fractured, indicates that the column is no longer serviceable due to accident damage. Do not expose the Procon-Ten column tube to temperatures in excess of 100°C (212° F), or to cleaning solvents, which may affect the bonding agent.

15 To dismantle the column, remove the upper lockwashers and spring. It may be necessary to grind away the edges of the lockwashers in order to remove them.

16 Remove the column from the tube.

17 The bearing may be removed from the tube using a suitable drift except on Procon-Ten-equipped models, where the bearing forms an integral part of the tube.

18 Reassembly and refitting are a reversal of

dismantling and removal, but note the following additional points. A special tool like the tool shown in Fig. 10.16 is required to press the lockwashers onto the top of the column. On the standard manual steering

13.8 Lower steering column and bulkhead rubber boot (arrowed)

10

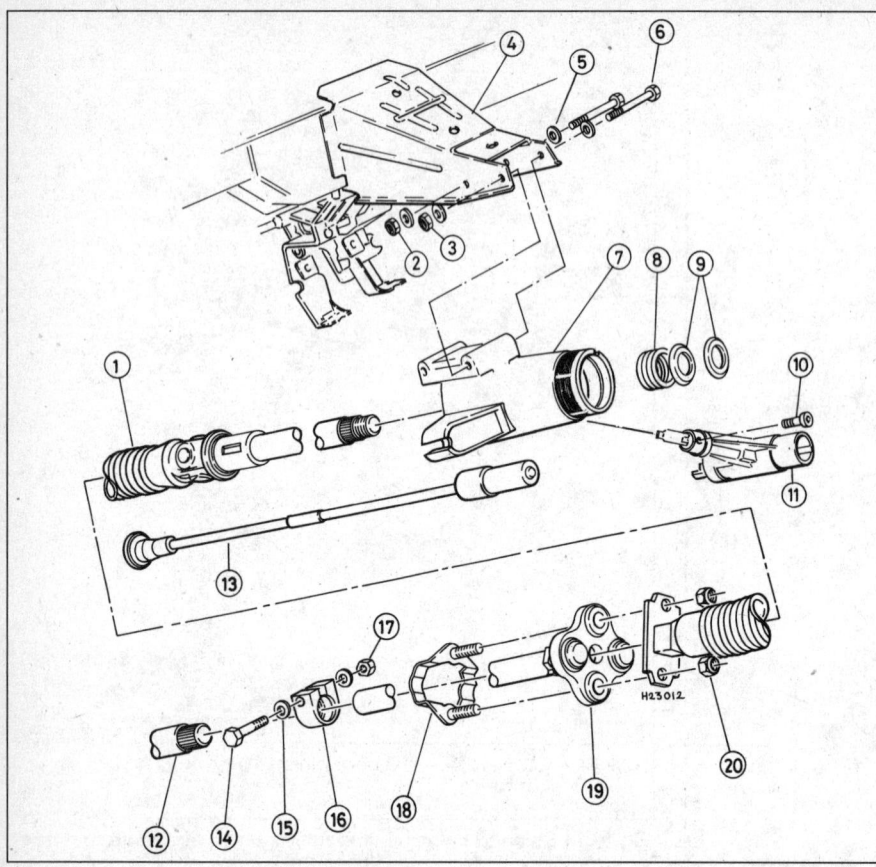

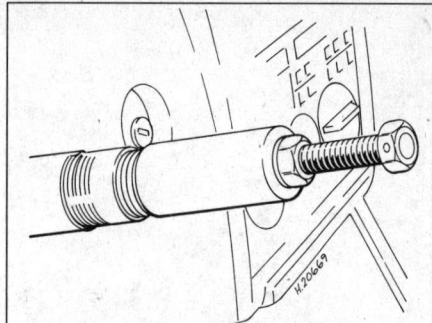

Fig 10.16 Using special tool to fit column lockwashers (Sec 13)

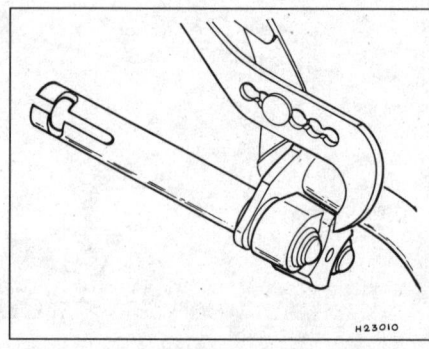

Fig 10.17 Holding the flange tube and column (Sec 13)

Fig 10.15 Steering column components for models with Procon-Ten safety system (Sec 13)

1	Inner column	6	Bolt	11	Lock housing	16	Clamp
2	Nut	7	Tube	12	Pinion	17	Nut
3	Washer	8	Spring	13	Procon-Ten cable	18	Shackle
4	Bracket	9	Lockwashers	14	Bolt	19	Flange tube
5	Washer	10	Bolt	15	Washer	20	Nut

version, hold the flange tube and column together with water pump pliers as shown in Fig. 10.17, then adjust the column position until the dimension shown in Fig. 10.18 is achieved. Secure the column to the pinion. Before tightening the threaded shackle securing the tube to the bulkhead, make sure that the tube is correctly aligned with the inner column.

plate, and separate it from the inner ends of the tie-rods.
4 Remove the tie-rod.
5 The tie-rod end may be removed from the tie-rod if necessary. To do this, first measure the distance between the inner bush and tie-rod end, and note this dimension. Loosen the locknut and unscrew the tie-rod end. The adjuster may also be removed if necessary.

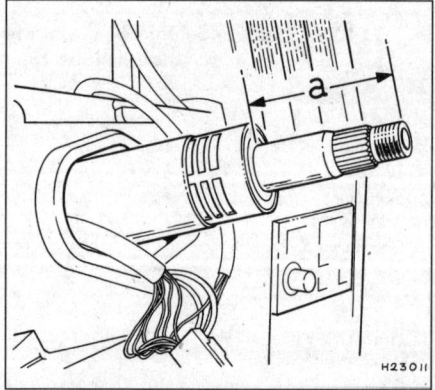

Fig 10.18 Column adjustment dimension (Sec 13)
$a = 67.5 \pm 1.0mm (2.66 \pm 0.04 in)$

14 Tie-rod - removal and refitting

1 Apply the handbrake, jack up the front of the car, and support on axle stands. Remove the front wheel from the relevant side of the car.
2 Unscrew the balljoint nut from the outer end of the tie-rod, and use a separator tool to detach the tie-rod from the strut steering arm (photo).
3 Unscrew the nuts on the front of the rack carrier plate (photo), then push out the stud

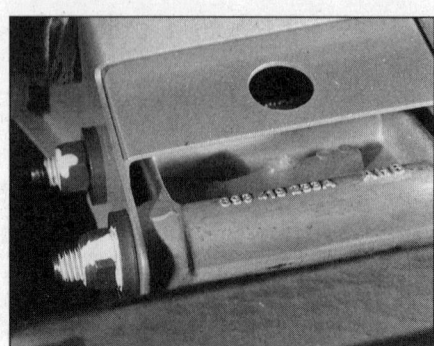

13.11 Upper column mounting bolts

14.2 Steering tie-rod end and nut

14.3 Tie-rod inner end mounting nuts on the rack carrier plate

6 Refitting is a reversal of removal, but renew all self-locking nuts, and tighten them to the specified torque. Delay fully tightening the stud plate nuts until the weight of the car is on the suspension. If removed, set the tie-rod end to the previously-noted dimension. Make sure that the adjuster is fitted centrally between the tie-rod and tie-rod end, so that equal amounts of thread are visible on each side of the central shoulder. On completion, check and adjust the front wheel alignment as described in Section 22. Make sure that the adjustment locknuts on the tie-rod are tightened fully.

15 Steering gear - removal and refitting

Note: *Repair of the steering gear is not possible. If the unit is worn excessively, its action will be weak, and the steering in general will transmit more road shocks to the steering wheel. A new, or reconditioned, unit should be obtained. Where the steering is heavy or stiff it may be worthwhile checking the steering damper for partial seizure (Section 16). For models with manual steering, refer also to Section 18 before condemning the steering gear.*

1 Apply the handbrake, jack up the front of the car and support on axle stands. Remove the front wheels.

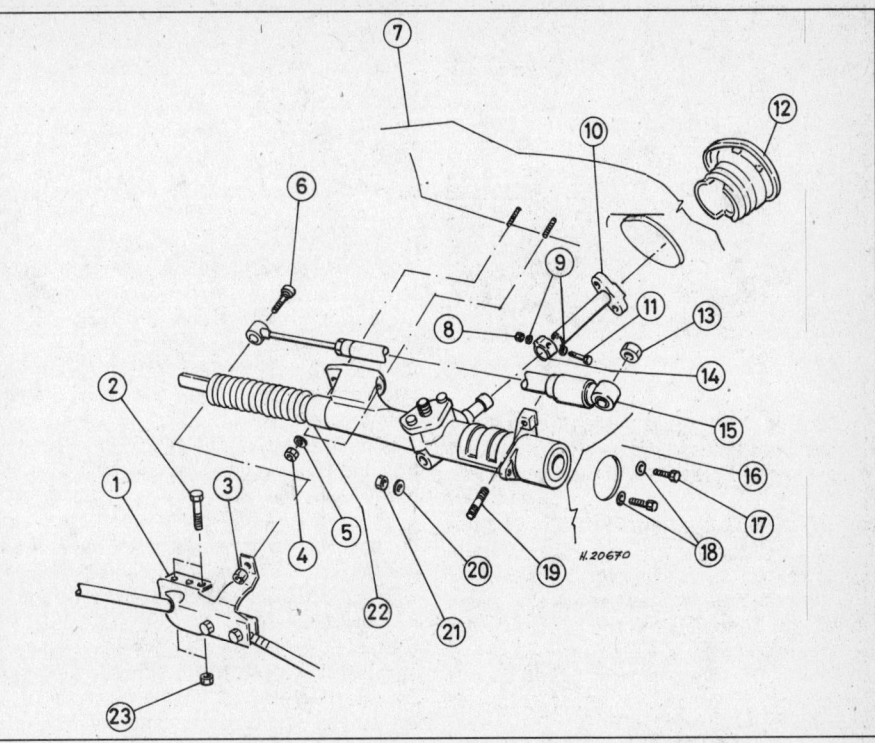

Fig 10.19 Steering gear external components (Sec 15)

1 Carrier	7 Bulkhead	13 Nut	19 Stud
2 Bolt	8 Nut	14 Clamp	20 Washer
3 Nut	9 Washers	15 Steering damper	21 Nut
4 Nut	10 Flange tube	16 Body	22 Steering gear
5 Washer	11 Clamp bolt	17 Bolt	23 Nut
6 Bolt	12 Rubber seal	18 Washer	

2 On manual steering models, unscrew and remove the bolt securing the steering damper to the carrier plate (photo).
3 Unscrew and remove the bolts securing the carrier plate to the steering rack (photo). Pull the carrier plate forwards.
4 Where applicable, remove the trim panel from under the facia panel over the steering column.
5 Disengage the rubber seal from the bulkhead and, on manual steering models, disengage it from the steering gear.
6 Unscrew and remove the clamp bolt securing the column flange tube to the

steering gear pinion, then, using a soft metal drift if necessary, tap the flange from the pinion.
7 On models equipped with power steering, place a suitable container beneath the steering gear to catch escaping fluid. Fit a hose clamp on the power steering flexible hoses. Unscrew the union nut and bolt from the supply and return lines, and detach them from the rotary valve housing on the steering gear.
8 Unscrew the mounting nuts securing the steering gear to the bulkhead and side panel, and withdraw it from the engine compartment (photos).

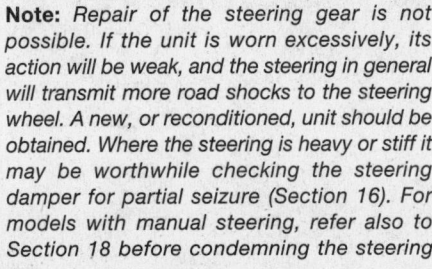

15.2 Steering damper-to-carrier plate mounting

15.3 Carrier plate-to-steering rack bolts

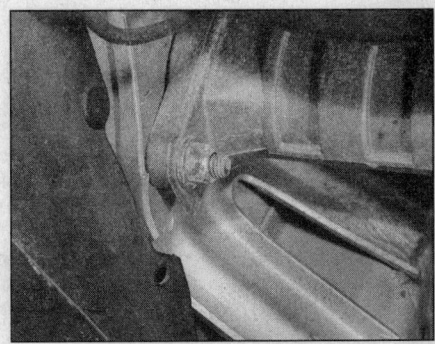

15.8A Steering gear side panel mounting . . .

10

15.8B . . . and bulkhead mounting (arrowed)

9 Unscrew the nut and detach the steering damper from the stud on the steering gear. If necessary, hold the stud stationary with an Allen key.

10 Refitting is a reversal of removal, but renew all self-locking nuts, and tighten all nuts and bolts to the specified torque. The bolts securing the steering gear to the side panel should be tightened **before** tightening the bulkhead bolts. Renew the power steering union washers where necessary. Top up and bleed the power steering circuit, with reference to Section 19.

16 Steering damper - testing, removal and refitting

1 A steering damper is fitted on manual steering models, and is connected between the tie-rod carrier and a mounting lug on the outer end of the steering gear housing.

2 To remove the damper, unscrew and remove the bolt securing the rod to the tie-rod carrier, then unscrew the nut and detach the damper from the outer mounting stud, while holding the stud with an Allen key.

3 With the damper removed, check that the movement of the piston rod is even and smooth over its complete stroke. Renew the damper if necessary.

4 Refitting is a reversal of removal, but tighten the nuts to the specified torque. If the self-locking nuts have been removed more than

18.3 Steering gear adjustment screw (arrowed)

two or three times, they should be renewed, otherwise the self-locking action will be insufficient. Renew them as a precaution, if in doubt.

17 Steering gear bellows - renewal

1 Unscrew and remove the bolts securing the tie-rod carrier plate to the steering rack. Support the plate above the rack using a block of wood.

2 Prise the bellows from the groove in the retaining ring on the rack, then slide the ring from the rack.

3 Loosen the clip and remove the bellows from the steering gear housing. Withdraw the bellows over the rack.

4 Scoop any remaining grease from inside the bellows, and smear it on the rack. If any grease has been lost, it should be replaced with the special Audi grease (part number AOF 063 000 04).

5 Locate the new bellows on the steering gear, and fit the clip, with the screw connection towards the bulkhead. Tighten the clip.

6 Push the outer ring fully onto the rack, then ease the bellows into the circular groove.

7 Locate the tie-rod carrier plate on the rack, then insert and tighten the two bolts to the specified torque.

18 Steering gear (manual) - adjustment

1 If there is any undue slackness in the steering gear, resulting in noise or rattles, the

steering gear should be adjusted as follows. An assistant will be required.

2 Have the assistant sit in the driver's seat and turn the steering wheel in alternate directions, about 30° either side of the central position. The front wheels should finally be set in the straight-ahead position.

3 Loosen the adjustment screw on top of the steering gear until there is noticeable slackness, and the rack movement is audible *from inside the car* (photo).

4 Slowly tighten the adjustment screw until the rack movement can no longer be heard *from inside the car*. If the adjustment screw is fitted with a locknut, ensure that it is tightened after the adjustment. Check also that the cover bolts are tight.

5 Turn the steering from lock to lock, and make sure that there are no 'tight' spots.

19 Power steering system - draining, refilling and bleeding

Draining and refilling

1 Position a suitable container beneath the fluid reservoir, then disconnect the pump supply hose and drain the fluid from the reservoir.

2 Position the container beneath the power steering pump, then unscrew the unions for the supply and pressure hoses and drain the fluid.

3 Check and if necessary renew the union sealing washers, then reconnect the hoses and tighten the unions. Reconnect the hose to the reservoir.

4 Unscrew the reservoir filler cap and remove

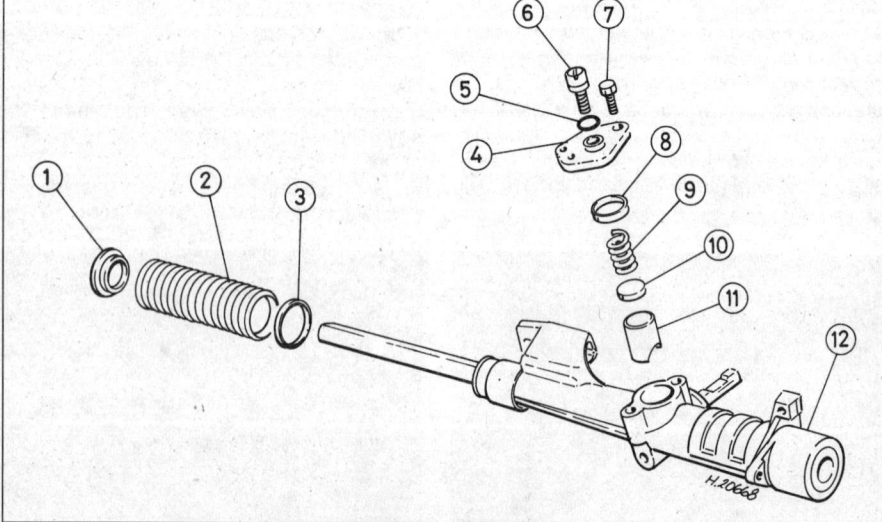

Fig 10.20 Steering gear internal components (Sec 18)

1 Retaining ring	4 Cover	7 Bolt	10 Thrust pad
2 Boot	5 O-ring	8 O-ring	11 Slipper
3 Clip	6 Adjusting screw	9 Spring	12 Housing

the filter, together with the spring, spring plate and sealing washer. Remove the components from the dipstick incorporated in the cap, then clean them with white spirit and allow to dry. Note that on models fitted with a hydraulic brake servo unit, the filler cap includes a low-level warning switch and the associated wiring.

5 Fill the system with fluid to the maximum level mark.

Bleeding

6 Apply the handbrake, then jack up the front of the car and support on axle stands.

7 With the engine switched off, turn the steering wheel sharply from lock to lock several times to allow air to be purged from the actuating cylinder. Top up to the fluid level.

8 Set the front wheels in the straight-ahead position, then run the engine at idling speed for approximately two minutes.

9 Switch off, and immediately check the fluid level in the reservoir. Top up the maximum level mark if necessary.

10 Repeat the procedure given in paragraphs 8 and 9 if it is noticed that air is still present in the reservoir fluid.

11 Finally, lower the car, and top up the fluid level. Refit the filler cap.

20 Power steering system - checking for leaks

1 With the engine running, turn the steering to full lock on one side and hold it in this position, to allow maximum pressure to build up in the system.

2 With the steering stiff at full lock, check all joints and unions for signs of leaks, and tighten if necessary (photos). To check the steering rack seal, remove the inner end of the rack bellows from the steering gear, and pull it back to reveal the seal.

3 Turn the wheel to full lock on the other side, and again check for leaks.

20.2A Power steering fluid supply pipe connection (arrowed) . . .

20.2B . . . and bracket (arrowed), located in front of the radiator

21 Power steering pump - removal, overhaul and refitting

1 Where applicable, unbolt and remove the radiator cooling fan cowling.

2 Loosen the pump adjustment, pivot, and mounting bolts (photos), swivel the pump towards the engine, and disconnect the drivebelt from the pulley.

3 Position a suitable container beneath the pump to catch escaping fluid.

4 Fit hose clamps to the pressure and return flexible hoses, then unscrew the union bolts and disconnect the hoses (photos). Recover the sealing washers. Where necessary, unscrew the hose support bracket bolt(s).

5 Remove the pivot and mounting bolts, and withdraw the pump from the engine.

6 Before overhauling the pump, check that it is possible to obtain spare parts. The cost of spare parts should also be taken into consideration, as it may well be better to obtain a new unit complete. The work must be carried out in a clean area, since the entry of dust and dirt will damage the internal components.

7 Clean the exterior surface of the pump.

8 Unscrew the studs and remove the rear cover. Mark both covers in relation to each other. Recover the O-ring seal.

9 Remove the spring and limiting valve, and lever out the securing element.

10 Remove the seal support, seal and channel plate.

11 Remove the stator, noting that the arrow is on the outer face.

21.2A Loosening the power steering pump adjustment bolt (arrowed) . . .

21.2B . . . pivot shaft (arrowed) . . .

21.2C . . . and mounting bolt (arrowed)

21.4A Unscrewing the power steering pump pressure line union bolt (arrowed). . .

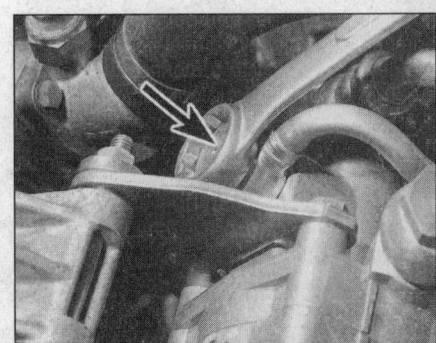
21.4B . . . and return line union bolt (arrowed)

10

12 Extract the circlip from the shaft, and remove the rotor. Extract the vanes, keeping them identified for position (ie with the shiny edges to the outside).

13 Remove the shaft from the rear cover, then use a screwdriver to prise out the oil seal.

14 Clean the components, and examine them for wear and damage. Spin the bearing by hand, and check it for roughness. Obtain a repair kit which consists of seals, seal support, and a circlip.

15 Reassemble the pump in reverse order, fitting the new components, but note the

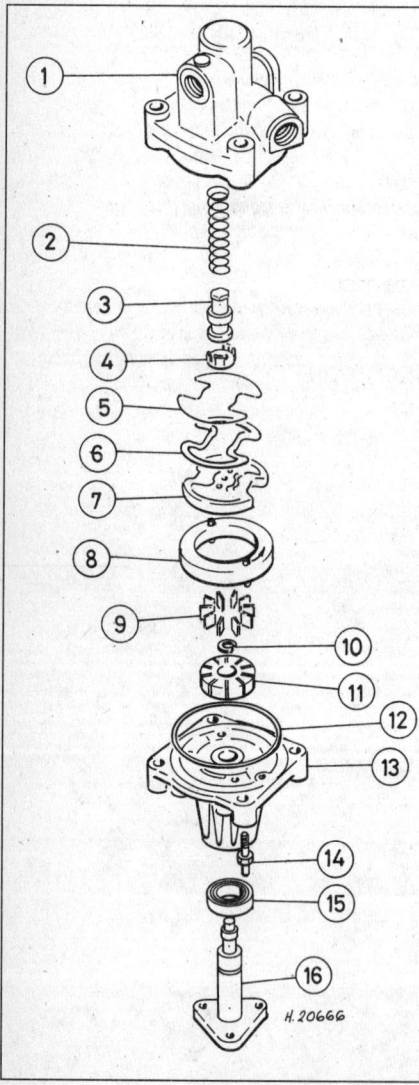

Fig 10.21 Exploded view of the power steering pump (Sec 21)

1	Rear cover	9 Vanes
2	Spring	10 Circlip
3	Pressure and flow	11 Rotor
	limiting valve	12 O-ring
4	Securing element	13 Front cover
5	Seal support	14 Stud
6	Seal	15 Seal
7	Channel plate	16 Shaft and drive
8	Stator	flange

following additional points. Dip the oil seal in the system hydraulic fluid, before driving it squarely into the housing using a block of wood. Press the securing element flush into the casing hole. The arrow on the stator must be outermost. The repair kit contains two types of circlip - only use the identical one to that removed. The oil holes in the casing halves must be correctly aligned. Apply locking fluid to the threads of the casing studs, before inserting and tightening them.

16 Refitting is a reversal of removal, but before doing so, it is recommended that the pump is filled with hydraulic fluid, and the air purged by turning the pulley by hand. Renew the sealing washers, and tighten the union bolts to the specified torque. Adjust the drivebelt with reference to Section 2, and refill the system with fluid, with reference to Section 1 9.

22 Wheel alignment - checking and adjusting

1 Accurate wheel alignment is essential for good steering and slow tyre wear. The alignment details are given in the Specifications and can be accurately checked by a suitably equipped garage. Front wheel alignment (toe) can be checked and adjusted, but checking and adjustment of the other steering angles is best left to your dealer due to the need for special gauges. For information purposes, camber is adjusted by moving the suspension lower wishbone balljoints within the tolerance allowed by their elongated fixing bolt holes. Castor is not adjustable, and any variation from the specified setting must be due to damage, or severe wear in the components. Rear suspension angles are not adjustable. Front wheel alignment gauges can be obtained from most motor accessory stores, and the method of using one is as follows.

2 Check that the car is only loaded to kerbside weight, with a full fuel tank, and the tyres correctly inflated.

3 Position the car on level ground, with the wheels straight-ahead, then roll the car backwards 4 metres (12 feet) and forwards again.

4 Using a wheel alignment gauge in accordance with the gauge manufacturer's instructions, check that the front wheel toe-in dimension is as given in the Specifications. If adjustment is necessary, loosen the locknuts on both tie-rods, and turn the adjusters by equal amounts. The amount of thread visible on each tie-rod should be the same, to ensure correct tracking on turns. Make sure that the tie-rod end balljoints are central in their arc of travel before tightening the locknuts.

5 If, after adjustment, the steering wheel spokes are no longer horizontal when the front roadwheels are in the straight-ahead position, then the steering wheel must be removed (see Section 12) and repositioned.

23 Wheels and tyres - general use and maintenance

Wheels and tyres should give no real problems in use provided that a close eye is kept on them with regard to excessive wear or damage. To this end, the following points should be noted.

Ensure that tyre pressures are checked regularly and maintained correctly. Checking should be carried out with the tyres cold and not immediately after the vehicle has been in use. If the pressures are checked with the tyres hot, an apparently high reading will be obtained owing to heat expansion. Under no circumstances should an attempt be made to reduce the pressures to the quoted cold reading in this instance, or effective underinflation will result.

Underinflation will cause overheating of the tyre owing to excessive flexing of the casing, and the tread will not sit correctly on the road surface. This will cause a consequent loss of adhesion and excessive wear, not to mention the danger of sudden tyre failure due to heat build-up.

Overinflation will cause rapid wear of the centre part of the tyre tread coupled with reduced adhesion, harsher ride, and the danger of shock damage occurring in the tyre casing.

Regularly check the tyres for damage in the form of cuts or bulges, especially in the sidewalls. Remove any nails or stones embedded in the tread before they penetrate the tyre to cause deflation. If removal of a nail does reveal that the tyre has been punctured, refit the nail so that its point of penetration is marked. Then immediately change the wheel and have the tyre repaired by a tyre dealer. Do not drive on a tyre in such a condition. In many cases a puncture can be simply repaired by the use of an inner tube of the correct size and type. If in any doubt as to the possible consequences of any damage found, consult your local tyre dealer for advice.

Periodically remove the wheels and clean any dirt or mud from the inside and outside surfaces. Examine the wheel rims for signs of rusting, corrosion or other damage. Light alloy wheels are easily damaged by 'kerbing' whilst parking, and similarly steel wheels may become dented or buckled. Renewal of the wheel is very often the only course of remedial action possible.

The balance of each wheel and tyre assembly should be maintained to avoid excessive wear, not only to the tyres but also to the steering and suspension components. Wheel imbalance is normally signified by vibration through the vehicle's bodyshell, although in many cases it is particularly noticeable through the steering wheel. Conversely, it should be noted that wear or damage in suspension or steering components may cause excessive tyre wear.

Out-of-round or out-of-true tyres damaged wheels and wheel bearing wear/mal-adjustment also fall into this category. Balancing will not usually cure vibration caused by such wear.

Wheel balancing may be carried out with the wheel either on or off the vehicle. If balanced on the vehicle, ensure that the wheel-to-hub relationship is marked in some way prior to subsequent wheel removal so that it may be refitted in its original position.

General tyre wear is influenced to a large degree by driving style harsh braking and acceleration or fast cornering will all produce more rapid tyre wear. Interchanging of tyres may result in more even wear, but this should only be carried out where there is no mix of tyre types on the vehicle. However, it is worth bearing in mind that if this is completely effective, the added expense of replacing a complete set of tyres simultaneously is incurred, which may prove financially restrictive for many owners.

Front tyres may wear unevenly as a result of wheel misalignment. The front wheels should always be correctly aligned according to the settings specified by the vehicle manufacturer.

Legal restrictions apply to the mixing of tyre types on a vehicle. Basically this means that a vehicle must not have tyres of differing construction on the same axle. Although it is not recommended to mix tyre types between front axle and rear axle, the only legally permissible combination is crossply at the front and radial at the rear. When mixing radial ply tyres, textile braced radials must always go on the front axle with steel braced radials at the rear. An obvious disadvantage of such mixing is the necessity to carry two spare tyres to avoid contravening the law in the event of a puncture.

In the UK, the Motor Vehicles Construction and Use Regulations apply to many aspects of tyre fitting and usage. It is suggested that a copy of these regulations is obtained from your local police if in doubt as to the current legal requirements with regard to tyre condition, minimum tread depth, etc.

Fault finding - suspension and steering

Excessive play in steering
- [ ] Worn steering gear
- [ ] Worn tie-rod end balljoints
- [ ] Worn tie-rod bushes
- [ ] Incorrect rack adjustment
- [ ] Worn suspension balljoints

Wanders, or pulls to one side
- [ ] Incorrect wheel alignment
- [ ] Worn tie-rod end balljoints or bushes
- [ ] Worn suspension balljoints
- [ ] Uneven tyre pressures
- [ ] Weak shock absorber
- [ ] Broken or weak coil spring

Heavy or stiff steering
- [ ] Seized steering or suspension balljoint, or steering damper
- [ ] Incorrect wheel alignment
- [ ] Low tyre pressures
- [ ] Leak of lubricant in steering gear
- [ ] Power steering faulty (where applicable}
- [ ] Power steering pump drivebelt broken (where applicable)

Wheel wobble and vibration
- [ ] Roadwheels out of balance
- [ ] Roadwheels damaged
- [ ] Weak shock absorbers
- [ ] Worn wheel bearings

Excessive tyre wear
- [ ] Incorrect wheel alignment
- [ ] Weak shock absorbers
- [ ] Incorrect tyre pressures
- [ ] Roadwheels out of balance

10

Notes

Chapter 11 Bodywork and fittings

Contents

Degrees of difficulty

Easy, suitable for novice with little experience	Fairly easy, suitable for beginner with some experience	Fairly difficult, suitable for competent DIY mechanic	Difficult, suitable for experienced DIY mechanic 	Very difficult, suitable for expert DIY or professional 

Specifications

Torque wrench settings	Nm	lbf ft
Door hinge bolts	30	22
Window regulator carrier	20	15
Door lock	16	12
Striker pin	50	37
Bumpers	23	17
Seat belts:		
Inertia reel mounting bolt	50	37
Stalk mounting bolt (rear)	50	37
Front seat belt upper mounting bolt	23	17
Front seat belt upper shouldered nut	50	37
Front seat stalk mounting bolt	60	44
Front seat belt lower mounting bolt	50	37

11

1 General description

The body is of all-steel unitary construction, and incorporates computer-calculated impact crumple zones at the front and rear, with a central safety cell passenger compartment. All panels are galvanized, and hot wax is injected into the internal cavities.

Some models may be fitted with a Procon-Ten safety system. Procon-Ten is an acronym for Programmed Contraction/Tension, and the system utilises steel cables connected to the front seat belt reels and steering column. In the event of a severe front end impact, the engine and gearbox will move rearwards and, since the cables are routed around the rear of the gearbox, this causes the front seat belt reels and steering column to be pulled forwards. This provides additional seat belt support, and also moves the steering column away from the driver.

2 Routine maintenance

Carry out the following procedures at the intervals given in 'Routine maintenance' at the beginning of the manual.

Check and adjust the air conditioner compressor drivebelt

1 Examine the full length of the drivebelt for fraying, deterioration and cracks, and for glazing of the pulley contact surfaces.
2 Check that the drivebelt deflection halfway between the two pulleys is approximately 5 mm (0.2 in), under firm thumb pressure.
3 If necessary, renew and/or adjust the drivebelt with reference to Section 36.

Lubricate the door check straps and bonnet lock

4 Apply a little multi-purpose grease to the door check straps on the lower door hinges, and to the bonnet lock striker and catch.

Lubricate the sliding sunroof

5 Open the sunroof and wipe clean the guide rails.
6 Spray the guide rails with multipurpose silicone lubricant.

Check underbody sealant

7 Raise the car and support on axle stands, or position it on a ramp.
8 Thoroughly check the underbody, sills and wheel housings for damage to the underbody sealant.
9 Where necessary, apply a new sealant after cleaning away any rust or dirt.
10 Lower the car to the ground.

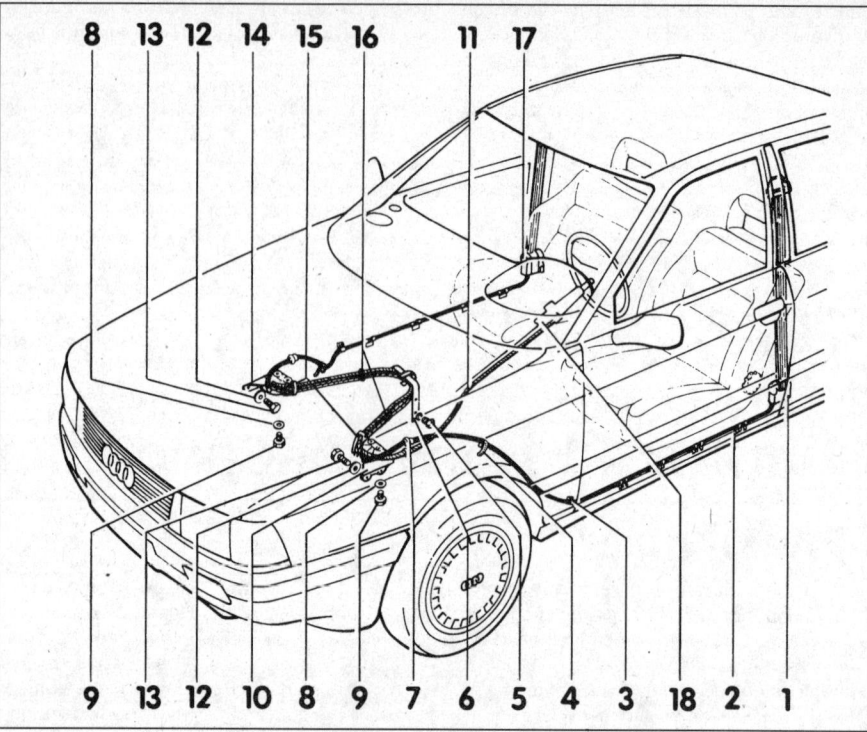

Fig 11.1 Procon-Ten safety system (Sec 1)

1 Seat belt inertia reel (LH)	7 Rubber grommet	13 Bolt
2 Clamp	8 Washer	14 Retaining bracket
3 Clip	9 Belt	15 Clip
4 Cable tie	10 Relay	16 Cable tie
5 Bolt	11 Cable for steering column	17 Seat belt inertia reel (RH)
6 Cable holder	12 Washer	18 Dovetail guide

3 Maintenance - bodywork and underframe

The general condition of a vehicle's bodywork is the one thing that significantly affects its value. Maintenance is easy, but needs to be regular. Neglect, particularly after minor damage, can lead quickly to further deterioration and costly repair bills. It is important also to keep watch on those parts of the vehicle not immediately visible, for instance the underside, inside all the wheel arches, and the lower part of the engine compartment.

The basic maintenance routine for the bodywork is washing - preferably with a lot of water, from a hose. This will remove all the loose solids which may have stuck to the vehicle. It is important to flush these off in such a way as to prevent grit from scratching the finish. The wheel arches and underframe need washing in the same way, to remove any accumulated mud, which will retain moisture and tend to encourage rust. Paradoxically enough, the best time to clean the underframe and wheel arches is in wet weather, when the mud is thoroughly wet and soft. In very wet weather, the underframe is usually cleaned of large accumulations automatically, and this is a good time for inspection.

Periodically, except on vehicles with a wax-based underbody protective coating, it is a good idea to have the whole of the underframe of the vehicle steam-cleaned, engine compartment included, so that a thorough inspection can be carried out to see what minor repairs and renovations are necessary. Steam-cleaning is available at many garages, and is necessary for the removal of the accumulation of oily grime, which sometimes is allowed to become thick in certain areas. If steam-cleaning facilities are not available, there are some excellent grease solvents available which can be brush-applied; the dirt can then be simply hosed off. Note that these methods should not be used on vehicles with wax-based underbody protective coating, or the coating will be removed. Such vehicles should be inspected annually, preferably just prior to Winter, when the underbody should be washed down, and any damage to the wax coating repaired. Ideally, a completely fresh coat should be applied. It would also be worth considering the use of such wax-based protection for injection into door panels, sills, box sections, etc, as an additional safeguard against rust damage, where such protection is not provided by the vehicle manufacturer.

After washing paintwork, wipe off with a chamois leather to give an unspotted clear finish. A coat of clear protective wax polish will give added protection against chemical pollutants in the air. If the paintwork sheen has dulled or oxidised, use a cleaner/polisher combination to restore the brilliance of the shine. This requires a little effort, but such dulling is usually caused because regular washing has been neglected. Care needs to be taken with metallic paintwork, as special non-abrasive cleaner/polisher is required to avoid damage to the finish. Always check that the door and ventilator opening drain holes and pipes are completely clear, so that water can be drained out. Brightwork should be treated in the same way as paintwork. Windscreens and windows can be kept clear of the smeary film which often appears, by the use of proprietary glass cleaner. Never use any form of wax or other body or chromium polish on glass.

4 Maintenance -  upholstery and carpets

Mats and carpets should be brushed or vacuum-cleaned regularly, to keep them free of grit. If they are badly stained, remove them from the vehicle for scrubbing or sponging, and make quite sure they are dry before refitting. Seats and interior trim panels can be kept clean by wiping with a damp cloth. If they do become stained (which can be more apparent on light-coloured upholstery), use a little liquid detergent and a soft nail brush to scour the grime out of the grain of the material. Do not forget to keep the headlining clean in the same way as the upholstery. When using liquid cleaners inside the vehicle, do not over-wet the surfaces being cleaned. Excessive damp could get into the seams and padded interior, causing stains, offensive odours or even rot.

 *If the inside of the vehicle gets wet accidentally, it is worthwhile taking some trouble to dry it out properly, particularly where carpets are involved. Do not leave oil or electric heaters inside the vehicle for this purpose.*

5 Minor body damage - repair

Repairs of minor scratches in bodywork

If the scratch is very superficial, and does not penetrate to the metal of the bodywork, repair is very simple. Lightly rub the area of the scratch with a paintwork renovator, or a very fine cutting paste, to remove loose paint from the scratch, and to clear the surrounding bodywork of wax polish. Rinse the area with clean water.

Apply touch-up paint to the scratch using a fine paint brush; continue to apply fine layers of paint until the surface of the paint in the scratch is level with the surrounding paintwork. Allow the new paint at least two weeks to harden, then blend it into the surrounding paintwork by rubbing the scratch area with a paintwork renovator or a very fine cutting paste. Finally, apply wax polish.

Where the scratch has penetrated right through to the metal of the bodywork, causing the metal to rust, a different repair technique is required. Remove any loose rust from the bottom of the scratch with a penknife, then apply rust-inhibiting paint to prevent the formation of rust in the future. Using a rubber or nylon applicator, fill the scratch with bodystopper paste. If required, this paste can be mixed with cellulose thinners to provide a very thin paste which is ideal for filling narrow scratches. Before the stopper-paste in the scratch hardens, wrap a piece of smooth cotton rag around the top of a finger. Dip the finger in cellulose thinners, and quickly sweep it across the surface of the stopper-paste in the scratch; this will ensure that the surface of the stopper-paste is slightly hollowed. The scratch can now be painted over as described earlier in this Section.

Repairs of dents in bodywork

When deep denting of the vehicle's bodywork has taken place, the first task is to pull the dent out, until the affected bodywork almost attains its original shape. There is little point in trying to restore the original shape completely, as the metal in the damaged area will have stretched on impact, and cannot be reshaped fully to its original contour. It is better to bring the level of the dent up to a point which is about 3 mm below the level of the surrounding bodywork. In cases where the dent is very shallow anyway, it is not worth trying to pull it out at all. If the underside of the dent is accessible, it can be hammered out gently from behind, using a mallet with a wooden or plastic head. Whilst doing this, hold a suitable block of wood firmly against the outside of the panel, to absorb the impact from the hammer blows and thus prevent a large area of the bodywork from being "belled-out".

Should the dent be in a section of the bodywork which has a double skin, or some other factor making it inaccessible from behind, a different technique is called for. Drill several small holes through the metal inside the area - particularly in the deeper section. Then screw long self-tapping screws into the holes, just sufficiently for them to gain a good purchase in the metal. Now the dent can be pulled out by pulling on the protruding heads of the screws with a pair of pliers.

The next stage of the repair is the removal of the paint from the damaged area, and from an inch or so of the surrounding "sound" bodywork. This is accomplished most easily by using a wire brush or abrasive pad on a power drill, although it can be done just as effectively by hand, using sheets of abrasive paper. To complete the preparation for filling, score the surface of the bare metal with a screwdriver or the tang of a file, or alternatively, drill small holes in the affected area. This will provide a really good "key" for the filler paste.

To complete the repair, see the Section on filling and respraying.

Repairs of rust holes or gashes in bodywork

Remove all paint from the affected area, and from an inch or so of the surrounding "sound" bodywork, using an abrasive pad or a wire brush on a power drill. If these are not available, a few sheets of abrasive paper will do the job most effectively. With the paint removed, you will be able to judge the severity of the corrosion, and therefore decide whether to renew the whole panel (if this is possible) or to repair the affected area. New body panels are not as expensive as most people think, and it is often quicker and more satisfactory to fit a new panel than to attempt to repair large areas of corrosion.

Remove all fittings from the affected area, except those which will act as a guide to the original shape of the damaged bodywork (eg headlight shells etc). Then, using tin snips or a hacksaw blade, remove all loose metal and any other metal badly affected by corrosion. Hammer the edges of the hole inwards, in order to create a slight depression for the filler paste.

Wire-brush the affected area to remove the powdery rust from the surface of the remaining metal. Paint the affected area with rust-inhibiting paint, if the back of the rusted area is accessible, treat this also.

Before filling can take place, it will be necessary to block the hole in some way. This can be achieved by the use of aluminium or plastic mesh, or aluminium tape.

Aluminium or plastic mesh, or glass-fibre matting, is probably the best material to use for a large hole. Cut a piece to the approximate size and shape of the hole to be filled, then position it in the hole so that its edges are below the level of the surrounding bodywork. It can be retained in position by several blobs of filler paste around its periphery.

Aluminium tape should be used for small or very narrow holes. Pull a piece off the roll, trim it to the approximate size and shape required,

11

then pull off the backing paper (if used) and stick the tape over the hole; it can be overlapped if the thickness of one piece is insufficient. Burnish down the edges of the tape with the handle of a screwdriver or similar, to ensure that the tape is securely attached to the metal underneath.

Bodywork repairs - filling and respraying

Before using this Section, see the Sections on dent, deep scratch, rust holes and gash repairs.

Many types of bodyfiller are available, but generally speaking, those proprietary kits which contain a tin of filler paste and a tube of resin hardener are best for this type of repair. A wide, flexible plastic or nylon applicator will be found invaluable for imparting a smooth and well-contoured finish to the surface of the filler.

Mix up a little filler on a clean piece of card or board - measure the hardener carefully (follow the maker's instructions on the pack), otherwise the filler will set too rapidly or too slowly. Using the applicator, apply the filler paste to the prepared area; draw the applicator across the surface of the filler to achieve the correct contour and to level the surface. As soon as a contour that approximates to the correct one is achieved, stop working the paste - if you carry on too long, the paste will become sticky and begin to "pick-up" on the applicator. Continue to add thin layers of filler paste at 20-minute intervals, until the level of the filler is just proud of the surrounding bodywork.

Once the filler has hardened, the excess can be removed using a metal plane or file. From then on, progressively-finer grades of abrasive paper should be used, starting with a 40-grade production paper, and finishing with a 400-grade wet-and-dry paper. Always wrap the abrasive paper around a flat rubber, cork, or wooden block - otherwise the surface of the filler will not be completely flat. During the smoothing of the filler surface, the wet-and-dry paper should be periodically rinsed in water. This will ensure that a very smooth finish is imparted to the filler at the final stage.

At this stage, the "dent" should be surrounded by a ring of bare metal, which in turn should be encircled by the finely "feathered" edge of the good paintwork. Rinse the repair area with clean water, until all of the dust produced by the rubbing-down operation has gone.

Spray the whole area with a light coat of primer - this will show up any imperfections in the surface of the filler. Repair these imperfections with fresh filler paste or bodystopper, and once more smooth the surface with abrasive paper. Repeat this spray-and-repair procedure until you are satisfied that the surface of the filler, and the feathered edge of the paintwork, are perfect. Clean the repair area with clean water, and allow to dry fully.

 **If bodystopper is used, it can be mixed with cellulose thinners to form a really thin paste which is ideal for filling small holes.**

The repair area is now ready for final spraying. Paint spraying must be carried out in a warm, dry, windless and dust-free atmosphere. This condition can be created artificially if you have access to a large indoor working area, but if you are forced to work in the open, you will have to pick your day very carefully. If you are working indoors, dousing the floor in the work area with water will help to settle the dust which would otherwise be in the atmosphere. If the repair area is confined to one body panel, mask off the surrounding panels; this will help to minimise the effects of a slight mis-match in paint colours. Bodywork fittings (eg chrome strips, door handles etc) will also need to be masked off. Use genuine masking tape, and several thicknesses of newspaper, for the masking operations.

Before commencing to spray, agitate the aerosol can thoroughly, then spray a test area (an old tin, or similar) until the technique is mastered. Cover the repair area with a thick coat of primer; the thickness should be built up using several thin layers of paint, rather than one thick one. Using 400-grade wet-and-dry paper, rub down the surface of the primer until it is really smooth. While doing this, the work area should be thoroughly doused with water, and the wet-and-dry paper periodically rinsed in water. Allow to dry before spraying on more paint.

Spray on the top coat, again building up the thickness by using several thin layers of paint. Start spraying at one edge of the repair area, and then, using a side-to-side motion, work until the whole repair area and about 2 inches of the surrounding original paintwork is covered. Remove all masking material 10 to 15 minutes after spraying on the final coat of paint.

Allow the new paint at least two weeks to harden, then, using a paintwork renovator, or a very fine cutting paste, blend the edges of the paint into the existing paintwork. Finally, apply wax polish.

Plastic components

With the use of more and more plastic body components by the vehicle manufacturers (eg bumpers, spoilers, and in some cases major body panels), rectification of more serious damage to such items has become a matter of either entrusting repair work to a specialist in this field, or renewing complete components. Repair of such damage by the DIY owner is not really feasible, owing to the cost of the equipment and materials required for effecting such repairs. The basic technique involves making a groove along the line of the crack in the plastic, using a rotary burr in a power drill. The damaged part is then welded back together, using a hot-air gun to heat up and fuse a plastic filler rod into the groove. Any excess plastic is then removed, and the area rubbed down to a smooth finish. It is important that a filler rod of the correct plastic is used, as body components can be made of a variety of different types (eg polycarbonate, ABS, polypropylene).

Damage of a less serious nature (abrasions, minor cracks etc) can be repaired by the DIY owner using a two-part epoxy filler repair material. Once mixed in equal proportions, this is used in similar fashion to the bodywork filler used on metal panels. The filler is usually cured in twenty to thirty minutes, ready for sanding and painting.

If the owner is renewing a complete component himself, or if he has repaired it with epoxy filler, he will be left with the problem of finding a suitable paint for finishing which is compatible with the type of plastic used. At one time, the use of a universal paint was not possible, owing to the complex range of plastics encountered in body component applications. Standard paints, generally speaking, will not bond to plastic or rubber satisfactorily. However, it is now possible to obtain a plastic body parts finishing kit which consists of a pre-primer treatment, a primer and coloured top coat. Full instructions are normally supplied with a kit, but basically, the method of use is to first apply the pre-primer to the component concerned, and allow it to dry for up to 30 minutes. Then the primer is applied, and left to dry for about an hour before finally applying the special-coloured top coat. The result is a correctly-coloured component, where the paint will flex with the plastic or rubber, a property that standard paint does not normally possess.

6 Major body damage - repair

Where serious damage has occurred or large areas need renewal due to neglect, it means that complete new panels will need welding in, and this is best left to professionals. If the damage is due to impact, it will also be necessary to completely check the alignment of the bodyshell, and this can only be carried out accurately by an Audi dealer using special jigs. If the body is left misaligned, it is primarily dangerous as the car will not handle properly, and secondly, uneven stresses will be imposed on the steering, suspension and possibly transmission, causing abnormal wear, or complete failure, particularly to such items as the tyres.

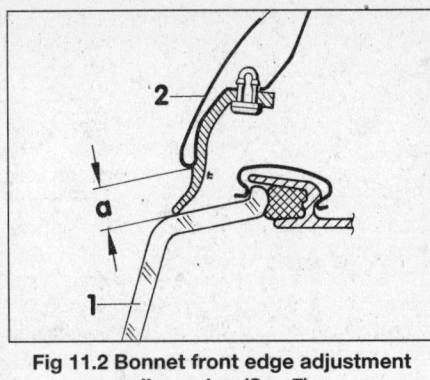

Fig 11.2 Bonnet front edge adjustment dimension (Sec 7)

1 Headlight   2 Bonnet
a = 9 + 2 mm (0.35 + 0.08 in)

7 Bonnet - removal, refitting and adjustment

1 Support the bonnet in its open position, and place some cardboard or rags beneath the corners by the hinges.

2 Push the windscreen washer jets rearwards, and pull them from the bonnet (photo). Disconnect the washer tubes and the washer heater wiring.

3 Disconnect the wiring for the engine compartment light.

4 Pull the wiring and tubes from the bonnet channel, and position them to one side (photos). As an aid to refitting, tie a piece of string or wire to the wiring before removing it, then leave the string in the channel.

5 If a gas-filled strut is fitted, disconnect it by pulling out the spring clip and pin. Support the bonnet.

6 Pull the plastic clips from the hinges (photo).

7 Mark the outline of the hinges on the bonnet with a pencil, or piece of chalk.

8 With the help of an assistant, unscrew the bolts and lift the bonnet from the car (photo).

9 Refitting is a reversal of removal, but adjust the bonnet so that it is level with the front wings. Forward and rearward adjustment is

7.2 Removing the windscreen washer jets

7.4B . . . and separate the connector

7.4D . . . and pull out the adaptor

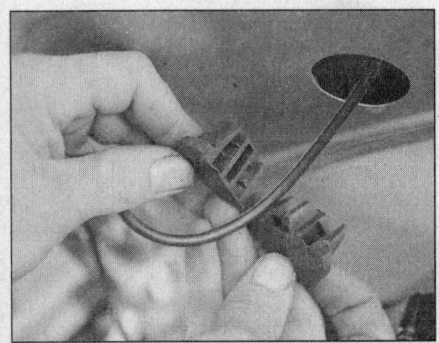

7.4F . . . and separate the holder halves

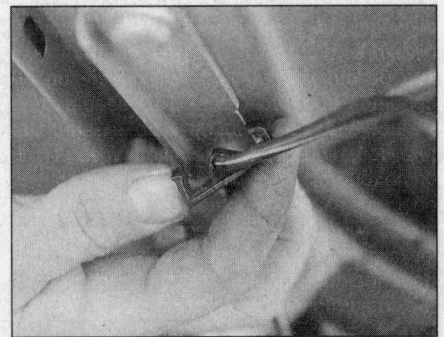

7.6 Releasing the clips from the hinges

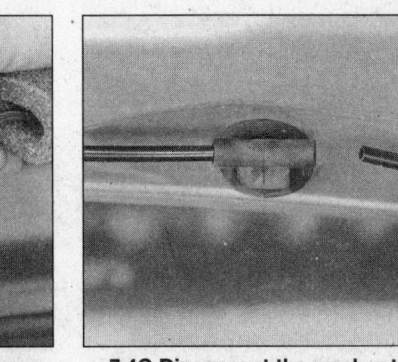

7.4A Remove the bonnet wiring . . .

7.4C Disconnect the washer tubes . . .

7.4E Pull out the washer tube holder . . .

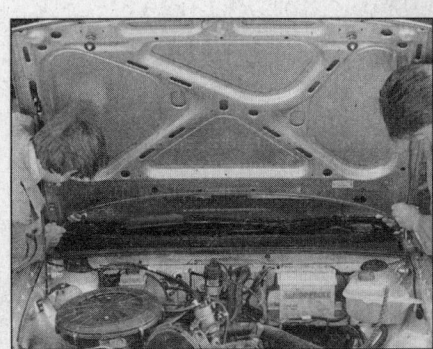

7.8 Removing the bonnet

11

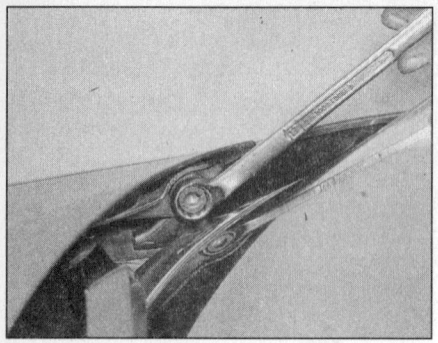
7.9 Adjusting the bonnet position

8.2 Bonnet opening lever

9.4 Bootlid hinge

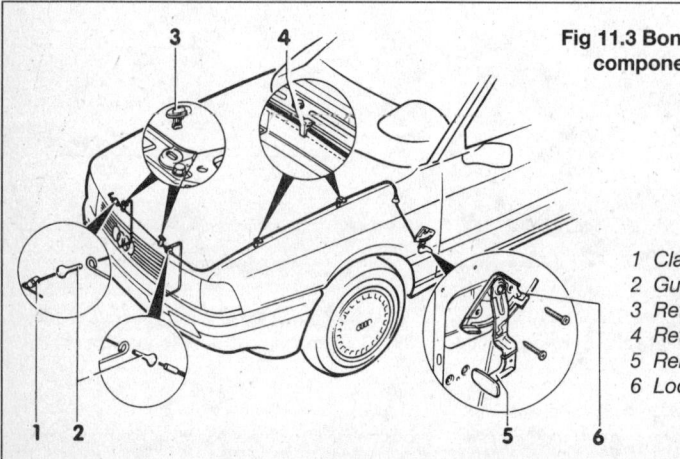
Fig 11.3 Bonnet lock cable components (Sec 8)

1 Clamping nipple
2 Guide sleeve
3 Retainer
4 Retaining clip
5 Release lever
6 Locking clip

made by loosening the bonnet-to-hinge bolts (photo). Height adjustment is made at the hinge pivot bolt, and by adjustment of the front rubber buffers and striker pins.

8 Bonnet lock cable - removal and refitting

1 Inside the car, remove the lower trim panel from under the steering column.
2 Unscrew the mounting screws from the bonnet opening lever, then disconnect the cable from the lever (photo).

3 Inside the engine compartment, unhook the cable from the lock control arms on the front crossmember.
4 Remove the special guides from the crossmember by turning the plastic retainers through 90°.
5 Release the cable from the clips on the front wing, and withdraw it through the bulkhead into the engine compartment.
6 Refitting is a reversal of removal. If a new cable is being fitted, transfer the guide sleeves and nipple to the new inner cable. Position the nipple on the cable so that there is no free play, then bend over the inner cable behind the nipple.

9 Boot lid - removal and refitting

1 Support the boot lid in its open position, and place some cardboard or rags beneath the corners by the hinges.
2 Disconnect the battery negative lead.
3 Disconnect the wiring loom and central locking hose.
4 Mark the position of the hinge on the boot lid with a pencil, or piece of chalk (photo).
5 Have an assistant support the boot lid, then remove the stops from each hinge by driving out the pins. If this action is not taken, it will be difficult to refit the support struts.
6 Extract the spring clips from the upper ends of the struts, and pull the struts from the ballpins.
7 Unscrew the mounting nuts and withdraw the boot lid from the car. If necessary, remove the fog, reversing and number plate lights with reference to Chapter 12. The hinges may also be unbolted from the body (photos).
8 Refitting is a reversal of removal, but check that the boot lid is positioned centrally. If necessary, reposition the hinges within the elongated mounting holes. The tail light clusters are also adjustable for position. Check also that the striker enters the lock centrally, and if necessary reposition the striker (photo).

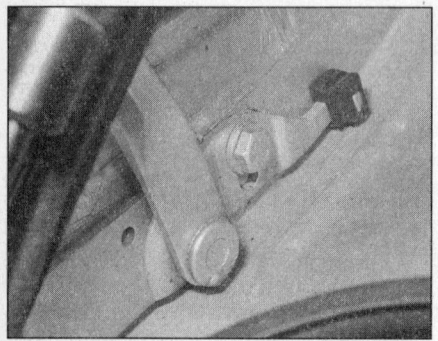
9.7A Bootlid hinge front bolt on body

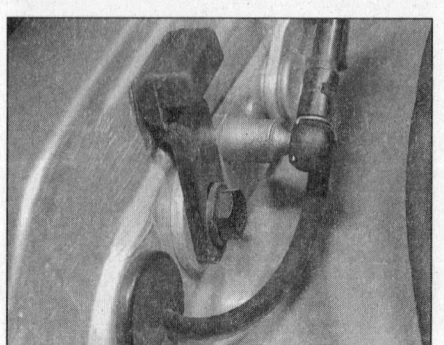
9.7B Bootlid hinge rear bolt on body

9.8 Bootlid lock striker

10.1 Removing the cover from the bootlid lock

10.3 Bootlid lock

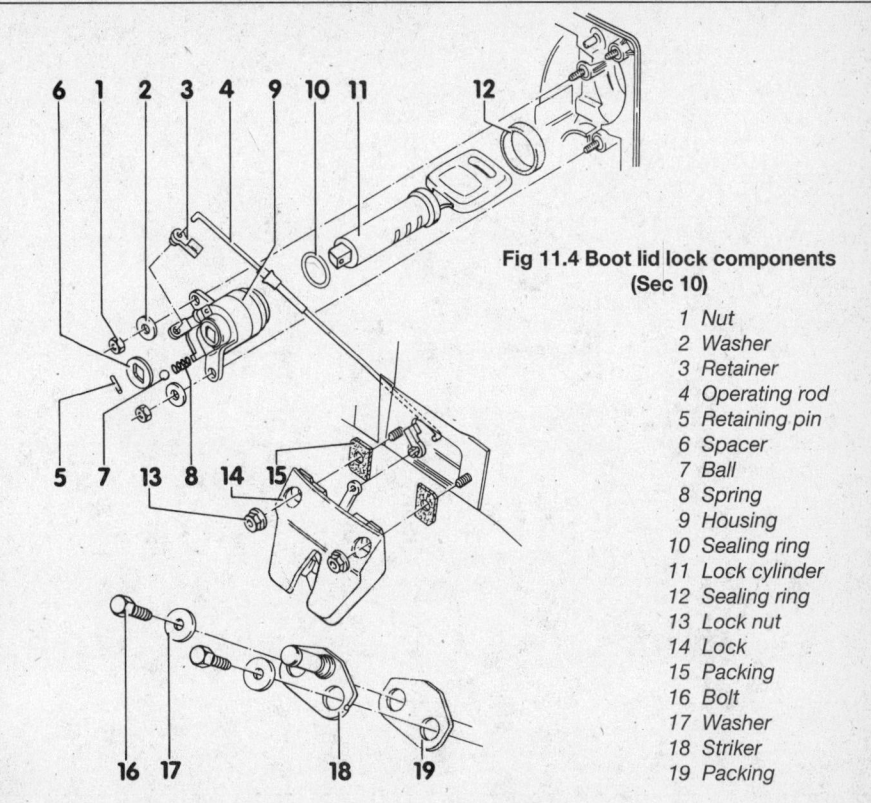

Fig 11.4 Boot lid lock components (Sec 10)

1 Nut
2 Washer
3 Retainer
4 Operating rod
5 Retaining pin
6 Spacer
7 Ball
8 Spring
9 Housing
10 Sealing ring
11 Lock cylinder
12 Sealing ring
13 Lock nut
14 Lock
15 Packing
16 Bolt
17 Washer
18 Striker
19 Packing

10 Boot lid lock - removal and refitting

1 Open the boot lid and remove the plastic covers from the boot lid and lock (photo).
2 Reach through the access holes, and disconnect the operating rod from the lock and private lock cylinder.
3 Unscrew the mounting nuts, and withdraw the lock from the boot lid (photo). Recover the packing if necessary, although this should be stuck to the lock.
4 To remove the lock cylinder, first insert the key, then use a small punch to drive out the retaining pin.

5 Remove the spacer, and recover the ball and spring on models with central locking.
6 Press out the lock cylinder, and recover the sealing ring and escutcheon.
7 Unscrew the mounting nuts, remove the washers, and withdraw the lock cylinder housing from the studs.
8 Refitting is a reversal of removal, however, observe the following points. On central locking models, apply a little grease to the ball located beneath the spring. If necessary, adjust the operating rod so that it enters the end bushes free of play, but without pretensioning the lock arm. The rod length is adjusted by releasing the sliding ring. Push the ring firmly into position after making the adjustment.

11 Boot lid and tailgate strut - removal and refitting

1 Support the boot lid/tailgate in its open position.
2 On the boot lid only, remove the stops from each hinge by driving out the pins, then open the boot lid to its limit.
3 Extract the spring clips from the upper and lower ends of the strut, and pull the strut from the ballpins (photos).
4 If the strut is being discarded, it is advisable to release the gas pressure as a safety precaution. To do this, mount the strut in a vice, on the area shown in Fig. 11.5. Using a hacksaw, cut through the strut cylinder to release the oil, but first wrap the cylinder with rag and wear protective goggles to prevent personal injury.
5 Refitting is a reversal of removal.

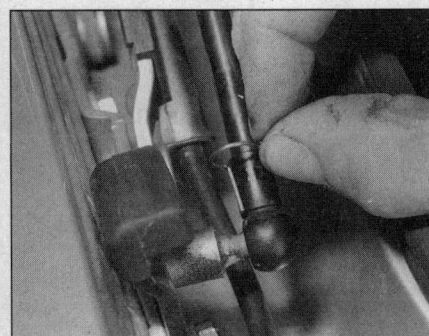

11.3A Extract the spring clip . . .

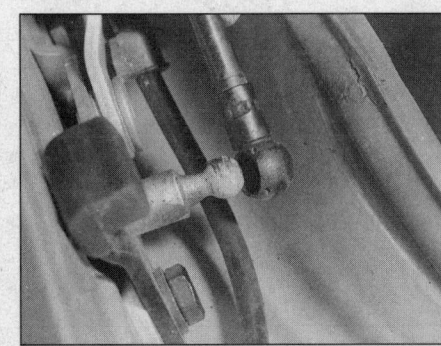

11.3B . . . and disconnect the strut

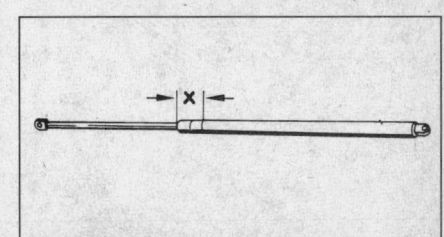

Fig 11.5 Strut mounting area (Sec 11)
x = 50 mm (2 in)

11

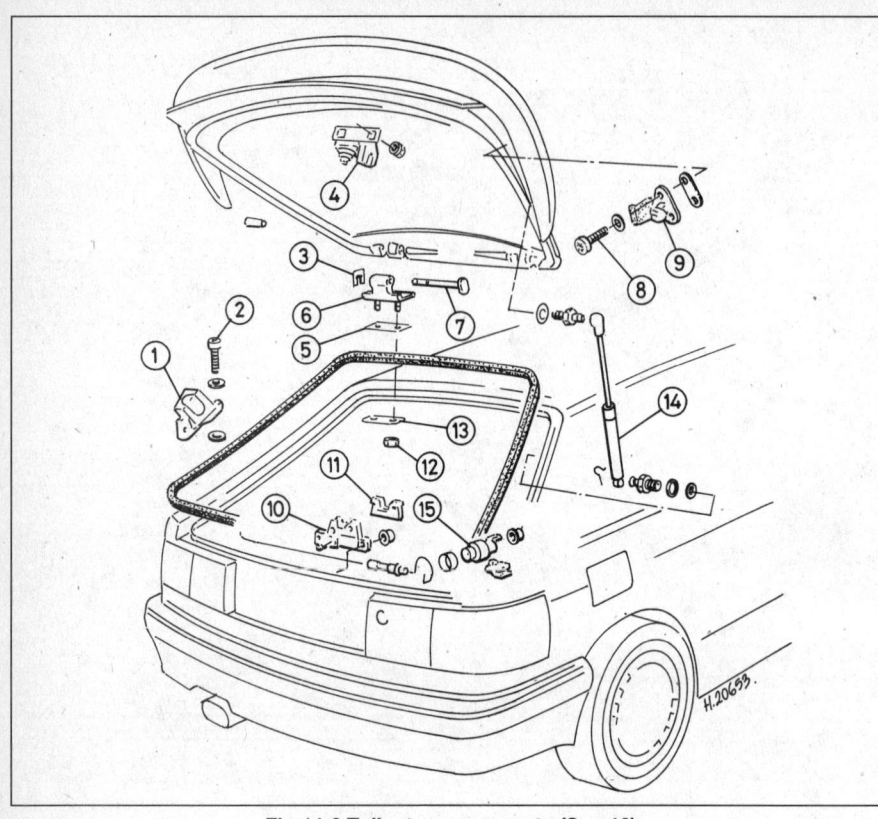

that the tailgate is positioned centrally. If necessary, reposition the hinges within the elongated mounting holes. Adjust the rubber buffers on the lower corners of the tailgate so that the tailgate rests firmly on them when shut. If necessary, reposition the striker so that it enters the lock centrally.

Fig 11.6 Tailgate components (Sec 12)

1 Rubber buffer	6 Hinge	11 Cover
2 Bolt	7 Hinge pin	12 Nut
3 Spring clip	8 Bolt	13 Gasket
4 Striker	9 Rubber buffer	14 Strut
5 Gasket	10 Latch	15 Private lock

13 Tailgate lock - removal and refitting

1 Open the tailgate and remove the trim from inside the rear panel.
2 Remove the cover from the lock.
3 Disconnect the operating rod from the lock and private lock cylinder.
4 On models fitted with central locking, disconnect the switch element operating rod.
5 Unscrew the mounting nuts and withdraw the lock from the rear panel.
6 To remove the private lock, unscrew the retaining nut.
7 Refitting is a reversal of removal.

14 Door trim panel - removal and refitting

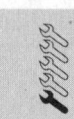

1 Open the inner door lever and unscrew the screw from the hinge plate (photo).
2 Press the fingerplate forwards and release it from the trim panel. Remove the seal, then prise out the cable clip and disconnect the inner cable from the lever (photos). Where applicable, disconnect the electrically-operated window wiring for the rear door.
3 On models with manually-operated windows, remove the regulator handle by prising off the knob, pulling off the plastic cover, and removing the retaining screw.
4 Remove the screws and withdraw the handle grip or switch panel. Disconnect the wiring where applicable, and detach the mirror adjustment mechanism on the front door (photos).

12 Tailgate - removal and refitting

1 Support the tailgate in its open position, and place some cardboard or rags beneath the corners by the hinges.
2 Disconnect the battery negative lead.
3 Remove the inner trim panel, and disconnect the tubing for the rear window washer jet. Also disconnect the wiring for the heated rear window and rear wiper.

4 Extract the spring clips from the upper ends of the struts, and pull the struts from the ballpins.
5 While an assistant supports the tailgate, extract the spring clips, then pull out the hinge pins. Withdraw the tailgate from the car.
6 The hinges may if necessary be removed from the roof panel by unscrewing the nuts, but mark their position with a pencil, or a piece of chalk, to ensure correct repositioning. Renew the sealing gaskets when refitting the hinges.
7 Refitting is a reversal of removal, but check

14.1 Fingerplate screw removal

14.2A Release the finger plate . . .

14.2B . . . remove the seal . . .

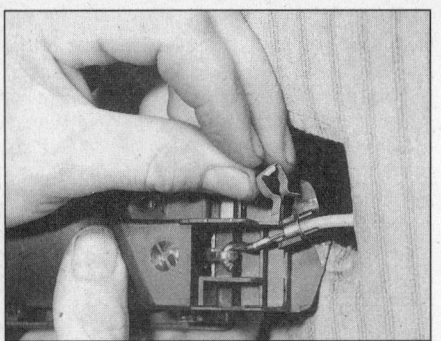

14.2C . . . extract the clip . . .

14.2D . . . and disconnect the cable

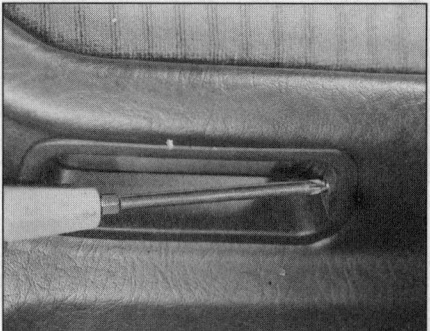

14.4A Remove the screw . . .

5 Unscrew the side screws from the upper corners, then push the trim panel upwards to release the plastic hooks from the door (photos). Withdraw the trim panel upwards over the locking knob.

6 Release the clips and remove the plastic-covered felt sheet from inside the trim panel (photo).

7 Refitting is a reversal of removal. Fit the window regulator handle with reference to Fig. 11.7. Check that the top edge of the trim is level with the outside window sealing lip, and if necessary adjust the screws on the regulator carrier plate.

14.4B . . . pull out the surround . . .

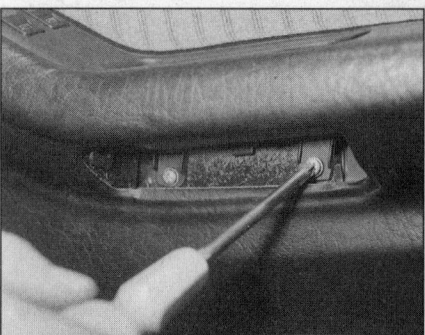

14.4C . . . remove the mounting screws . . .

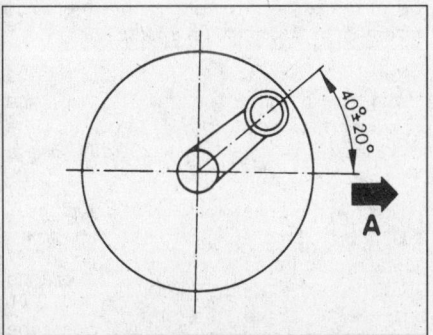

Fig 11.7 Window regulator handle closed position (Sec 14)
A = Front

14.4D . . . lever out the switch panel . . .

14.4E . . . and disconnect the wiring

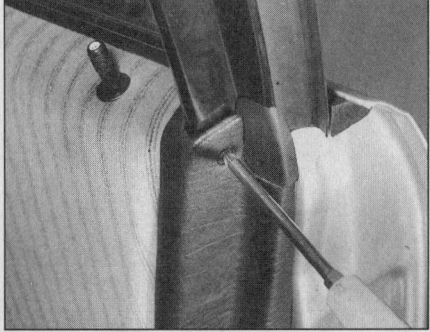

14.5A Remove the side screws . . .

14.5B . . . then release the trim panel plastic hooks (arrowed)

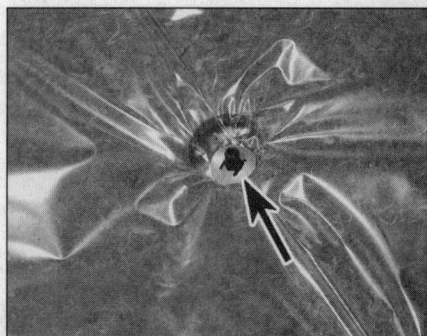

14.6 Inner trim panel clip (arrowed)

11

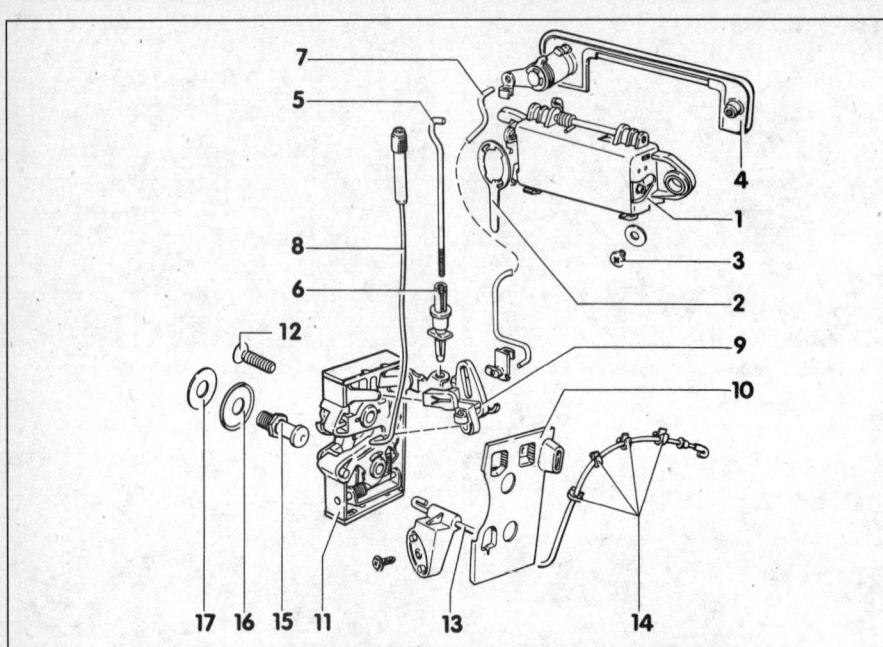

Fig 11.8 Front door lock components (Sec 15)

1 Exterior door handle	7 Securing rod	13 Interior door handle cable
2 Clip	8 Locking rod	14 Clips
3 Screw	9 Fastener	15 Striker
4 Cover	10 Seal	16 Dished washer
5 Operating rod	11 Door lock	17 Plastic washer
6 Clip	12 Screw	

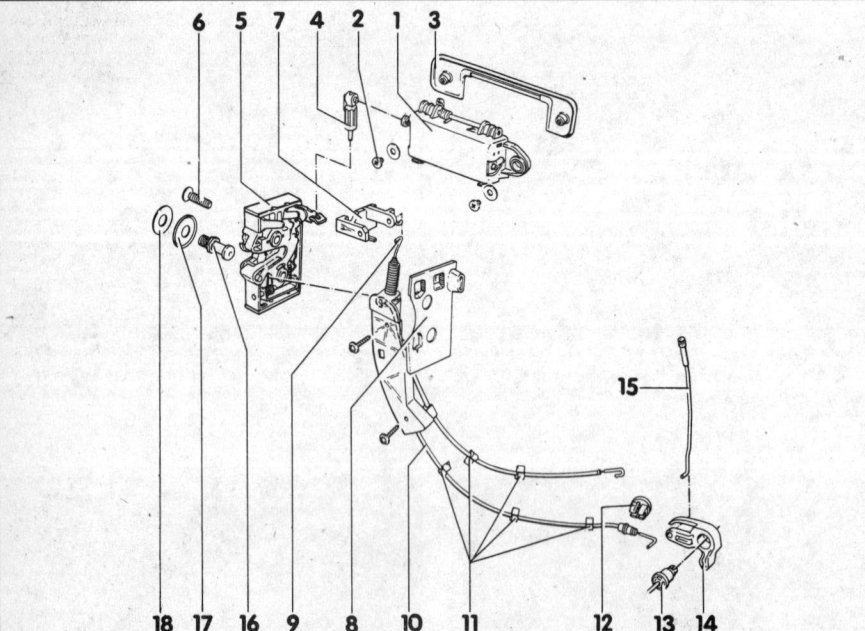

Fig 11.9 Rear door lock components (Sec 15)

1 Exterior door handle	8 Seal	13 Spreader clip
2 Screw	9 Interior door handle cable	14 Operating lever
3 Lever	end	15 Locking rod
4 Connector	10 Interior door handle cable	16 Striker
5 Door lock	11 Clip	17 Dished washer
6 Screw	12 Clip	18 Plastic washer
7 Fastener		

15.3 Door lock mounting screws (arrowed)

15 Door lock -
removal and refitting

1 Remove the door trim panel (Section 14).
2 Disconnect the locking knob and exterior handle operating rods from the lock.
3 Unscrew the lock mounting screws (photo).
4 Unhook the inner cable from the lock lever.
5 Withdraw the lock from the retainer, and recover the seal.
6 Refitting is a reversal of removal. To facilitate reconnecting the inner cable, hold the lock lever open by inserting a screwdriver through the hole shown in Fig. 11.10, then remove the screwdriver. Attach the operating rod to the exterior handle so that there is a maximum of 1.0 mm (0.04 in) free play.

16 Exterior door handle -
removal and refitting

1 Remove the door trim panel (Section 14).
2 Release the clip and disconnect the operating rod from the exterior handle.
3 Unscrew the handle mounting bolt, then turn the clip at the other end of the handle clockwise, and withdraw the handle from the door aperture.
4 Insert the key in the lock cylinder, then extract the circlip and remove the operating

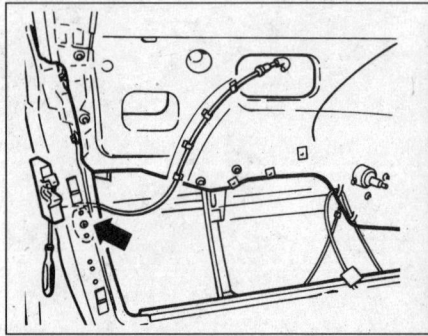

Fig 11.10 Refitting the door lock
(Sec 15)

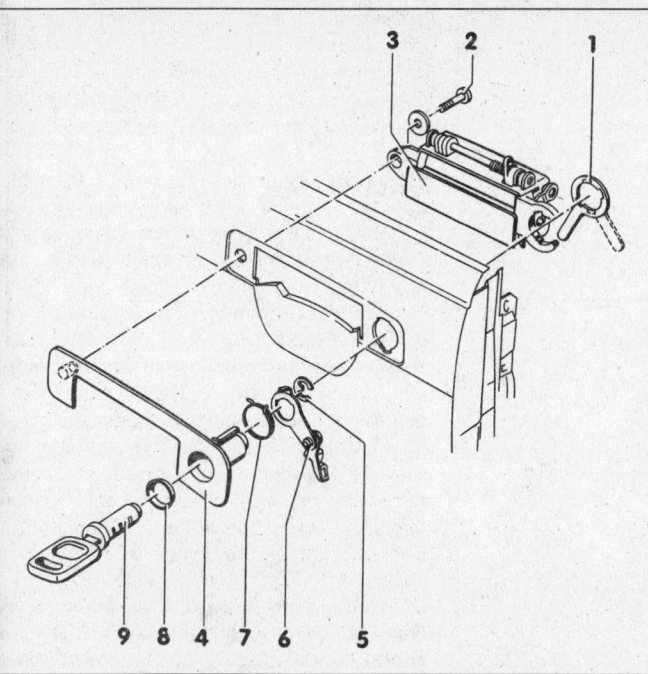

Fig 11.11 Exterior door handle components (Sec 16)

1 Pivoting clip	4 Cover	7 Spring
2 Screw	5 Circlip	8 Seal
3 Door handle	6 Operating lever	9 Lock cylinder

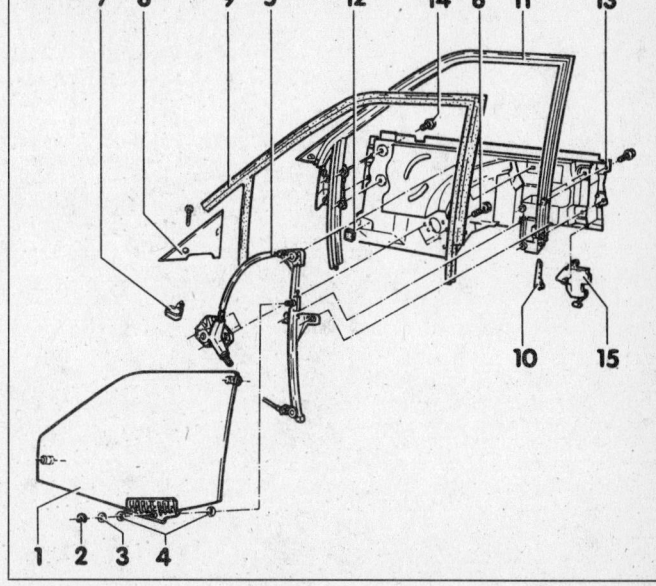

Fig 11.12 Window regulator components on Saloon models (Sec 17)

1 Window glass	6 Bolt	11 Door frame
2 Lock washer	7 Clip	12 Buffer
3 Washer	8 Cover	13 Carrier plate
4 Cushion	9 Seal	14 Bolt
5 Regulator	10 Plug	15 Door lock cover

lever and spring. Withdraw the lock cylinder and escutcheon from the handle.

5 Refitting is a reversal of removal, but make sure that the spring ends are positioned each side of the operating lever. Also make sure that the clip securing the handle is correctly seated.

17 Window regulator (Saloon) - removal and refitting

1 Remove the door trim panel (Section 14).
2 Mark the exact position of the carrier plate in relation to the door panel, then unscrew the mounting bolts, two at the front and two at the rear (photo).
3 Unclip the inner door handle cable and remove the carrier plate (photo).
4 Extract the circlip, and remove the washer and pad securing the window support to the regulator (photo). Disconnect the window support, and block it in the raised position with a length of wood.
5 Unclip the regulator cable.
6 Unscrew the nuts or bolts, and withdraw the regulator.
7 If necessary, remove the window glass from the door.
8 Refitting is a reversal of removal, but adjust the window stop so that the upper edge of the glass is in full contact with the weatherseal. The weatherseal lip should be compressed by at least 0.15 mm (0.02 in), but not excessive. The window stop is located on the centre guide of the regulator.

18 Window regulator (Coupé) - removal and refitting

1 The procedure is similar to that for the Saloon model, but the components are different as shown in Fig. 11.13.

19 Doors - removal and refitting

1 Remove the trim panel (Section 14).
2 If the door is to be refitted, mark round the hinges with a pencil, or a piece of chalk (photos).

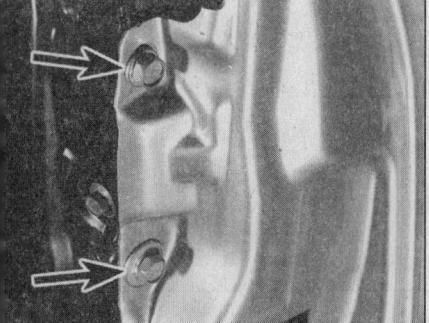

17.2 Carrier plate mounting bolts (arrowed)

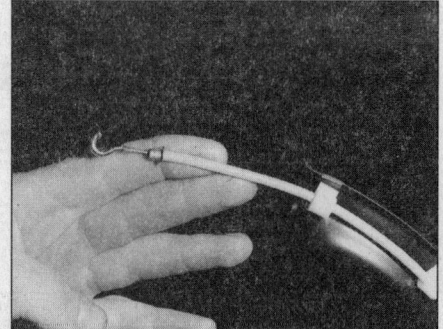

17.3 Inner door handle cable

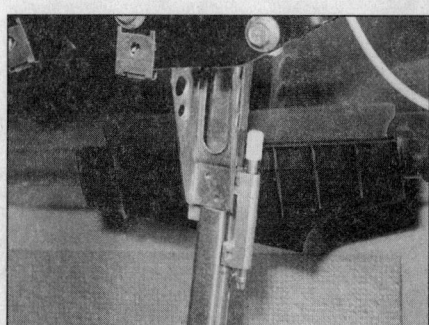

17.4 Window regulator support

11

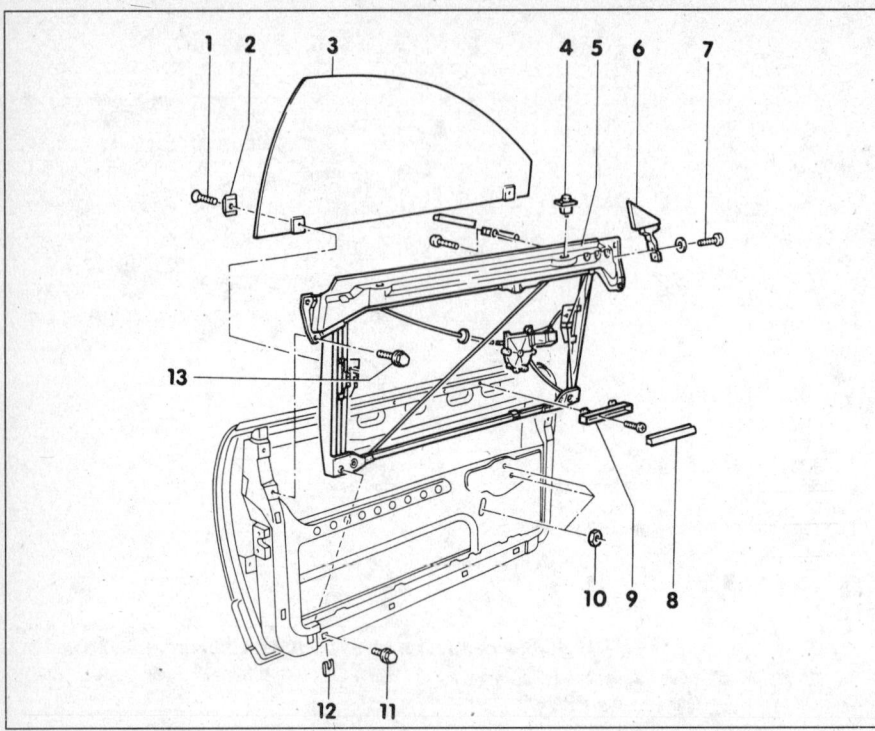

Fig 11.13 Window regulator components on Coupé models (Sec 18)

1 Screw
2 Pressure plate
3 Window glass
4 Adjusting clip
5 Carrier plate

6 Corner trim
7 Screw
8 Buffer
9 Retainer

10 Nut (on models with manual regulator)
11 Bolt
12 Spacer
13 Bolt

3 Disconnect all wiring and control cables from the door.

4 Support the door on blocks of wood.

5 Unscrew the bolts securing the door to the upper and lower hinges, and lift the door away.

6 If necessary, unbolt the hinges from the pillar.

7 Refitting is a reversal of removal, but apply a little grease to the door positioning spring and rollers, and adjust the door as follows. The clearance dimensions should be as shown in Fig. 11 .14.

8 To adjust the front edge of the door in or out, loosen the bolts on the hinges slightly, reposition the door, and then tighten the bolts. Fore and aft adjustment of the door is made by removing the inner pillar bolts loosening the outer bolts, then turning the special threaded bushes against the side of the pillar. Refit and tighten the bolts after making the adjustment.

9 To prevent wind noise, the rear edges of the doors should be adjusted so that they are approximately 1.0 mm (0.04 in) proud of the adjacent panel. This adjustment is made by loosening the striker (photo) and repositioning it, but make sure that it still enters the lock centrally.

10 Also check that the depth at which the striker enters the lock is correct, and if necessary, change the number of dished washers fitted beneath the striker head.

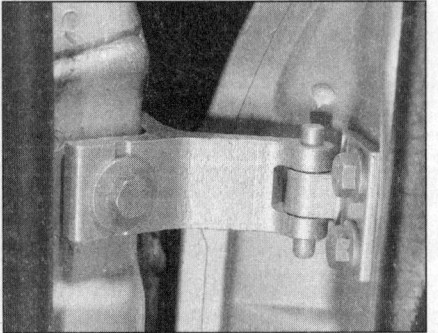

19.2A Upper door hinge

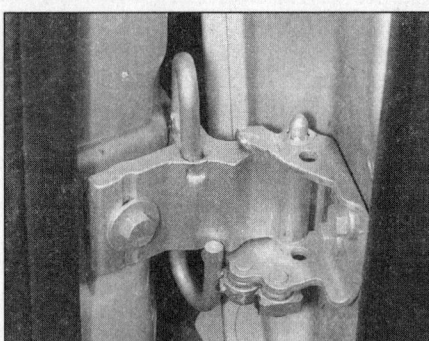

19.2B Front door lower door hinge

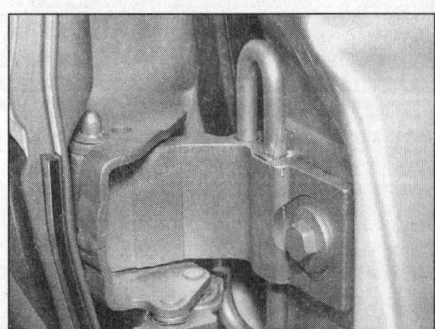

19.2C Rear door lower door hinge

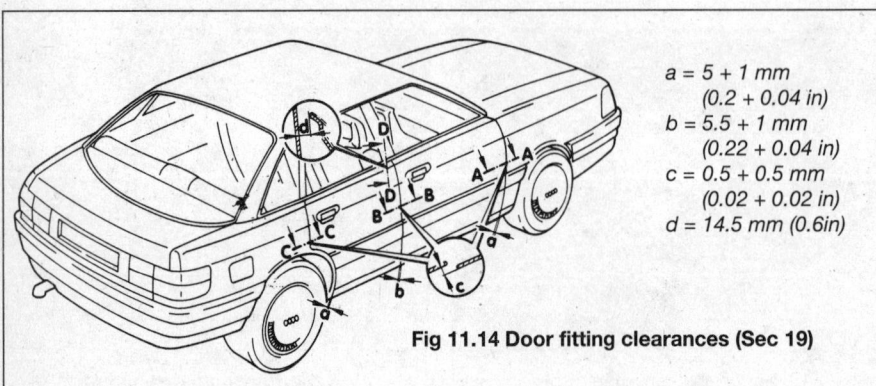

$a = 5 + 1\ mm$
$(0.2 + 0.04\ in)$
$b = 5.5 + 1\ mm$
$(0.22 + 0.04\ in)$
$c = 0.5 + 0.5\ mm$
$(0.02 + 0.02\ in)$
$d = 14.5\ mm\ (0.6in)$

Fig 11.14 Door fitting clearances (Sec 19)

19.9 Front door striker

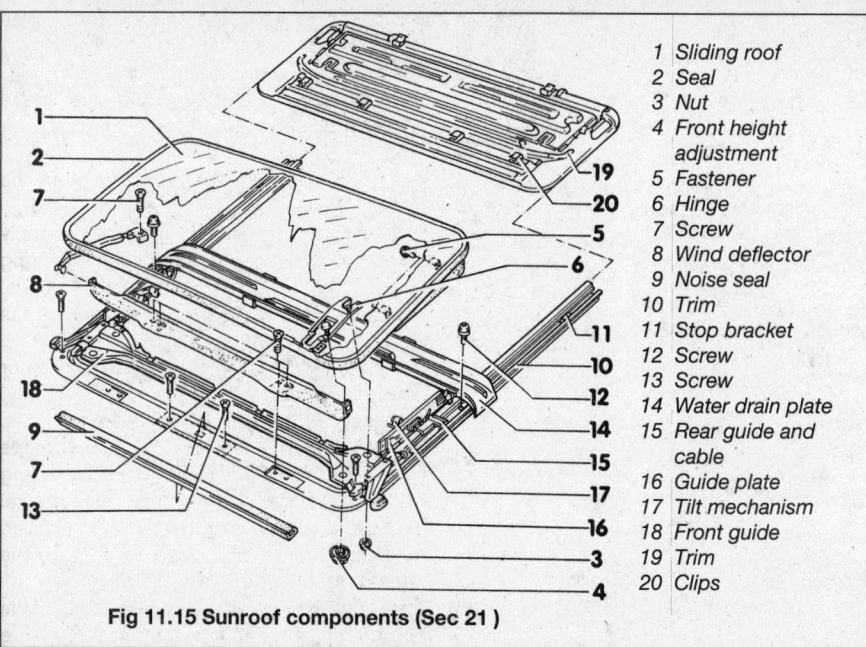

1	Sliding roof
2	Seal
3	Nut
4	Front height adjustment
5	Fastener
6	Hinge
7	Screw
8	Wind deflector
9	Noise seal
10	Trim
11	Stop bracket
12	Screw
13	Screw
14	Water drain plate
15	Rear guide and cable
16	Guide plate
17	Tilt mechanism
18	Front guide
19	Trim
20	Clips

Fig 11.15 Sunroof components (Sec 21)

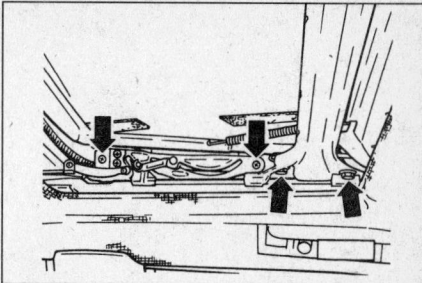

Fig 11.16 Sunroof mounting bolts (Sec 21)

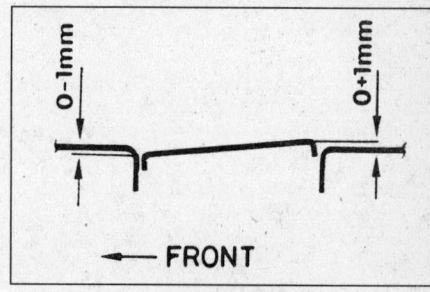

Fig 11.17 Sunroof height adjustment diagram (Sec 21)

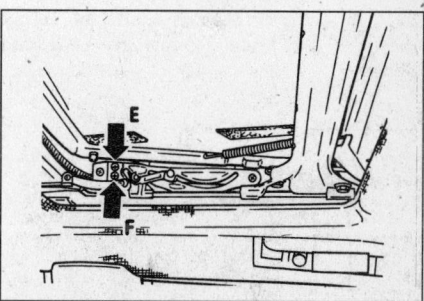

Fig 11.18 Sunroof front seal pressure adjustment screws (E and F) (Sec 21)

20 Windscreen, rear window glass, and rear side window glass - removal and refitting

The windscreen, rear window glass, and rear side window glass are directly bonded to the metalwork. Their removal and refitting requires the use of special tools not readily available to the home mechanic. This work should therefore be left to an Audi dealer, or a specialist glass replacement company.

21 Sunroof - removal, refitting and adjustment

1 Move the sunroof to its tilt position.
2 Press down the tilt flap then, using a 300 mm (12 in) long hook, disconnect the flap tension springs.
3 Reach into the flap recess, then push back and unclip the trim from the front guide. Do not lift the flap excessively, as it will touch the water drain plate.
4 Close the sunroof, and unscrew the mounting bolts indicated in Fig. 11.16 on each side to remove the sunroof.
5 Refitting is a reversal of removal. Make sure that the arrows on the guide plate and rear guide are aligned with each other, and that the water drain plate is engaged in the guide rails on both sides. If the mounting holes do not align, loosen the cross-head screws and move the guide plate as necessary. Check that the sunroof runs smoothly.
6 In the closed position. the front edge of the sunroof should be level with, or a maximum of 1.0 mm (0.04 in) lower than, the roof panel. The rear edge should be level with, or a maximum

of 1.0 mm (0.04 in) higher than, the roof panel. The adjustment points are shown in Fig. 11.16.
7 Note that the height adjustment nut (A) should have locking fluid applied to its threads before adjusting. When adjusting the height of the rear edge, tighten bolt (D) before bolt (C).
8 To adjust the pressure of the sunroof on the front seal, tilt the sunroof and loosen the screws shown in Fig. 11.18. Close the sunroof, open it approximately 50 mm (2 in) then close it lightly onto the front seal. Tighten screws E, then fully tilt the roof, and tighten screws F.

22 Sunroof water drain hoses - cleaning

1 If the sunroof water drain hoses become blocked with accumulated dust or leaves, they may be cleared by using a length of inner

speedometer cable approximately 2300 mm (90 in) long.
2 To clear the front hoses, open the sunroof and insert the cable through the hoses. The hoses terminate just above the lower door hinge positions in the A-pillars.

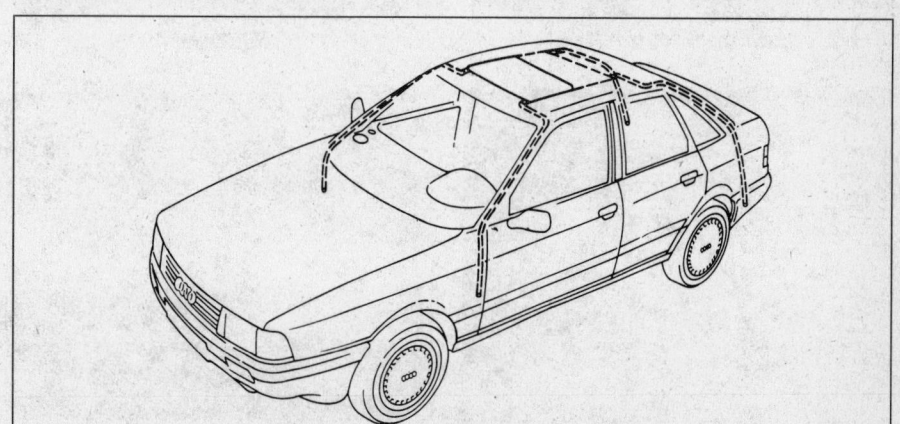

Fig 11.19 Routing of sunroof water drain hoses (Sec 22)

11

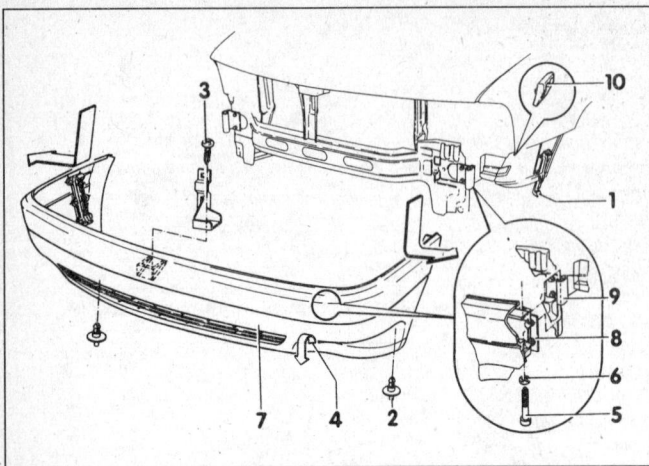

Fig 11.20 Front bumper components (Sec 23)

1 Guide	5 Bolt	9 Bracket
2 Expanding clip	6 Washer	10 Sliding spacer
3 Screw	7 Bumper	Arrows indicate
4 Cover	8 Bracket	direction of removal

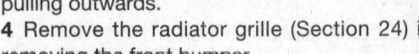

Fig 11.21 Rear bumper components (Sec 23)

1 Guide	6 Bracket	11 Rear end fitting
2 Screw	7 Spacer	12 Clip
3 Nut	8 Bumper	
4 Washer	9 Sliding spacer	Arrows indicate
5 Packing	10 Plastic nut	direction of removal

3 To clear the rear hoses, chock the front wheels, then raise the rear of the car and support on axle stands. Insert the cable through the hoses located in front of the rear bumper, and clear by pushing the cable upwards.

23 Bumpers - removal and refitting

1 Raise the front or rear of the car, and support on axle stands.
2 Where applicable, remove the foglight, with reference to Chapter 12.
3 Unclip the bumper ends from the side brackets by pressing down the end and pulling outwards.
4 Remove the radiator grille (Section 24) if removing the front bumper.
5 Refer to Figs. 11.20 and 11.21, and unscrew the mounting bolts and screws (photos). Withdraw the bumper.
6 Refitting is a reversal of removal. If a new rear bumper is being fitted, fit the self-adhesive seal in the position shown in Fig. 11.22. The clearance between the front bumper and panel strip should be 10 mm ± 1 mm (0.4 in ± 0.04 in), and between the rear bumper and side panel, 9 mm ± 1 mm (0.35 in ± 0.04 in). Adjustment is made by repositioning the mounting brackets.

24 Radiator grille - removal and refitting

1 Open the bonnet and unscrew the two screws holding the radiator grille to the front cross panel (photo).
2 Carefully release the radiator grille from the

Fig 11.22 Fitting position for self-adhesive seal in rear bumper (Sec 23)
Distance a = 280 mm (11 in)

23.5A Front bumper mounting bolt (arrowed)

23.5B Rear bumper mounting bolts

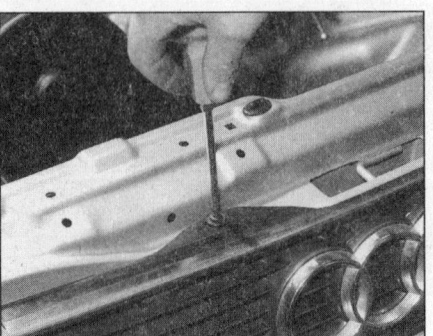
24.1 Removing the radiator grille upper mounting screws

24.2 Radiator grille corner clip (arrowed)

24.3 Radiator grille removal

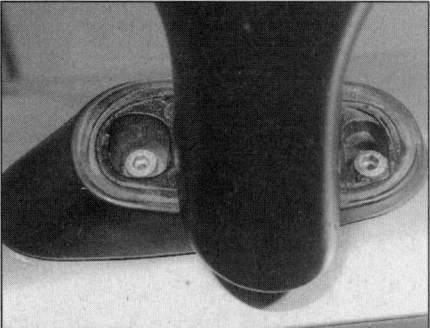

25.2 Electrically-operated exterior mirror retaining screws

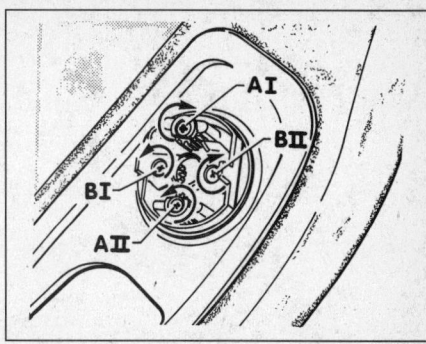

Fig 11.23 Exterior mirror adjustment – see text (Sec 25)

plastic clips on the upper corners using a screwdriver to depress the tabs (photo). It will help to slide the grille to alternate sides to do this, otherwise the plastic tabs may be broken.

3 Lift the radiator grille, and tilt the top outwards to release the lower tabs from the rail (photo). On models with air conditioning, disconnect the ambient air temperature sensor wiring.

4 Refitting is a reversal of removal.

25 Exterior mirror - removal and refitting

1 Remove the door trim panel (Section 14).

Electrically-operated mirror

2 Turn the mirror through 90° to expose the retaining screws (photo).

3 Unscrew the retaining screws, then disconnect the wiring and withdraw the mirror from the door. Refitting is a reversal of removal.

Manually-operated mirror

4 Mark the exact position of the window regulator carrier plate in relation to the door panel. Remove the front bolts, loosen the rear bolts, and move the carrier plate slightly forwards.

5 Release the clip and remove the adjusting head and cables from the carrier plate.

6 Turn the mirror through 90° to expose the retaining screws.

7 Unscrew the retaining screws, and withdraw the mirror from the door.

8 The mirror glass can be renewed separately by prising it out using a thin strip of plastic or wood. When fitting the new glass, press it onto the guide pins using a wad of cloth in the centre of the mirror.

9 Refitting is a reversal of removal, but if necessary adjust it as follows.

10 Centralise the mirror so that it is parallel to the housing. Pull off the control knobs. Refer to Fig. 11.23 and turn screw 'AI' clockwise until slight resistance is felt. Turn screw 'AII'

anti-clockwise until slight resistance is felt. Adjust screw 'BI' anti-clockwise, then screw 'BII' clockwise in the same manner. Refit the control knobs.

26 Interior rear-view mirror - removal and refitting

1 Press the complete mirror downwards to release it from the retaining plate on the windscreen.

2 To refit the mirror, locate it on the retaining plate at an angle of between 60° and 90° to the horizontal, then turn it clockwise until the spring clips engage.

27 Seat belts - removal and refitting

1 The seat belt anchorage points are shown in Fig. 11.24.

2 Access to the B-pillar anchorage points is gained by first removing the rear seat cushion (Section 31), then removing the screw securing the inner sill trim panel. Unscrew the special nuts and release the inner sill trim panel. Unbolt the bottom of the B-pillar trim panel, and unhook it at the top (photos). When refitting the panel, make sure that the height adjustment button engages with the B-pillar mechanism correctly.

3 Check that the height adjustment is heard

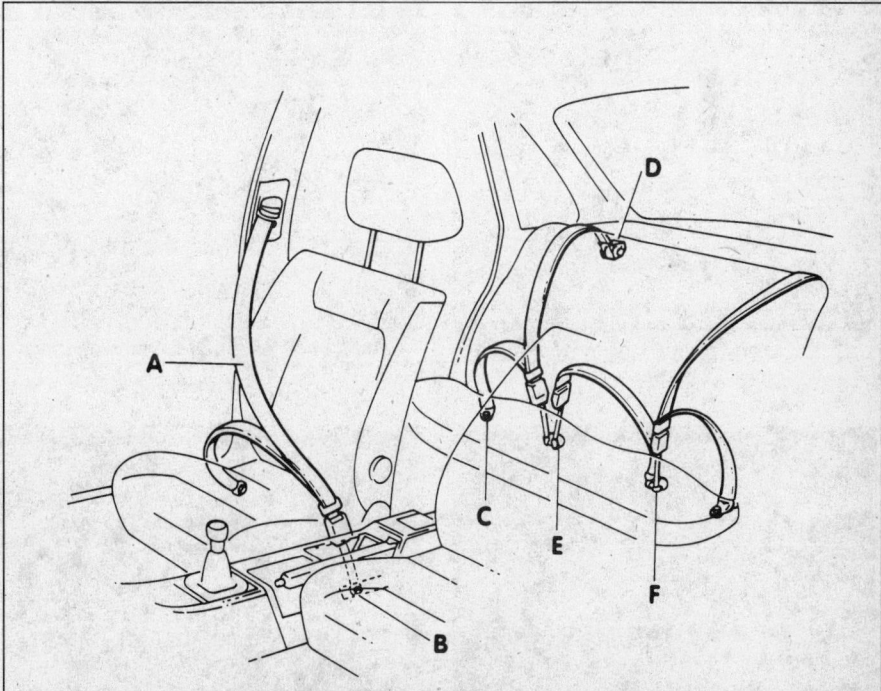

Fig 11.24 Seat belt anchorage points (Sec 27)

A Front seat belt
B Stalk-to-front seat attachment

C Rear seat belt outer floor mounting
D Rear inertia reel mounting

E RH rear stalk mounting
F LH rear stalk mounting

11

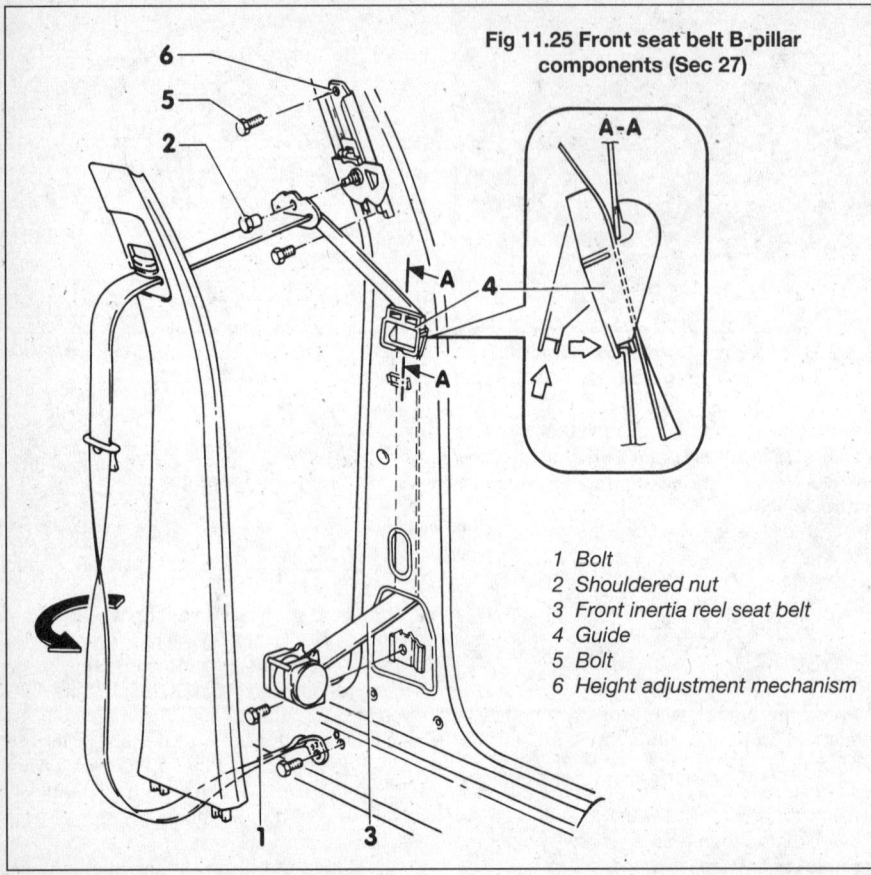

Fig 11.25 Front seat belt B-pillar components (Sec 27)

A-A

1 Bolt
2 Shouldered nut
3 Front inertia reel seat belt
4 Guide
5 Bolt
6 Height adjustment mechanism

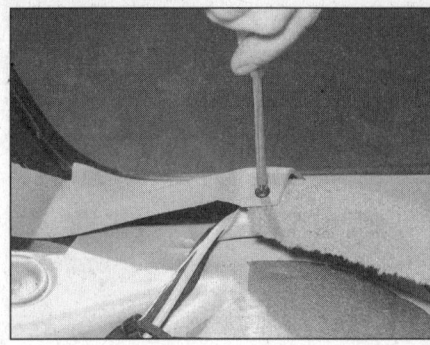

27.2A Remove the screw. . .

to engage the top position correctly, and that the adjustment button springs out fully when released in any position (photo).

4 Access to the rear seat belt anchorages is made by removing the rear seat cushion and backrest as described in Section 31. Unclip the D-pillar trim and withdraw upwards. Unbolt the seat belt from the floor bend up the metal tabs and withdraw the shelf forwards. Release the belt from the slot in the panel (photos).

5 Refitting is a reversal of removal, but tighten the anchorage bolts to the specified torque wrench settings.

6 On models fitted with the Procon-Ten safety system, note that the front inertia reels are attached permanently to the system

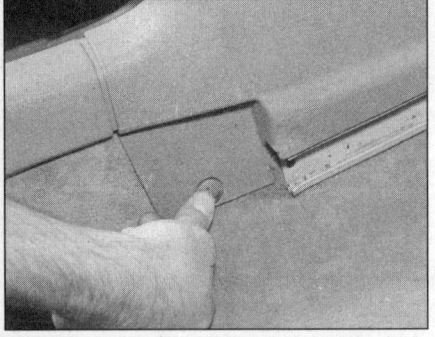

27.2B . . . and remove the inner sill trim panel

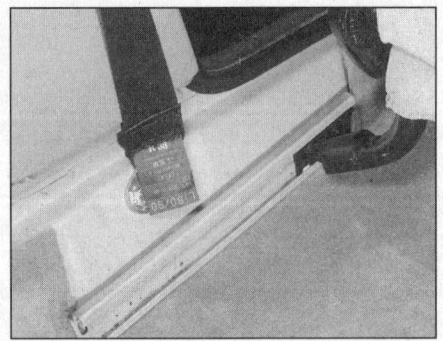

27.2C Front seat belt lower mounting

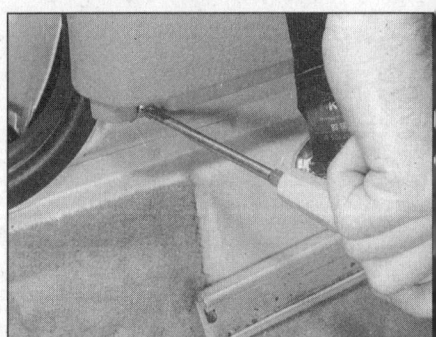

27.2D Remove the screw . . .

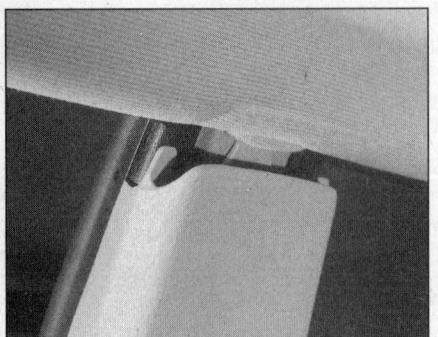

27.2E . . . and unhook the B-pillar trim panel

27.2F Front seat belt inertia reel

27.3 Front seat belt height adjustment mechanism

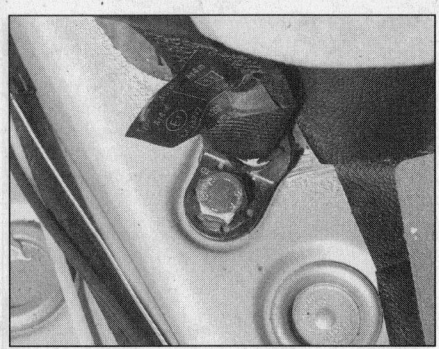

27.4A Rear seat belt lower mounting

27.4B Rear seat belt stalk mounting

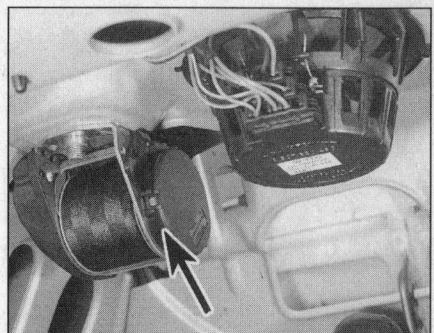

274C Rear seat belt inertia reel (arrowed)

cable. Therefore, the complete cable has to be removed, together with the seat belts. This involves removal of the A-pillar trim, manual choke control (if fitted), disconnection of the cable holder at the rear of the gearbox, and renewal of all the plastic guides. In view of the safety aspect, it is recommended that this work is performed by an Audi dealer, who will ensure that the system is fitted correctly.

28 Centre console - removal and refitting

1 Apply the handbrake, then use a screwdriver to prise out the lower trim from under the handbrake lever. Insert a screwdriver up through the handbrake lever hole to release the handgrip from the retaining lug, then pull off the handgrip. Pull off the lower trim (photos).
2 Disconnect the battery negative lead.
3 Remove the rear ashtray, then unscrew the centre console rear mounting bolts (photos).
4 Prise out the front trim cover and unscrew the mounting bolt (photo).
5 Lift the centre console and withdraw it forwards over the handbrake lever (photos).
6 Unscrew and remove the gearshift lever knob (photo).
7 Remove the single screw and release the gear lever boot over the gear lever (photos).

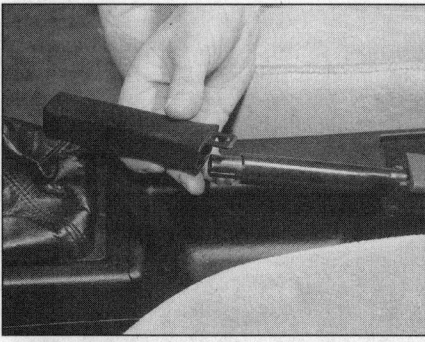

28.1A Removing the handbrake lever handgrip . . .

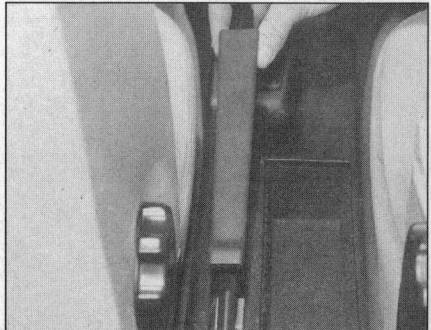

28.1B . . . and lower trim

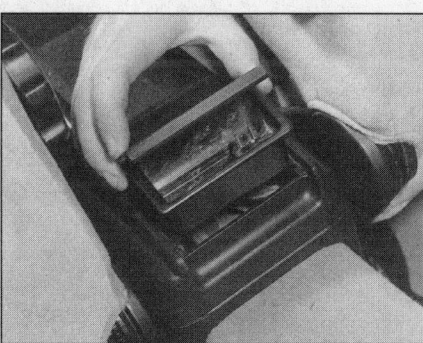

28.3A Remove the rear ashtray . . .

28.3B . . . for access to the centre console mounting bolts (arrowed)

28.4 Prising out the front trim cover – mounting bolt arrowed

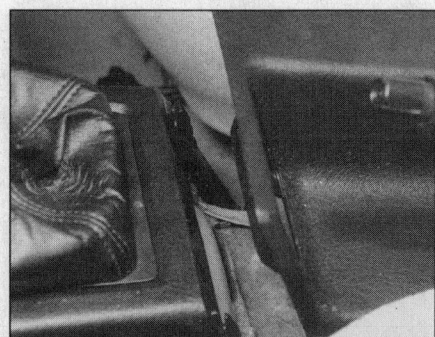

28.5A Lift the centre console . . .

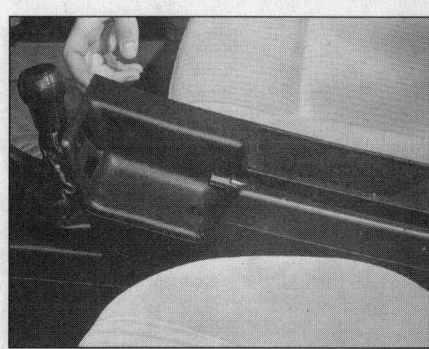

28.58 . . . and withdraw it forwards

11

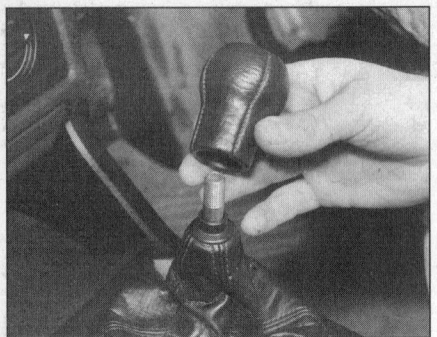

28.6 Gearshift lever knob

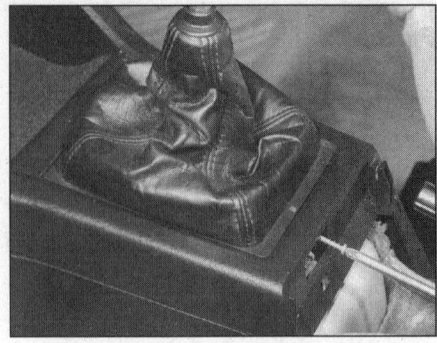

28.7A Remove the single screw . . .

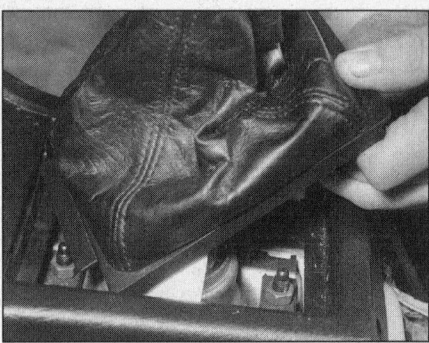

28.7B . . . and withdraw the gear lever boot

8 Push down the trim and remove the screws securing the console to the facia.
9 Withdraw the console from the clips on the bottom of the facia, and remove the console (photos).
10 Refitting is a reversal of removal.

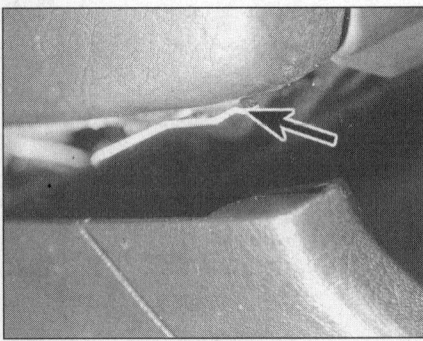

28.9A Withdraw the console from the front clips (arrowed) . . .

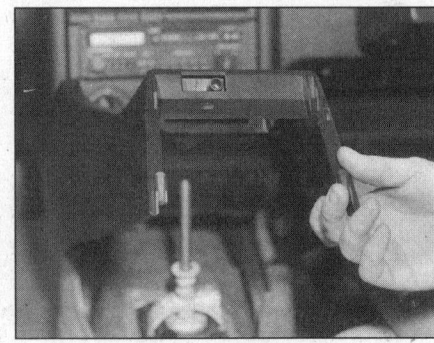

28.9B . . . and remove it

29 Facia panel - removal and refitting

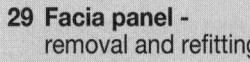

1 Remove the instrument panel (Chapter 12) and the centre console (Section 28).
2 Using a pair of pliers and a piece of card, carefully pull off the heater control knobs (photos).
3 Remove the screws from the knob recesses, and withdraw the surround panel (photos). On models fitted with air conditioning, the surround panel is clipped into position, without any screws.
4 Remove the screws securing the heater or air conditioning controls. Disconnect the multi-plug on air conditioning models.
5 Remove the radio (Chapter 12).
6 Unbolt the cover from the passenger side of the facia.
7 Unscrew the bolts from underneath the glovebox, then withdraw the glovebox (photos). On models fitted with air conditioning, unbolt the retaining strips, then press the glovebox towards the centre of the vehicle and lower it from the facia.

29.2A Using a pair of pliers and a piece of card . . .

29.2B . . . to remove the heater control knobs

29.3A Remove the screws . . .

29.3B . . . and withdraw the surround panel

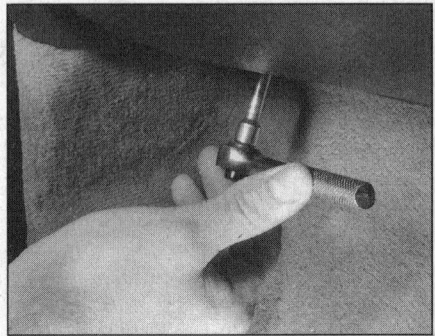

29.7A Unscrewing the bolts securing the glovebox

29.7B Glovebox mounting hinges

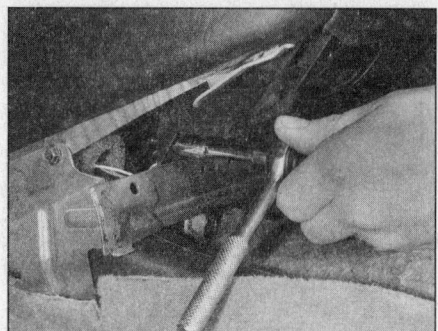

29.14 Facia centre mounting bolt removal

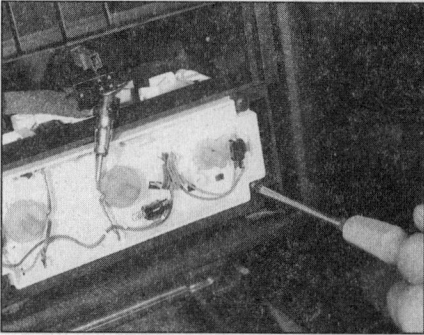

30.4 Heater control panel removal

8 Unbolt the lower trim panel on the driver's side.
9 On models with a manual choke control, depress the lug in the bottom of the choke knob, and remove the knob from the cable fitting. Unbolt the choke control from the facia panel.
10 Unbolt and remove the shelf (where fitted).
11 If not already done, disconnect the battery negative lead.
12 Disconnect the wiring loom multi-plugs beneath the steering column and beneath the centre of the facia.
13 Disconnect the wiring loom earth lead at the fusebox. The loom may remain connected to the switches if necessary.
14 Prise the plastic covers from each end of the facia panel, and unscrew the bolts. Also unscrew the centre mounting bolts on the centre tunnel (photo).
15 Unscrew the nuts from the heater housing, and remove the defroster duct screw.
16 Raise the defroster duct slightly, then withdraw the facia panel from the bulkhead, and remove it from the car.
17 Refitting is a reversal of removal. Press up the defroster duct connection, then attach the duct to the housing support. Make sure that the facia panel is correctly aligned before tightening the mounting bolts. The clearance between the facia and windscreen should be approximately 7.0 mm (0.28 in), and the top of the facia should align with the door trim panels with the doors shut.

30.5A Centre air vent removal

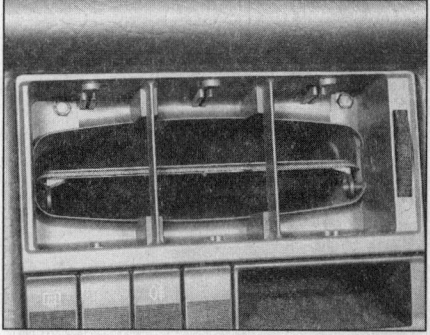

30.5B Air vent locations in centre section

30 Facia panel centre section - removal and refitting

1 Remove the centre console (Section 28).
2 Using a pair of pliers and a piece of card, carefully pull off the heater control knobs.
3 Remove the screws from the knob recesses, and withdraw the surround panel. On models fitted with air conditioning, the surround panel is clipped into position, without any screws.
4 Remove the screws securing the heater or air conditioning controls (photo).
5 Using a small screwdriver, carefully prise out the centre left and centre right air vents, inserting the screwdriver at the top edge first in each case (photos).

6 Press down the ashtray and remove the two screws exposed.
7 Remove the mounting screws located at each corner, and withdraw the centre section complete from the facia (photos). Disconnect the multiplugs from the switches and radio.
8 Refitting is a reversal of removal.

31 Seats - removal and refitting

Front seat

1 Move the seat fully rearwards and unscrew the front mounting bolt (photo).
2 Move the seat fully forwards and unscrew the rear mounting bolts (photo).

30.7A Remove the mounting screws . . .

30.7B . . . and withdraw the centre section

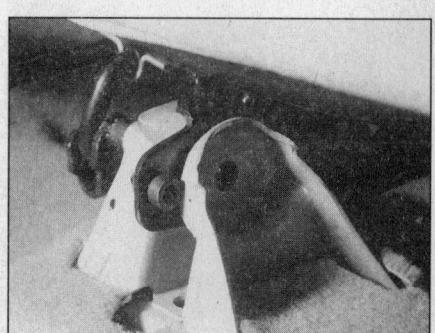

31.1 Front seat front mounting

11

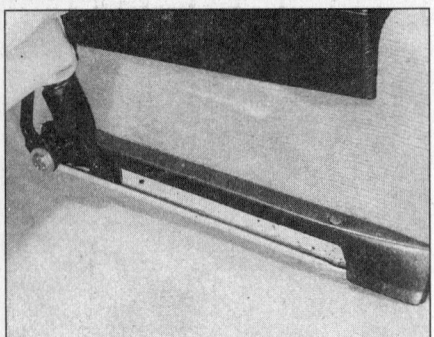

31.2 Front seat rear mounting

32.4 Central door locking switch/control element

3 Where applicable, disconnect the wiring for the seat heating element.
4 Remove the seat from the car.
5 Refitting is a reversal of removal.

Rear seat

6 Prise the covers from the mounting screws on the front edge of the cushion, then remove the screws (photo).
7 Lift the front of the cushion, and withdraw the cushion forwards.

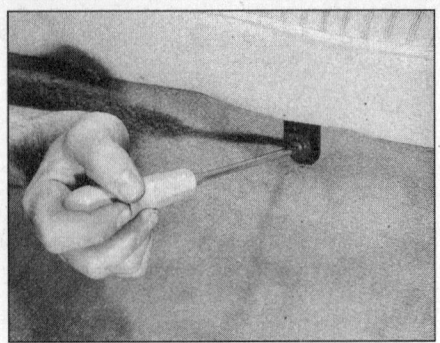

31.6 Rear seat cushion mounting screw removal

8 Bend out the two metal tags retaining the bottom of the backrest, release the backrest, then lift it upwards to free the two upper hooks from the shelf panel.
9 Refitting is a reversal of removal.

32 Central door locking system - general

1 Certain models are equipped with a central door locking system, which automatically locks all doors and the rear tailgate/boot lid in unison with the manual locking of either front door. The system is operated by a bi-pressure pump (photo), which supplies vacuum to lock the doors, and pressure to unlock them.
2 Should the system develop a fault, the condition and security of the hoses should first be checked. A leak will cause the bi-pressure pump to run longer than five seconds, and if it runs for thirty-five seconds, an internal control unit will automatically switch it off.
3 The bi-pressure pump is located on the right-hand side of the luggage compartment,

32.1 Central door locking bi-pressure pump

and is accessible by removing the inner trim. The pump is retained by a plastic cable tie.
4 The switch/control elements (photo) are accessible after removing the door trim panel, as described in Section 14. Check that the operating rod is in the upper (door open) position, before pressing down the locking ring and disconnecting the rod. Remove the mounting screws, and disconnect the air tube and wiring multi-plug.
5 Access to the boot lid switch element is made by removing the right-hand rear tail light inner trim. Thereafter, the removal and refitting procedure is the same as the door units. Make sure that the control air line is positioned between the inner skin and the operating rod (Fig. 11.27).
6 Access to the tailgate switch element is made by removing the rear inner trim panel.

33 Electrically-operated windows - general

1 Electrically-operated windows are fitted as standard to some Audi 80, 90 and Coupé

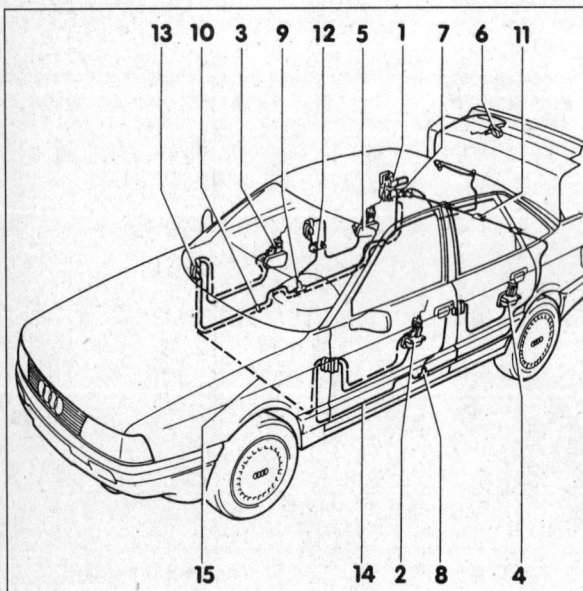

13 10 3 9 12 5 1 7 6 11

15 14 2 8 4

Fig 11.26 Central door locking system (Sec 32)

1 Bi-pressure pump
2 LH front control switch element
3 RH front control switch element
4 LH rear switch element
5 RH rear switch element
6 Bootlid switch element
7 Connector (X)
8 Connector (T)
9 Connector (T)
10 Cable tie
11 Cable clamp
12 Line guide
13 Bellows
14 Pressure line
15 Wiring harness

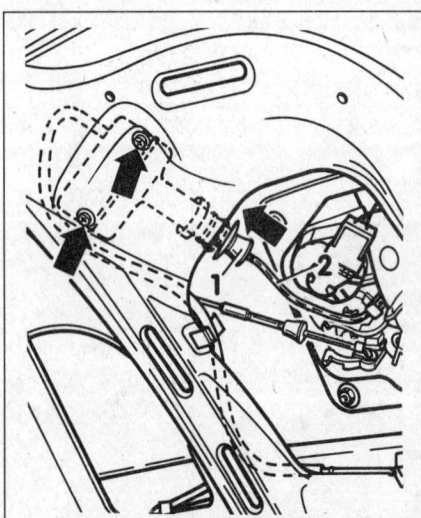

Fig 11.27 Bootlid switch element installation (Sec 32)

1 Locking ring   2 Operating rod

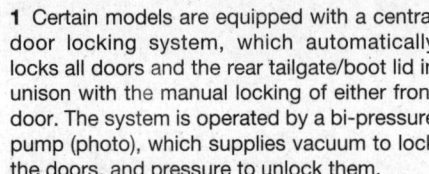
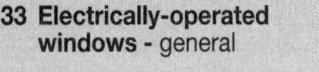

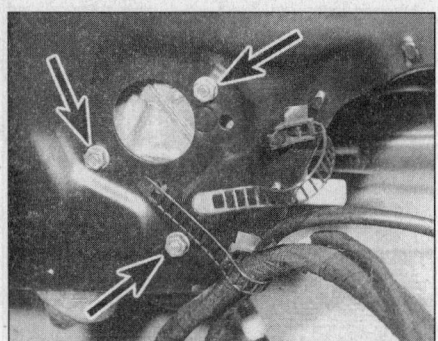

33.3 Electrically-operated window motor mounting nuts (arrowed)

models, and may be fitted as optional equipment on other models. The windows can be raised or lowered only when the ignition is switched on.

2 If a fault develops, first check that the thermal cut-out (circuit breaker) is not faulty. The location of the cut-out may be traced by referring to the wiring diagrams in Chapter 12.

3 The electric motors are attached to the window regulators, and can be removed with reference to Sections 17 and 18 (photo).

34 Heater - removal and refitting

1 Disconnect the battery negative lead.

2 Using a pair of pliers and a piece of card, carefully pull off the heater control knobs.

3 Remove the screws from the knob recesses, and withdraw the surround panel.

4 Remove the screws securing the heater controls.

5 Using a screwdriver, release the control cables from the heater, and disconnect the inner cables from the control levers (photos).

6 Remove the facia panel centre section (Section 30).

7 Remove the heater controls, radio and centre vent housing.

8 Disconnect the facia wiring loom from the fusebox and relay board, by first removing the fusebox, with reference to Chapter 12.

9 Unscrew the bolts from the centre air ducting and defrost ducting.

10 Remove the complete facia panel, with reference to Section 29.

11 Drain the cooling system, as described in Chapter 2.

12 Loosen the clips and disconnect the heater hoses at the bulkhead in the engine compartment (photos).

13 Remove the left-hand plenum chamber cover from just below the windscreen in the engine compartment.

14 Remove the heater air inlet (two screws) and recover the gasket.

15 Unscrew the mounting nuts located on the centre of the bulkhead.

16 Pull down the control unit, then withdraw the heater complete from inside the car.

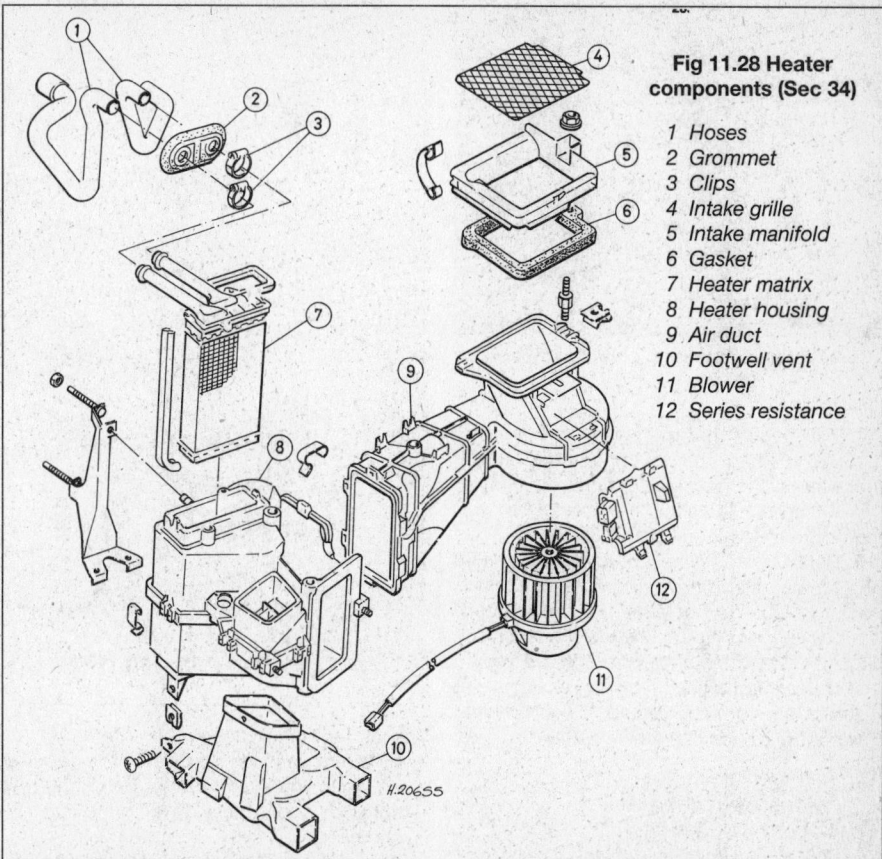

Fig 11.28 Heater components (Sec 34)

1 Hoses
2 Grommet
3 Clips
4 Intake grille
5 Intake manifold
6 Gasket
7 Heater matrix
8 Heater housing
9 Air duct
10 Footwell vent
11 Blower
12 Series resistance

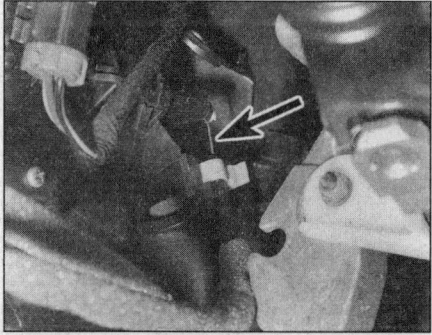

34.5A Right-hand heater control cable (arrowed)

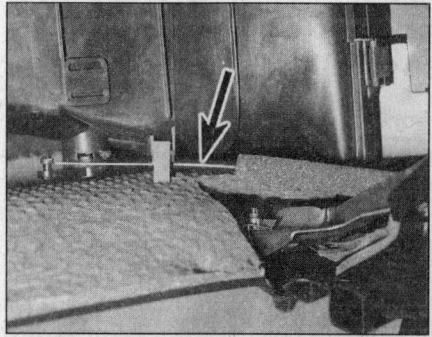

34.5B Left-hand heater control cable (arrowed)

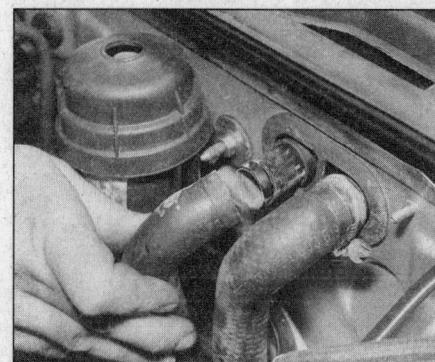

34.12A Heater supply hose removal

34.12B Heater return hose removal

11

35.2 Wiring connecting plate (arrowed) on the heater housing

17 The heater matrix may be removed by pulling it from the locating lugs, and if necessary, the housings may be dismantled by prising out the clips. Remove the blower unit with reference to Section 35.

18 Refitting is a reversal of removal, but note the following additional points. If the matrix locating lugs do not engage, use two self-tapping screws to secure the matrix. If the inner control cable ends break, fit a screw to the flap control arm. Check that all seals and gaskets are correctly seated. Make sure that the control cables operate smoothly.

35 Heater blower unit - removal and refitting

1 Unscrew the bolts from underneath the glovebox, then withdraw the glovebox.

2 Disconnect the wiring plug from the connecting plate on the heater housing (photo). The plate may be removed if necessary by pressing down and releasing the clip.

3 Using a screwdriver, push down the retaining lugs, then turn the blower unit clockwise to remove it from the housing.

4 Refitting is a reversal of removal.

36 Air conditioning system - precautions and maintenance

1 Never disconnect any part of the air conditioner refrigeration circuit unless the system has been discharged by your Audi dealer or a qualified refrigeration engineer.

2 Where the compressor or condenser obstruct other mechanical operations such as engine removal, then it is permissible to unbolt their mountings and move them to the limit of their flexible hose deflection, but not to

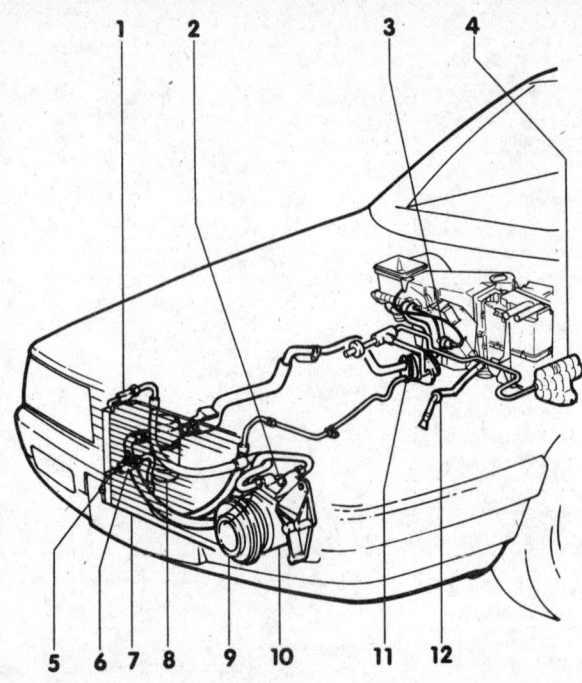

Fig 11.29 Air conditioner components (Sec 36)

1 High-pressure switch for magnetic coupling
2 Drain valve
3 Low-pressure switch for refrigerant circuit
4 Vacuum reservoir
5 Pressure relief valve
6 High-pressure switch for air conditioner
7 Condenser
8 Receiver
9 Magnetic coupling
10 Compressor
11 Restrictor
12 Water drain hose and valve

disconnect the hoses. If there is still insufficient room to carry out the required work, then the system must be discharged before disconnecting and removing the assemblies.

3 The system will, of course, have to be recharged on completion.

4 Regularly check the condenser for clogging with flies or dirt. Hose clean with water or compressed air.

5 Regularly check the tension of the compressor drivebelt. The belt deflection should be about 5 mm (0.2 in) at the centre point of its longest run. If adjustment is required on the four-cylinder engines, the quantity of spacers between the crankshaft pulley halves must be either increased to reduce the tension, or decreased to increase the tension. On the five-cylinder engines, the tension may be adjusted by loosening the two mounting bolts, then loosening the locknut and turning the adjusting nut as required. Tighten the locknut after making an adjustment.

37 Air conditioner blower unit - removal and refitting

1 Unscrew the bolts from underneath the glovebox, then withdraw the glovebox.

2 Disconnect the wiring.

3 Unscrew the bolts from the mounting plate, then remove the blower unit and mounting plate.

4 If necessary, separate the mounting plate from the unit.

5 Refitting is a reversal of removal, but first coat the mounting surfaces with a silicone rubber solution.

38 Air conditioner compressor magnetic coupling - adjustment

1 The air conditioner compressor is engaged by a magnetic coupling, which forms part of the drivebelt pulley. The coupling should not normally require adjustment, but if the pulley has been renewed, it will be necessary to check the clearance between the pulley and clutch plate as follows.

2 With the engine and air conditioner switched off, use a feeler blade to check that the clearance between the pulley and clutch plate is between 0.6 and 1.0 mm (0.024 and 0.040 in).

3 If necessary, unscrew the nut and remove the clutch plate, and adjust the number of shims accordingly. Refit the clutch plate and tighten the nut after making the adjustment.

Chapter 12 Electrical system

Contents

Degrees of difficulty

Easy, suitable for novice with little experience  | **Fairly easy,** suitable for beginner with some experience | **Fairly difficult,** suitable for competent DIY mechanic 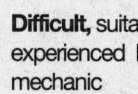 | **Difficult,** suitable for experienced DIY mechanic | **Very difficult,** suitable for expert DIY or professional

Specifications

System type .... 12 volt, negative earth

Battery
Capacity .... 45, 50, 54, 63 or 64 Ah

Alternator
Type .... Bosch
Output .... 65 or 90 amp
Minimum brush length .... 5.0 mm (0.2 in)
Regulated voltage .... 12.5 to 14.5 volts

Starter motor
Type .... Bosch pre-engaged
Commutator minimum diameter .... 33.5 mm (1.132 in)
Commutator maximum run-out .... 0.03 mm (0.001 in)
Commutator insulation undercut .... 0.5 to 0.8 mm (0.02 to 0.03 in)
Minimum brush length .... 13.0 mm (0.5 in)

12

Fuses

No	Function	Rating (amps)
1	Foglamps, front and rear	15
2	Emergency lights	15
3	Horn, brake lights, cruise control on 80 models	25
4	Clock, luggage compartment light, interior light, vanity mirror, cigarette lighter, on-board computer, reading lights. Air conditioner and anti-theft alarm on 80 and 90 models. Radio on 90 models	15
5	Radiator fan (full-load)	30
6	Tail and side lights (right)	5
7	Tail and side lights (left)	5
8	Headlight main beam (right), main beam warning light	10
9	Headlight main beam (left)	10
10	Headlight dipped beam (right)	10
11	Headlight dipped beam (left)	10
12	Instrument panel, reversing lights, auto-check system, ABS, differential lock, on-board computer. Cruise control on 80 models	15
13	Fuel pump, warm-up valve	15
14	Number plate lights, engine compartment light, glove compartment light	5
15	Windscreen wipers, radiator fan, air conditioner, direction indicators	25
16	Heated rear window, heated mirrors	30
17	Heater blower	30
18	Electric external mirrors. Rear window wiper on Coupé	5
19	Central locking. Heated door lock on 90 and Coupé models	10
20	Radiator fan (Stage 1). Fuel injector cooling where applicable	30
21	Rear cigarette lighter on 80 models	25
21	Self-diagnosis system on 90 and Coupé models	10
22	Not used	
23	Electric seat adjustment (and memory)	30
24	KE Jetronic control unit, on vehicles with catalytic converter, and closed-loop emission control on 80 models	10
24	Cruise control on 90 and Coupé models	5
25	Seat heating	30
26	Not used	
27	Engine management system 1 (electronic ignition with knock control)	10
28	Engine management system, 2 (lambda closed-loop system for vehicles with catalytic converter)	15

Wiper Blades

Wiper Blades .... Champion CS53-01

Bulbs

Bulbs	Wattage (W)
Headlamps:	
Main unit	60/55
Auxiliary unit (where fitted)	55
Direction indicators	21
Stop/tail lights	21/5
Front side lights	4
Number plate light	4
Front foglight	55
Interior lights	10
Map reading light	5
Luggage compartment light	5
Engine compartment light	10
Instrument panel lighting	3
Side marker light	5
Glovebox light	4

Torque wrench settings

	Nm	lbf ft
Alternator-to-engine (M 10)	45	33
Alternator-to-bracket (M8)	35	26

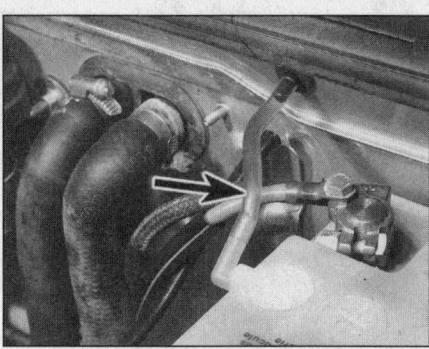
3.3 Battery vent tube (arrowed)

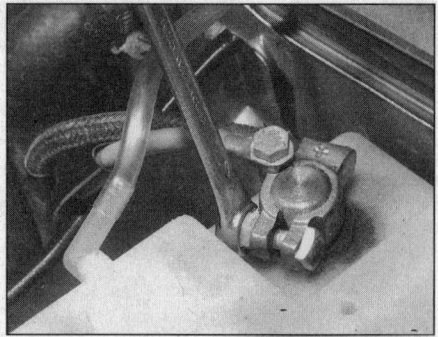
3.5 Disconnecting the positive battery lead

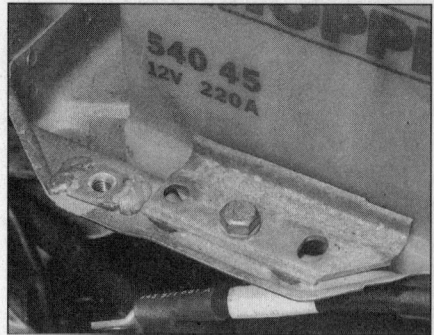
3.6 Battery holding clamp

1 General description and precautions

The electrical system is of 12 volt negative earth type, incorporating a belt-driven alternator with an integral voltage regulator. The starter is of pre-engaged type.

When working on the electrical system, the battery leads should always be disconnected, as a safety precaution against accidentally short-circuiting wires or terminals to earth. The system contains several computerised components, which can be damaged by incorrect voltages or excessive heat.

Before using electric-arc welding equipment on the car, disconnect the battery leads **and** the alternator leads. Never run the engine with a battery lead or alternator lead disconnected.

2 Routine maintenance

Carry out the following procedures at the intervals given in 'Routine maintenance' at the beginning of the manual.

Check operation of lights and horn

1 With the help of an assistant, check the operation of all lights, including stop-lights and direction indicator lights.
2 Check the operation of the horn.

Check wiper and washer systems

3 Check the operation of the wiper and washer systems. Where necessary, adjust the washer jets as described in Section 22.
4 Check the level of fluid in the washer reservoir(s) and top up as required.

Check battery electrolyte level

5 Refer to Section 4.

Check alternator drivebelt

6 Examine the complete length of the alternator drivebelt for cracking and deterioration, and renew if evident.

7 Check the drivebelt tension, and adjust if necessary, with reference to Section 6.

Check headlight adjustment

8 This is best carried out by an Audi dealer, who will have the necessary equipment.

3 Battery - removal and refitting

1 The battery is located in the engine compartment on the left-hand side, just in front of the bulkhead. On some models, it may be fitted with a protective cover.
2 Before disconnecting the battery leads, check if a security-coded type of radio is fitted. If so, make sure you have a record of the coded number which is necessary to switch on the security circuit.
3 Where fitted, disconnect the vent tube (photo).
4 Loosen the negative (-) terminal clamp bolt and disconnect the lead. Bend the lead away from the battery.
5 Loosen the positive (+) terminal clamp bolt and disconnect the lead (photo). Bend the lead away from the battery.
6 Unscrew the bolt and remove the battery holding clamp (photo).
7 Lift the battery from the platform, taking care not to spill any electrolyte.
8 Refitting is a reversal of removal. Make sure that the battery is fitted the correct way round, with the leads fitted to their correct terminals. Connect the negative (-) terminal last, and do not overtighten the clamp bolts. The curved side of the holding clamp must contact the base of the battery.

4 Battery - maintenance

1 Where a conventional battery is fitted, the electrolyte level of each cell should be checked every month and, if necessary, topped up with distilled or de-ionized water until the separators are just covered. On some batteries the case is translucent, and

incorporates minimum and maximum level marks. The check should be made more often if the car is operated in high ambient temperature conditions.
2 Where a low maintenance battery is fitted, it is not possible to check the electrolyte level.
3 Periodically disconnect and clean the battery terminals and leads. After refitting them, smear the exposed metal with petroleum jelly.
4 At the same time, inspect the battery clamp and platform for corrosion. If evident, remove the battery and clean the deposits away, then treat the affected metal with a proprietary anti-rust liquid, and paint with the original colour.
5 When the battery is removed for whatever reason, it is worthwhile checking it for cracks and leakage.
6 If topping up the battery becomes excessive, and the battery case is not fractured, the battery is being over-charged, and the voltage regulator will have to be checked.
7 If the car covers a very small annual mileage, it is worthwhile checking the specific gravity of the electrolyte every three months to determine the state of charge of the battery. Use a hydrometer to make the check, and compare the results with the following table.

	Normal climates	Tropics
Discharged	1.120	1.080
Half charged	1.200	1.160
Fully charged	1.280	1.230

8 If the battery condition is suspect, first check the specific gravity of electrolyte in each cell. A variation of 0.040 or more between any cells indicates loss of electrolyte or deterioration of the internal plates.
9 A further test can be made using a battery heavy discharge meter. The battery should be discharged for a maximum of fifteen seconds at a load of three times the ampere-hour capacity (at the 20 hour discharge rate). Alternatively connect a voltmeter across the battery terminals and spin the engine on the starter with the ignition disconnected (see Chapter 4), and the headlamps, heated rear window and heater blower switched on. If the voltmeter reading remains above 9.6 volts, the battery condition is satisfactory. If the

12

5.3A Loosening the alternator pivot bolt
(80 model)

5.3B Alternator adjustment bolt (90 model)

5.4 Removing the alternator drivebelt
(80 model)

voltmeter reading drops below 9.6 volts, and the battery has already been charged, it is faulty.

10 In winter when a heavy demand is placed on the battery (starting from cold and using more electrical equipment), it is a good idea to occasionally have the battery fully charged from an external source at a rate of 10% of the battery capacity (ie 6.3 amp for a 63 Ah battery).

11 The battery leads should be disconnected before connecting the charger leads. Continue to charge the battery until no further rise in specific gravity is noted over a four-hour period.

12 Alternatively, a trickle charger, charging at a rate of 1.5 amps can safety be used overnight.

5 Alternator - removal and refitting

1 On four-cylinder engines, the alternator is located on the left-hand side, above the timing cover. On five-cylinder engines, it is located on the bottom left-hand side of the engine.

2 Disconnect the battery negative lead - refer to Section 3, paragraph 2.

3 Loosen the alternator pivot and adjustment bolts, and swivel the alternator towards the engine (photos). For access to the alternator on five-cylinder engines, remove the plastic cover in front of the radiator, and the splash cover from under the engine.

4 Slip the drivebelt from the alternator pulley (photo).

5 Note the location of the wiring cables on the rear of the alternator, then disconnect them (photos). Where necessary, release the cables from the clips (photos).

6 Remove the pivot and adjustment bolts, and withdraw the alternator from the engine. On four-cylinder engines, the adjustment link may be unbolted from the cylinder head if desired (photos). Note also that it may be necessary to prise a plug from the timing cover for access to the pivot bolt.

7 If necessary, the mounting brackets may be unbolted, and on four-cylinder engines, the rubber bushes removed. When refitting the bracket on five-cylinder engines, the short bolt must be tightened first.

8 Refitting is a reversal of removal, but adjust the drivebelt as described in Section 6.

6 Alternator drivebelt - removal, refitting and adjustment

1 On five-cylinder engine models, remove the plastic cover in front of the radiator.

2 Disconnect the battery negative lead - refer to Section 3, paragraph 2.

3 Loosen the alternator pivot and adjustment bolts, and swivel the alternator towards the engine.

5.5A Remove the cap . . .

5.5B . . . and unscrew the terminal nut to disconnect the cable

5.5C Upper view of alternator on
90 models

5.6A Removing the alternator pivot bolt

5.6B Removing the adjustment link bolt

6.7A Adjusting the alternator drivebelt tension

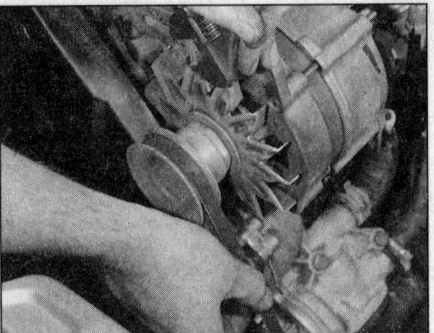

6.7B Checking the alternator drivebelt tension (80 model)

6.7C Checking the alternator drivebelt tension (90 model)

4 On models fitted with air conditioning and power steering, it will first be necessary to remove their associated drivebelts before removing the alternator drivebelt.

5 Slip the drivebelt from the pulleys.

6 Fit the new drivebelt onto the pulleys.

7 There are two methods of tensioning the drivebelt. With the first method, turn the tensioner rack nut to move the alternator away from the engine, until the drivebelt deflection half way between the pulleys is approximately 2.0 mm (0.08 in) under firm thumb pressure. If a used drivebelt is being refitted, the deflection should be 5.0 mm (0.20 in). Hold the tensioner rack nut in this position, then tighten the adjustment bolt, followed by the pivot and link bolts (photos).

8 A torque wrench is required for the second method. First check that the pivot bolt is loose, and that the alternator moves freely.

Tighten the tensioner rack nut to 9.0 ± 1.0 Nm (6.6 ± 0.7 lbf ft) using a torque wrench, and mark the position of the alternator in relation to the adjustment link.

Tighten the pivot bolt, and check that the rack nut remains in the same position. If necessary, re-position the nut using an open-ended spanner. Tighten the adjustment bolt, and if necessary the link bolt.

7 Alternator brushes - checking and renewal

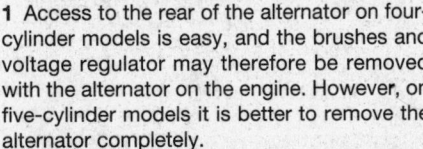

1 Access to the rear of the alternator on four-cylinder models is easy, and the brushes and voltage regulator may therefore be removed with the alternator on the engine. However, on five-cylinder models it is better to remove the alternator completely.

2 Disconnect the battery negative lead (refer to Section 3, paragraph 2) as a safety precaution on four-cylinder models.

3 Unscrew and remove the cross-head screws securing the brush holder and voltage regulator to the rear of the alternator (photo).

4 Withdraw the brush holder and voltage regulator, turning it slightly as it is removed (photo).

5 Measure the length of the brushes protruding from the holder (photo). If the length of any brush is 5.0 mm (0.2 in) or less, the complete unit should be renewed.

6 Using a fuel-moistened cloth, clean the slip

rings inside the alternator by turning the pulley (photo). If they are very dirty, use fine glass paper to clean them.

7 Check that the brushes move freely in the holder, then insert the brush holder and voltage regulator into position on the alternator.

8 Insert and tighten the cross-head screws.

9 Re-connect the battery negative lead where applicable.

8 Starter motor - testing in the car

1 If the starter motor fails to operate, first check that the wiring cables are firmly secured to the terminals on the solenoid.

2 Connect a voltmeter or 12 volt test lamp between the large terminal on the solenoid (terminal 30) and a suitable earthing point. This terminal is connected directly to the battery, and therefore battery voltage should be registered, or the test lamp should light whether or not the ignition is switched on.

3 Disconnect the small wire from the spade terminal on the solenoid, and connect the voltmeter or tail lamp between the wire and earth. With the ignition switched on, battery voltage should be registered. If not, check the ignition switch and associated wiring. Reconnect the wire.

4 Connect the voltmeter or test lamp between the field terminal on the solenoid and

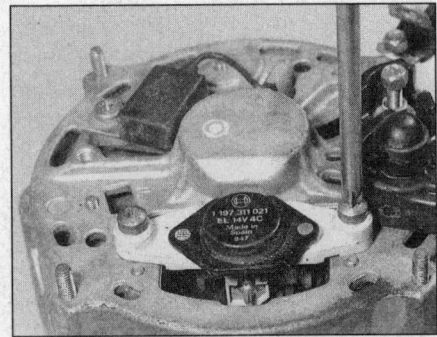

7.3 Remove the screws . . .

7.4 . . . and withdraw the brush holder and voltage regulator

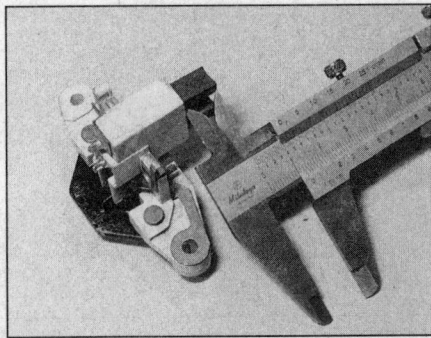

7.5 Measuring length of alternator brushes

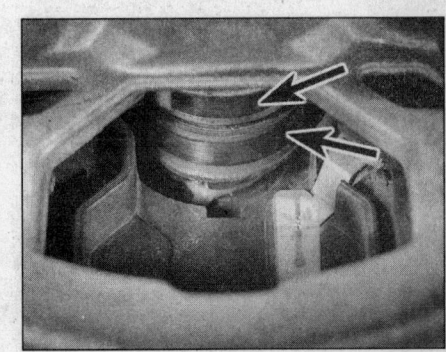

7.6 Alternator rotor slip rings (arrowed)

12

9.3 Starter motor and wiring (90 model)

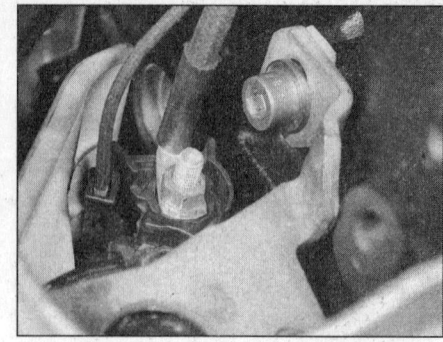

9.4 Starter motor front mounting bracket and bolt

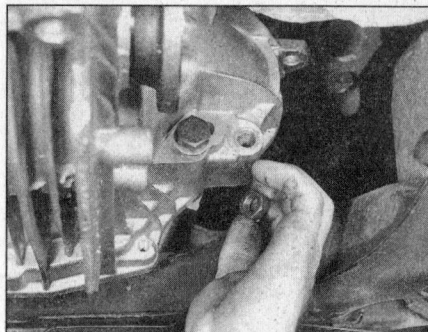

9.5A Remove the nuts . . .

earth. Switch the ignition key to the starting position, and check that battery voltage is registered. If there is no voltage, but the tests in paragraphs 2 and 3 prove positive, the contacts inside the solenoid are faulty. If there is battery voltage but the starter motor is not operative, then the fault lies in the starter motor windings, armature or brushes.

9 Starter motor - removal and refitting

1 Disconnect the battery negative lead - refer to Section 3, paragraph 2.
2 For better access, apply the handbrake, raise the front of the car and support on axle stands, then remove the splash cover from under the engine.
3 Note the location of the wires on the starter solenoid, then disconnect them (photo). Unscrew the nut to remove the main cable, and pull off the spade type connector for the solenoid trigger wire. There may also be an additional wire from the main cable terminal.
4 On four-cylinder engines, use an Allen key to unscrew the bolt securing the front mounting bracket to the cylinder block (photo).
5 Unscrew the mounting bolts/nuts, and withdraw the starter motor (photos).
6 Refitting is a reversal of removal. On four-cylinder engines, tighten the main mounting bolts first, then loosen the front bracket nuts, insert the front mounting bolt, and tighten the nuts, followed by the bolt.

10 Starter motor - overhaul

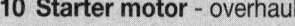

1 Mark the housings and mounting bracket (where fitted) in relation to each other.
2 Remove the nuts and washers, and withdraw the mounting bracket (photo).
3 Loosen the clips and remove the heat shield (where fitted) (photo).
4 Unscrew the nut and disconnect the field winding cable from the solenoid terminal (photo).
5 Unscrew the cross-head screws and withdraw the solenoid housing from the drive end housing (photos).
6 Unhook the solenoid core from the

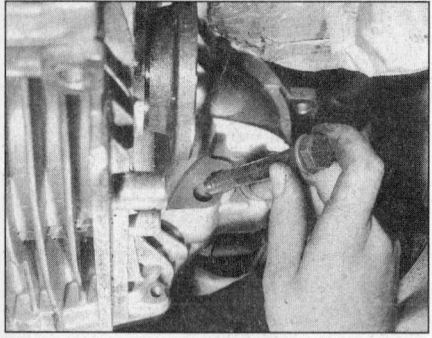

9.5B . . . and bolts . . .

9.5C . . . and withdraw the starter motor

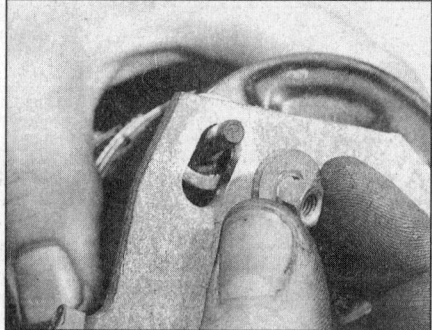

10.2 Starter mounting bracket removal

10.3 Starter heat shield removal

10.4A Unscrew the nut . . .

10.4B . . . and disconnect the field winding cable

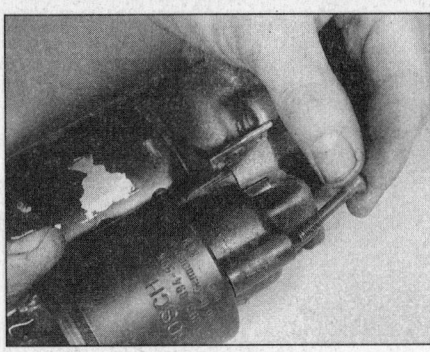

10.5A Remove the screws . . .

10.5B . . . and withdraw the solenoid housing

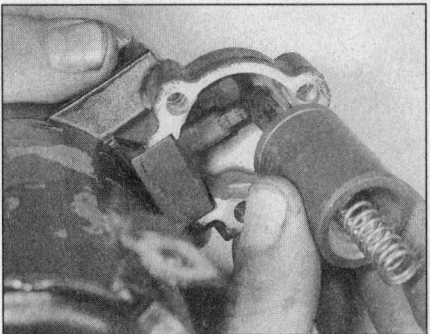

10.6 Unhooking the solenoid core

engagement lever (photo). Remove the spring if necessary.

7 Using a socket, unscrew the through-bolts and remove them from the bearing housing (photos).

8 Prise out the rubber pad over the engagement lever (photo).

9 Withdraw the drive end housing from the yoke, and at the same time prise out the engagement lever.

10 Disconnect the engagement lever from the armature slide ring (photo).

11 Remove the screws and withdraw the small end cover and gasket (photos).

12 Extract the C-clip and remove the shim(s), noting the exact number of shims, as they determine the armature endfloat (photos).

10.7A Unscrew the through-bolts . . .

10.7B . . . and remove them.

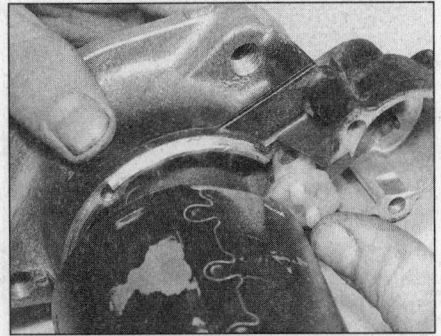

10.8 Removing the rubber pad

10.10 Engagement lever removal

10.11A Remove the screws . . .

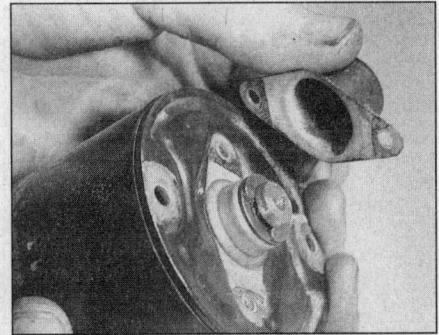

10.11B . . . and withdraw the small end cover and gasket

10.12A Extract the C-clip . . .

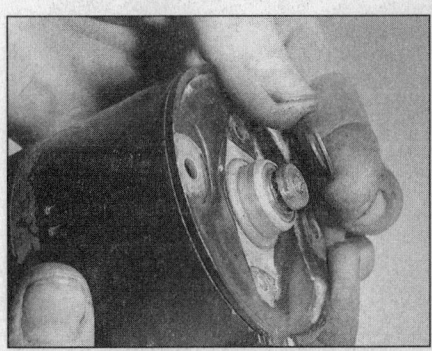

10.12B . . . and shims

12

10.13A Removing the commutator end bearing plate . . .

10.13B . . . and spacer

10.14 Removing the brush holder assembly

10.15A Engagement lever plate (arrowed)

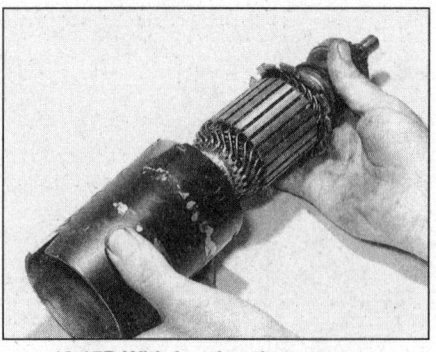

10.15B Withdrawing the armature

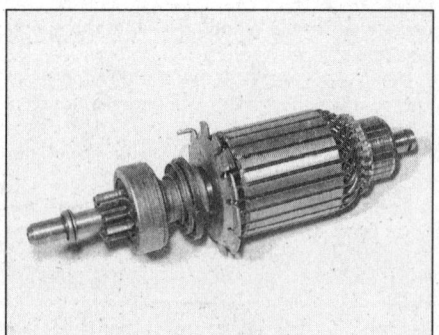

10.15C Armature assembly

13 Remove the commutator end bearing plate, followed by the spacer (photos).

14 Before removing the brush holder assembly, obtain a socket with a diameter approximately the same as that of the commutator. Locate the socket against the commutator, then slide the bushes and holder assembly onto the socket (photo).

15 Mark the engagement lever plate in relation to the yoke, then withdraw the armature (photos).

16 Using a metal tube, drive the stop ring off the circlip, then extract the circlip and pull off the stop ring (photo).

17 Slide the pinion drive from the armature.

18 Clean all the components in paraffin and wipe dry, then examine them for wear and damage. Check the pinion drive for damaged

teeth, and make sure that the one-way clutch only rotates in one direction. If the shaft bushes are worn they can be removed using a soft metal drift and new bushes installed. However, the new bushes must first be soaked in hot oil for approximately five minutes. Clean the commutator with a rag moistened with a suitable solvent. Minor scoring can be removed with fine glasspaper, but deep scoring will necessitate the commutator being skimmed in a lathe, and then being undercut. Check that the commutator diameter is not less than the minimum specified amount, using vernier callipers (photo).

19 Measure the length of the brushes. If less than the minimum amount given in the Specifications, fit new brushes. These will require

soldering into position, and care must be taken not to allow solder to run down the braided wire, as this may prevent the brushes moving freely in their holders.

20 Reassembly is a reversal of dismantling.

11 Fuses and relays - general

1 The fuses and relays are located in a box on the right-hand side of the bulkhead. The fuse numbers and relay locations are shown on the cover (photo). In addition, some relays are located behind the facia on the right-hand side, on a special relay board.

2 Always renew a fuse with one of identical

10.16 Stop ring (arrowed) on the armature shaft

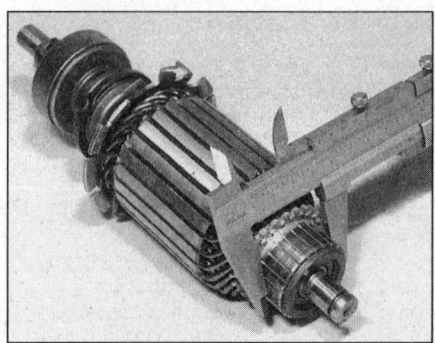

10.18 Checking commutator diameter

11.1 Fusebox cover

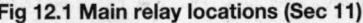

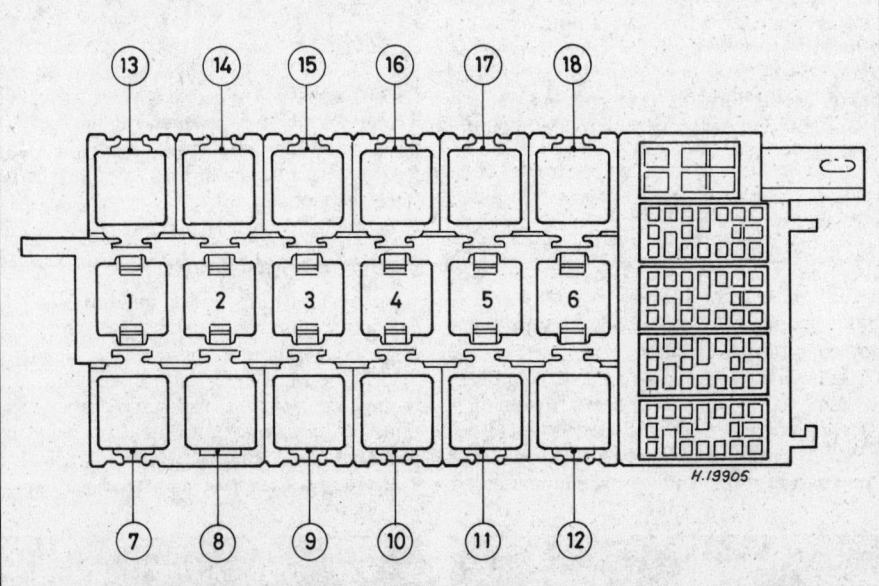

Fig 12.1 Main relay locations (Sec 11)

1 Foglamps
2 Radiator fan
3 Injector cooling fan
4 Headlight washer system
5 Relief terminal
6 Heater or air conditioner
7 Horn
8 Automatic transmission
9 Intermittent wash/wipe
10 Intake manifold pre-heating
11 Radiator fan (two speed)

Fig 12.2 Relay locations on relay board (Sec 11)

1 Anti-lock braking system
2 Radio and side light warning buzzer
3 Interior light switch-off delay
4 Air conditioner magnetic coupling
5 Rear window wiper (Coupé)
6 Oil warning
7 Alarm system for Taxi
8 Alarm system for Taxi
9 Automatic circuit breaker for electric windows, seats and sliding roof
10 Idling speed stabilisation
11 Idling speed stabilisation
12 Idling speed stabilisation, on automatic circuit breaker for electric windows, seats and sliding roof
13 Heated passenger seat
14 Heated driver's seat
15 Electric sliding roof, electric windows
16 Electric sliding roof and electric windows
17 Distribution adaptor
18 Town driving lights (dim-dip)

11.2A Fuses and relays

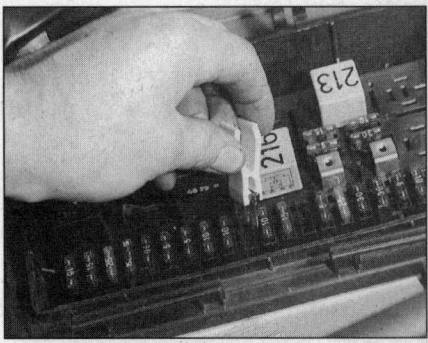

11.2B Removing a fuse with plastic tweezers

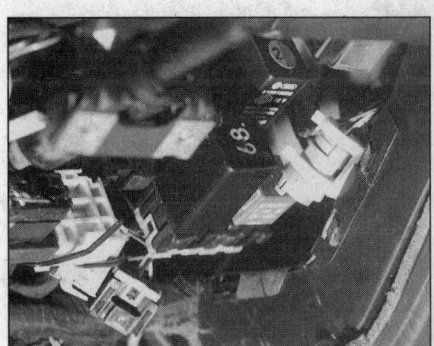

11.3 Relays located behind the facia

rating, and never renew it more than once without finding the source of trouble. A pair of plastic tweezers is provided in the fusebox to remove the fuses. Access to the fuses is gained by unclipping the front, then the rear, of the cover (photos).

3 The relays are of sealed construction, and cannot be repaired if faulty. The relays are of the plug-in type, and may be removed by pulling direct from their terminals. On some of the relays located behind the facia, it is necessary to prise the two plastic clips outwards before removing the relay (photo). The facia relay board may be removed by unscrewing the self-tapping mounting screws.

12

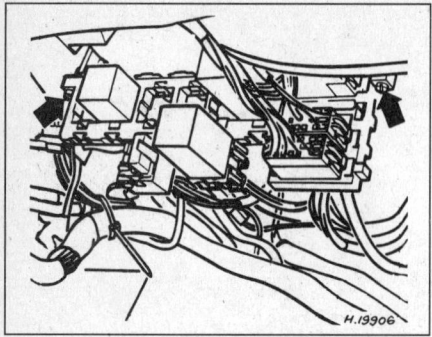

Fig 12.3 Relay board mounting screw locations – arrowed (Sec 11)

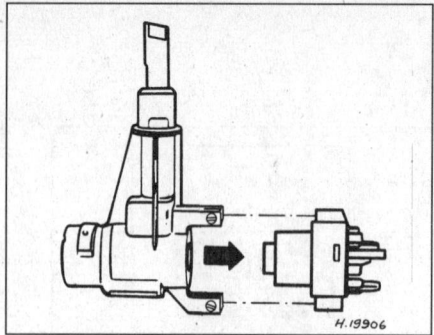

Fig 12.4 Removing the ignition switch from the lock housing (Sec 12)

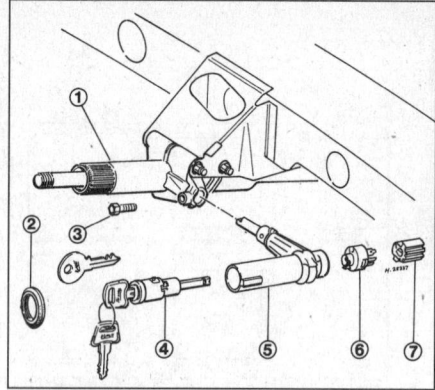

Fig 12.5 Ignition switch/steering column lock components (Sec 12)

1 Steering column	5 Lock housing
2 Grommet	6 Ignition switch
3 Mounting bolt	7 Connector
4 Lock cylinder	

12 Ignition switch/steering column lock - removal and refitting

1 Disconnect the battery negative lead - refer to Section 3, paragraph 2.
2 Remove the steering wheel (Chapter 10).
3 Using a screwdriver inserted through the hole in the bottom of the column shroud/combination switch, loosen the clip or unscrew the retaining screws, then withdraw the unit upwards.
4 Remove the instrument panel (Section 15).
5 Unscrew the Torx bolt securing the steering column lock housing to the column.
6 Unscrew and remove the two column upper

mounting bolts, then lower the column until the lock housing can be removed. Disconnect the wiring plug.
7 Scrape the locking paint from the grub screws, then unscrew them and pull out the ignition switch.
8 To remove the lock cylinder, it will be necessary to drill a 3 mm (0.12 in) diameter hole in the housing at the location shown in Fig. 12.6, to a depth of 1.5 mm (0.06 in). Using a small screwdriver inserted in the hole, depress the retaining pin and withdraw the lock cylinder.
9 Refitting is a reversal of removal. When refitting the ignition switch, insert the key in the cylinder, and turn fully anti-clockwise. Press the switch into the housing, tighten the grub screws and apply locking paint to lock them. Make sure that the steering column lower coupling is engaged correctly, and refer to Chapter 10 if necessary.

13 Combination switch - removal and refitting

1 Disconnect the battery negative lead - refer to Section 3, paragraph 2.
2 Remove the steering wheel (Chapter 10).
3 Remove the shroud covers from the steering column. On some models, these are retained by several screws, but on other models a clamp secures the cover unit to the

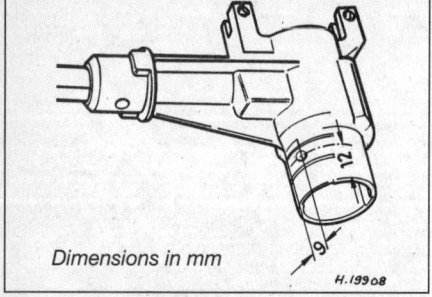

Dimensions in mm

Fig 12.6 Drilling location in the ignition lock housing for removal of the lock cylinder (Sec 12)

column, and a hole is provided for access to the clamp screw.
4 Disconnect the multi-plug.
5 Remove the screw(s) and withdraw the combination switch.
6 Refitting is a reversal of removal.

14 Switches - removal and refitting

Facia switch

1 Using a small screwdriver or similar tool, prise the switch out of the facia (photo).
2 Disconnect the multi-plug from the rear of the switch (photo).
3 Refitting is a reversal of removal.

Courtesy light switch

4 Prise off the rubber cover (photo).
5 Unscrew the cross-head screw (photo).
6 Carefully withdraw the switch from the door pillar (photo). Disconnect the wiring and remove the switch. Make sure that the wiring does not drop back into the door pillar, by using tape or string to secure it.
7 Refitting is a reversal of removal.

14.1 Removing a facia switch

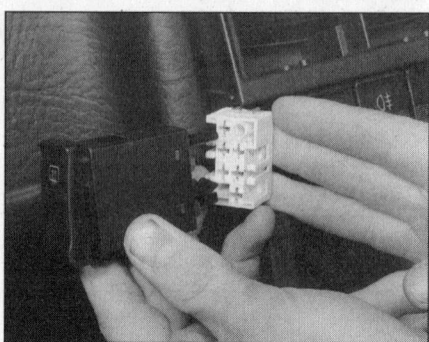

14.2 Disconnecting the facia switch multi-plug

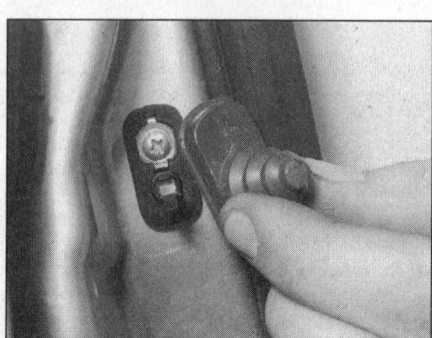

14.4 Remove the rubber cover ...

14.5 . . . unscrew the cross-head screw . . .

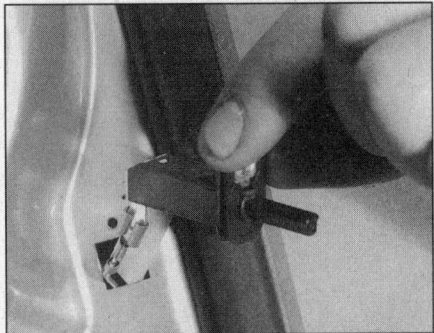

14.6 . . . and withdraw the courtesy light switch

14.8 Prise off the rubber cover . . .

Luggage compartment light switch

8 Prise off the rubber cover (photo).
9 Unscrew the cross-head screw (photo).
10 Withdraw the switch and disconnect the wiring (photo).
11 Refitting is a reversal of removal.

Handbrake warning switch

12 Remove the centre console (Chapter 11).
13 Unscrew the cross-head screw securing the switch to the floor beneath the handbrake (photo).
14 Disconnect the wiring
15 Refitting is a reversal of removal.

14.9 . . . remove the screw . . .

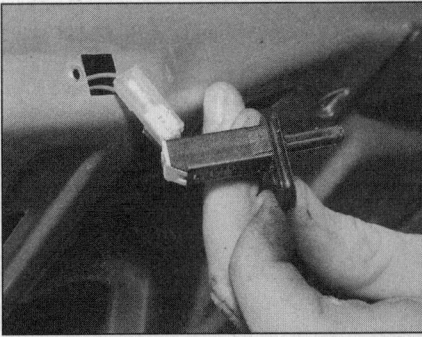

14.10 . . . and withdraw the luggage compartment light switch

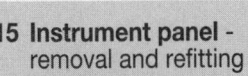

15 Instrument panel - removal and refitting

1 Disconnect the battery negative lead refer to Section 3, paragraph 2.
2 Remove the steering wheel (Chapter 10).
3 Remove the shroud covers or combination switch from the steering column.
4 Unscrew the two mounting screws from the bottom of the instrument panel (photo).
5 Place a cloth over the steering column, to prevent scratching the instrument panel.
6 Lift the bottom of the instrument panel and tilt it backwards. Withdraw the unit and disconnect the wiring multi-plugs (photos).
7 Refitting is a reversal of removal.

14.13 Handbrake warning switch (securing screw arrowed)

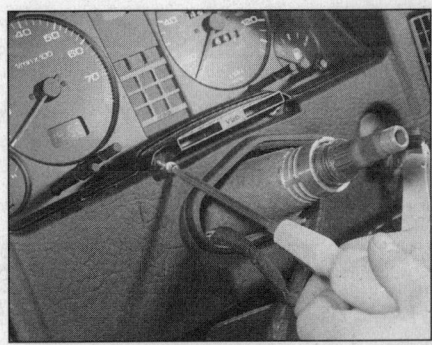

15.4 Instrument panel mounting screw removal

15.6A Withdraw the instrument panel . . .

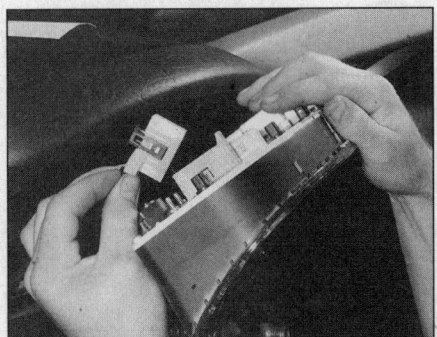

15.6B . . . and disconnect the right-hand multi-plug . . .

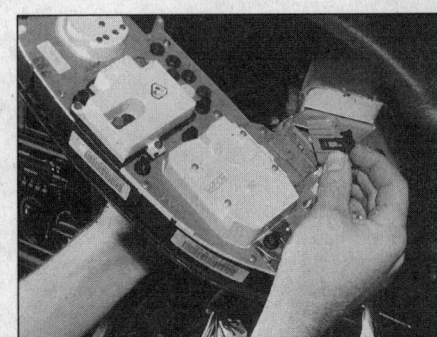

15.6C . . . and left-hand multi-plug

12

16.1 Instrument panel removed

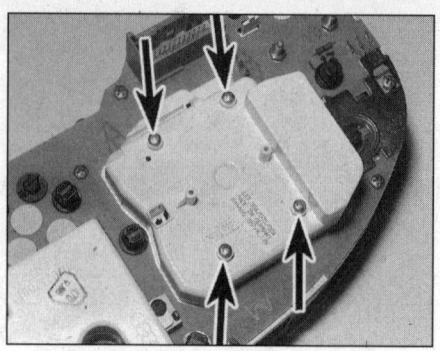

16.2 Speedometer retaining screws (arrowed)

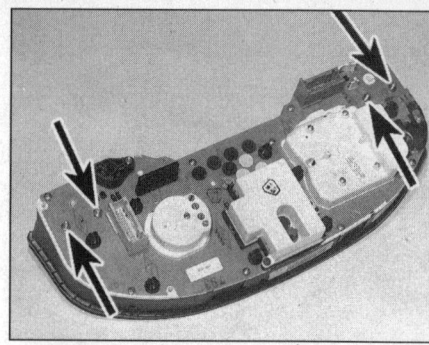

16.4 Rear view of the instrument panel, showing fuel and temperature gauge mounting bolts

Fig 12.7 Exploded view of the instrument panel (Sec 16)

1 Tachometer	10 Instrument carrier	21 Screws
2 Digital clock (where fitted)	11 Screw	22 Warning lamps
3 Speedometer	12 Printed circuit board	23 Voltage stabiliser
4 Screws	13 Corrugated washer	24 Cooling plate
5 Analogue clock (where fitted)	14 Nut	25 Nut
	15 Screws	26 Corrugated washer
6 Analogue clock pushbutton control	16 Rheostat	27 Screw
	17 Screws	28 Washer
7 Coolant temperature gauge	18 Analogue clock printed circuit board	29 Fuel gauge
8 Washer	19 Warning lamps	30 Fuel gauge adjusting pin
9 Control knob	20 Indicator unit	31 Felt washer

16 Instruments - removal and refitting

1 Remove the instrument panel as described in Section 15 (photo).
2 To remove the speedometer, unscrew the four retaining screws (photo) and lift it from the panel.
3 The analogue clock and tachometer are accessible after removing the printed circuit, which is retained by several cross-head screws. To remove the clock pushbutton control, press the lugs together at the end of the pin.
4 The fuel and temperature gauges are removed by removing the printed circuit board, then unscrewing the relevant mounting nuts (photo).
5 Refitting is a reversal of removal.

17 Headlamps and headlamp bulbs - removal and refitting

1 Access to the rear of the right-hand headlamp unit is gained by removing the air cleaner inlet hose. For access to the left-hand unit on 90 models, remove the radiator upper cover.
2 To remove a bulb on 80 models, turn the rear plastic cover anti-clockwise and remove it, then pull the wiring plug from the bulb terminals (photos).
3 On 90 models, release the spring clip and remove the rear plastic cover, then pull the wiring plug from the bulb terminals (photos).
4 Release the spring clip and remove the bulb from the headlamp (photo).
5 If the bulb is to be re-used, do not touch the glass with bare fingers. If the bulb is accidentally touched, clean it with methylated spirit.
6 To remove the headlamp, first remove the washer components (if fitted). Where an electric beam adjustment system is fitted, also disconnect the relevant wiring.
7 On 80 models, disconnect the wiring plug(s)

1 Connector
2 Control potentiometer
3 Connector
4 Servo motor
5 Headlight unit (80 models)
6 Direction indicator lamp
   (80 models)
7 Headlight unit (90 and
   Coupé models)
8 Earthing point
9 Commutator

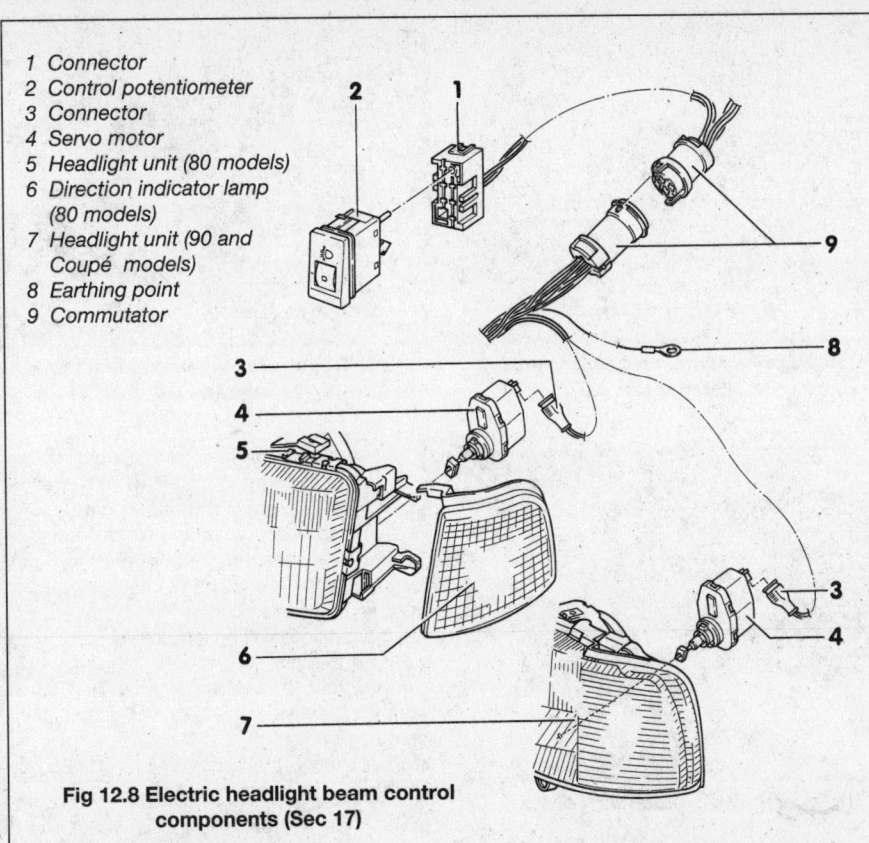

Fig 12.8 Electric headlight beam control
components (Sec 17)

17.2A Headlamp rear plastic cover removal
(80 models)

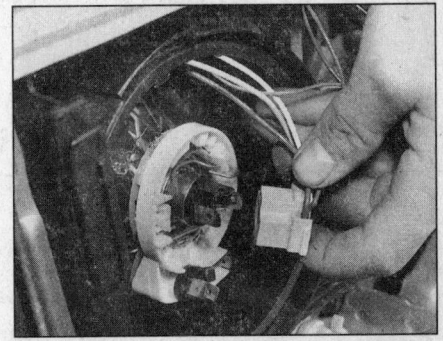

17.2B Headlamp wiring plug removal
(80 models)

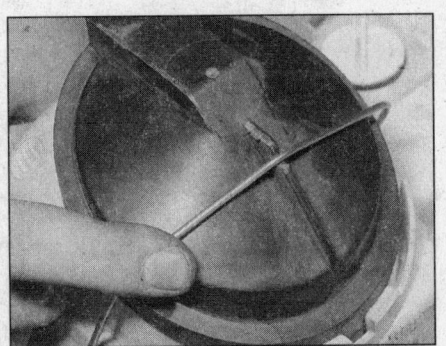

17.3A Release the spring clip . . .

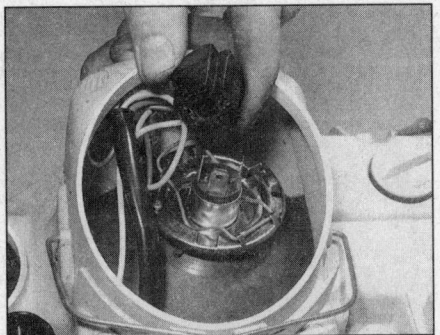

17.3B . . . and disconnect the wiring plug
(90 models)

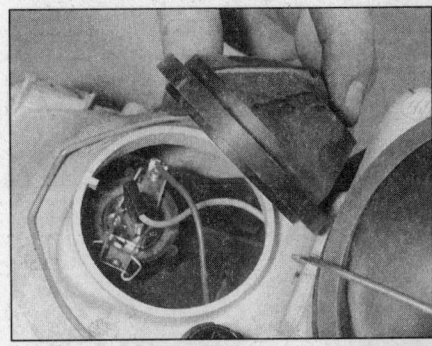

17.3C Auxiliary headlamp cover removal
(90 models)

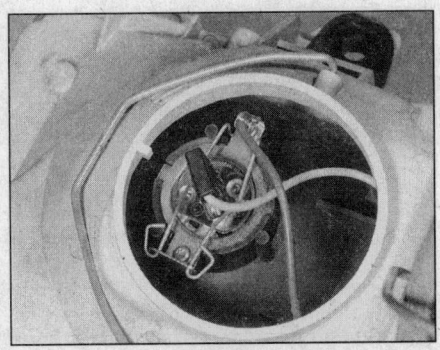

17.3D View of auxiliary headlamp bulb
(90 models)

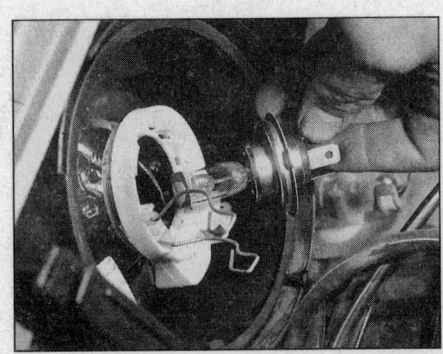

17.4A Removing the headlamp bulb
(80 models)

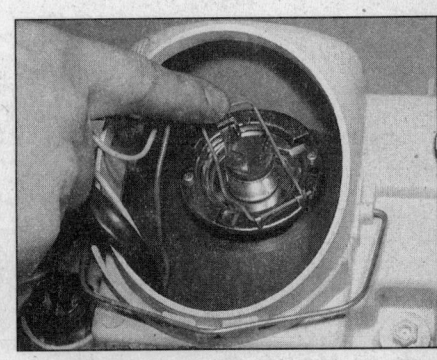

17.4B Release the spring clip . . .

12

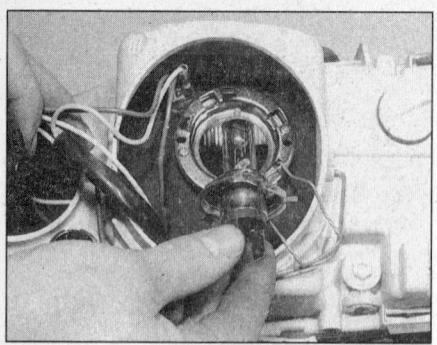

17.4C . . . and remove the headlamp bulb (90 models)

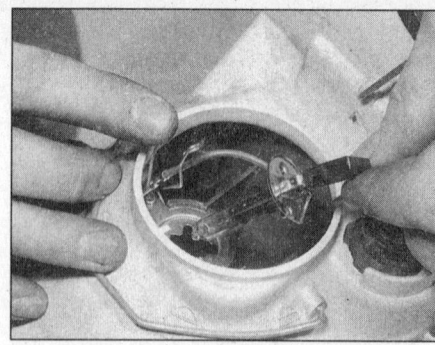

17.4D Auxiliary headlamp bulb removal (90 models)

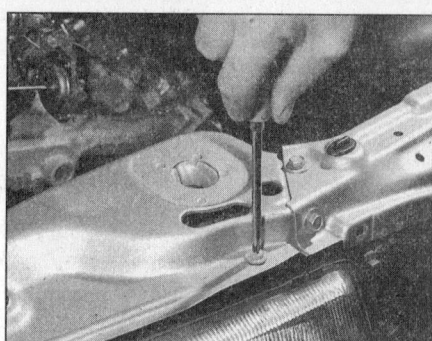

17.7A Remove the upper mounting screws . . .

17.7B . . . and lower mounting screws . . .

17.7C . . . trim strip mounting screws . . .

from the rear of the headlamp. The direction indicator lamp may be removed first if necessary. Unscrew the upper and lower mounting screws, and withdraw the headlight. For better access, the narrow trim strip may be removed from under the headlamp. If not already removed, unclip and remove the direction indicator lamp (photos).

8 On 90 models, disconnect the wiring plug from the rear. Unscrew the upper and lower mounting screws and withdraw the headlamp forwards (photos).

9 If necessary, the lens may be removed by prising off the spring clips with a screwdriver (photos).

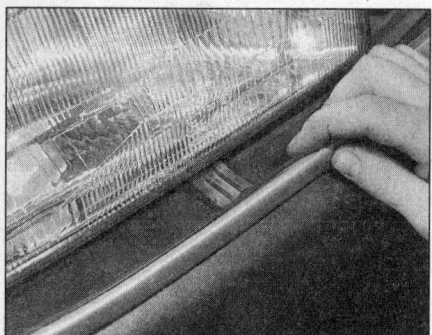

17.7D . . . and trim strip . . .

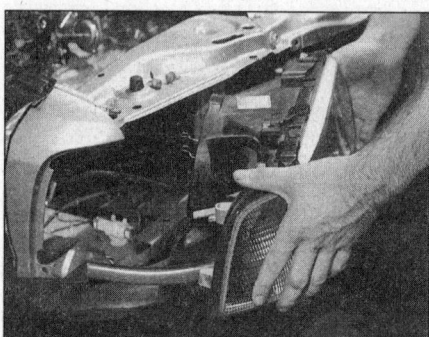

17.7E . . . and withdraw the headlamp (80 models)

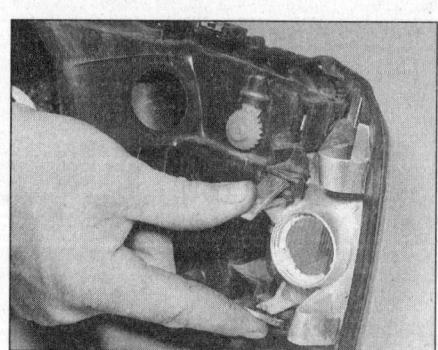

17.7F Unclip the direction indicator lamp . . .

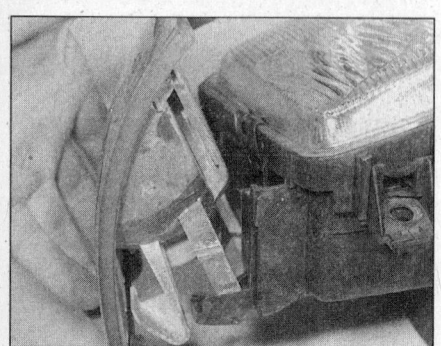

17.7G . . . and slide from the headlamp

17.8A Disconnecting the headlamp wiring plug (90 models)

17.8B Removing the headlamp (90 models)

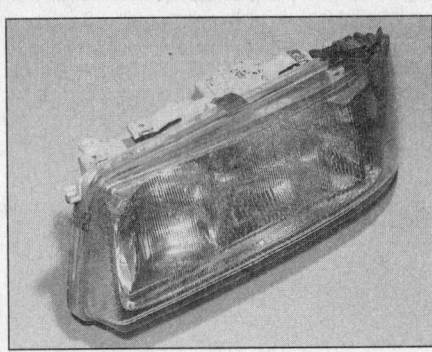

17.8C Headlamp unit removed (90 models)

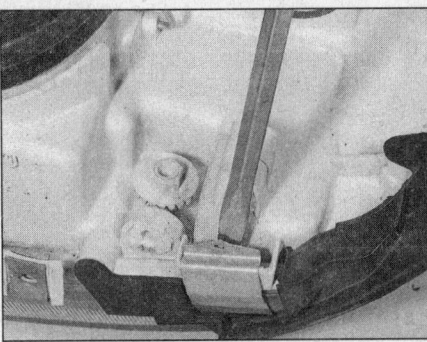

17.9A Prising off the outer . . .

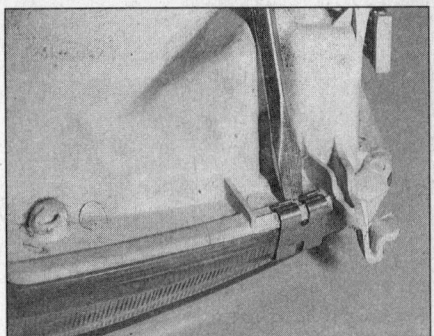

17.9B . . . and inner headlamp lens spring clips (90 models)

10 Refitting is a reversal of removal. When fitting the headlamp, tighten the upper mounting screws, then the lower screws. Adjust the headlamp as described in the following Section. When fitting the bulb, make sure that the centre one of the three terminals is positioned at the top, so that the bulb rim location lugs engage properly. Where the plastic cover is marked 'Oben', this should be uppermost when fitted.

18 Headlamps - alignment

1 Headlamp alignment should ideally be carried out by an Audi dealer, using a beam setter, but in an emergency, the following procedure will provide an acceptable light pattern.
2 Position the car (at kerb weight, and with tyres correctly inflated), on a level surface in front of, and at right-angles to, a wall or garage door.
3 Draw a horizontal line on the wall or door at headlamp centre height. Draw a vertical line corresponding to the centre-line of the car, then measure off points either side of this, on the horizontal line, corresponding with the headlamp centres.
4 Move the car back to a distance of approximately 10 metres (33 feet) from the wall or door. Switch on the main beam, and check that the areas of maximum illumination coincide with the headlamp centre marks. It will help to cover the remaining headlamp(s) while making the adjustment.
5 Adjust the headlamp using an Allen key through the upper access holes. The outer screw adjusts the height, and the inner screw adjusts the horizontal position (photos). Turning the outer screw clockwise lowers the beam. Note that some models are fitted with a height adjustment knob on the rear of the headlamp, for use when carrying heavy leads (photo). An electric beam adjuster system is also fitted to some models.

19 Bulbs - removal

Note: *Bulbs should always be renewed with ones of identical type and rating, as listed in the Specifications.*

Front sidelight

1 Remove the plastic cover from the rear of the headlamp (refer to Section 17 if necessary).
2 Disconnect the wiring plug (where applicable) (photo).
3 Pull the bulbholder from the reflector (photos).

18.5A Adjusting the headlamp horizontal position

18.5B Headlamp height adjuster – arrowed (headlamp removed)

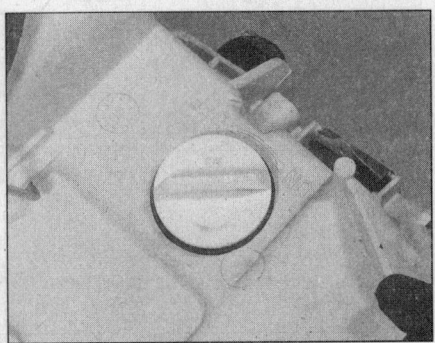

18.5C Headlamp height adjustment knob (90 models)

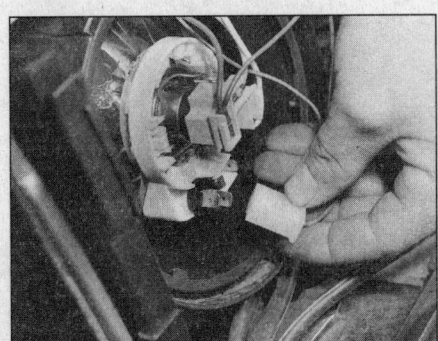

19.2 Disconnecting the sidelight wiring plug

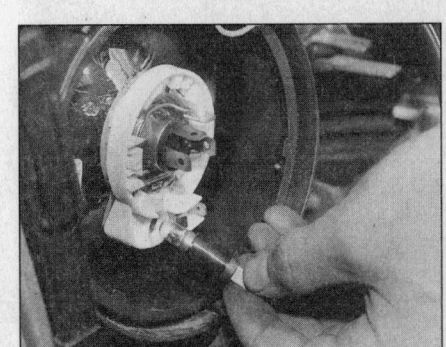

19.3A Sidelight bulbholder removal (80 models)

12

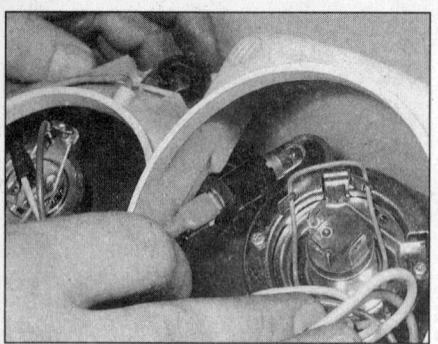

19.3B Sidelight bulbholder removal (90 models)

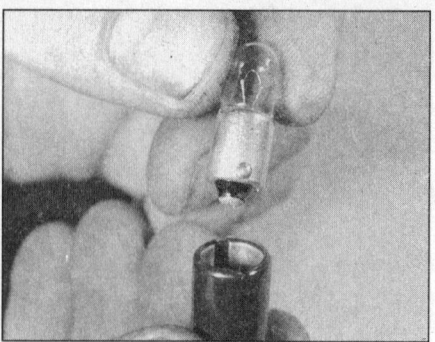

19.4 Sidelight bulb removal

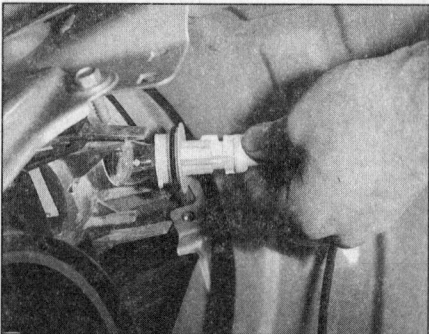

19.6 Removing the front direction indicator bulbholder (80 models)

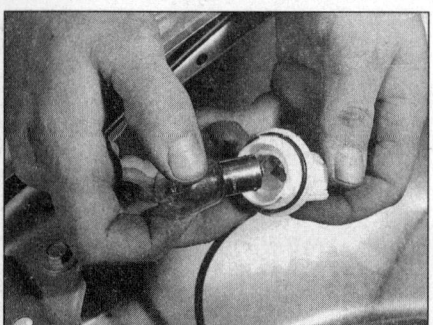

19.7 Front direction indicator bulb removal (80 models)

19.9 Front direction indicator lamp removal (90 and Coupé models)

4 Depress and twist the bulb to remove it.
5 Refitting is a reversal of removal.

Front direction indicators (80 models)

6 Turn the bulbholder on the rear of the lamp anti-clockwise and remove it (photo).
7 Depress and twist the bulb to remove it (photo).
8 Refitting is a reversal of removal.

Front direction indicators (90 and Coupé models)

9 Unscrew the cross-head screw and withdraw the front direction indicator lamp, releasing it from the foglamp at the same time (photo).
10 Turn the bulbholder anti-clockwise and remove it from the lamp (photo).
11 Depress and twist the bulb to remove it (photo).
12 Refitting is a reversal of removal.

Front foglamp (80 models)

13 Using a screwdriver, prise off the plastic frame.
14 Unscrew the cross-head screws, and withdraw the foglamp.
15 Disconnect the wire, then unhook the spring clip and remove the bulb.
16 Refitting is a reversal of removal, but make sure that the lugs on the bulb engage with the reflector correctly, and finally adjust the lamp using the cross-head screw provided. The procedure is similar to that described in Section 18.

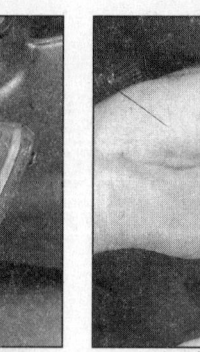

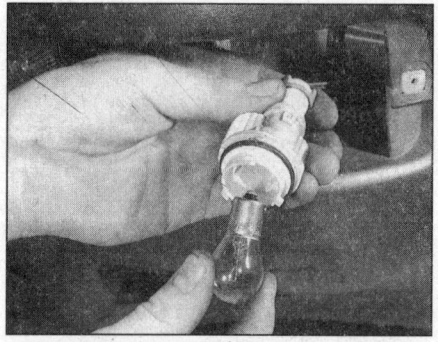

19.10 Removing the bulbholder from the front direction indicator lamp (90 and Coupé models)

19.11 Front direction indicator lamp bulb removal (90 and Coupé models)

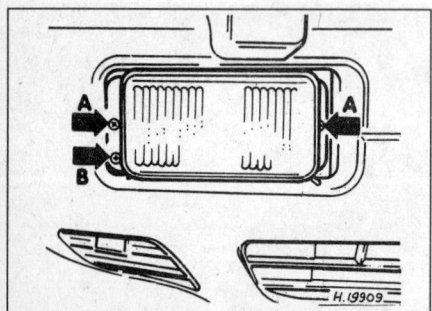

Fig 12.9 Front foglamp retaining screws (A) and adjustment screw (B) on 80 models (Sec 19)

H.19909

19.18A Remove the front foglamp mounting screws . . .

19.18B . . . and pull out the lamp . . .

19.18C . . . and unhook from the bumper

19.19 Disconnecting foglamp wiring plug

19.20A Unhook the wire clip . . .

Front foglamp (90 and Coupé models)

17 Remove the front direction indicator lamp as described in paragraph 9.
18 Unscrew the two cross-head mounting screws, pull out the lamp, and unhook it from the bumper (photos).
19 Disconnect the wiring plug (photo).
20 Unhook the wire clip and remove the lamp rear cover (photos).
21 Disconnect the wire leading to the bulb (photo).
22 Unhook the spring clip and remove the bulb from the reflector (photos).
23 Refitting is a reversal of removal, but make sure that the bulb is correctly engaged with the reflector.

Rear lamp cluster - boot lid (Saloon)

24 Open the bootlid and prise out the plastic cover (photo).
25 Turn the relevant bulbholder anti-clockwise, and remove it from the lamp (photo).
26 Depress and twist the bulb to remove it (photo).
27 If necessary, the lamp may be removed by unscrewing the retaining nuts. On the right-hand side, it is also necessary to disconnect the boot lock operating rods (photo).
28 Refitting is a reversal of removal.

19.20B . . . and remove the foglamp rear cover

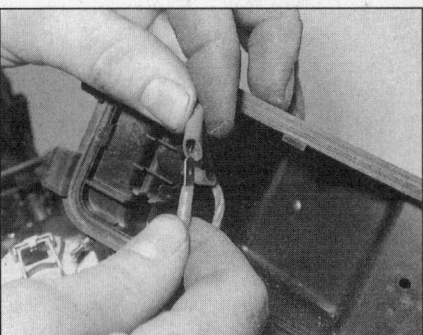

19.21 Disconnecting the foglamp supply wire

19.22A Unhook the spring clip . . .

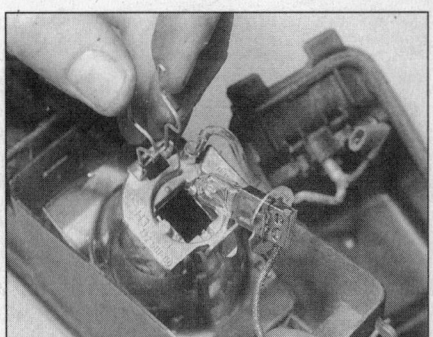

19.22B . . . and remove the foglamp bulb

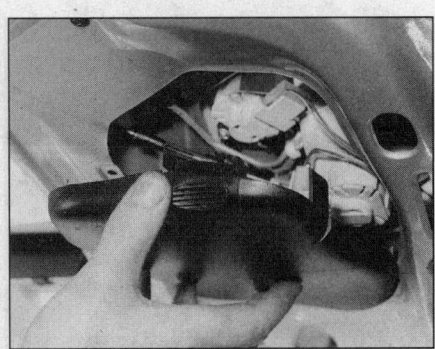

19.24 Remove the plastic cover . . .

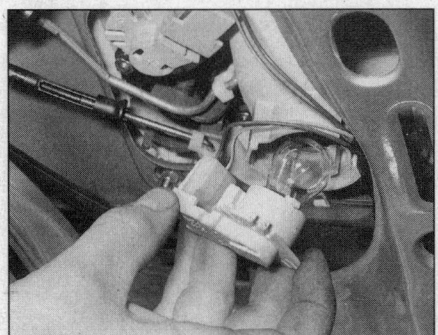

19. 25 . . . disconnect the bulbholder . . .

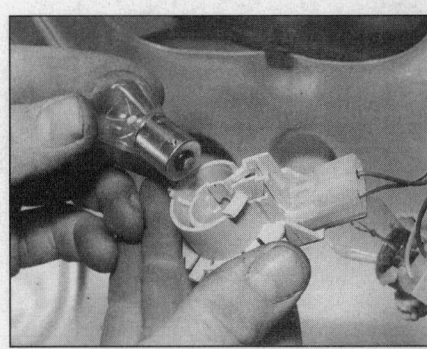

19.26 and remove the bootlid rear lamp cluster bulb

12

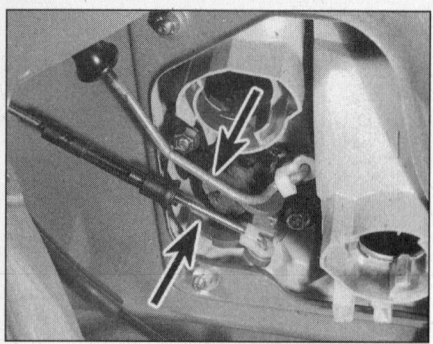

19.27 Inner view of bootlid rear lamp cluster, showing boot lock operating rod (arrowed)

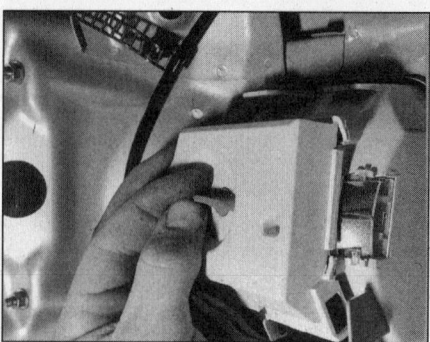

19.29A Release the catch . . .

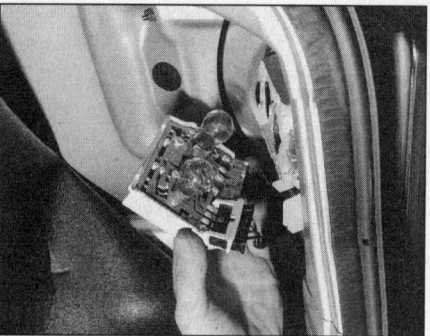

19.29B . . . and withdraw the rear side panel lamp cluster bulbholder

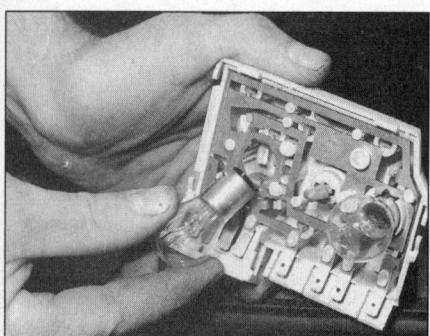

19.30 Removing a rear side panel lamp cluster bulb

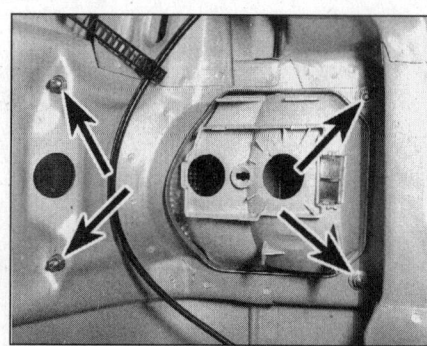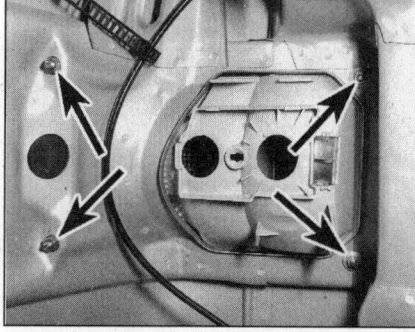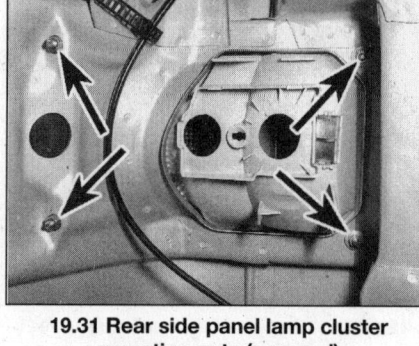

19.31 Rear side panel lamp cluster mounting nuts (arrowed)

Rearlamp cluster - rear side panel (Saloon)

29 Open the bootlid, then release the catch and withdraw the bulbholder (photos).
30 Depress and twist the bulb to remove it (photo).
31 If necessary, the lamp may be removed by unscrewing the nuts (photo).
32 Refitting is a reversal of removal.

Rear lamp cluster (Coupé)

33 Open the bootlid, then release the catches and withdraw the bulbholder.
34 Depress and twist the bulb to remove it.
35 Refitting is a reversal of removal.

Number plate light

36 Open the bootlid or tailgate as applicable.
37 Unscrew the cross-head screws and remove the lens, noting which way round it is fitted (photo).
38 Depress and twist the bulb to remove it from the lamp (photo).
39 Refitting is a reversal of removal, but make sure that the rubber seal is located correctly under the lens, and that the lug on the lens engages the cut-out in the lamp body.

Interior light(s)

40 Using a small screwdriver, prise the interior light from the headlining (photo).
41 Remove the festoon type bulb from the spring contacts (photo).

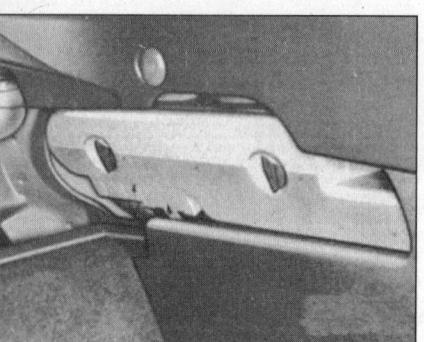

Fig 12.10 Rear lamp cluster inner view (Coupé) (Sec 19)

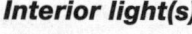

19.37 Removing the number plate light lens . . .

19.38 . . . and bulb

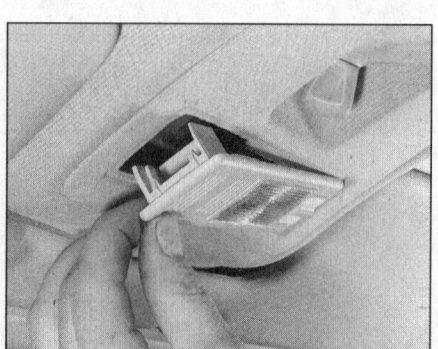

19.40 Removing the interior light . . .

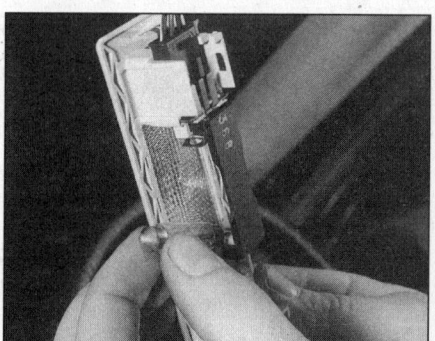

19.41 . . . and bulb

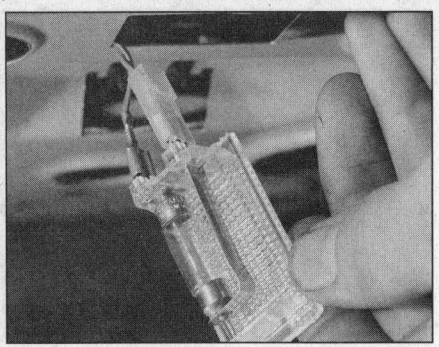

19.43 Luggage compartment light removal

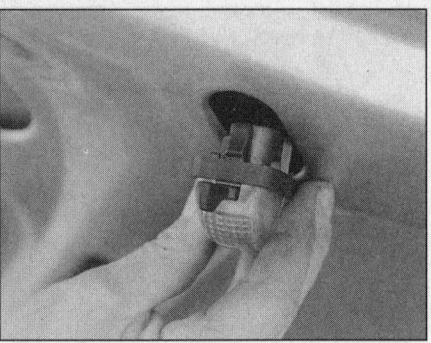

19.48A Removing the engine compartment light . . .

19.48B . . . and disconnecting the wiring

42 Refitting is a reversal of removal, but make sure that the spring contacts are tensioned sufficiently to hold the bulb firmly.

Luggage compartment light

43 Using a screwdriver, prise out the light lens (photo).
44 Remove the festoon type bulb from the spring contacts.
45 Refitting is a reversal of removal, but make sure that the spring contacts are tensioned sufficiently to hold the bulb firmly.

Engine compartment light

46 Squeeze the sides of the lens together, and remove the lens.
47 Depress and twist the bulb to remove it.
48 If necessary, prise the light from the bonnet and disconnect the wiring (photos).
49 Refitting is a reversal of removal.

Map reading light (Coupé models)

50 Hold the grab handle down, and unscrew the cross-head screws.
51 Remove the handle and light complete, and disconnect the wiring plug.
52 Remove the festoon type bulb from the spring contacts.
53 Refitting is a reversal of removal, but make sure that the spring contacts are tensioned sufficiently to hold the bulb firmly.

Side marker lamp

54 Push the lamp rearwards and release it from the location hole (photo).
55 Pull the bulbholder from the rear of the lamp (photo).
56 Pull the wedge type bulb from the bulbholder (photo).
57 Refitting is a reversal of removal.

Glovebox illumination lamp

58 Remove the glovebox as described in Chapter 11.
59 Pull the switch/bulbholder from its housing, then depress and twist the bulb to remove it (photos).
60 Refitting is a reversal of removal.

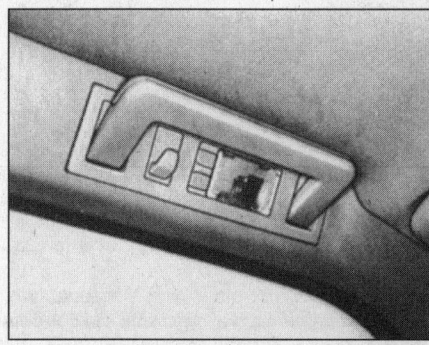

Fig 12.11 Map reading light (Coupé) (Sec 19)

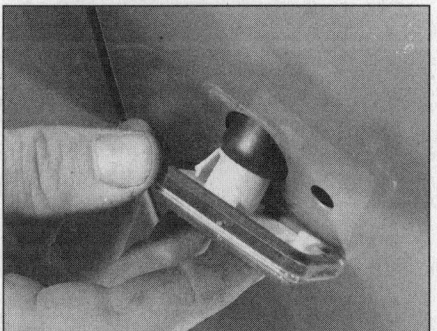

19.54 Release the side marker lamp . . .

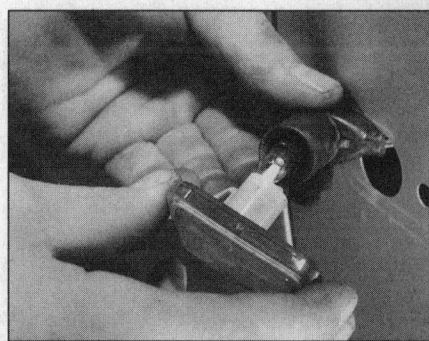

19.55. . . disconnect the bulbholder . . .

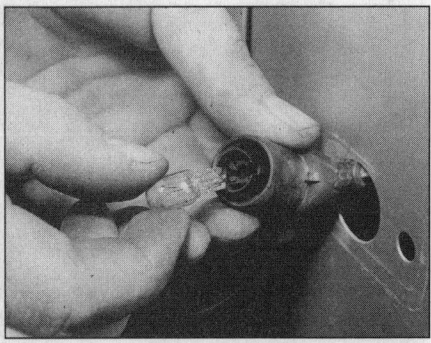

19.56. . . and pull out the wedge type bulb

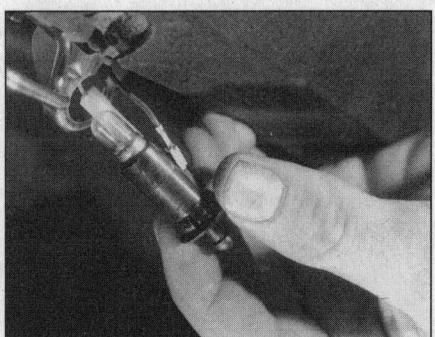

19.59A Removing the glovebox illumination lamp . . .

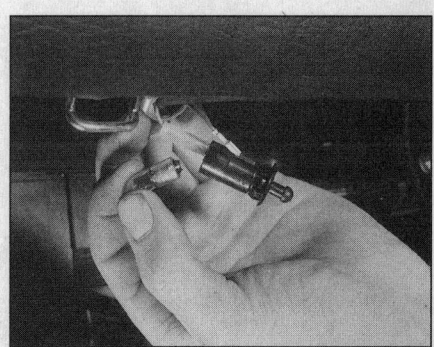

19.59B . . . and bulb

12

19.61 Prising out a facia switch cover

19.62 Using a piece of tubing to remove the facia switch illumination bulb

19.63 Fitting the facia switch illumination bulb

Facia switch illumination

61 Prise the cover from the switch with a screwdriver (photo).
62 Remove the wedge type bulb, using a piece of plastic or rubber tubing which is a tight fit over the bulb (photo).
63 Press the new bulb firmly into position, and refit the cover (photo).

Instrument panel illumination

64 Remove the instrument panel as described in Section 15.
65 Turn the bulbholder with a screwdriver, until the retainers are aligned with the cut-outs in the printed circuit board. Remove the bulbholder, and where applicable pull out the wedge type bulb (photos).
66 Refitting is a reversal of removal.

Heater control illumination

67 Remove the heater control knobs and surround panel, as described in Chapter 11, Section 30.
68 Remove the bulbholder from its retaining clip, then push and twist the bulb to remove it (photo).
69 Refitting is a reversal of removal.

20 Wiper blades and arms - removal and refitting

1 To remove a wiper blade, first lift the arm away from the windscreen and turn the wiper blade horizontal.

2 Lift the small spring clip, then slide the blade centre block down the arm, and withdraw the blade over the end of the arm (photos).
3 When refitting the blade, make sure that the spring clip engages correctly.
4 To remove an arm, prise off the cover and unscrew the spindle nut (photo). Remove the washer and ease the arm from the spindle by rocking it slowly from side to side.
5 If the wipers are not in their parked position, switch on the ignition, and allow the motor to automatically 'park'.
6 Refitting is a reversal of removal, but before tightening the spindle nuts, position the wiper blades as shown in Figs. 12.12 to 12.14, according to model.

19.65A Turn the bulbholder with a screwdriver . . .

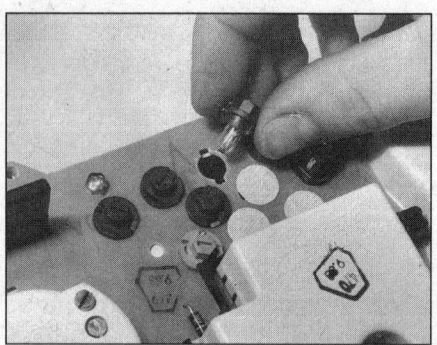

19.65B . . . and remove from the instrument panel

19.68 Heater control illumination bulb removal

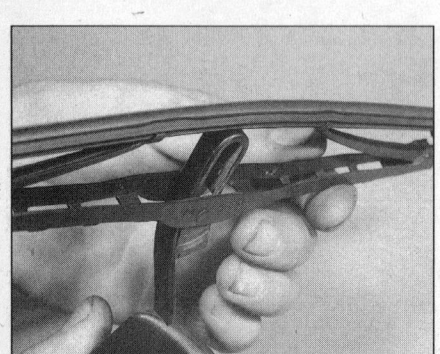

20.2A Release the wiper blade centre block . . .

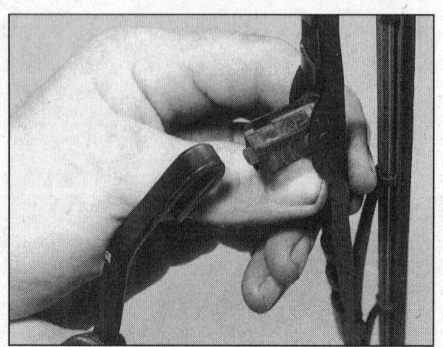

20.2B . . . and withdraw the blade over the end of the arm

20.4 Removing a wiper arm

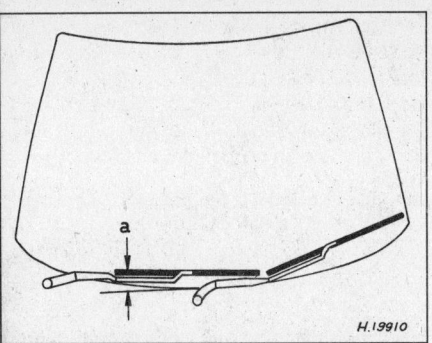

Fig 12.12 Parked position for windscreen wiper blades on 80 and 90 models (Sec 20)

a = 60 mm (2.4 in)

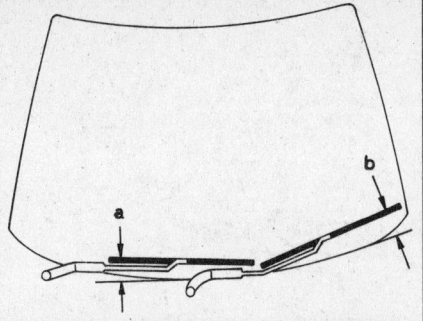

Fig 12.13 Parked position for windscreen wiper blades on Coupé models (Sec 20)

a = 65 mm (2.6 in)   b = 90 mm (3.5 in)

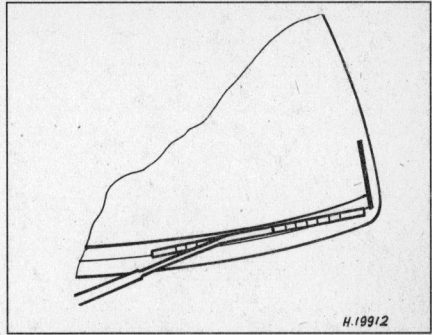

Fig 12.14 Parked position for tailgate wiper blade on Coupé models (Sec 20)

21 Windscreen wiper motor and frame - removal and refitting

Note: *It is not possible to remove the wiper motor separately from the frame.*

1 Switch on the ignition and the wipers, then switch off the ignition when the wiper blades are positioned as shown in Fig. 12.16.

2 Disconnect the battery negative lead.

3 With the bonnet open, use a screwdriver to turn the fasteners, then remove the plastic strip in front of and below the windscreen (photos).

4 Remove the wiper arms as described in Section 20.

5 Disconnect the wiring plug from the motor.

6 Unscrew the two side mounting screws and centre mounting bolt, and withdraw the wiper frame (photo).\

7 Lever the connecting rods from the crank on the motor, and also (if necessary) from the spindle assemblies.

8 Mark the crank in relation to the motor spindle, then unscrew the nut and remove the crank from the spindle.

9 Unscrew the three mounting bolts and remove the motor from the frame.

10 If the spindle assemblies are riveted to the frame, they may be renewed separately by grinding away the rivet heads and driving out the rivets. If the assemblies are pressed in, they cannot be renewed separately.

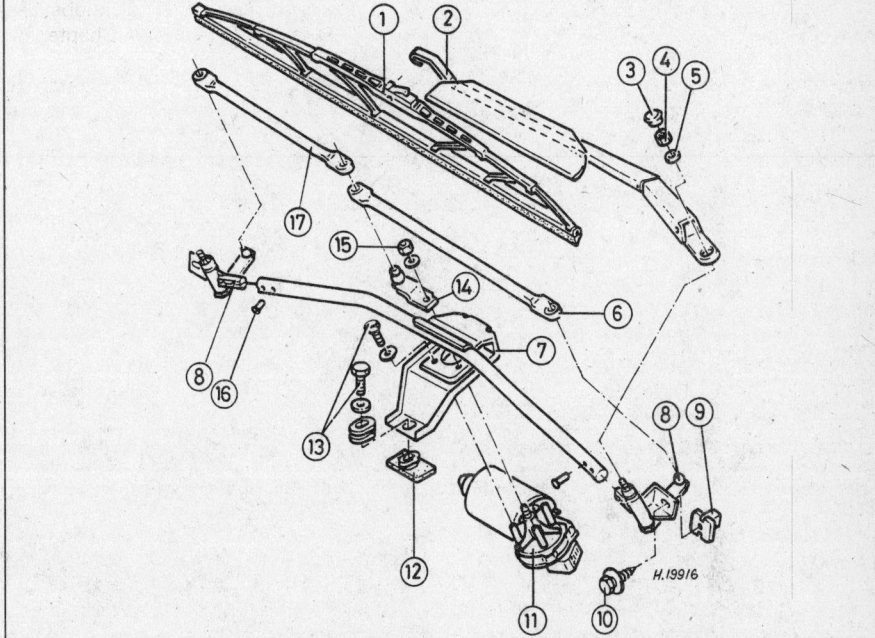

Fig 12.15 Windscreen wiper motor and frame components (Sec 21)

1 Wiper blade	7 Frame	12 Rubber packing
2 Wiper arm	8 Spindle assembly	13 Screw
3 Cap	9 Clip	14 Crank
4 Nut	10 Screw	15 Nut
5 Washer	11 Wiper motor	16 Rivet
6 Connecting rod		17 Connecting rod

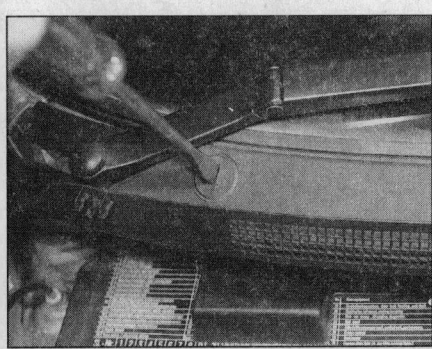

21.3A Turn the fasteners . . .

21.3B . . . and remove the plastic strip

12

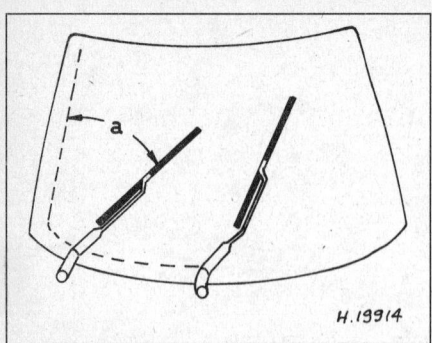

Fig 12.16 Windscreen wiper blade positions for removal of frame (Sec 21)
a = 45°

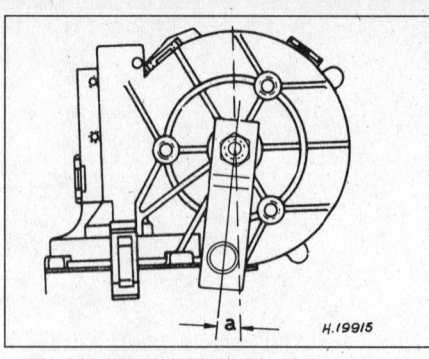

Fig 12.17 'Parked' position of crank on wiper motor (Sec 21)
a = 6°

11 Refitting is a reversal of removal, but lubricate the connecting rod bearings with a little molybdenum disulphide grease. If a new wiper motor is being fitted, fit the crank to the spindle in the position shown in Fig. 12.17, with the motor in its 'parked' position.

22 Washer system - general

1 All models are fitted with a windscreen washer system. Coupé models additionally have a tailgate screen washer system, and some models are fitted with a headlamp washer system.
2 The washer reservoir is located in the front left-hand corner of the engine compartment, and for the tailgate washer on Coupé models, on the right-hand side of the rear luggage compartment.
3 On 90 models, access is gained by removing the plastic cover in front of the radiator.
4 The electric pump is a push fit in a rubber seal located in the reservoir (photo).
5 To remove a jet from the bonnet, push the jet rearwards and lift the front edge. When fitting, insert the front first, then press down the rear until the plastic clip engages.
6 The jets should be adjusted to direct water as shown in Figs. 12.19 and 12.20, using a needle. Adjustment of the headlamp washer jets is only possible using VAG tool 3019 A.

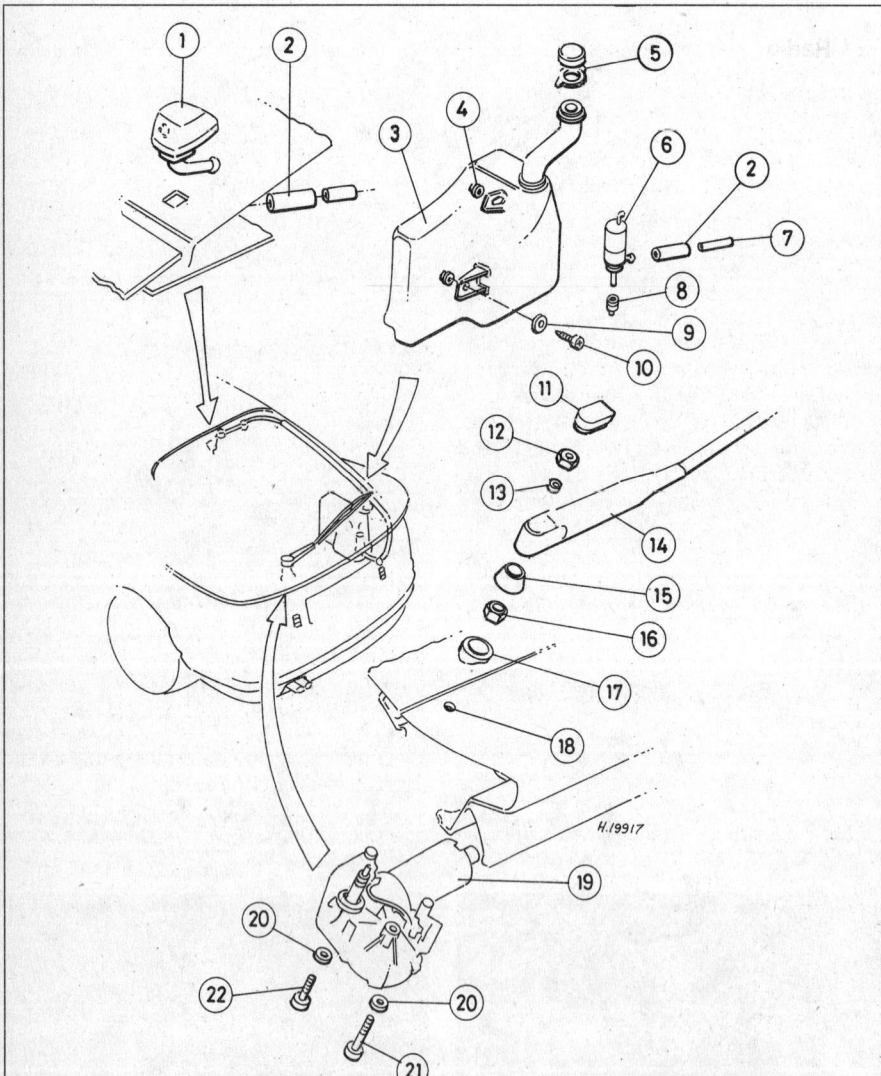

Fig 12.18 Rear window washer (and wiper) components (Coupé) (Sec 22)

1	Washer jet	7	Tubing	12	Nut	18	Tailgate
2	Hose	8	Seal	13	Spring washer	19	Wiper motor
3	Reservoir	9	Washer	14	Wiper arm	20	Spring washer
4	Nut	10	Screw	15	Cap	21	Bolt
5	Cap	11	Cap	16	Nut	22	Bolt
6	Washer pump			17	Spacer		

22.4 Windscreen washer reservoir and electric pump (arrowed)

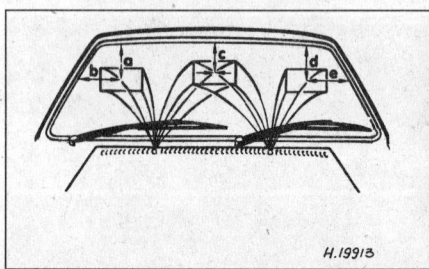

Fig 12.19 Windscreen washer adjustment (Sec 22)

a = 200 mm (7.9 in)   d = 180 mm (7.1 in)
b = 190 mm (7.5 in)   e = 180 mm (7.1 in)
c = 120 mm (4.7 in)

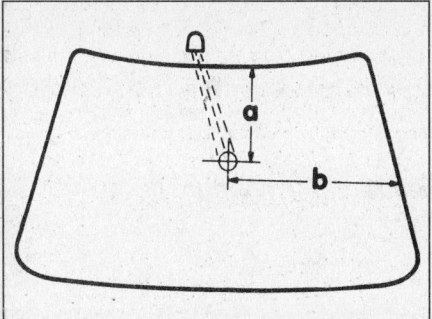

Fig 12.20 Rear window washer adjustment (Coupé) (Sec 22)

a = 300mm (11.8in)   b = 550mm (21.7in)

232 Horns and wiring

24.3 Removing the radio with the special rods

23 Horns - removal and refitting

1 Apply the handbrake, then jack up the front of the car and support on axle stands. Remove the splash guard from under the engine.
2 The horns are located under the left-hand front corner of the car (photo). First disconnect the wiring from the horn(s).
3 Unbolt the horn(s) from the underbody.
4 Refitting is reversal of removal - check for correct operation on completion.

24.4A Withdraw the radio . . .

24 Radio - removal and refitting

1 The radio is fitted with special mounting clips, requiring the use of special removal rods, which may be obtained from an in-car entertainment specialist. Alternatively, it may be possible to make up some removal rods.
2 Disconnect the battery negative lead - refer to Section 3, paragraph 2.
3 Insert the removal rods in the holes provided on each side of the radio front face, so that the spring clips are released (photo).
4 Withdraw the radio from the mounting case, then disconnect the loudspeaker, supply and aerial plugs (photos).
5 Refitting is a reversal of removal, but push the radio fully into its case until the spring clips are engaged. If the radio is of the security code type, it will be necessary to enter the code number before switching on the radio.

25 On-board computer - general

1 The on-board computer is located on the rear of the instrument panel. It has six display modes:

1 Instantaneous fuel consumption
2 Possible range with same driving style until fuel used up
3 Amount of fuel used since engine started
4 Driving time since last cancelled
5 Average fuel consumption since memory last cancelled
6 Average speed since memory last cancelled

2 If a fault occurs in the on-board computer, it is recommended that an Audi dealer is consulted.

26 Wiring diagrams - description

1 The wiring diagrams included at the end of this Chapter are of the current flow type where each wire is shown in the simplest line form without crossing over other wires.
2 The fuse/relay panel is at the top of the diagram and the combined letter/figure numbers appearing on the panel terminals refer to the multiplug connector in letter form and the terminal in figure form.
3 Internal connections through electrical components are shown by a single line.
4 The encircled numbers along the bottom of the diagram indicate the earthing connecting points as given in the key.
5 Restricted space means it has only been possible to include a typical selection of wiring diagrams.

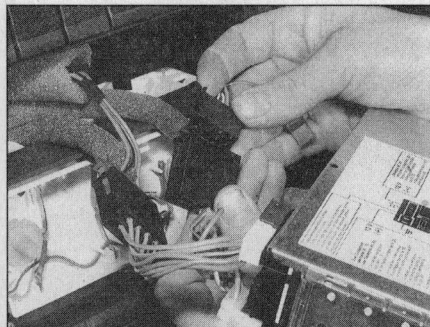

24.4B . . . and disconnect the loudspeaker multi-plug . . .

24.4C . . . supply multi-plug . . .

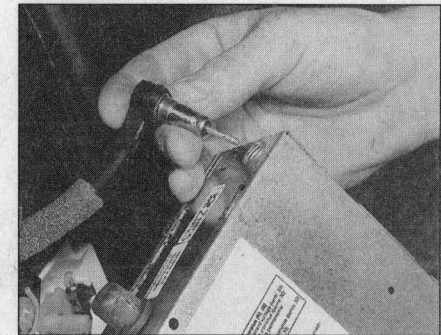

24.4D . . . and aerial plug

12

Fault finding - electrical system

Starter fails to turn engine
- [ ] Battery discharged
- [ ] Battery leads loose
- [ ] Starter motor connections loose
- [ ] Starter motor brushes loose, or dirty commutator

Starter turns engine slowly
- [ ] Battery discharged
- [ ] Starter motor connections loose

Battery will not hold charge
- [ ] Electrolyte level too low
- [ ] Alternator drivebelt slipping
- [ ] Alternator or regulator faulty
- [ ] Short in electrical circuit

Ignition light stays on
- [ ] Alternator drivebelt broken
- [ ] Alternator or voltage regulator faulty

Ignition light fails to come on
- [ ] Warning bulb blown
- [ ] Warning light open-circuit
- [ ] Alternator or voltage regulator faulty

Instrument readings increase with engine speed
- [ ] Voltage stabilizer faulty

Fuel or temperature gauge readings incorrect
- [ ] Voltage stabilizer faulty
- [ ] Sender unit faulty
- [ ] Wiring faulty

Lights inoperative
- [ ] Bulb blown
- [ ] Fuse blown
- [ ] Wiring faulty
- [ ] Switch faulty

Failure of component motor
- [ ] Commutator dirty
- [ ] Brushes sticking or worn
- [ ] Armature or field coils faulty
- [ ] Wiring faulty

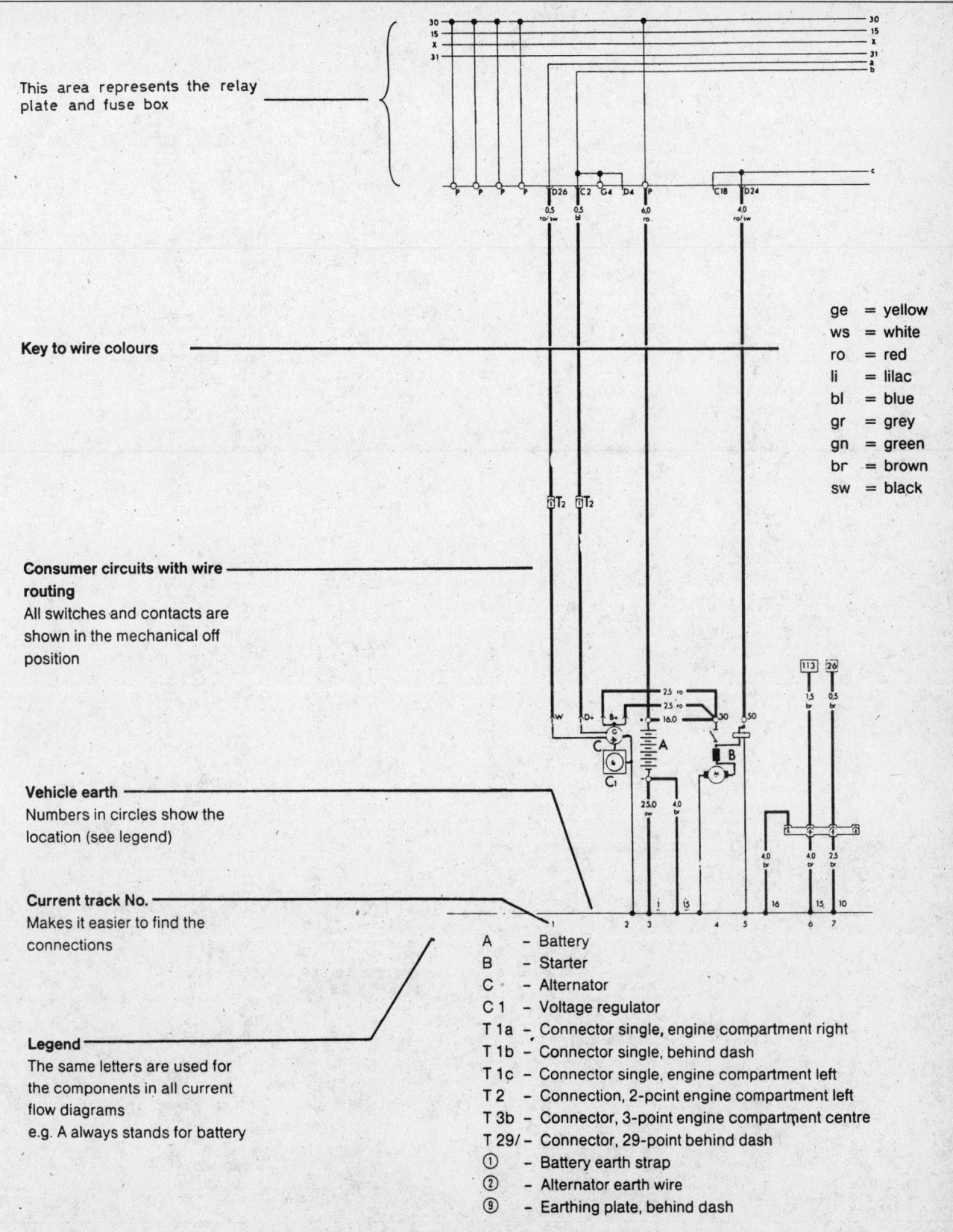

This area represents the relay plate and fuse box

Key to wire colours

ge = yellow
ws = white
ro = red
li = lilac
bl = blue
gr = grey
gn = green
br = brown
sw = black

Consumer circuits with wire routing
All switches and contacts are shown in the mechanical off position

Vehicle earth
Numbers in circles show the location (see legend)

Current track No.
Makes it easier to find the connections

Legend
The same letters are used for the components in all current flow diagrams
e.g. A always stands for battery

A – Battery
B – Starter
C – Alternator
C 1 – Voltage regulator
T 1a – Connector single, engine compartment right
T 1b – Connector single, behind dash
T 1c – Connector single, engine compartment left
T 2 – Connection, 2-point engine compartment left
T 3b – Connector, 3-point engine compartment centre
T 29/ – Connector, 29-point behind dash
① – Battery earth strap
② – Alternator earth wire
⑨ – Earthing plate, behind dash

Wiring diagrams – layout explanation and colour code

12

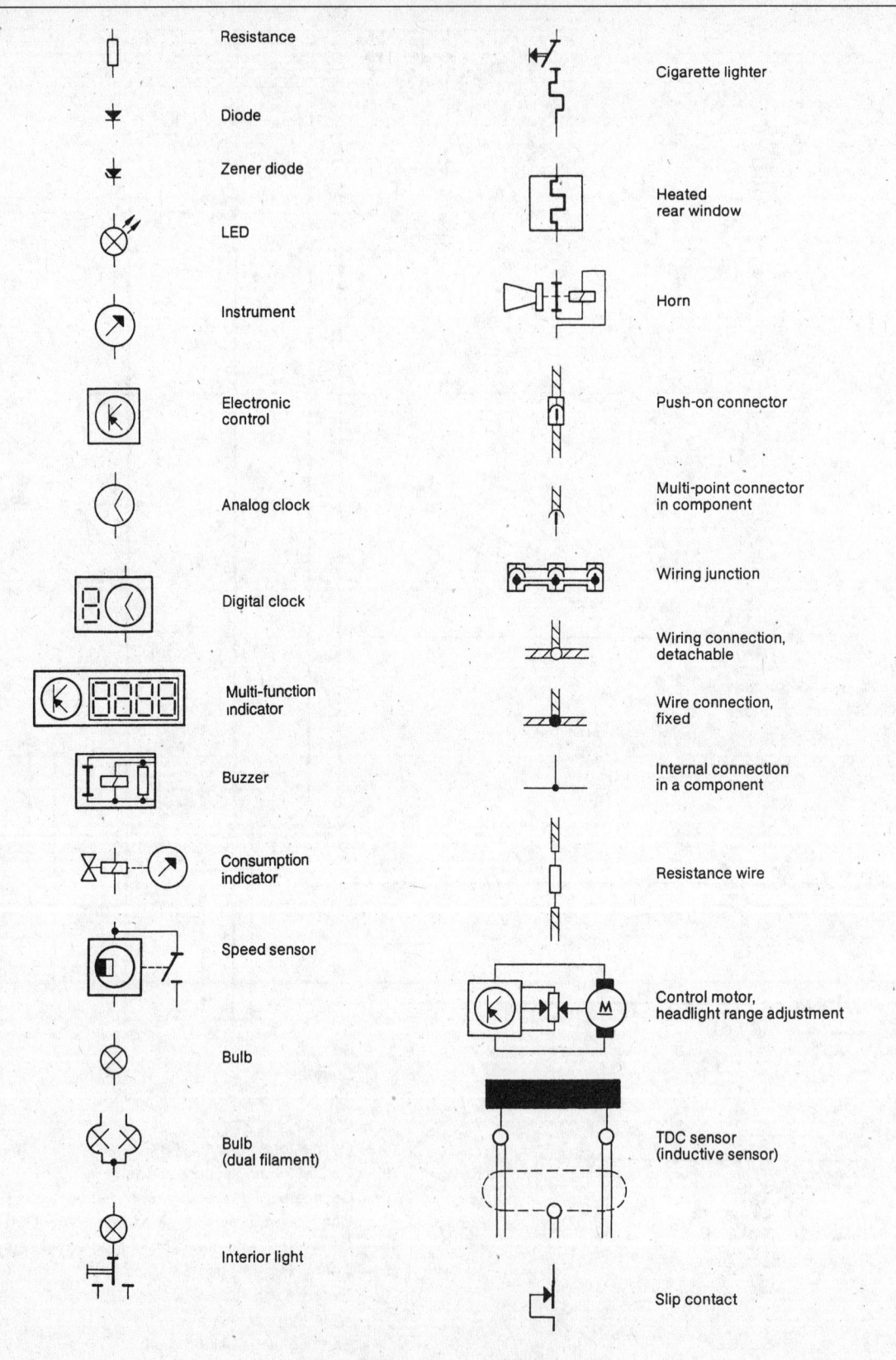

Resistance	Cigarette lighter
Diode	Heated rear window
Zener diode	Horn
LED	Push-on connector
Instrument	Multi-point connector in component
Electronic control	Wiring junction
Analog clock	Wiring connection, detachable
Digital clock	Wire connection, fixed
Multi-function indicator	Internal connection in a component
Buzzer	Resistance wire
Consumption indicator	Control motor, headlight range adjustment
Speed sensor	
Bulb	TDC sensor (inductive sensor)
Bulb (dual filament)	
Interior light	Slip contact

Symbols used on the wiring diagrams

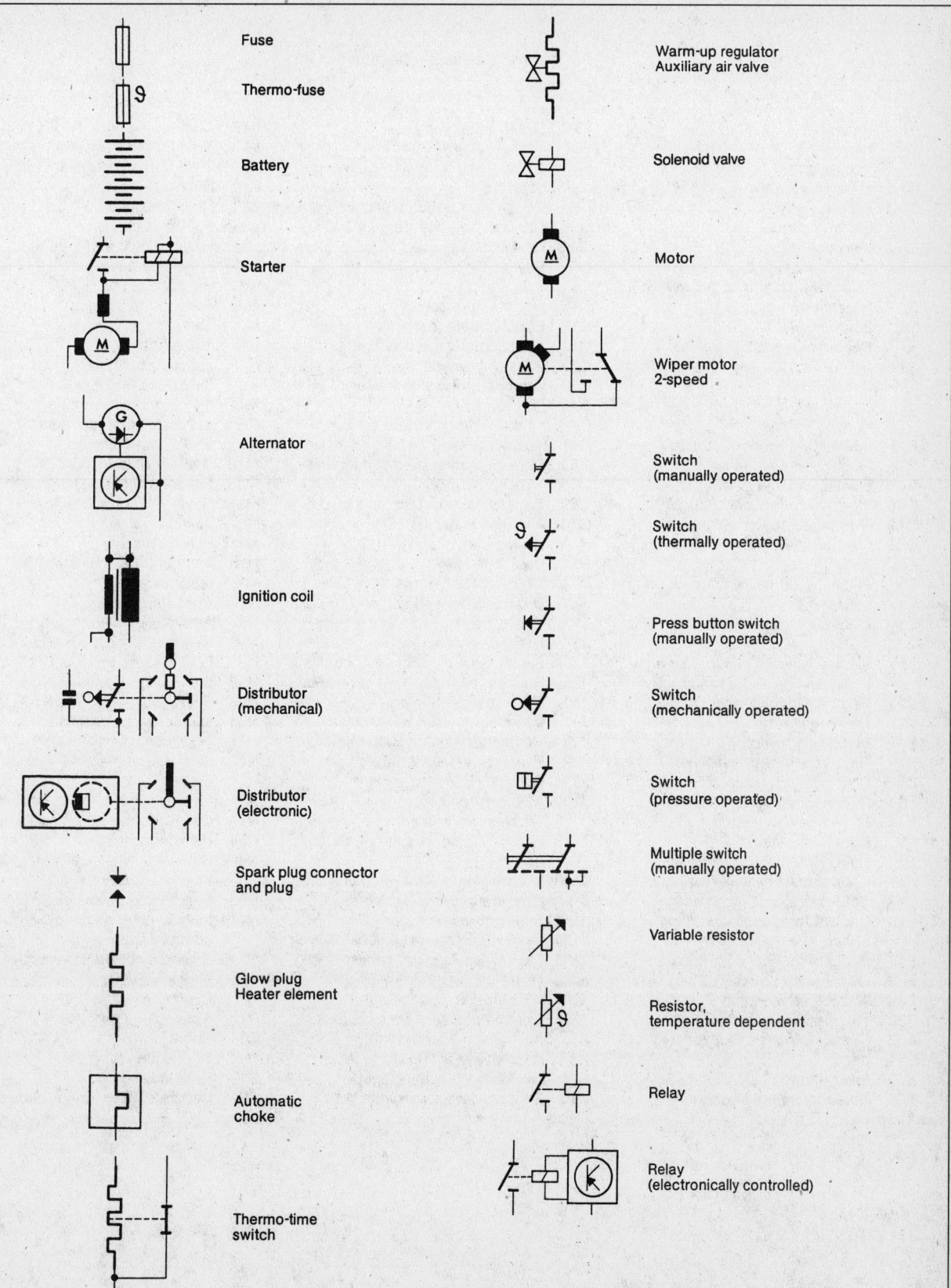

Fuse

Thermo-fuse

Battery

Starter

Alternator

Ignition coil

Distributor
(mechanical)

Distributor
(electronic)

Spark plug connector
and plug

Glow plug
Heater element

Automatic
choke

Thermo-time
switch

Warm-up regulator
Auxiliary air valve

Solenoid valve

Motor

Wiper motor
2-speed

Switch
(manually operated)

Switch
(thermally operated)

Press button switch
(manually operated)

Switch
(mechanically operated)

Switch
(pressure operated)

Multiple switch
(manually operated)

Variable resistor

Resistor,
temperature dependent

Relay

Relay
(electronically controlled)

Symbols used on the wiring diagrams (continued)

12

Key to all wiring diagrams

A	Battery
B	Starter
C	Alternator
C1	Voltage regulator
D	Ignition switch
E1	Lighting switch
E2	Indicator switch
E3	Hazard warning light switch
E4	Headlight dip and flasher switch
E7	Foglight switch
E8	Sunroof switch
E15	Heated rear window switch
E17	Starter inhibitor and reversing light switch
E18	Rear foglight switch
E19	Parking light switch
E22	Intermittent wiper switch
E39	Electric window switch
E40	Electric window switch, left
E41	Electric window switch, right
E43	Mirror adjustment switch
E52	Electric window switch, rear left, in door
E53	Electric window switch, rear left, in console
E54	Electric window switch, rear right, in door
E55	Electric window switch, rear right, in console
E107	Electric window switch in passenger's door
F	Brake light switch
F1	Oil pressure switch (1.8 bar)
F2	Door contact switch, front left
F3	Door contact switch, front right
F4	Reversing light switch
F5	Boot light switch
F10	Door contact switch, rear left
F11	Door contact switch, rear right
F12	Cold start warning contact
F14	Coolant temperature warning switch
F18	Radiator fan thermoswitch
F22	Oil pressure switch (0.3 bar)
F25	Throttle valve switch
F26	Thermotime switch
F59	Central locking switch (driver's door)
F60	Idle switch
F66	Low coolant level switch

F81	Full-throttle switch
F93	Vacuum timeswitch
F114	Central locking switch (passenger's door)
G2	Coolant temperature sender
G3	Coolant temperature gauge
G4	Firing point sender
G5	Rev counter
G6	Fuel pump
G18	Temperature sensor
G19	Potentiometer for airflow meter
G22	Speedometer sender
G28	Engine speed sender
G39	Lambda probe with heater
G40	Hall sender
G42	Intake air temperature sender
G61	Knock sensor 1
G62	Coolant temperature sender unit
G66	Knock sensor 2
G69	Throttle valve potentiometer
G70	Air mass meter
H	Horn control
H1	Dual tone horn
J2	Indicator flasher relay
J4	Dual tone horn relay
J5	Foglight relay
J17	Fuel pump relay
J21	Electronic fuel injection control unit
J26	Radiator fan relay
J30	Rear wash/wipe relay
J31	Intermittent wash/wipe relay
J39	Headlamp wash system relay
J59	Relief relay (for X-contact)
J89	Dim-dip changeover relay
J104	ABS control unit
J114	Oil pressure monitor switch unit
J139	Electric windows/sunroof switch unit
J140	Interior light delay switch unit
J 144	Cold start valve blocking diode
J152	Sidelight/radio buzzer
J154	Ignition control unit (knock control)
J192	Multi-point injection control unit
J202	Mono-Jetronic control unit
J204	KE-Motronic control unit
J221	Control unit, selector lever lock
K1	Main beam warning light
K2	Alternator warning light
K3	Oil pressure warning light
K15	Starting device warning light

K28	Coolant temperature warning light
L1	Twin filament headlight bulb, left
L2	Twin filament headlight bulb, right
L10	Dash insert bulb
L20	Rear foglight bulb
L22	Foglight bulb, left
L23	Foglight bulb, right
L29	Engine compartment light bulb
M1	Parking light bulb, left
M2	Tail light bulb, right
M3	Parking light bulb, right
M4	Tail light bulb, left
M5	Indicator bulb, front left
M6	Indicator bulb, rear left
M7	Indicator bulb, front right
M8	Indicator bulb, rear right
M9	Brake light bulb, left
M10	Brake light bulb, right
M16	Reversing light bulb, left
M17	Reversing light bulb, right
N	Ignition coil
N9	Warm-up valve
N10	Temperature sensor (NTC resistance)
N17	Cold start valve
N21	Auxiliary air valve
N30	Fuel injector, cylinder No 1
N31	Fuel injector, cylinder No 2
N32	Fuel injector, cylinder No 3
N33	Fuel injector, cylinder No 4
N34	Injector series resistance
N41	TCIH control unit
N70	Final output stage for ignition system
N71	Control valve for idle stabilisation
N73	Differential pressure regulator
N74	Resistance wire
N80	Solenoid valve, activated charcoal filter
N83	Fuel injector, cylinder No 5
N114	Ignition firing point adjustment control valve
N115	Solenoid cut-off valve, activated charcoal system
O	Distributor
P	Spark plug connector
Q	Spark plug
R	Connection for radio
S12	Fuse in fusebox
S27	Separate fuse, various circuits

Key to all wiring diagrams (continued)

S28	Separate fuse, various circuits	T3g	3-pin connector, right of engine compartment	T10c	10-pin connector, aux. relay carrier
T1	Single connector, various locations	T3h	3-pin connector, right of engine compartment	T26	26-pin connector, on dash insert
T1a	Single connector, various locations			T26a	26-pin connector, on dash insert
T1b	Single connector, various locations	T3l	3-pin connector, left of boot	V	Windscreen wiper motor
T1c	Single connector, behind dash	T3m	3-pin connector, left of boot	V5	Windscreen washer pump
T1d	Single connector, behind dash	T3n	3-pin connector, right of engine compartment	V7	Radiator fan
T1e	Single connector, behind dash			V11	Headlight washer pump
T1f	Single connector, behind dash	T30	3-pin connector, right of engine compartment	V12	Wiper motor
T1h	Single connector, behind dash			V13	Washer pump motor
T1x	Single connector, behind dash	T4	4-pin connector, various locations	V14	Window motor, left
T2	2-pin connector, various locations	T4a	4-pin connector, behind dash	V15	Window motor, right
T2a	2-pin connector, various locations	T4h	4-pin connector, left of engine compartment	V17	Mirror adjustment motor, driver's
T2b	2-pin connector, various locations			V25	Mirror adjustment motor, passenger's
T2c	2-pin connector, various locations	T5	5-pin connector, aux. relay carrier	V26	Window motor, rear left
T2d	2-pin connector, various locations	T5a	5-pin connector, aux. relay carrier	V27	Window motor, rear right
T2i	2-pin connector, behind dash	T5b	5-pin connector, left of engine compartment	V37	Central locking motor
T2j	2-pin connector, right of engine compartment			V60	Throttle vaive positioner
T3	3-pin connector, behind dash	T6	6-pin connector, aux. relay carrier	W	Interior light, front
T3a	3-pin connector, behind dash	T6a	6-pin connector, left of boot	W3	Boot light
T3b	3-pin connector, behind dash	T6d	6-pin connector, behind dash	W6	Glovebox light
T3d	3-pin connector, right of engine compartment	T7	7-pin connector, right of engine compartment	X	Number plate light
T3e	3-pin connector, right of engine compartment	T9	9-pin connector, in driver's door	Z1	Heated rear window
		T10	10-pin connector, aux. relay carrier	Z4	Heated mirror, driver's
T3f	3-pin connector, right of engine compartment	T10a	10-pin connector, aux. relay carrier	Z5	Heated mirror, passenger's
		T10b	10-pin connector, aux. relay carrier	Z19	Heating for Lambda probe

12

Earth connections

1	Battery earth strap
6	Alternator earth strap
17	On inlet manifold
32	Behind dash
50	Left of boot
69	Rear crossmember
81	Instrument loom
82	Front left loom
83	Front right loom
84	Engine block, front right loom
86	Rear loom
98	Bootlid/tailgate loom
100	Electric window/central locking/door contact switch loom
103	Electric window/central locking/door contact switch loom
105	Central locking loom
106	Exterior mirror loom

A1	Positive (+) connection in instrument loom
A2	Positive (+) connection in instrument loom
A10	Instrument loom
D1	Positive (+) connection in front right loom
D9	Positive (+) connection via fuse 27, in front right loom
D11	Positive (+) connection via fuse 28, in front right loom
Q9	Electric window loom
Q10	Positive (+) connection in electric window loom
S1	Positive (+) connection in central locking loom

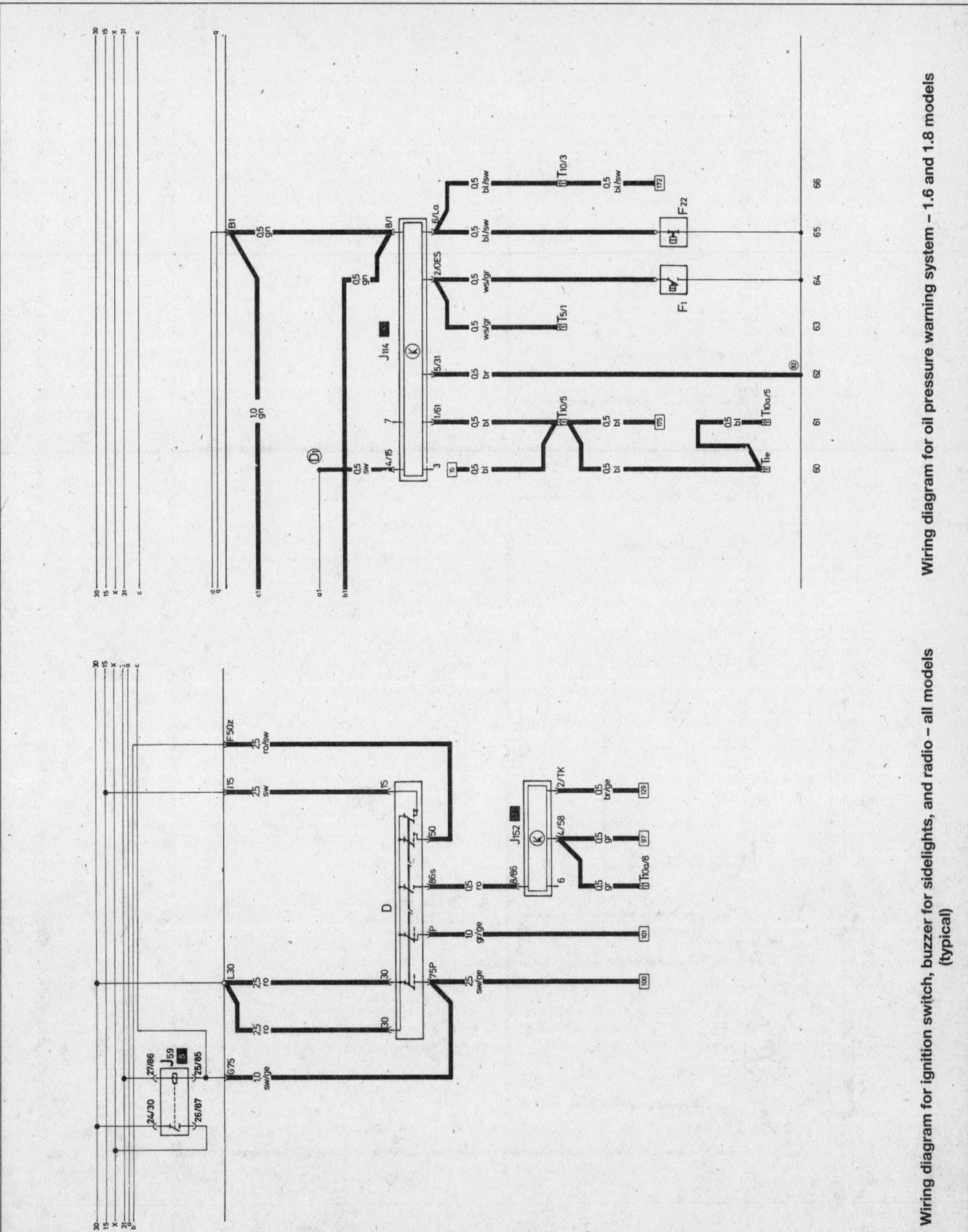

Wiring diagram for oil pressure warning system – 1.6 and 1.8 models

Wiring diagram for ignition switch, buzzer for sidelights, and radio – all models (typical)

12

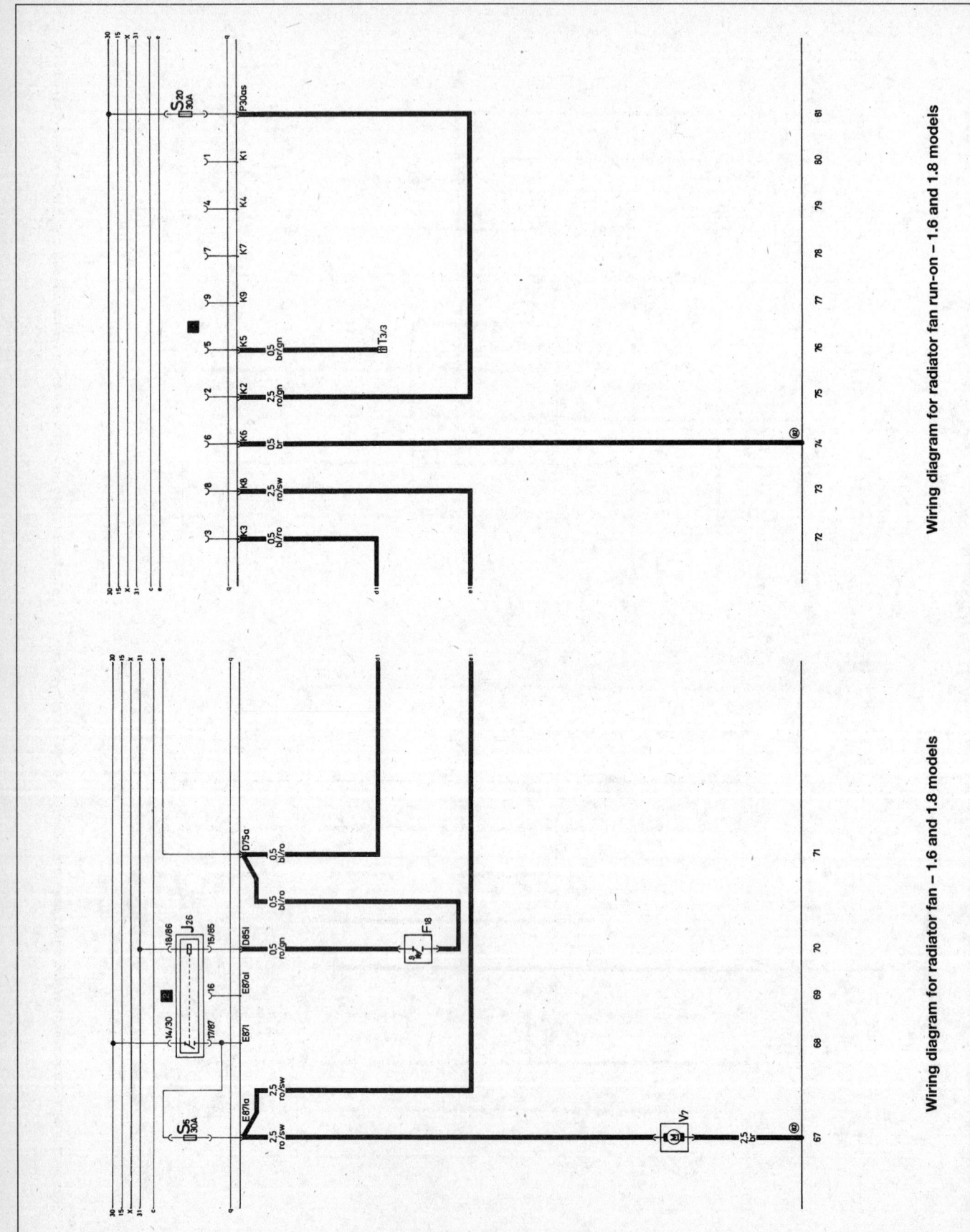

Wiring diagram for radiator fan run-on – 1.6 and 1.8 models

Wiring diagram for radiator fan – 1.6 and 1.8 models

Wiring diagram for lighting switch and headlight dip/flash switch - all models (typical)

Wiring diagram for headlights, tail lights and brake lights – all models (typical)

12

Wiring diagram for reversing lights – all models (typical)

Wiring diagram for sidelights, glovebox light, boot light and number plate light – all models (typical)

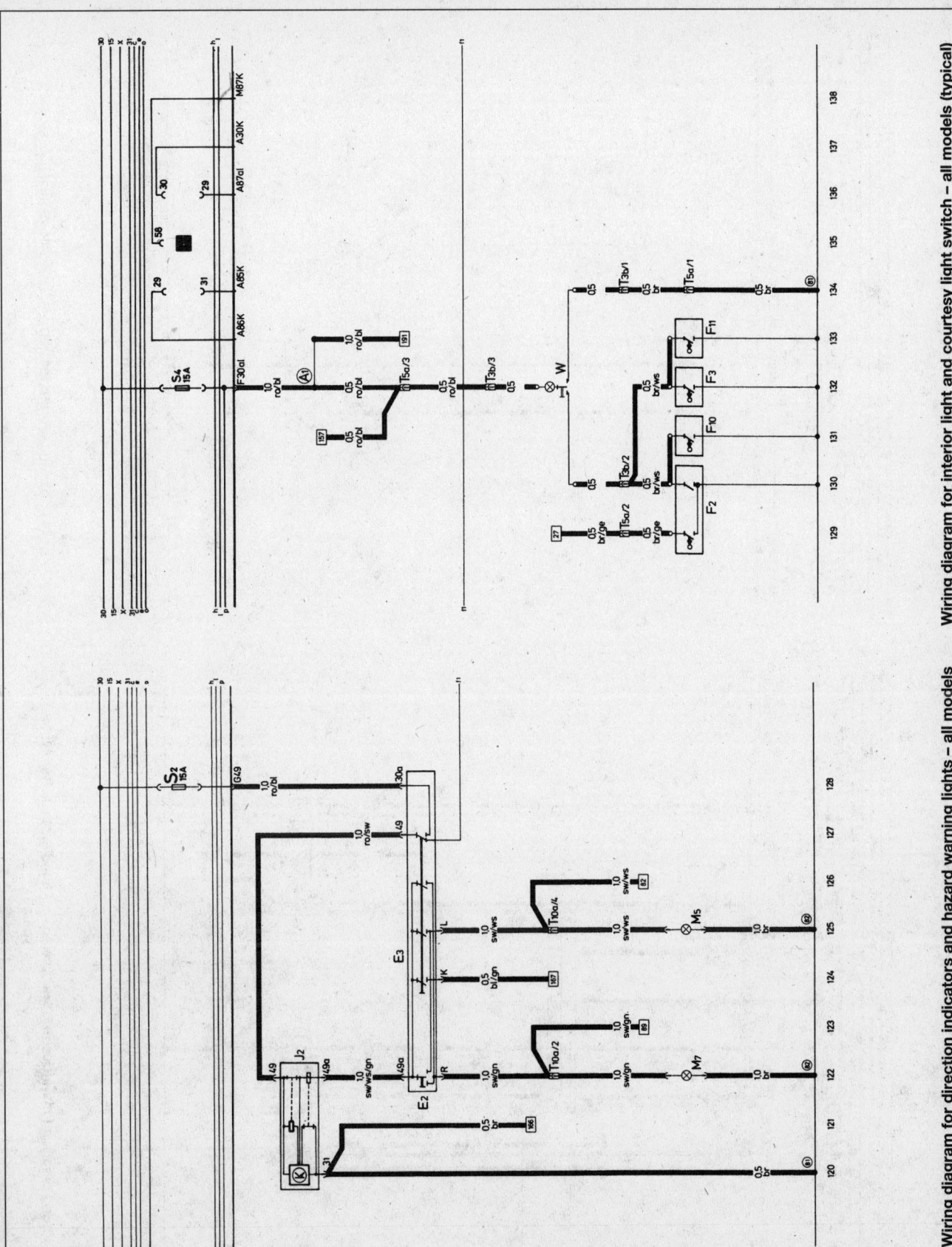

Wiring diagram for interior light and courtesy light switch – all models (typical)

Wiring diagram for direction indicators and hazard warning lights – all models (typical)

12

Wiring diagram for horn – all models (typical)

Wiring diagram for windscreen wash/wipe and headlight washer system – all models (typical)

Wiring diagram for battery, starter mtor and alternator – 1.6 models

Wiring diagram for heated rear window – all models (typical)

12

Wiring diagram for fuel system – 1.8 fuel injection models (K-Jetronic)

Wiring diagram for TCI-H ignition system – 1.6 models

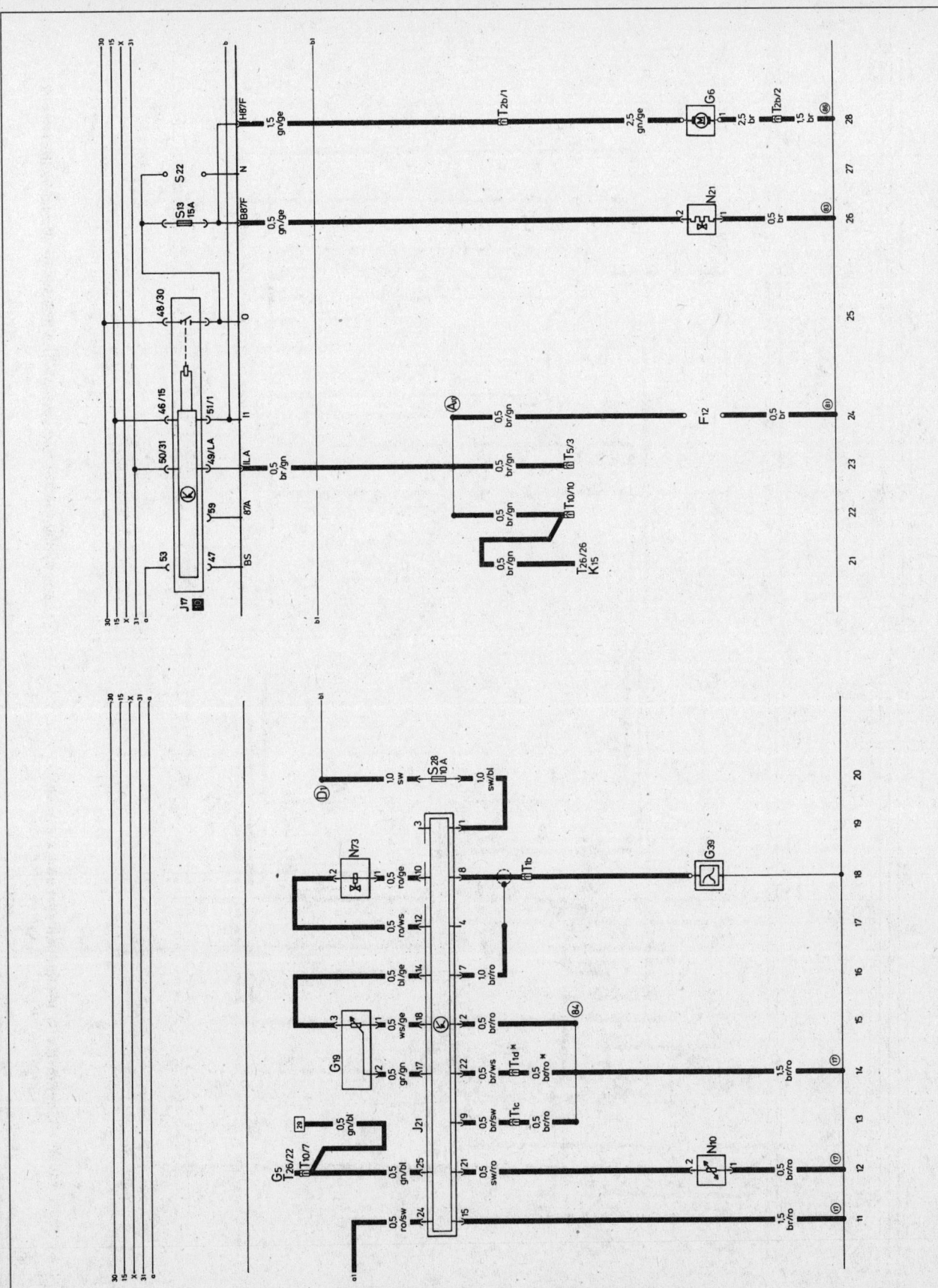

Wiring diagram for auxiliary air valve and fuel pump – 1.8 fuel injection models
(KE-Jetronic)

Wiring diagram for fuel system – 1.8 fuel injection models (KE-Jetronic)
*Automatic transmission models

12

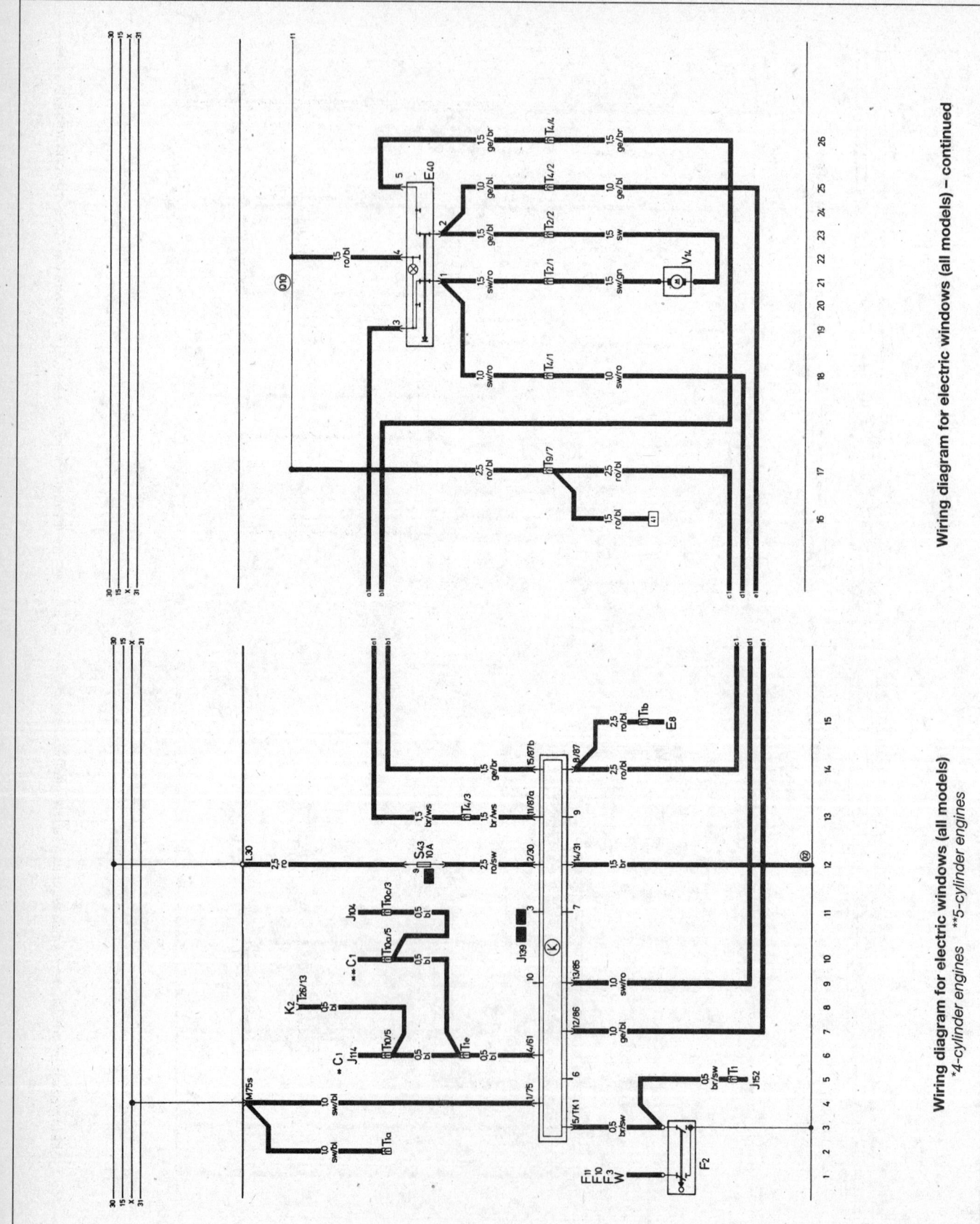

Wiring diagram for electric windows (all models) – continued

Wiring diagram for electric windows (all models)
*4-cylinder engines   **5-cylinder engines

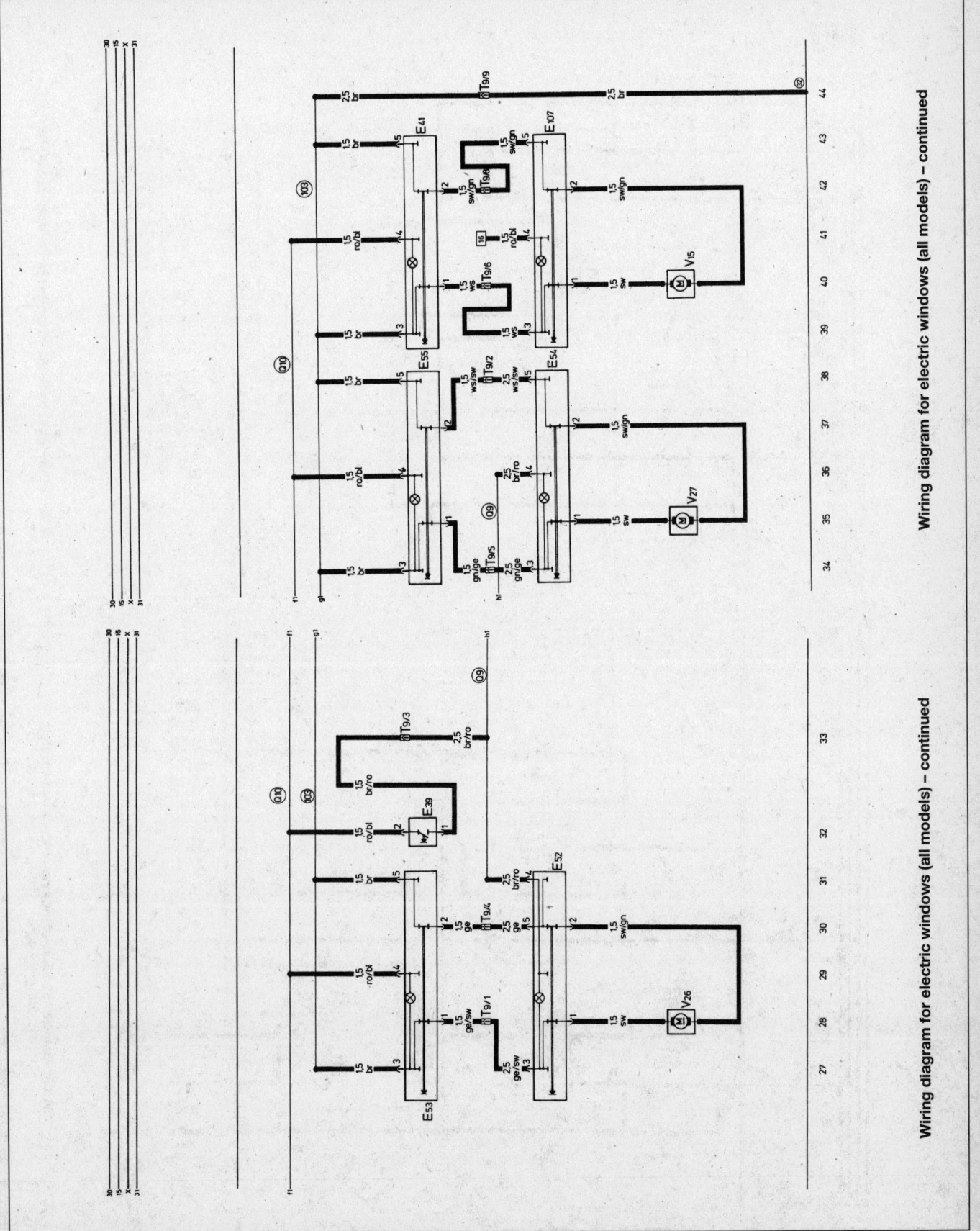

Wiring diagram for electric windows (all models) – continued

Wiring diagram for electric windows (all models) – continued

12

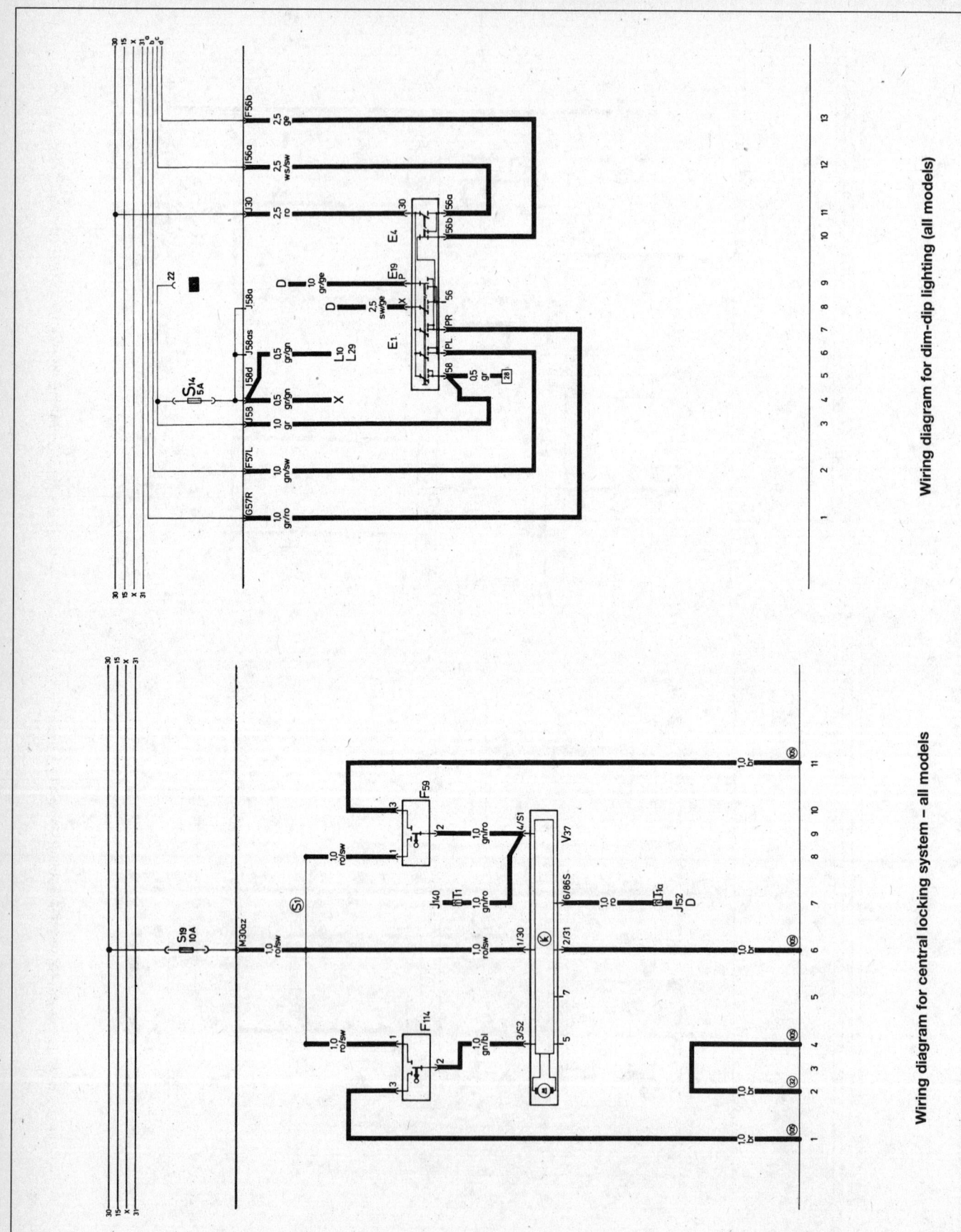

Wiring diagram for dim-dip lighting (all models)

Wiring diagram for central locking system – all models

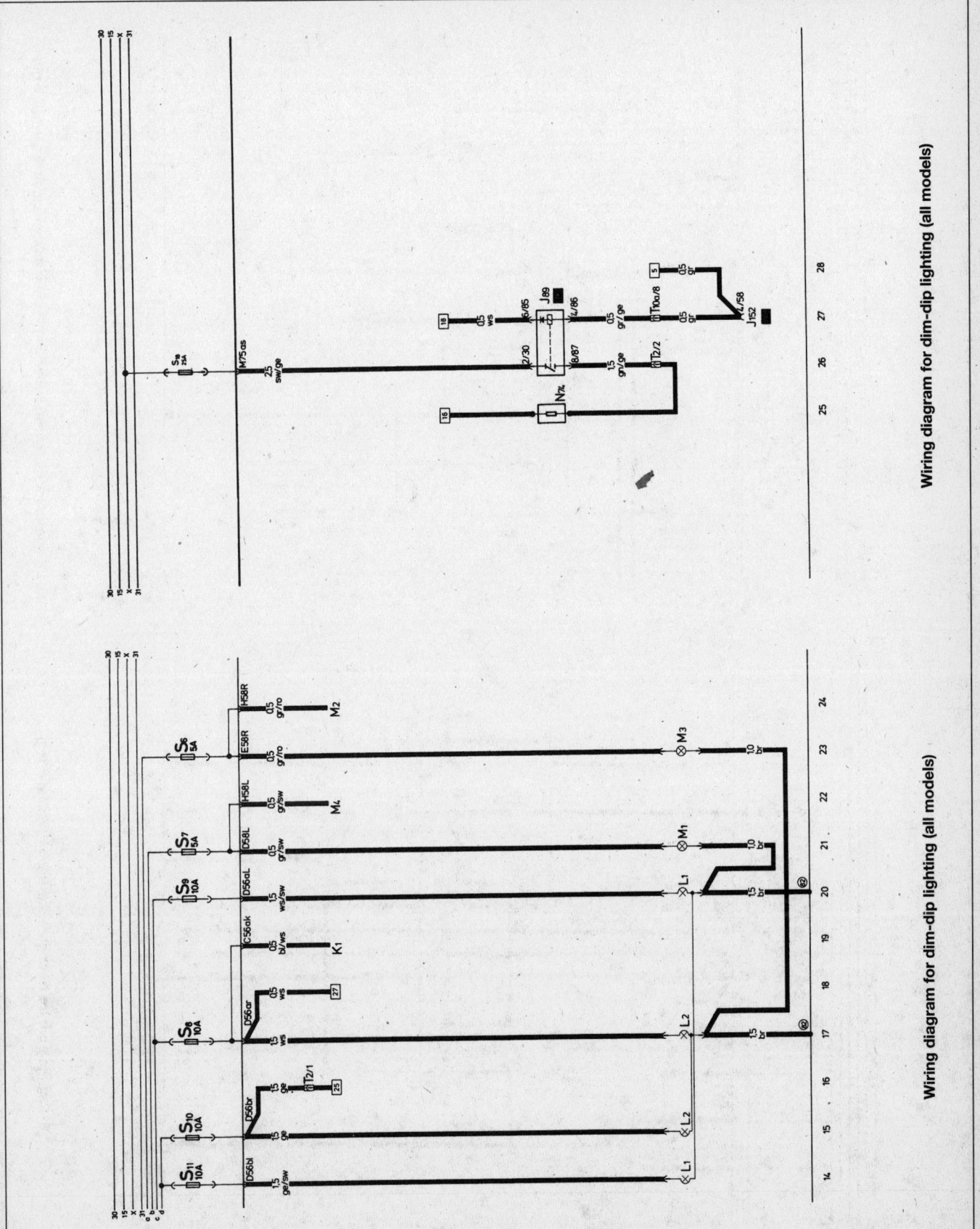

Wiring diagram for dim-dip lighting (all models)

Wiring diagram for dim-dip lighting (all models)

12

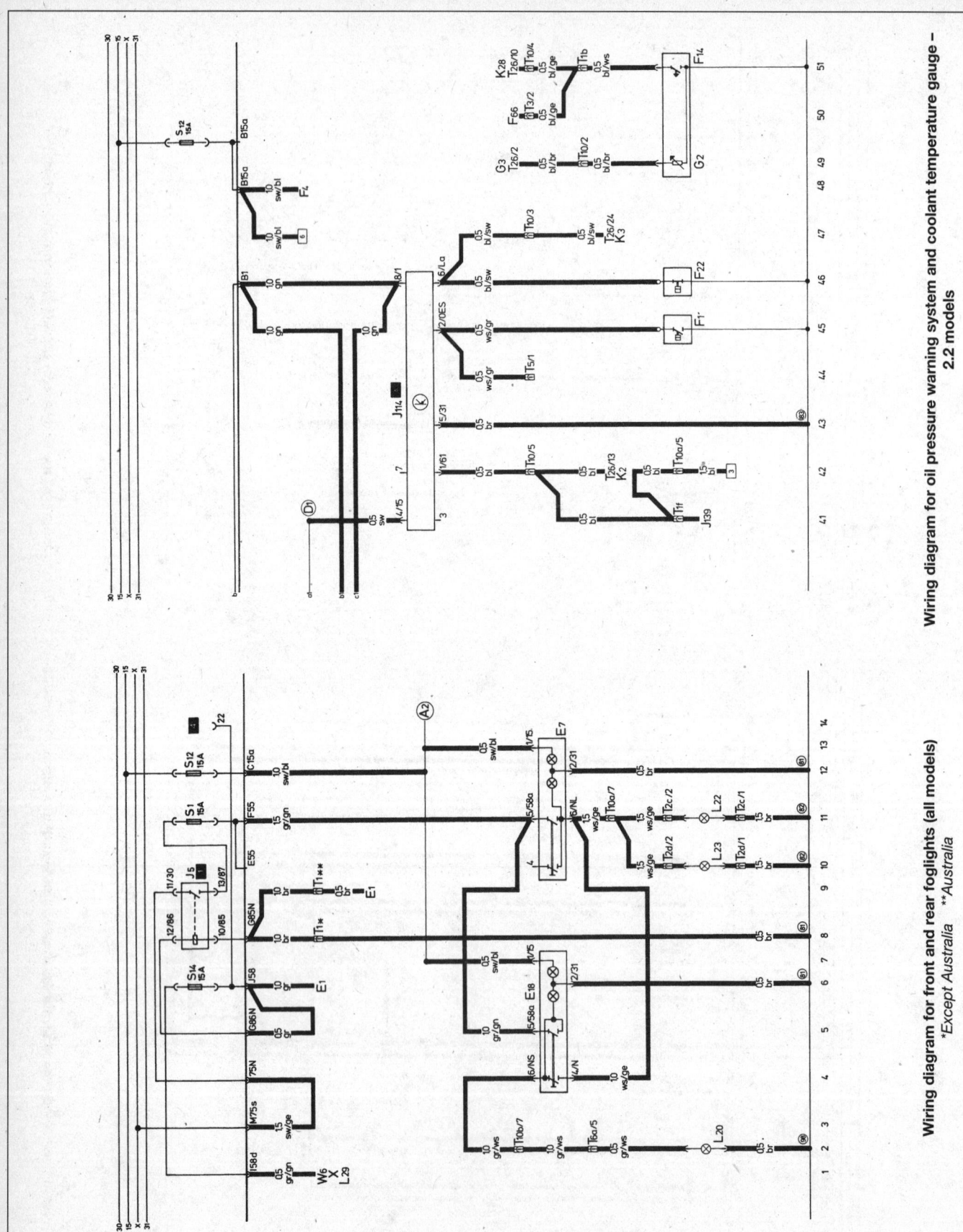

Wiring diagram for oil pressure warning system and coolant temperature gauge – 2.2 models

Wiring diagram for front and rear foglights (all models)
*Except Australia   **Australia

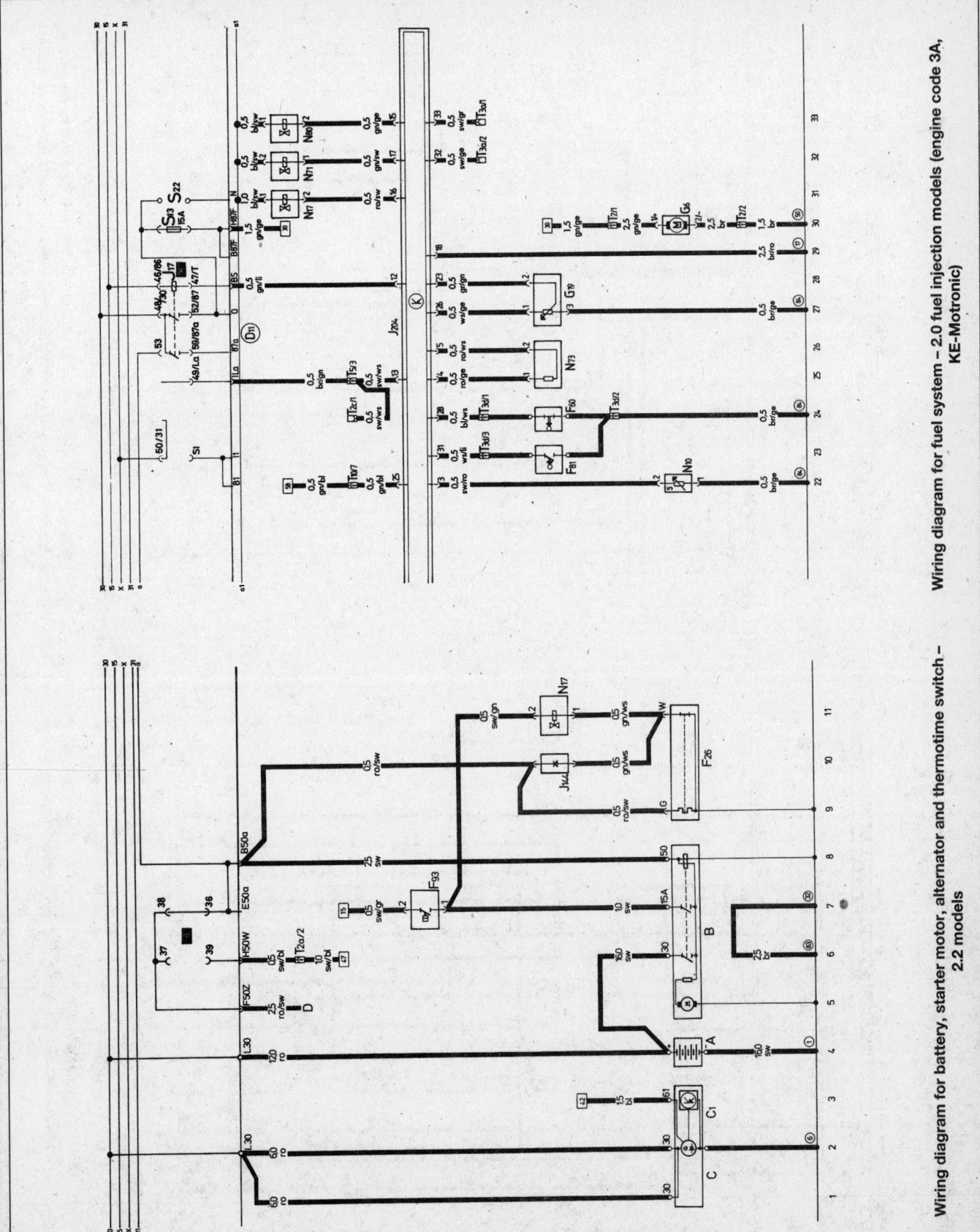

Wiring diagram for fuel system – 2.0 fuel injection models (engine code 3A, KE-Motronic)

Wiring diagram for battery, starter motor, alternator and thermotime switch – 2.2 models

12

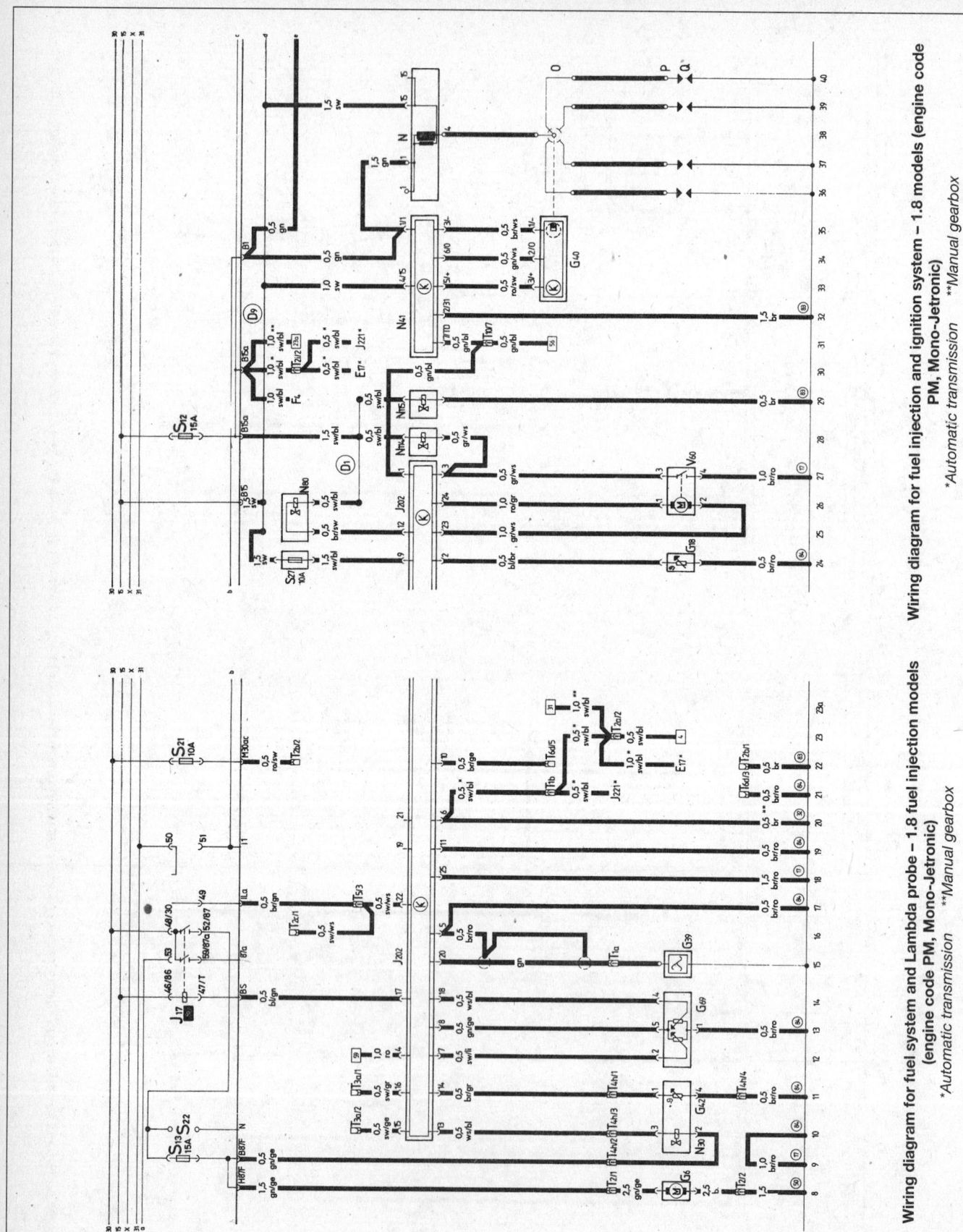

Wiring diagram for fuel injection and ignition system – 1.8 models (engine code PM, Mono-Jetronic)
*Automatic transmission
**Manual gearbox

Wiring diagram for fuel system and Lambda probe – 1.8 fuel injection models (engine code PM, Mono-Jetronic)
*Automatic transmission **Manual gearbox

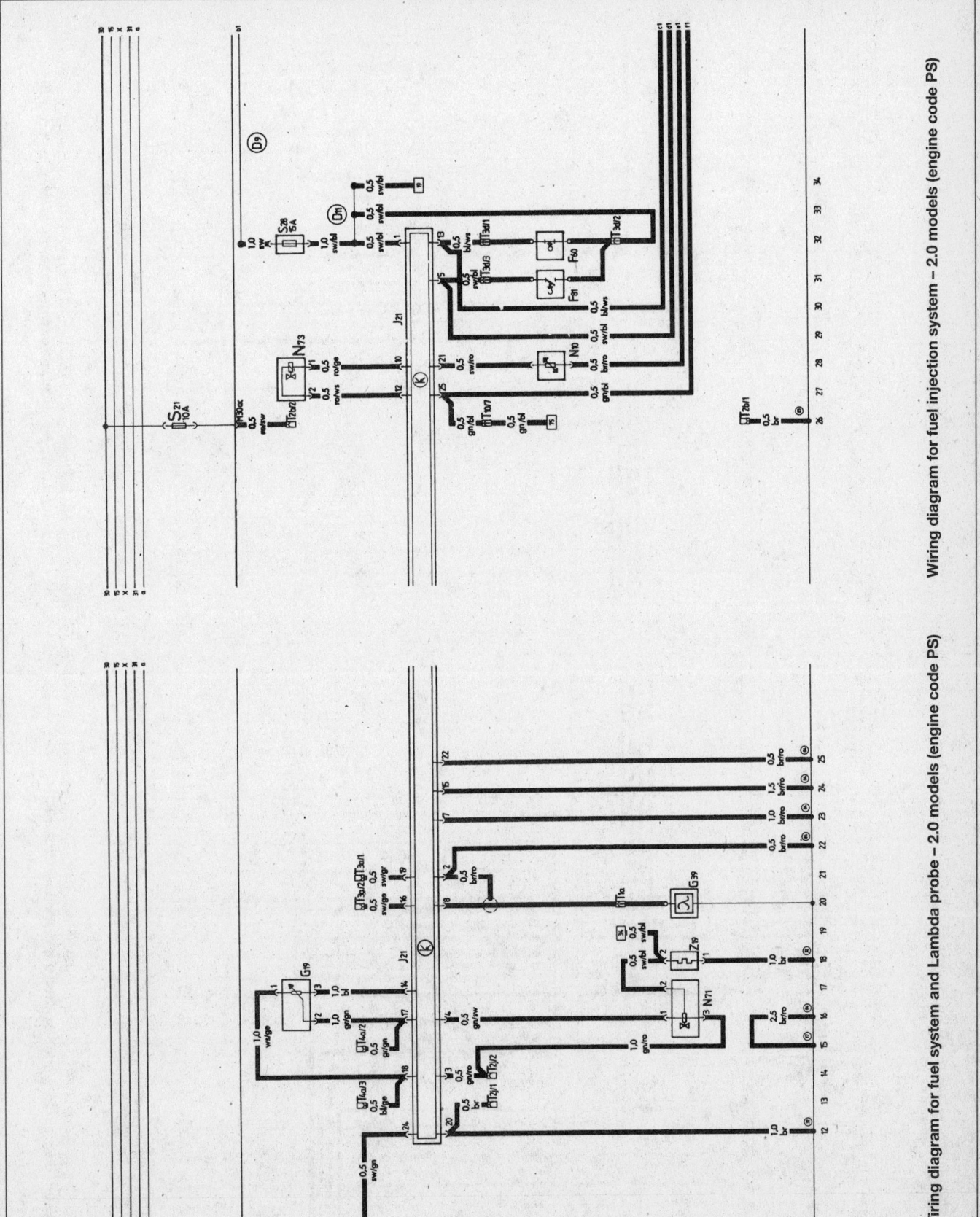

Wiring diagram for fuel injection system – 2.0 models (engine code PS)

Wiring diagram for fuel system and Lambda probe – 2.0 models (engine code PS)

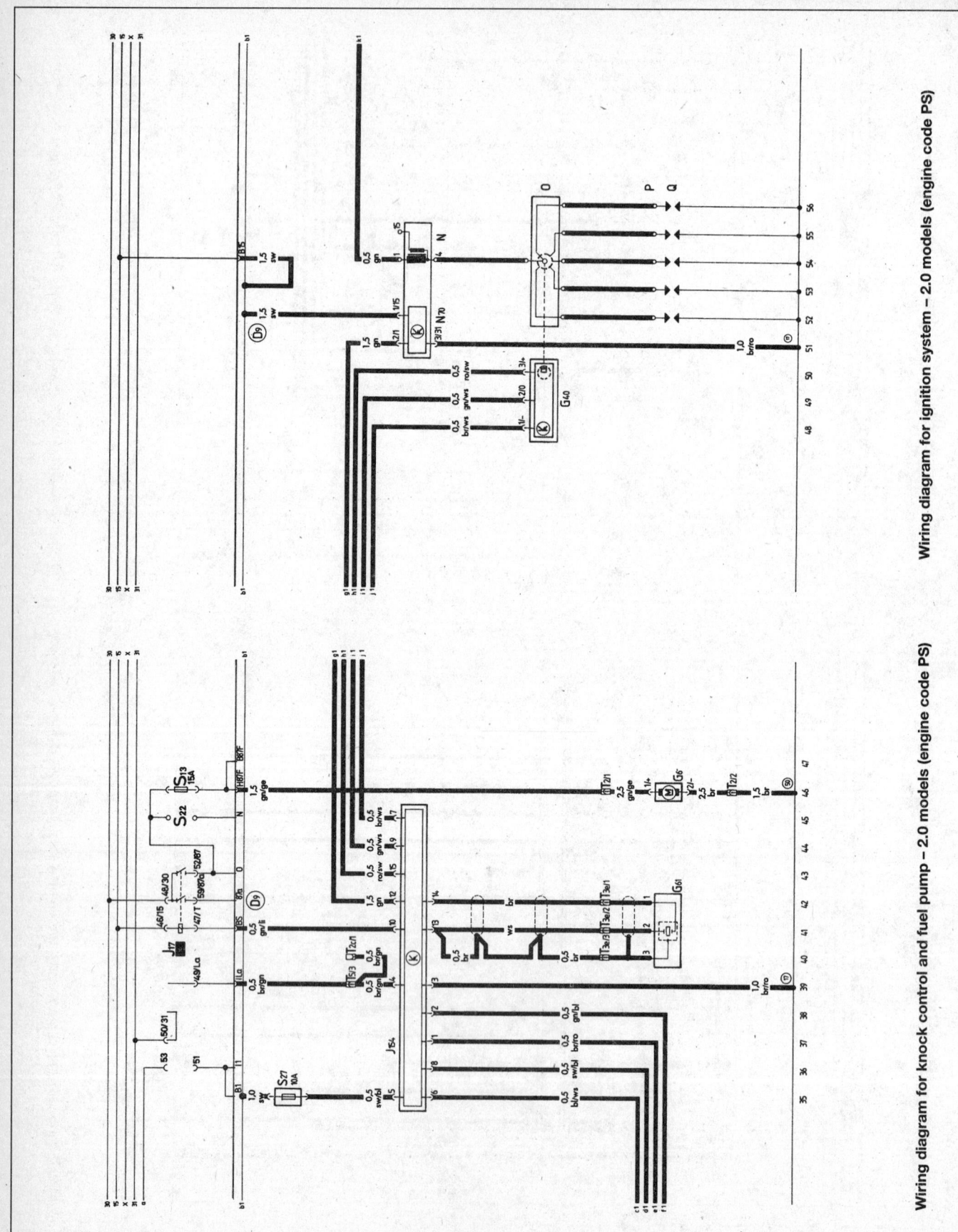

Wiring diagram for ignition system – 2.0 models (engine code PS)

Wiring diagram for knock control and fuel pump – 2.0 models (engine code PS)

Wiring diagram for fuel injection system – 2.3 models (engine code 7A)

Wiring diagram for fuel system and Lambda probe – 2.3 models (engine code NG)
*Automatic transmission   **Manual gearbox*

12

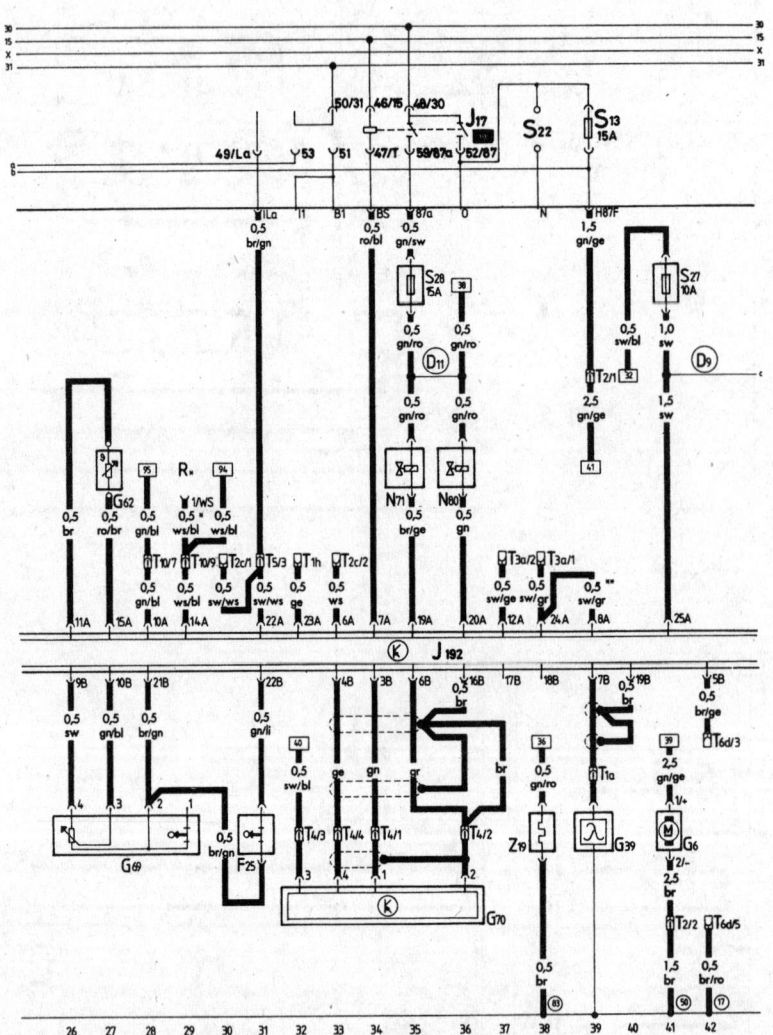

Wiring diagram for fuel system and fuel pump – 2.3 models (engine code 7A)
*Vehicles with preparation for radio installation
**Bridge connection, January 1989 onwards

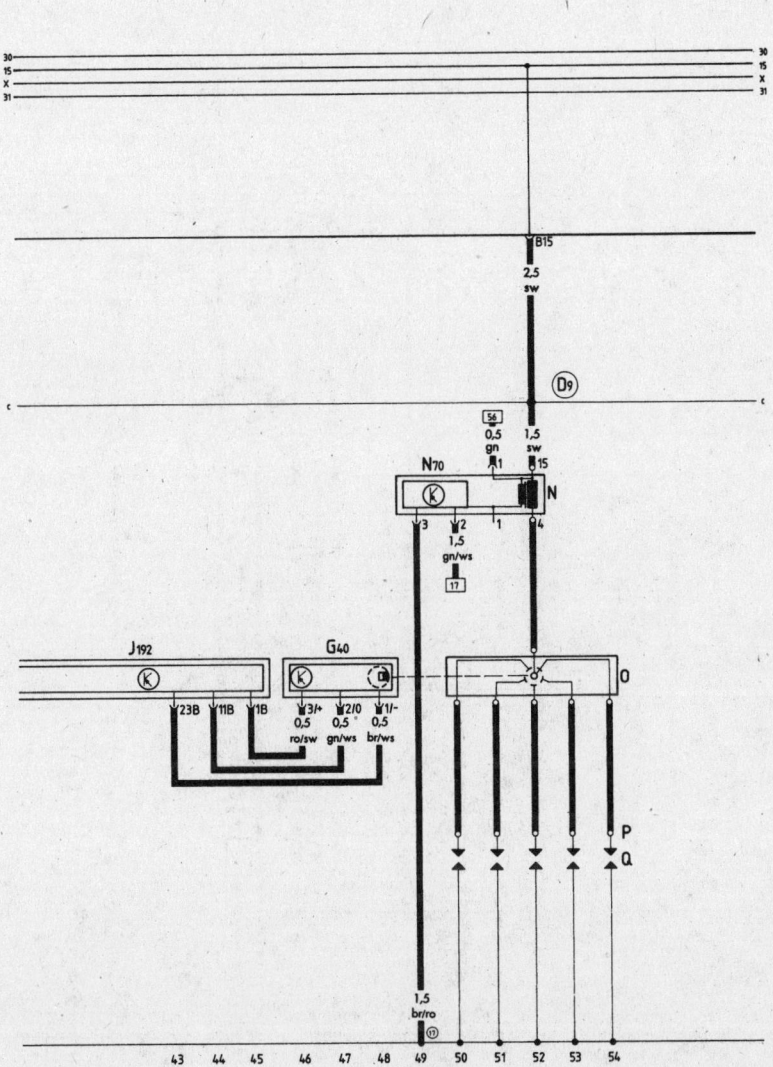

**Wiring diagram for fuel injection and ignition system – 2.3 models
(engine code 7A)**

12

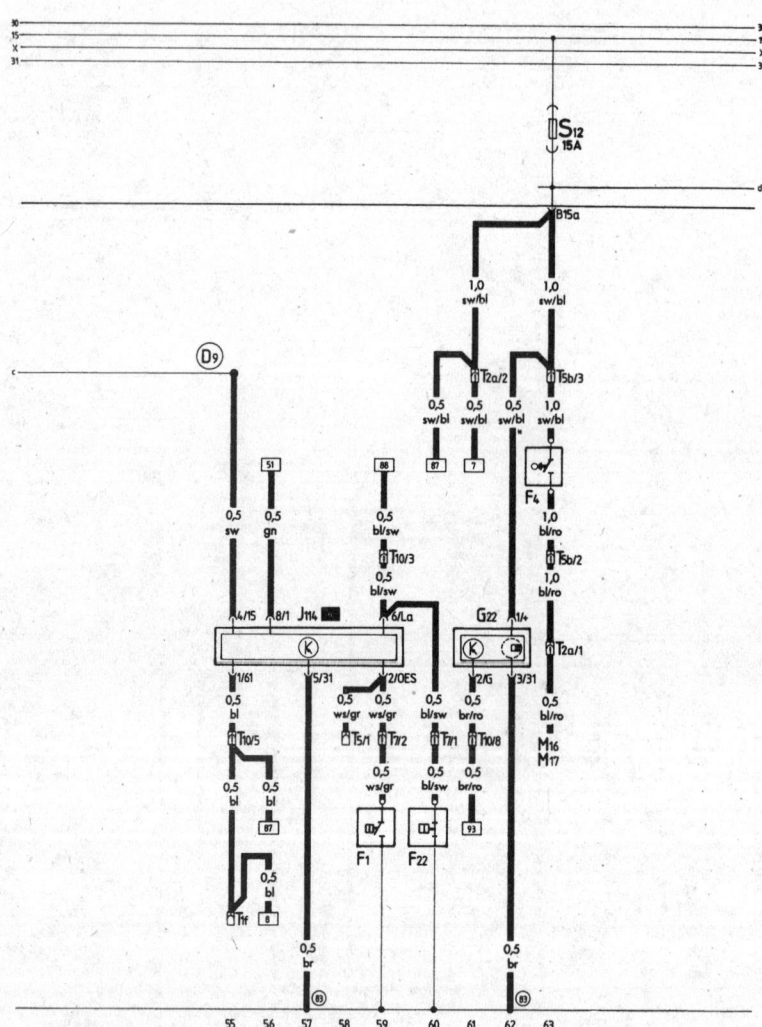

Wiring diagram for oil pressure warning system, speedometer and reversing lights – 2.3 models (engine code 7A)
*Automatic transmission   **Manual gearbox

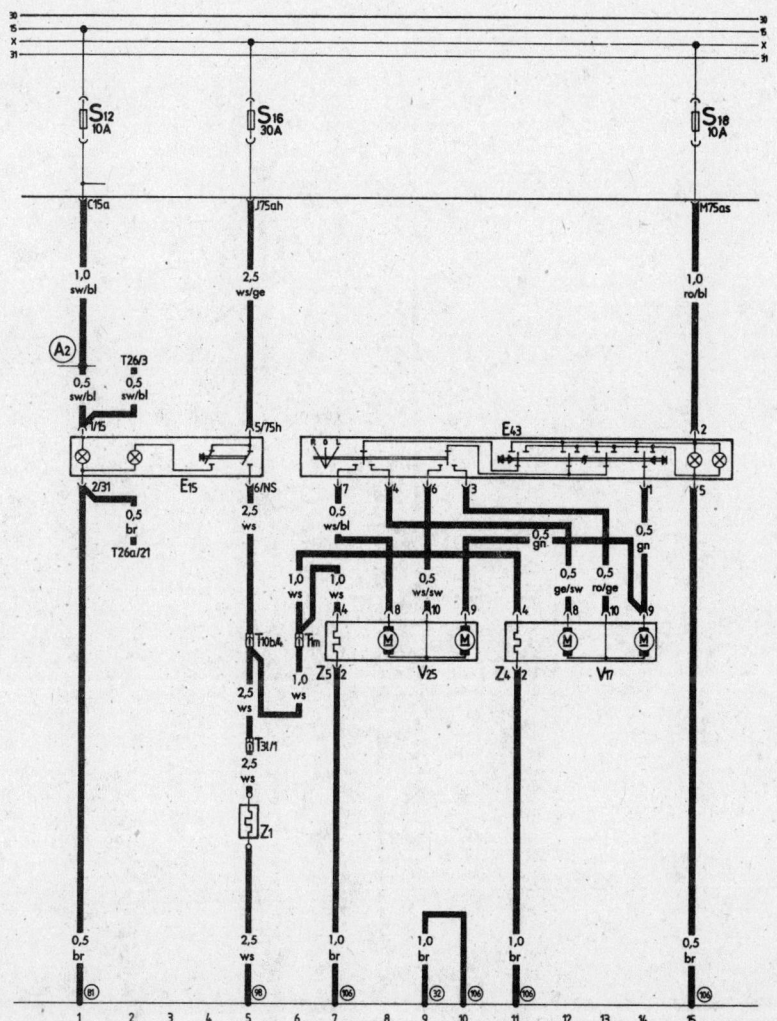

Wiring diagram for electric mirrors – Coupé models

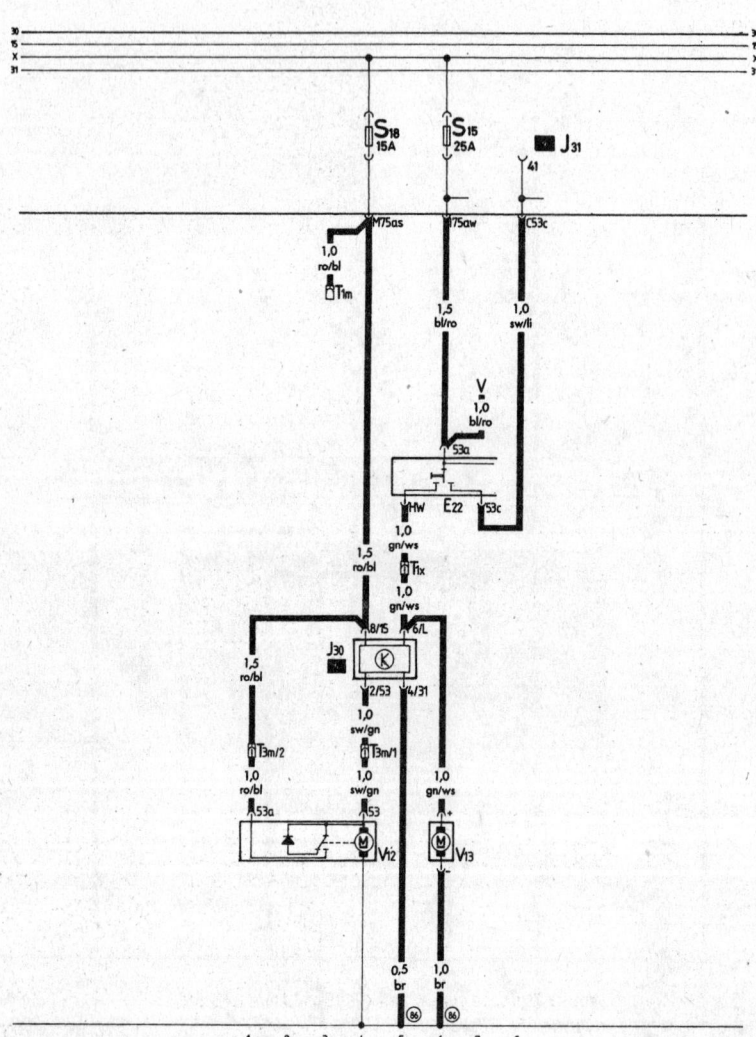

Wiring diagram for rear window wiper – Coupé models

This is a guide to getting your vehicle through the MOT test. Obviously it will not be possible to examine the vehicle to the same standard as the professional MOT tester. However, working through the following checks will enable you to identify any problem areas before submitting the vehicle for the test.

Where a testable component is in borderline condition, the tester has discretion in deciding whether to pass or fail it. The basis of such discretion is whether the tester would be happy for a close relative or friend to use the vehicle with the component in that condition. If the vehicle presented is clean and evidently well cared for, the tester may be more inclined to pass a borderline component than if the vehicle is scruffy and apparently neglected.

It has only been possible to summarise the test requirements here, based on the regulations in force at the time of printing. Test standards are becoming increasingly stringent, although there are some exemptions for older vehicles. For full details obtain a copy of the Haynes publication Pass the MOT! (available from stockists of Haynes manuals).

An assistant will be needed to help carry out some of these checks.

The checks have been sub-divided into four categories, as follows:

1 Checks carried out **FROM THE DRIVER'S SEAT**

2 Checks carried out **WITH THE VEHICLE ON THE GROUND**

3 Checks carried out **WITH THE VEHICLE RAISED AND THE WHEELS FREE TO TURN**

4 Checks carried out on **YOUR VEHICLE'S EXHAUST EMISSION SYSTEM**

---

1 Checks carried out **FROM THE DRIVER'S SEAT**

Handbrake

☐ Test the operation of the handbrake. Excessive travel (too many clicks) indicates incorrect brake or cable adjustment.

☐ Check that the handbrake cannot be released by tapping the lever sideways. Check the security of the lever mountings.

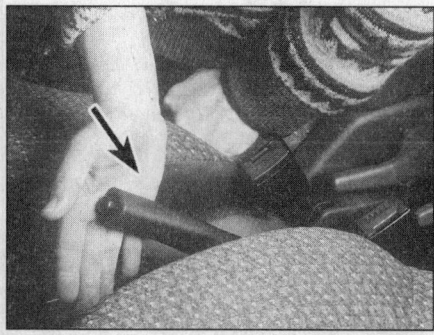

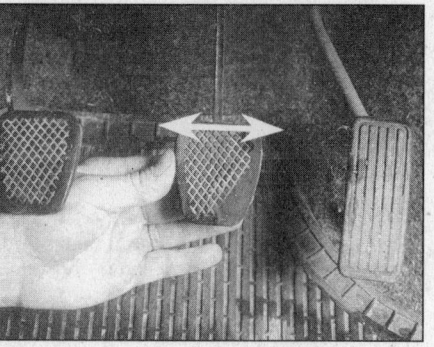

Footbrake

☐ Depress the brake pedal and check that it does not creep down to the floor, indicating a master cylinder fault. Release the pedal, wait a few seconds, then depress it again. If the pedal travels nearly to the floor before firm resistance is felt, brake adjustment or repair is necessary. If the pedal feels spongy, there is air in the hydraulic system which must be removed by bleeding.

☐ Check that the brake pedal is secure and in good condition. Check also for signs of fluid leaks on the pedal, floor or carpets, which would indicate failed seals in the brake master cylinder.

☐ Check the servo unit (when applicable) by operating the brake pedal several times, then keeping the pedal depressed and starting the engine. As the engine starts, the pedal will move down slightly. If not, the vacuum hose or the servo itself may be faulty.

Steering wheel and column

☐ Examine the steering wheel for fractures or looseness of the hub, spokes or rim.

☐ Move the steering wheel from side to side and then up and down. Check that the steering wheel is not loose on the column, indicating wear or a loose retaining nut. Continue moving the steering wheel as before, but also turn it slightly from left to right.

☐ Check that the steering wheel is not loose on the column, and that there is no abnormal

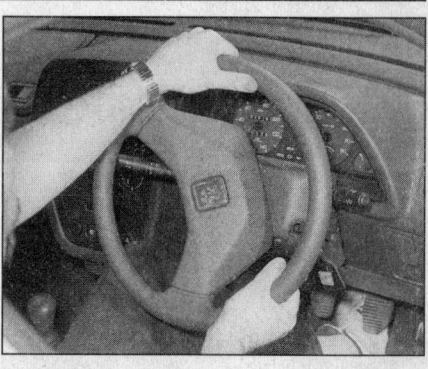

movement of the steering wheel, indicating wear in the column support bearings or couplings.

Windscreen and mirrors

☐ The windscreen must be free of cracks or other significant damage within the driver's field of view. (Small stone chips are acceptable.) Rear view mirrors must be secure, intact, and capable of being adjusted.

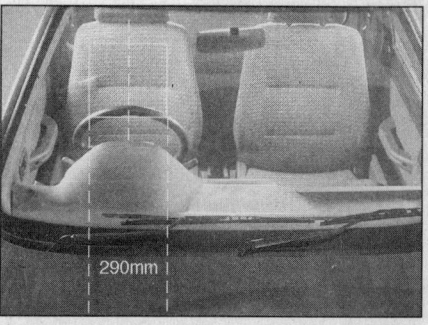

290mm

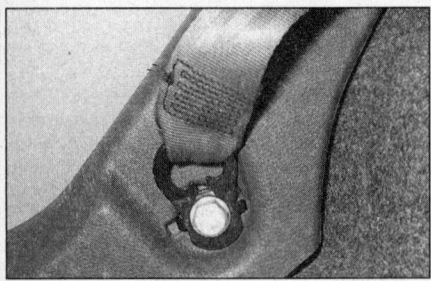

Seat belts and seats

Note: *The following checks are applicable to all seat belts, front and rear.*

☐ Examine the webbing of all the belts (including rear belts if fitted) for cuts, serious fraying or deterioration. Fasten and unfasten each belt to check the buckles. If applicable, check the retracting mechanism. Check the security of all seat belt mountings accessible from inside the vehicle.

☐ The front seats themselves must be securely attached and the backrests must lock in the upright position.

Doors

☐ Both front doors must be able to be opened and closed from outside and inside, and must latch securely when closed.

2 Checks carried out WITH THE VEHICLE ON THE GROUND

Vehicle identification

☐ Number plates must be in good condition, secure and legible, with letters and numbers correctly spaced – spacing at (A) should be twice that at (B).

☐ The VIN plate and/or homologation plate must be legible.

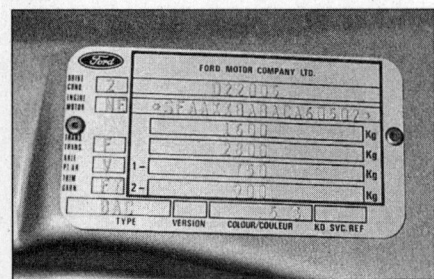

Electrical equipment

☐ Switch on the ignition and check the operation of the horn.

☐ Check the windscreen washers and wipers, examining the wiper blades; renew damaged or perished blades. Also check the operation of the stop-lights.

☐ Check the operation of the sidelights and number plate lights. The lenses and reflectors must be secure, clean and undamaged.

☐ Check the operation and alignment of the headlights. The headlight reflectors must not be tarnished and the lenses must be undamaged.

☐ Switch on the ignition and check the operation of the direction indicators (including the instrument panel tell-tale) and the hazard warning lights. Operation of the sidelights and stop-lights must not affect the indicators - if it does, the cause is usually a bad earth at the rear light cluster.

☐ Check the operation of the rear foglight(s), including the warning light on the instrument panel or in the switch.

Footbrake

☐ Examine the master cylinder, brake pipes and servo unit for leaks, loose mountings, corrosion or other damage.

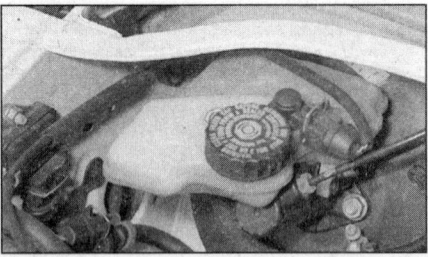

☐ The fluid reservoir must be secure and the fluid level must be between the upper (A) and lower (B) markings.

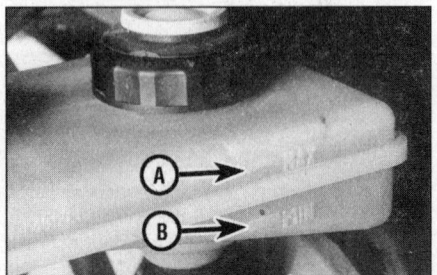

☐ Inspect both front brake flexible hoses for cracks or deterioration of the rubber. Turn the steering from lock to lock, and ensure that the hoses do not contact the wheel, tyre, or any part of the steering or suspension mechanism. With the brake pedal firmly depressed, check the hoses for bulges or leaks under pressure.

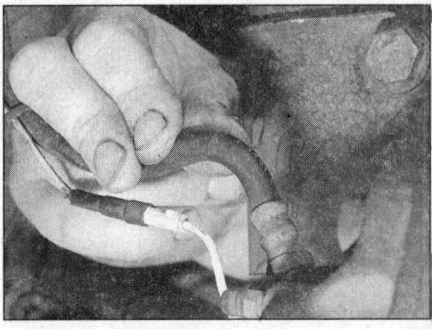

Steering and suspension

☐ Have your assistant turn the steering wheel from side to side slightly, up to the point where the steering gear just begins to transmit this movement to the roadwheels. Check for excessive free play between the steering wheel and the steering gear, indicating wear or insecurity of the steering column joints, the column-to-steering gear coupling, or the steering gear itself.

☐ Have your assistant turn the steering wheel more vigorously in each direction, so that the roadwheels just begin to turn. As this is done, examine all the steering joints, linkages, fittings and attachments. Renew any component that shows signs of wear or damage. On vehicles with power steering, check the security and condition of the steering pump, drivebelt and hoses.

☐ Check that the vehicle is standing level, and at approximately the correct ride height.

Shock absorbers

☐ Depress each corner of the vehicle in turn, then release it. The vehicle should rise and then settle in its normal position. If the vehicle continues to rise and fall, the shock absorber is defective. A shock absorber which has seized will also cause the vehicle to fail.

Exhaust system

☐ Start the engine. With your assistant holding a rag over the tailpipe, check the entire system for leaks. Repair or renew leaking sections.

3 Checks carried out **WITH THE VEHICLE RAISED AND THE WHEELS FREE TO TURN**

Jack up the front and rear of the vehicle, and securely support it on axle stands. Position the stands clear of the suspension assemblies. Ensure that the wheels are clear of the ground and that the steering can be turned from lock to lock.

Steering mechanism

☐ Have your assistant turn the steering from lock to lock. Check that the steering turns smoothly, and that no part of the steering mechanism, including a wheel or tyre, fouls any brake hose or pipe or any part of the body structure.
☐ Examine the steering rack rubber gaiters for damage or insecurity of the retaining clips. If power steering is fitted, check for signs of damage or leakage of the fluid hoses, pipes or connections. Also check for excessive stiffness or binding of the steering, a missing split pin or locking device, or severe corrosion of the body structure within 30 cm of any steering component attachment point.

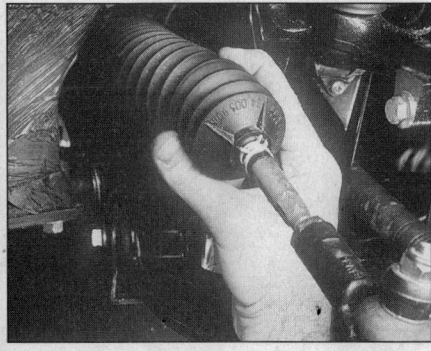

Front and rear suspension and wheel bearings

☐ Starting at the front right-hand side, grasp the roadwheel at the 3 o'clock and 9 o'clock positions and shake it vigorously. Check for free play or insecurity at the wheel bearings, suspension balljoints, or suspension mountings, pivots and attachments.
☐ Now grasp the wheel at the 12 o'clock and 6 o'clock positions and repeat the previous inspection. Spin the wheel, and check for roughness or tightness of the front wheel bearing.

☐ If excess free play is suspected at a component pivot point, this can be confirmed by using a large screwdriver or similar tool and levering between the mounting and the component attachment. This will confirm whether the wear is in the pivot bush, its retaining bolt, or in the mounting itself (the bolt holes can often become elongated).

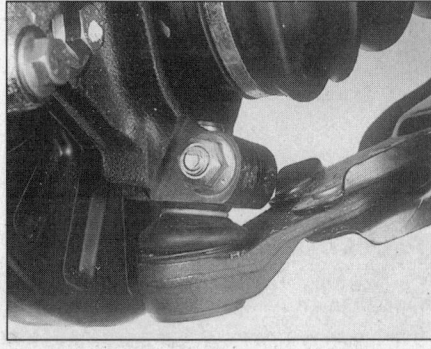

☐ Carry out all the above checks at the other front wheel, and then at both rear wheels.

Springs and shock absorbers

☐ Examine the suspension struts (when applicable) for serious fluid leakage, corrosion, or damage to the casing. Also check the security of the mounting points.
☐ If coil springs are fitted, check that the spring ends locate in their seats, and that the spring is not corroded, cracked or broken.
☐ If leaf springs are fitted, check that all leaves are intact, that the axle is securely attached to each spring, and that there is no deterioration of the spring eye mountings, bushes, and shackles.

☐ The same general checks apply to vehicles fitted with other suspension types, such as torsion bars, hydraulic displacer units, etc. Ensure that all mountings and attachments are secure, that there are no signs of excessive wear, corrosion or damage, and (on hydraulic types) that there are no fluid leaks or damaged pipes.
☐ Inspect the shock absorbers for signs of serious fluid leakage. Check for wear of the mounting bushes or attachments, or damage to the body of the unit.

Driveshafts (fwd vehicles only)

☐ Rotate each front wheel in turn and inspect the constant velocity joint gaiters for splits or damage. Also check that each driveshaft is straight and undamaged.

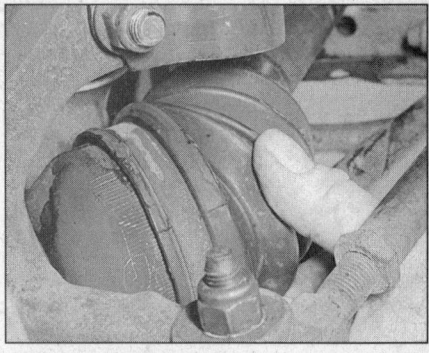

Braking system

☐ If possible without dismantling, check brake pad wear and disc condition. Ensure that the friction lining material has not worn excessively, (A) and that the discs are not fractured, pitted, scored or badly worn (B).

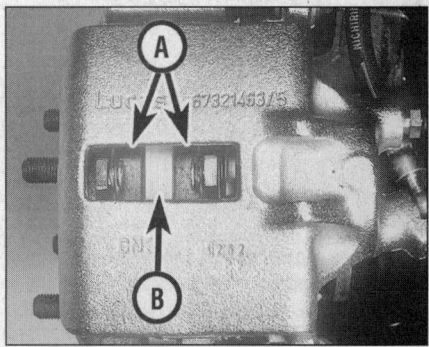

☐ Examine all the rigid brake pipes underneath the vehicle, and the flexible hose(s) at the rear. Look for corrosion, chafing or insecurity of the pipes, and for signs of bulging under pressure, chafing, splits or deterioration of the flexible hoses.
☐ Look for signs of fluid leaks at the brake calipers or on the brake backplates. Repair or renew leaking components.
☐ Slowly spin each wheel, while your assistant depresses and releases the footbrake. Ensure that each brake is operating and does not bind when the pedal is released.

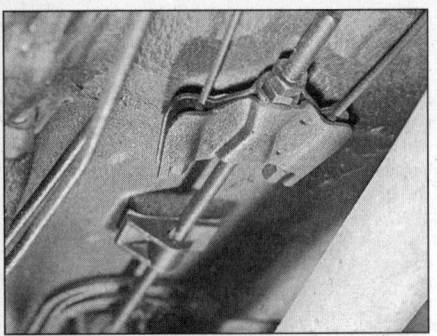

☐ Examine the handbrake mechanism, checking for frayed or broken cables, excessive corrosion, or wear or insecurity of the linkage. Check that the mechanism works on each relevant wheel, and releases fully, without binding.

☐ It is not possible to test brake efficiency without special equipment, but a road test can be carried out later to check that the vehicle pulls up in a straight line.

Fuel and exhaust systems

☐ Inspect the fuel tank (including the filler cap), fuel pipes, hoses and unions. All components must be secure and free from leaks.

☐ Examine the exhaust system over its entire length, checking for any damaged, broken or missing mountings, security of the retaining clamps and rust or corrosion.

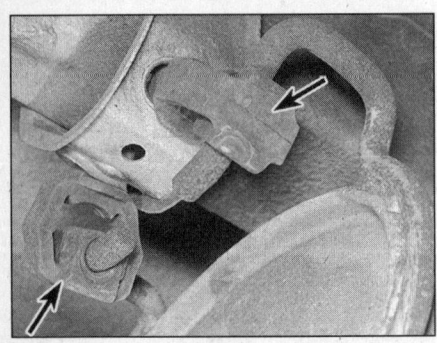

Wheels and tyres

☐ Examine the sidewalls and tread area of each tyre in turn. Check for cuts, tears, lumps, bulges, separation of the tread, and exposure of the ply or cord due to wear or damage. Check that the tyre bead is correctly seated on the wheel rim, that the valve is sound and

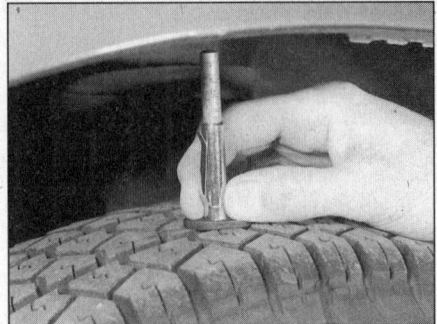

properly seated, and that the wheel is not distorted or damaged.

☐ Check that the tyres are of the correct size for the vehicle, that they are of the same size and type on each axle, and that the pressures are correct.

☐ Check the tyre tread depth. The legal minimum at the time of writing is 1.6 mm over at least three-quarters of the tread width. Abnormal tread wear may indicate incorrect front wheel alignment.

Body corrosion

☐ Check the condition of the entire vehicle structure for signs of corrosion in load-bearing areas. (These include chassis box sections, side sills, cross-members, pillars, and all suspension, steering, braking system and seat belt mountings and anchorages.) Any corrosion which has seriously reduced the thickness of a load-bearing area is likely to cause the vehicle to fail. In this case professional repairs are likely to be needed.

☐ Damage or corrosion which causes sharp or otherwise dangerous edges to be exposed will also cause the vehicle to fail.

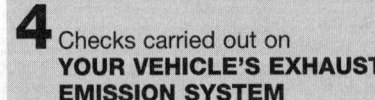

4 Checks carried out on
**YOUR VEHICLE'S EXHAUST
EMISSION SYSTEM**

Petrol models

☐ Have the engine at normal operating temperature, and make sure that it is in good tune (ignition system in good order, air filter element clean, etc).

☐ Before any measurements are carried out, raise the engine speed to around 2500 rpm, and hold it at this speed for 20 seconds. Allow

the engine speed to return to idle, and watch for smoke emissions from the exhaust tailpipe. If the idle speed is obviously much too high, or if dense blue or clearly-visible black smoke comes from the tailpipe for more than 5 seconds, the vehicle will fail. As a rule of thumb, blue smoke signifies oil being burnt (engine wear) while black smoke signifies unburnt fuel (dirty air cleaner element, or other carburettor or fuel system fault).

☐ An exhaust gas analyser capable of measuring carbon monoxide (CO) and hydrocarbons (HC) is now needed. If such an instrument cannot be hired or borrowed, a local garage may agree to perform the check for a small fee.

CO emissions (mixture)

☐ At the time of writing, the maximum CO level at idle is 3.5% for vehicles first used after August 1986 and 4.5% for older vehicles. From January 1996 a much tighter limit (around 0.5%) applies to catalyst-equipped vehicles first used from August 1992. If the CO level cannot be reduced far enough to pass the test (and the fuel and ignition systems are otherwise in good condition) then the carburettor is badly worn, or there is some problem in the fuel injection system or catalytic converter (as applicable).

HC emissions

☐ With the CO emissions within limits, HC emissions must be no more than 1200 ppm (parts per million). If the vehicle fails this test at idle, it can be re-tested at around 2000 rpm; if the HC level is then 1200 ppm or less, this counts as a pass.

☐ Excessive HC emissions can be caused by oil being burnt, but they are more likely to be due to unburnt fuel.

Diesel models

☐ The only emission test applicable to Diesel engines is the measuring of exhaust smoke density. The test involves accelerating the engine several times to its maximum unloaded speed.

Note: *It is of the utmost importance that the engine timing belt is in good condition before the test is carried out.*

☐ Excessive smoke can be caused by a dirty air cleaner element. Otherwise, professional advice may be needed to find the cause.

Introduction

A selection of good tools is a fundamental requirement for anyone contemplating the maintenance and repair of a motor vehicle. For the owner who does not possess any, their purchase will prove a considerable expense, offsetting some of the savings made by doing-it-yourself. However, provided that the tools purchased meet the relevant national safety standards and are of good quality, they will last for many years and prove an extremely worthwhile investment.

To help the average owner to decide which tools are needed to carry out the various tasks detailed in this manual, we have compiled three lists of tools under the following headings: *Maintenance and minor repair*, *Repair and overhaul*, and *Special*. Newcomers to practical mechanics should start off with the *Maintenance and minor repair* tool kit, and confine themselves to the simpler jobs around the vehicle. Then, as confidence and experience grow, more difficult tasks can be undertaken, with extra tools being purchased as, and when, they are needed. In this way, a *Maintenance and minor repair* tool kit can be built up into a *Repair and overhaul* tool kit over a considerable period of time, without any major cash outlays. The experienced do-it-yourselfer will have a tool kit good enough for most repair and overhaul procedures, and will add tools from the *Special* category when it is felt that the expense is justified by the amount of use to which these tools will be put.

Maintenance and minor repair tool kit

The tools given in this list should be considered as a minimum requirement if routine maintenance, servicing and minor repair operations are to be undertaken. We recommend the purchase of combination spanners (ring one end, open-ended the other); although more expensive than open-ended ones, they do give the advantages of both types of spanner.

- [ ] *Combination spanners: 8, 9, 10, 11, 12, 13, 14, 15, 16, 17, 19, 21, 22, 24 & 26 mm*
- [ ] *Adjustable spanner - 35 mm jaw (approx)*
- [ ] *Gearbox drain plug key*
- [ ] *Set of feeler gauges*
- [ ] *Spark plug spanner (with rubber insert)*
- [ ] *Spark plug gap adjustment tool*
- [ ] *Brake bleed nipple spanner*
- [ ] *Brake adjuster spanner*
- [ ] *Screwdrivers: Flat blade and cross blade – approx 100 mm long x 6 mm dia*
- [ ] *Combination pliers*
- [ ] *Hacksaw (junior)*
- [ ] *Tyre pump*
- [ ] *Tyre pressure gauge*
- [ ] *Grease gun*
- [ ] *Oil can*
- [ ] *Oil filter removal tool*
- [ ] *Fine emery cloth*
- [ ] *Wire brush (small)*
- [ ] *Funnel (medium size)*

Repair and overhaul tool kit

These tools are virtually essential for anyone undertaking any major repairs to a motor vehicle, and are additional to those given in the *Maintenance and minor repair* list. Included in this list is a comprehensive set of sockets. Although these are expensive, they will be found invaluable as they are so versatile - particularly if various drives are included in the set. We recommend the half-inch square-drive type, as this can be used with most proprietary torque wrenches. If you cannot afford a socket set, even bought piecemeal, then inexpensive tubular box spanners are a useful alternative.

The tools in this list will occasionally need to be supplemented by tools from the *Special* list:

- [ ] *Sockets (or box spanners) to cover range in previous list*
- [ ] *Reversible ratchet drive (for use with sockets) (see illustration)*
- [ ] *Extension piece, 250 mm (for use with sockets)*
- [ ] *Universal joint (for use with sockets)*
- [ ] *Torque wrench (for use with sockets)*
- [ ] *Self-locking grips*
- [ ] *Ball pein hammer*
- [ ] *Soft-faced mallet (plastic/aluminium or rubber)*
- [ ] *Screwdrivers:*
  Flat blade - long & sturdy, short (chubby), and narrow (electrician's) types
  Cross blade - Long & sturdy, and short (chubby) types
- [ ] *Pliers:*
  Long-nosed
  Side cutters (electrician's)
  Circlip (internal and external)
- [ ] *Cold chisel - 25 mm*
- [ ] *Scriber*
- [ ] *Scraper*
- [ ] *Centre-punch*
- [ ] *Pin punch*
- [ ] *Hacksaw*
- [ ] *Brake hose clamp*
- [ ] *Brake bleeding kit*
- [ ] *Selection of twist drills*
- [ ] *Steel rule/straight-edge*
- [ ] *Allen keys (inc. splined/Torx type) (see illustrations)*
- [ ] *Selection of files*
- [ ] *Wire brush*
- [ ] *Axle stands*
- [ ] *Jack (strong trolley or hydraulic type)*
- [ ] *Light with extension lead*

Special tools

The tools in this list are those which are not used regularly, are expensive to buy, or which need to be used in accordance with their manufacturers' instructions. Unless relatively difficult mechanical jobs are undertaken frequently, it will not be economic to buy many of these tools. Where this is the case, you could consider clubbing together with friends (or joining a motorists' club) to make a joint purchase, or borrowing the tools against a deposit from a local garage or tool hire specialist. It is worth noting that many of the larger DIY superstores now carry a large range of special tools for hire at modest rates.

The following list contains only those tools and instruments freely available to the public, and not those special tools produced by the vehicle manufacturer specifically for its dealer network. You will find occasional references to these manufacturers' special tools in the text of this manual. Generally, an alternative method of doing the job without the vehicle manufacturers' special tool is given. However, sometimes there is no alternative to using them. Where this is the case and the relevant tool cannot be bought or borrowed, you will have to entrust the work to a franchised garage.

- [ ] *Valve spring compressor (see illustration)*
- [ ] *Valve grinding tool*
- [ ] *Piston ring compressor (see illustration)*
- [ ] *Piston ring removal/installation tool (see illustration)*
- [ ] *Cylinder bore hone (see illustration)*
- [ ] *Balljoint separator*
- [ ] *Coil spring compressors (where applicable)*
- [ ] *Two/three-legged hub and bearing puller (see illustration)*

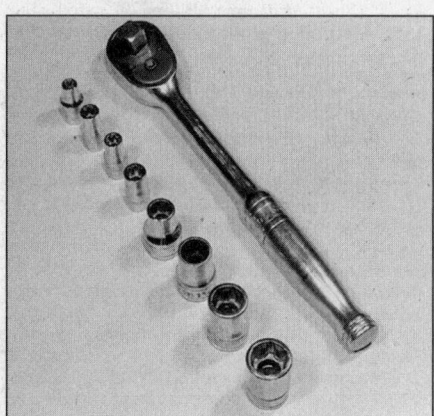

Sockets and reversible ratchet drive

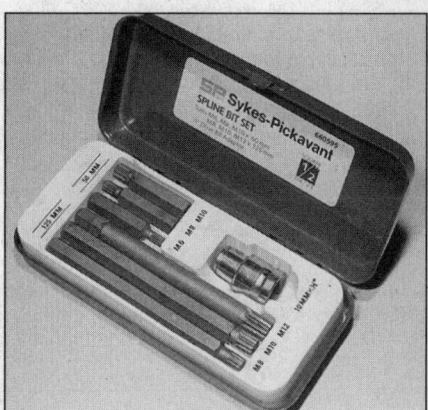

Spline bit set

Tools and Working Facilities

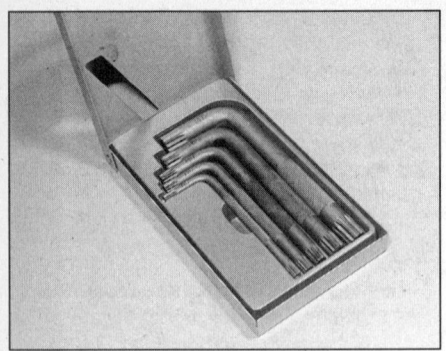

Spline key set

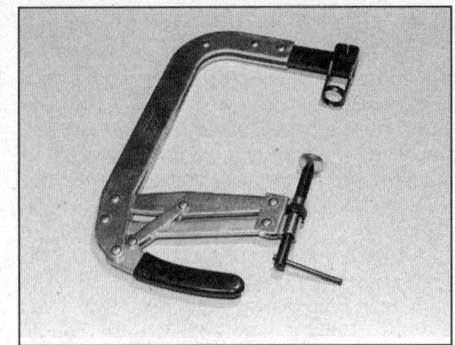

Valve spring compressor

Piston ring compressor

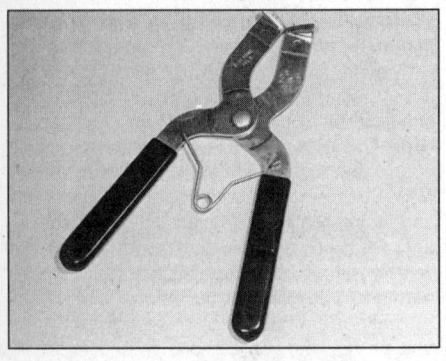

Piston ring removal/installation tool

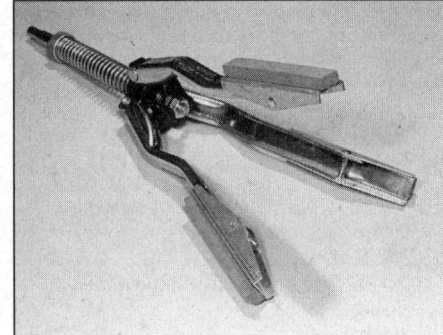

Cylinder bore hone

Three-legged hub and bearing puller

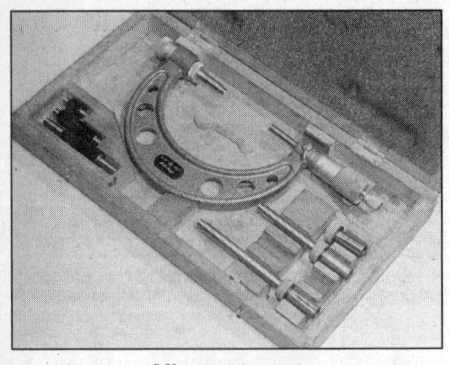

Micrometer set

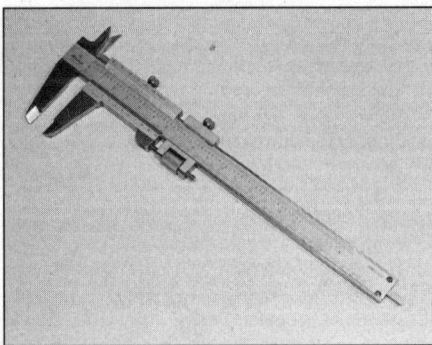

Vernier calipers

Dial test indicator and magnetic stand

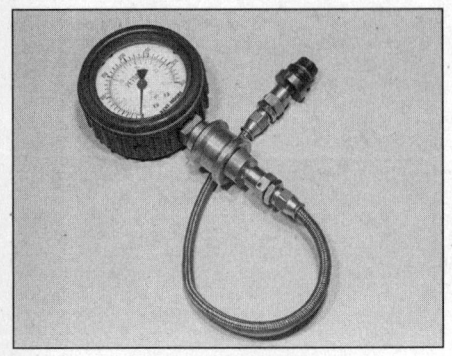

Compression testing gauge

Clutch plate alignment set

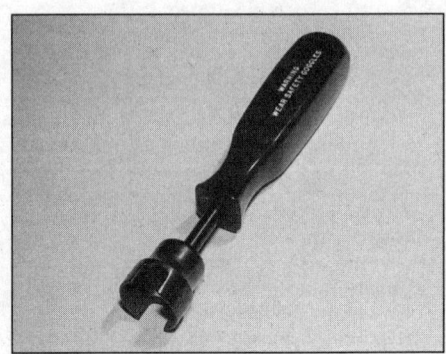

Brake shoe steady spring cup removal tool

- □ Impact screwdriver
- □ Micrometer and/or vernier calipers **(see illustrations)**
- □ Dial gauge **(see illustration)**
- □ Universal electrical multi-meter
- □ Cylinder compression gauge **(see illustration)**
- □ Clutch plate alignment set **(see illustration)**
- □ Brake shoe steady spring cup removal tool **(see illustration)**
- □ Bush and bearing removal/installation set **(see illustration)**
- □ Stud extractors **(see illustration)**
- □ Tap and die set **(see illustration)**
- □ Lifting tackle
- □ Trolley jack

Buying tools

For practically all tools, a tool factor is the best source, since he will have a very comprehensive range compared with the average garage or accessory shop. Having said that, accessory shops often offer excellent quality tools at discount prices, so it pays to shop around.

Remember, you don't have to buy the most expensive items on the shelf, but it is always advisable to steer clear of the very cheap tools. There are plenty of good tools around at reasonable prices, but always aim to purchase items which meet the relevant national safety standards. If in doubt, ask the proprietor or manager of the shop for advice before making a purchase.

Care and maintenance of tools

Having purchased a reasonable tool kit, it is necessary to keep the tools in a clean and serviceable condition. After use, always wipe off any dirt, grease and metal particles using a clean, dry cloth, before putting the tools away. Never leave them lying around after they have been used. A simple tool rack on the garage or workshop wall for items such as screwdrivers and pliers is a good idea. Store all normal spanners and sockets in a metal box. Any measuring instruments, gauges, meters, etc, must be carefully stored where they cannot be damaged or become rusty.

Take a little care when tools are used. Hammer heads inevitably become marked, and screwdrivers lose the keen edge on their blades from time to time. A little timely attention with emery cloth or a file will soon restore items like this to a good serviceable finish.

Working facilities

Not to be forgotten when discussing tools is the workshop itself. If anything more than routine maintenance is to be carried out, some form of suitable working area becomes essential.

It is appreciated that many an owner-mechanic is forced by circumstances to remove an engine or similar item without the benefit of a garage or workshop. Having done this, any repairs should always be done under the cover of a roof.

Wherever possible, any dismantling should be done on a clean, flat workbench or table at a suitable working height.

Any workbench needs a vice; one with a jaw opening of 100 mm is suitable for most jobs. As mentioned previously, some clean dry storage space is also required for tools, as well as for any lubricants, cleaning fluids, touch-up paints and so on, which become necessary.

Another item which may be required, and which has a much more general usage, is an electric drill with a chuck capacity of at least 8 mm. This, together with a good range of twist drills, is virtually essential for fitting accessories.

Last, but not least, always keep a supply of old newspapers and clean, lint-free rags available, and try to keep any working area as clean as possible.

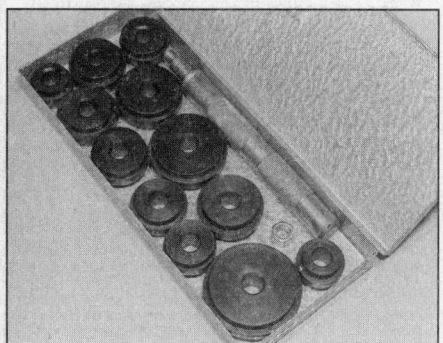

Bush and bearing removal/installation set

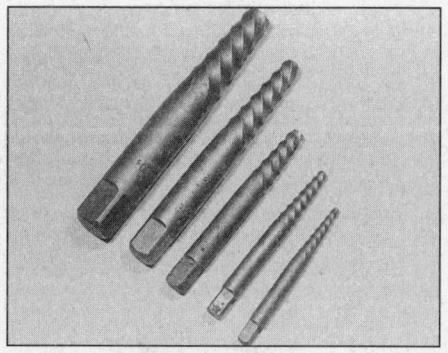

Stud extractor set

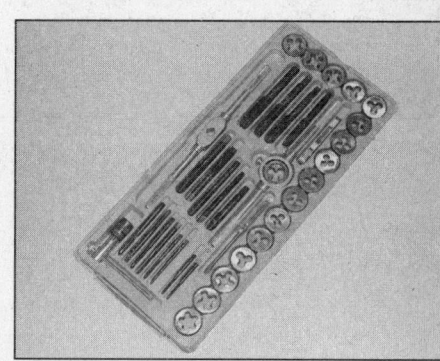

Tap and die set

Whenever servicing, repair or overhaul work is carried out on the car or its components, it is necessary to observe the following procedures and instructions. This will assist in carrying out the operation efficiently and to a professional standard of workmanship.

Joint mating faces and gaskets

When separating components at their mating faces, never insert screwdrivers or similar implements into the joint between the faces in order to prise them apart. This can cause severe damage which results in oil leaks, coolant leaks, etc upon reassembly. Separation is usually achieved by tapping along the joint with a soft-faced hammer in order to break the seal. However, note that this method may not be suitable where dowels are used for component location.

Where a gasket is used between the mating faces of two components, ensure that it is renewed on reassembly, and fit it dry unless otherwise stated in the repair procedure. Make sure that the mating faces are clean and dry, with all traces of old gasket removed. When cleaning a joint face, use a tool which is not likely to score or damage the face, and remove any burrs or nicks with an oilstone or fine file.

Make sure that tapped holes are cleaned with a pipe cleaner, and keep them free of jointing compound, if this is being used, unless specifically instructed otherwise.

Ensure that all orifices, channels or pipes are clear, and blow through them, preferably using compressed air.

Oil seals

Oil seals can be removed by levering them out with a wide flat-bladed screwdriver or similar implement. Alternatively, a number of self-tapping screws may be screwed into the seal, and these used as a purchase for pliers or some similar device in order to pull the seal free.

Whenever an oil seal is removed from its working location, either individually or as part of an assembly, it should be renewed.

The very fine sealing lip of the seal is easily damaged, and will not seal if the surface it contacts is not completely clean and free from scratches, nicks or grooves.

Protect the lips of the seal from any surface which may damage them in the course of fitting. Use tape or a conical sleeve where possible. Lubricate the seal lips with oil before fitting and, on dual-lipped seals, fill the space between the lips with grease.

Unless otherwise stated, oil seals must be fitted with their sealing lips toward the lubricant to be sealed.

Use a tubular drift or block of wood of the appropriate size to install the seal and, if the seal housing is shouldered, drive the seal down to the shoulder. If the seal housing is unshouldered, the seal should be fitted with its face flush with the housing top face (unless otherwise instructed).

Screw threads and fastenings

Seized nuts, bolts and screws are quite a common occurrence where corrosion has set in, and the use of penetrating oil or releasing fluid will often overcome this problem if the offending item is soaked for a while before attempting to release it. The use of an impact driver may also provide a means of releasing such stubborn fastening devices, when used in conjunction with the appropriate screwdriver bit or socket. If none of these methods works, it may be necessary to resort to the careful application of heat, or the use of a hacksaw or nut splitter device.

Studs are usually removed by locking two nuts together on the threaded part, and then using a spanner on the lower nut to unscrew the stud. Studs or bolts which have broken off below the surface of the component in which they are mounted can sometimes be removed using a proprietary stud extractor. Always ensure that a blind tapped hole is completely free from oil, grease, water or other fluid before installing the bolt or stud. Failure to do this could cause the housing to crack due to the hydraulic action of the bolt or stud as it is screwed in.

When tightening a castellated nut to accept a split pin, tighten the nut to the specified torque, where applicable, and then tighten further to the next split pin hole. Never slacken the nut to align the split pin hole, unless stated in the repair procedure.

When checking or retightening a nut or bolt to a specified torque setting, slacken the nut or bolt by a quarter of a turn, and then retighten to the specified setting. However, this should not be attempted where angular tightening has been used.

For some screw fastenings, notably cylinder head bolts or nuts, torque wrench settings are no longer specified for the latter stages of tightening, "angle-tightening" being called up instead. Typically, a fairly low torque wrench setting will be applied to the bolts/nuts in the correct sequence, followed by one or more stages of tightening through specified angles.

Locknuts, locktabs and washers

Any fastening which will rotate against a component or housing in the course of tightening should always have a washer between it and the relevant component or housing.

Spring or split washers should always be renewed when they are used to lock a critical component such as a big-end bearing retaining bolt or nut. Locktabs which are folded over to retain a nut or bolt should always be renewed.

Self-locking nuts can be re-used in non-critical areas, providing resistance can be felt when the locking portion passes over the bolt or stud thread. However, it should be noted that self-locking stiffnuts tend to lose their

effectiveness after long periods of use, and in such cases should be renewed as a matter of course.

Split pins must always be replaced with new ones of the correct size for the hole.

When thread-locking compound is found on the threads of a fastener which is to be re-used, it should be cleaned off with a wire brush and solvent, and fresh compound applied on reassembly.

Special tools

Some repair procedures in this manual entail the use of special tools such as a press, two or three-legged pullers, spring compressors, etc. Wherever possible, suitable readily-available alternatives to the manufacturer's special tools are described, and are shown in use. Unless you are highly-skilled and have a thorough understanding of the procedures described, never attempt to bypass the use of any special tool when the procedure described specifies its use. Not only is there a very great risk of personal injury, but expensive damage could be caused to the components involved.

Environmental considerations

When disposing of used engine oil, brake fluid, antifreeze, etc, give due consideration to any detrimental environmental effects. Do not, for instance, pour any of the above liquids down drains into the general sewage system, or onto the ground to soak away. Many local council refuse tips provide a facility for waste oil disposal, as do some garages. If none of these facilities are available, consult your local Environmental Health Department for further advice.

With the universal tightening-up of legislation regarding the emission of environmentally-harmful substances from motor vehicles, most current vehicles have tamperproof devices fitted to the main adjustment points of the fuel system. These devices are primarily designed to prevent unqualified persons from adjusting the fuel/air mixture, with the chance of a consequent increase in toxic emissions. If such devices are encountered during servicing or overhaul, they should, wherever possible, be renewed or refitted in accordance with the vehicle manufacturer's requirements or current legislation.

OIL CARE
FOLLOW THE CODE
OIL BANK LINE
0800 66 33 66

Note: It is antisocial and illegal to dump oil down the drain. To find the location of your local oil recycling bank, call this number free.

Introduction

The vehicle owner who does his or her own maintenance according to the recommended schedules should not have to use this section of the manual very often. Modern component reliability is such that, provided those items subject to wear or deterioration are inspected or renewed at the specified intervals, sudden failure is comparatively rare. Faults do not usually just happen as a result of sudden failure, but develop over a period of time. Major mechanical failures in particular are usually preceded by characteristic symptoms over hundreds or even thousands of miles. Those components which do occasionally fail without warning are often small and easily carried in the vehicle.

With any fault finding, the first step is to decide where to begin investigations. Sometimes this is obvious, but on other occasions a little detective work will be necessary. The owner who makes half a dozen haphazard adjustments or replacements may be successful in curing a fault (or its symptoms), but he will be none the wiser if the fault recurs and he may well have spent more time and money than was necessary. A calm and logical approach will be found to be more satisfactory in the long run. Always take into account any warning signs or abnormalities that may have been noticed in the period preceding the fault – power loss, high or low gauge readings, unusual noises or smells, etc – and remember that failure of components such as fuses or spark plugs may only be pointers to some underlying fault.

The pages which follow here are intended to help in cases of failure to start or breakdown on the road. There is also a Fault Diagnosis Section at the end of each Chapter which should be consulted if the preliminary checks prove unfruitful. Whatever the fault, certain basic principles apply. These are as follows:

Verify the fault. This is simply a matter of being sure that you know what the symptoms are before starting work. This is particularly important if you are investigating a fault for someone else who may not have described it very accurately.

Don't overlook the obvious. For example, if the vehicle won't start, is there petrol in the tank? (Don't take anyone else's word on this particular point, and don't trust the fuel gauge either!) If an electrical fault is indicated, look for loose or broken wires before digging out the test gear.

Cure the disease, not the symptom. Substituting a flat battery with a fully charged one will get you off the hard shoulder, but if the underlying cause is not attended to,the new battery will go the same way. Similarly, changing oil-fouled spark plugs for a new set will get you moving again, but remember that the reason for the fouling (if it wasn't simply an incorrect grade of plug) will have to be established and corrected.

Don't take anything for granted. Particularly, don't forget that a 'new' component may itself be defective (especially if it's been rattling round in the boot for months), and don't leave components out of a fault diagnosis sequence just because they are new or recently fitted. When you do finally diagnose a difficult fault, you'll probably realise that all the evidence was there from the start.

Electrical faults

Electrical faults can be more puzzling than straightforward mechanical failures, but they are no less susceptible to logical analysis if the basic principles of operation are understood. Vehicle electrical wiring exists in extremely unfavourable conditions – heat, vibration and chemical attack and the first things to look for are loose or corroded connections and broken or chafed wires, especially where the wires pass through holes in the bodywork or are subject to vibration.

All metal-bodied vehicles in current production have one pole of the battery 'earthed', ie connected to the vehicle bodywork, and in nearly all modern vehicles it is the negative (–) terminal. The various electrical components – motors, bulb holders, etc – are also connected to earth, either by means of a lead or directly by their mountings. Electric current flows through the component and then back to the battery via the bodywork. If the component mounting is loose or corroded, or if a good path back to the battery is not available, the circuit will be incomplete and malfunction will result. The engine and/or gearbox are also earthed by means of flexible metal straps to the body or subframe; if these straps are loose or missing, starter motor, generator and ignition trouble may result.

Assuming the earth return to be satisfactory, electrical faults will be due either to component malfunction or to defects in the current supply. Individual components are dealt with in Chapter 12. If supply wires are broken or cracked internally this results in an open-circuit, and the easiest way to check for this is to bypass the suspect wire temporarily with a length of wire having a crocodile clip or suitable connector at each end. Alternatively, a 12V test lamp can be used to verify the presence of supply voltage at various points along the wire and the break can be thus isolated.

If a bare portion of a live wire touches the bodywork or other earthed metal part, the electricity will take the low-resistance path thus formed back to the battery: this is known as a short-circuit. Hopefully a short-circuit will blow a fuse, but otherwise it may cause burning of the insulation (and possibly further short-circuits) or even a fire. This is why it is inadvisable to bypass persistently blowing fuses with silver foil or wire.

Spares and tool kit

Most vehicles are supplied only with sufficient tools for wheel changing; the *Maintenance and minor repair* tool kit detailed in *Tools and working facilities,* with the addition of a hammer, is probably sufficient for those repairs that most motorists would consider attempting at the roadside. In addition a few items which can be fitted without too much trouble in the event of a breakdown should be carried. Experience and available space will modify the list below, but the following may save having to call on professional assistance:

- [ ] *Spark plugs, clean and correctly gapped*
- [ ] *HT lead and plug cap – long enough to reach the plug furthest from the distributor*
- [ ] *Distributor rotor*
- [ ] *Drivebelt(s) — emergency type may suffice*
- [ ] *Spare fuses*
- [ ] *Set of principal light bulbs*
- [ ] *Tin of radiator sealer and hose bandage*
- [ ] *Exhaust bandage*
- [ ] *Roll of insulating tape*
- [ ] *Length of soft iron wire*
- [ ] *Length of electrical flex*
- [ ] *Torch or inspection lamp (can double as test lamp)*
- [ ] *Battery jump leads*
- [ ] *Tow-rope*
- [ ] *Ignition waterproofing aerosol*
- [ ] *Litre of engine oil*
- [ ] *Sealed can of hydraulic fluid*
- [ ] *Emergency windscreen*
- [ ] *Wormdrive clips*
- [ ] *Tube of filler paste*

If spare fuel is carried, a can designed for the purpose should be used to minimise risks of leakage and collision damage. A first aid kit and a warning triangle, whilst not at present compulsory in the UK, are obviously sensible items to carry in addition to the above. When touring abroad it may be advisable to carry additional spares which, even if you cannot fit them yourself, could save having to wait while parts are obtained. The items below may be worth considering:

- [ ] *Choke and throttle cables*
- [ ] *Cylinder head gasket*
- [ ] *Alternator brushes*
- [ ] *Tyre valve core*

One of the motoring organisations will be able to advise on availability of fuel, etc, in foreign countries.

Engine will not start

Engine fails to turn when starter operated

- [ ] Flat battery (recharge use jump leads or push start)
- [ ] Battery terminals loose or corroded
- [ ] Battery earth to body defective
- [ ] Engine earth strap loose or broken
- [ ] Starter motor (or solenoid) wiring loose or broken
- [ ] Automatic transmission selector in wrong position, or inhibitor switch faulty
- [ ] Ignition/starter switch faulty
- [ ] Major mechanical failure (seizure)
- [ ] Starter or solenoid internal fault (see Chapter 12)

Starter motor turns engine slowly

- [ ] Partially discharged battery (recharge, use jump leads, or push start)
- [ ] Battery terminals loose or corroded
- [ ] Battery earth to body defective

- [ ] Engine earth strap loose
- [ ] Starter motor (or solenoid) wiring loose
- [ ] Starter motor internal fault (see Chapter 12)

Starter motor spins without turning engine

- [ ] Flywheel gear teeth damaged or worn
- [ ] Starter motor mounting bolts loose

Engine turns normally but fails to start

- [ ] Damp or dirty HT leads and distributor cap (crank engine and check for spark)
- [ ] No fuel in tank (check for delivery at carburettor)

- [ ] Automatic choke faulty (carburettor engine)
- [ ] Fouled or incorrectly gapped spark plugs (remove, clean and regap)
- [ ] Other ignition system fault (see Chapter 4)
- [ ] Other fuel system fault (see Chapter 3)
- [ ] Poor compression (see Chapter 1)
- [ ] Major mechanical failure (eg camshaft drive)

Engine fires but will not run

- [ ] Automatic choke faulty (carburettor engine)
- [ ] Air leaks at carburettor or inlet manifold
- [ ] Fuel starvation (see Chapter 3)
- [ ] Ballast resistor defective, or other ignition fault (see Chapter 4)

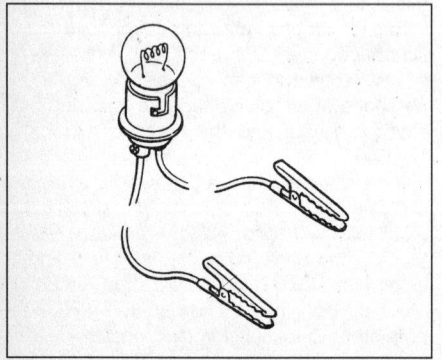

A simple test lamp is useful for checking electrical faults

Carrying a few spares may save you a long walk!

Engine cuts out and will not restart

Engine cuts out suddenly – ignition fault

☐ Loose or disconnected LT wires
☐ Wet HT leads or distributor cap (after traversing water splash)
☐ Coil failure (check for spark)
☐ Other ignition fault (see Chapter 4)

Engine misfires before cutting out – fuel fault

☐ Fuel tank empty
☐ Fuel pump defective or filter blocked (check for delivery)
☐ Fuel tank filler vent blocked (suction will be evident on releasing cap)
☐ Carburettor needle valve sticking
☐ Carburettor jets blocked (fuel contaminated)
☐ Other fuel system fault (see Chapter 3)

Engine cuts out – other causes

☐ Serious overheating
☐ Major mechanical failure (eg camshaft drive)

Crank engine and check for a spark. Note use of insulated tool

Engine overheats

Ignition (no-charge) warning light illuminated

☐ Slack or broken drivebelt — retension or renew (Chapter 2)

Ignition warning light not illuminated

☐ Coolant loss due to internal or external leakage (see Chapter 2)
☐ Thermostat defective
☐ Low oil level
☐ Brakes binding
☐ Radiator clogged externally or internally
☐ Electric cooling fan not operating correctly
☐ Engine waterways clogged
☐ Ignition timing incorrect or automatic advance malfunctioning
☐ Mixture too weak
Note: *Do not add cold water to an overheated engine or damage may result*

Low engine oil pressure

Note: *Low oil pressure in a high-mileage engine at tickover is not necessarily a cause for concern. Sudden pressure loss at speed is far more significant. In any event check the gauge or warning light sender before condemning the engine.*

Gauge reads low or warning light illuminated with engine running

☐ Oil level low or incorrect grade
☐ Defective gauge or sender unit
☐ Wire to sender unit earthed

☐ Engine overheating
☐ Oil filter clogged or bypass valve defective
☐ Oil pressure relief valve defective
☐ Oil pick-up strainer clogged
☐ Oil pump worn or mountings loose
☐ Worn main or big-end bearings

Engine noises

Pre-ignition (pinking) on acceleration

☐ Incorrect grade of fuel
☐ Ignition timing incorrect
☐ Distributor faulty or worn
☐ Worn or maladjusted carburettor
☐ Excessive carbon build-up in engine

Whistling or wheezing noises

☐ Leaking vacuum hose
☐ Leaking carburettor or manifold gasket
☐ Blowing head gasket

Tapping or rattling

☐ Incorrect valve clearances (where applicable)
☐ Worn valve gear
☐ Worn timing chain or belt
☐ Broken piston ring (ticking noise)

Knocking or thumping

☐ Unintentional mechanical contact (eg fan blades)
☐ Worn drivebelt
☐ Peripheral component fault (generator, water pump, etc)
☐ Worn big-end bearings (regular heavy knocking, perhaps less under load)
☐ Worn main bearings (rumbling and knocking, perhaps worsening under load)
☐ Piston slap (most noticeable when cold)

Conversion Factors

Length (distance)

Inches (in)	25.4	= Millimetres (mm)	x 0.0394	= Inches (in)
Feet (ft)	0.305	= Metres (m)	x 3.281	= Feet (ft)
Miles	1.609	= Kilometres (km)	x 0.621	= Miles

Volume (capacity)

Cubic inches (cu in; in³)	x 16.387	= Cubic centimetres (cc; cm³)	x 0.061	= Cubic inches (cu in; in³)
Imperial pints (Imp pt)	x 0.568	= Litres (l)	x 1.76	= Imperial pints (Imp pt)
Imperial quarts (Imp qt)	x 1.137	= Litres (l)	x 0.88	= Imperial quarts (Imp qt)
Imperial quarts (Imp qt)	x 1.201	= US quarts (US qt)	x 0.833	= Imperial quarts (Imp qt)
US quarts (US qt)	x 0.946	= Litres (l)	x 1.057	= US quarts (US qt)
Imperial gallons (Imp gal)	x 4.546	= Litres (l)	x 0.22	= Imperial gallons (Imp gal)
Imperial gallons (Imp gal)	x 1.201	= US gallons (US gal)	x 0.833	= Imperial gallons (Imp gal)
US gallons (US gal)	x 3.785	= Litres (l)	x 0.264	= US gallons (US gal)

Mass (weight)

Ounces (oz)	x 28.35	= Grams (g)	x 0.035	= Ounces (oz)
Pounds (lb)	x 0.454	= Kilograms (kg)	x 2.205	= Pounds (lb)

Force

Ounces-force (ozf; oz)	x 0.278	= Newtons (N)	x 3.6	= Ounces-force (ozf; oz)
Pounds-force (lbf; lb)	x 4.448	= Newtons (N)	x 0.225	= Pounds-force (lbf; lb)
Newtons (N)	x 0.1	= Kilograms-force (kgf; kg)	x 9.81	= Newtons (N)

Pressure

Pounds-force per square inch (psi; lbf/in²; lb/in²)	x 0.070	= Kilograms-force per square centimetre (kgf/cm²; kg/cm²)	x 14.223	= Pounds-force per square inch (psi; lbf/in²; lb/in²)
Pounds-force per square inch (psi; lbf/in²; lb/in²)	x 0.068	= Atmospheres (atm)	x 14.696	= Pounds-force per square inch (psi; lbf/in²; lb/in²)
Pounds-force per square inch (psi; lbf/in²; lb/in²)	x 0.069	= Bars	x 14.5	= Pounds-force per square inch (psi; lbf/in²; lb/in²)
Pounds-force per square inch (psi; lbf/in²; lb/in²)	x 6.895	= Kilopascals (kPa)	x 0.145	= Pounds-force per square inch (psi; lbf/in²; lb/in²)
Kilopascals (kPa)	x 0.01	= Kilograms-force per square centimetre (kgf/cm²; kg/cm²)	x 98.1	= Kilopascals (kPa)
Millibar (mbar)	x 100	= Pascals (Pa)	x 0.01	= Millibar (mbar)
Millibar (mbar)	x 0.0145	= Pounds-force per square inch (psi; lbf/in²; lb/in²)	x 68.947	= Millibar (mbar)
Millibar (mbar)	x 0.75	= Millimetres of mercury (mmHg)	x 1.333	= Millibar (mbar)
Millibar (mbar)	x 0.401	= Inches of water (inH₂O)	x 2.491	= Millibar (mbar)
Millimetres of mercury (mmHg)	x 0.535	= Inches of water (inH₂O)	x 1.868	= Millimetres of mercury (mmHg)
Inches of water (inH₂O)	x 0.036	= Pounds-force per square inch (psi; lbf/in²; lb/in²)	x 27.68	= Inches of water (inH₂O)

Torque (moment of force)

Pounds-force inches (lbf in; lb in)	x 1.152	= Kilograms-force centimetre (kgf cm; kg cm)	x 0.868	= Pounds-force inches (lbf in; lb in)
Pounds-force inches (lbf in; lb in)	x 0.113	= Newton metres (Nm)	x 8.85	= Pounds-force inches (lbf in; lb in)
Pounds-force inches (lbf in; lb in)	x 0.083	= Pounds-force feet (lbf ft; lb ft)	x 12	= Pounds-force inches (lbf in; lb in)
Pounds-force feet (lbf ft; lb ft)	x 0.138	= Kilograms-force metres (kgf m; kg m)	x 7.233	= Pounds-force feet (lbf ft; lb ft)
Pounds-force feet (lbf ft; lb ft)	x 1.356	= Newton metres (Nm)	x 0.738	= Pounds-force feet (lbf ft; lb ft)
Newton metres (Nm)	x 0.102	= Kilograms-force metres (kgf m; kg m)	x 9.804	= Newton metres (Nm)

Power

Horsepower (hp)	x 745.7	= Watts (W)	x 0.0013	= Horsepower (hp)

Velocity (speed)

Miles per hour (miles/hr; mph)	x 1.609	= Kilometres per hour (km/hr; kph)	x 0.621	= Miles per hour (miles/hr; mph)

Fuel consumption*

Miles per gallon (mpg)	x 0.354	= Kilometres per litre (km/l)	x 2.825	= Miles per gallon (mpg)

* It is common practice to convert from miles per gallon (mpg) to litres/100 kilometres (l/100km), where mpg x l/100 km = 282

Temperature

Degrees Fahrenheit = (°C x 1.8) + 32   Degrees Celsius (Degrees Centigrade; °C) = (°F - 32) x 0.56

Buying spare parts

Spare parts are available from many sources, Audi have many dealers throughout the country, and other dealers, accessory shops, and motor factors will also stock. Our advice regarding spare parts sources is as follows:

Officially appointed vehicle main dealers – This is the best source for parts which are peculiar to your car and are not generally available (eg complete cylinder heads, internal transmission components, badges, interior trim, etc). It is also the only place at which you should buy parts if your vehicle is still under warranty. To be sure of obtaining the correct parts it will always be necessary to give the storeman your vehicle engine and chassis number, and if possible, to take some 'old' parts along for positive identification. Remember that many parts are available on a factory exchange scheme – any parts returned should always be clean! It obviously makes good sense to go straight to the specialists on your car for this type of part for they are best equipped to supply you.

Other dealers and auto accessory shops – These are often very good places to buy materials and components needed for the maintenance of your car (eg oil filters, spark plugs, bulbs, fanbelts, oils and greases, touch-up paint, filler paste, etc). They also sell general accessories, usually have convenient opening hours, charge lower prices and can often be found not far from home.

Motor factors – Good factors will stock all of the more important components which wear out relatively quickly (eg, clutch components, pistons, valves, exhaust systems, brake cylinders/pipes/hoses /seals/ shoes and pads, etc). Motor factors will often provide new or reconditioned components on a part exchange basis – this can save a considerable amount of money.

Vehicle identification numbers

Modifications are a continuing and unpublicised process in vehicle manufacture. Spare parts manuals and lists are compiled on a numerical basis, the individual vehicle numbers being essential to identify correctly the component required.

The vehicle identification plate is located in the engine compartment, on the right-hand side of the air intake plenum chamber. Not all countries have this plate.

The engine number is stamped on the left-hand side of the cylinder block (photo).

The vehicle identification number (VIN or chassis number) is stamped on the bulkhead behind the engine.

The vehicle data sticker is located on the inside of the luggage compartment lid, on all models except the Coupé. On Coupé models, it is located under the cover of the storage recess on the right-hand side of the luggage compartment.

Engine number

A

ABS (Anti-lock brake system) A system, usually electronically controlled, that senses incipient wheel lockup during braking and relieves hydraulic pressure at wheels that are about to skid.

Air bag An inflatable bag hidden in the steering wheel (driver's side) or the dash or glovebox (passenger side). In a head-on collision, the bags inflate, preventing the driver and front passenger from being thrown forward into the steering wheel or windscreen.

Air cleaner A metal or plastic housing, containing a filter element, which removes dust and dirt from the air being drawn into the engine.

Air filter element The actual filter in an air cleaner system, usually manufactured from pleated paper and requiring renewal at regular intervals.

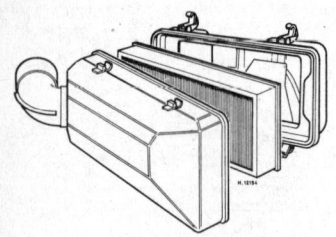

Air filter

Allen key A hexagonal wrench which fits into a recessed hexagonal hole.

Alligator clip A long-nosed spring-loaded metal clip with meshing teeth. Used to make temporary electrical connections.

Alternator A component in the electrical system which converts mechanical energy from a drivebelt into electrical energy to charge the battery and to operate the starting system, ignition system and electrical accessories.

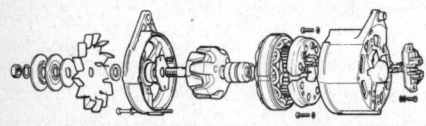

Alternator (exploded view)

Ampere (amp) A unit of measurement for the flow of electric current. One amp is the amount of current produced by one volt acting through a resistance of one ohm.

Anaerobic sealer A substance used to prevent bolts and screws from loosening. Anaerobic means that it does not require oxygen for activation. The Loctite brand is widely used.

Antifreeze A substance (usually ethylene glycol) mixed with water, and added to a vehicle's cooling system, to prevent freezing of the coolant in winter. Antifreeze also contains chemicals to inhibit corrosion and the formation of rust and other deposits that would tend to clog the radiator and coolant passages and reduce cooling efficiency.

Anti-seize compound A coating that reduces the risk of seizing on fasteners that are subjected to high temperatures, such as exhaust manifold bolts and nuts.

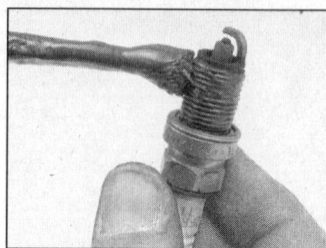

Anti-seize compound

Asbestos A natural fibrous mineral with great heat resistance, commonly used in the composition of brake friction materials. Asbestos is a health hazard and the dust created by brake systems should never be inhaled or ingested.

Axle A shaft on which a wheel revolves, or which revolves with a wheel. Also, a solid beam that connects the two wheels at one end of the vehicle. An axle which also transmits power to the wheels is known as a live axle.

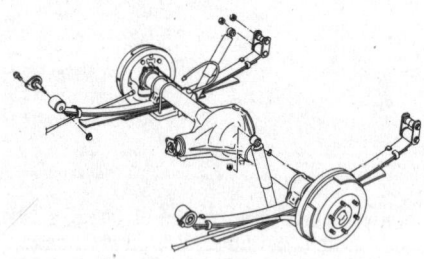

Axle assembly

Axleshaft A single rotating shaft, on either side of the differential, which delivers power from the final drive assembly to the drive wheels. Also called a driveshaft or a halfshaft.

B

Ball bearing An anti-friction bearing consisting of a hardened inner and outer race with hardened steel balls between two races.

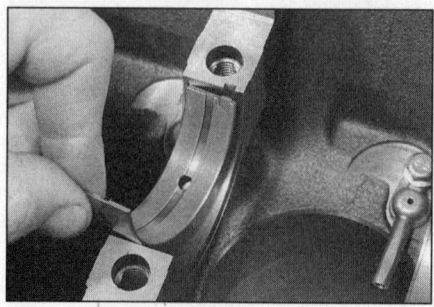

Bearing

Bearing The curved surface on a shaft or in a bore, or the part assembled into either, that permits relative motion between them with minimum wear and friction.

Big-end bearing The bearing in the end of the connecting rod that's attached to the crankshaft.

Bleed nipple A valve on a brake wheel cylinder, caliper or other hydraulic component that is opened to purge the hydraulic system of air. Also called a bleed screw.

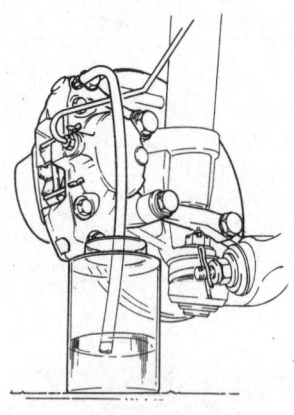

Brake bleeding

Brake bleeding Procedure for removing air from lines of a hydraulic brake system.

Brake disc The component of a disc brake that rotates with the wheels.

Brake drum The component of a drum brake that rotates with the wheels.

Brake linings The friction material which contacts the brake disc or drum to retard the vehicle's speed. The linings are bonded or riveted to the brake pads or shoes.

Brake pads The replaceable friction pads that pinch the brake disc when the brakes are applied. Brake pads consist of a friction material bonded or riveted to a rigid backing plate.

Brake shoe The crescent-shaped carrier to which the brake linings are mounted and which forces the lining against the rotating drum during braking.

Braking systems For more information on braking systems, consult the *Haynes Automotive Brake Manual*.

Breaker bar A long socket wrench handle providing greater leverage.

Bulkhead The insulated partition between the engine and the passenger compartment.

C

Caliper The non-rotating part of a disc-brake assembly that straddles the disc and carries the brake pads. The caliper also contains the hydraulic components that cause the pads to pinch the disc when the brakes are applied. A caliper is also a measuring tool that can be set to measure inside or outside dimensions of an object.

Camshaft A rotating shaft on which a series of cam lobes operate the valve mechanisms. The camshaft may be driven by gears, by sprockets and chain or by sprockets and a belt.

Canister A container in an evaporative emission control system; contains activated charcoal granules to trap vapours from the fuel system.

Canister

Carburettor A device which mixes fuel with air in the proper proportions to provide a desired power output from a spark ignition internal combustion engine.

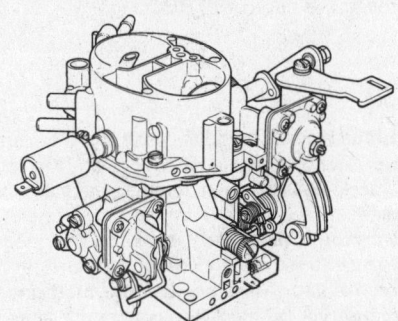

Carburettor

Castellated Resembling the parapets along the top of a castle wall. For example, a castellated balljoint stud nut.

Castellated nut

Castor In wheel alignment, the backward or forward tilt of the steering axis. Castor is positive when the steering axis is inclined rearward at the top.

Catalytic converter A silencer-like device in the exhaust system which converts certain pollutants in the exhaust gases into less harmful substances.

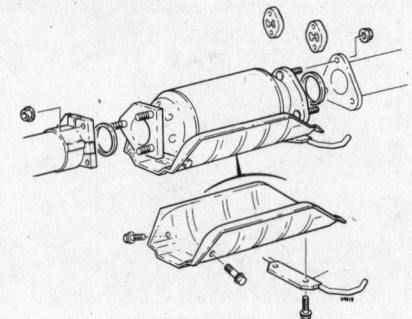

Catalytic converter

Circlip A ring-shaped clip used to prevent endwise movement of cylindrical parts and shafts. An internal circlip is installed in a groove in a housing; an external circlip fits into a groove on the outside of a cylindrical piece such as a shaft.

Clearance The amount of space between two parts. For example, between a piston and a cylinder, between a bearing and a journal, etc.

Coil spring A spiral of elastic steel found in various sizes throughout a vehicle, for example as a springing medium in the suspension and in the valve train.

Compression Reduction in volume, and increase in pressure and temperature, of a gas, caused by squeezing it into a smaller space.

Compression ratio The relationship between cylinder volume when the piston is at top dead centre and cylinder volume when the piston is at bottom dead centre.

Constant velocity (CV) joint A type of universal joint that cancels out vibrations caused by driving power being transmitted through an angle.

Core plug A disc or cup-shaped metal device inserted in a hole in a casting through which core was removed when the casting was formed. Also known as a freeze plug or expansion plug.

Crankcase The lower part of the engine block in which the crankshaft rotates.

Crankshaft The main rotating member, or shaft, running the length of the crankcase, with offset "throws" to which the connecting rods are attached.

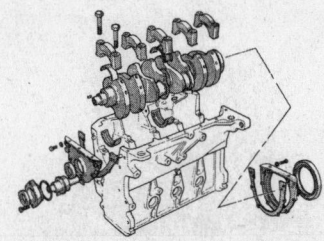

Crankshaft assembly

Crocodile clip See Alligator clip

D

Diagnostic code Code numbers obtained by accessing the diagnostic mode of an engine management computer. This code can be used to determine the area in the system where a malfunction may be located.

Disc brake A brake design incorporating a rotating disc onto which brake pads are squeezed. The resulting friction converts the energy of a moving vehicle into heat.

Double-overhead cam (DOHC) An engine that uses two overhead camshafts, usually one for the intake valves and one for the exhaust valves.

Drivebelt(s) The belt(s) used to drive accessories such as the alternator, water pump, power steering pump, air conditioning compressor, etc. off the crankshaft pulley.

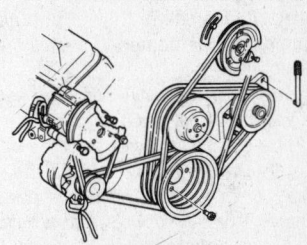

Accessory drivebelts

Driveshaft Any shaft used to transmit motion. Commonly used when referring to the axleshafts on a front wheel drive vehicle.

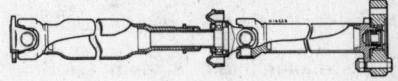

Driveshaft

Drum brake A type of brake using a drum-shaped metal cylinder attached to the inner surface of the wheel. When the brake pedal is pressed, curved brake shoes with friction linings press against the inside of the drum to slow or stop the vehicle.

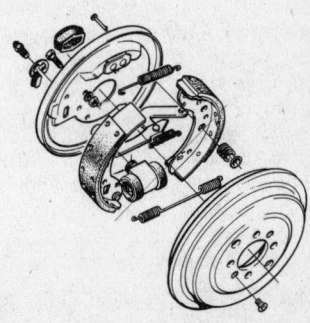

Drum brake assembly

E

EGR valve A valve used to introduce exhaust gases into the intake air stream.

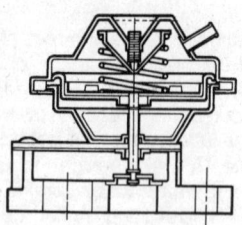

EGR valve

Electronic control unit (ECU) A computer which controls (for instance) ignition and fuel injection systems, or an anti-lock braking system. For more information refer to the *Haynes Automotive Electrical and Electronic Systems Manual*.

Electronic Fuel Injection (EFI) A computer controlled fuel system that distributes fuel through an injector located in each intake port of the engine.

Emergency brake A braking system, independent of the main hydraulic system, that can be used to slow or stop the vehicle if the primary brakes fail, or to hold the vehicle stationary even though the brake pedal isn't depressed. It usually consists of a hand lever that actuates either front or rear brakes mechanically through a series of cables and linkages. Also known as a handbrake or parking brake.

Endfloat The amount of lengthwise movement between two parts. As applied to a crankshaft, the distance that the crankshaft can move forward and back in the cylinder block.

Engine management system (EMS) A computer controlled system which manages the fuel injection and the ignition systems in an integrated fashion.

Exhaust manifold A part with several passages through which exhaust gases leave the engine combustion chambers and enter the exhaust pipe.

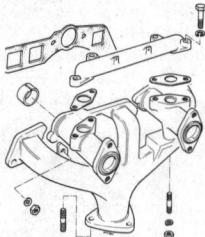

Exhaust manifold

F

Fan clutch A viscous (fluid) drive coupling device which permits variable engine fan speeds in relation to engine speeds.

Feeler blade A thin strip or blade of hardened steel, ground to an exact thickness, used to check or measure clearances between parts.

Feeler blade

Firing order The order in which the engine cylinders fire, or deliver their power strokes, beginning with the number one cylinder.

Flywheel A heavy spinning wheel in which energy is absorbed and stored by means of momentum. On cars, the flywheel is attached to the crankshaft to smooth out firing impulses.

Free play The amount of travel before any action takes place. The "looseness" in a linkage, or an assembly of parts, between the initial application of force and actual movement. For example, the distance the brake pedal moves before the pistons in the master cylinder are actuated.

Fuse An electrical device which protects a circuit against accidental overload. The typical fuse contains a soft piece of metal which is calibrated to melt at a predetermined current flow (expressed as amps) and break the circuit.

Fusible link A circuit protection device consisting of a conductor surrounded by heat-resistant insulation. The conductor is smaller than the wire it protects, so it acts as the weakest link in the circuit. Unlike a blown fuse, a failed fusible link must frequently be cut from the wire for replacement.

G

Gap The distance the spark must travel in jumping from the centre electrode to the side

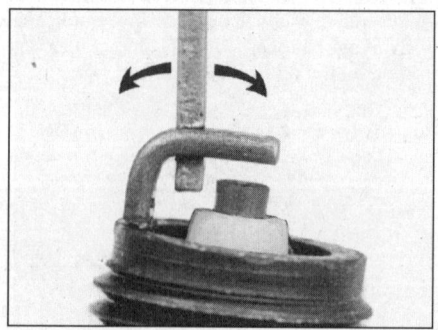

Adjusting spark plug gap

electrode in a spark plug. Also refers to the spacing between the points in a contact breaker assembly in a conventional points-type ignition, or to the distance between the reluctor or rotor and the pickup coil in an electronic ignition.

Gasket Any thin, soft material - usually cork, cardboard, asbestos or soft metal - installed between two metal surfaces to ensure a good seal. For instance, the cylinder head gasket seals the joint between the block and the cylinder head.

Gasket

Gauge An instrument panel display used to monitor engine conditions. A gauge with a movable pointer on a dial or a fixed scale is an analogue gauge. A gauge with a numerical readout is called a digital gauge.

H

Halfshaft A rotating shaft that transmits power from the final drive unit to a drive wheel, usually when referring to a live rear axle.

Harmonic balancer A device designed to reduce torsion or twisting vibration in the crankshaft. May be incorporated in the crankshaft pulley. Also known as a vibration damper.

Hone An abrasive tool for correcting small irregularities or differences in diameter in an engine cylinder, brake cylinder, etc.

Hydraulic tappet A tappet that utilises hydraulic pressure from the engine's lubrication system to maintain zero clearance (constant contact with both camshaft and valve stem). Automatically adjusts to variation in valve stem length. Hydraulic tappets also reduce valve noise.

I

Ignition timing The moment at which the spark plug fires, usually expressed in the number of crankshaft degrees before the piston reaches the top of its stroke.

Inlet manifold A tube or housing with passages through which flows the air-fuel mixture (carburettor vehicles and vehicles with throttle body injection) or air only (port fuel-injected vehicles) to the port openings in the cylinder head.

J

Jump start Starting the engine of a vehicle with a discharged or weak battery by attaching jump leads from the weak battery to a charged or helper battery.

L

Load Sensing Proportioning Valve (LSPV) A brake hydraulic system control valve that works like a proportioning valve, but also takes into consideration the amount of weight carried by the rear axle.

Locknut A nut used to lock an adjustment nut, or other threaded component, in place. For example, a locknut is employed to keep the adjusting nut on the rocker arm in position.

Lockwasher A form of washer designed to prevent an attaching nut from working loose.

M

MacPherson strut A type of front suspension system devised by Earle MacPherson at Ford of England. In its original form, a simple lateral link with the anti-roll bar creates the lower control arm. A long strut - an integral coil spring and shock absorber - is mounted between the body and the steering knuckle. Many modern so-called MacPherson strut systems use a conventional lower A-arm and don't rely on the anti-roll bar for location.

Multimeter An electrical test instrument with the capability to measure voltage, current and resistance.

N

NOx Oxides of Nitrogen. A common toxic pollutant emitted by petrol and diesel engines at higher temperatures.

O

Ohm The unit of electrical resistance. One volt applied to a resistance of one ohm will produce a current of one amp.

Ohmmeter An instrument for measuring electrical resistance.

O-ring A type of sealing ring made of a special rubber-like material; in use, the O-ring is compressed into a groove to provide the sealing action.

O-ring

Overhead cam (ohc) engine An engine with the camshaft(s) located on top of the cylinder head(s).

Overhead valve (ohv) engine An engine with the valves located in the cylinder head, but with the camshaft located in the engine block.

Oxygen sensor A device installed in the engine exhaust manifold, which senses the oxygen content in the exhaust and converts this information into an electric current. Also called a Lambda sensor.

P

Phillips screw A type of screw head having a cross instead of a slot for a corresponding type of screwdriver.

Plastigage A thin strip of plastic thread, available in different sizes, used for measuring clearances. For example, a strip of Plastigage is laid across a bearing journal. The parts are assembled and dismantled; the width of the crushed strip indicates the clearance between journal and bearing.

Plastigage

Propeller shaft The long hollow tube with universal joints at both ends that carries power from the transmission to the differential on front-engined rear wheel drive vehicles.

Proportioning valve A hydraulic control valve which limits the amount of pressure to the rear brakes during panic stops to prevent wheel lock-up.

R

Rack-and-pinion steering A steering system with a pinion gear on the end of the steering shaft that mates with a rack (think of a geared wheel opened up and laid flat). When the steering wheel is turned, the pinion turns, moving the rack to the left or right. This movement is transmitted through the track rods to the steering arms at the wheels.

Radiator A liquid-to-air heat transfer device designed to reduce the temperature of the coolant in an internal combustion engine cooling system.

Refrigerant Any substance used as a heat transfer agent in an air-conditioning system. R-12 has been the principle refrigerant for many years; recently, however, manufacturers have begun using R-134a, a non-CFC substance that is considered less harmful to the ozone in the upper atmosphere.

Rocker arm A lever arm that rocks on a shaft or pivots on a stud. In an overhead valve engine, the rocker arm converts the upward movement of the pushrod into a downward movement to open a valve.

Rotor In a distributor, the rotating device inside the cap that connects the centre electrode and the outer terminals as it turns, distributing the high voltage from the coil secondary winding to the proper spark plug. Also, that part of an alternator which rotates inside the stator. Also, the rotating assembly of a turbocharger, including the compressor wheel, shaft and turbine wheel.

Runout The amount of wobble (in-and-out movement) of a gear or wheel as it's rotated. The amount a shaft rotates "out-of-true." The out-of-round condition of a rotating part.

S

Sealant A liquid or paste used to prevent leakage at a joint. Sometimes used in conjunction with a gasket.

Sealed beam lamp An older headlight design which integrates the reflector, lens and filaments into a hermetically-sealed one-piece unit. When a filament burns out or the lens cracks, the entire unit is simply replaced.

Serpentine drivebelt A single, long, wide accessory drivebelt that's used on some newer vehicles to drive all the accessories, instead of a series of smaller, shorter belts. Serpentine drivebelts are usually tensioned by an automatic tensioner.

Serpentine drivebelt

Shim Thin spacer, commonly used to adjust the clearance or relative positions between two parts. For example, shims inserted into or under bucket tappets control valve clearances. Clearance is adjusted by changing the thickness of the shim.

Slide hammer A special puller that screws into or hooks onto a component such as a shaft or bearing; a heavy sliding handle on the shaft bottoms against the end of the shaft to knock the component free.

Sprocket A tooth or projection on the periphery of a wheel, shaped to engage with a chain or drivebelt. Commonly used to refer to the sprocket wheel itself.

Starter inhibitor switch On vehicles with an

automatic transmission, a switch that prevents starting if the vehicle is not in Neutral or Park.

Strut See MacPherson strut.

T

Tappet A cylindrical component which transmits motion from the cam to the valve stem, either directly or via a pushrod and rocker arm. Also called a cam follower.

Thermostat A heat-controlled valve that regulates the flow of coolant between the cylinder block and the radiator, so maintaining optimum engine operating temperature. A thermostat is also used in some air cleaners in which the temperature is regulated.

Thrust bearing The bearing in the clutch assembly that is moved in to the release levers by clutch pedal action to disengage the clutch. Also referred to as a release bearing.

Timing belt A toothed belt which drives the camshaft. Serious engine damage may result if it breaks in service.

Timing chain A chain which drives the camshaft.

Toe-in The amount the front wheels are closer together at the front than at the rear. On rear wheel drive vehicles, a slight amount of toe-in is usually specified to keep the front wheels running parallel on the road by offsetting other forces that tend to spread the wheels apart.

Toe-out The amount the front wheels are closer together at the rear than at the front. On front wheel drive vehicles, a slight amount of toe-out is usually specified.

Tools For full information on choosing and using tools, refer to the *Haynes Automotive Tools Manual.*

Tracer A stripe of a second colour applied to a wire insulator to distinguish that wire from another one with the same colour insulator.

Tune-up A process of accurate and careful adjustments and parts replacement to obtain the best possible engine performance.

Turbocharger A centrifugal device, driven by exhaust gases, that pressurises the intake air. Normally used to increase the power output from a given engine displacement, but can also be used primarily to reduce exhaust emissions (as on VW's "Umwelt" Diesel engine).

U

Universal joint or U-joint A double-pivoted connection for transmitting power from a driving to a driven shaft through an angle. A U-joint consists of two Y-shaped yokes and a cross-shaped member called the spider.

V

Valve A device through which the flow of liquid, gas, vacuum, or loose material in bulk may be started, stopped, or regulated by a movable part that opens, shuts, or partially obstructs one or more ports or passageways. A valve is also the movable part of such a device.

Valve clearance The clearance between the valve tip (the end of the valve stem) and the rocker arm or tappet. The valve clearance is measured when the valve is closed.

Vernier caliper A precision measuring instrument that measures inside and outside dimensions. Not quite as accurate as a micrometer, but more convenient.

Viscosity The thickness of a liquid or its resistance to flow.

Volt A unit for expressing electrical "pressure" in a circuit. One volt that will produce a current of one ampere through a resistance of one ohm.

W

Welding Various processes used to join metal items by heating the areas to be joined to a molten state and fusing them together. For more information refer to the *Haynes Automotive Welding Manual.*

Wiring diagram A drawing portraying the components and wires in a vehicle's electrical system, using standardised symbols. For more information refer to the *Haynes Automotive Electrical and Electronic Systems Manual.*

Note: *References throughout this index relate to Chapter•page number*

Haynes Manuals – The Complete List

Title	Book No.
ALFA ROMEO	
Alfa Romeo Alfasud/Sprint (74 - 88) up to F	0292
Alfa Romeo Alfetta (73 - 87) up to E	0531
AUDI	
Audi 80 (72 - Feb 79) up to T	0207
Audi 80, 90 (79 - Oct 86) up to D & Coupe (81 - Nov 88) up to F	0605
Audi 80, 90 (Oct 86 - 90) D to H & Coupe (Nov 88 - 90) F to H	1491
Audi 100 (Oct 82 - 90) up to H & 200 (Feb 84 - Oct 89) A to G	0907
Audi 100 & A6 Petrol & Diesel (May 91 - May 97) H to P	3504
Audi A4 (95 - Feb 00) M to V	3575
AUSTIN	
Austin A35 & A40 (56 - 67) *	0118
Austin Allegro 1100, 1300, 1.0, 1.1 & 1.3 (73 - 82) *	0164
Austin Healey 100/6 & 3000 (56 - 68) *	0049
Austin/MG/Rover Maestro 1.3 & 1.6 (83 - 95) up to M	0922
Austin/MG Metro (80 - May 90) up to G	0718
Austin/Rover Montego 1.3 & 1.6 (84 - 94) A to L	1066
Austin/MG/Rover Montego 2.0 (84 - 95) A to M	1067
Mini (59 - 69) up to H	0527
Mini (69 - Oct 96) up to P	0646
Austin/Rover 2.0 litre Diesel Engine (86 - 93) C to L	1857
BEDFORD	
Bedford CF (69 - 87) up to E	0163
Bedford/Vauxhall Rascal & Suzuki Supercarry (86 - Oct 94) C to M	3015
BMW	
BMW 1500, 1502, 1600, 1602, 2000 & 2002 (59 - 77)*	0240
BMW 316, 320 & 320i (4-cyl) (75 - Feb 83) up to Y	0276
BMW 320, 320i, 323i & 325i (6-cyl) (Oct 77 - Sept 87) up to E	0815
BMW 3-Series (Apr 91 - 96) H to N	3210
BMW 3- & 5-Series (sohc) (81 - 91) up to J	1948
BMW 520i & 525e (Oct 81 - June 88) up to E	1560
BMW 525, 528 & 528i (73 - Sept 81) up to X	0632
CITROEN	
Citroën 2CV, Ami & Dyane (67 - 90) up to H	0196
Citroën AX Petrol & Diesel (87 - 97) D to P	3014
Citroën BX (83 - 94) A to L	0908
Citroën C15 Van Petrol & Diesel (89 - Oct 98) F to S	3509
Citroën CX (75 - 88) up to F	0528
Citroën Saxo Petrol & Diesel (96 - 01) N to X	3506
Citroën Visa (79 - 88) up to F	0620
Citroën Xantia Petrol & Diesel (93 - 98) K to S	3082
Citroën XM Petrol & Diesel (89 - 98) G to R	3451
Citroën Xsara Petrol & Diesel (97 - Sept 00) R to W	3751
Citroën ZX Diesel (91 - 98) J to S	1922
Citroën ZX Petrol (91 - 98) H to S	1881
Citroën 1.7 & 1.9 litre Diesel Engine (84 - 96) A to N	1379
FIAT	
Fiat 126 (73 - 87) *	0305
Fiat 500 (57 - 73) up to M	0090
Fiat Bravo & Brava (95 - 00) N to W	3572
Fiat Cinquecento (93 - 98) K to R	3501
Fiat Panda (81 - 95) up to M	0793
Fiat Punto Petrol & Diesel (94 - Oct 99) L to V	3251
Fiat Regata (84 - 88) A to F	1167
Fiat Tipo (88 - 91) E to J	1625
Fiat Uno (83 - 95) up to M	0923
Fiat X1/9 (74 - 89) up to G	0273
FORD	
Ford Anglia (59 - 68) *	0001

Title	Book No.
Ford Capri II (& III) 1.6 & 2.0 (74 - 87) up to E	0283
Ford Capri II (& III) 2.8 & 3.0 (74 - 87) up to E	1309
Ford Cortina Mk III 1300 & 1600 (70 - 76) *	0070
Ford Cortina Mk IV (& V) 1.6 & 2.0 (76 - 83) *	0343
Ford Cortina Mk IV (& V) 2.3 V6 (77 - 83) *	0426
Ford Escort Mk I 1100 & 1300 (68 - 74) *	0171
Ford Escort Mk I Mexico, RS 1600 & RS 2000 (70 - 74)*	0139
Ford Escort Mk II Mexico, RS 1800 & RS 2000 (75 - 80)*	0735
Ford Escort (75 - Aug 80) *	0280
Ford Escort (Sept 80 - Sept 90) up to H	0686
Ford Escort & Orion (Sept 90 - 00) H to X	1737
Ford Fiesta (76 - Aug 83) up to Y	0334
Ford Fiesta (Aug 83 - Feb 89) A to F	1030
Ford Fiesta (Feb 89 - Oct 95) F to N	1595
Ford Fiesta (Oct 95 - 01) N-reg. onwards	3397
Ford Focus (98 - 01) S to Y	3759
Ford Granada (Sept 77 - Feb 85) up to B	0481
Ford Granada & Scorpio (Mar 85 - 94) B to M	1245
Ford Ka (96 - 99) P to T	3570
Ford Mondeo Petrol (93 - 99) K to T	1923
Ford Mondeo Diesel (93 - 96) L to N	3465
Ford Orion (83 - Sept 90) up to H	1009
Ford Sierra 4 cyl. (82 - 93) up to K	0903
Ford Sierra V6 (82 - 91) up to J	0904
Ford Transit Petrol (Mk 2) (78 - Jan 86) up to C	0719
Ford Transit Petrol (Mk 3) (Feb 86 - 89) C to G	1468
Ford Transit Diesel (Feb 86 - 99) C to T	3019
Ford 1.6 & 1.8 litre Diesel Engine (84 - 96) A to N	1172
Ford 2.1, 2.3 & 2.5 litre Diesel Engine (77 - 90) up to H	1606
FREIGHT ROVER	
Freight Rover Sherpa (74 - 87) up to E	0463
HILLMAN	
Hillman Avenger (70 - 82) up to Y	0037
Hillman Imp (63 - 76) *	0022
HONDA	
Honda Accord (76 - Feb 84) up to A	0351
Honda Civic (Feb 84 - Oct 87) A to E	1226
Honda Civic (Nov 91 - 96) J to N	3199
HYUNDAI	
Hyundai Pony (85 - 94) C to M	3398
JAGUAR	
Jaguar E Type (61 - 72) up to L	0140
Jaguar MkI & II, 240 & 340 (55 - 69) *	0098
Jaguar XJ6, XJ & Sovereign; Daimler Sovereign (68 - Oct 86) up to D	0242
Jaguar XJ6 & Sovereign (Oct 86 - Sept 94) D to M	3261
Jaguar XJ12, XJS & Sovereign; Daimler Double Six (72 - 88) up to F	0478
JEEP	
Jeep Cherokee Petrol (93 - 96) K to N	1943
LADA	
Lada 1200, 1300, 1500 & 1600 (74 - 91) up to J	0413
Lada Samara (87 - 91) D to J	1610
LAND ROVER	
Land Rover 90, 110 & Defender Diesel (83 - 95) up to N	3017
Land Rover Discovery Petrol & Diesel (89 - 98) G to S	3016
Land Rover Series IIA & III Diesel (58 - 85) up to C	0529
Land Rover Series II, IIA & III Petrol (58 - 85) up to C	0314
MAZDA	
Mazda 323 (Mar 81 - Oct 89) up to G	1608
Mazda 323 (Oct 89 - 98) G to R	3455
Mazda 626 (May 83 - Sept 87) up to E	0929

Title	Book No.
Mazda B-1600, B-1800 & B-2000 Pick-up (72 - 88) up to F	0267
Mazda RX-7 (79 - 85) *	0460
MERCEDES-BENZ	
Mercedes-Benz 190, 190E & 190D Petrol & Diesel (83 - 93) A to L	3450
Mercedes-Benz 200, 240, 300 Diesel (Oct 76 - 85) up to C	1114
Mercedes-Benz 250 & 280 (68 - 72) up to L	0346
Mercedes-Benz 250 & 280 (123 Series) (Oct 76 - 84) up to B	0677
Mercedes-Benz 124 Series (85 - Aug 93) C to K	3253
Mercedes-Benz C-Class Petrol & Diesel (93 - Aug 00) L to W	3511
MG	
MGA (55 - 62) *	0475
MGB (62 - 80) up to W	0111
MG Midget & AH Sprite (58 - 80) up to W	0265
MITSUBISHI	
Mitsubishi Shogun & L200 Pick-Ups (83 - 94) up to M	1944
MORRIS	
Morris Ital 1.3 (80 - 84) up to B	0705
Morris Minor 1000 (56 - 71) up to K	0024
NISSAN	
Nissan Bluebird (May 84 - Mar 86) A to C	1223
Nissan Bluebird (Mar 86 - 90) C to H	1473
Nissan Cherry (Sept 82 - 86) up to D	1031
Nissan Micra (83 - Jan 93) up to K	0931
Nissan Micra (93 - 99) K to T	3254
Nissan Primera (90 - Aug 99) H to T	1851
Nissan Stanza (82 - 86) up to D	0824
Nissan Sunny (May 82 - Oct 86) up to D	0895
Nissan Sunny (Oct 86 - Mar 91) D to H	1378
Nissan Sunny (Apr 91 - 95) H to N	3219
OPEL	
Opel Ascona & Manta (B Series) (Sept 75 - 88) up to F	0316
Opel Ascona (81 - 88) (Not available in UK see Vauxhall Cavalier 0812)	3215
Opel Astra (Oct 91 - Feb 98) (Not available in UK see Vauxhall Astra 1832)	3156
Opel Astra & Zafira Diesel (Feb 98 - Sept 00) (See Astra & Zafira Diesel Book No. 3797)	
Opel Astra & Zafira Petrol (Feb 98 - Sept 00) (See Vauxhall/Opel Astra & Zafira Petrol Book No. 3758)	
Opel Calibra (90 - 98) (See Vauxhall/Opel Calibra Book No. 3502)	
Opel Corsa (83 - Mar 93) (Not available in UK see Vauxhall Nova 0909)	3160
Opel Corsa (Mar 93 - 97) (Not available in UK see Vauxhall Corsa 1985)	3159
Opel Frontera Petrol & Diesel (91 - 98) (See Vauxhall/Opel Frontera Book No. 3454)	
Opel Kadett (Nov 79 - Oct 84) up to B	0634
Opel Kadett (Oct 84 - Oct 91) (Not available in UK see Vauxhall Astra & Belmont 1136)	3196
Opel Omega & Senator (86 - 94) (Not available in UK see Vauxhall Carlton & Senator 1469)	3157
Omega (94 - 99) (See Vauxhall/Opel Omega Book No. 3510)	
Opel Rekord (Feb 78 - Oct 86) up to D	0543
Opel Vectra (Oct 88 - Oct 95) (Not available in UK see Vauxhall Cavalier 1570)	3158
Opel Vectra Petrol & Diesel (95 - 98) (Not available in UK see Vauxhall Vectra 3396)	3523

* Classic reprint

Title	Book No.
PEUGEOT	
Peugeot 106 Petrol & Diesel (91 - 01) J to X	1882
Peugeot 205 Petrol (83 - 97) A to P	0932
Peugeot 206 Petrol and Diesel (98 - 01) S to X	3757
Peugeot 305 (78 - 89) up to G	0538
Peugeot 306 Petrol & Diesel (93 - 99) K to T	3073
Peugeot 309 (86 - 93) C to K	1266
Peugeot 405 Petrol (88 - 97) E to P	1559
Peugeot 405 Diesel (88 - 97) E to P	3198
Peugeot 406 Petrol & Diesel (96 - 97) N to R	3394
Peugeot 505 (79 - 89) up to G	0762
Peugeot 1.7/1.8 & 1.9 litre Diesel Engine (82 - 96) up to N	0950
Peugeot 2.0, 2.1, 2.3 & 2.5 litre Diesel Engines (74 - 90) up to H	1607
PORSCHE	
Porsche 911 (65 - 85) up to C	0264
Porsche 924 & 924 Turbo (76 - 85) up to C	0397
PROTON	
Proton (89 - 97) F to P	3255
RANGE ROVER	
Range Rover V8 (70 - Oct 92) up to K	0606
RELIANT	
Reliant Robin & Kitten (73 - 83) up to A	0436
RENAULT	
Renault 4 (61 - 86) *	0072
Renault 5 (Feb 85 - 96) B to N	1219
Renault 9 & 11 (82 - 89) up to F	0822
Renault 18 (79 - 86) up to D	0598
Renault 19 Petrol (89 - 94) F to M	1646
Renault 19 Diesel (89 - 95) F to N	1946
Renault 21 (86 - 94) C to M	1397
Renault 25 (84 - 92) B to K	1228
Renault Clio Petrol (91 - May 98) H to R	1853
Renault Clio Diesel (91 - June 96) H to N	3031
Renault Clio (May 98-01) R-reg onwards	3906
Renault Espace Petrol & Diesel (85 - 96) C to N	3197
Renault Fuego (80 - 86) *	0764
Renault Laguna Petrol & Diesel (94 - 00) L to W	3252
Renault Mégane & Scénic Petrol & Diesel (96 - 98) N to R	3395
ROVER	
Rover 213 & 216 (84 - 89) A to G	1116
Rover 214 & 414 (89 - 96) G to N	1689
Rover 216 & 416 (89 - 96) G to N	1830
Rover 211, 214, 216, 218 & 220 Petrol & Diesel (Dec 95 - 98) N to R	3399
Rover 414, 416 & 420 Petrol & Diesel (May 95 - 98) M to R	3453
Rover 618, 620 & 623 (93 - 97) K to P	3257
Rover 820, 825 & 827 (86 - 95) D to N	1380
Rover 3500 (76 - 87) up to E	0365
Rover Metro, 111 & 114 (May 90 - 98) G to S	1711
SAAB	
Saab 90, 99 & 900 (79 - Oct 93) up to L	0765
Saab 95 & 96 (66 - 76) *	0198
Saab 99 (69 - 79) *	0247
Saab 900 (Oct 93 - 98) L to R	3512
Saab 9000 (4-cyl) (85 - 98) C to S	1686
SEAT	
Seat Ibiza & Cordoba Petrol & Diesel (Oct 93 - Oct 99) L to V	3571
Seat Ibiza & Malaga (85 - 92) B to K	1609
SKODA	
Skoda Estelle (77 - 89) up to G	0604

Title	Book No.
Skoda Favorit (89 - 96) F to N	1801
Skoda Felicia Petrol & Diesel (95 - 99) M to T	3505
SUBARU	
Subaru 1600 & 1800 (Nov 79 - 90) up to H	0995
SUNBEAM	
Sunbeam Alpine, Rapier & H120 (67 - 76) *	0051
SUZUKI	
Suzuki Supercarry/Bedford/Vauxhall Rascal (86 - Oct 94) C to M	3015
Suzuki SJ Series, Samurai & Vitara (4-cyl) (82 - 97) up to P	1942
TALBOT	
Talbot Alpine, Solara, Minx & Rapier (75 - 86) up to D	0337
Talbot Horizon (78 - 86) up to D	0473
Talbot Samba (82 - 86) up to D	0823
TOYOTA	
Toyota Carina E (May 92 - 97) J to P	3256
Toyota Corolla (Sept 83 - Sept 87) A to E	1024
Toyota Corolla (80 - 85) up to C	0683
Toyota Corolla (Sept 87 - Aug 92) E to K	1683
Toyota Corolla (Aug 92 - 97) K to P	3259
Toyota Hi-Ace & Hi-Lux (69 - Oct 83) up to A	0304
TRIUMPH	
Triumph Acclaim (81 - 84) *	0792
Triumph GT6 & Vitesse (62 - 74) *	0112
Triumph Herald (59 - 71) *	0010
Triumph Spitfire (62 - 81) up to X	0113
Triumph Stag (70 - 78) up to T	0441
Triumph TR2, TR3, TR3A, TR4 & TR4A (52 - 67)*	0028
Triumph TR5 & 6 (67 - 75) *	0031
Triumph TR7 (75 - 82) *	0322
VAUXHALL	
Vauxhall Astra (80 - Oct 84) up to B	0635
Vauxhall Astra & Belmont (Oct 84 - Oct 91) B to J	1136
Vauxhall Astra (Oct 91 - Feb 98) J to R	1832
Vauxhall/Opel Astra & Zafira Diesel (Feb 98 - Sept 00) R to W	3797
Vauxhall/Opel Astra & Zafira Petrol (Feb 98 - Sept 00) R to W	3758
Vauxhall/Opel Calibra (90 - 98) G to S	3502
Vauxhall Carlton (Oct 78 - Oct 86) up to D	0480
Vauxhall Carlton & Senator (Nov 86 - 94) D to L	1469
Vauxhall Cavalier 1300 (77 - July 81) *	0461
Vauxhall Cavalier 1600, 1900 & 2000 (75 - July 81) up to W	0315
Vauxhall Cavalier (81 - Oct 88) up to F	0812
Vauxhall Cavalier (Oct 88 - 95) F to N	1570
Vauxhall Chevette (75 - 84) up to B	0285
Vauxhall Corsa (Mar 93 - 97) K to R	1985
Vauxhall/Opel Corsa (Apr 97 - Sept 00) P to W	3921
Vauxhall/Opel Frontera Petrol & Diesel (91 - Sept 98) J to S	3454
Vauxhall Nova (83 - 93) up to K	0909
Vauxhall/Opel Omega (94 - 99) L to T	3510
Vauxhall Vectra Petrol & Diesel (95 - 98) N to R	3396
Vauxhall/Opel 1.5, 1.6 & 1.7 litre Diesel Engine (82 - 96) up to N	1222
VOLKSWAGEN	
Volkswagen 411 & 412 (68 - 75) *	0091
Volkswagen Beetle 1200 (54 - 77) up to S	0036
Volkswagen Beetle 1300 & 1500 (65 - 75) up to P	0039
Volkswagen Beetle 1302 & 1302S (70 - 72) up to L	0110
Volkswagen Beetle 1303, 1303S & GT (72 - 75) up to P	0159
Volkswagen Beetle (Apr 99 - 02) W-reg onwards	3798

Title	Book No.
Volkswagen Golf & Bora Petrol & Diesel (April 98 - 00) R to X	3727
Volkswagen Golf & Jetta Mk 1 1.1 & 1.3 (74 - 84) up to A	0716
Volkswagen Golf, Jetta & Scirocco Mk 1 1.5, 1.6 & 1.8 (74 - 84) up to A	0726
Volkswagen Golf & Jetta Mk 1 Diesel (78 - 84) up to A	0451
Volkswagen Golf & Jetta Mk 2 (Mar 84 - Feb 92) A to J	1081
Volkswagen Golf & Vento Petrol & Diesel (Feb 92 - 96) J to N	3097
Volkswagen LT vans & light trucks (76 - 87) up to E	0637
Volkswagen Passat & Santana (Sept 81 - May 88) up to E	0814
Volkswagen Passat Petrol & Diesel (May 88 - 96) E to P	3498
Volkswagen Polo & Derby (76 - Jan 82) up to X	0335
Volkswagen Polo (82 - Oct 90) up to H	0813
Volkswagen Polo (Nov 90 - Aug 94) H to L	3245
Volkswagen Polo Hatchback Petrol & Diesel (94 - 99) M to S	3500
Volkswagen Scirocco (82 - 90) up to H	1224
Volkswagen Transporter 1600 (68 - 79) up to V	0082
Volkswagen Transporter 1700, 1800 & 2000 (72 - 79) up to V	0226
Volkswagen Transporter (air-cooled) (79 - 82) up to Y	0638
Volkswagen Transporter (water-cooled) (82 - 90) up to H	3452
Volkswagen Type 3 (63 - 73) *	0084
VOLVO	
Volvo 120 & 130 Series (& P1800) (61 - 73) *	0203
Volvo 142, 144 & 145 (66 - 74) up to N	0129
Volvo 240 Series (74 - 93) up to K	0270
Volvo 262, 264 & 260/265 (75 - 85) *	0400
Volvo 340, 343, 345 & 360 (76 - 91) up to J	0715
Volvo 440, 460 & 480 (87 - 97) D to P	1691
Volvo 740 & 760 (82 - 91) up to J	1258
Volvo 850 (92 - 96) J to P	3260
Volvo 940 (90 - 96) H to N	3249
Volvo S40 & V40 (96 - 99) N to V	3569
Volvo S70, V70 & C70 (96 - 99) P to V	3573
AUTOMOTIVE TECHBOOKS	
Automotive Air Conditioning Systems	3740
Automotive Brake Manual	3050
Automotive Carburettor Manual	3288
Automotive Diagnostic Fault Codes Manual	3472
Automotive Diesel Engine Service Guide	3286
Automotive Electrical and Electronic Systems Manual	3049
Automotive Engine Management and Fuel Injection Systems Manual	3344
Automotive Gearbox Overhaul Manual	3473
Automotive Service Summaries Manual	3475
Automotive Timing Belts Manual – Austin/Rover	3549
Automotive Timing Belts Manual – Ford	3474
Automotive Timing Belts Manual – Peugeot/Citroën	3568
Automotive Timing Belts Manual – Vauxhall/Opel	3577
Automotive Welding Manual	3053
In-Car Entertainment Manual (3rd Edition)	3363

* Classic reprint

CL12.10/01

CL12.10/01

Preserving Our Motoring Heritage

<
The Model J Duesenberg Derham Tourster. Only eight of these magnificent cars were ever built – this is the only example to be found outside the United States of America

Almost every car you've ever loved, loathed or desired is gathered under one roof at the Haynes Motor Museum. Over 300 immaculately presented cars and motorbikes represent every aspect of our motoring heritage, from elegant reminders of bygone days, such as the superb Model J Duesenberg to curiosities like the bug-eyed BMW Isetta. There are also many old friends and flames. Perhaps you remember the 1959 Ford Popular that you did your courting in? The magnificent 'Red Collection' is a spectacle of classic sports cars including AC, Alfa Romeo, Austin Healey, Ferrari, Lamborghini, Maserati, MG, Riley, Porsche and Triumph.

A Perfect Day Out

Each and every vehicle at the Haynes Motor Museum has played its part in the history and culture of Motoring. Today, they make a wonderful spectacle and a great day out for all the family. Bring the kids, bring Mum and Dad, but above all bring your camera to capture those golden memories for ever. You will also find an impressive array of motoring memorabilia, a comfortable 70 seat video cinema and one of the most extensive transport book shops in Britain. The Pit Stop Cafe serves everything from a cup of tea to wholesome, home-made meals or, if you prefer, you can enjoy the large picnic area nestled in the beautiful rural surroundings of Somerset.

>
John Haynes O.B.E., Founder and Chairman of the museum at the wheel of a Haynes Light 12.

<
Graham Hill's Lola Cosworth Formula 1 car next to a 1934 Riley Sports.

The Museum is situated on the A359 Yeovil to Frome road at Sparkford, just off the A303 in Somerset. It is about 40 miles south of Bristol, and 25 minutes drive from the M5 intersection at Taunton.
Open 9.30am - 5.30pm (10.00am - 4.00pm Winter) 7 days a week, *except Christmas Day, Boxing Day and New Years Day*
Special rates available for schools, coach parties and outings Charitable Trust No. 292048